# Reform Jewish Ethics and the Halakhah

## An Experiment in Decision Making

# Reform Jewish Ethics and the Halakhah

## An Experiment in Decision Making

Edited by
Eugene B. Borowitz

With An Introduction by
Louis Newman,
Carleton College

Behrman House, Inc.
New Jersey

Copyright 1988, 1989, 1990 and 1994 by Eugene B. Borowitz
Published by Behrman House, Inc.,
235 Watchung Ave., W. Orange, NJ 07052

## Library of Congress Cataloging-in-Publication Data

Reform Jewish ethics and the halakhah : an experiment in decision
  making / edited by Eugene B. Borowitz : with an introduction by
Louis Newman.
        P. 456
        ISBN 0-87441-572-1 : $29.95
            1.  Judaism and social problems.  2.  Reform Judaism.  3.  Jewish
law--Reform Judaism.  4.  Ethics, Jewish.    I.  Borowitz, Eugene B.
HN40.J5r38  1994
296.3'85--dc20                                                    94-22070 √
                                                                        CIP

To that untold number
of family and friends,
of donors named and anonymous,
of faculty, administration and support staff,
who generation after generation
have made it possible
for another group of students
to earn the title "rabbi"
at the
Hebrew Union College-Jewish Institute of Religion
and at other great centers of Jewish learning.

# Contents

# Preface:
# From Cognitive Dissonance to Creative Groping

Eugene B. Borowitz

For more than two decades now thoughtful Reform Jews have been grappling with the need to rethink their approach to ethical decisions-making. Since I have described the social and philosophic bases of that development elsewhere it need not be repeated here.* Suffice it to say that with political liberalism effectively challenged by ethical conservatism and with the liberalism's rational ("Kantian") academic underpinnings eroded, the identification of Jewish social ethics with a presumed universal human moral consciousness no longer evokes conviction. Besides, it seems odd that a religion which prides itself on its ethical emphasis has nothing distinctive to contribute to contemporary ethics other than an uncommonly large cadre of liberal ethical activists. For about two decades now, this change of mood has manifested itself at the New York School of the HUC-JIR by students linking their perennial dedication to ethics with an interest in "text" or "sources." By these charged terms they do not mean study of the Prophets but of classically authoritative Jewish teaching, *halakhah.*

This turn to the rabbis has increasingly plunged us into the current storm of problems clustering around the term "hermeneutics." Texts, we are continually reminded these days, do not read themselves or philologically disclose one true meaning. To read necessarily is to interpret and invest with meaning so academic rationality is not the only sure guide to The Truth but only another possible human hermenautic. We all "read" according to the presuppositions we bring to the document before us. While some of these can be stated, others remain implicit, perhaps to surface in a contest between rival readings. How, then, are we Reform Jews to read the rabbis? This is not merely an academic issue for us since unlikely literary or historical texts - themselves bedeviled by hermeneutic issues - we come to the rabbis seeking to define our religious duty. We grant them a certain authority over our lives (just how much being highly debated among us) so how they may properly help define our moral responsibility, our primary means of serving God, quickly becomes a critical human/religious issue for us.

Though I have called this an issue for "Reform Jews" that is true only on an organizational but not on a personal level. Only Reform Judaism has made informed, conscientious self-determination a formal part of ideology. In theory, Orthodox Jews follow the rules of the *rav*, Conservative Jews of their Commission on Law and Standards (or, in split decisions, their local rabbi's ruling), and Reconstructionists the democratic decisions of their community. In fact, most Jews, regardless of label, insist on personal autonomy, listening to their authorities but then making up their own minds. Crypto-Reform Judaism is the effective decision-making mode of most American Jews and this makes the issue under discussion far more than one movement's dilemma.

Once we grant autonomy pride of place in determining our obligations as Jews we cannot be satisfied with our older communal patterns of reaching decisions. The juristic model of the past fails us because great decisors, the *poskim,* are not expected to persuade the independent inquirer but only to rule for the faithful. For our liberal purposes it is troubling that they do not often go beyond legal reasoning to explain why they read just these texts and not certain others, emphasize some and play down others, arriving, therefore, at just this rather than another conclusion. Jewish tradition - like other legal systems - excuses the judge from significant hermeneutic self-disclosure. This system works as long as one can accept the decisor's special competence but only a minority today will regularly allow their faith in a given sage's scholarship and piety to override "conscience." The same reluctance to share the reasoning behind the "reading" characterizes decisions made by a group.

Modern Jews until recently avoided this problem by reading Jewish texts - insofar as they cared to do so - with the eyes of urban , liberal culture. The sophisticates did so by applying some version of neo-Kantian universal reason. But neither group granted Jewish texts any independent value in their deliberations. Rather they cited the Bible or the rabbis only to show that Judaism could agree with the enlightened conscience. The many texts which differed with the modern liberal consensus were ignored. The Conservative movement has made a valiant effort to overcome this problem by maintaining fealty to the *halakhah* but reading it with a sense of its historical and thus ever-developing nature. This strategy only postpones facing the hermeneutic issue. No one can tell us just what "the halakhic process" can and cannot allow. (And those who must study and live by it deny the authenticity of such Conservative views as have been put forward.) Moreover, no one can tell us when the claims of historic development must be recognized - as in women's rights - and when they must be rejected - as in the far better historical case for patrilineal Jewish identity.

The need to move toward a new hermeneutic for non-Orthodox Jewish ethics lead me to create a course at the HUC-JIR, New York, in which we would respond to the loss of deductive methodological clarity by proceeding inductively. First, students would render a Jewish religious decision on a contemporary ethical issue of some concern to them, doing so according to a schema I worked out (after some initial experience with the course.) Having done do, they would then reflect on the experience to see what it had taught them - and us all - about the living nature of Reform Jewish decision-making. I do not mean to suggest by this that ours was an exercise in pure induction, whatever that is. Rather, as will become clear in a moment, we began with certain rough affirmations - contemporary ethical pluralism; the "authority" of halakhic texts; and personal autonomy - and tried to see what would happen as we moved forward guided by them.

The course was began in the mid-1980's and by 1987 some of the students papers seemed to me of such substantive interest that in 1988 and then again in 1989 and 1990, the College made them available to interested alumni in desktop publishing form. The eight students in these three booklets evoked sufficient appreciation that I thought they should be made available in more permanent form. Fortunately the course work of 1991 and 1992 produced six more publishable studies and it is these fourteen efforts which comprise this volume.

After some experience I worked out a six-step schema for preceding that promised good results. First, students were to find a "fruitful" problem to study. This meant an issue of concern to them, on which the *halakhah* had something to say, preferably with some difference of opinion, and on which there was contemporary general literature, again preferably with differing views. Second, a preliminary survey of the general ethical literature would indicate where the ethical issue was thought to lie, thus clarifying what Jewish study would be specifically relevant. Third, students were to study the pertinent halakhic material as intensively as possible, paying particular attention to divergent views and disciplining themselves to ask what the sources they intuitively disagreed with might yet have to teach them. Fourth, the general ethical material was to be treated in similar fashion. Fifth, based on their study of the diverse Jewish and general sources, they were to render a decision on the issue. In setting this forth they were to explain best as they could their reasons for arriving at just this decision rather than another. That done, sixth, they were to step back and see what their work had taught them about a desirable method for responsible decision-making today.

It was quite a task for one semester's work, most students not only carry a full schedule with other courses but also being involved in their student congregations. Some of the pressure was alleviated by having students work in partnership, It was quite a task for one semester's work, most students not only carry a full schedule with other courses but also being involved in their student congregations. Some of the pressure was alleviated by having students work in partnership, *hevruta*, though a few preferred to work alone. Not all the students who took this course wanted to have their papers published. While

I briefly indicated to those who did what I thought they might do to make their papers more appropriate for publication, the final version is theirs. readers should keep an open mind that this is essentially a student publication.

In winding up this project I thought all of us would benefit by having someone not associated with it respond critically to what we had done. I therefore invited Professor Louis Newman of Carelton College, one of our most astute analyst of contemporary Jewish ethical activity, to react to these studies as he thought appropriate. I was delighted when he agreed to do so.

Copious thanks are do to the many people whose help made the publication of this volume possible. Chief of these are the students who worked to high standards under intense pressure. The project became practical because Dean Lawrence Raphael suggested we utilize our school's new laser printer for some desktop publishing and then loyally supported our efforts. Dean Norman Cohen supplied special help for our continuing publication. Professor Michael Chernick so regularly and generously guided students in their halakhic research that he is surely the unofficial sponsor of everything worthwhile in this effort. All of us remain very grateful to Dr. Philip Miller and his staff in the College Library for their gracious response to the exceptional demands which this effort imposed upon them. Special tribute must be paid to Henry Resnick of the Library staff for unstintingly sharing his wide knowledge of books and texts. Michael Cahana brought his computer literacy to bear on the problems connected with assembling all this material. I do not see how this volume would have been possible without the generosity and dedication of Paula Dubrow, a graduate student at the College. She graciously lavished her energy and talents as a graphic designer on this complicated effort. Seeing how her love of Judaism brought her to dedicate herself to the sacrificial task has been an inspiration to me. Then, too, the book exists because of Jacob Behrman's continuing love of things Jewish, particularly rabbinical students. Our association goes back over more than three decades now and I remain, as ever, enthralled by his special charm and honored by his unfailing friendship. This book finally became a reality because of Dan and Betty Golumb, involved leaders and enthusiastic supporters of Reform Judaism. Their quiet, generous gift to The Sanek Institute at HUC-JIR for the publication of the volume transformed a dream into a fact and we are deeply grateful. May God's blessing rest on the work and all involved in it.

**Note**

\*Exploring Jewish Ethics (Wayne State University Press, Detroit: 1990) pp. 22-25, but more particularly in papers No.2, "'Jewish?' 'Ethics?' 'Jewish Ethics?' - The New Problems." And No. 30, "Rethinking the Reform Jewish Theory of Social Action." The transition is described in Renewing the Covenant (The Jewish Publication Society, Philadelphia, 1991) pp. 9-52.

# Learning to be Led: Reflections on Reform Jewish Ethics and Halakhah"

Louis E. Newman
Carleton College

**C**ontemporary liberal Jews who turn to classical Jewish tradition for insight on current moral problems must address a number of questions. How can halakhic texts, which derive from distant times and places, speak to contemporary, often unprecedented, ethical issues? To what extent can these Jewish legal sources inform the ethical deliberations of those who do not see themselves as bound by the authority of those laws, yet who look to them for guidance? How can informed and sensitive liberal Jews resolve the conflict they often find between the norms embedded in Jewish tradition and those espoused by secular ethicists? The essays collected here attest to the seriousness with which the newest generation of Reform rabbis address these questions, as well as to their creativity and sincerity in searching for answers. In methodological terms, these exercises in developing a Reform Jewish ethic enable us to appreciate the formidable obstacles that liberal Jews encounter when they use halakhic sources in an endeavor which is explicitly not bound by *halakhah*. In all, they give us insight into the hearts and minds of those who firmly believe that the tradition has something of great value to teach them, but are certain neither what that is or whether, once discovered, it is the sort of guidance they are ready to follow. Thus, they display a profound willingness to engage the tradition, a determination to apply its norms to contemporary Jewish life, and yet, a deep reticence to be led by it.

## I. Turning to Tradition: The Challenges
There are two fundamental problems to which each of these essays in its own way constitutes a response. To appreciate these challenges – which I shall call the challenge of differentiating the "time-bound from the timeless" and that of balancing the "particular and the universal" – we must attend first to the presuppositions, shared by all these authors, which give rise to them. Like liberals in all religious movements, these writers believe that religious and moral truths (or at least our understanding of them) evolve over time. As liberal religious leaders, it is their task to separate the "wheat from the chaff,"

that which is timeless from that which is merely the misapprehension of an earlier age.

The first and perhaps most striking feature of these essays is that, without exception, they presuppose that classical Jewish texts, especially legal texts, are relevant sources of moral insight for late twentieth century Jews. Modest as this assumption may seem, it is by no means unassailable. Only a generation ago, Reform rabbis, under the still prevalent influence of classical Reform antinomianism, viewed *halakhah* as a largely antiquated remnant of an earlier age, of historical interest perhaps, but not particularly relevant to current moral issues. Certainly, Reform rabbis faced with moral questions from their congregants would not have been inclined to search medieval talmudic commentaries and responsa for guidance. (The work of Solomon Freehof represents a singular exception to this generalization.) In viewing *halakhah* in general as an aspect of the tradition which may contain timeless truths, these Reform rabbis demonstrate their willingness to take a broader view of tradition than did their predecessors.

Second, these essays all presuppose that Jews may have moral obligations particular to their own group, arising out of their own relationship with God, and so not necessarily shared by non-Jews. For many, the covenant between God and Israel is the foundation of these moral obligations or at least the context within which Jews will seek to understand those duties that they share with the rest of humankind. This, too, represents a significant departure from the view prevalent in an earlier period of Reform. Under the influence of Enlightenment thought, it had been assumed that ethical obligations by their very nature were universal, the same for Jews as for everyone else, and that they could be discovered through the proper use of reason. Of course, if all moral obligations are universal, then Jewish ethics is merely the particular Jewish articulation of these universal norms. These authors, by contrast, are open to the possibility that Jewish moral obligations may not coincide with those that would be recognized by moral philosophers as applicable to all people, thus Jewish ethics must be constructed (at least in part) out of particular Jewish sources.

These basic assumptions lead directly to two challenges. First, these authors recognize that, while the *halakhah* as a whole is a source of moral guidance and must be taken seriously, not every law or principle is equally valuable. Rather, they must delineate within *halakhah* between that which is timeless from that which is not. The former will be relevant to our moral situation, a source of moral insights and guidance, while the latter will be viewed as outdated or at least inapplicable to our current moral situation. Second, these authors recognize that those for whom they write are both Jews and human beings. Accordingly, they seek moral guidance which is both specifically Jewish and consistent with moral norms that apply universally. Unfortunately, Jewish and secular morals rarely coincide completely. This forces them to search for a balance between what they perceive to be their particular obligations as Jews and their universal obligations as human beings. As Kaplan and Memis put it, the dilemma that confronts every Jew in the postmodern world is "making sense of and valuing our own ethical system in terms of the existence of attractive competing systems."

These two challenges – how to distinguish within the *halakhah* between that which is relevant and that which is not, and how to resolve the incongruity between our moral obligations as Jews and as human beings – are inescapable given the liberal Jewish enterprise as these authors understand it. But, as their essays amply attest, these Reform rabbis are both fully cognizant of these challenges and deeply committed to facing them squarely. A number of approaches to these challenges can be discerned among these exercises in developing a Reform Jewish ethic.

## II. Turning to Tradition: Reform Approaches

In their effort to meet the challenges outlined above, these Reform rabbis utilize a number of familiar intellectual and exegetical strategies. This is most apparent in their efforts to discern those aspects of the tradition that speak to a contemporary moral problem. They most definitely do not begin by assuming *a priori* that certain types of texts, or texts of a certain period or by certain authors, are necessarily pertinent while others are not. Rather, much like their Orthodox counterparts, they search the breadth of biblical and rabbinic literature for legal precedents and the opinions of previous authorities on related questions. In doing so, they necessarily make judgments about which traditional cases are analogous, and much of the subsequent discussion depends upon how these judgments are made.

In some cases, such as the use of corporal punishment or the treatment of animals, the views of earlier rabbinic authorities are directly and self-evidently relevant. In many other instances, the connection is far more tenuous, as when Wiener and Elkin extend rules governing the ancient Temple to the modern synagogue, or when Balin and Panken apply rabbinic advice about choosing a spouse to questions of germ cell gene therapy. Drawing analogies of this sort, while necessary, is always potentially controversial. There are no rules to determine when and how to use a particular traditional precedent, how far to extend an analogy, or when slight differences between two cases render the legal inference invalid. While the same can be said for Orthodox legalists engaged in the same enterprise, the problem is even more acute for Reform rabbis who, by their own admission, are outsiders to the world of halakhic decision-making. The only criteria for success in this regard might be creativity and attentiveness to detail, both of which are much in evidence here. In this connection I am impressed by the efforts of Groffman and Millstein to find precedents for issues of hazardous waste disposal and Levin's attempt to apply rabbinic texts to right-to-work laws. The legal arguments of Reform ethicists will be most convincing when the authors are explicit about the analogies on which they rely and, more importantly, when they have reflected on the possible limitations of those same analogies.

A further strategy for extracting the relevant moral meaning from classical halakhic texts, and one much in evidence here, is to rely less on specific legal precedents and more on broad moral-theological principles. Indeed, this approach is especially appealing to these writers insofar as it allows for the greatest flexibility of interpretation and also facilitates the comparison between Jewish and secular ethics (the latter relying largely on philosophical principles). True to their education as western intellectuals and as religious liberals, these authors are most comfortable when they can ground their moral judgments about a particular situation in a broader principle. The appeal of general statements or values over specific case law is expressed forcefully by Brazen and Freeman in their discussion of intervening in the life of an alcoholic:

"...we believe halakhic principles work within a system of Jewish values upon which we can ground a Jewish decision. These values are implicit rather than explicit and are gleaned from whatever we have accumulated in our study and living of Judaism. Examples of these kind of values include sanctity of life, social responsibilities, and the dignity of the individual."

The effort to rely upon general moral principles is by no means incompatible with close attention to cases and precedents; indeed, they often go hand in hand. Often these writers proceed to derive ethical guidance from the tradition by discerning a general principle that appears to underlie a series of traditional rulings and even an entire area of the law. In such cases, these writers often feel that Jewish tradition mandates following the general principle, even if this leads to ignoring a precedent which might otherwise govern the case. This strategy is most apparent when the traditional case law appears to go against the perceived values of the tradition. Pomerantz and Stern speak directly to this in the context of their treatment of employee rights.

"While principles such as *b'tzelem elohim* and *matan torah* undergird *halakhah*, *halakhah* does not always take these concepts as far as we would like. ...Recent trends towards changing the structure and definition of the employment relationship ...extend workers' rights farther than *halakhah* found necessary. Thus while meta-halakhic principles such as *b'tzelem elohim* have a primary role in shaping our conclusions, the further development of such principles in the general ethical literature and in court rulings ... represents an enhancement of the halakhic position."

In general, then, when basic moral principles within Jewish tradition appear to conflict with the thrust of halakhic rulings, these Reform ethicists will tend to favor the principles.

The last major tool for discerning the morally applicable aspects of *halakhah* relies on sensitivity to historical context and especially to historical change. In distinguishing those aspects of the tradition that are relevant from those that are not historical judgment plays a critical role. To the extent that these authors discern an historical development within the traditional sources, they take this as license to endorse a moral position still further along the same trajectory. The treatment by Lieber and Symons of corporal punishment in schools offers a case in point.

"We acknowledge that the *halakhah* permits, and according to some, encourages the use of corporal punishment. However, we see a chronologically progressive trend towards a more liberal point of view. Were the *halakhah* to be written today, taking into account the nature of the American public school system, we believe that it would firmly decry the use of corporal punishment in public schools."

Such inferences, of course, rely upon a number of assumptions and judgments which cannot be verified. They assume that the thrust of tradition is uni-directional, that halakhic authorities of the past would not have considered reversing that trend rather than continuing it. By the same token, they assume that our historical situation is sufficiently different from that dealt with in the past that the same principles employed to reach one conclusion then would support a different conclusion today. There is no way to confirm or disconfirm such inferences, it is simply important to note that they play an important role in all such appeals to historical development.

The appeal to historical context takes other forms as well. Many of these authors interpret or dismiss certain traditional views as products of an historical situation that no longer exists. Thus, Kraus concludes his discussion of child custody arrangements by acknowledging that gender roles today are significantly different than they were in earlier times. "Contemporary Jews might co-opt the tradition's concern with the young child's primary need for physical stability and constant nurture without co-opting the assumption that a woman, by definition, is the more appropriate choice to meet that need." Similarly, Joselow and Stone recognize that the advanced state of current medical technology undermines some of the distinctions that traditional authorities were able to make with respect to care of the dying. They summarize their approach as follows: "Here we value the Reform approach, which seeks to carefully balance the halakhically informed Jewish approach with our sense that the human understanding of how best to manifest the divine in our world may be sometimes better informed through science, even if it flies in the face of traditional teaching." Thus, we always discern God's will in a specific historical context. Given the scientific age in which we live, our knowledge of the world may lead us to assess our moral choices very differently than did rabbis of earlier times.

Even after these rabbis have determined which portions of the tradition, which texts and which interpretations of them, speak to us on a given issue, they still face a second challenge. Jewish teaching rarely coincides completely with our perceived moral duties either as human beings or as Americans living in a multi-religious, multi-ethnic society. To be sure, there is often extensive overlap and these rabbis are reassured when they discovery that Jewish tradition and secular ethics instruct them to follow similar paths. So, Groffman and Millstein note that Jewish and secular teachings about hazardous waste point in similar directions, albeit for different reasons. At times, the differences too can be illuminating. Thus Cohen, Dantowitz and Schloss conclude, "...this process has taught us the value of drawing from both the secular and Jewish worlds. ...The process of forming a liberal Jewish ethic allowed us to benefit from the lenses that each tradition provided. The result is thus richer because it draws from the different concerns and sensitivities of each."

More troubling are those instances in which Jewish teaching directly challenges deeply held secular, liberal values. When this happens, the tensions between particular Jewish and general human responsibilities must be mediated. This often requires significant reinterpretations of Jewish values and it is here that the rabbis' creativity is most in evidence. In discussing the ethics of being truthful with terminally ill patients, Kaplan concludes, "Another strategy we have used is to address aspects of a value not considered in the *halakhah*; we took comfort and turned it into a motive on behalf of telling rather than as a motive for not telling. Finally, we took a value, redemption, that seemed obsolete and reinterpreted it along lines meaningful to a modern Jew." Evidently, then, the tension between opposing values can stimulate these writers to delve more deeply into both worlds so as to develop a moral position which is at once recognizablv Jewish and consonant with their own moral intuitions. This reflects, not an effort to ignore or minimize genuine moral conflicts, but rather a search for wholeness. It bespeaks a profound belief that our lives as Jews and as human beings ultimately must be unified.

This belief is strongly attested throughout these essays; indeed, it could be said to be the most deeply and widely held conviction of all. And yet, there is much in these exercises that points in quite another direction. It may be that the emphasis on finding common ground between Jewish and secular ethics belies widespread anxiety about whether such a unity really exists. In closing, I want to draw attention to the ambivalence that appears to underlie these essays and to the challenge implicit within it.

### III. Turning to Tradition: Authority vs. Freedom
In cases of significant conflict, virtually without exception the authors give preference to liberal, humanistic values over more conservative, traditional Jewish values. The reasons for this are complex and, I suspect, only partly revealed in the essays themselves. The most com-

monly offered rationale for such choices is the value of autonomy and the corresponding freedom of human choice and expression that is so basic to a modern liberal perspective. This, of course, underlies the oft-repeated admission that for Reform Jews the *halakhah* after all is instructive, but not authoritative; it guides, but cannot command. Thus, one is free as a matter of principle to demur when one finds halakhic rules and values morally objectionable.

The deeper question, however, and the one less directly addressed by the rabbis, is why a moral principle that restricts personal freedom and autonomy is objectionable. If these writers stand, as they claim, between two worlds, drawing moral guidance (equally) from each, we would expect that at least some of the time Jewish values would override even these cardinal secular values. The fact that this rarely happens (Brazen and Freeman's decision to intervene in the life of an alcoholic is perhaps the only exception) requires interpretation. Part of the explanation may be found in the following methodological reflections by Joselow and Stone:

"We find ourselves, then, advocating the libertarian position regarding this issue: ultimately, each one of us must have the right to exercise autonomy over our own lives. If we find *halakhah* instructive, that is all to the good, for it teaches respect for life and compassion for the human condition. We reserve the right, however, to weigh its injunctions against the information we receive outside its boundaries, and to judge it as equally valid in the formulation of our final decision. This is the hardest decision-making process of all, and the one modeled for us by respondents such as Isserles and Feinstein: to gather all the information available, even that which conflicts with ones prejudiced perspective; not to rely on the recitation of precedent, but to create new ones for each new case; to ever be responsive to the unique human needs of each new situation. For us, this situational approach reflects the ultimate morality, demands the deepest degree of intellectual and emotional honesty, and presents the highest level of difficulty."

In short, for these and many of the other authors here, halakhic considerations contribute to a process of ethical decision-making, but do not necessarily influence the nature of the process itself. That process is, of course, non-halakhic in the sense that Reform Judaism does not recognize the binding authority of Jewish law. But it is also non-halakhic in a deeper sense, for it presupposes values which themselves may be at odds with those of Jewish tradition. Autonomy and personal freedom are not merely secular values which, if challenged by *halakhah*, may be overridden; they are embedded in the very process by which both *halakhah* and secular perspectives are weighed and interpreted and through which a Reform Jewish ethic is constructed.

It does not necessarily follow from this that the value of autonomy is supreme in all cases. But these Reform ethicists clearly begin with a presumption in its favor, and this (together with personal experience and moral intuitions) shapes their perceptions of moral situations and their readings of the tradition. A more cynical critic might seize upon this fact as evidence that these Reform thinkers have not taken *halakhah* seriously after all and are being disingenuous when they claim to have done so. And while I concede that there is always the danger that one is not being fully honest with oneself, I prefer to judge the matter differently.

The relationship between Reform Jewish ethics and *halakhah* as evidenced by these essays reflects the ultimate situation of modern, liberal Jews. They wish to preserve their tradition, but not at the cost of abandoning their modern, intellectual commitments. They look to their tradition for instruction, but are not prepared to sacrifice their freedom to its authority. It follows that when they enter the world of halakhic discourse, they do so on their own terms; insofar as they do not share the presuppositions of that world, they could be said to work with the sources, but not in them. To expect that they approach *halakhah* "halakhically" is to expect them to be something other than what they are: Reform Jews. Their efforts to appropriate halakhic values and categories in the development of a Reform Jewish ethic, then, must be judged by other criteria – the extent to which they respect and understand those sources, think creatively about them, and finally are honest about the very process in which they are engaged. And, while the various contributors to this volume have not all succeeded equally in this respect (nor should we have expected them to), there is, as I have indicated, abundant evidence here of resourcefulness, critical thought, and sensitivity.

But this analysis does not quite answer the question I raised earlier. Granted that Reform Jews will necessarily begin their investigations of tradition with a prior commitment to personal freedom and autonomy, there is no reason to suppose that this must be an absolute value in Reform Jewish ethics. To put the question more forcefully: under what circumstances might a Reform ethicist engaged in serious study of the tradition set aside his or her commitment to autonomy in favor of embracing the *halakhah's* less liberal perspective? No clear answer emerges from these essays in part, I suspect, because the question has not been fully addressed. It is here I believe that *halakhah* presents its most serious challenge to Reform. For while no one expects Reform rabbis to abandon the value of autonomy, it is not unreasonable to expect them to consider its limitations.

In the end it seems that as these rabbis draw upon the *halakhah*, they come face to face with the problem of religious authority. As they grapple with specific issues, they are quite capable of appropriating halakhic texts and in this way they find significant moral guidance within the tradition. In a more general way, however, they seem unwilling or unable to acknowledge a source of authority outside of themselves, whether in *halakhah* or elsewhere. Thus the greatest challenge, over and above a willingness to take halakhic perspectives seriously and to draw out their implications in specific cases, is to take seriously what the *halakhah* represents: a source of transcendent authority. To do so would mean to entertain the possibility of surrendering one's autonomy to halakhic precedent some of the time (which is far different from the Orthodox insistence that it is a requirement to do so all of the time). To do less, I submit, is to shy away from the deepest, most meaningful challenge that *halakhah* presents to Reform Jews.

These essays, then, attest to what is most enduring about modern liberal Judaism, its commitment to making traditional values speak to modern Jews. They also demonstrate the abilities of this generation of Reform rabbis to interpret halakhic texts responsibly and creatively. But even as they find great value and insight in their tradition, they remain unwilling to relinquish authority to it. *Halakhah* provides important guidance, but these Reform Jews at least insist on retaining control of how and when it will enter into their ethical deliberations. *Halakhah* can instruct them and help them to see their moral choices in a new light, but they will not permit it to lead them to a conclusion they find unacceptable on other grounds. They have opened themselves up to the message of traditional texts, but not to their authority. Insofar as personal freedom remains paramount, *halakhah* can be incorporated comfortably within Reform ethics alongside other value systems. But *halakhah* as a value system forces upon them another question, under what circumstances can modern liberal Jews allow themselves to be led or, what amounts to the same thing, recognize the existence of a moral authority which limits their autonomy. That question, it seems to me, remains to be answered.

# Inter-
# personal
# Issues

# Corporal Punishment in Public School:

## A Responsible Reform Jewish Ethical Decision

Valerie Lieber
and Ronald B. B. Symons

You are rabbi of a Chicago congregation. Corporal punishment is legal in the state of Illinois. According to the legislation, each individual school district may choose to limit the use of corporal punishment beyond the limits of the state, or it may choose to abolish it all together. One of your congregants, a member of the local school board which is currently reviewing the question of corporal punishment in the district, approaches you seeking your rabbinic advice concerning the issue.

Is corporal punishment allowed according to Jewish Law? If so, under what circumstances may it be used? What methods of corporal punishment are allowed and forbidden?

Her questions reach beyond the scope of halakhic concerns. As a Reform Jew, she seeks your advice with regard to general ethical concerns as well. What are the psychological effects of corporal punishment? Has it been found to be an effective educational tool? Are there alternative methods which yield the same or better results?

## Methodological Concerns

In order to approach this question, we need to examine both pre-halakhic and halakhic material. Although the former, specifically Bible, was not considered binding by earlier generations, it clearly informed the world view of the Rabbis.

In this particular case, we find no legalistic biblical material because during the biblical era the responsibility of educating children was still on the father, and there was no formal communal educational system. The closest legal material that we have is that of the rebellious son.[1] Since all later rabbinic traditions discounted the possibility of such an extreme case, and limited the parameters of such a case in order to prevent its occurrence, we have excluded it from our discussion.

Therefore, with regard to biblical references to corporal punishment, we will be using both wisdom literature and narrative to begin our discussion. As the texts proceed chronologically, the issue of corporal punishment expands in the halakhic material to include the realm of the communal school where the teacher serves *in loco parentis*. The weight of our discussion is on this later material.

In both the halakhic and general ethical material, the masculine pronoun is assumed for both teacher and student. This in no way reflects our opinion of the gender of those who administer or receive corporal punishment. We have decided to use this same language in order to be consistent with both the halakhic and American legal texts. We do not intend the masculine pronoun to suggest universality.

## The Halakhic Discussion

### Bible

As far as children go, Eli the priest had it bad. He would have liked sons who followed in his footsteps, but they didn't. Not only did they abuse the privileges of the priesthood, but all the people of Israel knew about it, and Eli heard the rumors. He was outraged when he reprimanded his sons,

> Why do you do such things? I get evil reports about you from the people on all hands. Don't, my sons! It is no favorable report I hear the people of the Lord spreading about.[2]

But, his heartfelt plea fell on deaf ears and they continued in their evil ways.[3]

What alternatives did the aging Eli have? Obviously his verbal rebuke did no good. According to God's later judgement, the fault lay with Eli himself.

> And I declare to him [Eli] that I sentence his house to endless punishment for the iniquity he knew about – how his sons committed sacrilege at will - and he did not hit them (*khihah bam*).[4]

God withdrew the priestly dynasty from Eli because he chose to speak to his children instead of hitting them!

Corporal punishment and verbal rebuke went hand in hand in biblical days. "Rod and reproof produce wisdom, but a lad out of control is a disgrace to his mother."[5] Eli's mistake was that he used just one of the two acceptable disciplinary methods.

Yet, it seems that the authors of the Bible were aware of the fact that corporal punishment is often more effective than verbal rebuke. "Discipline (*yasair*) your son and he will give you peace; he will gratify you with dainties."[6]

It appears that the Bible sets no limits with regard to corporal punishment. Disciplining a child is a way of saving that child from future sin. Fear of the child's death at the hand of the rod is no deterrent.

Apply your mind to discipline (*lamusar*)

And your ears to wise sayings.

Do not withhold discipline from a child;

Beat him with a rod

And you will save him from Sheol.[7]

## Mishnah

The Rabbis of the Mishnah (who lived no later than the 3rd century C.E.) focused their discussion of corporal punishment on the very issue of limitations. Assuming that the common manner of corporal punishment remained the rod, we can identify the Tanayim as continuing in the tradition set forth in the Book of Proverbs.

The issue of excessive corporal punishment is discussed in connection to those who must flee to a city of refuge. The biblical source of the discussion is based on an accident in the woods.

For instance, a man goes with his neighbor into a grove to cut wood; as his hand swings the ax to cut down a tree, the ax-head flies off the handle and strikes the other so that he dies. That man shall flee to one of these cities and live.[8]

So, if one accidently committed homicide he may flee to a city of refuge in order to escape the blood avengers.

In the Mishnah, the comparison is made between the woodcutter and the father who hits his son, the teacher who strikes his students, and the court representative who performs his duty; in all cases, death accidentally results from the blow. In these three latter cases, the "killer" is not liable for his actions and need not flee to a city of refuge.[9]

What exempts the father, teacher, and court representative from liability? Rabbi Ovadiah Yarei of Bartenura (15th century Italy) comments on the exemption of "the father who hit his son" that this is "surely a positive commandment" (for the father to hit his son). Rabbi Yomtov Lippmann Heller (16th/17th century

Germany) comments that this case is one when the father is attempting "to direct his son to the truthful path." (He attributes this statement to Rashi.) Neither comments about the case of the teacher.[10]

The Mishnah continues: "The father goes into exile because of his son, and the son goes into exile because of the father."[11] This contradictory statement needs explanation. Bartenura comments that the father must go into exile, i.e. is liable for the death of his son, "when he hit him for an ulterior motive aside from teaching him Torah, morals (*musar*), or his primary craft (*omanut*)." Yomtov Lippmann Heller questions the commentary of Bartenura looking for proof texts for both morals and primary craft. But, he does not suggest a proof text for the teaching of Torah, perhaps because there is no dispute over it (especially in his day). Whether it be father or teacher who accidently kills a child at the time of Torah instruction, neither is liable for the death of the child.[12]

The only commentary on the Mishnah which does comment on the case of the teacher fatally striking a student is that of the 20th century Hanoch Albeck. Commenting on the word "strike" (*rodeh*), Albeck explains that this is to be done with "a strap."[13]

The anachronisms are abundant. First of all, Albeck speaks of a strap while the only instrument of corporal punishment spoken of up to the time of the Mishnah is a rod. The strap, as we will see, is an injunction of later traditions. Second, up until this point, there has been no definition of the circumstances in which a father may strike his son. Bartenura, with the textual support of Yomtov Lippmann, reads later values into an earlier text which has made no such claims.

At this point, through biblical and mishnaic times, we only know three things about corporal punishment. Corporal punishment was a favored means of discipline. A rod was used to carry out the task. Under certain circumstances (which are unclear) both father and teacher were exempt from liability should the child accidently die at their hands.

The rest of Rabbinic literature continues to deal with the extreme case of accidental death, but more attention is given to the parameters which regulate the administration of corporal punishment.

## Talmud

The Rabbis of the Talmud (who lived between the 3rd and 6th centuries) had a way of framing this entire discussion. "The left hand should always repel while the right hand draws close."[14] According to their perspective, assuming a right-handed dominant society, the weaker left hand repels while the stronger right hand draws close. One's stronger inclination should be to draw close.

It was during the talmudic period that restrictions were put on the instrument of discipline.

> Rav said to Rav Samuel the son of Shilath: Before the age of six do not accept pupils; from that age you can accept them, and stuff them with Torah like an ox. Rav also said to Rav Samuel the son of Shilath: When you punish (*ki maḥit*) a pupil, only hit him with a shoe strap (*b'arkata dimasne*).[15]

This discussion is clearly framed in a communal educational setting. The talmudic era was the time when formalized community education of children began.[16] We know that the children about whom we are speaking are at least six years old. The Rabbis have clearly moved away from the tradition of using a rod to discipline children. Why a shoe strap? Later, Rashi (12th century) would explain that the reason for using a shoe strap is that it will inflict "a light hit that will not cause damage."[17] We learn through Rashi's comment that the result of corporal punishment should be temporary pain as opposed to long term physical damage. Therefore, the strap is the preferred instrument.

Regarding the passage, "When you punish a pupil...," the text does not demand that the teacher should punish a pupil. Rather, it begins to explain the parameters for corporal punishment at a time when the teacher deems it necessary. We are not told when corporal punishment is necessary; we are only told what instrument to use.

This passage becomes the standard for two indisputable halakhic principles. First, children do not enter school before the age of six; and second, corporal punishment is administered through the use of a small leather strap resembling that of a shoe (most probably a sandal strap).

### Mishneh Torah

Maimonides (12th century) addresses the issue of corporal punishment in the school in two separate discussions. He concurs with the above passage in *Baba Batra* with regard to the age of the child. The child should be no less than six or seven when he begins his formal education. He elaborates on the issue of corporal punishment.

> The teacher hits (*makeh*) them [the students] in order to instill them with fear (*aimah*). But he does not hit them with a vengeful hit (*makat oyaiv*) or an excessive hit (*makat akhzari*). Therefore, he shall not hit (*yakeh*) them with whips (*shutim*) nor sticks (*maklot*); rather with a small strap (*retzuah kitanah*).[18]

Maimonides clearly adds to the development of the *halakhah* the issue of "instilling fear" upon the students. But he specifically remarks that the teacher must be in complete control of his own state of mind at the time of the punishment. This is not an opportunity for the teacher to vent his own anger or frustration, nor his own personal dislike for a specific student. The administration of corporal punishment should be carried out with an unbiased disposition. We still don't know under what circumstances a child is to be hit, but we do know that whips and sticks are clearly prohibited by Maimonides.

While commenting on this passage, Rabbi Abraham diBoton of 18th century Salonika explains that

> ...those who can read, shall read; and those who can't read shall join together with a peer [who can read]. That is to say: He [the teacher] hit (hakah) them with a small strap and the child who will listen because of the hit will read. But he who will not listen and will not read will be joined together with a peer. That is to say: At least he will be there in the group and he will understand a little of what the others say.[19]

Are Abraham diBoton's assumptions implicit in Maimonides' understanding of corporal punishment? This is not clear. Maimonides does not elaborate on the circumstances under which the teacher should administer corporal punishment. All that we know is that an 18th century Jew made this comment. We don't know under what circumstances Maimonides advises teachers to use corporal punishment.

Nonetheless, according to this 18th century comment, corporal punishment was used as a motivation and a method of self-discipline in order to encourage better reading skills. There is no evidence of it being used solely in reaction to misbehavior; however, it seems to be used in order to keep the student on task. While this is the written "learned" tradition, we wonder whether the "lived" tradition was different. Was corporal punishment also used simply as a reaction to misbehavior and not as an initial motivational tool?

In another discussion about the case of accidental death, Maimonides continues the tradition found in the Mishnah.

> The son who accidently kills his father goes into exile just as the father who accidently kills his son. With regard to what is this referring? This refers to [an incident] that did not happen at a time of studying or if he [the father] was teaching him [the son] a secondary craft (omanut aheret) for which he [the son] has no use. But, if he [the father] punished (yasar) him [the son] in order to teach him Torah, philosophy (hokhmah), or his primary craft (omanut) and he [the son] died, then he [the father] is exempt

> [from exile and is not liable for the son's death]. And so it is with the rabbi (*rav*) who strikes (*makeh*) his student or the representative of the court who strikes the litigant who refuses to come to judgment and accidentally causes him to die, [both] are exempt from exile as it is written concerning the woodcutter and the issues of domain (*divrei har'shut*), "The father who hits his son, the rabbi who strikes his student, and the representative of the court," for alas, his unintentional act and the resultant death was at the time of the performance of a commandment.[20]

The assumption is that if accidental death occurs at the time of the performance of a commandment, then the "killer" is not liable for the death. All of the commentators comment with regard to the issue of the court representative, but no one questions the role of the rabbi and his student.[21]

### Arbaah Turim

In his brevity, Jacob ben Asher (13th/14th century) only gives us one line regarding the issue of the teacher using corporal punishment on his student. While he does agree with Maimonides in method of punishment, there is a subtle difference in the use of language. "And the teacher will hit (*yakeh*) them in order to instill fear upon them...."[22]

Is the difference between "hits" (*makeh*) (as found in Maimonides) and "will hit" (*yakeh*) instructive or just trivial? Is Jacob ben Asher instructing us that the teacher should hit his student without provocation?

If we assume that both Maimonides and Jacob ben Asher intend corporal punishment to be used as a motivational tool, (as Abraham diBoton would have us believe), then the difference between Maimonides' present tense and Jacob ben Asher's future tense is inconsequential. Supposedly, if all of he students in the class could read, then there would be no need to administer corporal punishment.

However, if Jacob ben Asher disagreed with the Abraham diBoton's later claim, then the language difference is significant of a larger attitudinal shift. Perhaps the teacher "shall hit" the student on a regular basis regardless of the reading issue.

### Shulḥan Arukh

By the 16th century, Joseph Caro narrowed the instruction even more.

> The teacher shall not hit (*lo yakeh*) him with a vengeful hit (*makat oyaiv*) or with deadly chastise-

ment (*musar akhzari*); not with whips nor a stick, rather with a small strap.[23]

Caro did not instruct the teacher to hit the student, rather he framed the entire discussion in the negative. Perhaps this is exemplary of a small change in opinion.

While commenting on this passage, Rabbi Abraham Tzvi Hirsch Eisenstadt (19th century) added his bias to the discussion.

> See the responsum entitled *Kerit Hinah* section 23 concerning the ruling of a teacher who hit his student and broke his leg. He is obliged for five things and is excommunicated until he placates for the disgrace of his unintentional act.[24]

The 18th century responsum cited is based on the following Mishnah:

> He who injures his fellow is liable to [compensate] him on five counts: injury, pain, medical costs, loss of income [lit.: loss of time], and indignity. ...He who injures them [including a minor] is liable.[25]

This is a radical deviation from the norms already established. This teacher might have been acting within the regulations of corporal punishment, but he went one step too far. His excommunication and apology are indicative of his guilt even if this unintentional act occurred while he was performing a commandment.

## Summary

The general consensus within the *halakhah* is that corporal punishment is an accepted means of discipline. In the post-mishnaic literature, everyone agrees that only a small strap should be used (to the exclusion of a stick or whip) and that the teacher must be in control of his emotions at the time of administration.

The only clear opinion concerning the circumstances under which corporal punishment may be administered is that it can be used to motivate students to improve their reading skills. Maimonides' desire to instill fear upon the students can be read as another circumstance under which it may be used.

Both the desire to protect the rights of the teacher and the student are present. The latest opinion is that in the case of an abuse of the right to administer corporal punishment, the student's rights outweigh those of the teacher.

## The General
## Ethical Discussion

### An Overview of the Approaches

General ethics regarding corporal punishment in the schools can be characterized by three competing approaches.[26]

*The Conservative Approach:* There is a small group usually represented by religious fundamentalists mostly in southern states in rural areas[27] which supports the complete authority of the teacher over the student in which the interests of the student are altogether subordinated. According to this approach the teacher is thought to be *in loco parentis*, has ultimate rights and responsibilities to assert his authority, and should demand fear and respect.

*The Moderate Approach:* There is a large group which favors limited corporal punishment based on the principle that educators have duties to the student that have as their ultimate goal raising the child to fulfill some religiously, socially, and professionally agreed upon state that may not necessarily represent the direct self-interests of either the teacher or the child.

*The Liberal Approach:* There is a rapidly growing and already powerful group, led by the author of Teacher Effectiveness Training, Thomas Gordon; Adah Mauer, founder of the group "End Violence Against the Next Generation"[28]; and the United Nations, which favors the abolishment of corporal punishment in schools (and in the home). They argue that the student has individual interests and needs that must be given consideration and expression apart from those of educators. In other words, a child's personal emotional development should be considered before any other needs of the class, teacher, or society.

The moderate and liberal approaches may overlap to some degree in that some liberals whose guiding principle is identical with that of the moderate group, favor abolishment of corporal punishment in their own school district.

### The Legality of Corporal Punishment

As of February 1990 corporal punishment was banned in 19 states: Alaska, California, Connecticut, Hawaii, Iowa, Maine, Massachusetts, Michigan, Minnesota, Nebraska, New Hampshire, New Jersey, New York, North Dakota, Rhode Island, Vermont, Virginia, and Wisconsin. In the other 31 states corporal punishment is permitted in public schools. In these latter states, school boards of a number of major cities have abolished corporal punishment. Moreover, movements to abolish corporal punishment in public schools are currently underway in Maryland, Montana, Ohio, Tennessee, and Texas. Four of those states which permit corporal punishment (Florida, Georgia, Nevada, and West Virginia) mandate specific procedures to be followed in the administration of corporal punishment.[29]

### In Loco Parentis

The *in loco parentis* doctrine was imported to the United States from Great Britain, although it obviously has earlier roots in the halakhic material cited previously. The doctrine has evolved over time to become more restrictive of a teacher's rights, but in different geographical locations, the doctrine ranges in its permissiveness of teachers to administer corporal punishment.[30]

The legal doctrine of *in loco parentis* guides much of the American legal discussion of corporal punishment in public schools. Accordingly,

> A school teacher, to a limited extent at least, stands *in loco parentis* to pupils under his charge and may exercise such powers of control, restraint, and correction as may be reasonably necessary to enable him properly to perform his duties as a teacher and to accomplish the purposes of education.

> ...it has been said that when a pupil enters the school, the authority of the parent ceases and that of the teacher begins.[31]

### Regulations Concerning Corporal Punishment

Like the *halakhah*, the American legal discussion attempts to set limits on corporal punishment. In contradistinction to the *halakhah,* the American legal discussion speaks clearly with regard to a situation in which corporal punishment may be used.

> A teacher has the power to punish a pupil for all acts which are detrimental to the good order and best interests of the school, and for the breach of any regulations which it is within the power of the school authorities to adopt... But a pupil cannot properly be punished for breach of a regulation which is unreasonable, or with which it is beyond his power to comply.[32]

While the discussion of the "reasonableness" of the school regulations protects the rights of the student, ambiguity in the legislation allows for divergent interpretations.

In certain geographic areas, the issue of corporal punishment is regulated either by statute or school board regulations. As a result,

School boards and administrators have the power to promulgate and to enforce reasonable regulations governing students in attendance, with the power to impose reasonable nondiscriminatory corporal punishment for breaches thereof, without violating any federally protected constitutional rights of pupils.[33]

The American legal discussion, along with the *halakhah,* recognizes the need for limitations set upon the teacher. The language in both discussions is strikingly similar.[34]

While teachers are clothed with a discretionary authority with respect to the infliction of corporal punishment on their pupils, the punishment must be reasonable and confined within the bounds of moderation; that is, it must not be cruel or excessive, and the teacher must not act wantonly or from malice or passion.[35]

Despite this, it is asserted that no specific rules can be established that will govern every instance of corporal punishment.

However, no precise rule can be laid down as to what is excessive or unreasonable punishment. Each case must depend on its own circumstances. The punishment should be in proportion to the gravity of the offense, the apparent motive and disposition of the offender, and the influence of his example and conduct on others.[36]

The halakhic discussion of "instilling fear" on the student[37] can parallel 'the influence of his example and conduct on others'.

The principle that 'no precise rule can be laid down as to what is excessive or unreasonable punishment' in the American legal discussion, extends to the instrument of corporal punishment. There is no mention of an appropriate instrument. In practice, "Although a wooden paddle is the most frequent method for inflicting pain, numerous other instruments are used, for example, belts, sticks, etc."[38] While a concern such as Rashi's[39] would go unheard in the Supreme Court, certainly those from the moderate camp would support Rashi's comment in their own local legislation.

The purposes of corporal punishment are made clear.

The legitimate object of chastisement is to inflict punishment by the pain which it causes, as well as the degradation it implies. It does not follow, therefore, that because pain is produced, a chastisement is either cruel or excessive. Teachers exceed the limits of their authority when they cause lasting harm, but act within their limits when they inflict temporary pain.[40]

Clearly the halakhic ruling concerning the teacher who broke the foot of his student[41] concurs with the above. But, the sensitivity with which the *halakhah*, as interpreted by Eisenstadt, approaches the issue of degradation[42] is not heard in the American legal discussion.

In sum,

> A teacher is responsible for the discipline in his school, and for the progress, conduct, and deportment of his pupils. It is his duty to maintain good order and to require of the pupils a faithful performance of their duties. To enable him to discharge such a duty effectually, he must necessarily have the power to enforce prompt obedience to his lawful commands. For this reason he may inflict corporal punishment on refractory pupils.[43]

When spoken of in terms of ensuring "progress," corporal punishment can be administered in the way that Abraham diBoton understood it.[44]

## The Conservative Approach

This group, though shrinking over the past century, has regained some momentum from a few who teach in public inner-city schools where discipline is practically non-existent and violence among students and against teachers mounts daily. This opinion is fueled by the idea that a teacher serves *in loco parentis*. The teacher can and should strike the students to instill fear and respect for the teacher and rules of the classroom. Only then can discipline be maintained in the classroom so that students are able to learn effectively and teachers are able to teach effectively without fear of violence or insubordination.[45]

As demonstrated above in the legal material, there are many limits on a teacher in carrying out corporal punishment. However, because even these laws are vague and difficult to enforce, conservatives have been able to get away with harsher punishments, and more teacher authority. They maintain that the doctrine is intended to protect teachers who see the need to punish their students. As late as 1963 a case before the highest court in Indiana reasoned that

> ...the teacher's authority and the kind and quantum of punishment employed to meet a given offense is measured by the rules, standards and requirements as fixed and established for parents.[46]

In other words, a teacher could do anything to punish a student as long as the punishment did not violate the constitutional rights of the child.

Besides a strict interpretation of the *in loco parentis* doctrine, the strongest argument of the conservative group is that students, parents, and teachers expect and favor corporal punishment. Many students understand no other form of discipline. Many parents want the teacher to physically discipline the child both as a motivational tool and as a method of punishing misbehavior in the classroom. Teachers find that this is the method that is the simplest, quickest, most cost effective, and "it works."[47]

**The Moderate Approach**
This group remains active across the country, with the Supreme Court as one of its most effective mouthpieces. In regard to the discussion of the *in loco parentis* doctrine, they take a more moderate approach. They do not accord a teacher as full and unlimited authority over their students as the Law grants parents over their children. This opinion is best expressed by the following judgment of the highest court in Tennessee:

> The power to inflict punishment thus delegated to and vested in the school teacher is not the full extent of the parent's right because the power of correction, vested in parents, is little liable to abuse, being continually restrained by natural affection.[48]

They question the motives of a teacher in punishing a child, and support setting explicit limits on the method and state of mind of the teacher at the moment of administering punishment.

Those in the moderate group frown upon using corporal punishment often, and believe that most teachers use physical punishment only as a last resort. However, they argue that the lag time between the infraction and the administration of other alternative punishments, such as detention or suspension, may render these alternatives far less effective than an immediate paddling by the teacher. This is why cases brought before the United States Supreme Court which claim that corporal punishment violates a student's Fourteenth Amendment Right of due process are dismissed. The Court adjudicates that a student's procedural due process would only interfere with the goal of school (i.e. to teach) by wasting the time of teachers and administrators if they needed to conduct hearings prior to administering corporal punishment. Thus the procedural due process clause of the Fourteenth Amendment does not require advance notice or hearing prior to physical punishment.[49]

The Court, a voice of moderation, does, however, grant that a student's substantive due process may be violated if a beating

> was so disproportionate to the need presented, and was so inspired by malice or sadism, rather than merely careless or unwise excess of zeal that it amounted to a brutal and inhumane abuse of official power literally shocking to the conscience.[50]

If a punishment is unrelated to the educational goals of the school, then in some cases the court deems such punishment illegal and punishable.

The moderates want to keep corporal punishment as a legal option for teachers. Although they agree it may not be the best method of discipline for all students, some students desperately need this sort of discipline. In cases of neglect where children receive no discipline in the home from parents, a teacher may be the only person who cares enough to lovingly chastise the student. When done in a loving, manner, corporal punishment can be a very effective tool for altering poor behavior and expressing concern for the well-being of a student. Some students even favor corporal punishment because they know it is the only way they will be motivated to learn and pay attention.[51]

### The Liberal Approach

This group holds as its guiding principle that the rights of the child should be considered above all. These rights include not only the right to a good education, the right to be educated in a spirit of peace, the right to affection and freedom from unnecessary physical punishment, but also a right to enjoy these rights regardless of race color, sex, religion national or social origin.[52]

This group seeks to limit the *in loco parentis* doctrine even further than the moderate position embodied in the Law. Although they support a teacher's responsibility "...for the discipline in his school, and for the progress, conduct, and deportment of his pupils,"[53] they do not agree that corporal punishment is the best way to do this. In fact, they argue that it is an inappropriate way to ensure that a student learns.

When education was not mandatory and a parent could choose a teacher, that relationship was one of trust. The teacher was trusted and given permission to physically punish a child according to the agreed upon values of the parent and teacher. Now, however, when education is mandatory, and a parent has no chance to choose the public school or the teacher, a teacher should not automatically be given any authority to physically punish a child based on his [the teacher's] values and behavioral norms.

Many parents do not trust the judgment of public school teachers to consider properly the size, age and physical strength of the student as the Law suggests.

> Consideration must be given to the age, size , sex
> and physical strength of the pupil to be punished;
> and the instrument used must be one suitable to
> the purpose.[54]

From talmudic days and forward[55] the *halakhah* has prescribed that the only instrument of punishment is the small strap. Here, in the American legal discussion, we read that 'the instrument used must be suitable to the purpose'. It is generally assumed that the preferred means of inflicting corporal punishment is through the use of the paddle.[56] Clearly the *halakhah* and the American legal discussion disagree on this issue.

Furthermore, a parent may not agree with the moral judgment of a teacher who may punish a student for some behavior which the parent considers appropriate or merely a minor infraction. Because this liberal group disfavors the use of corporal punishment by parents on their own children (even in a spirit of love), they find that allowing teachers the authority to physically punish a student by a so-called *in loco parentis* doctrine, is completely inappropriate.

Those who espouse the liberal argument against corporal punishment in public schools do agree that discipline in the classroom is crucial. Yet they assert that there are alternative ways to ensure that order is maintained so that children can learn. They argue against the use of corporal punishment on the grounds that it is damaging to physical health, social competence, and emotional health.[57]

Addressing the issue of physical damage to a student, the Supreme Court only rarely even considers cases of abuse of the students by teachers. The Court argues that the school is not under Supreme Court jurisdiction because schools may set their own rules.

In the 1976 Ingraham v. Wright case, when the issue of cruel and unusual punishment as in the Eighth Amendment of the Constitution was addressed, the Court adjudicated that "the Eighth Amendment's proscription against cruel and unusual punishment did not apply to school discipline."[58] Furthermore, when the Fourteenth Amendment was brought up, the Court also dismissed it saying "the infliction of a paddling did not subject a school child to a grievous loss for which the Fourteenth Amendment (procedural) due process should be applied."[59]

In fact, the Law states,

> A school regulation that does not provide for notice, hearing, and the right of representation, before corporal punishment is administered, is not violative of the constitutional right of procedural due process of law guaranteed by the Fourteenth Amendment of the Constitution.[60]

Children's rights advocates argue that it is a disgrace that we accord criminals more rights than schoolchildren. One psychiatric social worker comments,

> We need to question the whole principle of allowing educators to beat children. Do we really want to be a society that treats kids who disrupt classes more harshly that hardened criminals?[61]

Whereas many of the moderates support corporal punishment because it is used as "a last resort" the liberals argue that it is often used first before any other action is taken to discipline a student. In some school districts expulsion and suspension are not allowed or available due to lack of supervision. Therefore, teachers have little recourse other than to use corporal punishment as discipline.[62] In many districts where money and staff are minimal, administrators are unwilling or unable to help teachers find effective alternatives to corporal punishment, and so teachers fall back on the method with which they are familiar – corporal punishment.

Whereas moderates argue that the threat of corporal punishment is useful in protecting a teacher from violence, the liberals counter with the fact that most corporal punishment is used against elementary school aged children who are rarely capable of committing harm to a teacher. One professor of psychology asks, "who is going to hit a 200-lb high school senior?"[63]

Addressing the issues of damage to social competence and emotional health, liberals argue that physical punishment causes students to focus on their failures rather than their successes. They lose self esteem and emerge with impaired social skills. First, an atmosphere of fear and anxiety is not conducive to good learning,[64] and second, sometimes the short-term goal of the teacher is reinforced such that it creates unworthy long-term results: the student becomes overly compliant, submissive, and yielding even outside of the classroom.[65] In some cases the use of corporal punishment causes the exact opposite to occur. A student who learns that violence gives someone control, (but not influence, according to Gordon) may rely on violence too often, and this leads to abuse. Corporal punishment leads to a cycle of violence in society that is difficult to reverse.[66]

One of the other arguments against corporal punishment is that some teachers abuse the right of corporal punishment and use it to discriminate against minority students. When families of punished students bring cases like this to court in order to collect damages under an equal protection clause, they can rarely prove discrimination because of loopholes in the Law.[67]

The liberal camp does propose many alternative methods of discipline in the classroom. Thomas Gordon suggests that we need to shift our thinking from seeing discipline as a "verb" to seeing discipline as a "noun." As a verb, "to discipline" implies externally imposed control over a student, which does not teach a student a sense of responsibility for his own actions.[68] Teaching a child "self-discipline" (used as a noun) may be more difficult, time consuming, and costly in the short run, but its long term results are far better than imposing physical punishment to keep a classroom quiet and under control. Gordon and others support rewards system rather that punishment systems as the ideal approach to maintaining good conduct in class and motivating students to learn. These rewards may include praise, attention, extra recess time, and access to particular toys. He admits that rewards systems, also referred to as 'behavioral modification' or 'positive reinforcement', may not work alone, but in tandem with other methods, they create a classroom atmosphere which best fosters learning.

Among the methods to be used in tandem with rewards systems are suspensions, expulsions, social isolation, verbal reprimands, and parent-teacher conferences.

It should also be emphasized that much of the need for discipline may arise from lack of preparedness by school people. Well-prepared and interesting lessons may prevent the need for behavior modification techniques.[69]

They argue that an engaged student rarely gets bored enough to disrupt the class.

## Conclusion

Should we find ourselves in the position of the rabbi described above, we would advise our congregant to vote to abolish corporal punishment in public schools.

The underlying ethical principle of the *halakhah*, regarding the use of corporal punishment in the school, is the importance of uncompromised excellence in education informed by the most effective methods of teaching school children.

We acknowledge that the *halakhah* permits, and according to some, encourages the use of corporal punishment. However, we see a chronologically progressive trend towards a more liberal point of view. Were the *halakhah* to be written today, taking into account the nature of the American public school system, we believe that it would firmly decry the use of corporal punishment in public schools.

In its day, the *halakhah* was familiar with an overall legal system that allowed for community imposed corporal punishment of adult criminals. In light of the advances in the treatment of adult criminals, under the protection of the Eighth and Fourteenth Amendments, we believe that an 'American halakhic system' would extend those rights to school children; especially, since an 18th century responsum leans in this direction.

We clearly see ourselves agreeing with the liberal approach described above. Incorporating the obvious focus of the *halakhah* on the importance of motivating students to learn, over discipline for its own sake, we condemn the use of corporal punishment when used by default. We would encourage the local, state, and federal governments to allocate sufficient funds to instruct teachers on alternative methods of discipline; and to staff the schools with enough qualified personnel to allow for the proper implementation of these alternatives. As teachers, we know that the best motivational tool is an engaging learning experience. We need to better train our public school teachers in order to create such an experience.

We are appalled by the decision of the Supreme Court to allow teachers the opportunity to accidently injure a student through the use so called "careless or unwise excess of zeal."[70] We don't trust the judgement of teachers who are allowed to be careless in the administration of corporal punishment. As Jews, we don't necessarily trust the value judgments of teachers of other religions whose ethics may differ from ours. We would expect the school board of our local district to apply the Eighth Amendment Right forbidding cruel and unusual punishment to students abused under the name of corporal punishment.

While we do agree with the liberals, we also find validity in some of the arguments of the moderates. Parents should be allowed to use limited corporal punishment on their own children if they so choose. We would expect that the child's rights, as delineated by the United Nations, would not be infringed upon. The halakhic standard of using a small strap should serve as a ceiling for the type of instrument used. We in no way encourage the use of such a strap, but find immense value in the principle of inflicting only temporary pain. We would prefer the open bare hand on the bare bottom, if necessary, but favor other non-physical methods of punishment as a rule.

# The Process of Making a Responsible Reform Jewish Ethical Decision

We are not *halakhic* Jews. While the body of *halakhah* informs us, we are not bound by it. In our study of corporal punishment, we could have selected to study only those aspects of the *halakhah* which agreed with our previously under informed liberal position. For example, we could have just taken the decision of Eisenstadt based on Mishnah *Baba Kama* 8:1/4[71] and ignored the competing opinions within the *halakhah*. By studying more than just this one stream, we learned of the spectrum of halakhic opinion.

While the halakhic and general ethical discussions literally and metaphorically speak in different languages, the basic issues addressed by both are the same. We would like to think that a halakhic Jew who absorbs the entire halakhic discussion would find himself agreeing with the moderate approach, but we acknowledge that differing interpretations might place him among the conservatives.

Since we, as Reform Jews, are not bound by the *halakhah*, but informed by it, we are able to place ourselves somewhere between the liberal and moderate positions while still claiming to be informed by the *halakhah*.

We can differ with the opinion of the halakhic Jew because we believe that ethics, including the ethics of *halakhah*, are relative. They depend upon the context in which they develop. It is a *sine qua non* of the responsible Reform Jew to seek out the intersection of the ethics inherent in the *halakhah* and the ethics ascribed to the general community (whether the two concur or disagree). So often, as Reform Jews, we only rely upon the ethics of the general community. It is our mandate to reclaim and grapple with the *halakhah* as testament of the history of our people's attempt to access the Holy through community standards.

As Reform Jews, we need to look beyond the surface of halakhic arguments to extrapolate and crystallize the ethics which underlie the *halakhah*. In this process, we may find it necessary to differ with a clear statement of the *halakhah*. In such cases, armed with the knowledge of the entire spectrum of halakhic opinion and general ethics, we may find it necessary to extend an underlying ethical principle found within the *halakhah* to circumstances of our own day of which the *halakhah* was unaware. Such "creative *halakhah*" is the highest form of a responsible Reform Jewish ethical decision.

While the expression 'creative *halakhah*' uses the traditional term '*halakhah*', it should not be understood as binding on any other person aside from the one who accepts it as binding. Of course, there are some general norms which must be agreed upon by society at large in order for it to function.

We believe that a Reform Jew is most true to his "Jewish Self" when he makes such a decision. In this way, he addresses the history and the future of the Jewish people. Such a process is an attempt to hear the commanding Divine Voice.

# Bibliography

*American Jurisprudence*. 2nd edition, Volume 68: "Schools"

Babylonian Talmud.

Bauer Gordon B., Richard Dubanoski, Lois A. Yamauchi, Kelly Ann H. Honbo. "Corporal Punishments and the Schools", *Education and Urban Society*, May 1990,

Bible.

Caro, Joseph. *Shulḥan Arukh.*

Frishtik, Mordecai. "Physical Violence by Parents Against Their Children in Jewish History and Jewish Law," unpublished ms. for *The Jewish Law Annual*, vol. IX

*Gould's Family Law Handbook of New York*, Gould Publications, Binghamton, New York: 1990.

Gordon, Thomas. "Crippling Our Children With Discipline," *Journal of Education.* Boston University School of Education, Volume 163, Number 3, Summer 1981.

Gudemann, M. "Education," *The Jewish Encyclopedia.* KTAV Publishing House, N.Y. Volume 5.

Henderson, Donald H. "Constitutional Implications Involving the Use of Corporal Punishment in the Public Schools: A Comprehensive Review," *Journal of Law and Education.* Volume 15, Number 3, Summer 1986.

Jacob ben Asher. *Arbaah Turim.*

Kessler, Gail. "Spanking in School: Deterrent or Barbarism," *Childhood Education.* Volume 61, Number 3. Jan-Feb 1985.

Maimonides. *Mishneh Torah.*

Matzner-Beckerman, Shoshana. *The Jewish Child: Halakhic Perspectives.* KTAV Publishing House, Inc. New York.

*Mishnah.* Commentary by Hanoch Albeck. The Bialik Institute, Jerusalem. 1988.

Mishnah.

Pross, Maureen N. "To Paddle or not to Paddle," *Learning 88.* October 1988.

Steinfels, Margaret O'Brien. "Children's Rights, Parental Rights, Family Privacy, and Family Autonomy," in *Who Speaks for the Child.* eds. Willard Gaylin & Ruth Macklin. Plenum Press, NY 1982.

*Supreme Court Reporter.* Volume 97A, October Term 1976. 430 U.S. 651. West Publishing, St. Paul, Minn. 1979.

*United Nations Declaration of the Right of the Child.*

Zirkel, Perry A., Henry F. Reichner. "Is *In Loco Parentis* Doctrine Dead?" *Journal of Law and Education.* Volume 15, Number 3. Summer 1986.

# Notes

1. Deuteronomy 21:18-21.

2. I Samuel 2:23-24.

3. Ibid. verse 25.

4. I Samuel 3:13.

5. Proverbs 29:15.

6. Ibid. 29:18.

7. Ibid. 23:12-14.

8. Deuteronomy 19:5.

9. Mishnah *Makot* 2:2.

10. Ibid. 2:2.

11. Ibid. 2:3.

12. Ibid. 2:3.

13. Hanoch Albeck, *Mishnah Makot* 2:2.

14. *Sotah* 47a.

15. *Baba Batra* 21a.

16. M. Gudemann, "Education," *The Jewish Encyclopedia.* KTAV Publishing House, N.Y. Volume 5, p. 43.

17. *Baba Batra* 21a.

18. *Mishneh Torah, Sefer Mada Hilkhot Talmud Torah* 2:2.

19. *Lekhem Mishneh.*

20. *Mishneh Torah, Sefer Nezikin, Hilkhot Rotzeaḥ Ushmirat Nefesh* 4:5.

21. Ibid.

22. *Arbaah Turim, Yoreh Deah Hilkhot Talmud Torah* 245.

23. *Shulḥan Arukh, Yoreh Deah Hilkhot Melamdim* 245:10.

24. *Pitḥei Teshuvah.*

25. *Mishnah Baba Kama* 8:1/4. This passage was not used in connection with the discussion of corporal punishment before the 18th century.

26. The categories are adapted from Margaret O'Brien Stienfels, "Children's Rights, Privacy and Family Autonomy," *Who Speaks for the Child?* Willard Gaylin and Ruth Macklin, eds., Plenum Press, 1982. pp. 232-235.

27. Gordon B. Bauer, et al. "Corporal Punishment and the Schools," *Education and Urban Society.* Vol. 22, No. 3, May 1990, p. 288.

28. Ibid. p. 295.

29. Mitchell L. Yell. "The Use of Corporal Punishment, Suspension, Expulsion, and Timeout with Behaviorally Disordered Students in Public Schools: Legal Considerations," *Behavioral Disorders.* Volume 15, Number 2, February 1990, p. 101.

30. Perry A. Zirkel and Henry F. Reichner. "Is *In Loco Parentis* Doctrine Dead?" *Journal of Law and Education.* Volume 15 Number 3, Summer 1986, pp. 274-275.

31. *American Jurisprudence,* 2nd Edition, p. 584.

32. Ibid. p. 585.

33. Ibid. p. 586.

34. See note 18.

35. *American Jurisprudence*, p. 586.

36. Ibid.

37. See note 18.

38. Bauer et. al. p. 285.

39. See note 17.

40. *American Jurisprudence,*. p. 587.

41. See note 24.

42. See notes 24 & 25.

43. *American Jurisprudence,*. pp. 585-586.

44. See note 19.

45. Maureen N. Pross, "To Paddle or Not to Paddle," *Learning 88.* October 1988, pp. 42-43.

46. Zirkel and Reichner, pp. 274-275.

47. Pross, p. 42.

48. Zirkel & Reichner, p. 275. This is a 1934 ruling.

49. Donald H. Henderson. "Constitutional Implications Involving the Use of Corporal Punishment in the Public Schools: A Comprehensive Review," *Journal of Law and Education.* Volume 15 Number 3, Summer 1986, p. 259.

50. Ibid. p. 261.

51. Pross, p. 49.

52. *United Nations Declaration of The Rights of the Child.* (Source unknown.)

53. *American Jurisprudence,* p. 585.

54. Ibid. p. 586.

55. See note 15.

56. See note 38. The use of the paddle has also been accepted as a proper means of inflicting corporal punishment by the United States Supreme Court. See Ingraham vs. Wright, 1977.

57. Thomas Gordon. "Crippling Our Children With Discipline," *Journal of Education.* Volume 163 Number 3, Summer 1981, p. 228.

58. Henderson, p. 257.

59 Ibid.

60. *American Jurisprudence,* p. 587.

61. Gail Kessler. "Spanking in School, Deterrent or Barbarism?" *Childhood Education.* Volume 61 Number 3, January-February, 1985. p. 176.

62. Pross, p. 43. (Personal interview.)

63. Kessler, p. 175. (Personal interview.)

64. Bauer et. al. p. 289.

65. Gordon, pp. 229 & 235.

66. Pross, p. 48. Bauer et. al. p. 290.

67. Henderson, pp. 265-269.

68. Gordon, p. 229. Kessler. p. 175.

69. Bauer et. al. p. 294.

70. Henderson, p. 261.

71. See notes 24 and 25.

# The Challenge of Child Custody

## At the Intersection of Jewish Law and Ethics

Stuart Weinberg Gershon
and Jonathan Kraus

It has become a truism to observe that divorce is a wide-spread and growing plague in 20th century American society. Estimates that as many as 40% of marriages end in divorce are not uncommon. Clearly, divorce has become an integral part of our general culture. Contemporary television, literature, newspapers, drama, music and art abound with images and stories of broken commitments, loves gone sour and shattered lives. Very few of our families have not been touched by divorce in some way. The profound tragedy inherent in the end of a marriage is powerful because it precisely reflects the sacred potential inherent in a family's creation. In no area is this observation more true than in the case of children. While the victims of divorce include the spouses, their families of origin and the society at large, children are the most critical victims. For their world, their self-understanding and their future is most dependent on the stability and character of the family structure. Of all the losses attendant upon a divorce, the loss of the sacred opportunity to share the nurture and guidance of new lives, of the next generation of Jews, may be the most tragic loss.

Not surprisingly, therefore, one of the most painful and complex phenomena surrounding divorce is the issue of determining child custody. But it is also one of the most critical issues. The present work is first an attempt to survey both the general, secular and the Jewish ethical guidelines for determining child custody.

In the former realm, one looks to both secular legal and psychological discussions of child custody. In the latter world, one looks to the Jewish legal-ethical tradition regarding custody. As "citizens" of both worlds, we have the challenge and the opportunity to bring their combined insights and values to bear upon this issue and to arrive at a position which grows out of both. In the concluding section of the paper, therefore, each of the authors attempts to articulate an approach to determining child custody that reflects what he has learned and integrated from these two worlds.

# A Brief Historical Overview

To understand the significance of recent developments in secular, American child custody determinations, it is helpful to place these changes in historical context. The history of custody determination moves generally from a presumption favoring the father, through one favoring the mother, to a situation in which, increasinginly, judges use many different factors in an attempt to decide which custody arrangement is in the best interests of the child.

To begin with, in both ancient Roman law and English common law the father had absolute power over his children. The law regarded children as the father's property and, therefore, his responsiblity (Roman law even allowed a father to sell his children or to condemn them to death).[1]

This absolute presumption for the father is still evident in American law as late as the mid 19th century. An 1860 New Hampshire opinion noted:

> It is a well-settled doctrine of the common law, that the father is entitled to the custody of his minor children, as against the mother and everybody else; that he is bound for their maintenance and nurture, and has the corresponding right to their obedience and services.[2]

According to this ruling, the father's right to the "custody," "obedience" and "services" of his children is a reciprocal result of his responsibility for their "maintenance and nurture." In fact, the strength of this reciprocal relationship was such that if, following divorce, the mother received custody instead of the father, "the father becomes entirely absolved from the common law obligation which previously rested upon him to support such a child."[3]

In addition to the paternal presumption and the reciprocity of support and custody, 19th century American law was characterized by a pronounced tendency to use "fault" for the divorce as a determinant of custody. This tendency was especially pronounced in cases involving adultery – whether on the part of the husband or the wife.[4] An 1858 court wrote: "a woman who has been guilty of adultery is unfit to have the care and education of children, and more especially of female children, nor is she entitled to the support of her husband's estate."[5]

The tendency to use culpability for divorce as a determinant of custody reflected four significant realities. First, as seen above, it reflected concern with the parent as moral model for his/her children. Second, the use of culpability reflected concern with whether a person who had had difficulty in accepting responsibility for one domestic relationship would be able to accept responsibility for another such relationship.[6] Third, it reflected society's desire to punish, or, at least, to avoid rewarding behavior which it considered immoral.[7] Fourth, the use of culpability rendered a potentially complex and painful decision relatively simple. The court had only to award custody to the parent not "at fault" for the divorce.[8]

As America entered the 20th century, the most significant change in child custody determination was a gradual shift to presumption favoring the mother. Three major changes in American society helped influence this trend. The shift from an agrarian, rural economy to an industrial, urban one decreased the economic interdependence of the family.[9] An increased interest in children as human beings and in childhood as a special phase of human development (epitomized by the introduction of child labor laws, public education and children's aid societies) began to focus attention on children's special needs.[10] And finally, the changing role and perception of women in American society (reflected in their new right to vote, to own property and to be employed on their own) gave women unprecedented levels of economic independence.[11]

These socioeconomic and cultural changes paralleled three, interrelated changes in the process of determining custody. The first change was the perpetuation of a principle known as the "best interests of the child" doctrine. The second change was the separation of the responsibility for support from the right to custody.[12] The third change was a new and dominant understanding of the importance of maternal care, especially for children of "tender years" (a doctrine consequently referred to as the "tender years" presumption).[13]

In theory, the "best interests of the child" principle led judges to take the special needs of childhood and of particular children into account when rendering custody decisions. In practice, however, the "best interests" doctrine served as a euphemistic justication for awarding custody to the mother rather than the father. The application of this principle during this period did not necessarily indicate more detailed attention to the particular child's needs or the particulars of a custodial situation.[14]

Similarly, the separation of responsibility for support from right to custody was generally used to ensure that women would have sufficient income to care for children placed in their custody. Increasingly, the courts required non-custodial fathers to provide support for their children.

It is clear, therefore, that both of these changes were subsidiary to the emerging consensus regarding the importance of maternal care for young children. A 1921 opinion noted:

> For a boy of such tender years, nothing can be an adequate substitute for mother love – for that constant ministration required during the period of nurture that only a mother can give because in her alone is duty swallowed up in desire; in her alone is service expressed in terms of love. She alone has the patience and sympathy required to mold and soothe the infant mind in its adjustment to its environment. The difference between fatherhood and motherhood in this respect is fundamental.[15]

This presumption remained a powerful influence, at least into the 1960's when the courts observed: "there is no substitute for the love, companionship and guidance of a good mother .... she has the time and opportunity of providing care and comfort to the children at times when normally the father is away from home."[16] The strength of this perspective can be seen in the estimation given by some sources that as much as 90% of custody awards went to the mother during the 1960's.[17] However, during the 1970's, important questions were raised which challenged the tender years presumption and the use of parental culpability and led to an increased effort to define the "best interests" of the child.

Three related factors account for the diminished influence of the tender years doctrine during the 1970's. The first factor was the wide-spread recognition that the presumption favoring the mother was based on outdated social stereotypes. As women entered the work force in record numbers, it simply became inaccurate to presume that women, by definition, had more time and opportunity to nurture their children.[18] The second factor was the question of the constitutional legality of any gender-based presumption. Insofar as the Fourteenth Amendment guarantees "equal protection under the law" to all American citizens, legal authorities began to ask whether a gender-based presumption such as the tender years doctrine represented a case of sex discrimination.[19]

A third factor which helped to undermine the tender years presumption during the 1970's was the movement for equality of the sexes.[20] An implied corollary to ideals such as equal pay and equal opportunity was that of equal rights and responsibilities in child custody. One result of the influence of the equal rights movement was to increase custody awards to the father, who was seen as having an equal right to raise his children.[21] A second significant outcome of this movement for equality was an increasing tendency to award "joint custody" to the parents (an arrangement in which the parents, minimally, share decision-making and support responsibilities for the child and, maximally, alternate residential custody).[22]

Even with all these undermining influences, however, it would be quite inaccurate to claim that the tender years presumption became obsolete during the 1970's. In truth, as written legal opinions demonstrate, its impact continues to be felt.[23]

As to the diminished tendency to use culpability for the divorce as a determinant of custody, this change reflected, in part, a general legal tendency towards "no-fault" divorce. However, the decreased emphasis also reflected a more permissive society, which felt less desire to "punish" the parent "at fault" and which had real questions about whether the behavior leading to the divorce would, in fact, have significant negative impact on the children. Like the tender years presumption, culpability remains a potent force in child custody adjudication, but it has generally become just one among many significant factors that judges consider.[24]

With the diminished emphasis on both the tender years presumption and the use of culpability during the 1970's, the courts turned increasingly towards attempts to define and protect the child's needs and "best interests." One outgrowth of this trend was the practice of providing a child with some independent legal representation during a custody proceeding.[25] A second product of this trend was legislative guidelines that attempted to shape custody proceedings so that they would result in decisions that protected the child's best interest.

One example is the 1974 Unified Marriage and Divorce Act (UMDA), which was endorsed by the American Bar Association and has been accepted as a whole or in part by many jurisdictions.[26] To pro-tect the child's need for stability, the UMDA includes a provision which prohibits a change of custody unless a child is endangered in the existing environment and the advantages of a change outweigh the harm of uprooting the child.[27] And, in an attempt to include all factors relevant to the child's well-being in custody decisions, the UMDA lists five factors which are to be considered including: the parents' wishes, the child's wishes, the quality of child's present relationships with all significant individuals, the child's adjustment to his home, school and community and the mental and physical health of all individuals involved.[28]

Obviously, the weight given to each of these factors and the methods of measuring them will vary from jurisdiction to jurisdiction and from case to case. Nonetheless, this legislation represents an important attempt to define and protect the child's "best interests."

In addition to legislative attempts, in recent years the courts have made increasing use of social science research and experts during custody proceedings. We will turn to the findings of that research shortly. At this point, suffice it to say that the in-creased interest in such research, like the legislation just described, represents an attempt to determine what it is the child's best interest as a response to the diminished reliance upon gender-based or culpability-based presumptions.

In summary, unlike their predecessors in ancient Rome, contemporary judges and advisors have far less certainty about what constitutes the most appropriate custodial arrangement. As a consequence, individuals who seek to help resolve these complex and painful situations have far greater latitude and, inevitably, bear far greater responsibility for the consequences of their decisions.

# Contemporary Ethical Perspectives on Child Custody

## Legal Ethics

Currently, the dominant legal standard for child custody determinations is the "best interests of the child."[29] Two characteristics of the best interests of the child standard are:l) it is focussed on children's rights rather than parental rights; 2) it is sex-neutral, making no custodial presumptions on the basis of sex (of parent or child).[30]

However, traditional age/sex-based presumptions, such as the tender years and same sex doctrines, are still operative within the court system.[31] In the last decade, the joint custody option at one time reached the level of a presumption under the best interests standard.

In l973, the "least detrimental alternative" was proposed by Goldstein, Freud, and Solnit as a serious alternative to the "best interests" standard.[32] According to this standard, custody would be awarded to the child's" psychological parent." The child's psychological parent was presumed to be "less detrimental" than any other option.

In its day, the "least detrimental alternative" was  a seminal effort to reformulate child custody determinations based upon the combined insights of psychology and psychiatry.  In the late l970's, the "least detrimental alternative" was regarded as a serious competitor to the" best interests" standard. However, in the current literature it appears to be mentioned more as an historical footnote than as a viable, contemporary alternative.

The legal criteria for what constitute the best interests of the child have never been precisely defined. The legal system allows judges to make highly individualized custodial assessments based on multiple factors which, taken together, are presumed to constitute the best interests of the child.[33]

Some of the criteria currently employed by the courts[34] are self-evident. They include: parental abuse and neglect, alcohol and drug problems, mental instability. Two unexpected factors, which can actually be determinative of custody are: perjury and interference with visitation. That is, a parent who commits perjury will automatically be denied custody. A temporary or permanent custodian who obstructs the visitation rights of the noncustodial parent may lose custody. Other important factors currently used by the courts in making child custody determinations are: automatic maternal preference, primary caretaker, time available to spend with child.

"Automatic maternal preference" has become problematic on both legal and psychological grounds. Presumptions based on sex are highly suspect of being unconstitutional under the equal protection and due process clauses (the 14th Amendment) of the U.S. Constitution.[35] It is also the current majority opinion within the field of psychology that there is no substantial empirical evidence to justify child custody determinations based on sex-based presumptions.[36] As a result of these problems, a more common use of the automatic maternal preference is as a tie-breaker.[37]

"Primary caretaker" is a highly significant factor. Whichever parent has served as the child's caretaker has already demonstrated commitment to the child and is experienced in meeting the child's needs. The child may also have become very attached to the primary caretaker.

"Time available to spend with child" is also a highly significant factor because it measures which parent will have the capacity and the lifestyle to be the child's future primary caretaker.

In a 1982 study of the factors used in deciding 241 child custody cases by the appellate courts,[38] Atkins found that fathers have made substantial progress in obtaining equal treatment with mothers. Fathers obtained custody in 51 percent of the cases and mothers obtained custody in 49 percent.

Atkinson also found that the most frequently cited criteria by the appellate courts were: 1) Maintenance of stable environment; 2) Nonmarital heterosexual relationships (lose custody); 3) child's custodial preference.

Parental "maintenance of stable environment" is an ambiguous term. Sometimes it is used to refer to physical stability. At other times it is intended to mean interpersonal stability and continuity. In this study, it was used in the latter sense. Atkinson states, "Custody usually will go to the parent with whom the child has had a more stable and secure relationship."[39] It is also worthwhile to note that the term "stability" has been interpreted by the courts to include the child's academic performance and health care. That is, if one parent can better help the child with academic performance or special health problems that parent usually will obtain custody.

The issue of parental "nonmarital heterosexual relationships" is currently the most tangled area of the law. Many courts presume that a nonmarital sexual relationship is automatically harmful to the child.[40] The Illinois Supreme Court ruled in Jarrett vs. Jarrett (1980) to modify custody, giving the father custody of 3 daughters, based upon his complaint that the mother had a live-in boyfriend. The court stated that the mother had engaged in conduct which was "injurious to the moral well being and development of the children" and "could well encourage the children to engage in similar activity in the future."

Other courts have rejected this presumption unless proof of harm can be demonstrated. The Pennsylvania Supreme Court stated (1982):

> "We have repeatedly held that if one of the parties is involved in a nonmarital relationship, the court must not presume that the relationship will have a bad effect on the children. Instead, the court must examine the facts of the particular relationship and on the basis of those facts determine what the effect the relationship has had on the children."[41]

Nevertheless, most courts agree that a person who flaunts a nonmarital relationship and places a child in embarrassing situations is likely to be denied or lose custody. On the other hand, most courts also agree that a parent who maintains a discreet relationship, with or without the child's knowledge, is not likely to be denied or lose custody.[42]

The weight given to the child's "custodial preference" varies with the court's assessment of the child's age, intelligence, and maturity. Courts have accepted a child's preference as young as age 4 and ignored it as old as 14. In West Virginia, the preference of a child 14+ is actually binding.[43]

From an ethical perspective, the process of *how* child custody decisions are made has as many ethical ramifications as the content of that process. Both the legal and psychological literature stress the problems and limitations of the adjudication process.

The adjudication process itself is, ironically, not in the best interests of the child. It is an adversarial process in which "whichever parent can show by the preponderance of evidence that it would be in the child's best interest to be in his or her custody obtains custody, even if the difference is very slight."[44] The intrinsically adversarial nature of the process may exacerbate interparental strife which is held by many mental health practitioners to be the single, most highly correlated factor in childhood disorder after divorce.[45]

The adjudication process is unjust insofar as it violates one of Rawls' central principles of justice: like cases ought to be decided in like ways.[46] In the late 1960's, the best interests standard came under fire as "conspicuously vague," and "amorphous." Critics argued that custody decisions were, in effect, largely a matter of the judge's personal value judgements and highly subjective impressions. The present adjudication process does not provide adequate safeguards to protect against the intrusion of judges' personal biases. In fact, the broad discretionary power given to judges requires them to operate out of a subjective hierarchy of values, whether implicit or explicit.

Mnookin argues that the results of the current system of child custody adjudication are, at best, indeterminate and speculative about the "best interests" of the child. This inherent indeterminacy of the system is due, according to Mnookin, to our inability to make predictions about human behavior and our lack of consensus with regard to values.[47]

Mnookin conceptualizes the judge's role in a custody determination as a problem of rational choice among alternatives. According to decision theory, a rational decision requires four consecutive operations: 1) Specify the possible outcomes of alternative courses of action; 2) Determine the probability of the possible outcomes actually occurring; 3) Assign utility to each of the alternative courses of action; 4) Select the course of action which "maximizes" the desired utility.[48]

Based on this decision theory of rational choice, "the judge would wish to compare the expected utility for the child of living with his mother to that of living with his father and choose the alternative that "maximizes" what is in the best interests of the child."[49] However, Mnookin demonstrates that the current system of child custody adjudication cannot fulfill these requirements:[50]

1)  The specification of possible outcomes under alternativ-custodial arrangements requires substantial information about the child's family life and parental behaviors. Judges do not have the necessary information.

2)  The determination of the probability that expected consequences of alternative custody arrangements will actually occur requires the capacity to predict human behavior. At the present time, the science of psychology cannot provide reliable predictions about human behavior or the consequences of various custodial arrangements.

3)  The assignment of value to each of the alternative custodial arrangements requires the application of a set of

values. But contemporary American culture does not offer a clear consensus on a hierarchy of values or on the "good life" for children.

Hence, Mnookin concludes that the present system of child custody adjudication "may yield something close to a random pattern of outcomes."[51] He contends,"Individualized adjudication means that the results will often turn on a largely intuitive evaluation based on unspoken values and unproven predictions."[52] Mnookin claims "We would more frankly acknowledge our ignorance and the presumed equality of the natural parents were we to flip a coin."[53] Nevertheless, Mnookin concludes that the present system of child custody adjudication, for all its problems and limitations, is the best system currently available.

## Summary
The best interests of the child is currently the dominant standard for child custody determinations. The courts are increasingly moving away from traditional age/sex-based presumptions, such as the tender years and same-sex doctrines, which are still operative within the legal system, but no longer function as serious competitors to the best interests standard as they once did. The contemporary debate about legal presumptions has shifted to the issue of whether parental nonmarital heterosexual or homosexual relationships are automatically harmful to the child. This appears to be the new (negative) presumption of the 1990's.

Although the legal criteria for what constitutes the best interests of the child have never been precisely defined, the legal system takes into consideration a multitude of sophisticated psychological and non-psychological variables. The principal criteria employed by the court system in making child custody decisions are: parent-child relationship, stability of physical/interpersonal environment: primary caretaker; parental capacity and time to fulfill parental role; children's custodial preference.

The process of child custody adjudication has serious problems. The very process itself may be incompatible with the child's best interests. It is subject to the intrusion of judges personal biases and other unfair practices. The results of the process may be speculative, at best, about the child's best interests. Nevertheless, no other available process, including mediation and the least detrimental alternative, have provided sufficiently compelling reasons to serve in place of the present system of child custody adjudication.

## Psychological
## Perspectives

The courts have turned to the social sciences, particularly psycho-logical research, to supply empirical evidence upon which new stan-dards for child custody determinations can be built.

This phenomenon is due to several parallel factors. The recognition of children as persons has compelled the inclusion of high-ly sophisticated psychological considerations into the best interests standard.[54] Secondly, as we observed above in the brief overview, the courts have historically employed certain presumptions of one kind or another with regard to child custody determinations. Each of these presumptions (whether paternal, maternal, or joint custody) has been discredited by the social sciences, leaving the courts with-out the benefit of any automatic determinants and few presumptions.

Finally, we live in a society characterized by competitive and frequently changing cultural values, in which there is no fixed hier-archy of values upon which the court system can rely. For all these reasons, the legal system has been left with a profound void, namely, the loss of overarching standards by which to make child custody determinations.

The science of psychology has conducted clinical and em-pirical research on 1) general issues of child development relevant to child custody determinations and 2) the specific variables of chil-dren's postdivorce adjustment. Only some of the current criteria used by the courts under the best interests standard have been sys-tematically examined by psychological research.

Before reviewing this data, it should be stated at the outset that much of this research is subject to clear methodological limita-tions.[55] Most of the clinical research has been based solely upon maternal custody families. Many of these studies have been criti-cized for faulty methodological controls. An adequate body of research on paternal custody families is sorely lacking. In the last decade,the initial attractiveness of joint custody among judges, lawyers, psy-chologists, and parents, sparked numerous studies. We now turn to a brief review of psychological research on the validity of some of the criteria used under the best interests standard.

### Age and sex
### of the child

It is the current majority opinion within the field of psychology that there is no substantial empirical evidence to justify child custody determinations based upon age/sex-based presumptions, such as the tender years or same sex doctrines.[56] According to this majority opinion: 1) Children create equally significant bonds with both par-ents. It should not be presumed that "mothering" is more important than "fathering."[57] 2) Mothers and fathers are equal in their capacity to parent. The District of Columbia Court of Appeals stated:

> Eminent child psychiatrists have demonstrated that
> what a child needs is not a mother, but someone who
> can provide 'mothering' ...And the ability of a per-
> son to provide 'mothering' does not necessarily cor-
> respond to the gender of the parent or the biological
> relationship between adult and child."[58]

Rohman, Sales, and Lou report substantial evidence pointing to an inverse negative relationship between the child's age and
adjustment problems. That is, the younger the child is at the time
of divorce, the greater the emotional problems following divorce.[59]

**Affectional
Ties**

In 1973, Goldstein, Freud, and Solnit published a seminal work, *Beyond the Best Interests of the Child*, in which they proposed an alternative set of custody standards, based solely on psychoanalytic theories.[60] Goldstein et al called for the replacement of the best interests
standard with the "least detrimental alternative." They proposed that
a child should always be placed in the custody of his/her "psychological parent," defined as "the one who, on a continuing day to day basis,
through interplay, and mutuality, fulfills the child's psychological
needs for a parent, as well as the child's physical needs." Goldstein et
al called for speedy and permanent custody placements in consideration of the child's sense of time. Finally, Goldstein et al proposed that
the psychological parent be granted complete control over the noncustodial parent's future access to the child.

Objections to the least detrimental alternative concept and
its related ideas coalesce into 3 groups: 1) Goldstein et al did not
cite any empirical data to validate their approach. It is based solely
on psychoanalytic theory; 2) the concept of psychological parent helps
only with the easiest cases. It fails to provide any guidance with
normal and difficult cases in which the child has some relationship
and psychological attachment to each parent; 3) the proposal that
custody placements be permanent and under the total control of
the psychological parent underestimates the value of the child's
access to the noncustodial parent and does not protect against retaliation by the custodial parent.

In a 1985 survey of 104 Kentucky mental health practitioners, Lowery found that the most critical factor in making child custody determinations was the quality of parent-child relationships
and the parent's ability to function well in a parental role.[61] The
principal criteria used by clinicians in making determinations of
child custody according to Lowery's survey were: 1) Quality of the
parent-child relationship, 2) Parent's sense of responsibility to the

child, 3) Parent's mental stability, 4) Parent's skill in parenting, 5) Amount of parental contact with the child; 6) Parent's affection for the child.

The survey also showed that the second most important consideration for the clinicians was the quality of the secondary social support network available to the child (i.e., child's access to peers and other relatives, stable community involvement, amount of contact with the non-custodial parent.

## Child's Custodial Preference

Current research exists which can help in determining the age at which a reliable custodial preference can be elicited from a child.[62] Some data suggest that the child's level of cognitive/emotional development is a more reliable indicator of the child's capacity to express a meaningful custodial preference than age. However, many studies point to age 12 or older, in general, as the transition point at which a reliable level of cognitive/emotional development becomes operational.

## Evidence from Clinical and Empirical Research

We now turn to the clinical and empirical research on *children's postdivorce adjustment*. The current state of knowledge in the science of psychology cannot make reliable predictions about the consequences of various custodial arrangements.[63] Weithorn and Grisso emphasize:

> "the lack of any methodologically sound empirical evidence allowing psychological predictions as to the effects of various types of custodial placements on children, or whether joint custody, in general, is a better option than single parent custody."[64]

Nevertheless, Weithorn and Grisso go on to declare:

> "our general knowledge in psychology may provide a scientific basis for the testimony of a psychologist on more limited questions of considerable relevance to the court. For example, we have a relatively firm base describing psychological functioning, characterizing interpersonal interactions and relationships, and making limited inferences about the current and possible future impact of certain conditions and situations upon the well-being of a child."[65]

Hence, no single custody arrangement presents itself as clearly in the best interests of the child. Rather, Felner and Terre point to a growing awareness among clinicians and social scientists that the form of custodial arrangement may be less significant to child adjustment following divorce than several other variables.[66] These variables, called contextual mediators of adjustment or prognostic indicators, provide some ideas as to what circumstances and conditions will enhance or harm children's post-divorce adaptation.

The most widely attested mediator is the level of interparental conflict.[67] An amicable interparental relationship helps both parents to adjust to the divorce and tends to increase the frequency of visitation by the noncustodial parent. The absence of excessive conflict between parents appears to facilitate the child's adjustment for reasons that are not totally clear. However, it is speculated that the absence of interparental hostility allows children to benefit from access to both parents, in which each relationship is emotionally less conflicted.

Another mediating factor is the quality of parent-child relationships.[68] The parent-child relationship is one of the most critical aspects of child development in general. More specifically, it has been found that close and satisfying contact with caring adults buffers children from the negative impact of divorce.

A third mediating factor is interpersonal stability and continuity with the non-custodial parent. Reppucci reports that "A somewhat consistent finding in research of divorced families is that what is most important to children – even with very young preschoolers – is free access to and continued relationships with both parents after divorce."[69] Hence, the quality of parent-child relationship applies to the noncustodial parent as well as the custodial parent. Contact between noncustodial fathers and children has regularly been associated with more positive adjustment. Rothman, Sales, and Lou point to several lines of research which establish that "maintenance of positive relations between the child and both parents is more strongly indicative of child adjustment during the postdivorce period than either the degree of interparental harmony or the family structure."[70]

A fourth mediator is the level of parental psychological functioning. Felner and Terre state that a number of studies have suggested that the level of parental adjustment to divorce is directly correlated with the frequency of either the child's depression or aggressive behavior.[71] Parental stress may also impact child-rearing practices. It may also be the case that it is parental stress from financial worries, rather than the actual economic circumstances, which have been correlated with post-divorce adjustment problems.

**Summary**
Significant psychological research has been conducted on some of the criteria currently used by the courts under the best interests standard to make child custody determinations, and on specific

variables related to children's postdivorce adjustment. The conclusions of this research are subject to contrary data and alternative minority opinions.

Psychological research indicates that children create significant emotional bonds with both parents and that mothers and fathers are equal in their capacity to parent. According to the current majority opinion, there is no substantial empirical evidence to justify making child custody decisions on the basis of sex-based presumptions, such as the tender years and same sex doctrines.

The current state of knowledge in the science of psychology cannot make reliable predictions about the consequences of various custodial alternatives. No single custody arrangement is clearly in the best interests of the child. Rather, the empirical evidence is increasingly pointing to the conclusion that the form of custodial arrangement is less significant than the status of several contextual mediators of adjustment: interparental relationship, quality of parent-child relationships, access and continued relationship with the noncustodial parent, and parental psychological functioning.

# Jewish Sources on the Determination of Child Custody

The Jewish legal tradition regarding child custody reflects a gradual and complex evolution. The following review presents the sources in general chronological order, beginning with the Talmudic texts and proceeding through contemporary decisions of Israel's Rabbinical authorities. The choice of a historical/chronological presentation reflects both the authors' post-Enlightenment intellectual heritage and their sense that the material can be meaningfully organized into historical categories. This research project does not constitute an exhaustive treatment of the subject. This study is based on the major citations in classic Jewish sources.

## Talmudic Texts
### *Ketubot* 101b-103a
*Ketubot* 101b-103a clearly concludes that following divorce, a daughter, regardless of her age, belongs with her mother. This *mishnah* tells us that a woman has divorced her second husband, who had agreed in their *ketubah* to provide maintenance for her daughter from the first marriage. According to the text, the man "must forward her maintenance to her at the place where her mother [lives]." This Talmudic passage affirms the second hus-

band's obligation to provide maintenance for his ex-wife's daughter, even though she lives with her mother and not with him.

In Rav Hisda's words, this passage "implies that [the place of] a daughter must be with her mother." Hisda's words provide the foundation for maternal custody in the case of daughters. However, the subsequent text asks, perhaps Rav Hisda's rule only refers to a daughter who is still a minor? After all, we know that a widow was once awarded custody of her child based on a previous case in which custody of a minor had been given to his potential heirs and they killed the child. If the daughter was an adult, this precedent would not apply.

In response, the text answers that the daughter's age is irrelevant. Insofar as the present rules specifies that the maintenace be sent to the daughter "at the place where her mother [lives]" and does not say, "wherever she (the daughter) lives," the Talmudic passage concludes that a daughter's proper place is with her mother, regardless of the girl's age. Thus *Ketu*bot 101b-103a establishes the rule of maternal custody for daughters after divorce.

### *Eruvin* 82a-b

*Eruv*in 82a-b discusses the young child's dependence on and preference for his mother as well as the age through which these characteristics generally endure. The context of the discussion, however, is not custody determination. The text describes the communal establishment of an *eruv* to extend the prescribed *Shabbat* boundaries and the age at which a child becomes obligated to participate in establishing such an *eruv*.

At the outset of the passage in question, Rav Assi cites a ruling that a six year old boy, who has neither ritually accepted the *eruv* for himself nor had it explicitly accepted in his name, fulfills the obligation (of acceptance) by virtue of his mother's acceptance of the *eruv*.[72] There follows a discussion of Assi's ruling in which the text cites an objection that the relevant criteria for applying this exemption is not the chronological age of the child (i.e., six years) but the fact of this dependence upon his mother. Several authorities offer alternative opinions as to the age through which a child is generally dependent and how one determines dependence.

Rav Joshua then provides an alternative interpretation to Rav Assi's statement. He takes *yotzey b'eruv imo* as a literal reference to physical behavior and argues that Rav Assi's statement speaks of a situation in which a six year old boy must choose to "go out" by either his father's *eruv* or mother's *eruv*. According to Rav Joshua, Assi's ruling teaches that the boy would "go out by his mother's *eruv*" because "even a child of six prefers his mother's company."

Thus, this Talmudic text teaches that age six is an important transition point in a child's development. Prior to this age, boys are clearly dependent upon their mothers. By age six, boys are deemed independent enough to fulfill the *mitzvah* of *eruv*, even though most boys would still "prefer" to be in their mother's company.

### *Ketubot* 65b

*Ketubot* 65b is concerned with the issue of child support. We learn that fathers are obligated to support their very young children (both boys and girls) until they reach age six. To show that six is an authoritative boundary for the duration of a father's obligation to provide support, the text cites Rav Assi's statement that "a child of six is exempt by his mother's [acceptance of the] *eruv*."

Rav Assi's statement regarding the *mitzvah* of *eruv* is applied to the context of paternal child support in order to establish the minimal duration of obligation. The Talmudic text does not provide a reason why fathers are responsible to support their children until age six.[73] The text teaches that age six not only marks a significant transition point in a child's development but also in paternal child support.

### *Baba Batra* 21a

*Baba Batra* 21a establishes a father's obligation to begin Torah study for sons at age six. The text reminds us that fathers are responsible to instruct their sons in Torah (based on Deut. 11:19). However, since the Rabbis saw that boys without fathers were not receiving such an education, the passage describes a series of legislative efforts to appoint teachers who could fulfill this role.

The last of these legislative efforts was a response to the fact that students were beginning their Torah educations at age 16 or 17 and, apparently, even then, adolescent boys were difficult to teach. In response, Joshua ben Gamla decreed that boys should begin their Torah studies at the age of six or seven.

Thus, this Talmudic text teaches, again, that age six is a significant point of transition, primarily for boys, with respect to education.

### Summary

With one notable exception, the Talmudic texts do not give explicit rules for deciding which parent should be awarded custody following a divorce. The only definitive rule of custody found in Talmudic sources is that a daughter, regardless of age, ought to placed with her mother. We find no definitive rule for the custody of boys in these Talmudic texts. Instead, we repeatedly find that age six is a significant point of transition mostly for boys with respect to education, the *mitzvah* of *eruv*, and paternal support. For girls, age six is only significant with respect to paternal support. Finally, we have only one statement which offers a reason why age six is a major transition point (Rav Joshua's psychological rationale that even a six year old still prefer's his mother's company).

## Geonic Texts
### Otzar Hageonim,
### Ketubot, Teshuvah 434
This responsum discusses a case in which an infant's mother has died and his father has moved away. Both sets of grandparents sought custody of the baby. The Geonim ruled:

> "It seems that one ought to investigate what will be for the good of the child (*tivuta d'tinok*), whether he is accustomed to one set of grandparents, recognizes them, is happy with them (*v'smach bo*) [if so], they ought to take the child, since his mind will be more settled with them (*d'bei tapai mitaba da'atai*)."[74]

Shochetman believes this Geonic responsum may be the earliest use of a term equivalent to the "best interests of the child."[75] In the case of an infant, the "good of the child" appears to be defined as the most familiar environment for the child. If, however, the child was not more familiar with either set of grandparents, the Geonim went on to rule that the court should compare the couples: 1) financial resources, 2) level of knowledge, 3) and the availability of women to carry and feed the baby. These factors seem to have constituted a second level of variables which define the "good of the child."

### Otzar HaGeonim,
### Ketubot, Teshuvah 435
In this responsum the Geonim ruled that a six year old boy should be placed with his widowed father rather than with his maternal grandmother because it is the father's responsibility to teach the boy Torah and prepare him for a profession:

> "When he reached the age of six, one places him with the father to bring him up, since the son can follow after his mother only until six years ...all the more so after the death of his mother, that one does not place him with his grandmother but rather with his father who can teach him Torah and teach him a trade, as our Rabbis have taught ...for what do women know of Torah study and preparation for a profession?"[76]

This Geonic source provides the first definitive rule about the custody of boys, before and after six years of age. It also provides a reason, directly linking the determination of custody with the father's responsibility to teach his son both Torah and a trade.

## Summary

The Geonic sources reflect further development and specification of the Talmudic law. There is now a general rule for the custody of boys, as well as girls. Boys are placed in the custody of their fathers at age six. Perhaps, the Geonim inferred this rule from the Talmudic concern for the education of boys (*Baba Batra* 21a).

Similarly, we hear for the first time of the concept of the "good of the child." At least one Geonic authority defined the "good of the child" as, primarily, the child's familiarity and contentment with his/her environment, and secondarily, with the capacity of that potential custodial environment to provide the child with financial and practical resources as well as female caretakers. However, we cannot declare the "good of the child" a general criterion for determining the custody of children, since the case involved two special variables. Perhaps, this concept of the " good of the child" would not have been invoked if either parent were available or if the child were not an infant. It may be the case that the concept of the "good of the child" became operative only when the two custody rules could not be applied.

## Medieval Codes

### *Mishneh Torah,*
### *Hilkhot Ishut* 21:16-18

Maimonides codified several important rules for determining child custody after divorce. With regard to infants, Maimonides ruled that the father is obligated to provide for their care, even if the mother has custody. The mother, however, is free to choose whether or not she will nurse her infant children. If the mother agrees to nurse her children, the father must pay her a fee. If the mother chooses not to nurse her children, the father must provide a wet nurse and provide for the infant's other material needs.

However, the mother's freedom of choice to nurse is limited if the child needs the mother to survive. If an infant recognized its mother, even a blind infant, Maimonides ruled that the mother was obligated to nurse the baby for two years. Hence, the *Mishneh Torah* teaches that the principle of *pikuaḥ nefesh*, saving life, overrides the mother's right to refuse to nurse.

With regard to children, Maimonides ruled that girls are always in the custody of their mothers. Maimonides also ruled that mothers may retain custody of their young sons:

> "If the months of nursing are completed and the child is weaned, the rule is as follows: If the divorced woman is willing to keep the child with her, it should not be separated from her until it is fully six years old, and the father should be compelled to provide

maintenance for the child while it remains with its
mother."[77]

So far, Maimonides' opinion is consistent with the Geonic ruling we
have already discussed. However, Maimonides' ruling about boys is
somewhat ambiguous:

> "After the six years, the father may say, 'if he will be
> with me, I will provide him with maintenance; but if
> he remains with his mother, I will provide no main-
> tenance for him."[78]

Maimonides did not explicitly require a transfer of custody for boys
at age six, in contrast to the Geonic ruling. Instead, he stated that
the father is not obligated to support a boy after age six, should he
remain in the custody of his mother. The threat of loss of paternal
economic support may have had some coercive influence in favor of
such transfer of custody. Yet it appears that Maimonides did not
make mandatory the transfer of custody of boys at age six. It seems
clear that Maimonides recognized the possibility that boys at age
six or older might still be in the custody of their mothers.

The Rabad (12th c.)[79], however, argued against Maimonides
that the mandated separation of a father from his son until the age
of six was unacceptable. Insofar as a father is responsible to begin
his son's Torah education at the age of four or five, Rabad asked
rhetorically, how is the father to do so when the boy grows up among
the women? Rabad's statement echoes the Geonic linkage of the
father's educational responsibilities to his son with the determination of custody. Implicit in Rabad's rhetorical question is the view
that custody of a son as young as four or five ought to be given to the
father for the purposes of Torah education. But from Rabad's comment, it is also clear that at the time of the *Mishneh Torah* (c. 1170),
the Geonic rule regarding custody of male children who had reached
six years of age had not achieved the status of recognized law.[80]

In further support of this last point, Maggid Mishneh (14th
c.),[81] argued against Rabad that he could find no halachic basis for
a paternal obligation to begin Torah study *before* the age of six.
The only source he found in this connection was the previously
mentioned text from *Baba Batra* 21a, which Maggid Mishneh presented as proof of the father's responsibility to begin Torah education at age six. In any case, Maggid Mishneh added, the father could
fulfill his educational obligations without having custody – when
the child would come to visit. Thus, Maggid Mishneh separated the
determination of custody from the issue of child support and Torah
education.

It should be remembered that the context of this discussion
is a rule in the *Mishneh Torah* regarding paternal support – not
custody. The entire discussion grows out of the implications of the

support rule for custody determination. As mentioned above, there clearly was no fixed and accepted rule regarding custody of male children who had reached age six. For authorities who accepted the Rabad's objection, the father's responsibility to begin educating his son in Torah was a critical consideration for the determination of custody. But from Maggid Mishneh's rebuttal, it is clear that even in the 14th century, not all authorities saw that responsibility as determinative.

### Toldot Adam V'havah

This lesser known medieval codification records an interesting alternative viewpoint to that of Maimonides. The text first cites the well-established rule regarding custody of daughters. However, it continues by pointing out that the Geonim wrote:

> ". ...but a son [ought to be placed] in the father's home, even [if] younger than age six. And it is permitted to compel him [father] to take custody of his son, because just as the mother teaches the daughter the practice of women (ma'aseh b'not), so the father teaches the son that which is appropriate to him (raui lo)."[82]

Just as a mother must teach her daughter "the practice of women," a father must teach his son "that which is appropriate to him" – presumably, the practice of men. As it was in the Rabad's opinion, concern with the father's educational responsibilities seems to have been a determinative factor in the custody of sons for some authorities. In fact, if we accept the text's Geonic attribution, we have additional evidence that some authorities held this position as early as the Geonic period.[83] However, if this is an authentic, Geonic opinion, it had not gained the force of recognized law by the medieval period – at least, not as far as Maimonides was concerned.

### Summary to
### Medieval Codes

Maimonides codified a rule favoring the mother as custodian for children younger than six years, particulary during the first years of life, on the grounds of concern for the infant's physical dependence and survival. After weaning, the mother has the option whether or not to retain custody, with the father's support guaranteed. In Rambam's code, consistent with the Talmudic rule, daughters remain with their mothers. But the custodial rule for sons, particularly those who have reached age six, is rather ambiguous. Maimonides ruled only that, after age six, a father is no longer required to support a son not in his custody. Halakhic authorities differed on the implications of this support rule for custody. A few authorities, such as Rabad and Toldot Adam V'havah seem to have felt that the father's responsibility to begin the child's Torah education necessitated a ruling for paternal custody. However, it is clear that there wasn't consensus regarding this point.

## Medieval Responsa
### Responsum of the Rashba
The Rashba (1235-1310) cited a responsum attributed to Ramban[84] in which a widowed mother requested that the administrators of her husband's estate provide support for her children. The administrators, who were relatives of her husband's, replied that they would do so if two of the children were given into their custody. The woman objected that she wanted custody of her children.

In the responsum, citing *Ketubot* 102b, custody of the daughter is left with the mother in order that the mother will "accustom the daughter and teach her the way of women (*derekh nashim*), so that she will not accustom herself to sexual impropriety." But custody of the son is given to the male relatives, since they will "accustom him and teach him the way of study (*derekh ha'limud*) and the way of men (*derekh anashim*), more than the mother."[85] In addition, the responsum points out, "the ways of widow's sons are strange (*darkham derekh zar*)."

In this decision, the Rashba holds that it is appropriate and necessary for children to have teachers and role models of the same gender. Girls need to be with their mothers in order to learn *derekh nashim*, in general, and sexual propriety, in particular. Boys need to live with men in order to learn *derekh anashim*, in general, and *derekh ha'limud*, in particular. Clearly, Rashba understands these concerns to be gender-specific. The mother is the appropriate teachers of "women's ways" and male relatives ("more than the mother") are the appropriate teachers of "men's ways" and "*derekh halimud*."[86]

In terms of the evolution of Jewish law, Rashba adds two items to the list, admittedly limited, of halachic concerns which are potentially determinative of custody. Previously, Geonic authorities have cited as determinative a mother's responsibility to teach the "practice of women" and the father's responsibility to train his son for a livelihood and to study Torah. Rashba adds particular concern with the mother teaching her daughter about sexual propriety and male relatives teaching the son "the way of men." Although it is difficult to be certain of the intended meaning, the added observation that the ways of widow's sons are strange may be meant to emphasize the importance of a role model of the same gender. When widowed women raise their male children alone, the boys tend to be "strange." As always, though, it is important to be cautious of anachronistic projection.

In addition to its ruling in this particular case, however,

Rashba's responsum is also important because it establishes a critical general principle of *tikkun* with regard to the *Beit Din's* role in custody decisions. The responsum states:

> "Always, in general, in these matters, it is necessary for the *Beit Din* in each place to examine carefully what [arrangement], in their view, has more benefit (*tikkun*) for orphans, since the *Beit Din* is [like] the orphan's father – looking after their well-being (*tikkunan*)."

The significance of this principle will be discussed in the summary to this section.

### Responsum of the Radbaz

The Radbaz (1479-1573) was asked to rule on a case in which a sick, male infant's mother had died and the child was living with the maternal grandmother.[87] Both the father and grandmother wanted custody of the child. Radbaz ruled that the grandmother should be given custody of the sick infant.

As discussed in the statement set forth by the Rashba, the guiding principle for this ruling, was the child's well-being (*takkanat havalad*) – defined both by the presumption that the grandmother would be more likely to have compassion upon the infant than would others and by the father's unfitness as a custodian. According to Radbaz, since "one's grandchildren are like one's children," the grandmother, like the mother, would have more compassion on the child than anyone else. As added support, Radbaz cites the *Eruvin* statement that "even a child of six prefers his mother's (and, by analogy, his grandmother's) company." In addition, for Radbaz, the child's poor health raised concerns about dangers to its life if placed in the father's custody – as we have seen, a major determinant of custody.

This concern was especially prevalent given the father's demand for custody in which he said: "Give the child to me and I will do what I wish and if he dies, he dies" – a statement the Radbaz characterized as "demented" (*shoteh*). The concern was further amplified by the fact that the father had not remarried and had no wife (presumably, to care for the child in his absence). In fact, according to Radbaz, had the father remarried, he rightfully *should* have received custody. Thus, while there were other considerations, the overriding determinant seems to have been the absence of a female caretaker in the father's household. In the end, Radbaz declared, the general rule in such matters was that everything depended upon the *Beit Din's* view of which "place" (*makom*) most promoted the child's well-being (*takkanat havalad*).

## Summary to
## Medieval Responsa

It is not absolutely clear whether Rashba's principle of *tikkun* and Radbaz's principle of *takkanat havalad* apply to regular custody situations between two biological parents or only to special custody situations in which one biological parent is dead. Both Rashba and Radbaz appear to be making statements about general custody determinations. Yet the immediate context in both cases concerns a dispute over custody between the sole remaining biological parent and a non-biological potential custodian.

The ambiguity emerges from the texts themselves. When Rashba states,"always, in general, in these matters," do the words "in these matters" refer to all custody determinations or to all custody determinations of "orphans"? The language seems to refer to general custody determinations but then Rashba specifically links the process of *tikkun* with orphans. Similarly, Radbaz's language about *takkanat havalad* also appears to refer to all custody cases in general. But throughout the responsum, Radbaz appears to be struggling with the problems specific to *this* case. Custody ought to go to the mother, but the mother is dead:

> "It is quite clear our Rabbis said the son should be with the mother and not with the grandmother. But if the *Beit Din* saw that it was for the benefit of the child that he reside with the grandmother, since she would have more compassion for him than others, they can place him with the grandmother."

It appears either that Radbaz had no definitive rule for this kind of situation or that the child should go to the father. Repeatedly, Radbaz justified awarding custody to the grandmother, rather than the biological father, on the basis of *takkanat havalad.*

Without additional data, we believe the decisions of both the Rashba and the Radbaz should be interpreted according to a minimal and a maximal position. The minimal position is as follows: The concept of *tikkun,* at this time period, applies only to custody situations where one parent is dead. That is the immediate context in both Medieval responsa, and we have no other evidence from this time period in which it can be clearly demonstrated that the principle of *tikkun* applies to regular custody situations.

According to this interpretation, both Rashba's principle of *tikkun* and Radbaz's principle of *takkanat havalad* are limited not only in application – to cases where at least one biological parent is deceased – but they are also limited in authority. It is significant that both Rashba's and Radbaz's rulings do not deviate from what would most probably have been the outcome according to the normal custody rules, had the deceased biological parents been alive. In Rashba's case, the normal custody rule would place a non-minor son in the custody of the father. Rashba grants custody to the closest available male relatives who could fulfill the deceased father's paternal responsibility to educate the boy in Torah and the ways of men. Also, in Radbaz's case, the normal custody rule would place an infant, especially a sick one, in the custody of the mother. Radbaz grants custody to the closest available female (the father had not remarried) relative who could fulfill the deceased mother's maternal responsibility to guard the infant's health and show the child compassion.

From this perspective, the function of Rashba's concept of *tikkun* and Radbaz's concept of *takkanat havalad* may not have been to establish a new legal principle at all, but rather to conserve and perpetuate the normal custody rules by resolving a technical problem within them: Do the normal custody rules apply when one biological parent is deceased? Underlying this technicality is a serious legal and ethical issue. Does the sole remaining biological parent obtain custody by default, or does the *Beit Din* have the authority to take a child away from the sole remaining biological parent and place it with a non-biological custodian?

Both Rashba and Radbaz ruled that the *Beit Din* does have *this* authority. The *Beit Din* can extend the normal custody rules to cover cases where one biological parent is deceased. In this view, the principle of *tikkun / takkanat havalad* at this time period may denote the authority of the *Beit Din* to award custody, by extending the normal custody rules, to a non-biological custodian. As such, the principle of *tikkun / takkanat havalad* does not yet establish the authority of the *Beit Din* to set aside the normal custody rules with regard to any custody cases. If this thesis is correct, then these principles actually functioned to conserve and extend the normal custody rules.

The maximal position is as follows: The principles of *tikkun / takkanat havalad* have significance well beyond the particulars of their cases. Both Rashba and Radbaz establish an important precedent regarding the right and responsibility of the *Beit Din* to exercise judicial discretion in deciding *all* custody cases. According to Rashba, the *Beit Din* ought to see itself as the child's guardian. The *Beit Din* must look to the particulars of each case and determine which custodial arrangement most insures the well-being or *tikkun* of the child. The application of *takkanat havalad* enabled Radbaz to make a custody determination which was not, as he observed, prescribed by the rules (awarding custody to the grandmother over the father), but which took account of extenuating circumstances (the child's illness combined with the father's unfitness and the fact that he had not remarried) and of the values inherent in the law (concern for proper care of infants and *pikuaḥ nefesh*, for instance).

According to this interpretation, the principles of *tikkun / takkanat havalad* were not limited in application or authority. The principles applied to all custody cases and allowed the *Beit Din* to deviate from the normal custody rules when circumstances seemed to require it. From this perspective, Rashba's concept of *tikkun* and Radbaz's concept of *takkanat havalad* may have served an an overarching criterion by which to assess the applicability of the custody rules.

While both Rashba and Radbaz defined the child's *takkanah* according to well-established halakhic values (instruction in sexual propriety, preparation for Torah study, importance of fe-male care for infants, concern with the preservation of life), each chose relevant Jewish values to define a child's *takkanah* according to the particulars of the case before him. These values, in turn, were used to assess the applicability of the rule for custody of girls and the general guidelines for boys (girls and young boys with their mothers and older boys with their fathers).

## Early Modern Texts
### *Shulḥan Arukh*
### *Even Haezer* 82:7

In the *Shulḥan Arukh*, Karo essentially repeated Maimonides' legislation regarding child custody and support.[88] However, Isserles' gloss notes an important exception to the rule regarding custody of daughters. Isserles qualified the presumption favoring maternal custody and noted that this was the rule only insofar as:

> It seems to the *Beit Din* that it is good for the daughter (*tov labat*) to live with her mother. However, if it seems to the *Beit Din* that it is better for her (*tov yoter lah*) to be placed in her father's house, the mother can not force the father to relinquish custody nor, if the mother is dead, can the maternal grandmother.[89]

Isserles codified the concept (at least for the Ashkenazim of his time) that the *Beit Din* has both the right and the obligation to exercise judicial discretion if it feels that the prescribed custody arrangement would not be best for a daughter.

Unfortunately, however, Isserles does not provide explicit criteria for deciding when it is better for a daughter to be placed in her father's custody than in her mother's custody. Isserles left it to individual *Batei Din* to define what is *tov* for a daughter.[90]

However, it is clear that the Talmudic rule for maternal custody of daughters serves as a legal presumption for Isserles. At least in his view, the rule may be set aside in the event that the *Beit Din* decides the presumed arrangement is not what is best for the daughter. Isserles' gloss reflects a willingness towards using halakhic values (though, admittedly, unspecified values) to assess the applicability of the maternal custody rule. Whether Isserles would allow the same latitude in deciding custody of male offspring is not clear from the text.

### Sh'elot Uteshuvot
### Darkhei Noam[91]

Mordechai ben Judah HaLevi provides the first formal acknowledgement that a custody rule for older boys had crystallized by the 17th century:[92]

> Speaking generally, the sages of the Talmud said that in the general case (*s'tam milta*), the daughter [should be placed] with the mother as should the son, in his earlier years, and later be with his father[93]. ...that all this is [for] the good of the child (*tikkun ha'yeled*) in the general case.

*Darkhei Noam* goes on to assert the strongest statement we have so far regarding the authority of the *Beit Din* to deviate from the normal custody rules:

> But if the *Beit Din* saw that the child's well-being is not in this [pattern of arrangements], rather, on the contrary, [it is] harmful, they should alter their decision in accordance with their [the children's] well-being, as it appears to the judges. And all the halakhic authorities (*poskim*) have agreed to this – that everything depends on the *Beit Din*'s view of what is best for the child (*tikkun lavalad*).[94]

*Darkhei Noam* clearly interprets the custody rules as legal presumptions which may be overturned if they do not provide that which is best for the child. Furthermore, if we take *Darkhei Noam* at his word, by the 17th century, all *poskim* subscribed to this view.[95]

In another section of this same responsum, we are given a specific example of the authority of the principle of *tikkun havalad*:

> If the *Beit Din* saw that [it was for] the well-being of the young child (*tikkun havalad*) to be in his father's home or, even, in the home of his father's relatives,' they [are permitted] to remove him [the child] from the mother and give him to the father, or to the father's relatives, from what we said: "his mother's company is preferable for him" — meaning that we should do that which is good (*tov*) and preferable for the child (*noah lavalad*).[96]

As against, for instance, the *Mishneh Torah*'s general rule providing for maternal custody of young children, the *Darkhei Noam* allows even a young male child to be placed in the custody of the father or his relatives if the *Beit Din* sees that arrangement as "better" for the child. *Darkhei Noam* does not define what is *tov* or *noaḥ* or *tikkun lavalad*. Similar to Isserles, the *Darkhei Noam* left it to individual *Batei Din* to define these terms according to the particulars of the case before them.

## Summary to
## Early Modern Texts

The rule of paternal custody for older boys was finally crystallized by the early modern period (17th century). Based on the texts we've seen, this rule appears to be a part of an increasing propensity to award custody of all children to the father in the early modern period. Under the appropriate circumstances, the *Shulḥan Arukh* would place a girl in the custody of her father rather than her mother. The *Darkhei Noam* would place a young boy in the custody of the father or even the father's relatives rather than the mother.[97] Similarly, the *Noda Biyehuda* ruled that a divorced father has the right to take custody of his son prior to age six, when the mother had decided to move to another city, in order to fulfill his paternal responsibility to provide Torah education.

It is noteworthy that in both of our early modern texts, the application of the principle of *takkanat havalad* resulted in paternal custody in opposition to the normal custody rules. It can be speculated that the concept of *takkanat havalad* may have functioned, at least in part, to challenge the presumption for maternal custody (which had been the norm for girls since the Talmudic period and for young boys since the Geonic period).[98]

Both the *Shulḥan Arukh* and the *Darkhei Noam* (and perhaps also the earlier Medieval responsa) reflect a growing tendency to use particular halachic values (*pikuaḥ nefesh*, Torah education, training for a profession, sexual propriety, behavior appropriate to each gender) to assess the applicability of the custody rules. For the *Shulḥan Arukh* and the *Darkhei Noam* the custody rules seem to function only as legal presumptions which may be set aside if, in a particular case, it seems to a *Beit Din* that the presumed custody arrangement will not promote their carefully defined understanding of the child's well-being. It is quite clear that the principle of *takkanat havalad* now applies to all custody cases and that the term denotes extensive judicial authority to deviate from the custody rules.

## Contemporary Rulings
## of the
## Rabbinical Courts
## of Israel

Israel's former Chief Rabbi, Ben-Tzion Meir Hai Uziel, in a responsum on the appropriate legal procedure for determining child custody,[99] articulated an interesting perspective on the significance of both parenthood and children. He wrote that children ought not be regarded as commodities, currency or beasts that can be purchased or traded. Rather, the Chief Rabbi wrote, "children are God's inheritance (*nakhalah*) to their parents, in order that they may raise them, educate them in Torah and *mitzvot* and in the way of life." Presumably, for the Chief Rabbi, this vision of parenthood and of children provides a framework of values within which custody decisions ought to be made. He would probably favor the custody arrangement which most effectively insures the fulfillment of this ideal parental role.

A brief analysis of several decisions of the Israeli Rabbinic Courts reveals an expanded willingness to assess the applicability of the halakhic guidelines/rules for custody according to definitions of what is best for the child. Interestingly, these contemporary definitions reflect not only halakhic values but related psychological values, as well. To note but a few cases: a mother was given custody of her son, who was older than six, because of the father's mental instability;[100] a mother, who had committed adultery was still given custody of her thirteen year old son, since the father was unwilling to raise and educate his son;[101] a father was given custody of a two and a half year old son and allowed to leave Israel for six months because he was the primary caretaker and the child's "psychological parent;"[102] and a mother of a thirteen year old boy was given custody based upon the boy's preference.[103]

According to both Warburg and Schaffer,[104] the child's best interests is the governing standard for child custody determination in contemporary Israel. From the proceeding cases, it is clear that the "best interests" standard of the Israeli Rabbinical Courts includes contemporary psychological considerations such as the "psychological parent," the child's preferences, and the parent's attitude towards parenting. Thus, contemporary halakhic authorities in Israel appear to exercise even more discretion in assessing the applicability of the rules/guidelines in accordance with their sense of what is best for the child.

**Summary**

The general perspective of the modern Israeli courts, which, as have seen, evolved from the medieval period to the present, is summarized in two decisions of the court. These decisions cite both the Rashba's responsum and the opinion of *Darkhei Noam* (see above), empowering and obligating the *Beit Din* to determine custody on a case by case basis, according to what is best for the child. The rulings concluded: "Thus, there is no fixed rule regarding placement of the children, only a general guideline if there is no contra-indication."[105] This statement nicely summarizes the halakhic state of affairs in contemporary Israeli rabbinical courts.

## General Summary

From the Talmudic period until the medieval period, Jewish law reflected only a rule regarding custody of daughters and several varied opinions as to the custody of sons. Maimonides codified both the rule regarding girls and a rule that mothers have the right to retain custody of young boys. However, as regards older boys, Maimonides codified only an ambiguous rule regarding the father's obligation for support. There was considerable disagreement regarding the interpretation of Maimonides ruling. However, eventually, at least according to the evidence at hand, a preference for paternal custody of older boys became authoritative. Aside from a Geonic ruling which neither the *Mishneh Torah* nor the *Shulḥan Arukh* seem to accept, the present study found no explicit, general statement of a rule regarding custody of older boys until *Darkhei Noam* (17th century).

From the early modern period onward (perhaps even as early as the medieval responsa), we noted an increased willingness to assess the applicability of these rules/guidelines based on the court's understanding of what was best for the child. One's view of the period in which this transition took place depends on whether or not one sees general application and overarching authority of the principle of *tikkun/takkanat havalad* in the late medieval or early modern periods.

According to Mnookin, custody determinations necessarily involve value judgements about the "good life." He stated, "deciding what is best for a child often poses a question no less ultimate than the purposes and values of life itself."[106] Until very recent times, the Jewish understanding of what was "good" for the child generally grew from a halakhic vision of the most ideal custody arrangement for a young person being trained for a particular role in the adult, halakhic community. None of the authorities attempted to provide an overarching definition of criteria for determining what was "best" for the child. However, in the collection of decisions, certain halakhic values did emerge with some consistency. Among these, the importance of preservation of life and physical health, Torah education and training in a profession for boys, training in sexual propriety for girls and instruction in gender-appropriate behavior for all children stand out. These values help to define "the good life" in Jewish Law.

It is of note that the values which were considered determinative seem to have varied with the age of the child. For instance, while physical survival and well-being was often of determinative importance for the infant child, in the cases dealing with older children, the importance of Torah study, training in sexual propriety and instruction in gender-appropriate behavior seem to have taken precedence. Thus, Jewish law seems to reflect some sensitivity to the nuances of child development – at least, insofar as it recognizes that children at different ages have different needs and abilities.

It is also of note that approaching the modern period, and, particularly, in contemporary decisions, Jewish legal authorities demonstrated a willingness to include not only a limited group of well-established halakhic values but related psychological values in their determination of what constituted the well-being of the child. However, even as the scope of the courts' latitude to determine what is best for a child and to judge the applicability of the rules/ guidelines has widened, the burden of its responsibility has in-creased. As a judge's values system for determining what is "best" for a child becomes broader or less well-defined, his responsibility for the decision becomes much heavier. In this respect, contemporary Israeli rabbinic law (and the contemporary liberal Jew) confront a problem somewhat analogous to that faced by secular legal authorities. As Mnookin observed," there is in our society no apparent consensus about the good life for children."[107]

# Mediation –
# Jonathan Kraus

In my initial attempt to mediate between the general ethical and the Jewish insights and presumptions regarding child custody, I confronted an important irony. I found myself willing to accept the validity and truth (albeit, with appropriate qualifiers) of the general ethical sources without much question. But the Jewish sources didn't seem to yield much that added to or improved on "contemporary" wisdom. In fact, the sexist assumptions undergirding many of the Jewish texts alienated me and almost moved me to dismiss Judaism's contribution in this area of concern. But after returning for a second look at the Jewish sources, I have revised that estimation. I begin there.

What has Judaism taught that might prove of assistance in the present endeavor? The halakhic tradition has displayed an evolving willingness to assess the validity of various custody arrangements based on the understanding, which emerges from its values system, of what is best for the child. By analogy, we, too, might establish guidelines for custody, based not on gender and traditional halakhic roles, but on a similar, general understanding of the "Jewish" meaning of parenthood and childhood.

For Judaism, as we have seen, the parent is primarily teacher, role model and caretaker. The child, correspondingly, is being prepared for Jewish adulthood and is in need of instruction, role models and care. But, relatively early on, Judaism seems to understand that the child's needs and the importance of these parental roles vary at different developmental stages.

As one example, we've observed the halakhic authorities' sensitivity to the fact that the infant's needs are quite different from that of the six year old, whose needs differ from that of the thirteen year old. Contemporary Jews might co-opt the tradition's concern with the young child's primary need for physical stability and constant nurture without co-opting the assumption that a woman, by definition, is the more appropriate choice to meet that need.

As the contemporary Israeli judgements testify, therefore, psychological insights, such as the infant's need for stability or men's ability to be "maternal," do not necessarily subvert and may even enrich a 'Jewish' understanding of the "best interests of the child." However, in any approach to custody that is truly grounded in Judaism, the values and perspective that define parenthood and childhood must be used as the guide.

In this connection, the insight of Israel's former chief rabbi, Ben-Tzion Meir Hai Uziel, is both inspiring and enlightening. As will be recalled, he wrote that children ought not be regarded as merchandise that can be purchased or traded. Rather, he wrote, "children are God's inheritance (naḥalah) to their parents, in order that they may raise them, educate them in Torah and mitzvot and in the way of life." For the present author, from a Jewish perspective, parents' consciousness that children are a sacred "gift" and their willingness and ability to assume the responsibilities that such an inheritance requires would provide a meta-ethical framework for the complex and painful work of determining child custody.

It should be admitted, however, that my understanding of a parent's duties to that naḥalah probably differ from the Chief Rabbi's understanding. The primary difference would seem to be that while education in "Torah and mitzvot" has an important and honored place in my understanding of the meaning of parenthood, my understanding of such education is neither as particular nor as determinative a consideration as it probably was for the Chief Rabbi. For me, as for Judaism, there is a rough hierarchy of needs and concerns that define the "best interests of the child," priorities in caring for the naḥalah. Again, I note, that, for me, this definition need not exclude, and, may well embrace and be amplified by the insights of psychology and secular law.

Borrowing a model from Abraham Maslow, the hierarchy of needs/values for determining custody takes the form of a pyramid (see Figure I). At the bottom of the pyramid are fundamental, general concerns such as the capacity to maintain the child's physical health and well-being. If, for some reason, either potential custodian is entirely unable to meet these needs, I would be unlikely to advise awarding custody to that individual. However, to say that these concerns are the most basic is to not to say that they are either the most important or, necessarily, the most determinative factors.

More critical, in my mind, are a range of psychological variables. These factors include the quality of the parent-child relationship, which parent has thus far served as the primary caretaker, psychological health of the potential custodians and the child, the probable quality of the parents' post-divorce relationship, the child's adjustment to and significant relationships in the present environment and, depending upon the child's developmental sophistication, his/her custodial preference.

As the ambiguity of the psychological evidence testifies, some of these factors will be extremely difficult to assess with certainty. Nonetheless, in order to maximize the child's psychological adjustment and well-being following this drastic change, I believe they ought to be taken into account. Incidentally, believing that healthy human beings combine characteristics commonly associated with both genders, the gender of the custodian is not of much concern to me. In any case, I would advocate the input of mental health professionals as well as the use of interviews with all significant individuals. However, as with the preceding factors, these aspects of the situation are very important but may not, necessarily, be determinative. There is still a third higher level of concern.

The "top" level is dependent upon and includes the preceding two categories. However, its concerns and values extend beyond them. A parent's responsibility as spiritual/ethical guide and teacher are here. At this level, a significant question is which custodian best emulates God-like qualities in his/her approach to children. As God's surrogate, which parent will cherish, care for and guide this child most in accordance with Jewish values and priorities? Here, we are concerned not only with the child's physical and psychological well-being but his/her growth towards Jewish adulthood and wholeness. Clearly, these factors will be even harder to assess than the psychological variables. But that does not make them less important in my view.

While the parents' Jewish knowledge, commitment and self-understanding might be among the factors considered here, I would want to exercise caution in using these variables to make a judgement. The God-like qualities sought on this level may include Jewish knowledge, community involvement and self-awareness. However, there are individuals who understand these matters intuitively and provide powerful models and instruction by virtue of this intuitive feeling for the sacred importance of parenthood.

In general, as Rashba suggested in Ramban's name, I would hope that judges or rabbinic advisors would exercise caution and look at every case on its own merits, judging what would most benefit the child, the family and the community – whether it be maternal, paternal or joint custody. The categories and levels described above function as a frame of reference. The over-arching concern is with which custodial arrangement most fulfills the vision of parents as caretakers and heirs of God's *naḥalah* to them and to the Jewish people. The following case study tentatively suggests how this approach might function in a particular custody decision.

## Case

> A family in the congregation is going through a divorce proceeding. There is one child, an eight year old girl who has expressed a desire to live with her father. The father has a live-in girlfriend. The mother wants to move to Los Angeles and work towards a doctorate at the University of Southern California. While the mother is a committed Reform Jew, the father is apathetic and indifferent to Jewish identity. Both parents have expressed a desire to receive custody of their daughter. They have come to you as rabbi, seeking your help in resolving the situation.

Beginning with the first level of the pyramid, it is unclear whether the mother will be able to support the daughter and still return to university. One would want to find out if the mother could afford to care for the daughter and, for that matter, how both parents feel about providing support for the child even if they do not have custody. For the present purpose, we'll assume that both parents could maintain the daughter at an acceptable level.

Moving to the second level, we note that the child is young but, since girls mature faster than boys, she may be at a developmental level where her preference for paternal custody should weigh significantly. In addition, as some psychological evidence suggests, being a girl, her adjustment to whatever custody arrangement is chosen may be easier. For this and other reasons, one would need to get a sense of "who" the child is.

Also important, however, are factors such as the probable quality of the parents' post-divorce relationship (somewhat promising, since they came to see you together), the psychological adjustment of each parent and which parent has been the primary caretaker thus far. Again, for the present purposes, let us assume that the parents are both reasonably well-adjusted and that the father and his girl-friend have been the primary caretakers recently.

Moving into the third level, it is clear that the mother is more committed and identified with a Jewish world view and perspective. Nonetheless, since the father desires custody and has been the primary caretaker recently, he, too, may well have some appreciation for the sacred potential of parenthood – albeit, not identified as such. Clearly, however, the mother would provide the best Jewish role model and would be most likely to initiate the child's Jewish education.

I would approach this case as follows. Presuming that the quality of relationship between the parents is sufficiently positive and that their shared concern for the child's well-being is strong, I would first encourage them to try and avoid adjudication. Their shared concern and willingness to work at a solution together may prove to be the most important factor for the child's well-being. Adjudication, by definition, seems to undermine those qualities.

Given that the daughter would prefer to remain in the father's custody and that she is already eight, I would probably be inclined to give that preference some weight. If the father is, indeed, a committed and caring parent, if the daughter has a decent relationship with the girlfriend and presuming that the daughter is fairly well-adjusted to the present environment, I would probably award custody to the father rather than forcing the child to go, against her will, to California.

However, if the mother is willing to seek her degree here,[108] a choice I would urge her to consider, several preferable alternatives open up. The first would be joint custody – an option which, it seems to me, is as good as the quality of the parents' post-divorce relationship. Given recent psychological evidence, however, I suspect that this arrangement is not the most preferable. More preferable, it seems to me, is to award custody to the father but to encourage him to allow the mother liberal visitation rights in order, among other things, that she may provide for the child's religious education (an arrangement which, ironically, reverses the situation we observed in several Jewish sources).

There are no simple, formula solutions to these problems. They are extremely complex – as all human relationships and systems are inclined to be. Nonetheless, at the intersection of Jewish law and ethics, one finds guideposts which can help to make the journey through this painful but increasingly vital terrain maximally productive, healthy and consistent with Judaism's vision of parenthood and childhood.

---

FIGURE I:
## Kraus' Hierarchy of Needs/Values

**PARENT AS CARETAKER
FOR
GOD'S "NAHALAH"**

---

**PSYCHOLOGICAL FACTORS:**

Quality of parent-child relationships

Primary caretaker
Child's preference

Child's adjustment
to present environment

Psychological health
of all significant individuals

Quality of probable future relationship
between parents

---

**CAPACITY TO MAINTAIN THE CHILD'S HEALTH
AND PHYSICAL WELL-BEING**

---

# Mediation –
# Stuart Weinberg

The mediation between the legal/ethical perspectives on on child custody determinations and Jewish Law will be worked out through a hypothetical custody case.

The details of the case:  1) Both parents want custody of their 8 year old girl; 2) The child's preference is to be with her father; 3) The mother intends to relocate to LA in order to study for her doctorate; 4) The father has a live-in girlfriend; 5) The father is indifferent to his Jewish identity.  The mother is a committed ·Reform Jew.

1) I begin my evaluation of the case with the belief, supported by the majority of current scientific research, that fathers and

mothers are equally important for a child's development. "Fathering" is no less important than "mothering." Children form strong emotional bonds with both parents.

Jewish Law was definitely tilted in favor of the maternal relationship (until the early modern period). I think the weight that Jewish Law has given to the tender years presumption is demonstrated by the fact that, despite the fundamental paternal obligation to instruct his sons in Talmud Torah, Jewish Law did not require a mandatory transfer of boys to the custody of their fathers at age 6 until the 17th century. It was possible for younger boys to remain in the custody of their mothers, and the father would teach them Torah when they came to visit. Jewish Law allowed the principle of tender years to prevail over Talmud Torah.

While Jewish Law had certainly given fathers many economic and educational responsibilities toward their children, I think it had underestimated (until the early modern period) the extent to which we now believe children need to emotionally bond with their fathers. I therefore welcome the value of parental equality and I would like to see its inclusion within Jewish Law.

The lack of a determinative presumption compels me to even more rigorously examine the quality of the child's psychological relationships with each parent. From the child's perspective, I want to know what the child feels toward each parent and what kinds of interactions they have. From the parents' perspective, I want to know whether the parent feels affection and responsibility toward the child.

Not unexpectedly, the psychological perspective is almost totally focussed on intrapsychic and interpersonal considerations. In this context, I think the legal perspective offers a necessary corrective. While the everwidening circles of the child's interpersonal relationships (with custodial parent, noncustodial parent, friends and relatives) are critical, they cannot be the sole criteria for child custody determinations.

The courts take into consideration a multiplicity of both psychological and non-psychological variables. Many of these non-psychological variables focus on parental characteristics (mental stability, moral fitness, parenting skills) and on situational factors (parental time availability,stability of living arrangments, financial resources). The courts child custody criteria can be characterized as focussed upon pragmatic considerations.

I think Jewish Law has steered a somewhat balanced course between psychological and non-psychological criteria in its custody determinations. However, my reading of the sources would place Jewish Law, overall, closer to the pragmatic considerations of the legal perspective. We see much concern in the Geonic and Responsa literature for situational factors and parental characteristics. I don't believe we find equal evidence in Jewish Law for intrapsychic or interpersonal psychological considerations (other than the most basic concerns for physical and emotional welfare until the modern period.

The Israeli Rabbinical Courts have included sophisticated psychological considerations into their custody determinations under the best interests standard. I am in favor of including such psychological criteria into Jewish Law. I should add that I perceive the sources as being more unaware of psychological considerations than opposed to them. However, I think Jewish Law would be opposed to the consideration of exclusively psychological criteria in determining child custody, and with this I also agree.

For our hypothetical case, let us presume that the child's relationship with both parents is good and that both parents are fully capable of the parental role.

2) Our sources appear to be silent on the issue of children's custodial preference. However, the argument from silence does not constitute proof that Jewish Law opposed the consideration of the child's custodial preference. In any case, I believe that the recognition of children as persons entails the consideration of a child's preference.

Psychological research informs us that the reliability of a child's preference is dependent not upon age, but upon the child's level of cognitive/affective development. However, it is generally accepted that the appropriate level of development becomes operational in children at age 12.

For this hypothetical case, let us assume that the child's preference is reliable even though she's only 8 years old, and she has good reasons for the preference. Hence, the child's preference is an important factor in support of awarding custody to the father.

3) One of the most interesting values that emerges from my reading of the sources, is that the family after divorce, although restructured, is not dissolved. Jewish Law seems to be concerned to preserve the child's free access and continued relationship with both parents. Ongoing relationship with the noncustodial father was maintained (even compelled) by paternal obligations. The noncustodial father must still educate his sons and financially support his daughters.

This Jewish value also appears as a contextual mediator of postdivorce adjustment in the psychological literature. The mother's intention to relocate to Los Angeles violates this value and could create problems with other contextual mediators as well. For example, the relocation might exacerbate strife between mother and daughter, increase hostility between the mother and father. All of these factors could retard the child's postdivorce adjustment.

In addition, the mother's intent to pursue a full time doctoral program would undoubtedly diminish the time and energy she would have available for her daughter. Even if we presume the mother had been the child's primary caretaker, an important factor in the mother's favor, its value is made moot since the the mother's future capacity to fulfill that role is doubtful.

The mother's intention to relocate is the single most critical factor against her receiving custody.

4) The legal system is divided on the issues of parental non-marital sexual relationships. Some courts presume automatic harm to the child. Other courts refuse to accept this presumption and argue that each case must be examined on its own merit.

Psychological research, while inconclusive, suggests that nonmarital sexual relationships are not harmful to the child. Jewish Law, certainly, is opposed to such relationships.

I believe the answer lies probably somewhere in the middle. I reject the presumption that nonmarital sexual relationships are either automatically harmful or automatically nonharmful to the child. The actual impact of the parent's relationship on the child must be ascertained and not presumed.

Clearly, if the nonmarital relationship is a poor one, the child should not be exposed to it. But if the parent is involved in a genuine, loving relationship, then the child may actually benefit from the experience. The girl will now have the benefit of both a man and a woman in the home. While I believe that male and female parenting is equally important, I don't deny that they are different. And that a child, optimally, should be given the opportunity to experience both.

For our hypothetical case, let us presume that the father's nonmarital relationship is a good one, and that the girlfriend is close to the child. Hence, the father's nonmarital relationship is a positive factor in the father's favor.

5) Another value which emerges from Jewish Law is the paternal obligation to teach his sons Talmud Torah. As a believer in egalitarianism, I immediately amend Jewish Law to include mothers and girls in this value. In the contemporary world, this value of Jewish law, as well as several other values, would be better served by the adoption of an egalitarian ethic. For the simple fact is, as illustrated by our hypothetical case, that frequently it is not the father, but the mother, who will be the child's catalyst for Jewish identity and education. We need to differentiate between the value and its traditional role bearers, and promote the former.

I abstract from this value a superordinate meta-halakhic value with regard to custody determinations: It is a privilege to be a Jew. The existence of Judaism enriches the world. Hence, I consider the mother's strong Reform Jewish identity to be a critical factor in support of awarding custody to the mother.

Finally, I believe there is one other superordinate meta-halakhic value which emerges from these sources, particularly from the responsum of the Radbaz. The Radbaz was particularly concerned with who would show *raḥamim* – compassion – to the child, repeating the concern several times. I believe that underlying Radbaz's concern for compassion stands the meta-halakhic value of *imitatio dei*. After all, God is *Haraḥaman*, the Compassionate One.

The relevance of this meta-halakhic value to child custody determinations is this: God, as our ultimate Parent, is the ultimate custodial role model. The way God relates to the world – with justice, with compassion, with self sacrifice – is the way a custodian should behave toward his/her child, and the way in which the process of making child custody decisions should be conducted. For example, the adversarial, unjust, and subjective process of child custody adjudication is incompatible with the meta-halakhic principle of *imitatio dei*.

## Conclusion

My ideal preference would have been to award custody to the mother, provided she will find another way to fulfill her educational pursuits without relocating.

The decision is based on the value that "it is a privilege to be a Jew." The mother's obligation to teach her daughter Talmud Torah prevails over all other considerations except one – the child's ongoing free access to the prized relationship with her father – which must also be accomodated.

Hence, this decision is also based on the value of *imitatio dei*. Just as God self sacrificed and went through a process of contraction in order to create the human world, so I believe the mother should make a sacrifice and contract her educational expectations. Such a sacrifice would allow the child continued free access to the prized relationship with her father.

If the mother could not or would not change her relocation plans, then I would award custody to the father, provided that he make a commitment to educate himself and his daughter in Judaism.

This decision is based on the principle of *imitatio dei*. Just as God shows compassion for the human world, so I would demonstrate compassion for the daughter and not allow her to be deprived of her cherished relationship with her father. Nor would it be compassionate to place the child with her mother in a foreign city with a mother who is unable to fulfill her parental role due to her academic responsibilities. The value of compassion prevails over all other considerations except one – the principle of "it is a privilege to be a Jew" – which must also be accomodated.

Hence, this decision is also based on the principle of "it is a privilege to be a Jew." Hopefully, the father would accept with joy the proviso to undertake the study of Talmud Torah. But even if he regarded it as an act of self-sacrifice that too would be necessary under the principle of *imitatio dei*. The father's act of *tzimtum* would allow his daughter free access to Judaism, which is her prized inheritance.

Ultimately, the ethics of child custody determinations revolve around the meaning of parenthood. From one Jewish perspective, children are an inheritance from God, to be shown by their parents the joys of Torah, *mitzvot*, and the way of life. From another Jewish perspective, parents are copartners with God in the act of creation. Parenthood is the imitation of the ways of the ultimate Parent.

# Bibliography

### Geonic Sources
*Otzar Hageonim*: writings and decisions of the "Geonim," heads of the academies from 7th-10th centuries.

### Medieval Sources
*Mishneh Torah:* famous Jewish legal code of Maimonides (c. 1178), Rabbi Moshe ben Maimon, physician, scholar, *poseq* and philosopher.

"Rabad:" Rabbi Abraham ben David of Posquierre, 12th century, one of standard commentators on the *Mishneh Torah*, who frequently challenges Maimonides' rulings.

*Sh'elot Uteshuvot Harashba Hameyuhasot L'haramban*: responsa of Rabbi Solomon ben Abraham Adret (1235-1310), Sephardic legal authority and student of Nachmanides (1194-1270), to whom many of the responsa in this collection are attributed.

*Toldot Adam V'havah*: codification by Jeroham ben Meshullan (1290-1350), arranged according to events in the life-cycle.

"Maggid Mishneh:" Rabbi Vidal Yom Tov, 14th century, another standard commentator on the *Mishneh Torah*, who generally refers to the Talmudic sources of Maimonides' rulings.

*Sh'elot U'teshuvot Haradbaz*: Responsa of Rabbi David ben Solomon Ibn Abi Zimri (1479-1573), Sephardic halakhic authority.

### Early Modern Sources
*Shulhan Arukh*: Joseph Karo's classic Sephardic legal code c. 1564. The glosses of Moses Isserles (1525-1572), which are incorporated into the text, add the Ashkenazic point of view.

*Sh'elot U'teshuvot Maharashdam*: Responsa of Rabbi Samuel of Medina (1506-1589), who was a leading halakhic authority for the community of Salonika.

"Mabit:" Rabbi Moses ben Joseph Trani, 1550-1580, legal authority and scholar, whose work on Maimonides is called, *Kiryat Sefer.*

Rabbi Isaac of Molina: a 16th century Egyptian *posek* of Spanish descent, who wrote several relatively unknown responsa.

*Sh'elot U'teshuvot Darkhei Noam*: responsa of Rabbi Mordecai ben Judah HaLevi (17th century), a respected Egyptian rabbinical legal authority who was also known as *"Darkhei Noam."*

*Sh'elot U'teshuvot Noda Bihuda*: responsa of Ezekiel ben Judah Ha'Levi Landau (1713-1793), perhaps the most famous Ashkenazic authority at the close of the classical Ashkenazic period. His work is divided into two sections, of which *"Mahadura Tinyana"* is the second.

### Contemporary Israeli Sources

*Sh'elot U'teshuvot Mishpetei Uziel*: responsa of Ben-Tzion Meir Hai Uziel (1880-1953), Sephardic chief rabbi of Israel during the formative years of the state.

*Piskei Din Rabbani*: (also known as *Piskei Ha-Din Shel Batei Ha-Din Ha-Rabbani'im Ha-Eyzori'im b'Yisrael*) are summary reports of the decisions of Israel's contemporary rabbinical courts, published in nine volumes.

### Secular Sources

Atkinson, Jeff. "Criteria for Deciding Child Custody in the Trial and Appellate Courts." *Family Law Quarterly* 18:1 (1984).

Benedek, Elissa P., & Benedek, Richard S. "Joint Custody: Solution or Illusion." *American Journal of Psychiatry* 136:2 (1979).

Bentovim, Arnon & Gilmour, Lorna."A Family Therapy Interactional Approach to Decision Making in Child Care, Access, and Custody Cases." *Journal of Family Therapy* 3 (1981).

Derdeyn, Andre P. "Child Custody Contests in Historical Perspective." *The American Journal of Psychiatry* 133:12 (1976).

Derdeyn, Andre P. "Child Custody: A Reflection of Cultural Change." *Journal of Clinical Child Psychology* 7:3 (1978).

Duquette, Donald. "Child Custody Decision-Making: The Lawyer-Behavioral Scientist Interface." *Journal of Clinical Child Psychology* 7:3 (1978).

Felner, Robert D., & Terre, Lisa. "Child Custody Dispositions and Children's Adaptation Following Divorce," in *Psychology and Child Custody Determinations.* ed. Lois A. Weithorn. Lincoln: University of Nebraska Press, 1987.

Felner, Robert D., Terre, Lisa., Farber, Stephanie S., Primavera, Judith &

Bishop, T.A."Child Custody: Practices and Perspectives of Legal Professionals." *Journal of Clinical Child Psychology* 14:1 (1985).

Felner, Robert D., Terre, Lissa. "Party Status of Children During Marital Dissolution: Child Preference and Legal Representation in Custody Decisions." *Journal of Clinical Child Psychology* 14:1 (1985).

Franklin, Robin L., & Hibbs, B."Child Custody in Transition." *Journal of Marital and Family Therapy* 6:3 (1980).

Kolata, Gina."The Children of Divorce: Joint Custody is Found to Offer Little Benefit," in *The New York Times,* March 31, 1988.

Lowery, Carol R. "Child Custody Evaluations: Criteria and Clinical Implications." *Journal of Clinical Child Psychology* 14:1 (1985).

Marafiote, Richard A. *The Custody of Children: A Behavioral Assessment Model.* New York. Plenum Press, 1985.

McDermott, John F. Jr., Tseng, Wen-Shing, Char, Walter F., & Fukunaga, Chantis S. "Child Custody Decision Making." *Journal of Child Psychiatry* 17:1 (1978).

Mnookin, Robert. "Children's Rights: Beyond Kiddie Libbers and Child Savers." *Journal of Clinical Child Psychology* 7:3(1978).

Mnookin, Robert. "Child-Custody Adjudications: Judicial Functions in the Face of Indeterminacy." *Law and Contemporary Problems* 39:3 (1975).

Musetto, Andrew P. "Standards for Deciding Contested Child Custody." *Journal of Clinical Child Psychology* 10:11 (1981).

Reppucci, N. Dickon. "The Wisdom of Solomon," in *Children, Mental Health, and the Law.* ed. N. Dickon Reppucci & Lois A. Weithorn. Beverly Hills. Sage Press, 1984.

Rohman, Linda Whobrey., Sales, Bruce D., & Lou, Mimi. "The Best Interests of the Child in Custody Disputes," in *Psychology and Child Custody Determinations.* ed. Lois A.Weithorn. Lincoln: University of Nebraska Press, 1987.

Roth, Allan. "The Tender Years Presumption in Child Custody Disputes." *Journal of Family Law* 15 (1977).

Saxe, David B. "Some Reflections on the Interface of Law and Psychiatry in Child Custody Cases." *Journal of Psychiatry and Law* 3 (1975).

Schaffer, Sylvan. "Child Custody: *Halacha* and the Secular Approach." *Journal of Halacha and Contemporary Society* 6 (1983).

Schochetman, Eliyav. "The Essence of the Principles Governing The Custody of Children in Jewish Law." *Sh'nation Hamishpat Haivri* 5 (1978): [Hebrew].

Warburg, Ronald. "Child Custody: A Comparative Analysis." *Israel Law Review* 14:4 (1979).

Weithorn, Lois A., & Grisso Thomas,"Psychological Evaluations in Divorce Custody: Problems, Principles, and Procedures," in *Psychology and Child Custody Determinations.* ed. Lois A.Weithorn. Lincoln: University of Nebraska Press, 1987.

Wyer, Melissa M., Gaylord, Shelley J., & Grove, Elizabeth T. "The Legal Context of Child Custody Evaluations," in *Psychology and Child Custody Determinations.* ed. Lois A. Weithorn. Lincoln: University of Nebraska Press, 1987.

# Notes

1. Andre P. Derdeyn, M.D., "Child Custody Contests in Historical Perspective," *American Journal of Psychiatry,* 133:12 (December, 1976), p. 1369 (hereafter, cited as Derdeyn, "Contests"). Derdeyn, who is our primary source for this section, provides a coherent, concise summary of the historical data that we found in a variety of sources. See also, below note 19.

2. Derdeyn, "Contests," p. 1370.

3. Ibid.

4. Ibid., p. 1372.

5. Ibid.

6. Ibid.

7. Ibid., p. 1373.

8. Ibid.

9. Ibid., p. 1370.

10. Ibid., p. 1371.

11. Ibid.

12. Ibid., p. 1372.

13. Ibid.

14. Ibid.

15. Ibid., p. 1372.

16. Ibid.

17. Ibid.

18. Ibid., p. 1373.

19. Andre P. Derdeyn, "Child Custody: A Reflection of Cultural Change," *Journal of Clinical Child Psychology*, 7:3 (Fall, 1978), p. 170 (Hereafter, cited as Derdeyn, "Change").

20. Derdeyn, "Change," p. 170.

21. Ibid., p. 170

22. Ibid., p. 172.

23. Ibid., p. 170.

24. Ibid., p. 172.

25. Derdeyn, "Contests," p. 1373.

26. Melissa M. Wyer, Shelley J. Gaylord, and Elizabeth T. Grove, "The Legal Context of Child Custody Evaluations," in *Psychology and Child Custody Determinations*, ed. Lois A. Weithorn (Lincoln: University of Nebraska Press, 1987), p. 10.

27. Derdeyn, "Change," p. 172.

28. Uniform Marriage and Divorce Act 1979, sec. 402 as cited in Lois A. Weithorn and Thomas Grisso, "Psychological Evaluations in Divorce Custody: Problems, Principles and Procedures," in *Psychology and Child Custody Determinations*, ed. Lois A. Weithorn (Lincoln: University of Nebraska Press, 1987), p. 158.

29. Jeff Atkinson, "Criteria for Deciding Child Custody in the Trial and Appellate Courts," in *Family Law Quarterly*, Volume 18, No. 1, Spring 1984, p. 4; Linda Rohman, Bruce Sales and Mimi Lou, "The Best Interests of the Child in Custody Disputes," in *Psychology and Child Custody Determinations*, (Lincoln: University of Nebraska Press, l987), p. 62.

30. Robert Mnookin,"Children's Rights: Beyond Kiddie Libbers and Child Savers," in *Journal of Clinical Child Psychology*," Volume 7, No. 3, Fall 1978, p; 163; Atkinson, p. 62; Rohman, Sales, and Lou, p. 63; Mnookin, "Child-Custody Adjudications: Judicial Functions in the Face of Indeterminacy," in *Law and Contemporary Problems*, Volume 39, No. 3, Summer 1975, p. 231, 284.

31. According to Atkinson, judges get around the best interests standard by either equating their presumptions with the child's best interests, keeping their presumptions implicit, or by simply ignoring the standard. See Atkinson, pp. 12-13.
    The tender years doctrine maintains that mothers are inherently better able than fathers to meet the needs of young children. The Mississippi

Supreme Court ruled in 1982 that,"We have held and it is generally conceded that children of tender age should be in the care and custody of their
mother. It is commonly accepted that the best interest and welfare of a
small child is promoted by love and care from the mother." See Atkinson,
p. 12.
    The same-sex doctrine maintains that mothers are inherently better
able than fathers to meet the needs of older girls and fathers are inherently better able than mothers to meet the needs of older boys. One Iowa
judge gave custody of 2 boys, aged 9 and 11, to the father on the basis that
the father "will be able to engage in various activities with the boys, such
as athletic events, fishing, hunting, mechanical training and other activities that boys are interested in." See Atkinson, p. 13, n. 31.

32. For this entire discussion, see Mnookin, "Indeterminacy," pp. 283-285
and the section of this paper on "Psychological Perspectives on Child
Custody Determinations."

33. Mnookin, "Indeterminacy," p. 227.

34. Atkinson, pp. 1-2.

35. Ibid., p. 13.

36. Mnookin, "Indeterminacy," p. 284. See also the section in this
paper,"Psychological Perspectives on Child Custody Determinations."

37. Atkinson, p.12.

38. Ibid., pp. 9-10.

39. Ibid., p. 22.

40. Ibid., pp. 29-32.

41. Ibid., p. 31.

42. Ibid., p. 29

43. Ibid., p. 35.

44. Ibid., p. 5

45. Andrew P. Musetto, "Standards for Deciding Contested Child Custody,"
in *Journal of Clinical Child Psychology*, Volume 10, No. 1, Spring l981, p.
52; Donald Duquette, "Child Custody Decision-Making: The Lawyer-
Behavioral Scientist Interface," in *Journal of Clinical Child Psychology*,
Volume 7, No. 3, Fall 1978, p. 192.

46. Mnookin, "Indeterminacy," p. 263. For example, two Louisiana courts
of appeal (1982), within a 3 month period, gave similar cases opposite rulings. One concluded, "A child of tender years can be better cared for by the

mother," The other concluded, "Father and mother stand on equal footing." See Atkinson,p.16.

47. Ibid., pp. 228-229.

48. Ibid., pp. 256-257.

49. Ibid., p. 257.

50. Ibid., pp. 257-260.

51. Ibid.,p. 291.

52. Ibid., 289.

53. Ibid., p. 289.

54. Derdeyn comments, "The child's interests may have more importance in the courts at present because of the trend toward equalization of the rights of parents. With fewer parent-oriented formulas available as guidelines, courts appear to be inclined to try to learn more about the needs of the child." Derdeyn, "Contest," p. 1374.

55. Robert Felner and Lisa Terre, "Child Custody Dispositions and Children's Adaptation Following Divorce," in *Psychology and Child Custody Determinations*, (Lincoln: University of Nebraska Press, 1987), pp. 106-153.

56. Jeff Atkinson, "Criteria for Deciding Child Custody in the Trial and Appellate Courts," in *Family Law Quarterly*, Volume 18, No. 1, Spring 1984, p.15. Some research suggests that same-sex custody is preferable. However, this research is based solely upon observations within one year of divorce that mothers experience more stress with sons than with daughters. Other studies have failed to find that opposite sex parent-child pairs are more stressful than same sex parent-child pairs. See Linda Rohman, Bruce Sales, and Mimi Lou," The Best Interests of the Child in Custody Disputes," in *Psychology and Child Custody Determinations,* (Lincoln. University of Nebraska Press, 1987), pp. 68-69.

57. Carol Lowery, "Child Custody Evaluations: Criteria and Clinical Implications," in *Journal of Clinical Child Psychology*, Volume 14, No. 1, 1985, p. 39.

58. Atkinson, p. 15

59. Some research suggests that boys have a tendency to be more seriously affected by divorce than girls. However, other studies suggest that the severity of boys' emotional response to divorce may not be due to sex but to other variables. These studies show that boys are more likely to be exposed to parental conflict and are less likely to receive positive support and nurture than girls. See Rohman, Sales, and Lou, pp. 67-68.

60. N. Dickon Reppucci, "The Wisdom of Solomon," in *Children, Mental Health, and the Law*, (Beverly Hills: Sage Annual Reviews of Community Mental Health, 1984), pp. 64-66.

61. Lowery, p. 38

62. Rohman, Sales, and Lou, pp. 75-76.

63. See Robert Mnookin, "Child-Custody Adjudication: Judicial Functions in the Face of Indeterminacy," in *Law and Contemporary Problems*, No.39, 1975, p. 258.

64. Weithorn and Grisso, p. 161. However, joint custody is a different matter. Current studies reveal that joint custody, in amicable divorces, is no more effective than sole parent custody, and may be potentially more harmful to the child in several ways: 1) joint custody may increase interparental conflict; 2) joint custody may mitigate against a stable environment for the child, due to the constant alternation between homes, caregivers, and lifestyles; 3) joint custody may encourage relitigation and ongoing custody battles. Moreover, there is clear evidence that joint custody is harmful to the child where there exists a high degree of interparental hostility.Felner and Terre, pp. 126-144; Gina Kolata,"The Children of Divorce: Joint Custody is Found to Offer Little Benefit," in *The New York Times*, March 31, 1988.

65. Ibid., p. 161

66. Felner and Terre, pp. 115-122; 144.

67. Ibid., p. 115; Lowery, p. 35; However, the Kentucky clinicians ranked interparental relationship as only a factor of moderate importance. See Lowery, p. 39.

68. Felner and Terre, pp. 116-119.

69. Reppucci, p. 63; Felner and Terre, pp. 117-119. However, the Kentucky clinicians ranked the child's contact with the noncustodial parent as only of moderate importance. See Lowery, p. 35, 39.

70. Rohman, Sales, and Lou, p. 78.

71. Felner and Terre, pp. 121-124; 144.

72. Soncino's translation takes *yotzey* literally – "goes out by his mother's *eruv.*" However, in the context of a discussion of the ritual obligation to formally "accept" an *eruv*, the understanding of *yotzey* as having fulfilled the halakhic obligation seems preferable.

73. However, Rashi, in his commentary does forge a link between a child's right to paternal support and his dependence upon his mother. Rashi cites Rav Joshua's interpretation of Rav Assi's statement that a child would pre-

fer to go out toward his mother's *eruv*. But then Rashi makes a stronger psychological statement declaring that the child at age six is still dependent upon his mother. Just as the father is obligated to support the mother, so too, the father is obligated to support the children who depend upon her. Hence, the Jewish equivalent of a "tender years" doctrine emerges in the Medieval period.

74. As quoted by Shochetman, p. 292.

75. Shochetman, p. 292.

76. As quoted by Shochetman, p. 298.

77. Maimonides, *Mishneh Torah, Hilkhot Ishut*, 21:17.

78. Ibid.

79. Rabad on *Mishneh Torah, Hilkhot Ishut* 21:17. For a brief description of the sources and authorities cited in this section, see the Bibliography

80. In support of this observation, Schaffer, p. 39, cites three different interpretations of Maimonides' ruling about support for a male child who reaches age six. Isaac of Molina (16th c.), for instance, was among those who understood Maimonides to say that the father may not remove the child against the mother's will but is no longer responsible for support. Mabit (16th c.), on the other hand, interpreted Maimonides to mean that a son may be removed to his father's custody through the age of thirteen [presumably, because, at that point, the son is no longer a minor].

81. Maggid Mishneh, *Mishneh Torah*, Ibid.

82. *Toldot Adam V'Ḥavah* 23:3 (197a) as cited in Shochetman, p. 293.

83. In support of the attribution, see above, *Otzar Ha'geonim, Ketubot, Teshuvah*: 435. In that geonic text, we observed that the authorities not only made a custody ruling on the basis of paternal educational responsibilities, they defined those responsibilities in terms of Torah education and training for a livelihood. These dual concerns may, in fact, define what the present text meant when it referred to a father teaching his son "that which is appropriate for him."

84. *Sh'elot U'teshuvot Harashba Hameyuchasot L'haramban*, #38.

85. The responsum raises and dismisses the potential objection implicit in the *Ketubot* 102b story, discussed above. In that story, a minor child, placed in the custody of male relatives who were also his heirs, was killed by his custodial heirs. However, the responsum points out that in a case such as this one, in which there is no such fear, either because the son is not a minor or the male relatives are not potential heirs, custody should be given to male relatives rather than the mother.

86. The text does not say whether or not Rashba would also award custody of very young boys to male relatives. As discussed in note 7, the responsum only rules that minor male children ought to be placed in the custody of their male relatives, presuming that the latter are not potential heirs. Whether "minor" male children is intended to include sons younger than six or, even, male infants is unclear. Given the determinative importance of Torah study for Rashba and the view that such study should commence somewhere around the age of six, it would seem safe to guess that only very young male children, if even they, would be placed in the custody of their mothers.

87. *Sh'elot U'teshuvot Ha'Radbaz*, #123.

88. It is to be noted that Karo changes the wording for the non-custodial father's right to refuse support after age six. Maimonides wrote: "After age six, the father may say: If he lives with me, I will support him but if he lives with his mother, I will not support him." But Karo writes: "After age six, the father may say: If he does not live with me, I will not support him." Perhaps, the implied presumption for custodial transfer to the father is more striking in Karo's formula since the possibility of maternal custody is acknowledged only as a negative case ("if he does not live with me"). But the difference may only reflect Karo's more concise summary of Maimonides' formula.

89. Perhaps, in his concern to limit the custodial claims of the maternal grandmother, Isserles has reference to the case discussed in the responsum of the Radbaz, see above.

90. Given several of the prior justifications for the maternal custody rule, perhaps Isserles has in mind a case in which the mother is an inappropriate teacher of sexual propriety or of adult female practice. But this explanation is speculative.

91. It is to be noted that Schochetman and Schaffer have cited only a portion of the responsum. In addition, since we do not know how these citations compare with whatever other data exists for the same time period, the present authors are not certain that this text represents the dominant halakhic perspective of the early modern period. Insofar as we are dependent upon these authors for our data, scholarly caution is clearly mandated.

92. *Sh'elot U'teshuvot Darkhei Noam, Even Haezer* 26, as cited in Schaffer, pp. 40-41.

93. The present authors found no explicit Talmudic statement of a custody rule regarding male children. In fact, aside from the Geonic texts discussed above, we have yet to find any explicit, authoritative statement of a rule for the custody of older boys. Either *Darkhei Noam* knows of a Talmudic source or, by the 17th century, the halakhic preference for awarding custody of older sons to fathers and younger sons to mothers had taken on the same authority as the rule regarding daughters and he simply assumed that these preferences were also Talmudic.

94. Schaffer, pp. 40-41.

95. In further support of the prevalence of this approach, Shochetman, p. 294, discusses a responsum in *Sh'elot U'teshuvot Noda Biyehuda* of Ezekiel ben Judah Halevi Landau (18th century). There, Landau apparently ruled that based on his responsibility to provide Torah education, a divorced father has the right to take custody of his son prior to age six, when the mother had decided to move to another city. This later responsum is interesting both for its implied presumption favoring maternal custody for sons younger than six and, its willingness to set aside that presumption based upon circumstances which would prevent the father from fulfilling his responsibility to provide Torah education. For Landau, as for Rabad and others previously, the father's obligation for Torah education is an important and, sometimes, determinative value.

96. *Sh'elot U'teshuvot Darkhei Noam, Even Haezer* 26, as cited in Shochetman, p. 293, note 37.

97. In this passage the *Darkhei Noam* insists that the Talmudic principle "a child prefer's its mother's company" means only that "we should do that which is good and pleasant for the child." This seems like an attempt to reject the Jewish equivalent of the tender years doctrine.

98. We may have an historical analogy for this process in American custody law. Derdeyn points out that in the early twentieth century the concept of the "best interests of the child" was used to make inroads into traditional paternal custody and was virtually synonymous with maternal custody:

> "The best interests of the child test, although it did signal an enhanced consideration of the child's needs, had more significance in that it reflected the strengthening of the mother's right to custody. When the best interests test came into use in the early years of the twentieth century, the courts were well along in the process of giving the mother the advantage in custody decisions...the best interests of the child test has throughout most of its existence primarily supported the mother's claim."

The very same process may have been going on in Jewish Law in the 17th century, except that the beneficiary of the principle of *takkanat havalad* was the father and not the mother.

99. *Sh'elot U'teshuvot Mishpetei Uziel, Even Haezer*: 91 (Jerusalem, 1964) as cited in Shochetman, p. 312.

100. *Piskei Din Rabbani* 1:65, 76 as cited in Warburg, p. 491.

101. *Piskei Din Rabbani* 1:55, 63 as cited in Warburg, p. 492.

102. *Piskei Din Rabbani* 1:173, 175 as cited in Schaffer, p. 41.

103. *Piskei Din Rabbani*, 1:55, 61 as cited in Warburg, p. 497.

104. Warburg, p. 491; Schaffer, p. 38.

105. *Piskei Din Rabbani* 1:55, 61 as cited in Schaffer, pp.40-41.

106. Mnookin, "Children's Rights," p. 164.

107. Ibid., p. 164.

108. I am indebted to Rachel Cowan, who opened our eyes to this possibility – yet, another proof that one needs to bring creativity and openness to these problematic situations.

# The Intersection of Jewish Law and Ethics:

## Intervening in the Life of an Alcoholic

Judith Brazen
and Susan Freeman

The question addressed in this paper is: what is my Jewish ethical obligation to intervene in the life of an alcoholic? The nature of alcoholism is elusive – it is characterized by physical, emotional, and social symptoms. *Halakhah* does not deal with "alcoholism" as the contemporary world has labeled it, and even in the modern world this so-called "disease" is difficult to pin down. Rather than deal with generalities, a specific case is focused on. From this case an effort will be made to suggest principles on which Jewish ethical responses to the dilemma of intervention are based. The following subcategories are addressed in this paper: 1) How is alcoholism defined? 2) Should I intervene? 3) If so, when? 4) How? These questions are examined in light of what both Jewish law and modern ideas have to say.

## The Case

You are a Jewish man in your 30's. A 35 year-old single Jewish man has been your co-worker at an investment banking company for five years. You met him two years prior and have been good friends with him ever since. You both work and socialize with him. He is smart, witty, and generous. In another year he will be transferred to another branch of the company, likely on the other side of the country.

Lately, you have been bothered by your growing certainty that your friend is an alcoholic. He has a fully-stocked liquor cabinet that seems to "empty" quickly; drinks heavily at restaurants and parties often becoming loud and irrational; has a reputation for lateness to morning appointments at work; and sometimes won't answer the phone when you know he is home. Once when you were with him, he detoured to a liquor store to get his "nightcap supply" which he claims helps him to sleep. He is very private about his family. You have never seen or heard about his being "completely wasted."

You've mentioned the problem to a couple of his friends who have noticed he drinks a lot but aren't terribly concerned. They don't feel it is their business to intrude especially since he is such a "private person." His girlfriend won't talk about the issue. You have brought up the issue three times as sensitively as possible to your friend. He denies he has any problem with alcohol and becomes angry. These "compassionate confrontations" have resulted in a negative and distancing feeling between you and your friend for several weeks following.

## How is Alcoholism Defined in Jewish Law?

As mentioned previously, "alcoholism" as such is not addressed directly in traditional Jewish law. In Jewish law references are made to the consumption of alcohol in ways that suggest a continuum – from acceptable to "problematic." Perfectly acceptable is the consumption of wine for *kiddush* on *Shabbat*, holidays, and life cycle events. A greater quantity of wine is drunk on Passover in which, during the course of the *seder*, Jews are directed to drink four cups of wine. Drinking at this level is for purposes of consecrating holidays and special events which come about at regular intervals (though not every day).

Greater quantities of wine may be drunk during times of mourning:

> Ten cups are drunk in the house of mourning, two before the meal, five during the meal, and three after the meal. After the mourner's blessing, and after comforting the mourners, and after deeds of lovingkindness, another three [cups are drunk] (*Semachot* 14:14).

Though a greater quantity of alcohol is allowed, the consumption in this case is more restricted than *kiddush* insofar as frequency is concerned.

Another time in which a greater quantity of alcohol is allowed, but it is restricted to a particular time is Purim:

> Rava said: It is the duty of a person to become cheerful from the effects of wine on Purim until that person cannot tell the difference between "cursed be Haman" and "blessed be Mordecai" (*Megillah* 7b).

The examples of *kiddush*, mourning, and Purim, occasions that occur more to less frequently, still all fall on the side of the continuum of fully acceptable drinking.

Terminology used for the "problematic" side of the continuum are *shatui, shikur,* and *shikur kelot* for: tipsy or "under the influence," drunk, and "smashed." This side of the continuum is termed "problematic" rather than "prohibited" because there are no direct prohibitions against drinking, rather prohibitions surrounding drinking have to do with consequences. For example, if a person is *shikur* (drunk), that person may be prohibited from participating in a particular activity. Detailed examples follow.

Specific quantities of alcohol are given in order to define *shatui* and *shikur:*

> Who is [called] *shatui*? Anyone who has drunk a quarter-*log*. [Who is called] *shikur*? One who drank more than that (*Y. Trumot* 1:4).

A quarter-*log* is approximately 2.9 ounces, or three drinks by contemporary standards. In other words someone who has had three drinks is, according to this ruling, considered tipsy and more than three drunk.

Besides straight definitions, Jewish sources are descriptive as to what characteristics typify someone at the various stages of drunkenness. A person's ability to speak coherently is one such characteristic:

> "What is to be understood," one of them began, "by one who is '*shatui*' and what by one who is '*shikur*?'" The former is one who is able to speak in the presence of a king, the latter is one who is unable to speak in the presence of a king (*Erubin* 64a; also *Y. Trumot* 1:4).

How well a person can walk is another indication as to a person's state of drunkenness:

> We learned... that a journey causes the effects of wine to be removed... Italian wine is different since its powers of intoxication are greater. But did not R. Nachman state in the name of Rabbah b. Abbuha, "This applies only to one who has drunk one quarter of a log, but if one has drunk more than a quarter, a walk would only cause that person more fatigue..." (*Erubin* 64b).

In other words someone who has drunk about three drinks (*shatui*) would experience a journey as sobering; whereas, someone who has either drunk more (*shikur*) or drunk a particularly potent alcoholic beverage (such as Italian wine) will become more fatigued by walking.

There are other physical indications of the *shikur* referred to in Jewish sources. One is heaviness of limbs – which would make slaughtering an animal in the proper way difficult.[1] Another is drowsiness (*Y. Trumot* 1:4) and difficulty in focusing.[2] As far as the third more extreme category of *shikur kelot* ("as drunk as Lot") is concerned, we can assume that at the very least the same physical indications are in effect as for the *shikur*.

Besides physical indications, Jewish sources refer to the mental condition of someone who has been drinking. Someone who is drunk is regarded as having impaired judgment:

> A blind person and a drunkard [may not separate heave-offering] because they are unable to [distinguish between better and worse quality in order to] separate heave-offering from the best [of their produce] (*Y. Trumot* 1:4; also *Trumot* 1:6).

Furthermore, a comment is made on Proverbs 31:4 which indicates that those who are involved in matters which require serious thought must not become drunk:

> Why drink no wine? – R. Aha b. Chanina said, "Scripture states, "It is not for princes to say, Where is strong drink?' [i.e.] those who are engaged in [unravelling] the secrets of the world must not become drunk." *(Sanhedrin* 42a).

In midrashic literature as well there is reference to mentally debilitating effects of alcohol:

> When the wine goes in intelligence takes its leave. Wherever there is wine there is no intelligence. When the wine enters the secret (*sod*) comes out; the numerical total of wine (*yayin*) is seventy and the total of *sod* (secret) is seventy (*Numbers Rabbah* 10:8).

Besides being descriptive as to some of the physical and mental characteristics typifying someone who has drunk certain quantities of alcohol, *halakhah* delineates consequences of drinking. The implications of these consequences are in terms of how an individual may or may not be allowed to participate in certain religious and civil activities.

One of the areas in which a person who has been drinking is restricted is instruction (*horaah*). From a Biblical verse – "wine and liquor you shall not drink, you and your sons, when you come to the Tent of Meeting" (Leviticus 10:9) – more detailed and explicit laws developed. Exactly what restrictions would be in effect would depend on the state of drunkenness (from *shatui* to *shikur*). An excerpt and good summary of these laws is provided by Maimonides:

> Just as it is prohibited for a priest to enter the Sanc-

tuary because of intoxication, so is it prohibited for anyone, priest or layman, to offer normative instruction (*horaah*) when drunk... unless he is instructing on a point we can assume is obvious to everyone already (*Mishneh Torah, Hilkhot Biat Hamikdash* 1:3).

Another area in which restrictions are advised is that of ritual slaughter (*shehita*):

A drunkard (*shikur*) who has become as drunk as Lot (*shikur kelot*) – his judgment is like that of an idiot. If he has not become as drunk as Lot, *prima facie*, he may slaughter (*Shulhan Arukh, Yoreh Deah* 1:8).

As a continuation of the above a modest dialectic takes place. A second opinion asserts that a drunkard is liable to perform an unfit slaughter (*darsa*). At the least this text points to the notion that it is unadvisable for someone who is drunk to perform ritual slaughter.

Someone who has been drinking is restricted in prayer (the "Eighteen Benedictions," the *Amidah*):

Abba bar R. Huna says, "A *shatui* (tipsy person) should not pray [the *Amidah*]. But if that person prays, the prayer is deemed a [valid] supplication. A *shikur* (drunkard) should not pray. And if that person prays, the prayer is deemed blasphemy (*Y. Trumot* 1:4).

Also in civil cases there are consequences as a result of drinking. One of the areas is liability (*hovel*):

A person is always deemed forewarned whether acting inadvertently or deliberately, whether awake, asleep, or drunk (*shikur*), and if that person wounds another or causes damage to another's property, compensation must be paid from the best of that person's property (*Mishneh Torah, Hilkhot Hovel Umazik* 1:11).

In other words if a drunk person wounds someone or damages someone else's property, that person is still responsible.

There is, however, a dialectic of opinion as to the degree people who are "as drunk as Lot" are held accountable for their actions:

If a [drunk person] (*shikur*) committed a transgression involving the penalty of death, that person is to be executed; and if [a drunk person] committed one involving flogging, that person is to be flogged – the general rule being that [a person] is regarded as sober in all respects with the exemption of prayer...

> R. Hanina said: This applies only to one who did not
> reach the stage of Lot's drunkenness, but one who
> did reach such a stage is exempt from all responsi-
> bilities (*Erubin* 65a).

In other words the anonymous rule does not distinguish between
being drunk (*shikur*) and being "smashed" (*shikur kelot*). But R.
Hanina would say that if someone is "smashed" (as drunk as Lot),
that person would not be put to death or flogged for crimes deserving of that punishment. If the person is less than "smashed," presumably *shatui* or *shikur*, that person would be deemed responsible
and would be put to death or flogged in the same instances as
would a sober person.

There is discussion throughout *halakhah* as to whether a
person who has been drinking can serve on a rabbinic court (*beit
din*). Some say those who are intoxicated are prohibited from judging cases in which death penalty is involved. Others extend this
prohibition to include cases involving monetary issues as well.
Others take the restriction even further – not only are those who
are *shikur* prohibited from judging cases, but also those who are
*shatui*, (who have drunk up to 2.9 ounces).[3]

## The Jewish Definition
## As It Relates
## to The Case Study

The Jewish man in the case study does not fall on the side of the
"continuum" of drinking which is perfectly acceptable in Jewish law.
His drinking is not limited to holidays and special occasions; however, "as drunk as Lot" does not describe the man either. The information his friend has makes him suspect that the friend drinks
regularly at least to the level of what, analogously, may be called *shatui*. What is unclear but possible is that the friend drinks to the
extent of *shikur* (drunkenness) regularly.

The friend drinks in a way that seems "problematic" from
the perspective of Jewish law. The most significant areas that are
potentially problematic are physical changes (though Jewish
sources do not label these changes as "damaging"), impaired judgment and ability to instruct (in Jewish law, formal rulings on the
law), and liability when drunk. The religious consequences, especially as they have to do with prayer and offerings, would make the
man consider that his friend's drinking would be regarded in Jewish
law as unholy and objectionable to God in some way. The extent of
this objection as it relates to the quantities drunk by the friend is
not clear, neither is whether a business relationship, which becomes
a friendship, involves the man in his friend's religious observance.

## Should I Intervene?
## The Role of
## Jewish Tradition

Alcoholism may be considered a form of self-injury, or *haḥovel be-atzmo*. Biblical and rabbinic law prohibit any form of self-injury. According to Deuteronomy 4:9: "Take utmost care and watch yourselves scrupulously..." and according to Deuteronomy 22:8: "When you build a house, you shall make a parapet for your roof so that you do not bring bloodguilt on your house if anyone should fall from it." Any act which incurs long term self-destruction, either physical or psychological, might be considered as a form of self-injury. According to Maimonides, placing one's life even in potential danger clearly is prohibited:

> The following are the acts prohibited: People may not put their mouths to a flowing pipe of water and drink from it, or drink at night from rivers or ponds, lest they swallow a leech while unable to see. Nor may they drink from water that has been left uncovered, lest they drink from it after a snake or other poisonous reptile has drunk from it, and die... Nor should they put a dish of food under their seats even during a meal, lest something harmful fall into it without their noticing it... Similarly, they should not walk near a leaning wall or over a shaking bridge or enter a ruin or pass through any such dangerous place.[4]

Both injuring oneself intentionally and unintentionally are prohibited according to Jewish law. Furthermore, self-injury is not considered a private affair determined by individual discretion. According to Maimonides:

> Many things are forbidded by the Sages because they are dangerous to life. If one disregards any of these and says, "If I want to put myself in danger, what concern is it to others?" or "I am not particular about such things," disciplinary flogging is inflicted upon [that person].[5]

According to *halakhah*, a Jew is obligated to restrain another Jew from performing a forbidden act. As has been delineated above, injuring oneself (*haḥovel beatzmo*) is forbidden (*asur*). By analogy, insofar as excessive alcohol consumption results in self-injury, it is forbidden. There is a principle in Jewish law regarding the obligation of Jews' to assist fellow Jews who are unknowingly doing something forbidden, (injuring oneself being forbidden or *asur*). This principle is *efroshey meisura*. A primary example of this principle is in *Kilayim* 10:29:

> If you see someone unwittingly wearing a garment
> containing a forbidden mixture of threads, you must
> inform the person that *kilayim* is being worn in order
> to save the person from doing wrong. If it is being
> worn deliberately, you must tear it off the person,
> even in public.

According to some rabbis, one even may strike fellow Jews in order
to restrain them from wrong. It must be stressed, however, that
any discussion of alcoholism as "wrong-doing" must be limited,
from a halakhic perspective, to the category of self-injury.

The command to "love your neighbor as yourself" (Leviticus
19:18) gives rise to a halakhic principle applicable to the question
of intervening in the life of a fellow Jew. That is, your love and
sympathy for your neighbor should be as your love and sympathy
for yourself insofar as both your neighbor's body and wealth are
concerned (*Mishneh Torah, Deot* 6:3). This principle specifically
points out the obligation of a Jew to be concerned about a fellow
Jew's body; therefore, on a halakhic basis the man in the case study
could argue that his concern about his friend's physical well-being
justifies and even obligates him to intervene.

## The Modern
## Therapeutic Perspective

From a modern perspective this case scenario is problematic. It
appears as if the friend is attempting to cope with the stresses in
his life with excessive alcohol use. The decision to intervene is not
evident since self-destructive and potentially damaging behavior is
to some extent a subjective judgement. Alcohol problems are particularly difficult to discern in modern society due to the degree to
which drinking is a socially acceptable behavior in modern America.
It would help our ethical analysis later if we clarify what modern
studies have taught us about alcoholism.

Alcoholism has been defined as a process and "a set of complex and interacting psychobiological dynamics."[6] The most widely
accepted definition of alcoholism, that of the World Health Organization, is as follows: "Alcoholics are those excessive drinkers whose
dependence upon alcohol has attained such a degree that it shows a
noticeable mental disturbance or an interference with their bodily
and mental health, their interpersonal relations, and their smooth
social and economic functioning; or those who show the [prelimi-
nary] signs of such developments.[7] According to Stephen Jay Levy
and Lester Futernick, addiction to alcohol is evident when alcohol
causes a persistent problem in any area of living and is based upon
three components: 1) compulsion, the desire to use the drug which
begins to creep into one's thoughts and actions on a more and more

persistent basis, 2) negative consequences in a person's life as a direct result of substance abuse, including social, vocational, emotional, marital, and physical consequences... and , 3) loss of control, to the extent that the person can no longer accurately predict when he or she will use the substance, how much he or she will use or what the actual effects on his or her behavior will be.[8] The Committee on Alcohol Related Disabilities include these following essential elements of alcoholism:

> "...increased tolerance to alcohol, repeated withdrawal symptoms, repeated relief or avoidance of withdrawal symptoms by further drinking, subjective awareness of a compulsion to drink, and reinstatement of the syndrome after abstinence.[9]

It is also relevant to our case to note that alcoholism has been identified as a disease of isolation. Denial is a fundamental component in every alcoholic adjustment. According to Light, "alcoholism represents a fundamental failure to assume personal responsibility for who one is and what one's circumstances in life may happen to be."[10] Thus "all addicts and their families lead double lives, including a public life in which great secrecy about the cover up of the addictive pathology is maintained at all costs."[11] Light explains: "Because of overdetermined reaction formation to and denial of [their] own deep feelings of unworthiness, inadequacy and guilt, [they] may go to elaborate lengths to present an opposite facade to the world and to [themselves], hoping desperately to hide [their] fundamental flaws. Alcohol facilitates this denial and permits temporary escape from [their] own ambivalent and obsessive ruminations about [themselves] and [their] imagined and real shortcomings."[12]

Unlike Jewish tradition, which speaks of drinking as a matter of will and decision, most current psychological studies understand alcoholism as a disease. Alcoholics Anomymous defines alcoholism as a disease which can never be cured, but which, like some other diseases, can be arrested. According to this definition, alcoholics can not control their drinking because they are ill in their bodies and in their minds.

The modern therapeutic perspective would encourage the man in the case study to question his friend's excessive need for privacy and his particular discomfort concerning his drinking. It is difficult to discern whether the friend is actually an alcoholic,[13] however. While he exhibits several typical symptoms of addictive behavior, it is difficult to prove that his drinking prevents him from functioning socially and professionally. The modern therapeutic perspective might sensitize the man in this case about the role of denial in alcohol addiction and lead him to be skeptical of his friend's recognition of his own behavior.

## Should I Intervene?

Literature on alcoholism tends not to address ethical issues of intervention in their full complexity; while, ethical literature does not necessarily deal with the practical consequences of applying philosophical precepts to alcoholism. The discussions of ethical approaches presented do not mutually exclude each other; in fact, it is difficult to discuss one approach without considering another. The purpose of the material that follows is to elucidate at least some of the ethical issues at stake when considering intervention.

## Should I Intervene?
## A Libertarian Response

A Libertarian perspective upholds in the most rigorous way respect for the individual and the notion of privacy. Libertarians would feel no moral obligation to intervene in a friend's life. They consider every individual to be the owner of his/her own life.

> I have no right to decide how you should spend your time or your money. I can make that decision for myself but not for you, my neighbor. I may deplore your choice of lifestyle, and I may talk with you about it provided you are willing to listen to me. But I have no right to use force to change it... Where do my rights end? Where yours begin. I may do anything I wish with my own life, liberty and property without your consent, but I may do nothing with your life, liberty and property without your consent. If we recognize the principle of [human's] rights, it follows that the individual is sovereign of the domain of his[/her] own life and property, and is sovereign of no other domain.[14]

From the above perspective it is clear how a libertarian might respond to the friend in the case study. The libertarian might "deplore the lifestyle" of his friend and might choose to talk with him about it, but he would not see it as his responsibility to intervene. In the final analysis even though the friend seems to have an alcohol problem, the friend has a right to live his life the way he chooses, and the libertarian has no right to dictate how that should be.

## Should I Intervene?
## The Ethics of Human/ Social
## Responsibility

On the side of the "ethical spectrum" opposite that of libertarianism is human/ social responsibility. This ethic advocates the position that human beings must take responsibility for one another.

This responsibility encompasses both concern for the welfare of the individual and the welfare of society.

Concern for the welfare of the friend in the case study would include primarily his physical and emotional health, his ability to function in social relationships (with his girlfriend, friends, and co-workers), and his ability to manage the requirements of his job. Concern for the welfare of society would require an evaluation of what responsibility needs to be assumed in order to preserve the safety and well-being of the rest of society. Might the friend pose physical danger to others; for example, by driving a car while under the influence of alcohol? Might the friend pose a financial threat to others, by making unwise investments for people at times when his judgment is not at its sharpest? Might he be an emotional threat to people who are close to him by being insensitive, irrational, and/or intimidating? Will he continue to be a contributing member of society if he doesn't curb his intake of alcohol, and will the "problem" get to the point where society will be forced to support him (on welfare, through a rehabilitation program, etc.) Ethical implications raised by the questions above would move the man in the case, if he is a person who advocates human/ social responsibility, to intervene.

There is, however, an ethical position on the side of human/ social responsibility which would inform the man not to consider intervention. The issue of privacy would be given more weight. If the man advocates human/ social responsibility, but not intervention, he would say something such as this: "My responsibility to my friend is to respect his privacy. His other friends and girlfriend also think they have no business intruding. Furthermore, when I've tried to bring up the issue of drinking, my friend denies he has a problem and becomes angry. Obviously, he doesn't want to talk about this, and I have a responsibility to respect his wishes." Another reason the man might not intervene but still consider himself socially responsible is that he would say, "Everyone has different ways of coping with the pressures and confusion of every day life. I must allow my friend to get himself through each day in what-ever way works for him. He has found a way that seems to work on some level, and my responsibility is to be supportive of his decision to drink, whether that decision is a conscious one or not." Furthermore, my friend still seems capable of functioning professionally. Since the company's supervisors have not found my friend's drinking habits troubling enough to dismiss him from his position, maybe I should just mind my own business.

Supposing the man seriously wants to consider intervention, the following question arises: At what level of relationship is he required to intervene – immediate relative, distant relative, friend, Jewish friend, co-worker, acquaintance...? If the man decides that Jewish friend and co-worker is a relationship that requires him to consider intervention, two general approaches to making his ethical decision are available to him. One of these approaches is deontological ethics, based on principles, and the other is teleological ethics, based on consequences.

From the perspective of deontological ethics, the man would make his decision to intervene or not based on what he felt to be his duty. If he upholds certain principles, he would feel obligated to intervene; other principles might lead him not to intervene. Similarly, in teleological ethics, consideration of the consequences of intervention may or may not lead him to intervene. The next few paragraphs will present mini-monologues based on four ethical possibilities. These monologues would be the imagined arguments the man in the case might make in order to support the various possibilities – 1) Based on my principles I must intervene; 2) Based on my principles I should not intervene; 3) Based on the probable outcome it is best to intervene; and 4) Based on the probable outcome it is best not to intervene. (At this stage the arguments are based solely on the modern ethical systems without taking into account Jewish considerations.)

## 1. Based on my principles I must intervene:

These are the principles upon which I will base my decision to intervene: 1) the worth of each person; 2) the responsibility of each person for another; 3) those who can help have a special obligation to do so, (i.e., I see the problem, my friend doesn't).

My friend likely is an alcoholic, a condition modern medicine and psychology consider to be a "disease." Human beings who have diseases should not be ignored. I, as a close friend and co-worker, see it as my duty to get involved, not to take the chance that my friend will continue harming himself and potentially others as well. Even though denial is a difficult symptom of alcoholism, I can't let it deter me. I shouldn't limit my efforts on account of even a slight chance my friend will respond positively to my intervening and change his self-destructive behavior. Since we know that no single method (of learning to live a sober life) works for every alcoholic,[15] it is not for me to judge what the consequences might be of my intervention. I have to do what I know to be right at the present moment, even if that requires some self-sacrifice of time and emotional energy – which is to take responsibility for those who I care deeply about, especially since it is known that alcoholics have little control over their addiction and resultant lifestyle.

## 2. Based on my principles I should not intervene:

These are the principles upon which I will base my decision not to intervene: 1) respecting others' privacy; 2) freedom of choice in lifestyle as long as others aren't being hurt, 3) present behavior, not potential results must be dealt with.

My primary concern for other human beings has do with respecting their privacy and the way they have chosen to live their lives as long as no one else is being hurt by their choices, (since I have a responsibility to the rest of society as well). Furthermore, I believe in helping others, but my first duty is to myself – it is not my responsibility to get involved in a situation which makes demands on my own time and emotional energy which deprive me of my right to privacy and well-being. Unless someone's actions and behavior *presently* pose life-threatening danger to self and/or others, it is not my place, my "duty" to get involved.

## 3. Based on the probable outcome it is best to intervene:

In order to "calculate" the best action to take in face of my friend's alcohol problem, I must consider these questions: 1) What might happen if I don't intervene? 2) If a crisis happens, will that destroy my friend or give him the necessary impetus to change?[16] 3) What is the likely physical and emotional damage he might cause to himself and others? 4) What is more critical to his well-being – protecting his privacy or openly trying to encourage him to change through compassionate confrontation? 5) Will the likelihood of him responding positively to continued efforts to intervene outweigh my own self-sacrifice of time and emotional energy? 6) Will he value my friendship more because I tried to help or less because I butted in on what is none of my business? 7) Since much of the current literature on alcoholism says that self-help must be sought by alcoholics,[17] is it worth it for me to make an effort?

After weighing the above considerations, I may or may not think it is worth taking the risk of intervening. However, after calculating that it is worth it, I plan to do so. In the long run, I assess that intervening will be the best thing for myself, my friend, and the rest of society.

## 4. Based on the probable outcome it is best not to intervene:

After weighing the considerations outlined in the section above, I have decided it is not worth intervening. In the long run, that will be the best thing for myself, my friend, and the rest of society. Or, at least it will be the best thing for myself and probably for my friend, and since it is not clear how his drinking will affect the rest of society, I can't base my decision on that factor. I can't take a risk that has such an uncertain outcome. Furthermore, my attempting to intervene may just arouse resentment in my friend and cause him to completely cut me off. As a result, not only will I lose his friendship, but I also may give up the possibility of ever having any "sobering" influence on him. Because denial is so much a part of alcoholism, the effect of my intervening likely would be negligible, but would be disastrous for our relationship and my emotional well-being. All things considered, it makes little sense to intervene.

The deontological and teleological arguments developed above are approximate. There are different nuances by which these arguments might be shaped. Still, the general thrust of the ethical considerations of these arguments should be clear – do I decide based on my principles or my calculations? Once I have decided on my ethical system, do I decide yes or no to intervention?

The libertarian position as well as all four arguments based on the postion of human/social responsibility have aspects to them which are compelling. Since the issue of interest in this paper is *Jewish* ethics, there is more information to draw upon in order to make a final decision as to what is "my *Jewish* ethical obligation to intervene in the life of an alcoholic."

## Conclusion

**Process of decision-making:** In the process of decision-making in which we have immersed ourselves, we find it difficult to separate Jewish considerations as opposed to modern ones. Often one consideration impacts on another. We feel it is necessary to realize that often the reason we might consider some aspect of Jewish tradition is because of some knowledge we bring with us from modernity, and vice versa. For instance, we consider the halakhic prohibition against self-injury (Jewish tradition) because from recent scientific research (modernity) we accept that self-injury is a serious consequence of excessive alcohol consumption. In other words, a certain back and forth between Jewish tradition and modernity must take place as each piece of the "ethical puzzle" is considered.

Furthermore, when considering Jewish ideas, we don't feel we have to restrict ourselves to the specifiations of halakhic principles stated directly; rather, we believe halakhic principles work within a system of Jewish values upon which we can ground a Jewish decision. These values are implicit rather than explicit and are gleaned from whatever we have accumulated in our study and living of Judaism. Examples of these kind of values include sanctity of life, social responsibilities, and the dignity of the individual. For instance, the principle of *pikuah nefesh* in a halakhic context deals with saving life. We feel justified in saying that this principle reflects the value of the sanctity of human life (even though we may not find a halakhic source that will state that value explicitly). We are influenced by this value. Though from a Jewish perspective "sanctity of life" may have its roots more in homiletics than in *halakhah*; nevertheless, it informs the ethical decisions we make, and it is based in "Jewish tradition." The danger of this kind of decision-making is that it is "slippery;" that is once permission is given to derive more general ideals, the permission may be distorted in all kinds of ways. Who knows what the source value is for any halakhic principle? Nevertheless, this is the risk we take, particularly as liberal Jews – by valuing autonomy in interpreting our heritage, we reap the benefits of an open system, but also take the risk that all kinds of ethical postions based on "Jewish tradition" can be justified. We are willing to take that risk because to do anything but that would be dishonest – we are influenced by the Jewish values taught to us and which continue to ring true as we immerse ourselves more in depth in scholarly issues.

In order to make our ethical decision we feel the responsibility of considering all relevent resources, both Jewish and modern. In the case study presented we don't feel there is a conflict between Jewish ethical requirements and what speaks to us from modern ethics generally; the exception is an extreme libertarian considerations. The reasons we don't accept an extreme libertarian postion are related to each other: 1) This position goes against our intuitive moral sensibilities which are formed by our upbringing, social conditioning, and personalities, and related to this. 2) The position goes against what is fundamentally valued in Judaism, (ie. communal social responsibilities). If our intuitive moral sensibilities conflicted with what is fundamentally valued in Judaism, we would extract from both what we find to be a position most respectful of human dignity.

**The decision:** We believe the friend has a Jewish ethical obligation to intervene as a result of his friend's drinking behavior. He has an obligation to do whatever he can in order to deter his friend's self-destructive behavior. Jewish tradition guides us that there are times when drinking is socially acceptable, but there are limitations. These limitations have to do with a person's ability to carry out responsibilities. We have learned from our modern research that drinking to the extent that the friend does may injure his health as well as endanger others' well-being.

From Jewish sources relevent to intervention, we conclude that the man is obligated to do what he can in order to prevent his friend from injuring himself. But as a result of physical and psychological factors which we glean from modern research, (i.e., addiction and denial), at a certain point *active* intervention may not be efficacious, and even may be counter-productive.

Even though in the context of alcohol consumption, Jewish sources do not refer to self-injury, as mentioned modern research claims that self-injury is involved in excessive intake of alcohol. *Halakhah* explicitly forbids self-injury. This prohibition is the basis for our Jewish considerations. We also based our considerations on *efroshey meisura, ahavat Yisrael,* and *pikuah nefesh. Efroshey meisura* is keeping a person from doing something forbidden. We infer from this principle that the man must prevent the friend from the prohibition of injuring himself. *Ahavat Yisrael*, loving a fellow Jew, applies because the man is concerned about his friend injuring himself. The principle applies indirectly because the friend may potentially risk his financial well-being. This principle of love requires intervening because it seems the friend is not adequately caring for himself. We make the presumption that the man has a more balanced perception of his friend's drinking problem than does the friend. We base this presumption on what we have learned from modern material that drinking alters a person's self-perception. We feel the principle of *pikuah nefesh*, saving another's life, applies because of our interpretation that underlying this principle is the sanctity and worth of human life. From our evaluation of the case study, we conclude that the friend is not in the process of "saving himself;" therefore, outside intervention must be considered seriously.

From the modern ethical systems we mediate between deontological and telelogical factors. While we take into account privacy and autonomy, we would not take these factors to the extent that a libertarian would. As compelling as the principle of intervention may be, we feel we cannot assess its desirability without considering the consequences of its application. We think the man's primary goal should be to help his friend; whatever means achieves this goal most effectively is the one he should assert. (In order for this man to discern what might be an effective means, we would advise the man to consult professionals who deal with addictive behavior.)

# Bibliography

Galanter, Marc; editor. *Recent Developments in Alcoholism*, Volume I, New York and London. Plenum Press, 1983.

Haugen Light, William J. *Psychodynamics of Alcoholism*, Springfield, IL. Charles C. Thomas Publisher, 1986.

Levy, Stephen Jay; editor. *Addictions in the Jewish Community*, Commission on Synagogue Relations, Federation of Jewish Philanthropies of New York, 1986.

Mann, Marty. *Marty Mann Answers Your Questions about Drinking/Alcoholism*, New York. Holt, Rinehart, and Winston, 1970.

Shaw, Stan; Cartwright, Alan; Spratley, Terry; Harwin, Judith. *Responding to Drinking Problems*, Baltimore. University Park Press, 1978.

Steiner, Claude M. *Healing Alcoholism*, New York: Grove Press, Inc., 1979.

Machan, Tibor A.; editor. *The Libertarian Alternative*, Chicago: Nelson-Hall Company, 1974.

Whitney, Elizabeth D. *Living with Alcoholism*, Boston: Beacon Press, 1968.

# Notes

1. *Encyclopedia Talmudit*, "Darsa," footnote #121.

2. *Encyclopedia Talmudit*, "Birkat Hamazon," footnote #499.

3. Sanhedrin 42a with Tosafot, *Sh'elot U'teshuvot* of *Bayit Ḥadash*, #41.

4. Maimonides *Mishneh Torah, Hilkhot Rotzeaḥ* 11:4.

5. *Mishneh Torah, Nezikin, Rotzeah V'shmirat Nefesh*, translated by Hyman Klein, New Haven. Yale Judaica Series, Volume IX, Section XI, 1954, p. 227.

6. Haugen Light, William. *Psychodynamics of Alcoholism,* Springfield. Charles C. Thomas Publisher, 1986, p.148.

7. Mandell, Wallace. "Types and Phases of Alcohol Dependence Illness" in *Recent Developments in Alcoholism*. Edited by Marc Galanter. NY. Plenum Press, 1983, p.415.

8. Futernick, Lester; Levy, Stephen Jay "Drinking and Drugging Among Jews" in *Addiction in the Jewish Community*. Edited by Stephen Jay Levy NY: Commission on Synagogue Realtions, Federation of Jewish Philanthropies of New York, 1986, pp. 184-185.

9. Galanter, Marc. *Recent Developments in Alcoholism*, NY. Plenum Press, 1983, p. 417.

10. Light, p. 168.

11. Ibid., p. 135.

12. Ibid., pp. 117-119.

13. Steiner, Claude M. *Healing Alcoholism*, NY. Grove Press, Inc., 1979, p. 195.

14. Hospers, John. "What Libertarianism Is" in *The Libertarian Alternative*, Edited by Tibor R. Machan. Chicago. Nelson-Hall Company, 1974, p. 6

15. Steiner, p. 195.

16. Whitney, Elizabeth D. *Living with Alcoholism*, Boston. Beacon Press, 1968, p. 70-71.

17. Steiner, p. 121.

# Bio-medical Issues

# Ethics of Animal Experimentation

Daniel M. Cohen,
Faith Joy Dantowitz
and Janine Schloss

In exploring the ethics of animal experimentation, we chose to focus on the following question: Is it ethically permissible to use animals for medical experimentation? To reach this phrasing, many topics were explored and considered. This section discusses the parameters that we chose for our study as well as the justification for them.

Selecting the ethics of medical experimentation narrowed our subject so that it concentrates on one specific area of ethics with respect to animal experimentation. For example, we do not include experimentation on animals for the sake of testing cosmetic products. We feel that the connection between animal research for cosmetic products and saving lives is unclear. Furthermore, we feel that the ethical discussion of such animal use would involve a vastly different array of issues than we can discuss in the scope of this paper.

In addition, we will not cover the area of animal use for food in the course of this paper. Our issue does concern when humans can use animals for their benefit. However, we chose to limit our focus and not include every category in which animals are involved.

Another element that we chose to limit from our study is the use of animals for monetary gain. We feel that the matter of monetary gain involves a different set of ethical concerns. This would make the paper too broad and thus will not be covered.

As we begin our exploration into the ethics of animal use for medical experimentation, it is interesting to note how many animals are involved. In the United States, it is estimated that 10-100 million animals are used each year.[1] Perhaps the best data available is from the United States Department of Agriculture / Animal Plant Health

Inspection Service (USDA/APHIS) report that states that in 1983, 17-22 million animals were used in research and testing in the United States. Approximately 12-15 million of these were rats and mice.[2] Use of these animals helps researchers advance knowledge and discover cures to human illnesses. Medical experimentation is performed with the intention of promoting healing, which can result in either direct or indirect saving of human lives.

This paper represents the process through which we reach our own liberal Jewish ethic regarding the issue of animal use in medical experimentation. Section II examines general ethical issues: In our studies, we found three dominant positions, representing the spectrum of debate. One extreme represents those who believe that all life is sacred. Therefore, humans do not have the right to 'use' animals. The opposite extreme believes that animals may be used by humans since humans are superior to animals. The middle position draws from both extremes. All lives have value, but being superior to animals, humans have the right to use them for their benefit. While permitting use of animals, this position also emphasizes careful consideration of numbers of animals used and tests performed in order to minimize animal suffering and promote the role of humans as caretakers.

Section III follows the development of our position and explains the ways in which halakhic sources approach this issue. Here, we state our assumptions and understanding of important terms and we examine a number of relevant halakhic passages to determine their applicability to our question. While the *halakhah* deals with law rather than ethics, by generalizing the halakhic stance, we attempt to reveal the meta-ethics within the halakhic text.

Section IV evaluates the preceding two sections. It summarizes the main points of two distinct areas of study and compares and contrasts them.

The final section of the paper includes our own conclusions. We are honest about our biases and indicate how we feel we were influenced by the general ethics and halakhic material. Following that, we consider how we can apply this process to the creation of a liberal Jewish ethic.

## General Ethics

To understand the general ethics of animal experimentation, we must consider the topic from a number of different perspectives. Our discussion of the general ethics of animal experimentation proceeds in the following manner: First we look at the positions held by those who are against animal experimentation and those who support animal experimentation. Then we look at the middle position, which developed between these two extremes. This leads us into a discussion of how current legal statements about animal experimentation follow this middle position. Finally, we present the alternatives to animal experimentation.

Our discussion of the different approaches to animal experimentation focuses on five important issues. The first issue, the hierarchy of life, deals with two questions: whether human beings are superior to animals and whether human life and animal life are equally sacred. Each group's (referring to the positions on the spectrum) answers to these questions reflect their opinions about humanity's role with respect to animals. It is important to note that this issue is greatly informed by religious beliefs, particularly those expressed in the Hebrew Bible. The opinions based on these religious concepts still fall under the heading of general ethics, however, because they completely permeate the thinking of our secular society.

The second issue, that of "ends versus means," asks whether the end goal of saving human lives justifies the means of causing pain and suffering to animals through experimentation. The third issue, social morality, confronts the possibility that animal experimentation may encourage immoral social behavior, such as stealing, cruelty, and desensitization to the value of life. The fourth issue revolves around the question of sentience, used here to refer to the ability of an animal to feel pain and experience suffering.[3] Finally, the fifth issue questions the statistical validity of experimentation using animals. This last issue covers topics such as alternatives, unnecessary repetition of experiments, the importance of animal experimentation to the development of science, and the question of whether the results of experiments with animals can be reliably applied to human beings. These topics and others will be explicated more fully in the course of the following discussion.

## Anti-Animal Experimentation: One Extreme View

We begin with the positions of the anti-animal experimentation group. Some of those who do not believe in animal experimentation base their opinions on a belief in the equality of humans and animals. They believe that there is no hierarchy of life; rather the lives of human beings and animals are equally sacred. Some suggest that this viewpoint was shaped by the Greek school of animism, which believes that animals and humans have the same type of indestructible, interchangeable souls.[4] Others point to the influence of the Methodist belief that animals will share immortality with humans.[5]

Another group of people who are against animal experimentation base their opinion on a different assumption about the hierarchy. They assert that human beings are superior to animals. Yet they go on to explain that this higher position does not give human beings the right to use animals any way they wish. To the contrary, this superiority gives humans the responsibility to protect and care for animals. As David O. Wiebers writes,

> Humankind's superior intelligence and capacity for making moral judgments do not confer upon us the right to exploit other species (or for that matter other humans with lesser intellectual capacity), but rather a responsibility to show compassion for them and assist them.[6]

These two approaches to the hierarchy of life both lead to the same position with regard to the question of ends versus means. Those who are opposed to animal experimentation maintain that the end goal of saving human lives does not in any way justify the means of animal experimentation. This viewpoint is expressed by the motto of the American Anti-Vivisection Society: "You cannot do EVIL that GOOD may result."[7]

The anti-animal experimentation group also believes that animal experimentation will morally corrupt society. For example, this group suggests that animal experimentation will desensitize society to the value of life and encourage people to be cruel to both animals and people.[8] Similarly, they maintain that animal experimentation will corrupt society by encouraging people to steal. The extent of this problem is unclear. However, public outcry over stolen pets that were sold for use in laboratories prompted Congress to pass the Animal Welfare Act in 1966.[9] The group against animal experimentation therefore suggests that animal theft will result from the permissibility of animal experimentation.

Furthermore, with regard to the issue of sentience, the anti-animal experimentation position maintains that animals can undoubtedly feel pain.[10] We should thus refrain from animal experimentation because it will cause animals to suffer.

Those who are against animal experimentation also base their opinions on their understanding of facts about the actual validity of experiments using animals. They claim, first of all, that the scientific community has not yet adequately proven that results from experiments with animals can be applied to humans. For example, they point to "the tragic birth defects caused by Thalidomide [which] occurred because of reliance on animal testing. Conversely, aspirin can kill a cat and penicillin is highly toxic to guinea pigs."[11] Secondly, they emphasize that alternatives are available that can allow experiments to be completed without using animals as subjects. The topic of alternatives will be addressed in more detail below.

Thirdly, this group criticizes the fact that many experiments using animals are unnecessarily repeated by different groups of scientists. The American Anti-Vivisection Society's pamphlet explains, for example, that a sampling of scientific journals between 1975 and 1982 indicated that tests involving the starvation of animals had been published at least 550 times, and those entailing asphyxiation had been performed at least 875 times. Coupled with the fact that many experiments are never even published in journals, this accounts for a great deal of repetitive and useless animal suffering.[12]

Lastly, some people who are against animal experimentation say that many "animal experiments are unjustified because the benefits to humans are small, or even negligible, in proportion to the costs in animal suffering."[13] Others go beyond the cost-benefit analysis to say that the results from animal experimentation have been insignificant and sometimes even detrimental to scientific progress. The American Anti-Vivisection Society, for example, makes the following argument:

> Researchers often... [exaggerate] claims of benefits to humans from animal experiments. Some have gone so far as to claim that 90 percent of all medical advances over the past century have resulted from animal research. Such statements are without foundation and obscure the fact that animal use has frequently retarded medical and scientific progress, due to the numerous obstacles posed by species variation.[14]

Based on this information, they go on to argue that if animal experimentation played such a small role in the history of scientific development, it would not hurt the pursuit of scientific knowledge to eliminate animal experimentation. The anti-animal experimentation group thus asserts that experiments using animals are invalid because their results cannot be reliably applied to humans, alternatives are available, tests with animals are repeated unnecessarily, and the results of experiments with animals are either not worth the suffering involved or have had a minimal effect on the progress of science.

We can see, therefore, that those who are against animal experimentation base their opinions on many important assertions:

animal life is sacred; humans have a responsibility to care for animals; the end goal does not justify the means; animal experimentation will corrupt society; animals can feel pain; and experiments using animals are invalid. There are a number of different organizations and people who, for many of the above reasons, are working to eliminate animal experimentation. Among the most important organizations are the American Anti-Vivisection Society, People for the Ethical Treatment of Animals, Animal Liberation Front, and World Society for the Protection of Animals. The most significant spokespeople for this opinion are individuals such as Peter Singer, Stephen R. L. Clark, Bernard Rollin, and Tom Regan. These and many others work to educate both the general and scientific communities in an attempt to bring about an end to animal experimentation.

## Pro-Animal Experimentation:
## Another Extreme View

On the other side of the spectrum is the group that supports animal experimentation. This group believes that human beings are superior to animals in the hierarchy of life, implying that humans have the right to use animals to serve humanity's needs. This viewpoint is supported by the Judeo-Christian tradition as can be seen in such texts as Genesis 1:28, in which God tells people to "fill the earth and master it; and rule the fish of the sea, the birds of the sky, and all the living things that creep on the earth."[15] Moreover, because human life is more sacred, the end goal of saving human lives justifies the means of animal experimentation.

With regard to the question of social morality, this group does not believe that animal experimentation encourages stealing or cruelty. Rather, it asserts that "Humans are morally obliged to each other to improve the human condition. In cases in which research with animals is the best available method to reach this goal, animals should be used."[16] In essence, if animal experimentation is a means to achieve the moral end of improving the human condition, then we are only encouraging positive social morality by experimenting with animals.

Those who support animal experimentation are divided on the issue of animal sentience. Some believe that animals feel pain but cannot suffer as humans do, so they are not concerned about causing an animal to suffer during experimentation.[17] The majority believe, however, that animals do feel pain and can suffer, but that the affliction of pain and suffering to animals during experimentation is necessary because of this group's other arguments.[18] In a sense, then, the pain that animals suffer during experimentation is viewed as a "necessary evil."

With regard to the validity of experiments using animals, those who are pro-animal experimentation make a number of important points. First, they explain that animal experimentation is necessary because it promotes healing and saves human lives. One group claims that "in the United States, animal experimentation has contributed to an increase in average life expectancy of about 25 years since 1900."[19] Similarly, the following breakthroughs have come about through animal experimentation: in 1908 the polio virus was isolated and studied in monkeys (the vaccine came from human tissue fifty years later); in 1981 the FDA developed a vaccine for Hepatitis B based on research with rhesus monkeys and chimpanzees; and in 1984 a monkey colony used to test antiviral drugs led to a breakthrough in Herpes research.[20] Similarly, Coronary Artery Bypass Graft Surgery,[21] now common in the United States, is due to animal experimentation, as are developments dealing with Multiple Sclerosis, muscle and sciatic paralysis, artificial insemination, and embryo transplants.[22]

Secondly, this group asserts that we have no choice but to use animals as subjects. Many people firmly believe that these experiments must be performed; therefore, since it is inappropriate to use humans as subjects of experimentation on the basis of theory alone, it becomes necessary to use animals.[23] Thirdly, those advocating animal experimentation believe that it is possible to apply to humans the results of research done on animals. For example, Wiebers writes that:

> the EEGs of animals are analogous to those of humans; in fact, the EEGs of gorillas and other primates are nearly indistinguishable from those of humans. This is not surprising given that the brain structure and other central peripheral nervous system structure and circuitry, down to the cellular level, are analogous in humans and other animals, particularly primates, where again they may be almost indistinguishable.[24]

Fourthly, this group formulated an important response to one of the suggestions made by those who espouse restricted use of animals in experimentation. Some people suggest that animals only be used in experiments predetermined to be valid and necessary. The pro-animal experimentation group explains, however, that many important scientific discoveries were made accidentally. It is therefore impossible to determine in advance which experiments are going to turn out to be valid and necessary. Since results cannot be known in advance, this group insists that restrictions should not be placed upon experiments based on predetermined conjecture about validity.[25]

Finally, this group also notes that the alternatives to animal experimentation are slower and too restrictive. There are some American researchers, for example, who claim that British researchers have suffered due to the restrictions placed on them by the British Cruelty to Animals Act of 1876. For example, some Americans believe that the British have not been on the cutting edge of many fields because they were unable to experiments with large animals.[26] As a result of sentiments such as these, many of those who support animal experimentation insist that such experiments cannot be replaced by alternatives. This group maintains that experiments using animals are valid because: they have been proven to help save human lives, we have no choice but to use animals as subjects, we can reliably apply their results to humans, they cannot be restricted in advance based on supposed validity, and the alternatives are slow and restrictive.

The pro-animal experimentation position is based on the following assertions: human life is more sacred than animal life, so humans can use animals to benefit humanity; the ends justify the means; humanity's moral obligation is to save human lives; animals cannot suffer the way humans do, or causing pain to animals through experimentation is a necessary evil; and experiments using animals are valid. Although there are organizations and people who hold many of these opinions, it is difficult to find anyone today who firmly believes in all of them. One group that seems to be closest to this approach, however, is the National Research Council's Committee on the Use of Laboratory Animals in Biomedical and Behavioral Research. Although this group certainly does not hold as extreme a view as was presented above, it does come out in favor of a very unrestricted environment for animal experimentation. Similarly, C. R. Gallistel stands out as an individual who believes strongly in unrestricted animal research.

**Restricted Animal Experimentation:**
**The Middle Position**
Between these two extremes lies a middle ground, one that is gaining popularity and legitimacy throughout the United States. This middle position maintains that animal experimentation is acceptable; however, it emphasizes that the experimentation must be restricted so animals do not suffer unnecessarily and the fewest numbers of animals are used.

Those holding this middle ground posit that human beings may be superior to animals in the hierarchy of life, but that humanity's rights as higher beings must be mediated by our role as caretakers. Moreover, while this position asserts that animal life is sacred, it determines that if a choice must be made, human life takes precedence. In order to respect the sacredness of animal life and to live up to our role as caretakers, this group suggests that we permit animal experimentation but impose on it serious limits and restrictions.[27]

With regard to the question of "ends versus means," the middle position agrees with the pro-animal experimentation group that the end goal of saving human lives does justify the means of animal experimentation. They mediate this position slightly, however, by adding that the ends do not justify the means when the means include animal abuse. According to this view, some animal experimentation is considered a "necessary evil." The problem then becomes defining which experiments constitute abuse. Michael Allen Fox expresses this point of view as follows:

> Since the use of animals for human ends is morally permissible [can be justified], we are not required by any principles of obligation to demonstrate our respect for animals and our reverence for nature by refraining from using them for our own ends – even when this involved taking their lives. We maintain our respect and reverence for the biosphere by considering what we do with the utmost seriousness and by conducting ourselves – as in experimentation on living animals – with the greatest degree of critical self-awareness and responsibility.[28]

He then goes on to discuss in detail the ways in which we can experiment on animals with respect and reverence, thus preventing abuse.

This middle position's opinion on the question of social morality acknowledges that stealing and cruelty may be by-products of animal experimentation. Yet these people do not agree that animal experimentation intrinsically leads to these immoral behaviors, nor do they agree that these challenges to society's social morality demand the elimination of animal experimentation. Rather, this group suggests that legislation and education can prevent these immoral by-products.[29] This would ensure that the acceptance of animal experimentation does not lead to a crisis of social morality.

The middle position takes a similar position with regard to the issue of sentience. The people who hold this middle ground agree that animals can feel pain, but they believe that many of the experiments are necessary. Therefore, they assert that it is the scientist's responsibility to minimize the amount of pain that an animal will suffer during an experiment, particularly through the use of analgesics, anesthetics, and euthanasia.[30]

Finally, on the question of the validity of experiments using animals, those in this middle position believe that some animal experimentation is necessary because it can promote healing, increase medical knowledge, and save lives. However, they maintain that not all experiments with animals are valid. Thus they suggest that we need to work to establish limits that will eliminate these invalid experiments.

In some cases, as we will see below, these limits are set in legislation. In other cases, however, they are suggested in codes of ethics. For example, the Canadian Council on Animal Care established in 1980 an Ethics of Animal Experimentation. The first principle in this work states:

> The use of any animal for experimental purposes should only be considered after all efforts to seek an alternative have been exhausted.
>
> Those using animals should recognize the need to use the best methods on the smallest number of appropriate animals required to obtain valid information. Proposed experiments must be justifiable in terms of the declared objectives. The experimental design must offer every practicable safeguard to the animal.[31]

In a sense, then, those who hold this middle ground agree with the pro-animal experimentation group that it is sometimes necessary to use animals as subjects, but at the same time they agree with many of the concerns put forth by the anti-animal experimentation group. Thus, although they maintain that experiments using animals are often valid and necessary, they promote the use of alternatives and insist that the most humane methods be used on the smallest numbers of animals possible.

It is interesting to note, however, that not everyone espousing this middle position believes that restrictive legislation is the answer to this problem. Michael Allen Fox, one of the spokespeople for this middle position, notes that highly restrictive legislation is clearly becoming more and more popular, but he believes that a restrictive environment will be harmful to scientific progress. He explains that severe curtailment of animal research by legislation or other means would amount to a de facto decision that the pursuit of knowledge in certain crucial areas cannot be allowed to continue. To many, this is also ethically unacceptable in a free society.[32]

He emphasizes that "if researchers want to preserve their independence and their proper role in society,"[33] they need to actively work to develop alternatives.

This middle position is based on the following opinions: a balance must be struck between humanity's superior position with regard to animals and humanity's role as caretaker of animals; the ends do not always justify the means; legislation and education can prevent moral corruption; animals can feel pain, so their suffering should be diminished whenever possible; and experiments using animals are often valid and necessary, but there need to be restrictions, and animal experimentation must be replaced as much as possible by alternatives.

As we will see in our discussion of the laws about animal experimentation in the United States, the trend in the general society today is toward this middle position. Although there are many organizations that support this position, a few have been particularly influential: National Institutes of Health (NIH); Scientists Center for Animal Welfare, led by W. Jean Dodds and F. Barbara Orlans; National Science Foundation; American Association for Laboratory Animal Science; and Canadian Association for Laboratory Animal Science. Similarly, some of the individuals who have figured most prominently in this area have been John Passmore, Michael Allen Fox, R. G. Frey, and Andrew N. Rowan.

## Legislation

We can see the way in which the general society has begun to adopt this middle position by looking at the laws about animal experimentation. The first federal legislation dealing with animal experimentation was the Laboratory Animal Welfare Act, passed in 1966. This Act states that its purpose is to protect the owners of dogs and cats, from the theft of such pets, to prevent the sale or use of dogs and cats that have been stolen, and to insure that certain animals intended for use in research facilities are provided humane care and treatment.[34]

The name of this law was changed to the Animal Welfare Act when it was amended in 1970, and it has been further amended in 1976 and 1985. It now regulates housing, feeding, animal care and husbandry, veterinary care, and appropriate use of anesthetic and analgesics. Moreover, while it requires that research facilities show that they are following acceptable standards with animals during experimentation, it does not give the U.S. Department of Agriculture, its regulatory authority, the power to regulate the design or performance of actual research or testing. It is also important to note that this Act does not cover "rats, mice, birds, and farm animals used in biomedical research, although rats and mice account for about 85 percent of the animals used in research, testing, and education."[35]

Almost twenty years after it was initially passed, greater enforcement of the Animal Welfare Act was provided by the Food Security Act of 1985. This Act established tighter regulations for laboratory animal care and worked to eliminate unnecessary repetition of experiments by encouraging better dissemination of information.[36]

Another important law passed in 1985 was the Health Research Extension Act, which mandates that all places conducting biomedical and behavioral research with Public Health Service funds establish animal care committees. This Act also transformed into law many of the guidelines set by the National Institutes of Health. These guidelines, revised in September of 1986 and entitled the Public Health Service Policy on Humane Care and Use of Laboratory Animals, include the following requirements:

> a. Procedures with animals will avoid or minimize discomfort, distress, and pain to the animals, consistent with sound research design.

b. Procedures that may cause more than momentary or slight pain or distress to the animals will be performed with appropriate sedation, analgesia, or anesthesia, unless the procedure is justified for scientific reasons in writing by the investigator.

c. Animals that would otherwise experience severe or chronic pain or distress that cannot be relieved will be painlessly sacrificed at the end of the procedure or, if appropriate, during the procedure.[37]

Another important document with regard to animal experimentation has been the Guide for the Care and Use of Laboratory Animals, revised most recently in 1985. The Guide was written for the National Institutes of Health by the National Research Council's Institute of Laboratory Animal Resources, and it is a statement of Government policy. The introduction states that "Nothing in the Guide is intended to limit an investigator's freedom – indeed, obligation – to plan and conduct animal experiments in accord with scientific and humane principles." Nevertheless, the Public Health Service "policy on the humane care and use of laboratory animals requires compliance with the Animal Welfare Act and its implementing regulations as well as with the current edition of the Guide for the Care and Use of Laboratory Animals."[38]

We can see how the emphasis of legislation and guidelines about animals used in experimentation has shifted over the years. This shift is particularly striking when one notes that these Acts that carefully ensure human care of animals stem from an Act that focused almost exclusively on stolen pets. Furthermore, the current policies now reflect the same balance which the middle position is trying to strike: an acceptance of animal experimentation balanced by a desire to minimize both unnecessary suffering and the number of animals being used.

## Alternatives

It is clear that the issue of alternatives has played an important role in much of the above discussion. To better understand this area, it is important for us to take a brief look at the theories behind alternatives and the different options that are currently available. Since, we do not have the expertise to make any further judgments about these alternatives, what follows is thus a general introduction to the topic.

Many experts have suggested that there are "3 R's" for alternatives.[39] The first is Replacement, using either invertebrate animals or models to replace vertebrate animals. Second is Reduction by using fewer animals. The third R is Refinement, which is trying to reduce the pain and distress caused to animals.

These 3 R's are put into practice through different alternatives, which the Office of Technology Assessment has divided into four main divisions.[40] The first is continued but modified animal use, where one uses fewer animals; substitution of species so we use an increased number of lower species such as rodents, reptiles, or fish; and reduction of pain. The second is the use of living systems in biomedical research. In this area one would promote in vitro research, the use of invertebrates, research on micro-organisms, and the use of plants. The third area is the use of non-living systems, such as chemical and physical systems and epidemiology, in biomedical research. The fourth area is computer simulation.

The issue of alternatives is clearly of great importance to the future of animal experimentation, for the development of alternatives will increasingly influence the conclusions that we can draw about the necessity of using animals as experimental subjects. For those who are interested in a more in-depth look at alternatives, we suggest turning to Alternatives to Animal Use in Research, Testing, and Education, put out by the Office of Technology Assessment of the United States Congress.[41]

## Conclusions about General Ethics

Opinions on the issue of animal experimentation fall at many points along a spectrum. On one end are the views of those who oppose any sort of animal experimentation, and on the other end are the views of those who support unrestricted animal experimentation. Over the years, however, society has tended toward a middle position. This position allows for some animal experimentation, but it maintains that one should use the most humane methods on the fewest animals possible. Moreover, to attain these goals the middle positions argues for restrictions and the further development of alternatives. It is also clear that the legislation and guidelines of the last twenty-five years have reflected this shift toward the middle ground. Therefore, despite the diversity of strongly-held convictions, it is possible to generalize and conclude that this middle positions reflects today's societal consensus about animal experimentation.

## Halakhic Sources

Before entering into a discussion of the various halakhic texts that bear on the issue of animal experimentation, there are a number of initial points that must be made. First, the entire question of performing specific experiments on animals in order to effect healing, or at least to increase the future possibility of effecting healing, presumes that human life is sacred. This sanctity of life is certainly the case within Jewish tradition. For example, *pikuah nefesh* demands that all but three commandments (idolatry, murder and sexual misconduct) must be broken in order to save a human life.

A second consideration holds that it is not permissible to cause pain and suffering to an animal. The Encyclopedia Judaica defines the category, known as *tzaar baalei hayim* as:

> Moral and legal rules concerning the treatment of animals are based on the principal that animals are part of God's creation toward which [humanity] bears responsibility. Laws and other indications in the Pentateuch and the rest of the Bible make it clear not only that cruelty to animals is forbidden but also compassion and mercy to them are demanded of [people] by God.[42]

*Tzaar baalei hayim* can be problematic, however. First of all, its origins are unclear. For example, there is considerable debate in the Tosafot (Baba Metzia 32b) and elsewhere as to whether it is Biblically or Rabbinically prescribed. Moreover, the parameters of *tzaar baalei hayim* and the specifics of its applicability vary depending on the halakhic source, as will be explicated further in the course of our discussion. Rabbi J. David Bleich comments that, "it is nevertheless probably incorrect to conclude that concern for *tzaar baalei hayim* is predicated upon a legal or moral concept of animal 'rights.'"[43] After reviewing the development of this issue within the *halakhah*, we will be able to return and evaluate this significant point. Yet despite the lack of clarity with regard to the origin and applicability, *tzaar baalei hayim* is a central issue in the discussion of animal experimentation from the vantage point of the Jewish legal system. In the case of animal experimentation, the requirement to heal comes into direct conflict with the ban on intentionally causing pain to non-human living beings. It is this tension between the obligation to save human lives and the relationship of humanity to God's other creatures that is central to our legal discussion.

### Biblical Texts

There are many Biblical texts that seem to relate to this issue. Few of them, however, are actually cited by the later halakhic authorities. While we might, as generalists and liberals, begin with our conclusion and strive to find quotes to employ as proof texts, this is not the appropriate method for approaching our traditional texts. Therefore, we will only cite those Biblical texts that are quoted by later authorities or form the foundation of their position.

Two significant verses from Genesis help form the basis of

the Rabbinic view of the relationship between humanity and the animal world. When God creates the first people, they are told "Be fertile and multiply, fill the earth and master it; and rule the fish of the sea, the birds of the sky and all the living things that creep on earth."(Gen 1:28) Later, they are told "Every creature that lives shall be yours to eat; as with the green grasses, I give you all these." (Gen 9:3-4) Clearly, the Biblical world-view inherited and adopted by the *halakhah* was one in which humanity was given dominion over the animal world. However this is itself problematic since dominion can infer both free usage and responsible guardianship. As we will see later, both aspects of this relationship find their way into the halakhic material. A final significant Biblical verse states "When in your war against a city you have to besiege it a long time in order to capture it, you must not destroy its trees" and has been generalized and interpreted as the basis of the prohibition against *bal taskhit*, wanton destruction of all property or animals. Thus, Talmud *Hullin* 7b notes that the killing of animals for no purpose is prohibited based on this verse and Maimonides extends the verse to include all needless destruction in *Mishneh Torah, Melakhim* 6:10. These three Biblical verses and the prohibition against *tzaar baalei ḥayim*, whether Biblically or Rabbinically based, establish the basic tension between human domination of the world, the sanctity of human life and the responsibility of humanity toward the world. It is this tension that is the root of the struggle within the later source material.

**Talmudic Texts**
The first important Talmudic text for determining the permissibility of animal experimentation from a Jewish legal perspective comes from *Kidushin* 82b. The text states, "R. Simeon b. Eleazar said, In my whole lifetime I have not seen a deer engaged in gathering fruits, a lion carrying burdens, or a fox as a shopkeeper, yet they were created only to serve me." Similarly, in *Berakhot* 6b the Gemara asks what is the meaning of the phrase "the whole of man" in the verse "The end of the matter, all having been heard: fear God and keep His commandments, for this is the whole of man." (Eccl. 12:13) In response Rabbi Eleazar states, "The Holy One, blessed be He, says, The whole world was created for his [man's] sake only." These texts maintain that animals were created for the purpose of human usefulness. From these statements we see a Rabbinic continuation of the Biblical understanding that human beings have dominion over animals. In addition, there is an added Rabbinic concept that animals were, in fact, created for the purpose of serving people. While these comments do not deal specifically with the issue of vivisection, they do help to establish firmly the Rabbinic concept that there is an implicit, God-created "hierarchy of being"

in which humans are above all other animals, leading to both responsibility as caretakers as well as permissibility of use.

This position vis a vis humanity and the animal world is further extended by a Talmudic statement from Shabbat 77b that notes that animals were created for specific medicinal uses for the sake of effecting human cures.

> Rabbi Judah said in Rav's name: Of all that the Holy One, blessed be He, created in His world, He created everything with a purpose, He created the snail [to heal] a scab, He created a fly [to heal] a wasp [sting], a mosquito [to heal] a snake [bite], and a snake [to heal] an eruption, a spider [to heal] a scorpion [sting]. How is this done? You take one white one and one black, boil them and rub them in.

The illustrations in this text indicate that insects can be killed for the purpose of healing human ailments. Therefore the phrase, "created everything for a purpose" means that everything was created to serve people through healing. The medical use of insects is therefore permitted.

There are two interesting and potentially important observations that can be made regarding this text. First, the creatures referred to here and used for human healing are "lower forms" such as insects. However, both the Tosafot and later commentaries make it clear, as we will see, that this statement of permitted use applies to all *baalei ḥayim*, all living beings. Second, these creatures are killed outright for healing rather than being used in experiments and caused to suffer over a period of time. This remains an important text from which later sources base their cases.

A fourth Talmudic text introduces the issue of *tzaar baalei ḥayim* and its relationship to the restrictions of Shabbat activity. Shabbat 128b states that an individual may touch objects deemed *muktzeh*[44] and may carry on the Shabbat for the benefit of an animal. This is the case since the laws of Shabbat are Rabbinic and in this opinion, *tzaar baalei ḥayim* is Biblical.

If an animal falls into a dike, one brings pillows and bedding and places [them] under it. *Tzaar baalei ḥayim* is Biblical law, so the Biblical law comes and supersedes the [law] of the Rabbis.

These texts indicate that there are occasions when *tzaar baalei ḥayim*, like the mandate of *pikuaḥ nefesh*, conflicts with existing prohibitions such as the laws of Shabbat observance. Thus an action that would normally be prohibited is permitted in order to relieve an animal of its suffering. It is important to note that implicit in this text is the assumption that animals are sentient beings. It is not clear if they experience pain in the same way as humans;[45] however, the pain is significant enough to warrant the supersession of Shabbat restrictions.

## Medieval Texts

An important medieval text is Tosafot's commentary on Talmud Baba Metzia 32b. The Talmudic passage deals with the issue of *tzaar baalei hayim*. The Tosafot enter into a discussion of whether the precept of *tzaar baalei hayim* is a Biblical injunction or a Rabbinic one. Three different opinions are offered. The first states that it is Biblical, while the second maintains that it is Rabbinic. The third agrees that it is Rabbinic but adds that causing pain to an animal is only problematic and prohibited if the resultant pain is without any benefit *(toelet)*. Rabbi J. David Bleich understands this to mean that "Tosafot apparently regards *tzaar baalei hayim* in a similar light, i.e., as forbidden only when wanton in nature, but permissible when designated to achieve a legitimate goal."[46] Therefore, it is acceptable to inflict pain on animals when this is done for a specific goal. In this we may see a clear loosening of the restrictions engendered by *tzaar baalei hayim*, such that animal experimentation may not even be considered as *tzaar baalei hayim*. This text adds an important dimension to the discussion of humans using animals for their benefit. Such behavior must be motivated by a specific need and done to achieve a definite end. Experimentation to provide cures for human ailments would clearly fall into this category as acceptable.

The 13th century text *Sefer Hahinukh* carries on the discussion of the tension between the use of animals for human benefit and the prohibition against causing suffering to animals. While all three of the key texts deal with the specific issue of *shehita* (ritual slaughter), the discussions are relevant since in both *shehita* and animal experimentation there is, as we have seen, a general permissibility of human use of animals. These texts, however, add an important dimension by stating that there are reasons, despite the legal permissibility of causing pain to animals in specific cases, why we as Jews should refrain from such actions. This is clearly seen in *Sefer Hahinukh* #451 which states:

> It is said as the reason for slaughter at the neck, and that the knife is examined, in order that we will not cause suffering to animals more than is necessary, for the Torah permitted them to man by virtue of his import in the hierarchy, to sustain himself, and all his needs, but not for their needless suffering; and the sages have already spoken at length regarding the prohibition of *tzaar baalei hayim* in *Baba Metziah* and *Shabbat*. Since it is forbidden Biblically, the punishment is the same as for any Biblical infraction.

The author of this text recognizes and accepts the legal right of humans to kill animals for food, survival and "all his needs." However, he notes that there is a specific way in which this should be done in order to keep the pain and suffering to a minimum.

A second statement from *Sefer Haḥinukh*, #186, extends this discussion of the tension between human needs and the pain to animals, which often accompanies it:

> The Holy One did not permit the flesh of animals to people only for atonement or for the needs of human beings (to live), for instance sustenance, or healing or any other matter of need which a person has. However, to kill them without any benefit (*to-elet*) at all, there is in such a case wasteful destruction and it is called *shofekh dam*. And even though this is not like the spilling of blood of a person, for people have been elevated over animals and animals are lower; in any case it is called *shofekh dam*, since the Torah did not permit spilling (blood) without benefit. However, there is in this matter harm (when it is spilling of blood) for he has transgressed the commandment of his Creator, and therefore Scripture punishes him with *karet* (cutting off from the community).

In this case, the issue is that there be direct benefit (*toelet*) drawn from the use of the animal in order that it be acceptable. If, according to the text, there is benefit drawn from the suffering or killing of the animal, the action is Biblically permitted. This position is based on the belief that humans are elevated over all other creatures and therefore have use of them. If, however, there is no benefit from the suffering or killing caused, it is prohibited and is punishable. Here we see the answer to a question raised above. Is elevation over the animal world a warrant to use them without regard or is it an obligation to protect them? According to this authority, it is both. The Torah permits use of animals for human benefit, but it does not permit abuse or use with total disregard for the consequences. We learn from this that we can kill and use animals, but purposeless, wanton killing is tantamount to "shedding blood." There is an underlying assumption that the concept of the "hierarchy of being" might lead to the conclusion that people are permitted to abuse animals. An element of responsible action is thus introduced into the human right of use.

A third and final statement from *Sefer Haḥinukh*, #596, extends this discussion even further by stating:

> with regard to beasts, even though they were only created to serve us, we should be merciful to them, to apportion to them ..; (by) accustoming the soul in this way, (it leads people) to be good to human beings. Thus is the path which is worthy for a holy chosen people.

Once again we see the permissibility of using animals for human benefit. However, an additional and potentially stricter consideration is added to the discussion. The letter of the law may permit this action, but the pursuit of holiness requires that we restrain from such behavior. An important consideration is whether this additional restriction is the result of a sensitivity to the legal question of *tzaar baalei hayim* or if there is a "quasi-ethical" level at play here. The use of such terms as "holiness" and "holy chosen people" point to the latter, although numerous scholars have shown that the halakhic authorities did not speak in terms of "ethics."

### Shulhan Arukh

Two texts from the 16th century *Shulhan Arukh* further this discussion. In both cases, however, the position taken by Isserles in his Mapa is of particular interest.

The Caro text of *Hoshen Mishpat* 272:9 discusses whether one should unload an animal that is over-burdened.[47] If it is an Israelite animal but the load belongs to a Gentile, the animal must be unloaded and the load carried by hand. The text continues to comment that if the animal and the load belong to a Gentile, it does not have to be unloaded. Caro thus stated that there are times when an animal is left under a painful burden. Isserles comments:

> One must unload (an over-burdened animal) even if the Gentile is not there because of (the ban on) pain inflicted on animals, as it is written in the Torah. And thus, in any case where one is (legally) exempt from unloading (an over-burdened animal) – in this case (one unloads the animals anyway) because of (the ban on) pain inflicted on animals (*tzaar baalei hayim*). Someone who is obligated (to unload an over-burdened animal) and fulfills this obligation is one who can receive a reward.

Isserles recognizes that there are times when it is halakhicly permissible to leave an overburdened beast in pain. However he notes that despite this permissibility, *tzaar baalei hayim* should motivate different action and the cause of the pain should be removed. We thus see here the clear limiting of a legally permissible act due to the consideration of *tzaar baalei hayim*.

A similar consideration and mitigation of permissible actions is found in *Even Haezer* 5:14. The Caro text discusses that it is forbidden for a gentile to mutilate an Israelite animal, but it is acceptable under Jewish law for him to mutilate a gentile animal. Caro goes on to maintain that, "anything that is necessary in order to effect cure or for other [similar] matters does not entail [a violation] of the prohibition against *tzaar baalei hayim*." As in Talmud *Shabbat* 77b, Caro notes that non-human, living beings can be used to heal human ailments. He goes one step further, however, by relating this directly to the seeming contradiction between such a statement and the prohibition of *tzaar baalei ḥayim*. He notes that if such action is done for the purpose of healing, then it is not a violation of *tzaar baalei ḥayim*. Isserles then comments:

> Therefore it is permitted to pluck feathers from the skin of an animal [only in order to write a prescription] but one must consider [the ban on] pain inflicted upon animals [*tzaar baalei ḥayim*]; and in any case, one should always refrain [from doing it] because it is cruelty.

Once again Isserles maintains that while causing pain to animals is indeed permissible according to the letter of the law, *tzaar baalei ḥayim* should lead one to reject such action. Here is another case in which law mitigates law. Moreover, Isserles is either directly influenced by the text of *Sefer Haḥinukh*, or indirectly by the same concerns which shaped that document's position, which mediates between the permissibility of the law and what should actually be done. He thus notes that even if *tzaar baalei ḥayim* were not a legal category, a person should still refrain because of the undefined, "quasi-ethical" category of "cruelty." In both cases, Isserles restricts Caro's conclusions and bases his own opinion on both *tzaar baalei ḥayim* and a category he simply refers to as "cruelty."

## Responsa Literature

Up to this point the halakhic material has dealt with the tension between the permissibility of using animals for healing and the prohibition of *tzaar baalei ḥayim*. None of the texts, however, have dealt specifically with the issue of the permissibility of animal experimentation in order to effect a cure. In *Shevut Yaakov III* #71, written by Rabbi Jacob Reischer in the 18th century, however, we see this issue dealt with directly. Reischer addresses the following question:

> Is it permitted in order to do healing for us to put to death an impure animal like a dog or a cat because [of a case of] doubtful "*pikuaḥ nefesh*" because this [treatment] is still not tried and tested and one has to test it by means of a liquid, so [we give it] to a cat or a dog to see if it will die from it?

His response begins with a reiteration of previous statements. However, he extends the discussion to include research on animals in cases where healing is not necessarily a direct benefit.

> A rule that is carried into practice by rule of thumb is that everything that is needed, whether for heal-

ing of the body or for any financial benefit – one should not be anxious [that it is] forbidden according to the ban against *bal tashkit* or *tzaar baalei ḥayim* and it is not forbidden here even according to the [higher] "law of the pious."[48]

Even if healing is not ensured, he notes, an animal may be killed or given an experimental cure to increase the possibility of healing. Yet, since earlier texts had raised the issue of *tzaar baalei ḥayim* in relationship to such questions, Reischer is prompted to respond. He seems to take a similar posture to that of Caro in *Shulḥan Arukh, Even Haezer* 5:14, positing that it is not considered an action prohibited by *tzaar baalei ḥayim* if there is direct gain from the suffering caused to the animal. It is clearly legal to do whatever is needed in order to heal, and even the most pious of people would agree that healing must take precedence over consideration of the animal. Yet a short time later in the text Reischer takes the position held by Isserles and comments that while there may be legal justification for taking certain action, there are equally important reasons why these actions, justified though they are, should not be actualized.

Further on in this rich *teshuvah*, we read a comment indicating that the statement in *Shabbat* 77b is understood as applying to animals as well as to insects. We also see the application of the Talmudic permissibility of profaning the Shabbat in order to save a life.

Rav said: everything that God created in the world was only created for its purpose. God created the snail as a remedy for a scab, the fly to crush and apply to a hornet's sting, the mosquito is crushed and used to cure a serpent's bite. Thus it is permitted to kill an animal because of healing, and we should not worry about *bal taskhit* or *tzaar baalei ḥayim*, even if there is doubt about healing. Everything that is needed by a person is permitted: *Bal Taskhit* of an animal's body is preferable. Even because of *pikuaḥ nefesh* we defile the Shabbat.

*Shevut Yaakov* establishes that while both *tzaar baalei ḥayim* and *pikuaḥ nefesh* supersede the Shabbat, *pikuaḥ nefesh* supersedes *tzaar baalei ḥayim*. We also see the inclusion of the general Biblical principal of *bal tashḥit*, the prohibition against wanton destruction. The *teshuvah*, however, notes that, as in the case of *tzaar baalei ḥayim*, if the destruction is done in the name of healing, this legal category is not applicable.

In his conclusion to the *teshuvah*, Rabbi Reischer ties all of these apparently disparate strands together:

A rule that can be carried into practice is that it

> seems to me to be clear, as it is written, that one
> should not worry that anything which is needed is
> forbidden according to *bal tashḥit* or *tzaar baalei
> ḥayim*. And it is possible to do it even with premedi-
> tation but that the Rema finished there in *Orakh
> Ḥayim*...that with regard to plucking feathers, every-
> one restrains because of cruelty. *Davka* with pluck-
> ing feathers they were [doing] something with their
> hands, and the chicken feels the pain in its skin at
> the moment of each and every pluck. What has been
> said here in the topic that is before us is that it
> doesn't feel any pain at the time of eating or drink-
> ing it. It is only afterwards that it causes sickness
> and pain. But it is for the healing of human beings
> [therefore] it seems to me that one should not worry,
> even from a sense of piety, that it is forbidden.

In this passage he establishes a distinction between acts which
cause pain to animals directly and acts which cause indirect or delayed pain. Acts which cause immediate pain are prohibited because
they teach people cruelty, but it is permissible to cause delayed
pain to animals since this is not viewed as promoting cruelty. This
distinction makes it clear that his understanding of *tzaar baalei
ḥayim* has nothing to do with the fact that it will teach humans to
be cruel. J. David Bleich comments,

> Apparently, Shevut Yaakov feels that concern for
> developing a cruel disposition exists only when the
> human act is the immediate and proximate cause of
> perceivable pain, but not when the act is not imme-
> diately associated with the pain experienced by the
> animal.[49]

Thus, so long as the action will potentially yield healing, and will
not adversely affect the human beings involved, it is permitted.

A second relevant *teshuvah* comes from *Ḥelkat Yaakov* I,
#30 sec. 6 written by Mordecai Jacob Breisch in the early 1900's.
The *teshuvah* begins with the specific question of whether it is permissible to cause pain to animals through experiments done in the
name of increasing the scientific knowledge of healing. This is significant since this text deals with animal experimentation for the
purpose of increasing medical knowledge in order to heal rather
than animal experimentation for the sake of effecting a direct cure.
In responding, he bases his decision on the same distinction
between prohibited actions and actions that are permitted but
avoided because of other, non-legal reasons. Thus, this extends the
permissibility of animal experimentation to the realm of general
experimentation for the purpose of increasing knowledge.

Finally, in a contemporary responsum by Rabbi Dov Yitzhak
Bamberger, we find a further loosening of the constraints of *tzaar*

*baalei ḥayim*. Bamberger, quoted by R. Jacob Ettlinger, *Teshuvot Binyan Zion* #108, asserts that Isserles permits *tzaar baalei ḥayim* "when there is need for medical purposes even for a patient who is not dangerously ill."When the action is pursued for medical purposes, even to increase the medical knowledge of how to heal, it is permitted to use animals.

## Conclusions from Halakhic Sources

All of the sources examined maintain that the legal right to cause pain to animals in the pursuit of healing must be tempered by other concerns. When the pain and death is not entirely necessary it is considered wanton destruction and is prohibited. In raising this level of concern, the authorities often employed the non-legal categories of "piety" and "cruelty." While these are not "ethical" categories by our modern definition, they are outside the realm of the strictly legal and serve as limits on the legal "right" of animal use established by Jewish law. In addition, the authorities seem to show less concern for the well-being and suffering of the animal than for the effect that the act of causing pain to animals has on a human being. The commentators also specify that inflicting pain is not permitted in cases where pain and death are caused without gain, or when experimentation is done in excess of specific needs. Moreover, researchers must seek means to limit the pain caused to their subjects during necessary procedures.

This halakhic material provides an important lens through which to examine the issue of animal experimentation. The interplay between the issues discussed above and the specific question of animal experimentation is complicated, but some general statements can be drawn from it. First, animal experimentation is clearly permitted by Jewish law in order to save a human life. It is also permitted by some authorities if the experimentation is done in order to increase medical knowledge of healing and to save lives in the future. In these cases the pain is either a permitted form of *tzaar baalei ḥayim* or, because it is life-saving, it is not considered *tzaar baalei ḥayim*. Thus, it is clear that this halakhic warrant for performing animal experimentation does not give free reign to the scientist or to the physician to pursue any avenue of experimentation.

## A Comparison of the General Ethical and Halakhic Material

Study of either the secular or halakhic material alone provides a great deal to consider regarding the issue of animal experimentation. When viewed together, a much fuller perspective can be obtained. Common areas of concern are addressed in both, while there are also distinct differences. This section explores the similarities and differences as part of the process of determining what our liberal Jewish ethic should be.

In reviewing the secular and halakhic material, it is evident that the *halakhah* does not agree with either of the extreme secular positions. In no case does Jewish law entirely prohibit or fully permit the use of animals for experimentation. However, there is a great deal of overlap between the *halakhah* and the middle ground ethics positions. This is seen through an overview of the five key points present in the discussion of general ethics. (Further reference to the phrase "general ethics" will indicate the "middle ground position.")

The points to be discussed in this section are as follows. First, both the secular and the halakhic positions believe that there is a hierarchy of life in which humans are superior to animals. However, they agree that the rights of humans as the dominant species must be mediated by the human role as caretaker since all life has intrinsic value. For the second issue of ends versus means, both agree that it is permissible to use animals for worthy goals. We must point out, however, that abuse is forbidden. Regarding social morality, limits must be established so as not to encourage people to be cruel to either animals or people. The halakhic and the secular positions presume that animals are sentient beings. But, since it is already established that experimentation is permissible, the general ethics provide suggestions on how to cause the least amount of suffering, while the *halakhah* also shows sensitivity to the matter of suffering. As for the last topic, both have a strong concern for the validity of the experiments performed.

We continue, then, with the first point of agreement: The halakhic and general ethics positions begin with the common premise that it is permissible for people to use animals. This notion is drawn in part from the Biblical concept of hierarchy. Based on this, there is general acknowledgment that the end goal of saving human lives justifies the means of animal use in experimentation. While humans may be superior to animals in the hierarchy of life, they are still obligated to serve as their caretakers. This leads to a struggle to balance these two role. Thus, there is a dialectic between the human being who dominates animals or acts as their caretaker.

Another important topic is how the use of animals for experimentation affects society in general. The *halakhah* approaches this question by exploring how human acts of cruelty to animals can affect human behavior in general. While the *halakhah* allows animals to be used for experimentation, it promotes consideration of the moral issues as well as the legal ones. Compassion toward animals according to Judaism is a "moral imperative"[50] that involves treating the animals kindly even beyond the requirements of the law. The main concern is that if humans are cruel to animals, they will learn to be cruel to other humans.

On the other hand, the general ethics concern differs from the *halakhah*. The secular view speaks in terms of animal rights, a topic not addressed by the *halakhah*. This is done through government legislation, such as The Animal Welfare Act, as well as education. Though the reasoning for the two positions are different, they both reach the same conclusion: allow the use of animals in experimentation.

The tension between the roles of humans as dominant beings and caretakers is particularly difficult since both the halakhic and secular positions agree that animals are sentient beings. They agree that abuse such as wanton killing must be avoided. Knowing that the animals will experience pain as a result of the experiments motivates both positions to strive to cause the least amount of discomfort possible. The *halakhah* views this in part as applying the principle of *tzaar baalei hayim*. In addition, at least one rabbi considers it more appropriate to cause an animal delayed rather than immediate pain (e.g., giving the animal a liquid with delayed reactions rather than plucking feathers). This reflects the view that humans will learn how to treat other humans by seeing how animals are treated.

The general ethics position is also sensitive to the fact that animals feel pain. They propose that pain should be diminished through the use of anesthetics or other pain relievers. In addition, they believe that the number of animals used in experiments should be limited in order not to cause unnecessary suffering. When possible, lower level animals should be used. Finally, alternative methods of research (e.g., computer simulation) should be explored. As demonstrated before, the general ethics show a deep concern for the animal.

Regarding the validity of the experiments, the dominant position as seen through the halakhic and general ethics arguments is to promote human benefit through medical experimentation while maintaining the most humane treatment possible for the animals. Human benefit is understood to be anything that promotes healing. While use of animals is permitted in such cases, care must be taken at all times to protect the animals from unnecessary pain and limit wasteful use.

As is eminently clear by now, the halakhic and middle secular positions overlap in several categories. For each issue, both aim at providing safeguards for the animals. In other words, while the actual law may allow use of animals, it is of extreme importance that the animals not be mistreated. Rabbi J. David Bleich explains that within the *halakhah*,

[there] is a distinction between normative law and

ethical conduct above and beyond the requirements of law [lifnim mishurat hadin]. Jewish teaching recognizes that, ideally, man must aspire to a higher level of conduct. That higher standard is posited as a moral desideratum, albeit a norm which is not enforceable by human courts.[51]

Similarly, within the general ethics we see a mixing of legislation with prescriptive guidelines that support even further restrictions. Thus, while experimentation may be permitted by law, there are a number of factors that limit causing pain to animals.

We have clearly seen that both positions agree that humans are at the top of the hierarchy of life. Therefore, they have the right to use animals for their benefit and also have the moral responsibility to be caretakers for the animals. Humans must strive to treat animals humanely and if possible seek alternative methods of experimentation. The meta-ethics of the halakhah overlaps much of the general ethics. Most significant is the goal of both to set up precautions or safeguards in the act of animal experimentation. The halakhah and the general ethics struggle between what is permitted and what they feel should be done. The intersection of the halakhic and secular arguments direct us toward a modern liberal Jewish ethic of this issue, which is elaborated upon in the final section of this paper.

## Conclusion

Our liberal Jewish ethic on animal experimentation reflects the intersection between the middle position of the general ethics and the meta-ethics that underlie the halakhah. After much consideration, we find ourselves taking a general stand that use of animals for experimentation is permissible in order to save human lives and to increase the knowledge of healing. However, this permissibility must be mitigated by the implementation of safeguards against abuse. In particular, we emphasize restrictions that limit the quantity and types of animals used in animal experimentation, and regulations that minimize the pain caused to these animals. We also strongly affirm the significance of alternatives to animal experimentation.

Our justification for animal experimentation is based on three main points. First, we believe that human beings are superior to animals, but are also responsible to care for them. In addition, people are responsible to employ all avenues possible to achieve healing and to improve the human condition. Animal experimentation is currently one of the means toward achieving this end. However, we consider it to be a "necessary evil" and do not state our approval with any sense of satisfaction or joy. We look forward to when it will no longer be a "necessary evil" and when other means of research will provide the same results.

Since animal experimentation at this point is still necessary, we must strive to make it reflective of our ethics. We have seen throughout this work that the general ethics emphasize concern for animal rights, whereas the *halakhah* is concerned with the effects that inflicting pain on animals will have on human morality. In forming our opinion, we feel enriched by the ability to draw from both of these foci. From the perspective of animal rights, we therefore stress the importance of what have been termed the "3 R's": Replacement, Reduction, and Refinement. Furthermore, with respect to human morality, we encourage continued education and legislation that stress sensitivity to the value of all life.

Another important issue is that of alternatives. We maintain that emphasis must be placed on the development and implementation of alternatives to the use of animals in experimentation. We realize that the *halakhah* does not speak to the issue of alternatives. Nevertheless, since alternatives would allow us to achieve our goal of healing people without causing pain to animals, we presume that the rabbis would support this option since it would lessen *tzaar baalei hayim*.

The above conclusions stem from our grappling with the same issues that have for centuries confronted the secular and halakhic Jewish world. In order to respond to our specific question we, too, have sought a balance between saving human life and preventing cruelty to animals. The clash between these two values is particularly apparent in the issue of animal experimentation. In seeking the most ethical resolution to this dilemma as possible, we have been fortunate that both the general ethics and the *halakhah* have pointed in the same direction. This has greatly simplified our decision-making process with regard to our question of animal experimentation.

However, this has also complicated our ability to generalize about the decision-making process of liberal Jewish ethics. Our case has not taught us what to do when the two worlds in which we stand point us in substantially different directions. Moreover, we realize that we are limited in our ability to navigate and interpret our Jewish inheritance. Similarly, we are neither trained in general ethics nor, with regard to our case, in the specifics of scientific research. As a result, the development of a liberal Jewish ethic clearly requires the involvement of individuals who have a greater knowledge of the intricacies of these worlds.

On the other hand, this process has taught us the value of drawing from both the secular and Jewish worlds. Even though there was a great deal of overlap between the two, each also addressed issues not considered by the other. The process of forming a liberal Jewish ethic allowed us to benefit from the lenses that each tradition provided. The result is thus richer because it draws from the different concerns and sensitivities of each.

# Bibliography

"Animals, Cruelty to." *Encyclopedia Judaica.* 1971 ed.

American Anti-Vivisection Society. *Why We Oppose Vivisection.* Jenkintown, PA: Revised 5/90.

Bleich, J. David. *Contemporary Halakhic Problems,* Vol. III. New York: Ktav, 1989.

Bleich, J. David. *Judaism and Healing – Halakhic Perspectives.* New York: Ktav, 1981.

Brown, Les. *Cruelty to Animals: The Moral Debt.* Houndsmills: Macmillan Press, 1988.

Cohen, Carl. "The Case for the Use of Animals in Biomedical Research." *The New England Journal of Medicine.* Vol. 315, #14. October 2, 1985.

Cohen, Noah. *Tsaar Baale Ḥayim – The Prevention of Cruelty to Animals: Its Bases, Development and Legislation in Hebrew Literature.* Washington: Catholic University Press, 1959.

Feeney, Dennis M. "Human Rights and Animal Welfare." *American Psychologist.* June, 1987.

Fox, Michael Allen. *The Case for Animal Experimentation.* Berkeley: University of California Press, 1986.

Frey, R. G. (in an exchange with Sir William Paton). "Vivisection, Morals, and Medicine: An Exchange." *Animal Rights and Human Obligations.* Tom Regan and Peter Singer, eds. New Jersey: Prentice Hall, 1989.

Gallistel, C. R. "The Case for Unrestricted Research Using Animals." *Animal Rights and Human Obligations.* Tom Regan and Peter Singer, eds. New Jersey: Prentice Hall, 1989.

Gendin, Sidney. "The Use of Animals in Science." *Animal Rights and Human Obligations.* Tom Regan and Peter Singer, eds. New Jersey: Prentice Hall, 1989.

Jakobovits, Immanuel. "The Medical Treatment of Animals in Jewish Law" in *Journal of Jewish Studies,* Vol. VII, #324. Manchester: Institute of Jewish Studies, 1950.

Jakobovits, Immanuel. *Jewish Medical Ethics.* New York: Bloch, 1959.

Kerr, Frederick W. L. "The Investigator's Responsibilities in Research Using Animals." *Scientific Perspectives on Animal Welfare.* W. Jean Dodds and F. Barbara Orlans, eds. New Jersey: Academic Press, 1982.

Langley, Gill, ed. *Animal Experimentation: The Consensus Changes*. New York: Chapman and Hall, 1989.

National Institutes of Health. Office for Protection from Research Risks. *Public Health Service Policy on Humane Care and Use of Laboratory Animals*. Rev. ed. Bethesda, MD: U.S. Department of Health and Human Services, 1986.

National Research Council. Committee on Care and Use of Laboratory Animals. *Guide for the Care and Use of Laboratory Animals*. 5th rev. ed. Bethesda, MD: U.S. Department of Health and Human Services, 1985.

— Committee on the Use of Laboratory Animals in Biomedical and Behavioral Research. *Use of Laboratory Animals in Biomedical and Behavioral Research*. Washington, D.C.: National Academy Press, 1988.

Rollin, Bernard E. "The Moral Status of Research Animals in Psychology." *American Psychologist*. August, 1985.

Rosner, Fred and Tendler, Moshe D. *Practical Medical Halakhah*. Hoboken, NJ: Ktav, 1990.

Rowan, Andrew N. *Of Mice, Models, and Men: A Critical Evaluation of Animal Research*. Albany: State University of New York Press, 1984.

Schochet, Elijah Judah. *Animal Life in Jewish Tradition: Attitudes and Relationships*. New York: Ktav Publishing House, Inc., 1984.

Shapiro, Harvey M. "Animal Rights and Biomedical Research: No Place for Complacency." *Anesthesiology*, Vol. 64, #2. February, 1986.

*Tanakh: The Holy Scriptures*. Trans. New JPS. Philadelphia: The Jewish Publication Society, 1988.

United States. Cong. Office of Technology Assessment. *Alternatives to Animal Use in Research, Testing, and Education*. New York: Marcel Dekker, Inc., 1988.

Vaillancourt, Sharon. Student at the North Carolina State University College of Veterinary Medicine. Telephone interview. November 1991.

Welborn, Robert F. "Service on an Institutional Animal Committee." *HSUS News*. Fall 1991.

Wiebers, David O. "Healing Society's Relationship with Animals: A Physician's View." *HSUS News*. Fall 1991.

# Notes

1. There is a wide discrepancy in this range. It is interesting to see how different people and organizations have such different facts. We have decided to trust the figures provided by the USDA/APHIS.

2. United States, Cong., Office of Technology Assessment, *Alternatives to Animal Use in Research, Testing and Education* (New York: Marcel Dekker, Inc., 1988), p. 5. (Hereinafter United States)

3. Andrew N. Rowan, *Of Mice, Models, and Men: A Critical Evaluation of Animal Research* (Albany: State University of New York Press, 1984), p. 259.

4. Ibid., p. 251.

5. Ibid., p. 48.

6. David O. Wiebers, "Healing Society's Relationship with Animals: A Physician's View," *HSUS News.* Fall 1991, p. 27.

7. American Anti-Vivisection Society, *Why We Oppose Vivisection* (Jenkintown, PA. Revised 5/90), p. 17.

8. Gill Langley, ed., *Animal Experimentation: The Consensus Changes* (New York: Chapman and Hall, 1989), p 28. See also Michael Allen Fox, The Case for Animal Experimentation (Berkeley: University of California Press, 1989), p. 170.

9. United States, p. 13.

10. Fox, in an interesting discussion entitled "On Knowing When and How Much Animals are Suffering," begins by stating: "I assume that it is not necessary to prove to anyone that animals are capable of feeling pain or of suffering." [Fox 161.]

11. American Anti-Vivisection Society, p. 11.

12. American Anti-Vivisection Society, pp. 8-9.

13. Les Brown, *Cruelty to Animals: The Moral Debt* (Houndsmills: Macmillan Press, 1988), p. 119. Brown presents this view as one which is commonly held by others, and he then proceeds to argue against it.

14. American Anti-Vivisection Society, pp. 11-12. Species variation is the term for the differences between humans and animals. The anti-vivisectionists claim that this variation prevents animal research from being reliably applied to humans.

15. *Tanakh: The Holy Scriptures*, trans. New JPS (Philadelphia: The Jewish Publication Society, 1988), p. 4.

16. National Research Council, Committee on the Use of Laboratory Animals in Biomedical and Behavioral Research, *Use of Laboratory Animals in Biomedical and Behavioral Research* (Washington, D.C.: National Academy Press, 1988), p. 11.

17. Fox writes: "Pain and suffering are not equivalent, though many writers use them interchangeably. Pain is generally somatic in origin, whereas suffering is a more inclusive term, subsuming varieties of psychological

distress and disagreeable physical sensations. Clearly, some animals can suffer, but it seems most improbable that they all can, since a certain level of mental complexity is presupposed when we speak of suffering, as is implied in the meanings of such subsidiary notions as anxiety, stress, anguish, apprehensiveness, despair, sorrow, worry, grief, lamentation, upset, and the like." Fox 217 #2.

18. National Research Council, *Use of Laboratory*, p. 11.

19. Ibid., p. 3.

20. United States, pp. 90-91.

21. Ibid., p. 94.

22. Sharon Vaillancourt, a student at the North Carolina State University College of Veterinary Medicine, telephone interview, November 1991.

23. C. R. Gallistel, "The Case for Unrestricted Research Using Animals," *Animal Rights and Human Obligations*, eds. Tom Regan and Peter Singer (New Jersey: Prentice Hall, 1989), p. 210.

24. Wiebers, p. 26.

25. Gallistel, pp. 211-214.

26. Rowan, p. 55.

27. Fox, pp. 87-88.

28. Ibid., p. 196.

29. Ibid., pp. 200-203. Fox reminds his readers, however, that we cannot always legislate morality.

30. Many people believe that it is more humane to destroy an animal immediately after experimentation than to let it recover and feel the post-operative pain. R. G. Frey (in an exchange with Sir William Paton), "Vivisection, Morals, and Medicine: An Exchange," *Animal Rights and Human Obligations,* eds. Tom Regan and Peter Singer (New Jersey: Prentice Hall, 1989), p. 224.

31. Canadian Council on Animal Care, *Guide to the Care and Use of Experimental Animals,* 2 vols. (Ottowa: CCAC, 1980). Cited in Fox 207.

32. Fox, p. 193.

33. Ibid., p. 190.

34. Laboratory Animal Welfare Act of 1966 (P.L. 89-544). Cited in National Research Council, *Use of Laboratory*, p. 49.

35. Ibid., p. 50.

36. Ibid., p. 51

37. National Institutes of Health, Office for Protection from Research Risks, *Public Health Service Policy on Human Care and Use of Laboratory Animals*, Rev. ed. (Bethesda, MD: U.S. Department of Health and Human Services, 1985), p. 7.

38. National Research Council, *Use of Laboratory*, p. 54.

39. Ibid., p. 4.

40. Ibid., p. 7

41. Ibid.

42. *Encyclopedia Judaica,* III, p. 5.

43. Bleich, p. 203. This is consistent with the fact that Jewish law deals with human obligation, not human rights.

44. Objects that you are not allowed to touch on Shabbat.

45. *Tzaar* is used in relation to both human and animal pain.

46. Bleich, p. 219.

47. This is based on the verse, "When you see the ass of your enemy lying under its burden and would refrain from raising it, you must nevertheless raise it with him." *Exodus 23:5.*

48. This refers to the most scrupulous observers of the law.

49. Bleich, pp. 233.

50. Ibid., p. 195.

51. Ibid., pp. 230-231.

# Shall We Counsel Germ Cell Gene Therapy?

Carole Balin
and Aaron Panken

"In the attic, Rabbi Leib found the sacks with the clay and began to sculpt the figure of a man. Rabbi Leib did not use a chisel but his fingers to carve the figure of the *golem*. ... All day Rabbi Leib was busy in the attic, ... a large shape of a man with a huge head, broad shoulders, and enormous hands and feet was lying on the floor – a clay giant. ... He could never have mastered this without the help of Almighty ... Rabbi Leib engraved [the name of God] on the forehead of the *golem* in such small letters that only he himself could distinguish the Hebrew characters. Immediately, the clay figure started to show signs of life." – Isaac Bashevis Singer, *The Golem*[1]

"The procession advanced; one by one the eggs were transferred from their test tubes to the larger containers; deftly the peritoneal lining was slit, the morula dropped into place, the saline solution dropped in ... and already the bottle had passed, and it was the turn of the labellers. Hereditary, date of fertiliztion, membership of Bokanovsky Group – details were transferred from test-tube to bottle. No longer anonymous, but named, identified, the procession marched slowly on; on through an opening in the wall, slowly on into the Social Predestination Room." – Aldous Huxley, *Brave New World*[2]

**T**he conceptualization of human alteration of genetic outcome long preceded the recently-acquired medical expertise that will enable this procedure to occur. As early as the fifteenth century, Jewish storytellers wove tales describing automatons, or so-called *golems*, fashioned by kabbalistic methods.[3] The most famous legend of this ilk tells of Rabbi Judah Loew of Prague who created a *golem* out of clay and inscribed the four-letter divine name on its forehead, thus bringing the automaton to life and making it obedient to his will. Loew created the *golem* to do his bidding, but was forced to restore him to dust when the *golem* began to run amok and endanger people's lives. Despite its fictitious nature, *The Golem* demonstrates humans' desire to become their own makers.

A similar theme appears in Aldous Huxley's celebrated science fiction novel *Brave New World*. Here the foresighted author, writing in 1932, constructed a society that constructs itself. That is to say, drawing on futuristic technology, characters in Huxley's novel manipulated life-giving materials in order to form creatures optimally designed for their functions in life. For instance, those destined to become rocket plane engineers spent their embryonic stages in constant rotation in order to improve their sense of balance. In Huxley's made up society, the genetic make-up of human beings can be and is predetermined.

Recent scientific breakthroughs are bringing our own society closer to the imagined worlds of these storytellers. Fiction has become reality in a world where, for example, medical experts can now determine the gender of a child at pre-embryonic stages of gestation and where teams of scientists received governmental approval for experimental microsurgery that alters human genetic material.[4]

Customarily we ponder bioethical issues as they emerge, as a result of extant technology. In this case, however, we want to ask hypothetical questions and begin considering solutions, before the technology is created. We will attempt to deal with some of these issues in advance rather than after the fact, as usual, when we are confronted with a special and perhaps pressing controversy. As Jews seriously committed to listening to our heritage and as liberals raised in modern American society, we want to know what our religious responsibilities are in the area of genetic therapy. Before presenting and analyzing the halakhic and ethical considerations at work on this issue, we will provide the reader with a basic scientific introduction to our question.

## The Scientific Aspects of Genetic Engineering

Every human has a uniquely coded genetic make-up. The pieces which code for this individuality are called genes. Genes are made up of an alphabet of four substances called bases, which can bond into molecules in a tremendous number of possible configurations.[5] These combinations of bases are repeated millions of times in different sequences along the DNA molecule. The thousands of genes which make up a DNA molecule hold specific genetic codes, which tell the cell containing this DNA which proteins to produce. Thus, the codes control all the basic functions of the cell, since most basic functions occur through the interaction and development of proteins.

An analogy to the gene would be a dressmaker's pattern. The pattern is not actually clothing that one could wear, but the pattern which is used to make new clothing. While the pattern itself may be copied, and used over and over to make hundreds of outfits, it is unchanged by the process. Genes, too, do not play a tremendous part in the regular functioning of the cell – they are not used as "actual clothing." Genes may be used to make thousands of new proteins in thousands of new cells, but they remain unchanged by the process. And, as in the fashion world, where there are many different fashions, there are up to 100,000 genes in a DNA molecule that provide the human body with the patterns for the various types of cells necessary for the functioning of a living being.

Genetic engineering is defined as the intentional alteration of an organism's genetic make-up, by replacing a portion of current genetic material with new genetic material. This modification of the genetic pattern produces change in the organism, depending on the genes which are replaced and the new genes that are inserted. It's as if one type of sleeve could be removed from the dressmaker's pattern, and replaced with a new one, to produce dresses similar to the original ones but with different sleeves.

Our new-found ability to manipulate and replace genes promises a multitude of valuable applications. To date, the greatest effort has been exerted in the development of treatments for hereditary disease caused by a genetic abnormality. We currently know of 2,000 to 3,000 human genetic diseases, and at least six tend to appear more frequently among Jews of East European origin than other ethnic groups. Tay-Sachs disease occurs in approximately one out of every 6,000 Jewish births, as compared with one out of every 500,000 non-Jewish births in the United States.[6] Tay-Sachs is characterized by arrest of normal development, progressive visual loss and slowly occuring dementia. Children afflicted with Tay-Sachs do not survive past the age of three.

By one day locating and replacing defective genes in human cells, scientists are hoping to improve the health of the patient and/or the patient's progeny. "Gene therapy," as the process has come to be known today, has only recently taken a leap from the theoretical realms of the laboratory toward the real world of practicing medicine.[7] The procedure is currently in its infancy.

Geneticists make a distinction between two types of gene therapy: "somatic cell gene therapy" and "germ cell gene therapy." Somatic cells (from the Greek, *soma* or "body") refer to the cells present in one's body, which carry on the functions of everyday life. Somatic cells include all the cells in the body, except those which are reproductive cells. Ova (egg cells) and sperm cells, which make up the body's reproductive cells, are known as germ cells (from the Latin *germen*, for "bud" or "embryo"), since they are the basis for an embryo which can eventually develop into a child.

Somatic cell gene therapy is the genetic alteration of the somatic cells of the body, for the purpose of improving the health of a patient suffering with a disease. In somatic cell gene therapy, there is no change in the genetic make-up of the germ cells, and therefore no impact on the genetic make-up of future generations of descendants. Somatic cell gene therapy's impact is limited to the patient, and produces absolutely no change in the offspring. It changes the pattern of the dress at hand, but leaves all future dresses unaffected.

Somatic cell gene therapy can be extremely useful in treating many different diseases. As the process enters the human trial stage, it holds a tremendous amount of promise for treating cancers and other diseases which might be repaired by changing the cells in charge of production of other cells. There is limited debate over the use of somatic cell gene therapy, since it treats diseases without risk of eternal change to the gene pool. In this respect, it has been compared to other medical and surgical procedures. For the purposes of this paper, we intend to look at the other process, that of germ cell gene therapy, since with it the ethical and halakhic concerns are more challenging.

For germ cell gene therapy, also called germ *line* gene therapy, the medical process involved is virtually the same as somatic cell gene therapy. The significant difference is in the cells that are affected. The reproductive cells or gametes of the human are removed, changed and then reinserted. It is also possible, through surgical methods, to remove a fertilized egg, after conception has taken place, and alter it during its earliest pre-embryonic stages, when it consists of only eight or sixteen cells.[8] The difficulty with changing the gamete or the pre-embryo, is that the change will affect it, *as well as all of its future offspring.* Any descendant of that embryo or gamete will exhibit the change, and this is where the controversy arises.

There are three *potential* applications of germ cell gene therapy:

1. **Genetic Therapy** – once a genetic defect is found, a doctor could locate the specific gene, replace it in the sex cells, and then all future descendants would carry the corrected gene.

2. **Genetic Enhancement** – The genetic make-up of all future descendants could be enhanced, changing "bad" genes to "better" genes, in the patient and all of his/her descendants. A case might be made, for example, that brown eyes see better than blue eyes, and thus all genes for blue eyes could be changed.

3. **Eugenics** – Human genes would be altered to provide the best genetic make-up for all future human beings.

In the interest of limiting this paper, we will concentrate only on the first application of germ cell gene therapy, for that is the possibility which will most likely develop first. In addition, enhancement and eugenics offer the thorny problem of determining what is genetically "good" among all possible genetic combinations. Enhancement and eugenics, as potential consequences of genetic therapy, will play a peripheral role in the ethical discussion.

It is useful here to provide a brief overview of the basic concepts of human genetics. There are three ways for human genes to pattern their inheritance: dominant, recessive and x-linked. Human DNA is linked together in groupings called chromosomes. Each human has forty-six chromosomes full of genetic material, twenty-three from each parent.

Recessive genetics has direct relevance to this paper as we will be concerned with recessive genetic traits, such as Tay-Sachs disease and sickle cell anemia. In the case of recessive genetic traits, there are three states: (1) unaffected, (2) affected and (3) carrier. The unaffected human has two normal copies of the gene. There is neither disease nor a defective copy of the gene to pass on. The affected person actually has the disease, since he or she has two defective copies of the gene, one from each carrier parent. The carrier has only one defective copy of the gene. Since there is another copy, the body uses the normal copy in its replications and production of proteins. Therefore, though the person does not suffer with the disease, s/he is considered a carrier since the defective copy may be passed on to future generations.

In the case of two carrier parents, the following outcomes are possible: there is a twenty-five percent chance that offspring will have the disease, there is a fifty percent chance that offspring will be carriers, there is a twenty-five percent chance that the offspring will be unaffected. Thus, in a recessive genetic transmission, there is a seventy-five percent chance that the gene will be passed on if both parents are carriers. If only one parent is a carrier there is a fifty percent chance that the offspring will be a carrier, but no chance that the child will be born with the disease.

Before we present our final statement of the problem, one more important question remains. If genetic technology is still in its infancy, why be concerned about the issue of germ cell gene therapy at all? The answer is in the research that is currently taking place. In the past year, scientists established links between genes and certain diseases. Genes have been isolated that cause cystic fibrosis, kidney disease and colon cancer.[9] The National Institutes of Health and the Energy Department have allocated $87 million to fund the massive undertaking known as the Human Genome Project.[10] So far, two percent of human genetic material has been mapped. Over the next fifteen years, scientists hope to map all of it, thereby giving us undreamed of information, and a wide range of new possibilities for genetic engineering. In light of the ever-quickening pace of scientific development, it behooves us to begin the process of ethical analysis now before genetic engineering techniques are in place.

We will employ the following hypothetical case in making ethical decisions regarding germ cell gene therapy in this paper:

> **In the case of monogenic (i.e. single-gene) recessive disorders, such as Tay-Sachs disease, when both married parents are carriers, there is a twenty-five percent chance that the child will develop the disease. Let us assume that medical experts can identify the affected gene and, through the use of germ cell gene therapy, replace it with a healthy gene during the earliest stages of pre-embryonic formation (e.g. 8 or 16 cells). They would then reintroduce the pre-embryo into the mother through *in vitro* fertilization. As ethically responsible Jews can we endorse this procedure?**

The remainder of this paper will focus on the halakhic and ethical considerations in determining an answer to this controversial question.

# Halakhic Considerations

Determining whether or not to engage in germ cell gene therapy involves analyzing numerous halakhic issues, as explicated by such major Orthodox authorities as J. David Bleich and Moshe Tendler.[11] Others, too, have suggested the *halakhah* that must be considered when discussing human modification of genetic material: namely Moshe Drori, David Feldman, Ronald Green, Immanuel Jakobovits, Avraham Rabinowitz, Azriel Rosenfeld, Fred Rosner, and Herschel Schacter.[12] As culled from these authors, the halakhic matters that bear most directly on genetic engineering include:

1. wasteful emission of semen and/or removal of ova
2. the male's obligation to procreate
3. influences on the natural process of conception

We will concentrate on these three issues. Certain authors raised other considerations, but since they seem tangential to the body of the discussion, we will not include them in this paper.[13]

## Wasteful Emission of Semen and/or Removal of Ova

### Introduction to the basic problem

As discussed in the scientific overview above, in order to engage in germ cell gene therapy it is necessary, in most cases, to remove semen and ova from the body, identify and then correct any defective genes, artificially fertilize the ovum and then insert the fertilized ovum into the mother's uterus. The means employed in procuring sperm and ova for purposes of genetic engineering and *in vitro* fertilization pose a halakhic problem. Jewish law prohibits wasteful ejaculation. The question is the definition of "waste," that is whether or not semen and ova procurement intended to promote procreation is to be deemed "wasteful."

There are a variety of technical terms that Jewish texts employ to describe the "wasteful destruction of seed." The earliest term is found in the Torah in the description of Onan who, rather than fulfilling his obligation to have intercourse with his deceased brother's wife, "*v'shikhet artzah* – lets his seed go to waste." (Genesis 38:9) Because he engaged in *coitus interruptus*, God was displeased and took his life. In a related instance, the Book of Leviticus stipulates, "when a man – *tetze mimenu shikhvat zera* – has an emission of semen, he shall bathe his whole body in water and remain unclean until evening." (Lev. 15:16). Like Leviticus, the halakhic literature generally uses the term *hotzaat zera levatalah* to denote destruction of the seed.

### Hotzaat Zera L'vatalah in the *Halakhah*

Beginning in the talmudic period and extending to the fifteenth century when the *Shulḥan Arukh* was written, *hotzaat zera l'vatalah* was considered a vile act. According to Rabbi Yochanan, every man who wastes his seed is deserving of death. While Rabbis Yitzhak and Ami claim that wasting seed is a form of murder, Rabbi Asi adds that *hotzaat zera l'vatalah* is like idol worship. (*Niddah* 13a) Approximately seven hundred years later, Moses Maimonides wrote in his *Mishneh Torah*, "wasteful emission of seed is forbidden." (*Hilkhot*

*Isure Biah* 21:18) Those who behave in this way must be removed for they are like those who shed blood and are thus prohibited from remaining in the community. The same sentiment is expressed by Jacob ben Asher in the *Tur*. (*Even Haezer* 23:1)

Thus far, the proscription against wasting seed is directed toward men only. Judah ben Samuel Rosanes (1657-1727), who wrote a commentary to the *Mishneh Torah* in 1731, which is known by its title *Mishneh Lemelekh*, raises the issue for women; that is, must women similarly refrain from wasting their seed? In answer, he cites two different authorities (*Mishneh Lemelekh*, ad. loc.). The Spanish scholar Solomon ibn Adret (1235-c.1310), known as *Rashba*, reasons that since women, unlike men, are not obligated in the commandment of procreation, they are similarly not obligated in the prohibition of *hotzaat zera l'vatalah*. On the other hand, Moses ben Nahman (1194-1270), another Spanish authority, argues that women, like men, are prohibited from wasting their seed. The issue, as far as we can tell, has never been resolved.

The debate on *hotzaat zera l'vatalah* continues in this century as well, with respect to testing semem in cases of suspected male infertility and fertilizing ova outside the womb. Many halakhic authorities have written responsa, on both sides of this issue, detailing their decisions.

In 1935, the Sephardic chief rabbi of Israel, Ben-Zion Meir Hai Uziel, when asked if it is permitted to procure semen by unnatural means for the sake of enabling a couple to procreate, ruled restrictively (*Mishpetei Uziel, Even Haezer* 19:4). He argued that it is forbidden to use seed in this manner because there is always the possibility that some portion of the semen could be wasted. For him, a man is allowed to ejaculate only during heterosexual intercourse.

Rabbi Mordecai Jacob Breisch, writing in 1959, takes a more lenient approach to the issue. When asked if a barren woman may be artificially inseminated with her husband's sperm, Breisch answers that if "a woman is unable to become pregnant, and the doctor wants to take her husband's seed to put it within her womb through a new scientific invention, it is permitted at a time of pressing need as long as two other expert rabbis agree." (*Helkat Yaakov* II 24:23) In other words, it would seem that Breisch allows removal of semen as a last resort to fulfill the commandment of procreation despite the risk of *hotzaat zera l'vatalah*.

In making their decisions the halakhic authorities attempt to balance the risks and benefits involved. To Uziel, the risk of wasting seed outweighs the benefits of producing offspring. Breisch disagrees; he allows the man to fulfill his obligation to procreate even at the risk of wasting seed.

## The Male's Obligation to Procreate

### Introduction to the basic problem

As discussed in the scientific section of this paper, genetic disorders, such as Tay-Sachs disease, are fatal. The halakhic literature obligates a man to be fertile and increase. Thus, if a man fathers a child who dies of Tay Sachs disease or any other fatal genetic disorder, the question arises as to whether or not that man has fulfilled his obligation to procreate. With the aid of germ cell gene therapy, doctors could potentially correct genetic disorders, thereby enabling a child to be born healthy and guaranteeing that the father has fulfilled his obligation.

In a related issue, some Rabbis are concerned with the number and gender of the children necessary for a man to fulfill his obligation to *priyah urviyah*. Germ cell gene therapy could allow a father to pre-select the gender of his children, thus enabling him to produce the required number of males and females.

### *Priyah Urviyah* in the *Halakhah*

The halakhic discussions regarding the obligation to procreate are based on Genesis 35:11 where God tells Jacob to "*preh urveh* – to be fertile and increase." The Mishnah elaborates on this:

> A man must not refrain from having children unless he already has some. The school of Shammai says: At least two sons [based on the example of Moses]. And the school of Hillel says: At least one son and one daughter, because it is written (in Genesis 5:2) "Male and female (God) created them" (*M. Yevamot* 6:6).

Thus, the *halakhah*, following the house of Hillel, requires a minimum of one son and one daughter. The obligation is so important in Jewish law that a man may even sell a Torah scroll in order to gain funds to marry a woman and have children. (*Yevamot* 61b)

The Rabbis' argument over whether or not a man has fulfilled his obligation if his child dies gives insight into the Rabbis' perception of the purpose of procreation.

> It was stated, (if a man) has children and they die (has he fulfilled his obligation to procreate?) Rav Huna said: He has fulfilled *priyah urviyah*. Rabbi Yohanan said: He has not. Rav Huna said: He has fulfilled (it) because of Rav Asi who said: The messiah will not come until all the souls of the *guf* are used up. [*Guf* literally means "body," but in this context a better translation is "well" or "pool," as the *guf* is a holding place for unborn souls.] As it is said, "I also create the breath of life." (Isa. 57:16)

> And Rabbi Yohanan said: He has not fulfilled
> *priyah urviyah* [because of the verse] "He formed it
> to be inhabited." (Isa. 45:18) The [counter-] argu-
> ment is raised, "Grandchildren are like children."
> (*Yevamot* 62a)

The fundamental disagreement here centers on why a man
must procreate. Rav Huna, quoting Isaiah 57:16, claims that there
is a "pool" inhabited by souls of the unborn, known as the *guf*. With
the birth of a child, one soul is extracted from this "pool." When no
souls are left in the "pool," the messiah will come. Thus, until a man
has fulfilled his obligation with two children, regardless of the length
of their lives, he has not hastened the coming of the messiah.

On a more pragmatic level, Rabbi Yohanan uses Isaiah 45:18
to demonstrate that procreation is necessary to populate the earth.
God, he argues, formed the world for the purpose of being inhabited. Thus, a man who has a child who dies has not fulfilled his obligation because the earth's population has not properly increased.
However, if a deceased child leaves behind progeny, the father has
fulfilled his obligation since "grandchildren are like children." That
is to say, grandchildren can be counted toward a man's required
quota for childbearing because they aid in populating the earth.

So, for example, if a man has a child who dies at the age of
three of complications resulting from Tay-Sachs, Rav Huna would
rule that he has fulfilled his obligation because a soul has been
extracted from the *guf*. Rabbi Yohanan, however, would rule that
the man has not fulfilled his obligation because the world's population has not increased as a result of that birth, since no progeny
was left behind.

In his *Mishneh Torah*, Maimonides makes it clear that a
man is obligated in *priyah urviyah*, while a woman is not (*Hilkhot
Ishut* 15:2). Following the school of Hillel, the Rambam rules that a
man must have at least one male and one female child to fulfill his
obligation (15:4). Furthermore, Maimonides agrees with Rabbi
Yohanan who posited the purpose of procreation as populating the
earth (15:5). In the *Shulḥan Arukh*, the material is treated in the
same way:

> [If a man] has a male and a female child, he has ful-
> filled the *mitzvah* of *priyah urviyah*. ... if a male and
> a female were born to him and they die and they
> leave behind children, he has fulfilled the *mitzvah*
> of *priyah urviyah* (*Even Haezer* 1:5-6).

A responsum written by Rav Moshe Feinstein, on the question of
using contraception to prevent pregnancy in cases where numerous
children have died at a young age, significantly impacts on this
issue (*Igrot Moshe, Even Haezer*, No. 62). Feinstein argues that the

obligation to procreate is not suspended because of a statistical probability that some children may be abnormal. However, he does permit the use of contraceptive ointment or some other acceptable form of contraception if two previous children have died, provided that it is the woman who uses the contraception since she is not obligated in the *mitzvah*. A condom, though, is not an acceptable form of contraception to be used because the man is obligated in *priyah urviyah*. Feinstein bases his answer on a ruling by the Polish authority Rabbi Solomon ben Yehiel Luria (c.1510-1574), *Rashal*, who argued that one may use contraception for reasons of *tsaar gadol* (great suffering). The pain of losing children to illness is reason enough for the woman to use contraception, according to Feinstein.

Within his explanation, Feinstein quotes and agrees with Rav Huna who, in the name of Rav Asi, said that the purpose of procreation is to extract a soul from the *guf*. Therefore, Feinstein is able to rule: If a man has two children, and they die at an early age, he has still fulfilled his obligation of the commandment of *priyah urviyah* because two souls have left the *guf*. His wife may then use contraception in order to prevent more *tsaar gadol* in their lives.

In sum, the law is that a man (but not generally a woman) is obligated to procreate. He must have one male and one female child. From our reading, we would judge that the *halakhah* exhibits a tendency toward Rav Asi who claimed that the purpose of procreation is to deplete the pool of souls and thus speed the coming of the messiah. Consequently, modifying genetic material to avoid disorders that result in death at a young age cannot be justified halakhically as assisting a man in fulfilling *priyah urviyah*. However, since preventing the loss of the life of a child eliminates *tsaar gadol*, the *halakhah* could apparently allow genetic therapy to prevent great suffering.

## Pre-Conceptual Influence
### Introduction to the problem

Germ cell gene therapy directly influences the procreative process. The procedures described in the scientific portion of this paper involve modifying the genetic material of a pre-embryo or gamete, thereby effecting the type of child born. Germ cell gene therapy could one day allow doctors to change a child's genetic make-up, from correcting a disorder to pre-selecting for gender or intelligence. Though they lived centuries before the rise of modern medicine, the Rabbis wrote about the influence humans could have on the procreative process. The Rabbis suggested ways to avoid bearing children with, what were in their perception, disabilities. They discussed eugenic methods as well with the object of creating more intelligent or handsome children.

## Pre-Conceptional Influence in the *Halakhah*

Various opinions are found on the Rabbis' view of "genetics." They believed that there are three partners in the creation of a child: God, the mother and the father. As they put it in an *aggadah*:

> His father supplies the seed of the white substance out of which is formed the child's bones, sinews, nails, the brain in his head and the white in his eye; his mother supplies the seed of the red substance out of which is formed his skin, flesh, hair, blood and the black of his eye; and the Holy One, blessed be God, gives him the spirit and the breath, beauty of features, eyesight, the power of hearing and the ability to speak and to walk, understanding and discernment (*Niddah* 31a).

Although this charming description would not carry much weight in a scientific setting, in this passage, the Rabbis demonstrate an uncanny sense of how heredity works. As the Talmud shows, the Rabbis understood that parents with visual impairments do not necessarily create offspring with visual impairments and that one parent with some other disability does not necessarily create an off-spring with disabilities, which led to the conclusion: "It is obvious that the seed [of two parents] is mixed up." (*Hullin* 69a)

Eugenics, with the sense of choosing a spouse with the well-being of the progeny in mind, is also found in talmudic legislation.[14] A man is advised to choose a wife prudently. Evidence of adverse herditary factors resulted in a ruling against marriage into a family of epileptics or lepers, or, by extension, similar diseases:

> Raba said: ... a man should not take a wife either from a family of epileptics, or from a family of lep-ers. This applies, however, only when the fact had been established by the occurence of three cases (*Yevamot* 64b).

Both the *Rambam* and Joseph Caro echo this ruling (*Hilkhot Isurei Biah* 22:30 and *Even Haezer* 1:7). And in another talmudic context we find an aggadic statement by Resh Lakish:

> An abnormally tall man should not marry an abnormally tall woman, lest their offspring be [like] a mast. A small male should not marry a small female, lest their offspring be of the smallest size. A man abnormally white-complexioned should not marry an equally white-complexioned woman, lest their offspring be an albino. A very dark-complexioned man should not marry an equally very dark-com-plexioned women, lest their offspring resemble an earthenware pot (*Bekhorot* 45b).

A related matter of eugenics occurs in another *aggadah* that appears twice in the Talmud (*Berakhot* 20a and *Baba Metzia* 84a). The tale is told of Rabbi Yohanan who would go and sit at the gates of the *mikvah*. When asked why, he responded, "When the daughters of Israel ascend from the bath, they will look upon me so that they will bear children as beautiful and as learned as I."

We note the varying degrees to which different halakhic authorities allow humans to take charge of their own destiny. One could show by analogy that the *halakhah* would endorse the use of germ cell gene therapy to produce a healthy child, and would even allow for the creation of physically and mentally superior children. Yet, as the first descriptive piece reminds us, the *halakhah* teaches that God plays a crucial role in procreation. Rabbi Immanuel Jakobovits, while defending the use of genetic engineering for the prevention, cure or treatment of disease, makes the following comment on non-therapeutic purposes,

> Eugenic considerations are perfectly legitimate in the choice of marital partner affecting the normal generation of human life, but they do not justify the manipulation of human life and its constituents in contravention of the natural order as predetermined in the scheme of creation.[15]

Though important, halakhic considerations alone will not complete the process of ethical decision-making for a committed liberal Jew. To broaden our discussion, we will now turn to the general ethical literature on the subject of germ cell gene therapy.

# Ethical Considerations

The ethical literature on the use of germ cell gene therapy falls not-so-neatly into two categories. Those who argue for the use of germ cell gene therapy base their arguments on the prospect of human improvement of our own gene pool and the individual's right to choose.Others who argue against germ cell gene therapy, base their arguments on the idea that interruption of the natural process of genetic selection can be hazardous and that tampering with evolution is unacceptable.

## Technological Choice:
## Arguing for
## Germ Cell Gene Therapy

We will now review in detail the six arguments that support the use of germ line gene therapy.

### 1. The obligation to heal

With the continuing development of the techniques necessary for germ cell gene therapy, it will become safer and easier to manipulate those genes which cause disease. Once the technology is developed, one could argue that we ought to use it, as it is our ethical obligation to heal the sick. Clifford Grobstein suggests that repair of the germ line may be considered a part of maintaining reproductive health:

> ... if reproductive health includes the probability of having genetically normal offspring, that individual could claim an ethical right not to be deprived of germ line repair since, without it, all offspring would at least be carriers and, were two double recessive individuals to marry, all offspring would develop the disease.[16]

This is certainly a valid point to consider. We may be continuing a painful or fatal genetic disease for no reason, when we refuse to perform germ cell gene therapy on a gamete or pre-embryo.

Within our obligation to heal, we must contemplate one other factor. There are many genetic diseases for which no somatic cell gene therapy exists. These could be cured only through germ cell gene therapy. LeRoy Walters reminds us:

> A second rationale for the germline approach is that some genetic diseases may be treatable only by this method. For example, because of the blood-brain barrier, the brain cells involved in hereditary central nervous system disorders may be inaccessible to somatic cell gene therapy. Early intervention that affects all the cells of the future organism, including the germ cells, may be the only means available for treating cells or tissues which are not amenable to genetic repair after birth.[17]

Thus the value of reducing suffering and the obligation to heal may compel us to use germ cell gene therapy where there is no other viable solution.

### 2. The obligation to improve the gene pool

This argument begins with the notion of healing. If healing the sick brings the greatest good to society, then it follows that we have an obligation to "heal" our gene pool, and thus heal more sick people.

John Fletcher, in discussing the works of Bernard Davis, says:

> [Davis] used as an example the desirability of germ line therapy in Tay-Sachs disease, but his argument could also apply to any other serious recessive disorder. Each available option (i.e. somatic cell and germ cell gene therapies) has evolutionary consequences. But which option has the most favorable consequences for the affected families and society? ... Therapy in the germ line could both prevent the disease in the person and reduce the incidence of harmful genes.[18]

Reducing the number of harmful genes in the gene pool would certainly decrease pain and suffering, and thus do greater good, once all the cross-gene interactions are mapped and eliminated.

## 3. The efficiency argument: treatment of patient and progeny simultaneously

> The idea of seeking a long-term cure for a genetic disease by introducing new genes directly into human germ line cells is nothing less than revolutionary. It diverges from a long tradition in mainstream Western medicine of focusing therapy on somatic cells. Germ line therapy, in sharp contrast, would grant physicians the power to prescribe treatment not simply for a single ailing patient but for all his or her progeny.[19]

The idea of treating both patient and progeny at once provides a truly compelling motivation for engaging in germ cell gene therapy. If a doctor can repair a gene once, and avoid generations of effort, expense and suffering, then for the simple reason of medical efficiency, we should permit it. One must also consider the following argument:

> ... the birth and subsequent care of a seriously defective child may endanger the welfare of other family members by drastically reducing their chances for receiving appropriate material support for their basic needs. Under such circumstances parental rights of self-determination must yield to the more exigent claims of others.[20]

Economically, it would make more sense to treat a pre-embryo with germ cell gene therapy, then to place the whole family at risk, by the attempt to use somatic cell gene therapy on its descendants. Eve Nichols futher emphasizes:

> For most single-cell gene disorders, modern medicine and surgery have very little to offer. An effective therapy could have a very high one-time cost,

and still be more cost-effective than years of repeated hospitalizations experienced by children with
diseases such as severe combined immune deficiency and sickle cell disease.[21]

Thus, even with a very high treatment cost for germ cell
gene therapy, it would still be economically advantageous to treat
that one patient. This benefit is multiplied because the treatment
eliminates numerous potential patients.

### 4. Choice is natural

Among the most interesting of the deontological ethical arguments
is the debate over what is natural and what is not. These arguments
are based on the idea that evolution is a process of nature, but that it
is within our nature to influence this process. One supporter, H.
Tristam Engelhardt, Jr., states it this way:

> . . . here it is enough to observe that, if there is any-
> thing natural about us, it is the ability we have as
> persons to objectify our characteristics as human
> and to inventory their benefits and drawbacks. Far
> from human nature being sacrosanct, this ability
> would appear to call us to reflect regarding revising
> and remaking ourselves.

> The enduring significance of genetic engineering of
> the human germ line lies in the fact that it offers
> the possiblity of persons remaking their bodies in
> the image and likeness of their goals. One is left with
> the canons of prudence and care, since there is noth-
> ing sacrosanct about the particular deliverances of
> evolution, which we find currently in human nature.[22]

Engelhardt reasons that human beings, in the course of being
free persons, have the right and obligation to re-create themselves.
Until now, they could do it in a limited manner, with their minds.
With germ cell gene therapy, it now becomes possible to do what,
he feels, is highly desirable – to re-create humans bodily as well as
mentally. This could remove the limitations that bodies place upon
us, especially in the case of genetic disease.

Another author points out that we already engage in manipulation of evolution, every time we marry, or have an abortion.[23]
Robert Davis, quoted by C. Keith Boone in an article which hints at
the prospects of germ cell gene therapy, tells us:

> God has put into our hands the possibility of what
> has so long been demanded by the great world reli-
> gions, a change in man himself [sic] . ... To succeed
> will be to begin a new and glorious stage in the his-
> tory of what has been so defective a humanity.[23]

One who would argue for this "new and glorious stage" of human history would certainly support the idea of germ cell gene therapy as natural.

Another author points out that medicine as a whole interferes with nature, and sees genetic medicine as nothing more than a new form of medicine:

> A major difficulty is that the word natural has more than a dozen different definitions and connotations; it is a veritable semantic swamp. Awareness of this difficulty is usually more implicit than explicit in scientific discourse. Medicine is patently an interference with nature and natural processes (what theologians often speak of as "the created order"). We might even say medicine uses nature to outwit - to outwit such natural phenomena as deformity and disease. Medical genetics extends our medical capabilities.[24]

When we view the processes of the body as natural, medicine seems an interference, so germ cell gene therapy may be nothing more than an extension of this interference.

## 5. Genetics improves on evolution

While evolution works toward the perfect human in slow, random steps, some feel that human-controlled evolution would guide the process along more rapidly. Germ cell genetic therapy, as a part of this process, would help us to make a "more human," more perfect human being by eliminating defects:

> Evolution to be sure, is a long-term, hunt-and-peck process of biological change, whereas genetics can bring about changes instantly – by deleting, inserting, or splicing genes.[25]

This same author, in an earlier paper, goes so far as to define the human as more human, when s/he is designed by a human:

> Man [sic] is a maker and selector and a designer, and the more rationally contrived and deliberate anything is, the more human it is. Any attempt to set up an antimony between natural and biologic reproduction, on the one hand, and artificial or designed reproduction, on the other, is absurd. The real difference is between accidental or random reproduction and rationally willed and chosen reproduction. ... It seems to me that laboratory reproduction is radically human compared to conception by ordinary heterosexual intercourse. ... This is, of course, the case for planned parenthood. I cannot see how either

> humanity or morality are served by genetic
> roulette.[26]

Fletcher, the author of both of these statements, believes strongly
that human-controlled genetics will enable faster human development, with better results. Engelhardt wants to hasten and improve
evolution as well:

> One must indeed wonder what is so important about
> the results of evolution. Insofar as human evolution
> has been successful, it has produced us as a species
> well adapted to environments in which we no longer
> live, but it is a slow process which has done little to
> adapt us to industrial, urban environments. More-
> over, evolution does not have our goals and interests
> in mind. If one may speak metaphorically, it has
> been directed by the goal of maximizing inclusive
> fitness, which may or may not be truly associated
> with human pleasure, tranquility, and the moral
> goals humans celebrate.[27]

Engelhardt strongly supports the strategies, such as germ
cell gene therapy, which will improve the current course of inefficient evolution.

### 6. Individuals' Right to Choose

> There appear to be at least three [moral premises in
> our society that appear to be persuasive] – all domi-
> nant in the genetic engineering debate and, by no
> accident, decisive in carrying the day. The first is
> the principle of individual liberty, encompassing
> not only a right to be left alone, but also a right to
> seek that which one desires if there is no demon-
> strable harm to others.[28]

Here Daniel Callahan outlines the libertarian position. Libertarians
argue that each individual has the right to choose what is best for
him or herself, providing that the decision does not interfere with
the rights of others. Therefore, government may not legislate public policies that prevent individual choice. Thus, the decision to
employ germ cell gene therapy rests with the individual.

# Genetic Destiny:
# Arguing Against
# Germ Cell Gene Therapy

Opponents of germ cell gene therapy base their arguments on one
or more of the five following reasons for rejection of this technology.

## 1. Slippery Slope

The most common ground of resistance to germ cell gene therapy is the so-called slippery slope objection. One form of the objection is the claim that though the immediate results are acceptable, the ultimate consequences would be disastrous. Thus, while germ cell gene therapy offers access to a number of important immediate benefits such as preventing certain genetic diseases, it could escalate into a procedure of eugenics where we could start to screen out other "defects" from our population. Jeremy Rifkin, one of the leading exponents of this reasoning, says:

> Once we decide to begin the process of human genetic engineering, there is really no logical place to stop. If diabetes, sickle cell anemia, and cancer are to be cured by altering genetic makeup of an individual, why not proceed to other 'disorders:' myopia, color blindness, lefthandedness? Indeed what is to preclude a society from deciding that a certain skin color is a disorder?[29]

The distinction between curing disease and improving the human germ line is arbitrary and prone to subjective interpretation. There is an absence, even within the medical profession, of clear-cut definitions and consensus on what constitutes health and disease, normality and abnormality.[30] It is near impossible, some claim, to determine when we are repairing genetic disease and when we are pursuing goals of higher perfection for the human species.

Another form of the slippery slope argument is the claim that permission for one eugenic measure inevitably establishes permission for other eugenic measures.[31] Once this rationale is in place, we may engage in any genetic impulse. As Jews we are well aware of the horrors associated with eugenics. The Nazis justified killing Jews for eugenic reasons. And their "final solution" began with eliminating other "defects" first. To avoid reaching extremes such as these, one must not even take the first step over the brink of the slippery eugenic slope.

## 2. Respect for Life

Another argument against the use of genetic therapy is tied to respect for life. Proponents of this line of thinking argue that when we tailor life genetically, by changing its make-up at will, we degrade life. It is disrespectful of life itself to "manufacture" people by intervening in their genetic structure. Life is sacrosanct and thus we must not tamper with it. As one scholar puts it. "The respect-for-life argument is tied psychologically to the feeling that genetic mastery of life will destroy life's mystery, and that its mystery is essential for generating respect for it.

Similarly, several religious leaders have noted that germ cell gene therapy may reduce perceptions of humanity to mechanistic interpretations. This, they contend, may lead to diminished attention to social and moral values, and may threaten attitudes about the sanctity of life.[32] Immanuel Jakobovits eloquently captures the argument in a few poetic phrases:

> Human life ... may be reduced to a form of mechanisation [sic] in which the incomparable grandeur of the human spirit, the genius of the human mind and the noblest virtues of the human heart are asphixiated in the exhuast fumes of our technological wonders. Without constant reminders that man [sic] is more than a bundle of cells, manipulated at will, the awe for man's incomparable greatness may be lost, and the focus on human dignity may be distorted.[33]

In our time when technology threatens to de-humanize our species, Jakobovits' words are particularly apt.

### 3. Playing God

One of the most common objections to germ cell gene therapy concerns what the Greeks called hubris, that is, the presumptuousness of humans trying to "play God" and usurping what is proper to God alone. In this view, genetic control seems to lack humility, and is reminiscent of Icarus, who made himself wings to fly but tumbled to his death as a result.[34] As C. Keith Boone suggests,

> It is not the use of creativity that offends, but rather attributing power to one's own resources, denying its origin ... in God's continuing creation.[35]

### 4. Chance is the natural way of evolution

Closely related to playing God is the common notion that genetic manipulation is somehow against nature. Some view gene therapy as an interference with nature and natural processes. As David Suzuki and Peter Knudtson say, "imperfection is part of what makes us human."[36] They argue that there will always be new genetic sequences in the human genome that cause diseases. Genetic imperfection is an unavoidable characteristic of human hereditary processes.

Behind this argument lies the notion that nature has a prescribed end and a single program for reaching that end. By engaging in germ cell gene therapy we interfere with the random mutations and natural selection of our developing universe. "The humanity of human beings rests at its core on natural development, not on technical production," according to a report issued by the Enquette Commission of the Federal Republic of Germany's Bundestag.[37] To this extent human beings are products of chance, not choice.

## 5. Unknown and potentially irreversible changes in the gene pool

Scientists can only speculate about the possible effects germ cell gene therapy will have on the gene pool. Some argue against germ cell gene therapy on the grounds that tinkering with genes may result in more harm than good. There is current evidence that some genetic diseases confer an evolutionary advantage to those individuals who carry one copy of the aberrant gene. For instance, those who carry one copy of the sickle cell anemia gene are better able to combat malarial infections. The genetic disease is the price paid for the advantage for most of the population, mitigated only by the statistical rarity of having two abnormal genes (and thus the disease).[38] The story of sickle-cell anemia underscores the ironic capacity of a seemingly defective gene to simultaneously offer both advantages and disadvantages. Genes that cause other diseases may also serve a purpose that has yet to be discovered, and so elimination of such genes might prove deleterious to the human population in the long run. We may be unable to ascertain that delicate balance whereby certain "defective" genes have positive qualities.[39] When we alter the prevalence of some genes, we could cause irreversible harm to humanity.

On a similar tack, there is the issue of the inheritability of mistakes.[40] As noted above, by altering the germ cells of a person, scientists would be affecting all of that person's descendants. Therefore, genetic manipulation of human reproduction has the potential to multiply medical errors exponentially, affecting infinite numbers of people. Even assuming these repairs could be carried out successfully, we could never be sure that altering genes would not inadvertently disturb other, seemingly unrelated cellular processes.[41] For some, therefore, the possiblity of creating mistakes, even in the process of pursuing noble ends, precludes the use of germ cell gene therapy.

There has also been some concern that germ therapy might lead to a loss of human genetic diversity. If a single uniform view of the ideal man or woman were proposed and accepted, opponents suggest that genetic engineering might lead to a uniformity in humans that "would on the one hand be boring and on the other be dangerous by narrowly adapting us to a particular ecological niche."[42] Morevoer, a single model for humanness constrains the possibilities of what it means to be human. That is to say, by creating an ideal type, we fail to recognize the full range of possibilities for being human and instead impose an arbitrary definition.

# What Does a Responsible Jew Faced With This Issue Do?

## Carole Balin's Discussion of the Dilemma

I am a liberal Jew, that is a Jew who uses the *halakhah* for guidance rather than governance. I can strongly identify as a Jew, drawing on my tradition as it has come down to me, and live simultaneously as a modern ... often comfortably. The question we posed in this paper above is a particularly difficult one because, in answering it, I am forced to choose between Judaism and modernity. I am truly at the crossroads of Jewish law and ethics. As a result of the research and deep thinking poured into this paper, I have reached the decision not to endorse the use of germ cell gene therapy in the case of married parents who are both carriers of a monogenic recessive disorder. I base my opinion on pragmatic and spiritual grounds.

From a practical perspective, I reject the use of germ cell gene therapy by drawing primarily on the ethical literature. In my decision-making process, I must, in effect, weigh the immediate benefits of curing some people of their diseases against the potential and/or eternal harm to the overall human gene pool. Germ cell gene therapy holds out the promise of repairing genetic disorders for all time, for it modifies reproductive cells. But consequently, unknown and potentially irreversible and pernicious changes could occur in the gene pool. Seventy-five percent of babies born to two carrier parents are healthy, and the twenty-five percent who are affected may soon be candidates for somatic cell gene therapy, the effect of which is limited to that individual alone. Additionally, as the sickle cell anemia example illustrates, a seemingly malignant gene may harbor an evolutionary benefit. The humanist in me wants to sympathize with the *tsaar gadol* of parents whose child, born with a disease such as Tay-Sachs, will surely die. However I must take a strong corporate stand here as against individualism and personal choice.

On spiritual grounds as well, I am unable to sanction the use of germ cell gene therapy, even in the case where both parents are Tay-Sachs carriers. In order to come to a decision on this matter, I had to resolve what I see as the central conflict which emerges from this paper: the clash between humanity's progress and God's continuing influence over humanity. On the one hand, as a product of the twentieth century, I believe in the potential of human beings to improve their lot through the use of human advances in science and medicine. Hegel taught, and many have agreed since, that progress is improvement. Yet certain lessons of history have proven him wrong. On the other hand, as a faithful member of the Jewish community, I believe that God exists and has an impact on my life and the lives of all people. Ultimately, I conclude that God deserves our trust more than humanity. Human procreation, as expressed aggadically by the Rabbis entails the partnership of parents and God. When we employ germ cell gene therapy, we cross the line from being created in God's image to creating in God's image.

Counter to the rationalistic modes of thinking common today (though waning in many respects in my opinion), I can not endorse human intervention in the roll of the genetic dice. The risk to the human gene pool is too great at this time. God's guidance is too palpable in my own life to sanction human interruption of the genetic flow. For all these reasons, I do not endorse germ cell gene therapy in this case.

## Aaron Panken's Discussion of the Dilemma

The halakhic material that we reviewed indicates to me that the Rabbis had some basic understanding of human genetics. Their prohibitions on marriage into families of lepers and epileptics, and their simultaneous support of marriage of those with visual disabilities, shows awareness of the idea that some human qualities are genetically transmitted, while others are not. These selective prohibitions prove that they see positive and negative genetic combinations. As I understand the Rabbis, we have a right, and perhaps a responsibility, to strive for the best possible combination of genes in our offspring.

In other halakhic discussion, the Rabbis tried to pinpoint the purpose of procreation. The words of Rabbi Yohanan – that procreation's purpose is the settling of the earth – are accepted by Maimonides and Joseph Caro. Their reliance on this opinion sends the message that length of life is accepted as an halakhic priority. If we can lengthen someone's life and improve the quality of it, the *halakhah* would surely support this endeavor.

Since the ethical issues which impact on germ cell gene therapy are complex, it is very difficult to formulate a coherent ethical standpoint. Always there is another compelling argument, always a side of the subject unseen. In my attempt to arrive at a personal ethical solution, I incorporated the following ideas.

Unknown and eternal changes occur in the gene pool daily through random mutations and marriages. Individual worth and humanness are not threatened by these changes, nor will they be threatened by human-initiated therapeutic changes. When we make genetic change to eliminate a devastating disease from all future generations, we significantly improve the basic human condition. Curing disease, and helping the sick, are surely ways of confirming human worth.

In terms of playing God, we are, and always will be, limited in our knowledge. God retains the power to create the universe, yet we grow in our ability to work within divine bounds. Use of this therapy is not playing God any more than developing a new vaccine. While a new vaccine affects only the innoculated, it prevents transmission of disease to others who come into contact with the infected person. Thus, in vaccinating people, we are already making positive, eternal changes in public health. Are we playing in God's realm when we do this? No. The power to create the elementary components of the vaccine is God's, not ours. In germ cell gene therapy, the power to make the existing genes remains with God. There will always be a smaller particle we don't fully understand. This is the realm of God, and it is infinite. Human understanding will always be finite.

The slippery slope argument is truly troubling, but I feel that in this case, the therapy's advantages outweigh its risks, and the argument fails. Any new technology comes with a set of risks. If you look at a simple household match, the case might be made for destroying it, since I can use it to commit arson. But I can also use it for thousands of valuable purposes, such as cooking, lighting, or heating. While a match only burns once, genetic therapy can burn many times, and thus we have an added ethical responsibility due to the eternal nature of the changes to the gene pool. The difficult part of the ethical equation is the assurance that scientific knowledge will be used for good. When used within proper limits, I believe that germ cell gene therapy can safely be used for the common good.

I would propose limits on germ cell gene therapy research which would help to protect this valuable technology from misuse. My aim, in these restrictions, is not to prevent free inquiry, but to ensure that the Pandora's Box of eugenic tinkering remains shut. The diseases for which I would permit research fit the following criteria:

## 1. The disease is incurable by any other means.
All attempts at curing the disease, both surgical and medical, including somatic cell gene therapy must have failed. Due to the hazards to descendants involved in germ cell gene therapy, all other known methods which affect only the patient should be attempted first.

## 2. The disease must cause severe suffering or disability or lead to death at an early age.
Germ cell gene therapy research should only be allowed in cases where the disease has a significant impact on the health of the patient. This category should include Tay Sachs and other early debilitating diseases which destroy the developing child. It should not include sickle cell trait or any other genetic condition which does not cause a serious change in the health of the child. The safest route is to bring about genetic change which is reactive to genetic disease, rather than proactive to genetic disposition.

**3. Scientists must have reasonable proof that the alteration of the gene which causes this disease will not place future patients at higher risk.**
As we know, in some cases when one gene is changed, resistance to other diseases is altered as well. In the most expert opinion available, there must be reasonable proof that the use of germ cell gene therapy will not be placing future patients at higher risk. This would defeat the purpose of the process entirely.

In conclusion, I return to our case study. Tay Sachs disease appears to be a good prospect for germ cell gene therapy. However, the question remains as to the link between the Tay Sachs gene and resistance to tuberculosis. Ultimately because a child afflicted with Tay Sachs dies within three years of birth, the question of resistance to tuberculosis becomes insignificant. In this case, as an ethically responsible Jew, I would endorse the use of germ cell gene therapy.

# Final Reflections on the Process

We came to the initial stages of our research with no preconceived answer to the difficult question of whether or not to endorse germ cell gene therapy. Because of our ignorance on this subject, we were able to be guided by both the halakhic and ethical literature pertaining to this subject. Of course, the *halakhah* does not specifically consider this issue. However, in our final decisions, we found ourselves making use of the underlying principles of the *halakhah*. For example, Carole's reliance on the idea of corporate responsibility over individualism echoes the Rabbis' concern for the community as a whole and indifference toward individual rights. Rabbi Yohanan's argument regarding the purpose of procreation as populating the earth assisted Aaron in the formulation of his views.

Yet the critical question remains as to whether or not what we retroactively label as "halakhic guidance" constitutes it. That is to say, how does one hear the *halakhah*'s voice without interference. As Terry Eagleton says,

> The literary work itself exists merely as ... a set of 'schemata' or general directions, which the reader must actualize. To do this, the reader will bring to the work certain 'pre-understandings,' a dim context of beliefs and expectations within which the work's various features will be assessed.[43]

Like Eagleton, we believe that the way in which a text is understood derives from the combination of text *and reader*. Therefore, in our opinion, it is impossible for the *halakhah* to speak for itself; it speaks through its reader.

Having stood at the crossroads of Jewish law and ethics, we leave with the sense that *halakhah* alone is an incomplete system for offering the modern liberal Jew guidance. We discovered that when the *halakhah* as defined in Orthodox circles is complemented by other forms of Jewish sources and general ethical literature it is able to provide a stronger foundation for ethical decision-making. Throughout this process, we have been troubled by the limiting definition of what constitutes "Judaism's opinion" on a matter. In our minds Jewish tradition is not restricted to Jewish law. When deciding controversial issues, Jews ought to consider all available sources, from ancient to modern, from law to lore, from orthodox to liberal.

In retrospct, this process of applied ethics, filtered through the lenses of Judaism and modernity, has helped us to clarify and articulate internal convictions heretofore embraced but unspoken. For that reason, we recommend this valuable exercise to others.

# Bibliography

American Jewish Committee. "Conference on Genetic Engineering and the Family: Promise or Peril? – Summary of Proceedings." 1984.

Birch, Charles and Abrecht, Paul, eds. *Genetics and the Quality of Life.* Elmsford, NY: Pergamon Press, 1975.

Bleich, J. David. *Judaism and Healing.* New York: Ktav, 1981.

Boone, C. Keith. "Bad Axioms in Genetic Engineering." *Hastings Center Report.* 18 (August/September 1988).

Callahan, Daniel. "The Moral Career of Genetic Engineering." *Hastings Center Report.* (April 1979).

Capron, Alexander Morgan. "The Rome Bioethics Summit." *Hastings Center Report* 18 (August/September 1988).

Carey, John. "The Genetic Age." *Business Week*, May 28, 1990.

"Clerics Urge U.S. Curb on Genetic Engineering." *New York Times.* June 9, 1983.

Davis, Bernard D. and Engelhardt, H. Tristam Jr. "Genetic Engineering: Prospects and Recommendations." *Zygon* 19 (September 1984).

Drori, Moshe. "Genetic Engineering: Preliminary Discussion." *Tehumin* 1 (1980).

Eagleton, Terry. *Literary Theory.* Minneapolis: University of Minnesota Press, 1983.

Engelhardt, H. Tristam Jr. "Persons and Humans: Refashioning Ourselves in a Better Image." *Zygon* 19 (September 1984).

Feldman, David. *Health and Medicine in the Jewish Tradition*. New York: Crossroad, 1986.

Fletcher, John C. "Ethical Issues In and Beyond Prospective Clinical Trials of Human Gene Therapy." *Journal of Medicine and Philosophy* 10 (1985).

Fletcher, Joseph. "Ethics and Genetic Control." *In Medical Ethics: A Guide for Health Professionals,* pp. 3-11. Edited by John F. Monagle and David C. Thomasma. Rockville, MD: Aspen Publ., Inc., 1988.

"Gene Implant Therapy is Backed for Children with Rare Disease." *New York Times*. March 8, 1990.

"Gene Swap in Mice Offers Hope for Medical Gains." *New York Times*. April 19, 1990.

"Gene Therapy Moves Closer to Reality." *New York Times*. March 11, 1990.

"The Genetic Age," *Business Week*, May 28, 1990.

Goodman, Richard M. *Genetic Disorders among the Jewish People*. Baltimore: Johns Hopkins University Press, 1979.

"Great Fifteen-year Project to Decipher Genes Stirs Opposition." *New York Times*. June 5, 1990.

Green, Ronald. "Genetic Medicine in the Perspective of Orthodox Halakhah." *Judaism* 34 (Summer 1985).

Grobstein, Clifford and Flower, Michael. "Gene Therapy: Proceed with Caution." *Hastings Center Report*. (April 1984).

Huxley, Aldous. *Brave New World*. New York: Harper & Row, 1932.

Jacobovits, Immanuel. "Human Fertilisation and Embryology: Values and Safeguards." *L'eylah* 29 (April 1990).

_____. "Some Letters on Jewish Medical Ethics." *The Journal of Medicine and Philosophy* 8 (August 1983).

Lappe, Marc. "The Limits of Genetic Inquiry." *Hastings Center Report*. 17 (August 1987).

"A Major Operation of a Fetus Works for the First Time," *New York Times*, May 31, 1990.

McLaren, Anne. "Can We Diagnose Genetic Disease in Pre-Embryos?" *New Science* 16 (March 1987).

National Council of Churches of Christ. "Genetic Engineering: Social and Ethical Consequences." 1984.

Nichols, Eve. *Human Gene Therapy*. Cambridge, MA: Harvard University Press, 1988.

Rabinowitz, Avraham Tzvi. "Remarks Concerning the Halakhic Policy and its Implications for Genetic Engineering." *Tehumin*. 2 (1981).

Ramsey, Paul. "A Response to Daniel Callahan." *Hastings Center Report*. (December 1979).

"A Report from Germany." *Bioethics* 2 (1989).

Roberts, Leslie. "Ethical Questions Haunt New Genetic Technologies." *Science* 3 (March 1989).

Rosenfeld, Azriel. "Judaism and Gene Design." In *Jewish Bioethics*, pp. 401-8. Edited by Fred Rosner and J. David Bleich. Brooklyn: Hebrew Publishing Co., 1985.

_____. "Religion and the Robot." *Tradition*. (Fall 1966).

Rosner, Fred. "Genetic Engineering." In *Modern Medicine and Jewish Ethics*. New York: Ktav, 1986.

_____. and Bleich, J. David, eds. *Jewish Bioethics*. Brooklyn: Hebrew Publishing Co., 1985.

_____. "Test Tube Babies, Host Mothers and Genetic Engineering in Judaism." *Tradition*. 19 (1981).

Ruse, Michael. "Genesis Revisited: Can We Do Better than God?" *Zygon* (September 1984).

Schachter, Herschel. "Halakhic Aspects of Family Planning." *Journal of Halakhah and Contemporary Society* 4 (1982).

Schmeck, Harold M. "Battling the Legacy of Illness," *New York Times Magazine*, April 29, 1990.

"Scientists Identify Sex of Three-Day-Old Embryo." *New York Times*. April 19, 1990.

Singer, Isaac Bashevis. *The Golem*. New York: Farrar, Strauss, Giroux, 1982.

Suzuki, David and Knudtson, Peter. *Genethics – The Ethics of Engineering Life*. Cambridge, MA: Harvard University Press, 1989.

Tendler, Moshe D. "Genetic Engineering: A Composite of Ethical Problems." In *Pardes Rimmonim: A Marriage Manual for the Jewish Family*. New York: Judaica Press, 1979.

Twiss, Sumner B. "Parental Responsibility for Genetic Health." *Hastings Center Report* 4 (February 1974).

U.S. Congress, Office of Technology Assessment. *Human Gene Therapy: Background Paper*. Washington, D.C.: OTA, 1984.

Walters, LeRoy. "The Ethics of Human Gene Therapy." *Nature* 320 (March 1986).

Weatherall, D.J. *The New Genetics and Clinical Practice*. Oxford: Oxford University Press, 1985.

Wertz, Dorothy C. and Fletcher, John C., eds. *Ethics and Human Genetics*. Heidelberg, NY: Springer-Verlag Berlin, 1989.

# Notes

1. Isaac Bashevis Singer, *The Golem*, New York: Farrar, Strauss, Giroux, 1982.

2. Aldous Huxley, *Brave New World*, (New York: Harper & Row, 1932), p. 8.

3. According to Gershom Scholem, the motif of the *golem* as it appears in medieval legends originates in the Talmud (*Sanhedrin* 65b). The *Hasidei Ashkenaz* developed a mystical ritual in the 12th and 13th centuries that focused on the creation of the *golem*. In this festive rite, they took earth from the soil and made a *golem* out of it, walked around the *golem*, and recited the letters and secret name of God in accordance with detailed sets of instructions. As a result, the *golem* arose and lived. When they walked in the opposite direction and said the combination of letters in the reverse order, the *golem* returned to the earth from which he had come. Legends concerning the creation of the *golem* are also attributed to the prophet Jeremiah and his so-called son, Ben Sira. In the popular legend of the *golem* that began to appear among German Jews in the 15th century, the *golem* became an actual creature who served his creators and fulfilled tasks laid upon him. The best-known form of the popular legend is connected with Judah Loew of Prague. This legend has no historical basis in the life of Loew. For more information see Gershom Scholem, "The Idea of the Golem," in *On the Kabbalah and its Symbolism*, New York: Schocken Books, 1965, pp. 158-204.

4. Numerous reports have appeared in various publications in the past few months. The stories alluded to are only two of the many: "Gene Therapy Moves Closer to Reality," *New York Times*, March 11, 1990; "Gene Implant Therapy is Backed for Children with Rare Disease," *New York Times*, March 8, 1990; "Gene Swap in Mice Offers Hope for Medical Gains," *New York Times*, April 19, 1990; "Scientists Identify Sex of Three-Day-Old Embryos," *New York Times*, April 19, 1990; "Battling the Legacy of Illness," The Good Health Magazine of the *New York Times Magazine*, April 29, 1990; "The Genetic Age," *Business Week*, May 28, 1990.

5. Harold M. Schmeck, "Battling the Legacy of Illness," *New York Times Magazine*, April 29, 1990.

6. "Tay-Sachs," *Encyclopedia Judaica*, Vol. 13, p. 24.

7. "Gene Implant Therapy is Backed for Children with Rare Disease," *New York Times*, March 8, 1990.

8. "A Major Operation on a Fetus Works for the First Time," *New York Times*, May 31, 1990.

9. "The Genetic Age," *Business Week*, May 28, 1990, p. 71.

10. "Great Fifteen-Year Project to Decipher Genes Stirs Opposition," *New York Times*, June 5, 1990.

11. Before broaching the subject of genetic engineering itself, most halakhists must cope with issues that arise from the processes necessary for the modification of genetic material, such as *in vitro* fertilization, artificial insemination, and embryo experimentation. For introductory analyses of these particular issues see J. David Bleich and Fred Rosner, "Artificial Insemination and Jewish Law," in *Jewish Bioethics* (New York: Hebrew Publishing Company, 1979), pp. 105-117 and Lord Immanuel Jakobovits, "Human Fertilisation and Embryology: Values and Safeguards," *L'eylah* 29 (April 1990), pp. 2-3.

12. See Moshe Drori, "Genetic Engineering: Preliminary Discussion," *Tehumin* 1 (1980): 280-296 (in Hebrew); David Feldman, *Health and Medicine in the Jewish Tradition* (New York: Crossroad, 1986); Ronald Green, "Genetic Medicine in the Perspective of Orthodox Halakhah," *Judaism* 34 (Summer 1985): 263-277; Immanuel Jakobovits, "Some Letters on Jewish Medical Ethics," *Journal of Medicine and Philosophy* 8 (August 1983): 217-221; Avraham Tzvi Rabinowitz, "Remarks Concerning the Halakhic Policy and its Implications for Genetic Engineering," *Tehumin* 1 (1980): pp. 280-296 (in Hebrew); Azriel Rosenfeld, "Judaism and Gene Design," *Tradition* 13 (1972): pp. 71-80; Fred Rosner, "Genetic Engineering and Judaism," in *Jewish Bioethics* (New York: Hebrew Publishing Co., 1979), pp. 409-420; Herschel Schachter, "Halakhic Aspects of Family Planning, *Journal of Halakhah and Contemporary Society* 4 (1982): pp. 5-32; and Moshe D. Tendler, "Genetic Engineering: A Composite of Ethical Problems," in *Pardes Rimmonim: A Marriage Manual for the Jewish Family* (New York: Judaica Press, 1979), pp. 77-84.

13. In his article, "Judaism and Gene Design," *Tradition* 13 (1972), p. 402, Azriel Rosenfeld discusses submicroscopic surgery as being relevant. Immanuel Jakobovits discusses the relationship between the obligation to heal and genetic therapy in "Some Letters on Jewish Medical Ethics," *Journal of Medicine and Philosophy* 8 (August 1983), p. 221.

14. As cited by David Feldman, *Health and Medicine in the Jewish Tradition* (New York: Crossroad, 1986), p. 75.

15. Immanuel Jakobovits, "Some Letters on Jewish Medical Ethics," *Journal of Medicine and Philosophy* 8 (August 1983), p. 220.

16. Clifford Grobstein and Michael Flower, "Gene Therapy: Proceed with Caution," *Hastings Center Report* 14 (April 1984), p. 14.

17. LeRoy Walters, "The Ethics of Human Gene Therapy," *Nature* 320 (March 1986), p. 227.

18. John C. Fletcher, "Ethical Issues In and Beyond Prospective Clinical Trials of Human Gene Therapy," *Journal of Medicine and Philosophy* 10 (1985), p. 304.

19. David T. Suzuki and Peter Knudtson, *Genethics* (Cambridge, MA: Harvard University Press, 1989), p. 206.

20. Sumner B. Twiss, "Parental Responsibility for Genetic Health," *Hasting Center Report* 4 (February 1974), p. 10.

21. Eve Nichols, *Human Gene Therapy*. Cambridge, MA: Harvard University Press, 1988, p. 170.

22. H. Tristam Engelhardt, Jr., "Persons and Humans: Refashioning Ourselves in a Better Image and Likeness," *Zygon* 19 (September 1984), p. 286 and p. 293.

23. "A Report from Germany," *Bioethics* 2 (1988), p. 259.

24. Robert Davis, from a letter to the *New York Times* as quoted in C. Keith Boone, "Bad Axioms in Genetic Engineering," *Hastings Center Report* 18 (August/September 1988), pp. 12-13.

25. Joseph Fletcher, p. 10.

26. Ibid.

27. Here Fletcher quotes himself from a different article, pp. 776-783.

28. Engelhardt, pp. 283-4.

29. Daniel Callahan, "The Moral Career of Genetic Engineering," *Hastings Center Report* 9 (April 1979), p. 9.

30. As quoted in John C. Fletcher, "Ethical Issues In and Beyond Prospective Clinical Trials of Human Gene Therapy," *Journal of Medicine and Philosophy* 10 (1985), p. 293.

31. Twiss, p. 9.

32. Boone, p. 11.

33. Joseph Fletcher, p. 9.

34. In 1983, a group of 64 clergy, including members of the Synagogue Council of America, urged a curb on genetic engineering based on this very claim. See "Clerics Urge U.S. Curb on Genetic Engineering," *New York Times*, June 9, 1983, pp. A1, A19.

35. Immanuel Jakobovits, "Human Fertilisation and Embryology: Values and Safeguards," *L'eylah* 29 (April 1990), p. 3.

36. Joseph Fletcher, p. 9.

37. Boone, p. 10.

38. David Suzuki and Peter Knudtson, p. 205.

39. The Enquette Commission is part of the Committee for Research and Technology of the German Bundestag, and is made up of representatives of the political parties and a few scientists and professors. They published their report on January 6, 1987. The Commission recommended to the German Bundestag that it make it a criminal offense to use gene technology to intervene in the human germ line. Of particular note is the historical background against which this decision was made. An English translation of the report appeared in *Bioethics*, 2 (1988).

40. U.S. Congress, Office of Technology Assessment, *Human Gene Therapy: Background Paper* (Washington, D.C.: OTA, 1984), p. 32.

41. In a phone call on February 28, 1990 with geneticist Dr. Gloria B. Gertzman, she stated that scientists are conjecturing now that those who are Tay-Sachs carriers may have a higher immunity to tuberculosis.

42. John C. Fletcher, p. 304.

43. Suzuki and Knudtson, p. 206.

44. Engelhardt, p. 287.

45. Terry Eagleton, *Literary Theory*. Minneapolis: University of Minnesota Press, 1983, p. 77.

# When the Physician is Sero-H.I.V. Positive

Janise Poticha

The existence and spread of Acquired Immunodeficiency Syndrome (AIDS) has presented society with an issue, most recently and eagerly addressed by the media, as well as *poskim*, the American Medical Association (AMA), American Dental Association (ADA), and the Center for Disease Control (CDC). In 1988, the media reported the identity of a surgeon who had recently been diagnosed with AIDS. Although health authorities attempted to reassure the public, concern grew about surgeon-to-patient transmission of AIDS. The case is one of a very few in question of the transmission of AIDS from a health care professional to patient among the more than 175,000 cases reported to the C.D.C. since AIDS was discovered in 1981. The issues are extensive spanning from a physician's obligation to cure, a physician's/person's right to privacy, a physician's right to earn a living and not ruin their professional career, the degree of risk involved with physician to patient transmission of AIDS, to the responsibility not to put another person in "harms way."

## The Question

What is the responsibility the health care worker has to his/her patients if the health care worker is HIV positive, through the perspective of *halakhah* and contemporary ethics?

## Halakhic Perspective

### The Obligation to Heal

Judaism teaches that the value of human life takes precedence over almost all consideration. It is incumbent upon those learned persons to accept the responsibility to heal and preserve life.

The basis for the obligation to heal the sick comes from the verse found in Exodus 21:19 *v'rapo y'rapey* (heal and one shall be healed). According to Rabbi Baruch Halevi Epstein's *Torah Temimah*, it was taught at the school of Rabbi Ishmael that the verse "heal and one shall be healed" gives license to the physician to heal: *Mikan, shenatata rishut l'rofey l'rfot* (from here license is derived for a physician to cure).[1] By the emphasis expressed in the double wording *l'rofey l'rfot*, the Torah takes the opportunity to oppose any concern that the use of medical aid may exhibit a lack of trust and confidence in Divine healing. The Talmud *Baba Kamma* 85a interprets this duplication of healing as intended to teach us that not only was the physician permitted to practice medicine but that authorization was granted by God to the physician to heal. In this passage concerning personal injury, the Talmud *Baba Kamma* 85a states that the repetition of the word *v'rapo* (healed) means that the patient must be repeatedly healed if the illness or injury recurred or became aggravated. In this passage, the Talmud also requires that where ulcers have grown on account of the wound and the wound breaks open again, the offender would still be liable to heal it, i.e. pay the medical expenses, even repeatedly. (The Bible appears to take for granted the use of medicine, but a differing view is expressed in II Chronicle 16:12 "...yet in his (Asa's) disease, he sought not to God, but to the physicians."[2])

The obligation to heal is also derived from *vahashayvoto lo* (and you shall restore it to him) (Deut. 22:2). This sanction is qualified by Epstein in *Torah Temimah*, making human healing obligatory. In Maimonides' *Commentary on the Mishnah, Nedarim* 4:4, he states:

> "It is obligatory from the Torah for the physician to heal the sick and this is included in the explanation of the Scriptural phrase 'and you shall restore it to him,' meaning to heal his body."

The duties toward our fellow human beings are described in Lev. 19:11-16. According to S.R. Hertz, these precepts restate the fundamental principles of life in human society and are contained in the second set of the Ten Commandments. This Levitical passage culminates with the precept in verse 16 "...neither shall you stand idly by the blood of your neighbor." These principles of societal order permeated all phases of civil and criminal law. An example is given from Talmud *Sanhedrian* 73a:

> "Whence do we know that if a man sees his fellow drowning, mauled by beasts, or attacked by robbers, he is bound to save him? From the verse 'You shall not stand idly by the blood of your neighbor.'"

Maimonides supports this Talmudic passage in *Mishneh Torah Hilkhot Rotzeaḥ* 1:14:

> "Whoever is able to save another and does not save him transgresses the commandment 'neither shall

you stand idly by the blood of your neighbor.' Similarly, if one sees another drowning in the sea, or being attacked by bandits or being attached by a wild animal and is able to rescue ... and does not rescue him ... he transgresses the commandment 'neither shall you stand idly by the blood of your neighbor.'"

Not only was healing permissible, but its religious obligation (as we read in *Baba Kamma* 85a) is included in the category of *Pikuah Nefesh*, which is a supreme religious precept.[3] Fear of making a mistake or inadvertently causing death to the patient is no reason to refrain from treatment, as long as one is duly cautious, as is true in any procedure that involves risk of mortal results.[4]

Starting treatment quickly is considered praiseworthy, while refraining from treatment by the physician when called upon is tantamount to *shofekh damim* (spilling blood), causing death.[5] From this we may infer that every physician who possesses the knowledge and training is under obligation to heal. Joseph Karo's *Shulhan Arukh* supports this as long as there is no other physician of higher capability available.[6]

Great demands of conscience and perplexing decisions are imposed upon the physician. It is for these reasons that Nachmanides draws an analogy between a doctor and a judge. Nachmanides concludes the the physician who acts with the same concern and heed that is observed by a judge when applying the law in regard to capitol offenses, should be treated in the same manner as a judge who passes judgement with justice and truth. If they err unknowingly, both are exempt from punishment under both human and divine law.[7] There is one substantial area where the responsibility of the physician exceeds that of a judge. When becoming aware of an innocent mistake, the judge, acting under authority of the *Beit Din*, is exempt even under diving law. The physician who mistakenly errs and learns of the error, though exempt under human law, is liable under Divine law. If his error caused death, the physician must go into exile.

## Professional Secrecy/Confidentiality

Judaism holds the physician and medicine in high esteem. Accompanying this high regard for the professional are the severe restrictions of what information, received during the course of the professional relationship may or may not be revealed.

The prohibition from disclosing information is taken from Lev. 19:6: "You shall not go as a bearer-of-tales among your people." Such activity, under any condition, is prohibited.

Maimonides in his *Mishneh Torah* asks and responds to his question:

"Who is a tale-bearer? One who carries gossip going about from person to person telling: 'so and so said this, have heard so and so about so and so.' Even though he tells the truth, he ruins the world. There is a still worse iniquity that comes within this prohibition, namely: the evil tongue of the slander-monger who speaks disparagingly of ones fellow, even if the truth is told."

Maimonides in *halakhah* 5:

"It makes no difference whether someone deals out gossip in the presence or the absence of the party concerned. Anyone who tells things that, if transmitted from person-to-person, are likely to cause physical or financial harm to a fellow or merely to distress or frighten, is guilty of slander."[8]

Rabbi Israel Meir Kagen in his text *Hofetz Hayyim*[9] acknowledges that in certain circumstances professional confidences must be discloses. The circumstance explained by the *Hofetz Hayyim* concerns a person seeking disclosure of medical information of a prospective marriage partner. The text rules that in only four cases may medical information be disclosed:

1. the presence of a disease or physical defect; however a general weakness of deficiency which does not impede health may not be disclosed;
2. the nature of a disease or injury must not be exaggerated:
3. the only motivation prompting disclosure must be the benefit of the person to whom the information is supplied. No disclosure may be made when prompted, even in part, by personal animosity.
4. when there exists reasonable grounds for assuming that the information divulged will be the determining factor in terms of the contemplated marriage.

These restrictions also apply in regard to a prospective employer. Implicit in the *halahkah* is the difference between privacy and potential harm which may occur to the other party. Information may not be disclosed, at random or for the benefit of a third party, nor to complete a file. It then follows that information which has no bearing on job performance may not be disclosed.

According to Dr. J. David Bleich the respect for privacy and the inviolability of the professional relationship certainly do not take precedence over protection of the lives and safety of others. The overriding obligation to protect the lives of others is of sufficient weight to oblige the physician to take whatever measures may be necessary to eliminate the danger.[10] The recipient of private information is obliged to disclose information only in order to preserve the lives and property of others. But, if no danger exists, or if the danger can be prevented, the recipient may disclose any information.

A person is forbidden to wrongly or justifiably disclose information about another potentially marring and/or ruining their professional or personal status. We read in the *Shulḥan Arukh* the rule of how much money a person is allowed to give to *tzedakah*. A person is not allowed to put one's profession in jeopardy by giving more than what is explicitly required, based on their earnings. The prohibition against ruining one's self is directly related to self preservation.[11]

## Damage/Risk

The Rabbis understood Lev. 18:5 "you shall therefore keep my statues ... which if a person do, they shall live by them...," to suggest that the observance of a commandment must not jeopardize life, it is therefore prohibited to enter into a dangerous situation to fulfill a commandment.[12] *Safek sakana* (potential danger) is to be prevented. According to Rashi and *Torah Temimah* when discussing Deut. 22:8, one who builds a new house, must construct a *maakey*, (a parapet) or fence on the roof to protect all who are within its borders.

Maimonides is very forthright with his statement concerning rescue:

> "Whoever is able to rescue and does not do so violates the commandment: do not stand idly by the blood of your neighbor (Lev. 25:36). Also, one who sees his fellow drowning in the see, threatened by robbers, or wild animals coming upon him, and has the ability to save him...yet does not do so transgresses the commandment 'do not stand idly by the blood of your neighbor.'"[13]

Rabbi Joel Sirkes (d. 1640) points out that the Talmud states[14]:

> "Whence do we know that if a man sees a fellow drowning, mauled by beasts, or attacked by robbers, he is bound to save him? From the verse: 'you shall not stand idly by...' But is it derived from this verse? Is it not rather from elsewhere? Whence do we know (that one must save his neighbor from) the lose of himself? From the verse: 'and you shall restore him to himself' (Deut. 22:2). From that verse I might think that it is only personal obligation, (because 'you shall restore' implies 'you' in person), but that he is not bound to take the trouble of hiring men (if he cannot deliver him himself), therefore this verse teaches that he must."[15]

Maimonides' formulation makes it clear that the obligation to rescue exists only where there is no doubt involved as to the rescue; then the rescuer is to pursue the rescue and endanger himself, if need be. Rabbi Sirkes assumes that "no doubt involved" means that there is no doubt as to the safely of the rescuer. This obligation to rescue another person is most sacred. Failure to do so constitutes a direct transgression of: "you shall not stand idly by your neighbor" and of similar commandments in the following cases:

> 1. Where there is no danger to the rescuer, or where he can serve as a witness to someone facing criminal charges and does not do so;

> 2. Where the danger to the rescuer is minimal without placing himself in serious danger, and does not do so;

> 3. Where there is no clear and present danger to the intended victim, he is duty-bound to come to the intended victims rescue if he can;

> 4. Where someone is being pursued by an attacker intent on murder or rape, Scripture obligates anyone who is able to save the intended victim, even at the cost of the attackers life, if necessary for 'the blood of your neighbor' includes the irreparable harm inherent in rape as well as the lose of life. The obligation exists even when the rescuer would place his own life in jeopardy;

> 5. "However, if the possibility of death to the rescuer is close to certainty, he need not sacrifice his own life to save his fellow. Nay, if the possibility is more or less half favorable and half unfavorable (50%-50%), he is not obligated to sacrifice his life; for 'what makes you think your blood is redder, perhaps his blood is redder'.[16] Where the possibility is not half and half, rather tending toward safely and the rescuer will not be seriously endangered, if he does not strive to rescue, he had violated; 'you shall not stand idly by...'[17]

Further prohibition against risking potential danger to save a life is also found in the Talmud.[18] The story is of a town having a well as the sole water supply, sufficient only for the townspeople or for outsiders but not for both. Both sources agree that the needs of the townspeople; those of drinking, watering their animals and laundering override the needs of the outsiders. The sources agree even if the outsiders are in need of drinking water while the townspeople need it for purposes for laundry, the needs of the time supercede. Rabbi Jose favors the laundering of the residents due to the health dangers involved.[19] Rabbi Jose takes the view that one is not obligated to risk potential danger (not laundering) to save someone from certain danger.

The question of potential vs certain danger is further discussed in *Baba Metzia* 62a [20]:

> "If two are traveling on a journey (far from civilization) and one has a pitcher of water, if both drink, they will (both) die; but if one only drinks, he can reach civilization. The son of Patura taught: it is better that both should drink and die rather than one should be bold his companions death. Until Rabbi Akiva came and taught: that your brother may live with you,[21] my life takes precedence over his life."

The son of Patura requires the water-bearer to share, thus risking potential danger. Based on his theoretical-moral feelings, this also suggests that giving the water to his companion is tantamount to declaring that his companion's blood is redder than his. He is expounding a moral position whereas Rabbi Akiva, not risking certain danger, is professing a legal-ethical norm. It is interesting to note that Maimonides, the *Tur*, and the *Shulḥan Arukh* do not codify Rabbi Akiva's position.[22]

Rabbinic law exempts a person from the duty of self-sacrifice and absolves any moral blame. In the case of son of Patura, if both travelers drink the water, both of them will die. The status of a citizen who, above and beyond the call of duty, elects to give his life to save another is discussed with regard to martyrdom for any reason other than the prescribed religious law (avoidance of idolatry, incest and adultery or murder). Maimonides considered such sacrifice as sinful; the *Tosafot Avodah Zarah* 27b, regarded it as meritorious.[23]

The late Chief Rabbi of Israel, Rabbi Isser Yehudah Unterman was convinced that a person is obligated to come to the rescue of his fellow, even if by doing so, places his own life in potential danger.[24] He asks: how great must the possibility of danger be as to constitute an exemption from the Scriptural imperative: "you shall not stand idly by?" The question is a good one, but his response paralleling saving one's own precious possessions falls short of a person being duty-bound to save the life of another human being.[25]

When discussing how potential and clear risk applies to a medical practitioner, Rabbi Eliezar Yehudah Wallenberg of the Jerusalem Rabbinic court lists five criteria when a medical practitioner may put his life into jeopardy in order to treat patients with contagious diseases:

1. when there exists a question of contagion;
2. to extol the sanctity of the medical calling;
3. to distinguish between imminent physical danger (such as donating a vital organ);

4. to justify the employment of all people
   treating sick patients and;
5. to emphasis the extreme social benefit to
   society as well as the economic benefit to
   the doctor and the earning of a livelihood.

Rabbi Wallenberg comments on Rabbi David Ibn Zimra
(Radbaz), that a medical practitioner who could not take sufficient
measures to protect himself as well as the patient would be forbidden to treat a patient with a life-threatening disease. He adds that
his position applies to all medical practitioners and lay persons.

In *Berakhot* 33a we read the story of a person in the midst
of prayer who is perplexed as to the action to be taken when a reptile wraps itself around his leg. The text tells us that he cannot
interrupt his prayer if the reptile is a snake. Rav Shesheth limits
the rule to an innocuous reptile which will not bite unless provoked.
But a scorpion or other venomous sort one may interrupt. A snake
is considered dangerous only if it bites. But it may not bite; while the
scorpion more than likely will bite, the bite being fatal. The question,
once again is the nature of the risk.

Halakhic examples have been presented here concerning
the imperative to heal the ill; to take a speedy, active and ongoing
part to restore one's health; the command not to disclose information concerning another person unless the information is life-threatening or dangerous; a person's obligation not to ruin themselves professionally and the existence and degree of risk involved i.e. endangering one's own life. I would like to conclude this Halakhic presentation with a brief discussion of the risk a (healthy) person is allowed
to accept when donating one of their own organs to save the life of
another. To what extent, if any can one risk their own life by donating a kidney in order to save another life?[26]

Commentaries on Maimonides[27] and J. Karo[28] offer the
answer:

The Jerusalem Talmud concludes that one is obligated to place oneself even into a possible dangerous
situation (to save another's life). It seems logical
that the reason is that one's (death without intervention i.e. the kidney recipient) is a certainty whereas
his (the donor's) is only a possibility."[29]

The clearest understanding of risk involvement is the traditional
interpretation of Lev. 18:5 *vaḥai bahem* – one must observe the
commandments by "living by them."[30]

## Contemporary Perspective

The contemporary issues confronting the medical/dental industries concerning physicians/dentists diagnosed as sero-positive or HIV positive are extensive and emotional The issues range from AIDS activist and civil liberties groups opposing mandatory testing of anyone to the specific Florida case where Dr. Acer (deceased dentist) allegedly transmitted the HIV virus to Kimberly Bergalis in 1987. The issues concern the legal and ethical controversies of identifying and balancing risk and protection; privacy; personal and professional responsibility; and the right to know for the benefit of an individual and/or society. How does/could society approach the threat of a ultimately fatal transmissible disease in a time when individual liberties have been given new emphasis in law and ethics?

### Historic Development

American courts are familiar with the tensions between public health and civil rights. for years, as physicians fought against smallpox, yellow fever, leprosy, typhoid, tuberculosis and syphilis, the courts struggled to balance societal interests in controlling communicable disease against constitutional liberties due to each citizen.

By 1873 only 37 United States towns had established local health departments. The first permanent State Board of Health was not founded until 1869.

Between 1875 and 1910 all states had established boards of public health. During this same time, state and local governments instituted widespread vaccination and quarantine programs to control the spread of communicable disease. Citizens began to challenge the governments control over individual liberty. The courts responded rigorously to adopt stringent measures controlling contagious disease. They proclaimed public health to be "the highest law of the land"[31] and announced that all "constitutionally guaranteed rights must give way"[32] to its demands.

The courts did acknowledge their limited medical expertise and would defer decisions to health department. The courts believed that a social contract existed between a citizen and the government which simply suggested that an individual joined a society for security and to reap the benefits-in return the government could demand of the individual to make certain sacrifices. The social contract became an important protection for individuals. Excepting the notion that a person joined a particular society only if that society promised to further their survival, courts reasoned that the State could not kill or seriously injure an innocent citizen. Even if public health would benefit, the social contract did not allow the State to act as such.

The courts had a very limited concept of individual rights. The concept was that individuals did not posses a set of well-defined rights that could be weighed against conflicting social/communal needs. Individuals had the right to participate in any activity which offered no threat to other members of society. Once an action threatened some degree of danger to other people the individual lost their rights to continue the action.

The courts were concerned with determining whether a challenged health measure responded to a real danger. They did not distinguish between types of individual liberty; individual rights were not part of this system.

Between 1875-1910 two factors influenced the courts' disposition of challenges to control communicable disease:

1. judges uncomfortable with immigration, urbanization, and industrialization created new public health problems justifying stricter measures;
2. decisions reflected the courts' sympathy for free enterprise and commercial development.

The years between 1910 and 1940 carried on previous patterns. Courts enforced quarantine orders and upheld mandatory vaccination laws. But, two new measures of public health control were instituted:

1. mandatory testing for communicable disease and;
2. involuntary sterilization of the genetically unfit.

These mandates increased the tension between individual liberty and public health.

During this same time period many states organized widespread examinations of adults for venereal disease. Judges readily acknowledged that known pimps and prostitutes should also be examined. States also approved blood tests and other forms of examinations for couples seeking marriage licenses. But the courts did not compel those who did not break the law nor applicants for marriage licenses to submit to venereal disease tests. Although no state required the testing of adults, only one court indicated that such a program would be an "intolerable interference" with individual liberty.[33]

The courts were reluctant to examine non-prostitutes who may have been suspected of infection with venereal disease. Judges considered venereal disease testing more physically intrusive than other forms of examination. The blood test required was considered a "violation of the person."[34] The courts were also concerned that ordering a citizen to submit to such an exam would seriously endanger the citizen's reputation.

The health of school children and married couples was of much greater concern than citizens who neither planned to marry nor worked as prostitutes. The courts upheld compulsory testing for school children and premarital testing for venereal disease. One court characterized the transmission of venereal disease to innocent spouses as a "tremendous evil."[35]

These new decisions of public health control suggest that the courts were beginning to move away from their view that individual rights could never outweigh threats to the public health. By taking into account the intrusiveness of the test, the threat to the person's reputation, and the public need for the examination, judges conceded that the ethics of individual liberty may transcend concern for public health.

From 1940 through the 1980's judges continued to enforce public health needs: quarantines, vaccinations, mandatory health tests and in some cases sterilization. Three changes have transpired:

1. courts widened their perspective concerning individual rights. They redefined their concept of individual rights which held that individuals possess rights to engage only in activities that do not interfere in any way with the liberty of others with a more positive concept, i.e. the recognition that individuals retain certain fixed rights – even if the exercise of those rights endanger others. Under some circumstances the individual's liberty interests may be strong enough to outweigh health threats to others;
2. based on the courts increasing disillusionment with the democratic process they realized the democratic process did not work very well in certain cases;
3. judges became less willing to accept medical claims that particular person are dangerous or that certain procedures are essential to promote health. The courts became more interested in the proven history of illness than in medical theories concerning possibilities.

The changes in the court between 1940 and the 1980's exhibit the courts' new regard for individual liberty. But protection of public health is still considered a preeminent governmental function.

## Ethics...Confidentiality
The growth of AIDS has focused attention on not only the implicit ethical rights of an individual through public responses to disease, but also the explicit ethics involved.

For some, our question of the responsibility a physician has to his/her patients has already been answered. Because of their HIV infection or AIDS diagnosis numerous physicians, nurses and other health care workers have lost their practices, have been denied employment or discharged or have found their duties restricted. The cases to date are individual.

Certain elements must be factored into the equation before an answer is achieved; one of which involves morals and ethics. There is great conflict with this area. According to the Institute of Medicine, National Academy of Science's article entitled "Confronting AIDS-Update 1988," every professional code of ethics mandates some form of confidentiality for the person being provided services. To inform a third part of the existence of an illness in considered a violation of that ethical principle. Professional confidentiality generally holds a more stringent ethical obligation than does ordinary confidentiality; for example professional confidentiality may override the requirement to cooperate within the judicial system. It is also considered that physicians have an implicit ethical obligation to protect society from harm. To some, this suggests that those who could harm another individual should not receive the same degree of confidentiality. but at what point is an individual such a threat to someone else that confidentiality can be breached?

The debate rages on of maintaining confidentiality for individuals and protecting others from harm. The phrase often used "duty to warn" has added to the existing suspicion and fear. The connotation that this responsibility supersedes all others is a concept that "is in direct conflict with the ethical precept that the primary duty of physicians is to their patients."[36] According to Larry Gostin the Executive Director of the American Society of Law and Medicine,[37] HIV-infected practitioners should not be required to warn/disclose their HIV status to their patients. He agrees that it is unrealistic to expect professions to inform patients of the HIV status and still be able to practice. Disclosure would inevitably result in the ruination of the professional's career.[38] Such a serious invasion of human rights and ethics would be warranted only for purposes of a compelling public health benefit and no such unequivocal benefit has been demonstrated in these situations.[39]

Under the same rubric of confidentiality is the law of informed consent. This doctrine requires a physician to explain to a patient the risks and benefits of a particular treatment, drug or operation so that the patient is able to make an "informed decision" regarding the proposed medical action. In deciding what risks and benefits to disclose, the physician is to disclose all risks that a reasonable patient would find material.[40] Based on the information, the patient then decides whether or not to undergo treatment or surgery.

Personal information regarding the physician does not fit into this paradigm.[41] Requiring physicians to disclose their personal issues that may or may not effect their competence or performance creates a conflict of interest for both physician and patient.

A physician's responsibility is to inform the risks and benefits regarding new drugs, experimental treatments, or an operation. In contrast, the physician's responsibility is not to discuss those personal factors that may increase or decrease his/her competency.

Thus, according to Chai Feldblum's response to Larry Gostin[42] the doctrine of informed consent has not been applied to the disclosure of relatively remote risks associated with physicians – "nor should it be."[43] Instead, if a physician truly posses a real risk to the patient, the appropriate legal requirement would be to restrict the physician from practice. The solution is not to have a requirement that physicians disclose professional risks regarding themselves.

> "If the risks of contracting HIV were indeed significant in relation to particularly invasive procedures, then informing patients would not suffice...If a physician is impaired or there is a real risk of transmission of infection to a patient, then this is a problem that should be remedied by professional standards and licensing requirements."[44]

## Confidentiality...Blood Testing

The issue of confidentiality can not be fully discussed without noting the issues of blood testing. Blood tests are to detect the presence of antibodies to the HIV. The presence of these antibodies is evidence of infection but the converse is not necessarily true. The fact that antibodies may not appear in the bloodstream for six months after infection means that infected individuals may not be identified in this manner. Testing in this manner would not necessarily prevent transmission of the infection.

Mandatory testing raises a number of issues, not the least of which are ethical and civil rights issues. On a more pragmatic level, there is the very high cost associated with testing.; the cost of the testing not being proportional to the results. The result of mandatory testing and disclosure would have a threatening impact on the reputation of health care workers. Quoting Dr. James L. Nelson, an associate for the Hastings Center:

> "It will continue to erode something that is already under a great deal of pressure: which is, basically, the sense that medicine and health care in general isn't simply a job pursued for economic motives or because someone thinks it is intellectually interesting. Rather, that it has some element of a calling. That is in some ways an old fashioned notion that is under pressure for a lot of reasons, the AIDS epidemic is one of them. ...promote and create the conditions that allow and encourage and nourish health care providers to think of themselves this way."[45]

Gostin lists four adverse results caused by mandatory testing and disclosure:
1. the loss of career of dedicated professionals;
2 .the possible reduction in the willingness of professionals to care for infected patients;
3. the logistical problems of testing; and
4. the creation of a disincentive for honest reporting.

His response to these possible results is: "these serious costs... probably would be ameliorated once the ethical standard of avoiding invasive treatment becomes more accepted in the health professions."[46] Unfortunately, he never clarifies how these factors would be ameliorated over time, but does acknowledge that screening without consent is an invasion of human rights.

## Risk

Substantial public anxiety has been created concerning what is termed by some "minimal risk." In January 1991 the AMA reaffirmed its policy stating that the "medical profession as a matter of medical ethics...should err on the side of protecting patients" and that HIV-infected physicians "have an ethical obligation not to engage in any professional practice which has an identifiable risk of transmission" to patients.[47] Based on the uncertainty concerning transmission, the AMA suggests that "HIV-infected physicians should either abstain from performing invasive procedures which pose an identifiable risk of transmission or disclose their sero-positive status prior to performing a procedure and proceed only if there is informed consent."[48] They do support sero-positive, HIV positive physicians by acknowledging that they "have a right to continue their career in medicine in a capacity that posses no identifiable risk to their patients."[49]

There are two basic principles which the AMA's Council on Ethics and Judicial Affairs (which maintains the Code of Ethics that is generally regarded as the medical profession's code) offers as guidelines for the CDC and the medical profession. The first is, a physician who has a transmittable and fatal disease should not place his/her patients at risk. The risk of transmission from an HIV-infected physician during certain invasive procedures is very low, but real. "Some restraint on invasive procedures is necessary as a matter of the oldest precept of medical ethics-that the physician shall do not harm."[50] The second principle is the AMA opposing mandatory testing of physicians. "When the very low probability of a surgeon acquiring AIDS from an infected patient is multiplied by the even lower probability that the same physician would then transmit the infection to the patient, the risk to patients of becoming infected is virtually immeasurable, much lower than the risk that an already infected surgeon would transmit the disease."[51] If a physician performs significant invasive procedures, having some measurable risk of acquiring AIDS, they, according to the AMA, have an obligation to determine their HIV status. They have an "ethical obligation" to avoid any professional activity which has an identifiable risk of transmission of the infection to the patient.

According to the paper: "The HIV-Infected Health Care Profession: Employment Policy and Public Health"[52] the AMA "identifiable risk" standards is such that no physician could possible attain, since any physician could have a number of infectious conditions at any one time. In many cases, those conditions, a cold for example, might have little impact on patient health. In other settings, however, the normal infections and bacteria that all persons carry, could lead to more serious conditions. "Under the AMA's 'no identifiable risk' policy, therefore no surgeon could operate and by implication, no surgical nurse cold assist-the danger of infection, even the most minimal and remote danger-would disqualify all infected professionals from practice."[53]

In 1988 the New York State Legislature directed the State Department of Health to define "significant risk" for the transmission and contraction of HIV in occupational and other settings.[54] The Department adopted a formal definition of "significant risk" of HIV transmission, outlining blood-to-blood and blood-to-mucous membrane exposures. That definition of "significant risk" does not include occupational circumstances where individuals use scientifically accepted barrier techniques and preventive practices in circumstances which would otherwise pose a significant risk.

Congress, while offering a definition of "significant risk" indicated that a "speculative or remote risk" or a "merely elevated risk of injury" would not qualify as significant; that a case-by-case, individualized determination of risk was necessary; and the evaluation of risk should not be based on generalizations, misperceptions, ignorance, irrational fears, patronizing attitudes or pernicious mythologies."[55]

All available data point to an extremely low risk of transmission from medical care personnel to patient. The risk is described by the New York State Department of Health as remote but cannot be quantified precisely. As a general principle, limiting the practice of HIV-infected physicians is not necessary or justified unless there is clear evidence "that such workers pose a significant risk of transmitting infection through an inability to meet basic function control standards or unless they are functionally unable to care for patients."[56] Consequently, on the basis of existing evidence on the risk of HIV transmission from physician to patient, New York State Department remains "convinced that HIV-infected professionals should continue all professional practice for which they are qualified, with rigorous adherence to universal precautions and scientifically accepted infection control practices."[57]

The question remains: do we wish to tolerate "significant

risk?" We have noted the low-level risk presented by physicians. "In comparison with legal and public health treatment of other disabilities ... one would be forced to conclude that the risk from HIV-infected health professionals performing invasive procedures for which they are qualified has not yet been proven to be 'significant.'"[58] More importantly, since drug and alcohol use, psychiatric difficulties, and even fatigue and marital problems are much more common sources of impairment,[59] screening for those conditions also would be indicated, if a "no risk" policy similar to that of the AMA were applied consistently. Physicians, by the nature of their profession, incur some risk of contracting some infections from their patients. But, the risks they incur from HIV are no greater, and probably less than the risks from other contagious conditions or occupational hazards.

The risk of HIV perceived by physicians and the public are distorted because of the high mortality associated with AIDS. The changes of "contracting HIV are decidedly low, but the consequences are severe. The risks alone are distorted by societal perceptions of AIDS and its victim. It is not only that AIDS is a lethal disease it also engenders social prejudice and irrational fear."[60]

## Contemporary Conclusion

As the debate rages on concerning a physicians responsibility to his/her patients both the AMA and the ADA have revised their guidelines and recommendations. They are concerned that public attitudes, misperceptions about HIV-infected persons, and the stigma attached to HIV will ruin the livelihood of infected medical providers. But as their January 1991 statement declared:

> "Physicians who are HIV positive have an ethical
> obligation not to engage in any professional activity
> which has an identifiable risk of transmission of the
> infection to the patient ... the medical profession as
> a matter of medical ethics, should err on the side of
> protecting patients."[61]

The AMA guidelines allow the informed patient the right to choose. The AMA believe their guidelines will work because it reflects policy fundamental to the professional ethics by which the vast majority of physicians abide.

Conversely, on April 26, 1991, New Jersey Judge Phillip S. Carchman ruled: "The ultimate risk to the patient is so absolute, so devastating, that it is untenable to argue against informed consent combined with restrictions on procedures which present any risk to the patient."[62] The following week the Medical Society of New Jersey called for the testing of all hospital patients for the AIDS virus. Dr.

Joseph Riggs, the Society's President, said that he may also request that the State Legislature make HIV testing mandatory. Their resolution also called for regular testing of all health care professionals. A spokesperson for Lambda Legal Defense and Education Fund suggests that such a policy would institutionalize discrimination against people infected with the virus. "It is an invitation to segregate out a group of patients and expose them to discrimination and inferior treatment."[63] The debate rages on.

## How Does a Contemporary Jew Respond?

Immanuel Jakobovits, in his article: "Ethical Problems Regarding the Termination of Life" asked:

> "How does Jewish Law go to work in relating to very modern issues, many of which obviously are the result of spectacular advances in medicine that are of very recent times? How can we apply to contemporary perplexities insights that have their origin in the timeless traditions of our faith and are imbedded in virtually all the layers of our literature going back to earliest biblical times? How can we find principles enshrined in these early sources that have relevance and application to the highly complex questions that arise from these dramatic advances in medicine"?[64]

His questions could not be more aptly expressed as society continues to debate the complex controversies of the AIDS virus.

It was J. David Bleich who wrote:

> "In Jewish law and moral teaching the value of human life is supreme and take precedence over virtually all other consideration ... Human life is not a good to be preserved as a condition of other values but as an absolute basic and precious good in its own stead. The obligation to preserve life is commensurately all-encompassing."[65]

Rabbi Akiva was one of many who answered the Talmudic question of: "What is the fundamental principle of Judaism?" He responded: "You shall love your neighbor as yourself."

Judaism, as a system of law (*halakhah*) has much to say concerning the questions of bio-medical ethics. The Rabbis used specific methodology in reasoning through a problem to reach an ethical conclusion. Can a person, firmly rooted in Judaism, not living according to *halakhah*, understand its sociohistoric value and apply it to the question posed by this paper?

Judaism has throughout history emphasized the importance of maintaining the highest level of community safety. Jewish law has dealt with the issues arising from infectious disease as we read from *Ḥofetz Hayyim* concerning a person seeking disclosure of medical information of a perspective marriage partner.

The risk of contamination from early plagues which *halakhah* had to confront, was much higher then the risk a patient confronts if their physician is HIV positive. The need to define the level of risk/danger is paramount in the decision-making precess of Rabbi David Feldman, Rabbi J. David Bleich, and Dr. Fred Rosner. Each of these noteworthy *poskim* agree, although via different means, that the percentage of risk must be defined in order to make case by case decisions.

As we have seen there exists a conflict between the precept and obligation to heal the sick and the pain of making decisions of legal and ethical consequence. In the world of the *halakhah*, humanity's well-being can not be assured without preserving the special relationship with God. This special relationship, although not thoroughly discussed is implicit in every halakhic decision.

We have seen that Rabbinic Judaism's perspective is more of duty and obligation rather than rights: the physician is obligated to heal; a person is required to construct a parapet around a new house to keep people from danger; unless very specific life-threatening reasons exist one can not disclose information from a physician to patient relationship and if your neighbor is in trouble you must not "stand idly by."

As a liberal Jew I can use the *halakhah* as a foundation, as a guide, but not as an obligatory rule. Living in the modern world, I must find a way to integrate *halakhah* with modernity. A physician today is confronted with many more obstacles, hazards and risks than that of our ancestors.

The Rabbis were very much concerned with humanity's relationship with God. Medical decisions today are not always concerned with potential divine intervention or the integration of God and humanity.

As we read in the historic development section of this paper, our contemporary world has moved from stressing communal needs to the elevation and support of the rights of the individual. If a physician is HIV positive, the rights of two people, the physician and patient, must be considered.

The AMA and the ADA have offered guidelines and recommendations which take into account the rights of the physician and society. The guidelines offer safety to the community while protecting the rights, professionalism and privacy of the physician.

Using *halakhah* as a foundation, as a guide, I must respond to the question of what is a physician's responsibility to his/her patient if the physician is sero-HIV positive, as a liberal Jew, taking into consideration all issues previously address in this paper. My response to the question is four-fold:

1. information about the degree of risk of HIV transmission from a physician to patient is, to date, too low to restrict a physician from performing their duties (see kidney transplant discussion above);
2. the screening of physicians is unjustified as per the level of risk and would breach the code of confidentiality;
3. universal precautions optimizing precautionary steps for medical procedures should be taken (similar to building a parapet around a roof); and
4. the prohibited cost of testing is not proportionally worth the net information gained.

My response to the question has taken into account the multi-facets of human nature and the complexities of *halakhah*. Drawing finite borders around human responsibility is difficult at best. When deciding such a controversial issue as this one, I would recommend seeking out all available sources; sources having Jewish historic roots and following their transition through time to the present; as well as secular research that has a direct effect on the conclusion.

# Bibliography

American Medical Association, "Statement on HIV-Infected Physicians", Jan. 17, 1991.

Barnes, Mark. *Law, Medicine and Health Care*, "The HIV-Infected Health Care Professional: Employment Policies and Public Health," Vol. 18:4, Winter 1990.

Bleich, J. David. *Judaism and Healing-Halakhic Perspectives*, Ktav Pub. House, 1981.

Bleich, J. David. "Medical Questions," *Contemporary Halakhic Problems* 2, pp. 54-56, 74-80.

Elon, Menahem. *Israel Law Review* 4, "Jewish Law and Modern Medicine."

Feldblum, Chai. *Law, Medicine and Health Care* 4, "A Response to Gostin, 'The HIV-Infected Health Care Professional: Public Policy, Discrimination, and Patient Safety," Feb. 1991.

Feldman, David. Health and Medicine in the Jewish Tradition, Crossroads Publishing Co., 1986.

Gostin, Larry. *Law, Medicine and Health Care* 4, "The HIV-Infected Health Care Professional: Public Policy, Discrimination and Patient Safety," Spring 1991.

Kellner, Menachem. *Contemporary Jewish Ethics*, Sanhedrin Press, 1979.

Kirschenbaum, Aaron. " The Good Samaritan and Jewish Law," *Dine Israel* 7, Tel Aviv University, Faculty of Law, 1976.

*Maryland Law Review*, Number 1, vol. 48, 1989.

Meier, Levi. *Jewish Values in Bioethics*, Human Sciences Press, Inc., 1986.

Merritt, Deborah Jones. "The Constitutional Balance Between Health and Liberty," *AIDS:Public Health and Civil Liberties, a Hastings Center Report* – Special Supplement, Dec. 1986.

New York State Dept. of Health: Policy Statement and Guidelines-Health Care Facilities and HIV-Infected Medical Personnel, Jan. 29, 1991.

*New York Times*, Jan. 27, April 26, May 1, 1991.

Rosner, Fred. *Modern Medicine and Jewish Law*, Block Publishing Co., 1972.

Rosner, Fred. *Tradition* 12, "The Physician and the Patient in Jewish Law."

Silberstein, Arthur. *Israel Law Review* 10, "Liability of the Physician in Jewish Law."

Spero, Shubert. *Morality, Halakhah and the Jewish Tradition*, Ktav Publishing House, Inc., 1983.

# Notes

1. R. Baruch Halevi Epstein, *Torah Temimah*, Exodus 21:20.

2. Acknowledging the theological tension, the justification for the physician to heal is also substantiated in Nachmonides *Torat HaAdam, Shaar Hasakanah*, and *Tur, Yoreh Deah, Hilkhot Bikkur Ḥolim* 336.

3. The source of this among others is the *Jerusalem Talmud, Yoma* 8:5: "...and any matter of doubt as to danger to life overrides the prohibitions of *shabbat*."

4. *Tur: Yoreh Deah 336; Shulḥan Arukh, Hilkhot Bikkur Ḥolim 336; Arukh Hashulḥan, Dine R'fuot Harofim 336.*

5. *Ibid., Shulḥan Arukh.*

6. *Ibid,. Shulḥan Arukh.*

7. *Nachmanides, Torat Haadam.*

8. *Maimonides, Mishneh Torah, Hilkhot Deot 7:2,5.*

9. *Hofetz Hayyim, Hilkhot Issurei Rekhilut, 9:1.*

10. J.D. Bleich, "Professional Secrecy," *Judaism and Healing-Halakhic Perspectives,* Ktav Publishing House, Inc., 1981, pp. 35.

11. *Shulḥan Arukh, Yoreh Deah, Hilkhot Tzedakah 348.*

12. *Mishnah Yoma* 8:5-7, and Yoma 85a and 85b.

13. *Mishneh Torah, Hilkhot Rotzeaḥ* 1:14. It should also be noted that Maimonides' *Hilkhot Rotzeaḥ* 11:4 is interperted to mean the removal of all danger to one's physical being. Concerning the construction of an encircling ring or cover or pit... "any obstruction that is a danger to life must be removed as a matter of positive duty and extremely necessary caution."

14. *Tur, Ḥoshen Mishpat* 426:2, *Bayit Ḥadash.*

15. *Babylonian Talmud, Sanhedrin,* 73a.

16. *Bab. Yoma* 82b.

17. Rabbi David Ibn Zimra (Radbaz d. 1573), *Responsa.*

18. *Bab., Nedarim* 80b; *Pal., Shevi-it* 8:5 and *Nedarim* 11:1.

19. *Bab. Nedarim* 81a.

20. *Bab. Baba Metzia* 62a.

21. *Bab. Baba Metzia* 62a, Soncino: "with 'me' implies that my life takes first place, but that he too has a right to life after mine is assured."

22. Aaron Kirschenbaum, "The Good Samaritan and Jewish Law", *Dine Israel 7*, Tel Aviv University, Faculty of Law, 1976, pp. 25.

23. Ibid., pp. 28.

24. Based on Rabbi Unterman's accordance with *halakhah*, with the Palestinian Talmud and the 'proper understanding' of the Babylonian Talmud.

25. *Shevet Miyehvdah*, pp. 19-23; based on *Bab., Baba Metzia* 30b.

26. The example of kidney donation is used based on the human ability to live fully with one operative kidney, the level of risk involved is low.

27. Commentary on Joseph Karo, *Kesef Mishneh* on Maimonides' *Mishneh Torah, Hilkhot Rotzeaḥ* 1:14.

28. Commentary of *Meirat Ainayim* on Karo's *Shulḥan Arukh, Ḥoshen Mishpat* 426:1.

29. We will return to kidney transplants for Rabbi Eliezer Yehudah Wallenberg's response.

30. Rashi on *Leviticus* 18:5.

31. Beeks v. Dickinson County, 131 Iowa 244, 248, 108 N.W. 311, 312 (1906).

32. Ibid.

33. Rock v. Carney 216 Mich. 280, 298, 185 N.W. 789, 800 (1921).

34. Ibid.

35. Peterson v. Widule 157 Wis. 614, 647, 147 N.W. 966, 968 (1914).

36. *Maryland Law Review*, "Health Care Workers and AIDS," Number 1, Vol. 48, 1989.

37. Larry Gostin, *Law, Medicine and Health Care* 4, "The HIV-Infected Health Care Professional: Public Policy, Discrimination and Patient Safety." Spring 1991.

38. Gostin's response to a debate concerning his in press article (ibid), in an Association of Practitioners for Infection Control position paper: "The HIV-Infected Health Care Worker", given Feb. 21, 1991 in Atlanta, Georgia.

39. Ibid.

40. Chai Feldblum, "Informed Consent: Issues for Individuals with HIV Disease:, unpublished, Jan. 1990.

41. Ibid., #38.

42. Chai Feldblum,: "A Response to Gostin, The HIV-Infected Health Care Worker: Public Policy, Discrimination and Patient Safety", given at APIC testimony, 21-Feb-1991, Atlanta, Ga, and AMA testimony, Feb. 1991.

43. Ibid.

44. Gostin, Ibid. #37.

45. Dr. James L. Nelson, from the Hastings Center, quoted in New York Times, Jan. 27, 1991, "When the Doctor, too, May Have AIDS.

46. Ibid., #37.

47. American Medical Association, "Statement on HIV Infected Physicians, Jan. 17, 1991.

48. Ibid.

49. Ibid.

50. Ibid.

51. Ibid.

52. Mark Burns, Nicholas Rango, Gary Burke, Linda Chiarello, *Law, Medicine and Health Care*, "The HIV Infected Health Care Professional: Employment Policies and Public Health, vol. 18:4, Winter 1990.

53. Ibid.

54. *New York Public Health Law* 2786 (1) (1990).

55. *Code of Cong. and Admin. News Suppliment 6*, Sept. 1990, pp. 446-447.

56. New York State Dept. of Health, "Policy Statement and Guidelines of Health Care Facilities and HIV-Infected Medical Personnel," Jan. 29, 1991.

57. Ibid.

58. Ibid. #52.

59. *AMA, Journal of American Medicine,* A. 684, "The Council on Mental Health, The Sick Physician: Impairment by Psychiatric Disorders, Including Alcoholism and Drug Dependence," 1973.

60. *Maryland Law Review*, "Symposium on AIDS and the Rights and Obligations of Health Care Workers," Number 1, vol. 48, 1989.

61. Ibid., #47.

62. *New York Times*, April 26, 1991.

63. *New York Times*, May 1, 1991. The spokesperson for Lambda Legal Defense and Education Fund was Evan Wolfson.

64. Immanuel Jakabovits, "Ethical Problems Regarding the Termination of Life", published in Rabbi Meier: *Jewish Values in Bioethics,* Human Sciences Press , Inc, New York, 1986.

65. Shapira, "The Human Right to Die: Some Israeli and Jewish Legal Perspectives," pp. 366.

# Informing the Terminally Ill of Their Impending Death: A Jewish Answer

Karen Bookman Kaplan
and Amy Memis


In the area of bioethics, technology has forced a multitude of new ethical dilemmas and decisions to the fore. These include: prolongation of life of a "vegetable" and those in severe pain by means of respirators and other equipment, research using aborted fetuses, and many others. Some ethical questions, however, are timelessly problematic. From the most primitive ages to the present, they elude easy resolution. Even when a resolution appears to be at hand, new considerations and priorities arise which force one to reevaluate one's answer and possibly revise it. We have such a question before us: Should one inform a terminally ill patient of his or her impending death?


## The Perplexed Seeking Guidance

The answer to this has varied, even for one group, that of doctors, in a relatively short period of time. As Schimmel puts it, "up until about twenty-five years ago most doctors felt that, generally speaking, terminal patients should not be informed... However, more recent empirical studies of physicians' attitudes and behavior indicate a dramatic shift in their approach to this issue."[1] He backs this up with a survey of forty-five physicians. The first questions asks, if the terminal patient requests information about their condition, "do you feel they have an unqualified right to know the truth?" Eighty-seven percent said "yes."[2] This kind of finding matches our less provable, but nevertheless intuitive, perception that death is not as taboo a topic nowadays, and this includes more openness about telling people they are going to die. In addition, in most studies, over 80 percent of patients asked indicated that they would want to be informed of their diagnoses.[3]

Both the shifts of opinion regarding this question, plus the many pros and cons of answering "yes" presented below, suggest that the presence of two or more ethical values is what makes the question so difficult. Anytime two or more values simultaneously apply, an ethical dilemma is generated. Each value is desirable in its own right, but when making one value a priority over all the others, those others have to get sacrificed to some degree if not totally. Thus, our question is not easily settled, neither in general ethics (secular principles), nor in the realm of Jewish law, the *halakhah*.

Different values are addressed in these two areas, general ethics and *halakhah*, so they will be noted under each area as we come to it. Headings for each area directly follow this introduction. Although this holds the reader in suspense, it is wise to hold off on naming the values until we refine our question as stated above. As it stands, it is too vague. In its present form, one would have the right to answer it by responding, "Well it depends." Thus our next task is to explain upon what the answer depends. We call these "whats" our variables. Thus, among others, the answer depends on the following: the patient's age, emotional and physical state, when and how often the information would be given, how much information is given, how it is given, and who gives it.[4]

The question was raised in class discussion whether all of these variables had ethical consequences. The answer is yes, since they can affect the impact on the patient of telling the truth. Some are self-evidently a question of ethics. Telling the truth to a patient who is mentally ill may be cruel indeed. Telling a ten-year old child is different from telling an aged adult. Telling the truth bluntly and abruptly is different from telling it gently, which are both different from dropping broad hints about it. The ethical dimension of some of the remaining variables may be less obvious, but Veatch does a good job of showing the ethical impact of how much information is given. He brings up "the truthful lie". One instance of that phenomenon is jargon. A doctor will sometimes tell the truth in such a complicated way that the patient does not understand its import. (This addresses how it is given as well as how much is given. Another element involved in how information is given is the degree of optimism conveyed. A doctor may overemphasize the possibility of a miracle.)

Another ethical dimension arises in how much to tell when the patient is told he or she is terminal but does not know what the chances for survival are. Or suppose a patient is given a confusingly large amount of information, some of which is extraneous. "Who tells" becomes an issue when a stranger, for example, a nurse, tells when a close relative could have or wanted to. Robert Kavahaligh, a psychiatrist and former priest, best addresses who should tell a dying person of his/her impending death: "There is no proper person, only one brave and humble enough to try to bring the maximum of graciousness to a forbidding task.[5]

The complexity of our ethical question, "Should one inform a terminally ill patient of his or her impending death," is abundantly clear. This complexity becomes mind-boggling when the variables are all combined. An infinite number of hypothetical cases exist. For instance, it is one thing to be blunt (the "how to tell" variable) with a child as opposed to an adult (the age variable).

There are other variables, but apparently they do not make a difference on the ethical outcome. Feminists may ask whether it matters if the patient and/or the one telling or not telling is a woman. It is hard to imagine how gender would effect the ethics here. If telling the truth causes the patient mental anguish, then that discomfort is equally undesirable for a patient of either sex. Likewise, it would also be equally undesirable whether a man or a woman is doing the telling. Finally, there are other variables that might matter but are practically impossible to measure, such as the patient's past experience in dealing with bad news. Moreover, if we get too detailed, then our results will not be applicable to enough situations to make them genuinely useful.

We will now make our question more precise by specifying which variables are operative; we will then have a specific case study problem to analyze. The variables were chosen to generate the presumably "typical" case that we as rabbis will be confronting. Thus, according to the variables, we assume the following: the patient is an adult and is mentally or physically capable of absorbing and responding to the information. A close relative or doctor will be the one to tell or not to tell. If delivered, the information will be given gently but directly. So our case is as follows: *A congregant, who is a close relative of the terminally ill patient, comes to one of us and says, "Rabbi, should my seventy-five year-old mother be told that the doctors say that she has two weeks to live?"*

Below, we will indirectly answer this question according to two sources: general ethics and *halakhah*. This is an indirect approach in the sense that the cases addressed by these sources will not be the same as our case. In the concluding section of this paper, we will reexamine all the answers and then give our own answer for our specific case.

Before moving on to that task, it is necessary to define general ethics as opposed to *halakhah*. *Halakhah* is Jewish law as developed in rabbinic literature starting with the Mishnah and continuing in codes and responsa literature up to the present day. Much of the *halakhah* in this paper draws principally on the Babylonian Talmud and the *Shulḥan Arukh*. Other sources useful to our case include the *Tur*, Siftei Cohen's commentary on the *Shulḥan Arukh*, and *Ḥokhmat Adam*, a seventeenth century code by Abraham Danzig. The *Tanakh* and *midrashim* were consulted as well but are commented on briefly since neither is halakhic. We use the *halakhah*, then, as a basis for giving a Jewish, as opposed to a secular, answer to our question of the ethics of informing the terminally ill patient of his or her condition.

General ethics is a looser term than *halakhah*. We define it as any ethics developed in philosophical systems or in any non-religious entity such as the American Medical Association. Any conclusions reached on our question, even in a Jewish journal, will be deemed general ethics if it is based on secular studies.

In the next section, general ethics, we will list the pros and cons of telling the truth to the terminally ill patient, and how the variables chosen play into those pros and cons. We will also show what ethical values are being addressed. We will follow a similar procedure for the section on *halakhah*. In addition, we will dwell on the interrelationships among the *halakhah* in terms of our topic and see what effect those relationships have on our understanding of the *halakhah* as a system.

The concluding section of this paper contains our commentary on the fact that the *halakhah* and general ethics clash over the answer to our question, that is, to our case. We will compare, first of all, the list of values tapped into by each of the two areas. Some values are shared in common and some are not. Then we will compare the pros and cons that each area offers, looking for some common ground. As a last step, we will then formulate our own answer to our case. Our task, of course, is to defend that answer where it deviates from the halakhic, that is, the classic Jewish, position. Thus we will be playing out the dilemma that confronts every Jew in the postmodern world, namely, making sense of and valuing our own ethical system in terms of the existence of attractive competing systems.

## General Ethics

In this section we will study the general ethical material which addresses our topic of informing a dying person of his/her impending death. Our question, "should my seventy-five year old mother be told she has only two weeks to live?" revolves around the issue of telling her or not telling her. We will divide the following sources as either "pro" or "con." We define "pro" as: tell the truth to the patient of his/her impending death and "con" as: withhold the truth from the patient regarding the news of his/her impending death.

In the process of examining the following material, we will determine the underlying reasons why a given viewpoint is either pro or con. These reasons will essentially constitute the underlying ethical values. We will focus on the values which determine whether or not a patient is told of his/her impending death. The values are most important because the variables or other factors in our examples below may differ from those in our question, but the ethical values weighed in the decision made in those examples will be similar to our own. These general ethical values fall into five basic categories which we have labeled as (1) truth, (2) comfort of the patient, (3) prolonging life, (4) patient autonomy, and (5) trust. These values are also important, as we will be looking at similar ethics in our Halakhic analysis.

## Con

The first code of the American Medical Association (1847) raised the question of telling the truth to possibly terminal patients:

> A physician should not ... fail, on proper occasions, to give to the friends of the patient timely notice of danger when it really occurs; and even to the patient if absolutely necessary. This office, however, is so peculiarly alarming when executed by him, that it ought to be declined whenever it can be assigned to any other person of sufficient judgment and delicacy. For the physician should be the minister of hope and comfort to the sick...; The life of a sick person can be shortened not only by the acts, but also by the words or the manner of a physician. It is, therefore, a sacred duty to guard himself carefully in this respect, and to avoid all things which have a tendency to discourage the patient and to depress his spirits.[6]

This early code recognizes that there may arise an occasion in which a physician should inform a patient of danger (this may or may not imply death), but the overall tone implies that a physician generally should not say anything of a gloomy nature to a dying patient.

Early medicine did not address the issue of telling or not telling a patient the truth. According to Sissela Bok, Associate Professor of Philosophy at Brandeis University, "we find very few mentions of veracity in the codes and oaths and writings by physicians through the centuries."[7] The Hippocratic Oath makes no mention of truthfulness to patients about their condition, prognosis, or treatment. In one early oath, however, written in the 16th century by Amatus Lusitanus, a Jewish physician, included a section on honesty toward the patient:

> If I lie, may I incur the eternal wrath of God and His angel Raphel, and may nothing in the medical art succeed for me according to my desires.[8]

While Lusitanus confronted the issue of honesty and truth in medicine, others did not. The AMA's Principles of Medical Ethics (1957) still leaves the matter of informing patients up to the physician. "Given such freedom, a physician can decide to tell as much or as little as he wants the patient to know,"[9] or not to inform the patient at all. The ethical value of truth, or rather withholding the truth, is just one factor which has guided physicians in the past to not inform patients of their impending deaths.

One reason that physicians have chosen to withhold the truth from patients is that their mode of ethical reasoning is situational. "Any overreaching rule such as, 'always tell the truth' or 'truth for truth's sake' is unacceptable."[10] No physician can be certain that a given illness is terminal. It is hard to know whether a physician has been right in the first place in making a pessimistic diagnosis. Moreover, it goes against the grain of the physician's role as healer to deliver bad news, even when it is uncertain. Physicians therefore will defend that a "'truthful' statement could *turn* out to hurt patients unnecessarily."[11]

Another reason that physicians do not tell the truth of terminal illness or impending death to patients is that some patients do not want to know. While it is true that a majority of patients do want to know the truth that they have a terminal illness,[12] in our case we are not assuming that our congregant's mother wants to know either way. The purpose of leaving this factor unknown allows us to look at all the cons as well as the pros with fairness.

For those patients who do not want the truth, one concern might be that they just want to be kept comfortable.[13] This concept of comfort leads us into the next ethical value as to why doctors do not disclose the truth to patients regarding a terminal illness or an impending death. For many physicians, whether the patient will benefit, physically or psychologically, is the definitive factor for disclosing the news of one's impending death. We have labelled these physical or psychological benefits as the ethical value of a patient's comfort.

Bok specifically mentions the physical discomfort that can come from disclosure of news such as one's impending death. Another reason doctors do not want to tell a patient s/he is dying is that upon hearing bleak news, there is the possibility of the "triggering of physiological mechanisms which allow death to come more quickly... unhappy news, abruptly conveyed... could also bring on such a 'dying response.'"[14] There is little scientific proof to this response; nevertheless, doctors consider these possible physical reactions as factors in withholding the truth of a patient's impending death.

Also in support of withholding the truth, Schimmel mentions the emotional discomforts that could arise upon hearing the news of one's impending death. He recognizes that informing a patient of his/her impending death may trigger specific psychological reactions of "depression, anxiety and loss of hope for recovery."[15] These reactions might accelerate death, and "thus are counter to the goals of prolongation of life and avoidance of harm."[16] A physician's duty, after all, is to do whatever possible to (1) preserve life and (2) cause no harm to the patient. Many physicians, therefore, will allow the consequences of these two criteria to supersede the value of truth-telling.

The two types of comfort, physical and psychological, are not always easy to separate. Several physicians who are in favor of withholding the truth from a dying patient generalize these comforts in one category of "harm." Bernard Meyer, a physician who wrote in the 1960's on the ethics of what should be told to the terminal patient, believes a physician's role is to do what is best for the patient, not to merely tell the truth. He says,

> ours is a profession which traditionally has been guided by a precept that transcends the virtue of uttering the truth for truth's sake; that is, 'so far as possible to do no harm.'[17]

Harm, although undefined here, indicates the opposite of a physician's duty (which Schimmel referred to above as prolonging life and avoidance of harm). Bok points out that even the doctors who acknowledge a patient's right to have information, might still not provide it, for the same reason Meyer indicates. These physicians hold that "the information given might hurt the patient and...[is] therefore a threat to proper health care."[18] This general term, harm, includes not only the ethical value of physical and psychological comfort. Harm also includes another ethical value, which Schimmel touched upon, prolonging life.

Prolonging life thus becomes another ethical value in our question, "should my 75-year-old mother be told she has two weeks to live?" Failure to prolong life, in its most extreme case, would occur if a patient committed suicide upon hearing the news of his/her impending death. When persons are already ill physicians fear telling them of a very serious prognosis for they believe the news may cause the patients to commit suicide. Bok, however, notes, "the fear that great numbers of patients will commit suicide is unfounded."[19] Although doctors often use the possible attempt of suicide as a reason to withhold the truth from a dying patient, Veatch verifies that the claim of suicide to his knowledge is without documentation.

In examining the material which we have classified as con, in favor of withholding the truth from the dying patient, we found that the following ethical values are used in making a decision: (1) truth, (2) patient comfort, and (3) prolonging life. We also found that individuals in favor of withholding the truth are physicians and this is supported by documents of the American Medical Association. Telling the truth to the dying patient in the con cases is not always a given. Truth is merely one factor weighed by physicians in making a decision to tell the patient the bleak news. The other ethical values, patient comfort and prolonging life are also considered when a doctor chooses not to inform a patient s/he is dying. In the above con cases, it is the consequences of possible physical reactions and psychological repercussions that are more heavily weighed above merely telling the truth for truth's sake. The same is so for the value of prolonging life. In the examples we mentioned, many physicians believe telling the truth will reverse the effect of preserving or prolonging life, and therefore, they too will withhold the truth from the patient.

## Pro

The ethical value of truth has also been utilized by those who favor telling the truth to the dying patient. Those who believe in "truth for truth's sake," or "always tell the truth" follow the ethics of Immanuel Kant. Kant bluntly expresses this unconditional duty of being truthful, "The moral worth of an action does not depend on the result expected from it."[20] Those who would agree with this Kantian principle believe that the truth is a patient's right. "Withholding information is an omission for which one is responsible – because the patient has the right to expect such information to be transmitted."[21]

In the con examples above, which are not based on Kantian ethics, the physicians believed that there are possible harmful consequences that could result in telling the dying patient of his/her impending death. These harms outweighed the value of the truth. In the pro case, however, the balance reverses how the values are weighed,

> "According to those who follow the moral principle that there is a duty to tell the truth, even if withholding information from the dying patient would prevent harm or preserve life, one would still have to ask whether withholding or deceiving a patient is right."[22]

In discussing the value of truth in the con section, we also mentioned that sometimes the physician cannot be certain of the truth, or that a given illness is terminal. Even in the cases where the physician is not fully informed of the prognosis, there will be an

> "infinite range of possible facts about a patient's case [and this] will mean that the physician must do some selecting. There is no way around that, and some borderline pieces of information may be difficult to evaluate, but certainly the impending death of the patient can never be confused with such trivia."[23]

Those who support telling the patient the truth of his/her impending death, above and beyond the consequences that might come as a result of not telling the truth, do so because they believe that the physician has a moral duty to tell the truth and the patient has an inalienable right to hear the truth.

The ethical value of patient comfort has also been utilized by those who favor telling the dying patient the truth of his/her impending death. Bok challenges the assumption that the notice of bad news hurts the patient. She argues that the:

> "damages associated with disclosure of sad news or risks are rarer than physicians believe; and the benefits which result from being informed are more substantial, even measurably so."[24]

Schimmel, who noted above the psychological effects which result from telling a patient s/he is dying, also points out that a "lack of knowledge about one's medical condition produces anxiety that may be greater than the anxiety engendered by knowing of one's terminal condition."[25] Depending on which side of the fence one falls, one can utilize patient comfort, for or against telling the patient the truth of his/her impending death.

Dr. Elizabeth Kubler-Ross is at the forefront of informing a person of a terminal illness or a dying patient of his/her impending death. She believes, "the question should not be stated, 'Do I tell my patient?' but should be rephrased as, 'How do I share this knowledge with my patient?'"[26] Kubler-Ross is one step ahead because her goal focuses on the patient processing the five stages s/he will go through before death. Although Kubler-Ross has moved beyond our question of informing the patient, she asks her question, how one should inform a dying patient, based on the value of a patient's physical and emotional comfort.

Others who favor informing the dying patient of his/her impending death are concerned with the patient's right to tie up loose ends.

Practicing Roman Catholics, for example, have a duty, not merely a right, to prepare for death... other people also believe that they should prepare for imminent death. While this will not include last sacraments, it does mean preparing or reviewing wills, clarifying business arrangements, and perhaps making final reconciliation with family members.[27]

Thus a dying patient needs to hear the truth that s/he will die soon so that the patient can take care of his/her personal affairs such as preparing wills, family reconciliation, religious or spiritual preparation, and tying up business affairs. All these fall into one category which we have labeled as the patient's autonomy.

Also based on the value of autonomy, the "pro" viewpoint focus on knowing the truth as a patient's freedom. In the 16th century Michel de Montaigne, in his Essays, wrote how people should think about death and be prepared to accept it, "To be prevented by lies from trying to discern what is to come, hampers freedom – freedom to consider one's life as a whole, with a beginning, a duration, an end."[28] Knowing the truth of one's impending death is an

ultimate value in the mind of many individuals: "Freedom to control one's life... is fundamental to human nature and applies no less to
the dying."[29] A dying person's freedom, in addition to his/her right
to tying up loose ends, comprise a patient's autonomy. The pro view,
to inform the patient s/he is dying, thus introduces another ethical
value, that of patient autonomy.

Still others who favor telling the dying patient of his/her
impending death do so because honesty and trust must be at the
basis of the relationship between the physician and the patient.
"Each act of lying or withholding of information from the patient con-
tributes to general mistrust."[30] If the truth is not told to the patient,
then the dying patient (and patients in general) will lose trust in
health professionals and fail to cooperate in procedures which may
help them. In addition, "failure to disclose [the truth to the dying
patient] forces unnatural behavior on physicians and others. They
cannot relate to the patient honestly and openly express true feelings for him or her."[31] These two examples bring forward the last of
the five general ethical values, that of trust.

In examining the material which we have classified as pro,
in favor of telling the truth to the dying patient, we found that the
following values were used in making decisions: (1) truth, (2) patient
comfort, (3) patient autonomy, and (4) trust. In contrast to the con
examples, we found that individuals in favor of telling the truth were
not, for the most part, physicians, with the exception of Dr. Elizabeth
Kubler-Ross. On the pro side, telling the truth became a value weighed
more heavily than the physical or psychological consequences discussed in the con section. Truth is also considered a patient's right.
In the pro view regarding a patient's comfort, we found the exact
opposite to be true from the con view. According to the con, anxiety is
the result if a patient is informed of his/her impending death. In the
pro opinion, however, a patient incurs anxiety if s/he is not told of
his/her impending death. In addition, the pro examples introduced
two other ethical values of patient autonomy and trust. Based on
the ethical value of patient autonomy, telling the patient allows for
the dying person to tie up any loose ends before his/her death. The
value of trust for the pro supporters must exist not only between
the patient and physician, but also between the patient and other
professionals and non-professionals. Those who favor telling the
patient the truth based on the value of trust believe in the need for
honest communication among all parties involved with the dying
patients.

Having explored both the pro and con views based on some
similar and some differing ethical values, it is interesting to note
that there is a majority opinion in today's American society that
favors telling the dying patient the truth of his/her impending death.
This majority opinion, however, was not always the case. Up until
the early 1960's,

"most doctors felt that, generally speaking, terminal patients should not be informed of their condition, and this feeling guided prevailing medical practice. However, more recent empirical studies of physicians' attitudes and behavior indicate a dramatic shift in their approach to this issue."[32]

Physicians believed it was their duty to protect patients from harm, and should do so by withholding distressing information.

In the early 1970s, however, studies reveal that physicians views were beginning to change as well. The following survey from 1975 by Rea, Greenspoon, and Spilka indicates this change:

3% of the physicians acknowledge some negative feelings about informing dying patients of their condition.

97% of the physicians felt the patient must be told.[33]

The 1970's showed a gradual shift of physicians favoring the disclosure of the truth to their patients. Studies since 1979 report on average between 79 and 90 percent of physicians favor disclosure.[34] Other recent surveys of patients indicate that between 80 and 90 percent of patients would want to be told they have a fatal diagnosis.[35]

This gradual shift from con to pro does not take place without cause. Schimmel suggest five reasons as to why physicians attitudes have changed since the 1960's.

(1) Physicians have come to accept arguments in favor of disclosure as more compelling than arguments against it
(2) Patients have favored disclosure.
(3) There is a general trend in medical care towards providing patients with more information about their treatment.
(4) The advances in medical intervention require patient consent.
(5) Doctors fear legal consequences in cases where they fail to disclose.[36]

These reasons, although they do not indicate it specifically, show that the reason for the shift is due to a change in weighing the various ethical values. This shift toward the pro shows that the values of truth (or a patient's right to the truth), patient comfort (as a lack of anxiety from knowing the truth), trust (in the doctor-patient relationship), and most of all, the patient's right to autonomy are being weighed more heavily than any other values. Further evidence is noted in the AMA's Principle of Ethics revised in 1980, which states, "A physician shall deal honestly with patients."[37]

The conclusion of the general ethics section is that a majority of physicians and patients favor having the truth told to the patient that s/he is going to die soon. This conclusion is not a consensus, but rather a majority, for there are still traditional Hippocratic physicians who believe for ethical reasons in withholding the truth from the patients, and there are also some patients who ethically wish to have the truth withheld.

## *Halakhah*

In this section of our paper we will turn to the halakhic material which addresses our question, "should my 75 year old mother be told she has only two weeks to live?" We will also look at non-Halakhic material which address our question, but will not use the latter in reaching our final conclusion. We will explore the halakhic data, both in terms of chronological development and in terms of the ethical values listed below. Of interest in the chronological development is seeing which value takes precedence over which others, and how conflicting values are resolved at any given point. We will discuss the *halakhah* in chronological "batches;" that is, where halakhic texts refer to each other either explicitly or implicitly.

Similar to the General Ethics section, we will determine the underlying values of each passage we examine. These halakhic values also fall into five basic categories, similar to the general ethical values. We have labeled them as (1) redemption, (2) comfort, (3) truth, (4) prolonging life, and (5) autonomy.

## First Batch

The earliest text we found addressing the issue of telling a dying person the truth that s/he is going to die is in II Kings 8:10. It comes from the Prophets of the Bible and is therefore not halakhic material. Although it is non-halakhic, and never recurs in the halakhic material, the question and answer are quite clear, "Elisha said to him, 'Go and say to him, 'You will get well.' However, the Lord has shown me that he will surely die.'"[38]

Does one tell a dying person he is going to die? According to II Kings 8:10, clearly, no. In fact, tell him the opposite, that he will get better. The background on this scene concerns King Ben-Hadad, who is ill. He sends Hazael to ask the man of God if he will get well. Hazael goes and asks, but Elisha tells him to lie. Hazael returns and tells the King the lie, that he will recover. The next day, the King dies and Hazael succeeds him as king. The verse itself, as its surrounding text, does not mention any reasons or values taken under consideration for lying to the dying person. When God, via Elisha, gives direction no reasons or values are required.

While II Kings 8:10 does not appear again in the halakhic sources, it is worthwhile to note Gersonides' commentary on this verse.

> "Go and say to him you will get well." That is, that God already showed him that he would surely die, but in order that he (Hazael) will not say to him (King Ben-Hadad of Amram) (you will die), because of the fear of [hastening] death. [So instead] he (Hazael) said to him (King Ben-Hadad), 'You will get better.' And this is the vision of the prophets, because with this more truth will come to be in their prophecy.[39]

Gersonides "indicates that absolute candor might hasten the death of the patient."[40] The value Gersonides uses as reason to lie to the King is prolonging life. Gersonides infers that telling King Ben-Hadad the truth will hasten his death, which he already knew was coming soon, because God had told him.

The following charts illustrate these two passages and the emphasis the values they consider in the conclusion made as either pro or con.

**II Kings 8:10**

| | |
|---|---|
| Redemption | — not considered |
| Truth | — ignored if not blatantly violated |
| Comfort | — not considered |
| Prolonging life | — not considered |
| Autonomy | — not considered |

**Gersonides on II Kings 8:10**

| | |
|---|---|
| Redemption | — not considered |
| Truth | — ignored for the sake of comfort |
| Comfort | — not considered |
| Prolonging life | — primary value |
| Autonomy | — not considered |

Truth is concealed by Hazael in both the II Kings and the Gersonides passages, but Gersonides considers the added value of prolonging life in favoring withholding the truth from the dying person.

## Second Batch

The next earliest passage, which also comes from the Prophets, is Isaiah 38:1.

> In those days Hezekiah was sick and likely to die.
> The prophet Isaiah son of Amoz came to him and
> said, "So says the Lord, 'Set your affairs in order,
> for you are going to die; you will not get well.'"[41]

In this verse the answer is very clear, Hezekiah was sick,
and likely to die, and God told him to "Set your affairs in order for
you will die and not get well." The answer to our question in this
case, is tell the dying person the truth, that he is going to die. The
underlying reason is so that the person can tie up loose ends, and
literally, "set [one's] house in order." This reason is based on the
value we call in modern terms, autonomy.[42]

A second text which utilizes the passage from Isaiah 38:1 is
*Berakhot* 10a.

> "In those days Hezekiah was sick and likely to die.
> The prophet Isaiah son of Amoz came to him and
> said, "So says the Lord, 'Set your affairs in order, for
> you are going to die; you will not get well.'" ...He said
> to him, "The decree has already been declared." The
> other replied, "Son of Amoz, finish up your prophecy
> and be off. A tradition I have from the house of my
> ancestor is: Even if a sharp sword rests upon one's
> neck, he is not to prevent himself from praying.[43]

While the text comes from the Babylonian Talmud, the passage is aggadic. The first part of the text simply repeats the verse
and therefore one might designate this passage as in favor of
telling the truth to the dying person. The rest of the text, however,
is ambiguous on that point and depends on how one interprets the
"prayer" in which "he does not prevent himself from praying," even
at the point of death.

If his prayer is praying for redemption, then this passage
favors telling a dying person the truth. God already gave him the
decree he is going to die, this gives him time to pray for redemption
in the world to come. This concept is similar to halakhic passages
regarding confession (see below), in which a dying person is encouraged to be told the truth so that he has time to confess before he
dies. If, on the other hand, his prayer is for the prolonging of his
life, then this text would be seen as con. Even though God already
gave him the decree that he is going to die, he tries to get God to
reverse the decree by praying that he will live longer.

The underlying values in *Berakhot* 10a will vary according
to which way we read the passage. If praying is interpreted as a
prayer for redemption in the world to come, then redemption and
truth are the primary values which would lead one to telling the
dying patient the truth about his impending death. If, however
praying is interpreted as a prayer for life over death, then the
value of truth is joined by the value of prolonging life.

There is a third text which comprises the last text of this batch, *Ecclesiastes Rabbah* 5:6.1.

> And so is it found with Hezekiah, King of Judah. When Hezekiah was sick, God said to Isaiah, "Go and tell him, 'Set your house in order for you will die and not get well.'" Hezekiah said to Isaiah, "Isaiah, usually when a person is visiting the sick, he says to him, 'May mercy from heaven be upon you.' And the doctor comes to him and says to him, 'This you can eat, and this you cannot eat. Drink this, and do not drink that.' And even when he sees him at the point of death, he does not say to him, 'Set your affairs in order,' that one will not totally upset him. But you say to me, 'Set your affairs in order for you are dying and will not get well.' I pay no attention to what you say, and I will not listen to your advice."[44]

The first part of this midrash quotes the Isaiah passage, and one would think this passage would favor telling the dying person the truth. The second half of the passage, however, changes tone. In *Ecclesiastes Rabbah* 5:6.1, Isaiah is given a new set of instructions when he visits the sick:

> "...usually when a person is visiting the sick, he says to him, 'May mercy from heaven be upon you.' And the doctor comes to him...and even when he sees him at the point of death, he does not say to him, 'Set your affairs in order,' that one will not totally upset him."[45]

The value of autonomy has been over*tur*ned for the sake of comfort. Here are the charts of the last three passages which create a batch based on the text form Isaiah 38:1:

## Isaiah 38:1
| | |
|---|---|
| Redemption | — not considered |
| Truth | — assumed |
| Comfort | — not considered |
| Prolonging life | — not considered |
| Autonomy | — primary value |

## Berakhot 10a
| | |
|---|---|
| Redemption | — primary value if "praying" = a prayer for redemption in the world to come |
| Truth | —primary value if "praying" = a prayer for redemption in the world to come, —joined by prolonging life |

|  |  |
|---|---|
|  | if "praying" = a prayer for life over death |
| Comfort | —not considered |
| Prolonging life | —primary value if "praying" = a prayer for life over death |
| Autonomy | —overturned from Isaiah passage if "praying" = a prayer for redemption in the world to come, —overturned by prolonging life if "praying" = a prayer for life over death, it is a primary value as in Isaiah passage |

### Ecclesiastes Rabbah 5:6

|  |  |
|---|---|
| Redemption | — not considered |
| Truth | — assumed at beginning, refuted at end |
| Comfort | — supersedes truth and autonomy |
| Prolonging life | — not considered |
| Autonomy | — over*turn*ed and ignored |

## Third Batch

The next batch spans quite a large era. The basic text comes form *Moed Katan* 26b from the Babylonian Talmud. The other passage is from Abraham Danzig's *Hokhmat Adam*, which was written in the 1700s. The message in *Moed Katan* is clear.

> Our Rabbis taught: If there is someone close to the sick person who dies, they do not inform him (the sick one) that someone died, perhaps he will go mad. And they do not rend garments in his presence, and they keep the women silent in his presence.[46]

If one were not to tell a sick person of another's death, *kal v'khomer*, one would not tell another of that individual's own impending death. The reason, *"shema titaref daato,"* "lest he go mad," or "become insane."[47] In addition to not telling the patient the truth of this other person's death, others should not display any action which indicates mourning such as renting clothing or crying in this sick person's presence. The primary value considered in this case is that of patient's comfort, specifically his emotional state of mind.

The second passage, from Danzig's *Hokhmat Adam*, extracts the first phrase from *Moed Katan* 26b which does not favor telling a sick person of another's death, lest it drive him mad.

> If there is someone close to the sick person who dies, they do not inform him, lest he go mad. And even if it is made known to him, it is not the custom

for him to tear his garment in mourning, lest it increase his anxiety. Bewailing and lamentation [for the deceased] is not to be done in front of him [the sick person] whether the dead is kin or not, because even if the deceased is not a relative, we are afraid that the sick man too will die. The comforters are to remain silent even if there is no relative who through this [procedure of mourning] is called to mind by the death of the one who had died.[48]

Danzig adds that even in the case where the one who has died is a relative of the sick person, and one might expect to tell the sick person because of this; the truth, nevertheless is withheld from the sick person. As in *Moed Katan* 26b, Danzig heavily weighs the value of patient comfort, specifically emotional comfort. Danzig also includes another reason to withhold the truth, "*shefaḥad shegam hu yamot*," for the fear that the sick person will also die. In this case, his other underlying value is that of prolonging life. While *Moed Katan* 26b values only the patient's emotional comfort, Danzig adds the value of prolonging the patient's life in reaching the decision to withhold the truth from the dying person.

### *Moed Katan* 26b

| | |
|---|---|
| Redemption | — not considered |
| Truth | — avoided |
| Comfort | — primary value in that telling the truth will make the sick person go mad |
| Prolonging life | — not considered |
| Autonomy | — not considered |

### *Ḥokhmat Adam* 151:10

| | |
|---|---|
| Redemption | — not considered |
| Truth | — avoided |
| Comfort | — co-primary value |
| Prolonging life | — co-primary value |
| Autonomy | — not considered |

## Fourth Batch

This batch, the most extensive, contains four sources. In chronological order they are: *Shabbat* 32a from the Babylonian Talmud; the *Tur, Yoreh Deah* section 338; the *Shulḥan Arukh, Yoreh Deah* section 338:1; and Siftei Cohen's commentary on 338:1.

*Shabbat* 32a is our strongest statement in support of telling the truth to a person whose death is imminent.

The Rabbis taught: If one is sick, and at the point of

death (*natah lamut*), one should tell him to confess,
because all who are destined to die are to confess.
When a person goes into the street, he should imagine that he is on trial. When he has a headache, it
should be as if he were in chains. When he climbs
up into bed and goes to sleep, it should be as if he
were ascending a scaffold as punishment. Whoever
ascends a scaffold for punishment will be saved if
he has great advocates; if he does not, he will not be
saved. These are the advocates: repentance and good
deeds...[49]

Without any mention of hope for recovery, this *halakhah* advises one
to urge the patient to confess: "Confess, for all who are destined to
die must say their confession." Upon hearing this, the patient knows
without a doubt that as far as the one telling him this knows, his
death is close at hand. Not only that, this knowledge is supposed to
spur him on to repentance. He is to take commonplace occurrences
such as a headache and imagine they signify something much more
serious that is connected with being judged for his deeds. There is no
mention here of the patient's emotional comfort. There is more of a
concern that if the patient is not anxious enough, he will fail to
repent, or at least fail to repent in time. Thus, the value of ensuring
his redemption overrides the value of emotional comfort. *Shabbat*
32a also does not address the value of prolonging life, which is
addressed elsewhere in the literature. Apparently at all costs, even if
the anxiety of being told death is imminent shortens his life, the
main thing is to make him confess to achieve his redemption. Placing redemption as a value of the highest priority is to say that being
saved for life in the hereafter is more important than any other consideration. All else pales next to redemption.

How do the other values play into this? Autonomy is assumed, in that the patient is now equipped with information that
will allow him to exercise his will – the assumption is that he is a
good Jew who wants to do his duty before it is too late. The one
remaining value, telling the truth, is implicit as well. Here is a case
where it could potentially be suspended in consideration of other
values such as patient comfort but it is not. Telling the truth is
what best promotes ensuring redemption through confession.[50]
Therefore, according to this, our earliest *halakhah*, redemption is
the value which takes precedence. The other values are either
negated (comfort, prolong life) or follow as a natural consequence
(autonomy, telling the truth.)

Reference to *Shabbat* 32a appears in the *Tur*. It refers to it
in the sense that words are repeated from it verbatim in parts,
namely the exhortation to confess and the urgency of doing so as
one imagines commonplace occurrences as reminders of being judged
for one's sins.

One is to direct a sick person at the point of death (*natah lamut*) to confess, as it is the custom of all the doomed to do so. When a person goes into the street, he should imagine he is on trial. When he has a headache, it should be as if he were in chains. When he climbs up into bed and goes to sleep, it should be as if he were ascending a scaffold as punishment. Whoever ascends a scaffold for punishment will be saved if he has great advocates; if he does not, he will not be saved. These are the advocates: repentance and good deeds. In order not to break [the sick person's] heart (*shelo yishbar et libo*), tell him that many confess and do not die, and many who do not confess do die, and many of them [who were told to confess] had been [up and about]in the street. One should confess, because as a reward for your confessing, you [might] live. All who confess have a share in the world to come. If he can confess verbally, he shall do so, and if not, he shall confess silently [in his heart]. One who confessed, whether verbally or silently, does so alone, so that he shall remain cool-minded (*shetehei daato meyushevet alav*).[51] And if he does not know how to confess, they tell him, "Say: my death shall atone for all my sins." And all these things are not said in the presence of the ignorant, nor in the presence of women, nor in the presence of children, lest they cry and break his [the sick person's] heart (*veyishberu et libo*).[52]

So the first two paragraphs give us the same result as *Shabbat* 32a. But now another consideration comes along, the comfort of the dying person. A stratagem is set up whereby an attempt is made to satisfy both values, redemption and comfort. The idea is to get the patient to confess without the negative impact of "breaking his heart." This phrase might means loss of hope or indicate anxiety. It is clear that it means discomfort. The *Tur* mentions two ways of preventing the "breaking of his heart." The first way is to let the sick one know that many have confessed and lived. The second way is to refrain from telling certain people who would get emotional in front of the sick person, causing him discomfort.

Another point the *Tur* mentions which emphasizes the value of comfort is *"shetehei daato meyushevet alav,"* "that he (the sick person) shall remain cool-minded." Compared with *Shabbat* 32a, the value of redemption in the *Tur* is not as strongly in the forefront. It now is tempered in relation to another value, patient comfort. This is also done by mitigating another value, telling the truth. To say to a patient "that many confess and do not die" is at the very least to make the patient's status ambiguous to the patient. If the patient takes this at face value, then at most what he knows is that he might possibly be near death, but not necessarily. So this is a way of hedging the issue – one is not telling the truth, but one is not exactly lying either.

In order to accommodate the value of comfort, the value of redemption had to be balanced against it as opposed to being brought forward at all costs as in *Shabbat* 32a. Also, the value of telling the truth had to give up some ground, from telling it outright to being ambiguous, in order to ensure patient comfort. This, in turn, means some loss of patient autonomy, since he will not have the same opportunity to make decisions such as financial arrangements or settling loose ends with an estranged relative that he would have if he knew for sure what was happening. Finally, since the value of comfort is addressed, then by implication so is prolonging life. If the patient is not upset, this calm may prolong life. To compare the halakhic sources so far, examine the following charts:

**Shabbat 32a**

| | |
|---|---|
| Redemption | — primary value |
| Truth | — telling the truth assumed |
| Comfort | — not considered |
| Prolonging life | — not considered |
| Autonomy | — follows as a na*tur*al consequence of telling the truth |

**Tur**

| | |
|---|---|
| Redemption | — a very important value |
| Comfort | — almost as important as redemption |
| Truth | — compromised in order to ensure comfort |
| Prolonging life | — follows as a na*tur*al consequence of ensuring comfort, and is also aided by more ambiguous position on telling the truth |
| Autonomy | — somewhat less, as patient is not clearly told the truth |

Let us now see what happens to the five values in *Shulḥan Arukh Yoreh Deah* 338:1.

> When one is at the point of death (*natah lamut*), one should be advised to say the confession. He should be told, "many have confessed and not died, and many who have not confessed have died. And on account of your confessing, you might therefore live. All who confess have a share in the world to come."

And if he is unable to confess verbally, he shall confess silently (in his heart). All these things are not
said in the presence of the ignorant, nor in the presence of women, nor in the presence of children, lest
they cry and break his [the sick one's] heart (*veyishberu libo*).[53]

The *Shulḥan Arukh* repeats the admonition to confess as
well as the stratagem to not upset the patient with the truth. But
this time, the text dropped the details of the sick person's judgment
for the world to come and the specifics of atoning for one's sins. This
may be a way of placing redemption slightly in the background when
compared with the *Tur*. In the *Tur*, the concern with comfort is balanced by the redemptive language about the trial, chains and scaffold. Interestingly, the *Shulḥan Arukh* passage has also dropped
the concept of cool-mindedness which relates to comfort. With this
one phrase the *Shulḥan Arukh* seems to be holding back its value of
comfort, yet the text has more strongly given up its value of redemption.

The other values remain the same as in the *Tur*: autonomy
is compromised by not having the unambiguous truth, and prolonging life is aided by taking comfort into account. Telling the truth
has the same ambiguous status. In comparison with the *Tur*, we
have the following chart:

### *Shulḥan Arukh* 338:1

| | |
|---|---|
| Redemption | — important, but less force fully urged |
| Comfort | — slightly withdrawn as compared to the *Tur*, but given a stronger emphasis than redemption |
| Truth | — same ambiguous status as in the *Tur* |
| Autonomy | — same as in the *Tur*; com- promised by ambiguous truth value |
| Prolonging life | — same as *Tur*; aided by importance of comfort value |

The last source in our halakhic chronological batch is the
*Siftei Kohen's* commentary on 338:1.

"People advise him to confess because the custom of
all the doomed is to recite the confession." On the
*Tur* and *Shabbat* 32a passage, the BaH[54] writes:
"and its meaning applies specifically to one who is at
the point of death (*natah lamut*), but regarding one

who is not at the point of death, he is not told to confess, so as not to break his heart (*shelo yehei nishbar libo*)."

And even when he is told, "many sick [have now returned to] the street who had confessed," in general, when a person is told, "confess, for it is the custom of all who are doomed to confess," he knows he is in great danger. Otherwise, he would not have been reminded of his impending death and his heart will be broken (*veyihiyeh nishbar libo*). Therefore, one is not told to confess except if he is actually about to die.

It seems from his words [the BaḤ's], that he is told to confess, because it is the custom of all who are doomed to die to confess. To this effect one is only told to do as such if he is actually about to die...

And anyway, it seems for the one who is at the point of death they tell him to confess, otherwise he will think that he is in danger and this will break his heart (*veyishbar libo*). Or, if one is not at the point of death, he is not told as such, that behold he still has time when that he is able confess. But when one is at the point of death, one should sense that he will die suddenly without a confession.[55]

Here, the concern for comfort is heightened even more. He questions the effectiveness of the stratagem of telling the patient that both the non-dying and the dying are given the same advice. The implication is, whatever the good intention might be, the patient is being reminded of the possibility of death. Furthermore, he might have a reaction like, "Who are you trying to kid? If you are mentioning confession to me, you are talking about dying; I see through this ruse." *Siftei Kohen* asks the person who directs the patient to confess not to bring it up unless the person is actually about to die. This stratagem postpones telling the patient almost until the last possible moment. So now the values of redemption and comfort are more on a par with each other. Since comfort is now a more prominent value, prolonging life now assumes more importance as well.

Interestingly, in one way, telling the truth becomes a greater value and in another way a far lesser value. Since bringing up confession is the same as saying death is imminent and is therefore not ambiguous after all, then whoever is bringing up the subject of confession is telling the truth. But since this truth comes only if the patient is near the actual moment of dying, the issues involved such as comfort and prolonging life and autonomy scarcely apply. By putting off telling the truth so long, this amounts to dodging the other concerns that make truth-telling an ethical issue in the first place! The chart of values for *Siftei Kohen* compared to the *Shulḥan Arukh* looks like this:

**Siftei Kohen**

| | |
|---|---|
| Redemption | — more or less on a par with comfort |
| Comfort | — has become more important, since it is operative until nearly the last possible moment |
| Truth | — largely displaced by the value of comfort; since the patient is not told until the last moment, it is too late to be an issue; essentially, the patient is not told the truth |
| Autonomy | — somewhat displaced too, except at the last moment, where the patient does have the choice to ensure redemption through confession |
| Prolonging life | — like comfort, is even more in the foreground because the anxiety-provoking truth is withheld the longest possible time |

There is a progression in this chronological batch from valuing redemption and truth telling over comfort, to valuing comfort much more, redemption somewhat less, and truth-telling very little. In terms of our case, to tell or not to tell the seventy-five-year-old of her impending death, we move from telling her straight out with exhortations to repent (*Shabbat* 32a), to hedging and being ambiguous about the truth (*Tur* and *Shulḥan Arukh*) to not telling her the truth, unless they know she is actually going to die, which could be at almost the last possible moment. At this point then, telling or not practically ceases to be an ethical issue (*Siftei Kohen*).

## Fifth Example

There is one more *halakhah* that remains to be discussed, but it stands alone. It does not belong to a chronological batch, at least as far as our data go. This is our other excerpt from *Shulḥan Arukh*, *Yoreh Deah*, section 335:7.

One is to tell (the sick) that he is to attend to his affairs, whether he lent something or deposited it under someone else's care, or whether others lent him something or deposited something in his care. Because of this he should not fear death.[56]

Partly because we see it in the *Shulḥan Arukh* in isolation, and partly because the language is terse, it is hard to interpret in terms of whether it implies one should tell the truth or not. It does say to tell the sick person to tidy up his financial responsibilities, which could mean that he will pick up the implication that death is near. The puzzling sentence is the last: "Because of this he should not fear death." This carries at least 3 implications: (1) he will not be so upset as we think if told about his condition in this indirect way; (2) he will be at peace knowing his affairs will be in order, and so will not be afraid of death; and (3) he should not conclude from this type of talk that this means he will die.

The first two implications would fall on the side of telling the truth. The first addresses the comfort value, and the second the autonomy value of giving one control over one's affairs. But the third implication suggests that the sick one will remain in the dark yet get done what needs to be done. This is like the idea behind telling the patient that not all who confess will die; two benefits are achieved at once: getting the confession/getting the financial affairs done and retaining patient comfort. Since 335:7 is ambiguous, we must leave it and not draw any conclusions from it one way or the other.

# Conclusions

**Amy Memis**: In this paper, we pictured the following case, where a congregant came to the Rabbi and asks, "Rabbi, should my seventy-five year old mother be told that she has two weeks to live?" As this person's rabbi (let's say this person is female) I would tell her yes, your mother should be told. But I would not answer her without giving her reasons. My reasons for telling her yes are based most strongly on the values of truth, autonomy, comfort and redemption.

It is a general ethical value that it is a patient's right to know the truth. While the halakhic material did not overtly express a Kantian perspective of "tell the truth regardless of the consequences," truth acts as a "larger-than-life" value in Judaism. It is Jewish to tell the truth, and lying in most cases is a sin, though there are exceptions in tradition where one might tell an ugly bride she is beautiful. This example, however, is not a case of life and death, where the case of our congregant's mother is.

The value of autonomy, allowing a patient to tie up loose ends, is found both in the general ethics and the *halakhah*. This includes wills, family reconciliation, business affairs, spiritual preparation, etc. When we tell our congregant that yes, her mother should be told the truth of her impending death, we consider that her mother has a right as a patient to take control of her affairs and should know that she is dying so she can attend to them.

The third value, comfort, is probably the one to which our congregant will be most sensitive. Our congregant might be concerned that her mother's emotional state will be upset if she is told. If we were to look at the halakhic material, we would find several that agree with this sentiment. I might offer my congregant an alternative perspective based on the value of comfort. Perhaps her mother's mind will be put to ease if she does hear the truth, and as long as the truth is withheld from her, she might be filled with anxiety. If I were a patient, I believe I would feel this way.

The last value, redemption, is found only in the *halakhah*, and is not mentioned in the general ethics. Related to the mystery of God is the mystery of death and what happens to us after we die. Should our congregant's mother be told that she is going to die so that she will have time to confess and therefore be redeemed in the world to come? (*Shabbat* 32a, *Tur* 338, *Shulḥan Arukh* 338:1). As a rabbi, I would have to be honest in that I do not know if I believe in such a thing as redemption. But if I were using the *halakhah* that included saying confession, I would substitute "peace of mind" as a modern value which we could understand relates to confession and redemption. Our congregant's mother should be told she is going to die, not necessarily so that she should confess, rather so that she can have peace of mind, perhaps in her relationship with God, at the last moments of her life.

**Karen Bookman Kaplan**: Another way to translate "redemption" into modern sensibilities is to use the phrase "spiritual preparation." We do not know what happens after we die. But the spiritual state in which we find ourselves after our life's journey may somehow affect what happens in the hereafter, if there is one. Part of our autonomy, in a religious sense, involves working on our relationship with God, even during the last weeks of life. To deny a person their last spiritual phase through obfuscating the truth about their condition does more harm than the supposed increase in patient discomfort. After all, much of the later *halakhah* ended up discouraging us from telling the truth because of this concern for comfort. It is hard to know whether, when my time comes, the truth will "break my heart." Maybe I will be anxious or lose all hope and sense of meaning. My rejoinder to this argument is that lack of clear communication will make me feel more anxious and/ or depressed. Having everything up front, and thereby having as much control (autonomy) as possible over decision making and spiritual preparation, is to me the ultimate comfort. With *Siftei Kohen*, I agree with his opinion that the patient will see through ruses. With the general ethicists, I agree that for example between a doctor and patient, not telling the truth will strain their relationship and deny the patient full personhood. A phony atmosphere will result.

## On This Process

In terms of *halakhah* versus general ethics, the question before us is, How do we claim that the answer with which we concluded is a Jewish response? We have taken values introduced by the *halakhah* and weighed their relative importance to each other. As individuals living in a modern society, we give greater weight to autonomy, which looms large in our final decision to tell the truth. Another strategy we have used is to address aspects of a value not considered in the *halakhah*; we took comfort and *turn*ed it into a motive on behalf of telling rather than as a motive for not telling. Finally, we took a value, redemption, that seemed obsolete and reinterpreted it along lines meaningful to a modern Jew. In conclusion, we made a Jewish-based decision by confining ourselves to halakhic values, but we allowed ourselves to assign different weights to them, or add new aspects to them, or to "translate" them into modern terms.

# Bibliography

### General Ethics

Abraham, Abraham S. *Medical Halakhah for Everyone*. New York: Feldheim Publishers, 1979.

_____. *The Comprehensive Guide to Medical Halacha*. New York: Feldheim Publishers, 1990.

Alcalay, Reuben. *The Complete Hebrew-English Dictionary*. Tel Aviv/ Jerusalem: Massadah Pub., 1965.

Bleich, J. David. *Judaism and Healing*. Hoboken, N.J.: KTAV Publishing House, 1981.

Block, Richard A. "A Matter of Life and Death: Reform Judaism and the Defective Child." *CCAR Journal of Reform Judaism*, vol. 31, No. 4, Fall 1984.

Bok, Sissela. *Lying: Moral Choice in Public and Private Life*. New York: Pantheon Books, a Division of Random House, 1978.

Bokser, Ben Zion. "Problems in Bio-Medical Ethics: A Jewish Perspective." *Judaism*, Vol. 24, No. 12, Spring 1985.

Brody, Baruch A., and H. Tristram Englehardt, Jr. *Bioethics: Readings and Cases*. Prentice-Hall, 1987.

Cherkis, M.S., and P. Stinson. "Living and Dying." *Present Tense,* Vol. 11, Fall 1983.

*Encyclopedia Judaica.* Jerusalem: Keter Pub. 1972.

*Entziklopediah Talmudit. Jerusalem*: Talmudic Encyclopedia Pub. 1984.

Freehof, Solomon, B. "The Hospice." In *New Reform Responsa.* Cincinnati: Hebrew Union College Press, 1980, pp. 67-71.

*The Hastings Center's Bibliography of Ethics, Biomedicine, and Professional Responsibility.* Frederick, Maryland. University Publications of America in association with the Hastings Center, 1984.

Jakobovits, Immanuel. *Jewish Medical Ethics: A Comparative and Historical Study of the Jewish Religious Attitude to Medicine and Its Practice.* New York: Bloch Publishing Co., 1975.

Kubler-Ross, Elizabeth. *On Death and Dying.* New York: Collier Books, MacMillan Publishing Company, 1969.

Pollak, G. "Ethical Considerations in the Care of the Dying Elderly Patient." *Journal of Jewish Communal Service.* Vol. 43, Winter 1966.

Schimmel, S. "The Terminal Patient's Right to Know." *Journal of Jewish Communal Service.* Vol. 63, Winter 1986.

Silverman, William B. "'Remember Us Unto Death': The Rabbi Confronts Agonizing Dilemmas." *CCAR Journal,* Vol. 21, No. 2, Spring, 1974.

Steinsaltz, Adin. *Madrikh L'Talmud (Guide to the Talmud).* Jerusalem: Beit Hotsei Keter, 1984.

_____. *The Talmud: A Reference Guide.* New York: Random House, 1989.

Veatch, Robert M. Death, *Dying, and the Biological Revolution.* New Haven: Yale University Press, 1989.

Weir, Robert F., Ed. *Ethical Issues in Death and Dying.* 2nd ed. New York: Columbia University Press, 1986.

## Traditional Sources

*II Kings* 8:10

Isaiah 38:1 *Berakhot* 10a, Babylonian Talmud

*Shabbat* 32a, Babylonian Talmud

*Moed Katan*, Babylonian Talmud

*Ecclesiastes Rabbah* 5:6; 7-10th century

*Tur Yoreh Deah* 338; 14th century
Gersonides on II Kings 8:10; 14th century

*Shulḥan Arukh Yoreh Deah* 338:1 and 335:7; 16th century

*Siftei Kohen* on *Shulḥan Arukh* 338:1; 17th century

Abraham Danzig, *Ḥokhmat Adam* (18th C.) Title: Laws of Mourning - Subtitle: Laws of Visiting the Sick, Healing, and Those Soon to Die.

# Notes

1. S. Schimmel, "The Terminal Patient's Right to Know," *Journal of Jewish Communal Service,* vol. 63, (Winter 1986), p. 132. (Hereinafter Schimmel)

2. Ibid., p. 133.

3. Sissela Bok, *Lying: Moral Choice in Public and Private Life,* (New York: Pantheon Books, a Division of Random House, 1978), p. 76. (Hereinafter Bok)

4. William B. Silverman, "'Remember Us Unto Death': The Rabbi Confronts Agonizing Dilemmas," *CCAR Journal,* vol. 21, no. 2, (Spring 1974), p. 55; (Hereinafter Silverman). Robert M. Veatch, *Death, Dying, and the Biological Revolution,* (New Haven: Yale University Press, 1989), pp. 177ff. (Hereinafter Veatch)

5. Schimmel, p. 138.

6. Baruch A. Brody, and H. Tristram Englehardt, Jr., *Bioethics: Readings and Cases.* (Prentice-Hall, 1987), p. 347.

7. Bok, p. 75.

8. Ibid., p. 75.

9. Ibid., p. 75.

10. Veatch, p. 169.

11. Bok, p. 75.

12. Veatch, p. 150; Schimmel, p. 134.

13. Brody, p. 349.

14. Bok, p. 79.

15. Schimmel, p. 134.

16. Ibid., p. 134.

17. Bok, p. 75; Veatch, pp. 167-8.

18. Ibid., p. 78.

19. Ibid., pp. 78-79.

20. Veatch, p. 169.

21. Ibid., p. 181.

22. Ibid., p. 169.

23. Ibid., p. 179.

24. Bok, p. 78.

25. Schimmel, p. 136.

26. Elizabeth Kubler-Ross, *On Death and Dying*. New York: Collier Books, MacMillan Publishing Company, 1969., p. 36.

27. Veatch, p. 172.

28. Bok, p. 77.

29. Veatch, p. 172.

30. Ibid., p. 172.

31. Schimmel, p. 136.

32. Ibid., p. 132.

33. Veatch, pp. 183-84.

34. Ibid., p. 184.

35. Schimmel, p. 134.

36. Ibid., p. 133.

37. Veatch, p. 189.

38. II Kings 8:10

39. Gersonides on II Kings 8:10

40. J. David Bleich, *Judaism and Healing,* (Hoboken, N.J.: KTAV Publishing House), 1981, p. 29.

41. Isaiah 38:1

42. Autonomy as defined in the General Ethics section includes preparing wills, family reconciliation, religious or spiritual preparation, and tying up business affairs, as much as they are applicable to the halakhic and other texts. In the Biblical world this notion probably took the form of respect for persons and for their duties.

43. Babylonian Talmud *Berakhot* 10a

44. *Ecclesiastes Rabbah* 5:6.1

45. *Ecclesiastes Rabbah* 5:6.1

46. Babylonian Talmud *Moed Katan* 26b

47. Reuben Alcalay, *The Complete Hebrew-English Dictionary,* (Tel Aviv/Jerusalem: Massadah Pub.), 1965, p. 893.

48. Abraham Danzig, *Ḥokhmat Adam*: Laws of Mourning – Subtitle: Laws of Visiting the Sick, Healing, and Those Soon to Die, 151:10

49. Babylonian Talmud *Shabbat* 32a

50. One wonders that if lying turned out to be the best way to ensure confession, then perhaps the *halakhah* would have advocated not telling the truth.

51. Alcalay, p. 455.

52. *Tur Yoreh Deah* 338

53. *Shulḥan Arukh Yoreh Deah* 338:1

54. *Bayit Ḥadash*, a commentary to the *Tur*.

55. *Siftei Cohen*, commentator on the *Shulḥan Arukh*

56. *Shulḥan Arukh Yoreh Deah* 335:7

# The Challenge
# of the
# Persistent Vegetative State

Deborah Joselow
and Ariel Stone

**H**er name is Nancy Cruzan. If you were to walk into her hospital room, you would think she was asleep. She lies in the bed, her body curled in a near fetal position. There are no machines nor any frightening noises. The only sign of illness is a single tube which disappears discreetly beneath the blanket and whose one visible end is attached to a bottle labeled "FlexiFlo" suspended near the head of the bed.

Only after a closer look might you begin to question the tranquility of this scene. Nancy's eyes open frequently but they are blank and unseeing. Her hands are curled into fists and napkins are wedged inside them to prevent the nails from piercing the skin of her wrists. There is a peculiar rigidity to her limbs and muscles. She emits small sounds and occasionally her body moves as if reacting to the sterile world around her. If you were to follow the tube beneath the blanket you would find it implanted into her stomach. For seven years nothing has changed in this room. For seven years Nancy Cruzan has been lying in this bed minus the capacity to speak or think or feel or act. Nancy Cruzan has been diagnosed as being in a Persistent Vegetative State (PVS).

Only 25 years old when the accident which left her in this condition occurred, Nancy Cruzan had not given any specific instructions about her desires to have her life sustained or terminated should such a decision be required. Her friends and family remember passing comments, reactions she had to such well publicized cases as Karen Ann Quinlan, but there was never anything definite and certainly nothing in writing. For seven years her loved ones have hoped for a miracle. Now they want to let her die by disconnecting the tube which provides her with her only source of food and hydration.

The central dilemma of this paper is the ethicality of removing the naso-gastric feeding tube from this patient's stomach without a clear statement of her wishes. Our survey and conclusion are both specifically informed by our search for a Jewish answer to this situation. This paper consists of several parts. The first section is a review of the ethical literature pertaining to this case. The second section covers the pertanent halakhic material. The concluding pages are our attempt to reflect between the two "sides" and to advise the Cruzan family as Reform Rabbis.

## The Ethical Debate

A review of the ethics of removing food and water from a PVS diagnosed patient takes a certain amount of courage and mental fortitude. Long term health care for the hopelessly ill is in itself a "dangerous" topic because it involves decisions between life and death bringing human beings perilously close to a role which has always been relegated to the realm of God. Combined here with the dilemma of feeding and hydration the issue of the PVS patient becomes nearly explosive.

Although each case varies by degrees, the typical PVS patient retains many bodily functions which technically qualify the patient as living. The PVS label denotes the destruction of the cerebral cortex. A PVS patient is therefore physiologically incapable of all mental or cognitive functions. A PVS patient does not feel or think. Brain stem activity, such as reflexes and respiration, which when lost is the medical, technical basis for declaring a patient "brain dead," is, in a PVS patient, regular. Unlike some in comas, a PVS patient breathes independently. A PVS patient has an expected lifespan of thirty years beyond the date of diagnosis, depending upon age and general health at the time of the accident.

PVS patients do not recover. Their condition is considered permanent given all current medical experience and technology. As the report of the President's Commission for the Study of Ethical Problems in Medicine states "No return to an even minimal level of social or human functioning is possible. Disability is total."[1] After diagnosis, all clinical procedures have exclusively to do with maintenance of the patient's personal hygiene and nutrition. No measures are taken which are considered curative.

Those who argue for the ethicality of discontinuing food and water to a PVS patient fall into two categories. The first group adopts what might be called a "utilitarian position" and argues for stopping feeding and hydration based upon a prioritization of the social over the personal. By focusing on the public consequences of maintaining a regular program of nutrition for PVS patients, the utilitarian "school" shifts the debate from the patient to the community.

It is estimated that currently there are between five and ten thousand patients in the United States who are classified as PVS. It can be expected that this number will only increase as methods of accurate diagnosis are perfected and made more widely available. Although the cost of medical care varies from state to state, the medical bills for a single PVS patient range from eighteen to twenty thousand dollars a year. The total annual national health bill for PVS patients alone is estimated at between 120 million to 1.2 billion dollars a year.[2] In the Editorial Notebook of *The New York Times* the following comment was recorded as a reaction to Daniel Callahan's book, *What Kind of Life*: "How to spend finite funds on what seems as infinity of ills is what 'What Kind of Life' is about. How long can society afford to postpone the inevitable? One says society because, as the author points out, it is government that often pays for the extraordinary interventions that have become commonplace."[3]

# The Utilitarian Case: For Cessation

Those ethicists whom we have classified as utilitarian contend that the treatment of PVS patients is continued at an enormous cost to society. They state that the time has come for making a choice: the same money that is spent to keep patients alive with no hope of recovery, could be allocated to a variety of projects with greater social benefits. The President's Commission in its report on the care of PVS patients summarizes the dilemma in the following way:

> Measured against virtually any benefit/cost or cost/effectiveness standard, the case for allocating public funds for extended care of (PVS) patients is weak. This especially in a period of concern with the rapidly rising cost of health care and of cutbacks in public expenditures for a wide variety of more beneficial care. We endorse the government's responsibility to provide or fund health care for those unable to do so for themselves. We do not question this general responsibility, but only whether it extends to care of (PVS) patients."[4]

An actualization of this utilitarian position can be seen in the recent decision of the Oregon State legislature to ration health care so that the maximum number of people may be serviced by a limited amount of funds. The basis of this action was the recognition that "health care is already being rationed in this country – in inequitable, haphazard ways, mostly by ability to pay."[5] In describing the Oregon decision *Time* magazine reporters write: "After months of debate, state officials let a computer rank 1,600 medical procedures according to costs, benefits and patient's "quality of well-being. Last week they unveiled the first rough rankings... For the first time in American Public policy, somebody has looked reality in the face and said 'How do we buy the most health care for the those who can't afford it.'"[6] Put succinctly, "Economists are calculating a sort of social triage: at a time when infant mortality is scandalously high and public health care a shambles, does it make sense for taxpayers to spend tens of thousands of dollars a year to keep unconscious patients alive?"[7]

The social implications of continuing treatment to PVS patients must be recognized as a legitimate and worthy ethical case. The content of the utilitarian argument is not exclusively monetary. There is a strong human dimensions to this rationale. Put bluntly, the shortage of hospital beds leads to the possibility that a (PVS) patient who is designated for total physiological care for the indefinite future will be the direct cause of denial of access to such equipment for another patient who may actually have a chance to live and who will die because access was not available.

There are certain values cloaked in the figures of the preceding paragraphs that go beyond the numbers. Those who argue that nutrition to a PVS patient should be discontinued because of a social imperative are making certain "quality of life" judgments that many find repugnant. By advocating the removal of food and water they have defined life in such a way as to either completely exclude the PVS patient or to rule that the condition constitutes a form of life that is not worthy of preservation. For some of the utilitarian persuasion the PVS patient is "dead." For others these patients are alive but so minimally that only a medical technicality keeps them within the parameters of life.

There is no dilemma about refusing to feed a dead person. However, there is also no debate that according to the current medical definition the PVS patient is alive. Some may argue that the definition of "death" used in the medical community is faulty and should be revised based on the "new" medical reality of the PVS patient but that change is not yet actual and so has no bearing upon the ethical question being considered. Utilitarians argue their position by defining "life" from a social rather than medical perspective. Dr. John Swomley in his defense of the removal of feeding tubes states that in the case of the PVS patient "there is no relationship to what is normally associated with life ... In short, she is unable to express personhood as other humans do."[8] For him "living" depends upon a person's ability to "meaningfully interact with her environment."[9] A PVS patient cannot and does not meet these standards. Feeding is therefore not a medical or communal imperative. Dr. Swomley and others place the PVS patient in a separate category of life which allows them to recommend policies which would otherwise be morally and ethically untenable.

Somewhere between dead and alive are advocates of the category of dying. They insist that a PVS patient is in fact dying and so food and hydration would qualify as excessive and useless treatment. In the field of medicine a distinction is made between ordinary and extraordinary measures. The difference in how a procedure is categorized is not merely semantic. As a report from the University of Minnesota Center for Biomedical Ethics explains "the critical distinction has been that ordinary care is obligatory and extraordinary care is optional."[10] What is extraordinary is determined by asking if the care is *useless*, that is without the power to cure even the smallest symptoms of the illness.

Since the PVS patient cannot be cured by any means the utilitarians claim that feeding does qualify as a useless form of treatment. Some opponents insist that feeding does not however, qualify as a medical treatment, this position will be covered in a later section. The utilitarian response to opponents is to underscore the artificiality of the naso-gastric tube which places it in the realm of technology rather then nature. They declare that medical treatments share common characteristics: most basically they are all "prescribed by physicians and administered by health care professionals."[11] Furthermore, the naso-gastric tube in the PVS patient does not aim to quench thirst or satisfy hunger – two essential reasons for feeding – since the patient has lost both of these sentient abilities. For a utilitarian, because a tube cannot be medical or physiologically justified it is, in this instance, morally indefensible.

"The ordinary/extraordinary distinction, however, has been increasingly criticized as unclear and unhelpful."[12] Some thinkers suggest that "measuring" the burdens against the benefits of the procedure is "more morally relevant"[13] because it includes the elements of the case that are less easily quantified, the human elements, such as pain and suffering. The utilitarians find that this second equation, with its visceral components, supports their position as well.

Certainly "burden" cannot be considered as a physical category when discussing the treatment of a PVS patient. Since the patient cannot feel pain she does not suffer from the placement of the naso-gastric tube in her stomach. However, the emotional burden to the patients family must be considered as a burden of the equal order of physical pain. For seven years they have watched a loved one lying unresponsive in her bed. As one mother stated "it took a long time to accept she wasn't getting any better."[14] While the family of a PVS patient may not be paying for or experiencing the physical pain of the treatment procedures, they are suffering. Although their anguish cannot be quantified it must be considered because it is a present and real component of the patient's world. Given that there is no medical benefit to the PVS patient and no emotional benefit to her or her family derived from the feeding procedure, according to the utilitarians, nothing mitigates the burden of the situation. Feeding is, therefore, morally optional.

Utilitarians are aware that their most ardent opponents are those who argue that quality of life must not be a consideration in any case. They answer the opposition by citing such diverse pieces of American culture as capital punishment and slavery. To utilitarians our country has an established legal and social history of evaluating lives differently. As John Swomley states "The phrase 'sanctity of life' is an unfortunate myth that has little basis in reality. Although the state speaks about sacredness of life, it always holds some lives more sacred than others"[15]

# The Deontological Case: For Continued Maintenance

Those who argue for continuing to feed and hydrate the PVS patient can be classified as maintaining the "deontological" position. They stand in direct opposition to the utilitarians, answering the same questions with radically different presumptions and conclusions.

This group of thinkers begins with the assumption that life in all its forms is sacred. They would argue that the responsibility of both the state and the individual is to guard and preserve life without consideration of the social worthiness of the patient. As Gilbert Meileander writes " To be a human being one need not be exercising or capable of exercising the functions characteristic of consciousness. Those are capacities of human nature: they are not functions that all human beings can exercise."[16] In insisting on feeding, the principle that is being defended is an obligation that is felt to exist between human beings by virtue of being human. The giving of food and water is merely a subcategory of the larger issue of human moral responsibility. As Daniel Callahan, Director of the Hastings Center, explains in an early article on this issue, "Feeding of the hungry, whether because they are poor or because they are physically unable to feed themselves, is the most fundamental of all human relationships. It is the perfect symbol of the fact that human life is inescapably social and communal. We cannot live at all unless others are prepared to give us food and water when we need them. If the duty of parents toward infants provides a perfect example of inescapable moral obligation, the giving of nourishment is its first and most basic manifestation."[17] Callahan does not categorize feeding as medical care. While it may be the PVS patient's only form of treatment, it is so basic as to be ordinary.

In the case of this PVS patient, although she retains the ability to swallow and digest, she could not eat unless someone was willing to spoon food and pour liquid into her mouth. From the deontological perspective, the naso-gastric tube is simply an easier and more efficient way of insuring that the patient gets the proper nutrition and water at appropriate intervals. Although some argue that the tube is invasive from this ethical perspective it is critical to her life and therefore necessary and beneficial in the most ultimate of ways. Moreover since the tube is already in place and since the patient cannot feel pain there is nothing at all burdensome about this nutrition system. As Gilbert Meileander writes "When we stop feeding the (PVS) patient, we are not withdrawing from the battle against illness or disease; we are withholding the nourishment that sustains all life."[18] No human, no matter the condition, can survive without food and water. Withdrawal of the naso-gastric tube has important social as well as individual consequences. If such a measure were allowed, from the deontological position certain atrocities could become legitimate options. As Patrick Derr explains, "...modern Western societies can, and in our lifetime have, attempted to rid themselves of retarded, psychotic, senile, handicapped, and racially "undesirable" citizens by a systematic denial of food and fluids. ...The potential abusive consequences of a decision to permit the denial of food and fluids are incommensurably ... terrible... ."[19] One only needs to look backward fifty years to find the Holocaust as evidence of this kind of agenda.

The argument that the burden of the parents must be considered in the withdrawal of the tube is in this case unacceptable in that the determination of the medical treatment must be based solely upon the patient's condition not the condition of those around her.

According to advocates of the deontological position, removing the feeding tube is equivalent to murder since this action is done with the intent to kill. Medical experts may argue that the patient has no capacity to feel and so will not suffer, but there is no dispute that she will indeed die and the cause of death will be starvation and dehydration. Despite the absence of malice, to the deontologists no form of murder is praiseworthy even if the motives can be defended.

"Quality of life" is not a category which this group of thinkers applies. Based upon the medical evidence it is clear to them that the PVS patient is not dead or dying. She is, according to the current medical definition, alive and though her life may be "nothing" when compared to our own this does not legitimize her death. Gilbert Meileander explains that although the PVS patient is "neither dead or dying, her life is the sort no one would choose if given more normal possibilities. To see this, however, is to see the true nature of the choice to withdraw nutrition. In doing so we aim at no death-prolonging treatment; rather we aim at a life though to be of little or no worth. ...But it should be clear that in doing so we are not simply rejecting a treatment as useless or inadequate – but a life as unworthy."[20]

The deontological position does not ignore the trauma of the family. They simply refuse to vest them with unlimited authority for what is literally a life decision. Although this may seem presumptuous it is a position based on the understanding of the complexity of such a decision. Not only does the deontological position seek to protect the patient but the family of the patient as well. As Ira Ellman explains,

> Family members are often subject to pressures that conflict with the patient's interests. These pressures are not only financial. Prolonging the dying process may also prevent them from bringing their mourning to closure and extend their daily exposure to a close relative ravaged by disease. Meeting the patient's continued financial and emotional needs may impair the relatives' ability to meet their obligations to other family members, including their own children. Alternatively, family members are sometimes less able to accept the oncoming death than the patient, and may urge difficult or pointless treatment that the patient may not want. In short, the family's intimate involvement is at once both a powerful reason they are entitled to be heard and a powerful reason they may not be motivated solely by the patient's best interests.[21]

## The Libertarian Case: Deciding When No Clear Choice Has Been Made

The second group which defends the ethicality of withholding nutrition and hydration from PVS patients might well include the patient's parents. These thinkers assume what is called the "libertarian" position. What is most critical about their perspective is not how they answer the question of removing the naso-gastric tube. Rather they primarily concern themselves with resolving the dilemma of who has the right to make the decision for the PVS patient who has left no clear instructions.

The PVS patient is clearly incompetent to make decisions regarding her own treatment. The parties who claim competing rights as her surrogate are her parents, her doctors, and the state. For the libertarian, the state's argument, whether it be from the deontological or utilitarian perspectives, has no validity since the decision to remove the naso-gastric tube is a completely private matter into which the state cannot intrude. While understanding that the doctors have a moral obligation to the patient, they too, from a libertarian perspective, cannot impose their professional obligations on the moral decisions of the individual. As Giles Scofield, president of The Concern for Dying explains, "we seek guidance from the individuals' community and turn last to the state because the state should be least involved in defining individual values."[22] Where ethics compete, according to the libertarians, the individual ethic must always win. The ethical issues that the removal of the gastric tube generates are the exclusive territory of the individual.

If the libertarians were lawyers, they would argue their case as the patient's right to privacy. The Constitution of the United States maintains both the right of the individual and the right of the state. Libertarians are not denying the needs of the republic for some sort of communal morality. Rather they insist that any decision in the case of an incompetent patient be made on the basis of "substituted judgement and best interests analysis."[23] Undeniably the PVS patient cannot transfer her constitutional right to self-determination to another person but, the libertarians argue, the determination of her wishes should be the exclusive domain of the people that know her and love her best. As Richard McCormick, Professor of Ethics at Notre Dame, puts this argument "There are two good reasons for arguing this: First the family is normally in the best position to judge the real interests of the incompetent patient. The family knows those treatments that might be particularly disturbing and those that the patient may have accepted without distress in the past. Second, and more importantly, our society places great value on the family. The family is a basic moral community affirmed not only to have rights but responsibilities in determining how best to serve the interests of its incompetent members."[24]

## Epilogue

On June 25, 1990, the Supreme Court ruled against the Cruzan's petition to allow their daughter Nancy to be disconnected from her naso-gastric feeding tube. In a 5 to 4 ruling the majority of the justices endorsed a person's right to die but "regretfully" rejected their plea to set their daughter free because there was not enough clear evidence of Nancy Cruzan's express wishes. In the fall, the state of Missouri withdrew any objections to the family's wishes and, after some further litigation, the tube was withdrawn. Nancy Cruzan died December 26, 1990.

## Review of Halakhic Literature

The halakhic concept which occupies a central place in the contemporary Jewish consideration of euthanasia is *gesisah*, the period immediately preceding death. According to the classical definition offered by the Talmud and codes, a *goses* is one who will die within seventy two hours.[25] Talmudic stories dealing with *gesisah* demonstrate a sensitivity to the moral issues implied by intervention in the death process; they delineate a difference between acts of commission, "causing death," as opposed to those of omission, "allowing death to occur", on the part of anyone who is attending a *goses*, a dying patient.

Two early stories of death and intervention appear in the form of *aggadah*, not *halakhah*. This distinction is significant because, while *aggadah* does inform halakhic attitudes, it does not imply legal obligation. *Ketubot* 104a, which relates the death of Rabbi Judah HaNasi (from a painful intestinal disorder), indicates support for the actions of those who would seek to alleviate the pain of the irrevocably dying patient by shortening the dying process.

On the day of Rabbi [Judah HaNasi]'s death, the rabbis decreed a public fast, and prayed unceasingly all day; they proclaimed that whoever came to them and said that Rabbi had died would be run through by a sword. Rabbi's maidservant ascended to the roof, saying: "Those who are above seek Rabbi's soul, and also those who are below. May it be that those below will triumph over those above." But when she saw how many times he would go to the bathroom, taking his *tefilin* off and redonning them each time, and the pain he suffered, she said: "May it be that those above will triumph over those below." The rabbis had not ceased from praying. She took a pitcher, and threw it down from the roof to the ground. The rabbis momentarily ceased from praying, and Rabbi died.

No protest at the maid's action is recorded in the Talmudic or later commentaries on this passage. *Avodah Zarah* 18a reflects an even stronger sense of support for hastening the dying process for an irrevocably dying person, in the form of a *bat kol*, a voice from heaven. This *aggadah* relates the martyrdom of Rabbi Haninah ben Teradyon, who was sentenced by the Romans to burn at the stake; it illustrates the distinction drawn between shortening life (in this case, by one's own hand), and hastening the process of dying, which becomes the crux of the matter for later responsa:

> They took R. Haninah b. Tradyon and wrapped a Torah scroll around him, and encompassed him with faggots of vine branches, to which they set fire. They brought woolen tufts, soaked them with water, and laid them on his heart, so that his soul should not depart quickly. ...His disciples said to him: "Open your mouth that the fire may penetrate." He replied: "Better is it that He who gave the soul should take it, than that a man should do himself an injury." Then the executioner said to him: "Master, if I increase the flame and remove the woolen tufts from off your

heart, will you bring me to the life of the world-to-come?" "Yes," said Haninah. "Swear it," demanded the executioner. Haninah took the oath. Forthwith the officer increased the flame and removed the woolen tufts from over Haninah's heart, and his soul departed quickly; then the executioner threw himself into the flames. A voice from heaven proclaimed: "R. Haninah and his executioner are destined for the life of the world-to-come."

The earliest halakhic legislation on death and dying is found in the minor tractate *Semahot* 1.1-5. It sets forth the principle that a dying person is *"k'hai l'khol davar"*, considered for legal purposes (such as the issuance of a get, among others) to be "like one who is alive for every purpose." Accordingly, it is prohibited to do anything to the dying person which is done for the dead, to save time, or for any other reason. Unlike the unfortunate woman in William Faulkner's *As I Lay Dying*, under Jewish law no *goses* has to endure hearing the noise of the building of a coffin nearby. The dying person may not be moved or touched until it can be ascertained with certainty that the moment of death has arrived; one who touches the dying person is considered a murderer. The tractate records Rabbi Meir's comparison of the *goses's* life to a flickering candle, which may be put out with the slightest touch. No preparations for the funeral, even those of which the *goses* would be unaware, may be made while the dying person is still alive.

A thousand years later in the *Shulhan Arukh* (*Yoreh Deah* 339.1) Joseph Caro built upon the legal developments to his time. He repeats and expands on the Talmudic list of what may and may not be done with a *goses*, adding the words *"ayn shomtin hakar mitakhtav"*—among others things, "one may not move the pillow under the head" of the dying person. The gloss of Moses Isserles on this passage notes that these things are prohibited even though *"rov gosesin lemitah"*, the majority of those who begin the process of dying do die. He adds to Caro's statement that one may not hasten a dying person's death by such active means as moving him bodily. No form of shortening of life is permitted.

Action taken to shorten the dying process is a different matter. In the same gloss, Isserles quotes from the 13th century work *Sefer Hasidim*:

> if in the vicinity there is something which delays the dying person's death, such as a woodchopper working outside, or salt on the *goses'* tongue, it is permitted to remove these impediments to the soul's departure, for this is not a positive act, but only the removal of the impediment.[26]

In his commentary *Darkhei Moshe* to the *Arbaah Turim*

(*Yoreh Deah* 339), Isserles notes that the phrase *"ayn shomtin hakar mitakhtav"* seems to prohibit a custom which he knows is followed by some communities, in which exactly that is done to help the dying die more quickly. He explains that there is a folk belief that the feathers in pillows can cause an impediment to the dying process, and reports that R. Nathan Ish Agraye accordingly wrote an opinion allowing for this removal of the pillow. He concludes with another quote from the *Sefer Ḥasidim* which says, in part, that "it is prohibited to do that which prevents the dying person from dying quickly ... anything which impedes the dying process may be re-moved. But to do that which will cause death more quickly is prohibited."[27]

The halakhic definition of death is provided in the *gemara* to *Yoma* 65a, in which it is stated that if someone is buried under rubble, he or she must be uncovered, even on Shabbat, and the person's nose must be checked for signs of breathing. In his later summary of the halakhic development, Maimonides explains that one checks for even the faintest evidence of breathing with a feather or piece of thin paper. If there is no sign of breathing, the person is *"badin met,"* legally considered to be dead. This check must be done several times, as Rambam cautions in the *Mishneh Torah* (*Hilkhot Avel* 4.5): "wait a bit, perhaps he is just in a swoon."

The *Shulḥan Arukh* also notes the case of "those who are considered dead even while still alive" (*Yoreh Deah* 377) in its discussion of *Hullin* 21a (from *Ohalot* 1.6). Examples of such a person are:

> one whose neck is broken, and most of his flesh with it; and similarly, if [the flesh] is torn open on his back like a [filleted] fish. Even if he is still alive, he is considered as a dead person, and [contact with him] causes impurity. In contrast, [contact with] a *goses* does not cause impurity until his soul departs.

The specific context of this ruling is in regard to priestly vulnerability to ritual impurity through contact with a dead body. This source provides a legal exception to the general rule that one is considered dead when no evidence of breathing may be discerned, based, apparently, upon common sense, which dictates that a person so injured has no possible chance of recovery. This person, who is still alive, is nevertheless considered a source of the same ritual impurity which bars a cohen from the area of a dead body. This differentiation between categories of the dying is carried through as a distinction in the laws of murder and punishment in Jewish law. The halakhic codes which clearly forbid the murder of a *goses* also speak of the person who is called *treifah*, one who suffers from a condition which makes it plain that he will be dead within a year. In his *Hilkhot Rotzeaḥ* Maimonides states that one who kills a *treifah* is not liable to punishment by the *beit din*, though he is considered liable to judgement by the heavenly court at the time of the resurrection.[28]

The halakhic concepts which occupy a central place in the modern consideration of euthanasia are that of *pikuah nefesh*, the definition of *gesisah* and of death, and the distinction made between the prolongation of life and the shortening of the death process. The legislation reflects a sense of compassion for the dying patient's agony balanced against a concern to defend the patient's right to every moment of life, recognizing, as well, the status of human life as an overriding value in itself. Immanuel Jakobovits describes a "dialectical tension of the *halakhah* on this question."

> [There is] the inestimable value and priority attached to life itself. This is seen in the suspension of the Sabbath to preserve but one moment of precious life. ...[against] the concern to avoid needless pain even in the case of the worst criminal, for whom the *halakhah* is concerned to find the least painful form of execution. ...Whether pain is to be looked on as an instrument of divine punishment or not, it is clearly a curse ... consideration for a patient's pain is greater ... than the concern for his spiritual and temporal preparedness to die. Even the criminal walking to his execution was to be saved from unnecessary suffering ... hence the Talmud [*Sanhedrin* 43a, 45a; *Semahot* 2.8], followed by Maimonides [loc. cit.], insisted that he had to be drugged into insensibility during the final ordeal so that his feelings might be spared.[29]

In his *Iggerot Moshe*, Moshe Feinstein asserts that if the current state of medical knowledge provides a patient with treatment which cannot cure and only prolongs suffering, it should not be administered. He points out that if it were permissible to prolong life artificially despite suffering, Isserles would have required that more woodchoppers be brought instead of stipulating the removal of such a distraction. In his discussion of Isserles' ruling that impediments to death should be removed, he restricts application to the case of a *goses* who is suffering pain.[30] No overt act may be taken to hasten death, however.[31] In another responsum, he adds that "it is forbidden to maintain the life of a person "who is not fit to live" by artificial means. "If the intention of prolonging life is not to heal but merely to maintain, and if there is pain and suffering, it is forbidden. Even if a patient is comatose, it must be considered possible that there is pain."[32] Basing himself upon the traditional halakhic definition of death as the cessation of breathing, Feinstein prescribes an acceptable way to apply this criterion to a patient on a respirator. He explains that a working respirator may not be removed from a patient's mouth, for even this slight movement may cause his death.

> However, when the machine runs out of oxygen and stops [and must be refilled] the machine should not

be returned to the mouth [of the patient] until some
time has passed, for example a quarter of an hour;
if the patient is not alive he will cease to breathe
and they will know that he is dead. If he breathes,
but with difficulty, they return the machine to his
mouth immediately. This process should be repeated often, until he either improves or does not breathe
at all by himself, because he is dead.[33]

Eliezer Waldenberg states in his *Tzitz Eliezer* that life is to
be sustained regardless of its quality or brevity. He explicitly includes
the *goses:*

We are obliged to make every effort to save the life
of a *goses*, using every available means, even for the
sake of another hour of life. This is also true for a
*goses* who suffers greatly. It is prohibited to take
any action which will hasten the death of a *goses* at
any stage; one who acts in such a manner is considered a murderer.[34]

He is in agreement with Feinstein in ruling for the temporary
removal of a respirator in order to check for independent breathing.
He further states that a *goses* is allowed to pray for his own death,
although his relatives are not. (In traditional Judaism, petitionary
prayer is considered to be at least as efficacious a means of affecting
the natural order as is medicine.) Finally, the physician is permitted
to administer drugs which will alleviate the suffering of the *goses*,
even if they shorten his life; drugs may not, however, be administered
specifically in order to hasten death.[35]

In his discussion of the physician's responsibility toward a
dying patient, J. David Bleich argues that

passive euthanasia involving the omission of a therapeutic procedure, or the withholding of medication, which could sustain life is ... prohibited by
Jewish law. The terminal nature of an illness in no
way mitigates the physician's responsibilities. The
physician is charged with prolonging life no less than
with effecting a cure.[36]

Bleich also holds that the patient has no right to request the
cessation of treatment. "Even if the patient cries out, 'leave me be and
do not give me any aid because for me death is preferable' everything
possible must be done on behalf of the patient." This includes all levels of activity undertaken on the patient's behalf. For Bleich, the
*halakhah* does not permit "distinction between 'natural means,' such
as food and drink, and artificial means, such as drugs and medica-
tions." He cites the analogy drawn between medication and food and
water by Maimonides, and extends it to the use of modern medical
technology:

God created food and water; we are obliged to use them in staving off hunger and thirst. God created drugs and medicaments and endowed man with the intelligence necessary to discover their medicinal properties; we are obliged to use them in warding off illness and disease. Similarly, God provided the materials and the technology which make possible catheters, intravenous infusions, and respirators; we are obligated to use them in order to prolong life.[37]

In a discussion of the Quinlan case, he argued against the removal of life-sustaining mechanical equipment for a patient in a persistent vegetative state.

It is quite true that man has the power to prolong life far beyond the point at which it ceases to be either productive or pleasurable. Not infrequently, the patient, if capable of expressing his desires and allowed to follow his own inclinations, would opt for termination of a life which has become a burden both to others and to himself. Judaism, however, teaches that man does not enjoy the right of self-determination with regard to questions of life and death.[38]

Accordingly, Bleich holds that *halakhah* cannot sanction living wills or the Natural Death Acts that have been enacted by a number of state legislatures.

Judaism denies man the right to make judgments with regard to quality of life. The category of *pikuah nefesh* extends to human life of every description, including the feeble-minded, the mentally deranged, and even persons in a so-called vegetative state. ...Nor, in the final analysis, does the desire of the patient to have, or not to have, his life prolonged play a role in the halakhic obligation to initiate or maintain life-sustaining procedures. ...Judaism does not perceive the overriding obligation to preserve life to be in any way antithetical to "death with dignity". ...the struggle for life is never an indignity. ...Generations ago our Sages wrote, "against your will you live; against your will you die." (*Ethics of the Fathers* 4.22)[39]

There is one exception: citing Isserles, Bleich asserts that "while the death of a *goses* may not be hastened, there is no obligation to perform any action which will lengthen the life of the patient in this state."

The distinction between an active and a passive act applies to a *goses* and to a *goses* only. When a patient is, as it were, actually in the clutches of the angel of death and the death process has actually begun, there is no obligation to heal.[40]

He excludes a patient on a respirator from the category of *goses*.

> The physiological criteria of *gesisah* must be spelled out with care. It is surely clear that a patient whose life may be prolonged for weeks and even months is not yet moribund; the actual death process has not yet started to commence and hence the patient is not a *goses*.[41]

*Gesisah*, as a process which does not exceed three days, implies that "a *goses* is one who cannot, under any circumstances, be maintained alive for a period of seventy-two hours", i.e., not merely by natural means.

In his response to an article dealing with the halakhic definition of death vis-a-vis organ donation published in late 1989 by Bleich in the New York bimonthly *Jewish Review*, R. Moshe Tendler of Yeshiva University offered a different criteria for determining death, for which he draws upon a late responsum of his father-in-law, Moshe Feinstein (which itself is based upon *Iggerot Moshe* 2.74[42]):

> There is now a test in which a liquid is injected into the body through the veins in order to see whether the connection has been broken between the brain and the rest of the body and destruction of the brain has set in; this is the same as death by decapitation. ...If he can be made to breath [sic] by a respirator even though he has died, this does not declare him alive.[43]

Tendler insists that medically-ascertained brain death is the best indicator of death, since heart and respiratory activity can be sustained indefinitely with modern technology. He uses the term "organ perfusion system" instead of "life-support system" to illustrate his point that it is not life which is being sustained, but the function of a collection of individually operating human organs which are located within the same human body. After the brain is dead, they no longer constitute an integrated system.[44] Thus, the traditional halakhic definition of death, the cessation of breathing, is considered on a conceptual level: this was the most accurate way the ancients knew to ascertain death. However, modern technology has provided that our "most accurate way" is found in the electroencephalograph, and thus, the appropriate halakhic attitude would be to rely upon it rather than upon a feather held before the nose, as it were. Although Jakobovits will allow for the removal of insulin as an impediment to dying, he explicitly denies that the withholding of nutrition and hydration can be considered an act of removing an impediment to death, and states that "it is forbidden to starve a *goses* in order to hasten his death."[45] Only the statement of Moshe Feinstein, that it is forbidden to extend the life of one "who is not fit to live," seems to invite a certain flexibility of interpretation. It must be concluded, therefore, that to the majority of Orthodox respondents, the withholding of nutrition and hydration is beyond the pale of discussion of the limits of the permitted passive euthanasia which can be administered to a *goses*. The flexibility of the dialectic demonstrated in the general discussion of euthanasia is entirely absent in this area.

When the question is whether or not to initiate artificial respiration, Jakobovits argues that the *halakhah* would countenance inaction – *shev velo taaseh* – in order that nature might take its course: "there is no obligation to keep a hopelessly ill patient alive, and to lengthen his sufferings, by artificial means."[46] In his discussion of euthanasia, Isaac Klein points out that once the respirator is in operation, its removal "requires an act which may be forbidden." He describes the debate which took place in the rabbinic and Jewish medical ethics journals *She'arim* and *Assia*.[47] In their final decision, they relied upon Isserles:

> because there is no direct act involved here, only the removal of an obstacle – they ruled that the removal of a respirator is an analogous case and comes within the category of passive euthanasia.[48]

In a statement which, compared to others he has made (as quoted above), reflects Jakobovits' continuing effort to find the correct, flexible balance between *halakhah* and individual need:

> Any form of active euthanasia is strictly prohibited. ...At the same time, Jewish law sanctions, and perhaps even demands, the withdrawal of any factor – whether extraneous to the patient himself or not – which may artificially delay his demise in the final phase. It might be argued that this modification implies the legality of expediting the death of an incurable patient in acute agony by withholding from him such medicaments as sustain his continued life by unnatural means. ...Our sources advert only to cases in which death is expected to be imminent; it is, therefore, not clear whether they would tolerate this moderate form of euthanasia, though that cannot be ruled out.[49]

## Conclusion

This case involves not only a consideration of the traditional halakhic attitude toward euthanasia, but also of the rights of Nancy Cruzan and others like her, the responsibilities of physicians and legal guardians, larger social considerations, and the "quality of life" argument which proponents of euthanasia have put forward in the contemporary debate.

It is clear that objective halakhic consideration of this issue becomes difficult, due to religious sensitivity to the inestimable value of a human life, created as it is *b'tzelem Elohim*, as well as by the more primordial, fundamental and irrational human tendancy to recoil from a straightforward approach to any matter concerning human death. Traditionally, the choice has been not to interfere in the process, which is left between the dying person and God; nature has been allowed to take its course. Thus, the crucial distinction develops between aiding the natural process of dying, which is permitted, and hastening it, which is forbidden.

In our contemporary world, however, medical technology has advanced to the point that the distinction between natural and artificial processes of life and death is not always clear. In cases such as Miss Cruzan's, intervention in the natural process of her life and death began when she first received emergency treatment after her accident. The level of intervention reached its apex when the naso-gastric tube was inserted into her nose and stomach. The sophistication of the technologies we use today might themselves be seen as actualizing a reality which is contrary to God's will. Even as we are capable of acting against God's will when we transgress any given commandment, so too we might consider that we could be acting against God's will by hooking up a PVS patient to a naso-gastric tube. In her natural state, Miss Cruzan was incapable of independent life; in an earlier, less medically advanced age, she would have died at the scene of the accident. In the case of other PVS patients, dependent as they are upon others to feed and care for their most basic needs, we would not see such long periods of PVS existence as can be achieved by our modern technology. In such cases it would undoubtedly be observed that such is God's will. From this perspective, our sophisticated technology, practically speaking, enables us to defy what might be considered to be God's will. The argument that to remove someone's gastrostomy tube is to actively play God is only a partial view of the truth: we were playing God, in the best sense of the word, when we attempted to save a life by inserting it. The danger is that such mechanical maintenance of a human body will continue regardless of whether the patient will ever recover sentience; such treatment regards the life as human, even after that definition no longer applies. Richard A. McCormick has pointed out that the manner of the evidence "that biological death is imminent" has changed radically in the past decade with the advances of medical technology.

> This has tended gradually to shift the problem from the means to reverse the dying process to the quali-

ty of life sustained and preserved. The questions "is this means too hazardous or difficult to use?" and "does this measure only prolong the patient's dying?" while still useful and valid, now often become "granted that we can easily save the life, what kind of life are we saving?" This is a quality-of-life judgment. And we fear it. And certainly we should. But with increased power goes increased responsibility. Since we have the power, we must face the responsibility.[50]

This question of the "quality" of life is one which some respondents disparage as indicative of a lessening of the value which modernity places on the individual human's life. In his discussion of the Quinlan case, Bleich argued that "the *mitzvah* of saving a life is neither enhanced nor diminished by virtue of the quality of the life preserved."[51]

Within the general examination of the ethical issues involved in euthanasia, the case of the PVS patient presents a special difficulty. For some halakhic authorities, the ruling that a respirator may be considered an impediment to a normal dying process, and therefore removed, is defensible in terms of Isserles' gloss in the *Shulhan Arukh* and of the classic definition of death as an absence of independent breathing. But a PVS patient breathes naturally, and therefore, according to those criteria, s/he is alive. Given the possible span of thirty years of continued existence which some PVS patients have demonstrated, the classic definition of a *goses* also cannot apply.

Yet these patients are not, for some modern ethicists, alive in the sense in which we usually understand the concept. Proponents of euthanasia seek to delineate a difference between "life" and mere "existence" of the sort experienced by PVS patients. The question is worth asking: is life itself the good, or is it the medium by which we know and do the good? The argument they make is that life itself is not meant to be an end, but a means to the ends that define living: the ability to transcend the moment in thought, to interact with other human beings, to experience the input of the human senses, to know love, and thus to know life. In defense of his position against any form of euthanasia, Bleich repeats the rationale of Me'iri[52] that one must preserve the life of

> even the hopelessly ill ... although the moribund patient may be incapable of any physical exertion he may be privileged to experience contrition and utilize the precious final moments of life for the achievement of true repentance. ...No clinical experiment has ever been conducted to determine at what level of consciousness a comatose patient becomes incapable of remorse and repentence.[53]

It has been medically ascertained that the PVS patient is incapable
of this. McCormick argues:

> Life's potential for other values is dependent on two
> factors, those external to the individual, and the
> very condition of the individual. The former we can
> and must change to maximize individual potential.
> That is what social justice is all about. The latter we
> sometimes cannot alter. ...there comes a point where
> an individual's condition itself represents the nega-
> tion of any truly human – i.e., relational – potential.[54]

The purpose of life, as it may be derived according to Judaism's traditional teachings, is to do *mitzvot*, to work for *tikkun olam*
(in traditional terms, the coming of the Messiah), and to seek to
know God. Thus it may legitimately be asked: how does the permanently unconscious patient qualify as a living human being? For the
traditional Jewish respondent, human birth qualifies one as a human
soul, and only death indicates that soul's departure. They indicate,
explicitly or implicitly, that the decision about whether life is worth
living is God's alone. It must be noted, however, that in questions
of Jewish law, God's decisions are determined by those who are
appointed by their community to be God's representatives in any
given case; a legal ruling on an individual case is inevitably filtered
through the subjective and humanly limited understanding of the
individual respondent.

In addition, recognition must be accorded to the expressed
desires of those belonging to the "right to die" movement, illustrated in its creation of the "living will," which specifies the wish that
no heroic or extraordinary measures be taken to prolong life. The
morality of the right to die is denied in Jewish tradition; it is a matter
of straightforward Jewish law. In arguing this point, Bleich quotes
from the daily morning prayer, "my God, the soul that you have
given me is pure."[55] For Joseph Fletcher, the issue is not defined
legally but ethically: "it is harder morally to justify letting somebody die a slow and ugly death, dehumanized, than it is to justify
helping him to avoid it." He argues the superior morality of situational over deontological ethics:

> ...the belief that our moral acts, including suicide and
> mercy killing, are right or wrong depending on the
> consequences aimed at (we sometimes fail, of course,
> through ignorance or poor reasoning), and that the
> consequences are good or evil according to whether
> and how much they serve humane values. In the
> language of ethics this is called a "consequential"
> method of moral judgment.
>
> ...In duty-ethics what is right is whatever act obeys
> or adheres to the rules, even though the foreseeable

result will be inhumane. That is, its highest good is not human happiness and well-being but obedience to a rule – or what we might call a prejudiced or pre-determined decision based not on the clinical variables but on some transcending generality.

[For example], the sixth of the Ten Commandments, which prohibits killing, is a no-no rule for nonconsequentialists when it comes to killing in the service of humane values like mercy and compassion, and yet at the same time they ignore their "moral law" when it comes to self-defense. ...You may end your neighbor's life for your own sake but you may not do it for his sake! And you may end your own life for your neighbor's sake, as in an act of sacrificial heroism, but you may not end your life for your own sake.[56][57]

For the halakhist, the crux of any consideration of euthanasia lies with the difference carefully delineated between acts of comission vis-a-vis the patient, i.e. "causing death," vs. those of omission, i.e. "allowing death to occur." Fletcher argues against this distinction:

It is naive and superficial to suppose that because we don't "do anything positively" to hasten a patient's death we have thereby avoided complicity in his death. Not doing anything is doing something; it is a decision to act every bit as much as deciding for any other deed.[58]

The *halakhah* clearly reflects the emotional level of traditional Jewish sensibilities, beyond legislating, which inform the attitudes adopted and the decisions taken, for this is an issue pervaded with the ultimate human difficulty: the reality of death. Thus we find demonstrated throughout the available texts that while halakhic guidelines are clear, intervention is countenanced and even encouraged in specific examples, both in the aggadic paradigm and in the responsa literature.

For the writers of this paper, it seems clear that it is considerations of situational ethics, within the broad deontological framework, which govern the halakhic choices made and the rulings decided. This becomes obvious when one considers the very nature of halakhic responsa literature, which deals with individual cases. A practitioner of situational ethics considers each case individually, without attempting to formulate broad guidelines for support of individual decisions. The overriding consideration is for the suffering of the patient. According to the available medical evidence, we may hazard the guess that Miss Cruzan is not experiencing pain. But Feinstein argued that we must consider that such a patient does experience suffering; and medical experts concede that their understanding of a PVS patient's condition is incomplete. Following Isserles, therefore, we deduce that from a halakhic perspective, the removal of her gastrostomy tube should be considered the removal of an impediment to the normal dying process of a *goses*; it should be permitted. According to *Sefer Ḥasidim,* it might even be understood as mandated: "there is a time to die." Granted that Miss Cruzan is not a *goses* according to the strict interpretation of that category; it must be taken into account, however, that halakhic categories have undergone a certain amount of redefinition as new scientific information futher illuminates the traditional concepts of Jewish law (as indicated in Tendler's arugment for brain death to supersede the traditional halakhic definition of the absence of breathing to indicate death). The question hangs upon the respondent's judgement as to just how much "redefinition" is appropriate.

For Arthur J. Dyck, the appropriate respect for human life must extend to human death. He describes the modern dilemma:

> the arguments for euthanasia focus upon two human and significant concerns: compassion for those who are painfully and terminally ill; and concern for the human dignity associated with freedom of choice. Compassion and freedom are values that sustain and enhance the common good. The question here, however, is how these values affect our behavior toward the dying.[59]

In the case of a PVS patient such as Nancy Cruzan, the compassion must be more than the reflex stating of the deontological axiom that any form of life is a good which must be preserved; given the nature of the PVS patient's life, to offer such an answer to the complex questions of the case is to dismiss them. As the case analyses of traditional responsa indicate, compassion demands that the characteristics of each individual situation be respected. The Jewish approach seeks to realize the presence of the divine in life; all the more so in questions of life and death. For the writers of this paper, this approach is most appropriately represented when judgements and actions reflect our limited understanding of how best to respect the inherent dignity of the human manifestation of the divine image which is Nancy Cruzan.

The human dignity which is defended through freedom of choice (for the Cruzans, the essence of their legal battle) must be accorded to the patient and family. While we are convinced that the PVS patient should be considered a *goses* and therefore free to die, we find that the ethical crux of the matter, for us, is not what should be done, but who should make the decision. As her legal guardians, Miss Cruzan's parents have held her life in their hands from its beginning; why should they now be suspected of having less interest in their daughter than the state which seeks to prevent them from helping Nancy to complete the dying process? For R. Nahman this is the highest form of friendship, and of love: "choose for your friend a good death" *(Sanhedrin* 45a). The Cruzans have the right to make that choice, after thoroughly examining all of the medical, economic, and emotional dimensions of the issue, for their daughter. If they consider their religion an important part of their lives, they will also undoubtedly take the religious perspective of their faith into consideration. If they were Jewish, we feel that their ethical Jewish duty would be to do just what their suit in the Supreme Court seeks: to remove their daughter's feeding tube, and to allow her to complete the dying process. We feel intuitively that the logical thrust of the *halakhah* leads in this direction, but that the enunciation of such a position is politically dangerous at the current time. While Judaism has witnessed both major and incremental modifications in the halakhic process in the past, our time is more conservative, and, with good reason, less self-confident in the face of the radical pace of modern scientific advancement; a religious awareness indicates a more slowly incremental process of change. Here we value the Reform approach, which seeks to carefully balance the halakhically informed Jewish approach with our sense that the human understanding of how best to manifest the divine in our world may be some-times better informed through science, even if it flies in the face of traditional teaching. Miss Cruzan left no clear instructions, no living will, to help her parents make their difficult decision; but in the absence of any evidence that they harbor ulterior motives or malice toward her, we feel that they have a prior right to that of the state to determine their daughter's fate.

In summary, the writers of this paper would note that the halakhic material is flexible, to the degree that it can maintain a distinction between active and passive euthanasia, with the technical definition of the term *goses* insuring against confusion of the two categories. In practice, imminent death is usually easy enough to ascertain medically in a given case, and although all who are declared to be in a state of *gesisah* may not die exactly within seventy-two hours, precision does not seem to be the ultimate value here. Rather, it is clear that the underlying motivation of Jewish law is the intention to preserve and protect life, a direct derivative of God's command to choose life over death.

In general it is true that *halakhah* is a deontologically-based legal framework, in its insistence upon maintaining an ethic that is reflective of the highest possible moral standard. However, we have demonstrated with the responsa cited throughout this paper that, although traditional Jews will not speak of contradictions in divine law, it is possible to understand the divine will in various ways, and there are instances in which legal interpretations stand in opposition to each other. The halakhic process accords authority not only to what the texts say, but to what they are understood to mean in each age. The responsa literature underscores the importance of the particulars of each case in determining the appropriate legal ruling. While certain questions may rely on identical halakhic precedents, each answer is derived with a degree of independence which is recognized as necessary and valid. Precedent and environment mediate each other; this is the situational level within the deontological which keeps the system alive to the needs of its adherents. We value the *halakhah's* individual approach, with its refusal to set all-encompassing precedent from a single case, for the defense it erects against the concept of the "slippery slope".

As for our own position within the debate, we find the *halakhah* to be instructive, but not directive. We make no pretenses to be halakhic Jews. We are informed by the content of the halakhic material, but not bound by its parameters. We recognize the salutary effect of a legal code's guidance upon the development of a coherent community which seeks to shape its future as it seeks to manifest the divine in our world as part of the historical unfolding of Jewish destiny, by following one of the different, but related, normative Jewish paths. We are not, however, prepared to require halakhic observance upon that community, nor to impose its discipline beyond the group level. We cannot endorse legislating private lives or decisions once the parameters of liberal Jewish life are established; therefore, we would never presume to decide this, or any other, case. For us, human beings have the right to make their own choices, and families should not face obstruction in seeking to care for their own; failing that, such decisions belong to legal guardians within the private domain. They should fall to the public domain of the state only by default.

We find ourselves, then, advocating the libertarian position regarding this issue: ultimately, each one of us must have the right to exercise autonomy over our own lives. If we find *halakhah* instructive, that is all to the good, for it teaches respect for life and compassion for the human condition. We reserve the right, however, to weigh its injuctions against the information we receive outside its boundaries, and to judge it as equally valid in the formulation of our final decision. This is the hardest decision-making process of all, and the one modeled for us by respondents such as Isserles and Feinstein: to gather all the information available, even that which conflicts with one's prejudiced perspective; not to rely on the recitation of precedent, but to create new ones for each new case; to ever be responsive to the unique human needs of each new situation. For us, this situational approach reflects the ultimate morality, demands the deepest degree of intellectual and emotional honesty, and presents the highest level of difficulty. At the conclusion of their examination of the case of Nancy Cruzan and others like her, the writers of a recent article mused:

...in a sense, the abiding difficulty of these choices has a value of its own. It reflects the deep desire to do the right thing and respect the wishes of a loved one – and also an unshakable sense that life is neither to be taken nor relinquished lightly, even in mercy's name.[60]

In the case of a PVS patient, the balance which must be struck between these two ethical imperatives should be weighed anew in each new case; and that terrible deliberation should be the right of those only who have already been paying the consequences of suffering the loss of one they have loved, regardless of the decision which they make.

## Appendix

Modern biblical scholarship has discovered that the Decalogue, or Mosaic Covenant, is in the form of a treaty between a Suzerain and his people. The point of such a treaty is to specify the relationship between a ruler and his people, and to set out the conditions necessary to form and sustain community with that ruler. One of the most significant purposes of such a treaty is to specify constraints that members of a community must observe is the community is to be viable at all. Fundamentally, the Decalogue articulates the indispensable [sic] prerequisites of the common life.

Viewed in this way the injunction not to kill is part of a total effort to prevent the destruction of the human community. It is an absolute prohibition in the sense that no society can be indifferent about the taking of human life. Any act, insofar as it is an act of taking a human life, is wrong, that is to say, taking a human life is a wrong-making characteristic of actions.

To say, however, that killing is prima facie wrong does not mean that an act of killing may never be justified. For example, a person's effort to prevent someone's death may lead to the death of the attacker. However, we can morally justify that act of intervention only because it is an act of saving a life, not because it is an act of taking a life. If it were simply an act of taking a life, it would be wrong.

A further constraint upon human freedom with the Jewish and Christian traditions is articulated in a myth concerning the loss of paradise. The loss of Eden comes at the point where man and woman succumb to the temptation to know good and evil, and to know it in the perfect and ultimate sense in which a perfect and ultimate being would know it. To know who should live and who should die, one would have to know everything about people, including their ultimate destiny. Only God could have such knowledge. Trying to decide who shall live and who shall die is 'playing god.' It is tragic to 'play god' because one does it with such limited and uncertain knowledge of what is good and evil. (pp. 287-288)

Arthur J. Dyck, Professor of Population Ethics in the school of Public Health and Professor of Christian Ethics in the Divinity School, Harvard University, "An Alternative to the Ethic of Euthanasia", in Weir, pp. 281-296.

# Bibliography

Bleich, J. David. "Establishing Criteria of Death," *Contemporary Halachic Problems.*

——————. *Judaism and Healing: Halakhic Perspectives.* NY: Ktav, 1981.

Caro, Joseph. *Hilkhot Bikkur Ḥolim, Shulḥan Arukh, Yoreh Deah* 339.1-5 text; Isserles commentary 339.2; *Turei Zahav* 339.2; *Siftei Kohen* 339.1-3, 5.

Cohen, Haim H., "The Methodology of Jewish Law: A Secularist View," in Jackson, Bernard S., ed. *Modern Research in Jewish Law.* Leiden, The Netherlands: E. J. Brill, 1980.

Cranford, Ronald E. "The Persistent Vegetative State: The Medical Reality (Getting the Facts Straight)," *Hastings Center Report.* February/March 1988.

Dyck, Arthur J. "An Alternative to the Ethic of Euthanasia", 1973, in Weir, Robert F. ed. *Ethical Issues in Death and Dying.* NY: Columbia University Press, 1977.

"Euthanasia," *Encyclopaedia Judaica.*

Feinstein, Moshe. *Ḥoshen Mishpat* II, No. 74; *Yoreh Deah* II, p. 289, and III, No. 132, *Iggerot Moshe.*

Fletcher, George P. "Prolonging Life", 1967, in Weir, Robert F. ed. *Ethical Issues in Death and Dying.* NY: Columbia University Press, 1977.

Fletcher, Joseph. "Ethics and Euthanasia," 1973, in Weir, Robert F. ed. *Ethical Issues in Death and Dying.* NY: Columbia University Press, 1977.

Gibbs, Nancy, Priscilla Painter, and Elizabeth Taylor, "Love and Let Die," *Time Magazine,* March 19, 1990, pp. 62-71.

"Goses," *Encyclopaedia Talmudit.*

Herring, Basil F. *Jewish Ethics and Halakhah For Our Time.* NY: Yeshiva University Press, 1984.

Isserles, Moshe. *Darkhei Moshe* commentary to *Arbaah Turim, Yoreh Deah* 339.1.

Jakobovits, Immanuel. "A Ruling on Whether it is Permitted to Hasten the Death of a Hopelessly Ill Person Who Suffers Greatly," *HaPardes* 31 (1956), number 31.

Klein, Isaac. *A Guide to Jewish Religious Practice.* NY: Jewish Theological Seminary, 1979.

Maimonides. *Hilkhot Harotzeaḥ Ushmirat Nefesh, Mishneh Torah, Nezikin.*

McCormick, Richard A. "To Save or Let Die: The Dilemma of Modern Medicine," in Weir, Robert F. ed. *Ethical Issues in Death and Dying.* NY: Columbia University Press, 1977. pp. 173-184.

Newman, Louis E. "Woodchoppers and Respirators: The Problem of Interpretation in Contemporary Jewish Ethics," *Modern Judaism,* 10.1.

Rosner, Fred. "Jewish Attitude Toward Euthanasia," *Modern Medicine and Jewish Law.* NY: Yeshiva University, 1972.

*Talmud Bavli, Masekhtot: Avodah Zarah* 18a, *Ketubot* 104a, *Semachot* 1.1.

Tendler, Rav Moshe David. "Halakhic Death Means Brain Death," *Jewish Review.* Vol. 3, No. 3 (Jan-Feb. 1990), p. 6.

Waldenberg, R. Eliezer. *Hilkhot Rofim V'r'fuah.* Jerusalem: The Rav Kook Institute, 1978.

Weir, Robert F. ed. *Ethical Issues in Death and Dying.* NY: Columbia University Press, 1977.

# Notes

1. The President's Commission for the Study of Ethical Problems in Medicine and Biomedical and Behavioral Research, "The Care of Patients With Permanent Loss of Consciousness," staff discussion paper, December 12, 1981, p.19.

2. Cranford, Ronald E., 'The Persistent Vegetative State: The Medical Reality," *Hastings Center Report,* February/March 1988, pp.27-32.

3. Mary Cantwell, The Editorial Notebook, *The New York Times,* March 9, 1990.

4. The President's Commission for the Study of Ethical Problems in Medicine and Biomedical and Behavioral Research, p.36.

5. Beck, Melinda, "Not Enough For All," *Newsweek Magazine,* May 14, 1990, p.53.

6. Ibid., p.36.

7. Staff Writers, "The Right to Die," *Time Magazine,* March 19, 1990, p.64.

8. Swomley, Dr. John D., "The Cruzan Decision: A Confusion of Confusions," *Midwest Medical Ethics,* Winter/Spring 1989, p.16.

9. Ibid., p.16.

10. Priester, Reinhard, editor, "Withholding or Withdrawing Artificial Nutrition and Hydration," University of Minnesota Center for Biomedical Ethics, Biomedical Ethics Reading Packet #2, p.3.

11. Ibid., p.2.

12. Ibid., p.3.

13. Ibid., p.4.

14. Staff Writers, *Time Magazine*, March 19, 1990, p.62.

15. Swomley, Dr. John D., p.15.

16. Meileander, Gilbert, "On Removing Food and Water: Against the Stream," *Hastings Center Report*, December 1984, p.12.

17. Callahan, Daniel, "On Feeding the Dying," *Hastings Center Report*, October 1983, p.22.

18. Meileander, Gilbert, "The Cruzan Decision: A Moral Commentary," *Midwest Medical Ethics*, Winter/Spring 1989, p.7.

19. Derr, Patrick G., "Why Food and Fluids Can Never Be Denied," *Hastings Center Report*, February 1986, p.29.

20. Meileander, Gilbert, "The Cruzan Decision: A Moral Commentary," p.7.

21. Ellman, Ira, "Can Others Exercise an Incapacitated Patient's Right To Die?" *Hastings Center Report,* January/February 1990, p.49.

22. Scofield, Giles, "The Calculus of Consent," *Hastings Center Report*, January/February 1990, p.46.

23. Ibid., p.46.

24. McCormick, Father Robert A., "The Cruzan Decision," *Midwest Medical Ethics,* Albert Luper, editor, Winter/Spring 1989, p.4.

25. *Shulḥan Arukh, Yoreh Deah* 339.2.

26. Remah's commentary to *Shulḥan Arukh, Yoreh Deah* 339.1.

27. *Arba-ah Turim, Darkhei Moshe,* 339.1.

28. *Mishneh Torah, Hilkhot Harotzeaḥ Ushmirat Nefesh*, ch. 1.
29. Herring, Basil F. *Jewish Ethics and Halakhah For Our Times*, p. 79-88.

30. *Iggerot Moshe, Ḥoshen Mishpat* 74, p.311.

31. Herring, p. 84.

32. *Yoreh Deah* 2, p. 289.

33. *Yoreh Deah* 3.132, p. 398.

34. *Hilkhot Rofim V'r'fuah*, pp. 203-204.

35. Ibid.

36. Bleich, *Judaism and Healing*, p. 137.

37. Maimonides, *Commentary on the Mishnah, Pesahim* 4.9, cited in Bleich, *Judaism and Healing*, p. 138.

38. Bleich, "The Quinlan Case," in *Jewish Bioethics*, p. 269.

39. Ibid., p. 139.

40. Ibid., p. 140-141.

41. Ibid.

42. "Skilled physicians are able to ascertain by way of an injection into the veins if the link between the brain and the body is interrupted (*nifsak*)...so that it is clear that the brain no longer has any connection with the body, and the brain has already decomposed completely, it is as if the head had been cut off. ...otherwise, however, even if none of the other signs of life (response to pain, independent breathing) are present, the respirator is put in his mouth, even for a long time; only by way of this examination revealing that there is no connection between brain and body can they decide."

43. *Jewish Review*, Vol. 3 no. 3 (January-February 1990), p. 20.

44. Ibid., p. 6.

45. Jakobovits, cited in Feldman, David M. "Right To Life – Neonatal and Terminal," *Health and Medicine in the Jewish Tradition,* p. 18.

46. Ibid.

47. Moses Munk, Nov 1971, and Barukh J. Rabinowitz, no. 3, 1971, respectively.

48. Klein, p. 255.

49. Cited in Herring, pp. 124-125.

50. McCormick, in Weir, Robert F. ed. *Ethical Issues in Death and Dying*, p. 178.

51. Bleich, "Quinlan," p. 270.

53. Bleich, "Quinlan," pp. 273-274.

54. Richard A. McCormick, in Weir, pp. 180-181.

55. Bleich, "Establishing Criteria of Death," p. 393.

56 Joseph Fletcher, "Ethics and Euthanasia," pp. 355-357.

57. For another interesting perspective on the Jewish attitude toward killing, please see the appendix at the end of this paper.

58. Fletcher, p. 358.

59. Dyck, in Weir, p. 284.

60. Gibbs, p. 71.

# Social Issues

# The Autonomous Jewish Self Meets Solidarity Forever

## Should a Jew oppose a state's right-to-work laws?

Harry Levin

In this case, should the freedom of individuals to make personal choices supersede the coercive power of the majority to establish regulations for the common benefit? Are the strongly-documented positive consequences of labor unions in the workplace more important here than a modernistic vision of autonomous individualism? Should a worker be legally entitled to enjoy the benefits of a labor union without contributing financially to the union's efforts, a fundamental right and possibility in workplaces in right-to-work states?

A union security agreement, according to Max Zimny, general counsel of the International Ladies' Garment Workers' Union, is "a contract under which employees are compelled to pay union dues or an equivalent amount as a condition of continued employment."[1] In the language of lawyers for Senators Jesse Helms, Strom Thurmond, Dan Quayle and Steven Symms in their *amicus curiae* brief in support of Harry Beck against the Communications Workers of America: "Provisions in collective bargaining agreements that require 'union membership' are known as 'union security agreements'."[2] (Zimny's phrase "or an equivalent amount" refers to the circumstances in agency shops, as distinguished from union shops, a distinction which we will examine below.)

The Helms *amicus curiae* brief then relates that "twenty-one states have exercised their prerogative under section 14(b) of the National Labor Relations Act (NLRA) to outlaw union security agreements within their borders.[3] In the other twenty-nine states the question of union security is a mandatory subject of bargaining. An employer is required by law to negotiate with a union whether

■ 247

the collective bargaining agreement ultimately executed by the parties will require 'union membership' as a condition of employment."[4]

What does "union membership" mean in this context of American law? The National Labor Relations Act, also named the Wagner Act, in recognition of sponsoring Senator Robert Wagner, became law in 1935. The Taft-Hartley Act, adopted in 1947, "was built upon the framework of the Wagner Act."[5] Prior to the enactment of Taft-Hartley, the NLRA allowed majority unions to negotiate "closed shop" agreements requiring employers to hire only persons who were already union members.[6] But "only a dozen years after the passage of the NLRA, in the wake of the massive strikes that swept the country at the end of World War II, the national mood had changed dramatically."[7] The House of Representatives was ready to repeal the policy of the United States, as expressed in the language of the NLRA, of "encouraging the practice and procedure of collective bargaining."[8] Senator Taft altered the House's direction by offering legislation whose professed intent was "to balance" the power between unions and employers so that "the parties can deal equally with each other."[9]

The Congress was concerned that the closed shop, and abuses associated with the closed shop, "created too great a barrier to free employment to be longer tolerated."[10] But, as Justice William Brennan notes in the majority opinion handed down in the Beck case, "The 1947 Congress was equally concerned that without such agreements, many employees would reap the benefits that unions negotiated on their behalf without in any way contributing financial support to these efforts."[11] As understood in the Supreme Court decision in the case of NLRB versus General Motors Corporation, the Taft-Hartley Act was "intended to accomplish twin purposes. On the one hand, the most serious abuses of compulsory unionism were eliminated by abolishing the closed shop. On the other hand, Congress recognized that in the absence of a union-security provision, 'many employees sharing the benefits of what unions are able to accomplish by collective bargaining will refuse to pay their share of the cost.'"[12]

By the laws of a right-to-work state, a worker in a shop in which a union is the legally certified collective bargaining representative for all the workers does not have to join the union and does not have to pay any money at all to the union. Under section 14(b) of the Taft-Hartley Act, paralleling the section of the NLRA cited in the Helms brief, there is a specific sanction in favor of state laws that regulate union security agreements more strictly than does the federal act.[13] These state laws are known as right-to-work laws, perhaps because of the language of a state constitutional amendment adopted in Florida in 1944: "The right of persons to work shall not be denied or abridged on account of membership in any labor union or labor organization, provided that this clause shall not be construed to deny or abridge the right of employees by and through a labor organization or labor union to bargain collectively with their employer."[14]

The constitutionality of state right-to-work laws was upheld by the United States Supreme Court in 1949.[15] The agency shop, requiring non-union members working in a union shop to pay the equivalent of union dues (called "agency fees"), has been held unlawful under most states' right-to-work laws. In 1963, the Supreme Court ruled that an agency shop is lawful under Taft-Hartley. But, the Court also ruled that the sanction provided by section 14(b) of Taft-Hartley affirms the authority of states to outlaw agency-shop contracts. A state may declare an agency-shop contract illegal and enjoin the contract's enforcement.[16]

The Helms brief, citing language in Abood versus Detroit Board of Education, tells us: "Collective bargaining agreements that require 'union membership' as a condition of employment have historically been known as 'union shop' agreements. Contracts that require only the payment of fees to the union are called 'agency shop' agreements. Union shop and agency shop agreements are 'practical equivalent[s]' since only 'financial membership' can be required of dissenting employees under the authority of section 8(a)(3)."[17]

Section 8(a)(3) is also part of the Taft-Hartley Act. Section 8(a)(3) makes it an unfair labor practice for an employer "by discrimination in regard to hire or tenure of employment ... to encourage or discourage membership in any labor organization."[18] Justice Brennan notes: "The section contains two provisos without which all union security clauses would fall within this otherwise broad condemnation." The first proviso declares that nothing in the Act "preclude[s] an employer from making an agreement with a labor organization ... to require as a condition of employment membership therein" thirty days after the employee becomes employed.[19] The second proviso limits and balances the first: "[N]o employer shall justify any discrimination against an employee for nonmembership in a labor organization (A) if he has reasonable grounds for believing that such membership was not available to the employee on the same terms and conditions generally applicable to other members, or (B) if he has reasonable grounds for believing that membership was denied or terminated for reasons other than the failure ... to tender the periodic dues and the initiation fees uniformly required as a condition of acquiring or retaining membership."[20]

Citing NLRB v. General Motors, Justice Brennan writes: "Taken as a whole, section 8(a)(3) permits an employer and a union to enter into an agreement requiring all employees to become union members as a condition of continued employment, but the 'membership' that may be so required has been 'whittled down to its financial core.'"[21]

So we have come to understand that although section 8(a)(3) of the Taft-Hartley Act, as interpreted in NLRB v. General Motors, "permits" an agreement between union and employer which requires all employees to become union members, whose membership is defined as purely a financial participation, section 14(b) of the same Taft-Hartley Act permits states to enact laws which outlaw union security agreements altogether within their borders.

Section 14(b) sanctions state laws which more strictly regulate union security agreements than does federal law, and thus allows states to pass right-to-work laws which render 8(a)(3) essentially meaningless in those states' jurisdictions.

We have also seen that right-to-work laws can create circumstances in which employees would enjoy union-negotiated benefits without having contributed financial support to the union's efforts to win those benefits.

# The Question(s)

Twenty-one states have passed right-to-work legislation. Seven of those states have right-to-work guarantees in their constitutions. Twenty-nine states, then, still have not enacted right-to-work statutes. Now we will begin probing the specific question, here phrased as two questions because of this reality of current labor law in the United States: Should a Jew seek to repeal a state's extant right-to-work laws or constitutional amendments? Should a Jew oppose enactment of right-to-work legislation in states which do not as yet have such statutes or amendments on their books?

# The Halakhic Material

First, we will examine the status of labor unions in Jewish law. In *Baba Batra* 8b (Babylonian Talmud) we read: "*Reshain benei hair lehatnot al hamidot veal hashearim veal skhar hapoalim* (The city's people [or, townspeople] are legally entitled to fix weights and measures, prices, and workers' wages.)." The phrase *skhar hapoalim* merits attention. Jewish law makes a distinction between the *poel* and the *uman*. The *uman* is a craftsman or artisan – a goldsmith or a weaver or blacksmith or metalworker. The *poel* is a laborer: a farmworker, a stonecutter in a quarry, a donkey driver. Professor Michael Chernick has stated that since *poalim* are the lowest class of workers, the legal right of the townspeople to fix *skhar hapoalim* – the laborers' wages – can be interpreted as the right to set a minimum wage. [22] [23]

The sentence in *Baba Batra* stating that the townspeople are legally entitled to fix weights and measures, prices, and workers' wages, ends by declaring that the townspeople are also legally entitled *l'hasiah al kitsatan*, literally meaning "to remove their contempt", meaning the contempt of those people who would infringe the standards of weight, measure, price and wage established by the townspeople. Rashi's sense of the phrase *l'hasiah al kitsatan* is that the townspeople have the right *liknos et haover,* to punish anyone who transgresses their rules. [24]

In *Baba Batra* 9a, we find language limiting the townspeople's right affirmed in *Baba Batra* 8b:

> "There were two butchers who made an agreement with each other that if either worked on the other's day, the skin of the animal [which he slaughtered on the day when he had agreed not to be working] would be torn up [a penalty which would significantly diminish the transgressing butcher's profits for that day]. One of them went and worked on the other's day. The other tore up his animal skin. The one who had [torn up the skin] was called before Rava. Rava obligated him to make restitution. Rav Yemar bar Shlemaya reminded Rava [of the tannaitic material which we examined as it appeared in *Baba Batra* 8b, that the townspeople are legally entitled] *l'hasiah al kitsatan* [to punish those who transgress their established standards and practices]. Rava did not respond to him. Rav Papa said: "Rava was right not to respond to him. This regulation applies if there is no *adam hashuv* [no important man, a halakhic authority, in the town]. But where there is an important man, the townspeople do not have the right to make such regulations."

In *Tosefta* (*Baba Metzia* 11:24) we read: "*Reshain hatzmarin v'hatzvain* [The wool workers and the dyers are legally entitled] to say: 'All of us will participate in any business [meaning, in any work in our crafts] which comes into the city.' Bakers are legally entitled to establish agreements [*regi-ah*] amongst themselves."

In Maimonides' *Mishneh Torah*, we read: "*Reshain anshei umaniut* [Craftsmen, or fellow tradesmen, are legally entitled] to determine amongst themselves that one [of them] will not work on the day when his colleague is working, and so on, and they can punish anyone who might violate the condition." [25]

In a commentary to this passage in the *Mishneh Torah*, the *Maggid Mishneh* cites the Tosefta about the rights of bakers to make *regiah*, agreements, amongst themselves. To the Maggid Mishneh, *regiah* is *lashon margoa*, a term dealing with rest, "for this is a matter of *menuḥah*" [another word meaning "rest" or "tranquility"].

The sense of the Maggid Mishneh here is that craftsmen who practice the same craft are legally entitled to arrange amongst themselves a schedule of days off. [26]

In a responsum written five hundred years later, Hatam Sofer cites the language of the passage in *Baba Batra* 9a to substantiate the point – in answering a question regarding the propriety of a census of *sarsurim*, or agent/middlemen, in a given city – that fellow craftsmen or tradesmen have the right to set a limit on the number of people who can work at all in their trade in their city:

> "...(T)he agent/middlemen should not proliferate beyond the point of what is appropriate according to the city's business [climate], so that they can [all] make a living and not prevent each other from surviving. And so it is in all countries, that there exists a quota in all kinds of crafts, *omaniut*, limiting the number in that city who can work in that craft, so they don't do damage to one another."[27]

In Maimonides' *Mishneh Torah*, the *anshei hair*, the townspeople of *Baba Batra* 8b – have become *anshei umaniut*, "craftsmen." Incorporating the sense of *Baba Batra* 9a in his code, Maimonides says that the legal rights of craftsmen to make agreements amongst themselves and to punish those who violate those agreements apply if there is not a *ḥakham hashuv*, an important sage, to guide the city's inhabitants.[28]

In the *Tur*, written by Jacob ben Asher (1270-1340), the language concerning this issue is not appreciably different. *Baalei umaniut* serves as the the synonym for Maimonides' *anshei umani-ut*: "Craftsmen are legally entitled to establish regulations in regard to their work, in any way they want, and [are legally entitled] to punish anyone who violates their regulations."[29] Here also, *takana*, regulation, or communal enactment, has replaced *t'nai*, legal condition. The *Tur* repeats the primacy of the recognized or appointed sage, here "*adam gadol v'hashuv*," a great and important man; if the city has such a man, the craftsmen must yield to his ruling.

The language of the *Shulḥan Arukh* of Josef Karo (1488-1575) provides us with some important new material, and with material which welds the links between the codes we have been examining and the language of *Baba Batra* 8b. The commentary of Shabbetai ben Meir Hakohen (1621-1662), *Siftei Kohen*, to the *Shulḥan Arukh*, citing words of the Rosh (father of the author of the *Tur*), says: "*B'nei hair* are called *baalei umaniut* in matters having to do with work."[30] *B'nei hair* of the Babylonian Talmud are synonymous with *baalei umaniut* of Josef Karo's code, some one thousand years later. The right of craftsmen or tradesmen to organize themselves in guilds or unions has been affirmed again and again, from the Talmud through the codes.[31]

The *Shulḥan Arukh* here amalgamates the language and intent of *Baba Batra* 8b and 9a, of the *Tosefta* on *Baba Metzia* 11:24, of Maimonides' *Mishneh Torah*, of the *Tur*: "*Baalei umanut*"[32] are legally entitled, *reshain*, to establish regulations in matters regarding their work, such as determining amongst themselves that a person will not work on the day when his fellow craftsman is working, and so on. And they can punish anyone who violates their conditions."

But now the Rema, Moses Isserles (1488-1575), citing the *Bet Yosef's* (the commentary to the *Tur* by Joseph Karo) citation of the Ran (Rabbeinu Nissim, 14th century), inserts language which we have not yet seen within the central text of the *Mishneh Torah* or the *Tur*: "Craftsmen can establish regulations amongst themselves *hayinu kulam b'yaḥad*," "if they were all together" [that is, in agreement]. Is the Rema saying here that "craftsmen can establish regulations amongst themselves [only] if they are unanimous in their agreement"? The Rema continues: "But if [only] two or three of them [are in agreement], the agreement has no meaning."[33] This last mitigating statement would not be necessary if Rema intended to press an unrealistic demand for absolute unanimity in the decision-making process of a guild or a union.

The discussion continues into the current period. In *Iggerot Moshe*, immediately after citing virtually all the sources which we have examined above (Rosh, *Mishneh Torah*, *Tur*, *Shulḥan Arukh*), as he begins to respond to a request for guidance regarding the *halakhah's* views of workers' rights to strike, Rabbi Moshe Feinstein declares: "*Ufashut shetalui b'rovam*" – "And it is obvious that [the decision] depends on the majority of [the workers]." Rabbi Feinstein continues:

> "Even though the Rema wrote that 'craftsmen may make regulations amongst themselves *hayinu kulam b'yaḥad*,' he surely did not intend to demand unanimity, but rather that the minority of them may not [establish regulations]. And it is clear that not even if [exactly] half [of the workers agree can they establish regulations] ...*Tzarikh sheyaskimu harov* – the majority must agree to their regulations."[34]

The view of the twentieth-century Rabbi Feinstein, writing in New York, has a counterpart in a responsum of the Rashdam (Rabbi Shmuel de Medina) writing in Salonika in the sixteenth century, approving "all which *rov shel hakahal* [the majority of the community] will decree and agree upon concerning the needs of their community." In his responsum, the Rashdam supports the action of a "majority [which] acted against the will of *yehidim* [individuals] in doing something which the majority of the population could live with." The Rashdam concludes: "*Hay'ḥidim nikhna-im*

*tahat harabim* [The individuals yield to the majority], and must behave themselves according to their (the majority's) word in all matters, for the minority is to *anshei iram* [to the people of their city]
as all Israel is to the Great Bet Din [the Sanhedrin, the Great Rabbinic
Court]."35

In an article examining a decision by the Rabbinical Administrative Board of Torah Umesorah, The National Association of
Yeshivot and Day Schools, regarding teachers' rights to join national labor unions, Rabbi J. David Bleich, the contemporary halakhic
master, sums up the halakhic material we have examined:

> "It is a well-established principle of Jewish law that
> the residents of any town may promulgate rules
> and regulations for the common benefit of the
> townspeople. Rosh states that members of a partic-
> ular profession or craft may establish regulations
> which are binding upon all such professionals or
> artisans. The members of such professions or crafts
> are deemed to be 'townspeople' entitled to exercise
> coercive power upon members of their own 'society'
> for the common benefit. This principle is recorded
> by Maimonides, *Hilkhot Mekhirah* 14:10, and *Shulḥan
> Arukh, Ḥoshen Mishpat* 231:28. Hence, persons en-
> gaged in a common trade or profession are entitled
> to unionize and to impose organizational discipline
> upon one another."36

Right-to-work laws express a state government's intention
to frustrate labor union activity, to prevent the imposition of organizational discipline upon members of a common trade or profession. A strict constructionist might choose to interpret the halakhic
material presented here as binding only the minority of a *union's
membership* to live by the majority's vote. In my understanding,
halakhic masters through the centuries have been teaching us that
the majority of *workers* have the legal right to obligate *all workers*
in their trade (in an American context, all workers in their shop, at
minimum) to live by the majority's expressed standards concerning
the needs of their community.

# Consequences
# of Labor Unions

Why join a union, or even have unions? If a community of workers,
and a majority of individuals within that community, and even the
broader society within which that workers' collective lives, do not
benefit from labor unions, then state right-to-work laws would be

serving a positive social purpose by frustrating unions' existence. What are the consequences of having unions or not having unions?

The Helms brief allows some answers: "Congress has declared that the important governmental interest in industrial peace is furthered by collective bargaining."[37] Citing information from the United States Labor Department, published in 1980, on the characteristics of major collective bargaining agreements, the Helms brief reports that

> "(i)n states that have chosen to allow union security agreements, ninety percent of the collective bargaining agreements covering more than six million workers contain clauses ... (by which) an employer is required by law to negotiate with a union whether the collective bargaining agreement ultimately executed by the parties will require 'union membership' as a condition of employment."[38]

The Helms brief continues:

> "The sacrifice of individual rights resulting from exclusive representation and collective bargaining is therefore justified to the extent employees are compelled to accept a union as their collective bargaining agent.[39] Industrial peace is also enhanced to the extent that employees who share in the `benefits' of collective bargaining are required to share in the expenses associated with collective bargaining to eliminate the problem of the 'free rider.'"[40]

As Senator Taft explained: "The argument ... against abolishing the closed shop ... is that if there is not a closed shop, those not in the union will get a free ride, that the union does the work, gets the wages raised, then the man who does not pay dues rides along freely without any expense to himself."[41]

Supreme Court Justice Brennan writes that in section 8(a)(3) of the NLRA and its "statutory equivalent," section 2, Eleventh, of the Railway Labor Act, "Congress authorized compulsory unionism only to the extent necessary to ensure that those who enjoy union-negotiated benefits contribute to their cost."[42]

Free riding is legal in a right-to-work state. A worker, in a right-to-work state, working in a shop whose certified bargaining agent is a union, enjoys the union-negotiated benefits, but is under no legal obligation to contribute to their cost.

What are these "benefits" which unions negotiate for workers under their jurisdiction? Are there benefits for management (and for stockholders) when the employees of their companies are unionized? In a paper entitled "The Impact of Collective Bargaining: Illusion or Reality?", Richard Freeman and James Medoff (of Harvard University and the National Bureau of Economic Research) present "the results of recent research concerning the impact of unionism on certain key aspects of the labor exchange."[43]

Under the heading of "Compensation," citing the results of six different studies published between 1976 and 1981 (in "a partial listing of relevant references") Freeman and Medoff find that "all else (measurable) the same, union/nonunion hourly wage differential is between ten percent and twenty percent."[44] Citing six studies on fringe benefits, Freeman and Medoff find: "All else the same, union/nonunion hourly fringe differential is between twenty percent and thirty percent ...Looking at separate fringes, the largest union/nonunion percentage differentials on a per hour basis are for pensions, life, accident, and health insurance, and vacation pay."[45]

Citing four studies on wage dispersion, they find:

> "Wage inequality is much lower among union members than among comparable nonmembers ... Since their inception, unions in our country have been concerned with the structure as well as the level of wage rates. The practice which most exemplifies unions' efforts on this front is the long-standing policy of pushing for 'standard rates;' that is, uniform rates for comparable workers across establishments and for given occupational classes within establishments ... For blue-collar workers, wage inequality is substantially lower among union members than among similar nonmembers."[46]

Citing eight studies on wage structure, they find:

> "Wage differentials between workers who are different in terms of race, age, service, skill level, and education appear to be lower under collective bargaining."[47]

Citing eight studies on the cyclical responsiveness of wage rates, Freeman and Medoff find:

> "Union wages are less responsive to labor market conditions than nonunion wages ... Recent analyses of cyclical variation in wage rates have confirmed the earlier finding of Lewis that the union/non-union wage differential has tended to be greater during economic downturns, which suggests that the reduction in (the growth of) real wage rates in response to a reduction in product demand is smaller under trade unions."[48]

Under the general heading of "Internal and External Mobility," citing four studies on promotions, Freeman and Medoff find: "Seniority independent of productivity is rewarded substantially more in promotion decisions among union members than among otherwise comparable nonunion employees."[49] Freeman and Medoff, on the basis of eight studies, find that "the quit rate is much lower for union-ized workers than for similar workers who are nonunion ... (A)mong workers receiving the same pay, unions reduce employee turnover and associated costs by offering 'voice' as an alternative to 'exit.'"[50] "Terminations are more likely to be on a last-in-first-out basis among union employees."[51]

Freeman and Medoff report that

> "several recent studies examining the impact of unionism on the stated job satisfaction of workers have found union workers expressing less satisfaction, or in some instances no more satisfaction, with their jobs than similar nonunion workers, even when compensation is not held constant. At the same time however, union members are also more likely to state that they are 'unwilling to change jobs under any circumstance' or 'would never consider moving to a new job' than are their 'more satisfied' nonunion counterparts, even when the wage is fixed. One interpretation of these results is that the collective voice of unionism provides workers with a channel for expressing their preferences to management and that this increases their willingness to complain about undesirable conditions ... The extent to which stated job security grows with tenure is substantially greater under unionism."[52]

Freeman and Medoff also report that

> "a number of recent studies have attempted to isolate 'as well as is possible with existing data' the effect of trade unionism on the productivity of otherwise comparable workers using the same amount of capital. The Brown and Medoff study (1978), based on 1972 state-by-industry data for U.S. manufacturing, found that unionized enterprises had twenty-four percent higher productivity than otherwise comparable nonunion establishments. ... [What explains the apparent union impact on productivity?] One relevant finding is that roughly twenty-five percent of the union/nonunion productivity differential in the manufacturing sector can be explained by the union/nonunion differential in quit rates. Other evidence suggests that a significant piece of the union productivity effect can be explained by the union/nonunion differential in the quality of management practices."[53]

In a study entitled "Management Performance," D. Quinn Mills of Harvard University reports on what American managers perceive to be the negative consequences of unions:

"Executives generally agree that unions complicate managers' lives. Unions are believed to impose inefficient work practices, to extract pay increases beyond productivity improvements, which contribute to inflation and undermine the competitive position of a company, and to constitute a major factor opposing corporate interests in the legislative and judicial arena. [Mills asserts that] "broadly, among the majority of American managers who are in nonunionized enterprises, and to a large degree in enterprises which do deal with unions, the above attitudes are strongly held, and are repeated continually." [These American managers believe that] unions exist as a reflection of management failures in the current workplace. [They believe that] where managers are insensitive, the workers will vote for a union.[54] ... Unions were necessary, they concede, because of management failure during the 1930s and 1940s. But, they argue, that time is now past. Government regulation of employment practices with respect to health, safety, pension benefits and possible racial or sex discrimination, combined with a more enlightened management, have made unions obsolete as protectors of workers' interests. [55]

Mills cites three overall industrial relations objectives of management: to hold down labor costs, to encourage high employee productivity, and to preserve nonunion status wherever possible.[56] In trying to understand the consequentialist perspective of management in regard to unions, Mills remarks that

"in the end, what may be most surprising to an observer of American management is the degree to which opposition to unions seems to be a matter of general doctrine rather than of analysis of the specific situation involved. If there are, as is sometimes argued, benefits of being unionized in some instances, American managers do not seem to investigate them. Rarely does one find an investigation by a company measuring the potential benefits versus the costs of recognizing a union. Where potential costs of unionized versus nonunionized operations are compared, the estimates seem to be based more on assumptions than on careful surveys ... In the prevailing attitude in most of the business community, it appears to be an act of disloyalty to ask whether a third party – that is, a union – might not in some instances be, on balance, in a corporation's interest in dealing with its employees."[57]

In a study entitled "Large Nonunionized Employers," Fred K. Foulkes of Boston University analyzes "the impact that the union movement and the institution of collective bargaining has had on the policies of large nonunion companies." Foulkes declares:

> "Unions have clearly done a lot of good for workers who (work in large nonunion companies and thus) are neither members nor dues-payers to those organizations. Some of the large nonunion companies studied resembled the large unionized companies. Some, moreover, imposed upon themselves the policies that are more restrictive than those that may emerge or be imposed under union contractual arrangments. This is true not only with respect to pay and benefits, but, more importantly, with respect to the plant's operating rules."[58] ... [Foulkes concludes]: "One cannot escape noting that one driving force behind the policies described is (management's) fear of being unionized. To the extent that these approaches continue to be successful over time and spread to other companies, the portion of the U.S. workforce represented by organized labor will continue to decline, simply because these approaches seem to obviate the felt need on the part of at least a majority of the workforce for union representation."[59]

A significant perception contributing to managers' opposition to unions is that unions oppose corporate interests in the legislative and judicial arenas. Jack Stieber and Richard Block, of Michigan State University, write: "(U)nions have on occasion joined with management to lobby Congress and to appear before regulatory bodies and in state legislatures in support of protective legislation, steel trigger prices, loans for Chrysler, quotas on Japanese auto imports, and other common interests." However, "unions more often than not have been on the opposite side from management."[60] We have seen that "the collective voice of unionism provides workers with a channel for expressing their preferences to management." That collective voice also provides workers with a channel for expressing their preferences in the judicial and legislative arenas on issues of significance to those workers.

# Ethical Opposition to Unions

In the Beck case, Harry Beck Jr. and nineteen other employees who worked for an AT&T subsidiary in Maryland – not a right-to-work-state – and who had chosen not to become members of the Communications Workers of America, were challenging the CWA's use of their agency fees for purposes other than collective bargaining, contract administration or grievance adjustment. Justice Brennan writes: "Specifically, respondents alleged that the union's expenditure of their fees on activities such as organizing the employees of other employers, lobbying for labor legislation, and participating in social, charitable, and political events violated petitioners' duty of fair representation, section 8(a)(3) of the NLRA and the First Amendment."[61]

As the Helms brief notes, "the First Amendment protects against state or governmental action and not against wrongs done by individuals."[62] Since, according to the Helms brief, "a union is able to compel financial support from dissenting employees only by virtue of its statutory status as exclusive representative," Beck was, according to the Helms group, being wronged by governmental action. The Helms brief quotes Thomas Jefferson, who said that it is "sinful and tyrannical (to) compel a man to furnish contributions of money for the propagation of opinions which he disbelieves."[63] Language of West Virginia Board of Education versus Barnette (1943) affirms that "no official, high or petty, can prescribe what shall be orthodox in politics, nationalism, religion, or other matters of opinion."[64] James Madison, who authored the First Amendment, wrote, in defense of religious liberty: "Who does not see....(t)hat the same authority which can force a citizen to contribute three pence only of his property for the support of any one establishment, may force him to conform to any other establishment in all cases whatsoever?"[65] The Helms brief concludes: "The principle that all Americans should be free to choose the groups and political causes they support is basic to our concept of individual liberty."

The Supreme Court, with Justice Brennan writing the majority decision, in June of 1988, did rule in favor of Beck against the CWA – but *not* on First Amendment grounds. Opponents of unions claim, in the Beck case literature, that unions inhibit a worker's right to choose, and damage a worker's freedom of expression. But academic studies which we have reviewed above indicate that union members, more secure in their jobs, and provided with formal channels of communication, are more likely to express their dissatisfactions. These studies show that unions give workers a voice, in many arenas, where otherwise they would have none.

Writing on the Beck case, Reed Larson, president of the National Right to Work Committee and the National Right to Work Legal Defense Foundation, affirmed: "The Beck decision will not affect workers' rights in the twenty-one states that have right-to-work laws. In these states, you cannot be required to pay union dues as a condition of employment."[66] Workers in right-to-work states are not required to contribute a cent to unions who are their certified bargaining agents, not required to help meet the costs of collective bargaining, contract administration and grievance adjustment.

# Deontological/Libertarian Ethics and Right-to-Work Laws

Dr. Charles E. Rice, a professor of constitutional law at the University of Notre Dame Law School, writes: "If it were a question decided by reason, fairness, and objective law, it would be obvious that one cannot properly be said to have a right to do something unless one also has a right not to do it."[67] Developing a deontological stand, Dr. Rice continues: "The right to join a labor association has been recognized since at least the enactment of the Norris-LaGuardia Act in 1932 as a basic protected right. Its counterpart, the right not to join, should be treated as inseparable from it."

In his introduction to the anthology in which Dr. Rice's essay appears, Dr. John B. Parrish, a professor of economics at the University of Illinois, writes:

> "A major theme runs throughout these contributions. The authors are concerned with protecting the freedom of individuals to make personal choices. This should be a fundamental right. This right is suppressed under the various forms of compulsory unionism: the closed shop, the union shop, and agency shop."[68]

F.A. Hayek, who won the 1974 Nobel Prize in Economic Science, writes: To say that the workers have a right to form unions, however, is not to say that the unions have a right to exist independently of the will of the individual workers." Hayek insists that "the essential requirement is that true freedom of association be assured and that coercion be treated as equally illegitimate whether employed for or against organization, by the employer or by the employees."[69] (One cannot separate, I believe, the prescriptive deontological tone of Hayek's words from the libertarian language demanding true freedom of association and asserting all coercion – and perhaps all external prescription – to be equally illegitimate.)

Citing language from the case of NLRB versus Allis-Chalmers Manufacturing Company (1967), the *amicus curiae* brief of Helms, Thurmond, Quayle and Symms, in support of Harry Beck against the Communication Workers of America, states: "The federal policy of exclusive representation 'extinguishes the individual employee's power to order his own relations with his employer and creates a power vested in the [collective bargaining] representative to act in the interest of all employees.'"[70] Even state right-to-work laws cannot supersede federal laws which, as the Helms brief expresses it, "without regard to whether a collective bargaining agreement contains a `union shop' provision, compel all employees in a bargaining unit to associate with a certified collective bargaining agent to the extent that all employees must accept it as their bargaining agent."[71]

In sum, Professors Rice, Parris and Hayek assert that one cannot properly be said to have a right to join a union unless one also has a right not to join a union, that the freedom of individuals to make personal choices must be protected as a fundamental right, that true freedom of association be assured and coercion treated as thoroughly illegitimate. Individuals who support state right-to-work laws for these reasons will find their position in conflict with the federal legislation which compels even workers in a right-to-work state (who need not pay a cent to a union) to accept a union as their bargaining agent if that union is properly certified as bargaining agent according to federal standards.

# Coming to a Jewish Decision

Rabbi Bleich has expressed

> "the well-established principle of Jewish law that the residents of any town may promulgate rules and regulations for the common benefit of the townspeople. Rosh states that members of a particular profession or craft may establish regulations which are binding upon all such professionals or artisans. The members of such professions or crafts are deemed to be 'townspeople' entitled to exercise coercive power upon members of their own society for the common benefit. This principle is recorded by Maimonides [and in the *Tur*] and in *Shulḥan Arukh*. Hence, persons engaged in a common trade or profession are entitled to unionize and to impose organizational discipline on one another."[72]

The clear likelihood is that a Jew whose life is governed meticulously by *halakhah* will not support right-to-work statutes and amendments.[73] But how does a Jew, who lives a life not governed by *halakhah*, decide this question of personal choice versus majority power and a dominant collective reality, not as a "liberal general human self with its accretion of Jewish coloration,"[74] but as a decidedly Jewish self?: By probing the tensions between the autonomous Jewish self and the survival of the Jewish community.

Professor Eugene Borowitz's reading of Buber frames the tension:

> "The Buberian shift from liberal religion as ideas to religion as relationship ... transforms the notion of autonomy. Because every relationship manifests distance as well as communion, the self retains its full

identity even in its most intimate involvement with
the other ... Despite all that you and I now mean to
one another, neither of us must now surrender to
the other our power of self-determination."[75]

This sounds as if the autonomous self will choose to support
right-to-work laws, for even though the self finds fulfillment in community with others, that self will not yield its power of self-determination, and will not ask the other to yield its power. "Yet because
you are here with me, my self, formerly so potentially anarchic, now
has a sense of what it must choose and do." This sounds as if the
experience of community has drawn the self away from its focus on
self-determination, this self perhaps ready to endorse the community's power, and priority, and reject right-to-work laws. "This
interpretation of religious experience is too individualistic for any
orthodoxy" – **for compulsory union membership** – "and too
other-involved for anarchy" **free riding**.

"Religious experience?" Isn't this a process of ethical decision-making? Here, ethics are not independent of religion. To be
Jewish is to participate in a covenantal relationship with God. "In
the healthy Jewish self one detects no place, no matter how deeply,
one searches, where one can find the old liberal schizoid split
between the self and the Jew."[76]

What makes this Jewish self healthy? "In responding to
God out of the Covenant situation, the relationally autonomous
Jewish self acknowledges its essential historicity and sociality."[77]
The Jew whose life is not governed meticulously by *halakhah*
might not recognize the legal force of the "well-established principle of Jewish law ... that persons engaged in a common trade or
profession are entitled to unionize and to impose organizational
discipline upon one another."[78] But the healthy autonomous Jewish
self will recognize the sociohistorical force of that *halakhah*, and
will recognize the self's place in the social reality which that *halakhah* defines.

"With heritage and folk compelling values, with the Jewish
services of God directed to historic continuity lasting until messianic days, the Covenanted self acknowledges the need for structure to
Jewish existence. Yet this does not rise to the point of validating
law in the traditional sense, for personal autonomy remains the
cornerstone of this piety."[79] But in this case, the "compelling values" of Jewish historic continuity are asserted by a legal principle
which has been affirmed and reaffirmed throughout the history of
halakhic evolution. This legal principle in its essence commands
that individuals' resources be joined, together and in partnership
with God, to insure the community's historic continuity lasting until
messianic days. The compelling values of historicity and social reality – of Jewish survival – observed in the halakhic material presented

in this case, and felt in the covenantal richness of being a Jew, create for the autonomous self a way (*halakhah*) to affirm "the community which is so great a part of its selfhood."[80] In this case, opposing right-to-work laws can mean, for the autonomous Jewish self, choosing not to exercise the principle of personal choice. Here, personal choice would be exercised as pure principle (or as self-interest), opposing documentedly positive consequences for the community.

Traditional Judaism builds a fence around the Torah. Too often, Jewish autonomy has meant building a fence around the self. But by affirming the positive communal consequences of healthy trade unions, the autonomous Jewish self will be affirming the priority of collective benefit, without which there is only the vaguest sense to the philosophical primacy of a lone Jew's options.

What Jewish congregation will stomach non-payment of dues by a participating Jew who has the means to pay? Right-to-work laws, under which workers are legally entitled to enjoy communal benefits while not contributing financially, violate fundamental principles of Jewish communal participation.

Is it possible for a Jew who has decided that unions are beneficial, that unions should exist, to support right-to-work laws? My answer, in the pragmatic context of current trade union realities is: No. Reed Larson, president of the National Right To Work Committee writes: "Against the argument that right-to-work laws are anti-union must be placed the evidence that most such laws, now in force in the private employment sectors of twenty-one states, protect the right of employees either to belong or not to belong as a matter of voluntary choice."[81]

But in daily reality, right-to-work laws create and enhance an anti-union environment. A retired vice-president of the International Ladies' Garment Workers' Union, commenting on his experiences of "heartburn and heartache" in trying to organize workers in right-to-work states,declared: "The whole purpose of right-to-work laws and amendments is to destroy the trade union movement."[82] The weakening of labor unions means a weakening in the influence of Jewish law, and in the influence of a long-enduring Jewish social reality, on life in America.

# Closing Comments

In the Beck case, Thurgood Marshall sided with the majority of the Court, supporting Beck's challenging position against the Communication Workers of America. Marshall saw it as a worker's rights case. Union officials were astonished. Thurgood Marshall had come down on the same side as Jesse Helms and Strom Thurmond, Dan

Quayle and Steve Symms. Conservatives were surprised: Justices Scalia and O'Connor had sided with the dissenting Harry Blackmun in saying that, "in enacting section 8(a)(3) [of the Taft-Hartley Act] the 1947 Congress ... was not making inroads on a policy of full freedom of choice."[83]

Liberal Jews who find themselves Jesse Helms's adversary when they assert the principle of personal choice on the question of abortion, might have found themselves celebrating with Jesse Helms had they narrowly applied that principle of personal choice in developing a position on the Beck case. But also attending the celebration would have been Reed Larson, president of the National Right To Work Committee, who wrote these words:

> "First and foremost, unionism in the United States was not at any time a natural, organic element of society. It has always represented an alien product, imported with some of the millions of European refugees who came in the nineteenth century to escape various forms of political or religious tyranny ... The collectivist ethos implicit in unionism made these organizations, when they arose at all on American soil, a product of the Eastern seaboard urban areas where some had already begun to lose the sense of adventurous expansionism characteristic of America's early years ... Given the fact that a large portion of the urban population at the time was newly arrived from a milieu in which unions were a major dissenting force, it is not surprising that the union song sounded so sweet."[84]

Looking to the continuing evolution of this process of locating the places where Jewish law and Jewish ethics intersect (and locating also the moments of intersection, and perhaps even the languages in which those intersections might be communicated): We must try to develop categories, within this process, which will provide formal status – an effective angle of attack – for literatures other than halakhic literatures. Yes, liberal Jews have done this for years to prove that there should be no binding law, but only aggadic liberty. Can we find ways, as we develop our methodologies, our rules of metahalakhic engagement, to accept aggadic material as a more potent disciplining supplement to the legal material than old liberal tactics intended or than our current policy of devaluing (and excluding) *aggadah* permits? The redactors of *Bereishit Rabbah* seem to have been developing their midrashic literature as a buttress – or a pillar – at weak points of intersection between Jewish law (or Palestinian rabbis' presence in communicating the guiding forces which informed and girded that law) and a struggling community's absorption of that guidance. We should study rabbinic literatures that are other than halakhic, focusing on the points where those literatures intersect the halakhic, with the intent of grasping whatever strategies might structure that intersection, and with the hope of developing new strategies. But we must concentrate on resisting earlier tendencies of finding only freedom in the aggadic literature and not finding discipline.

How could the following aggadic material from the Babylonian Talmud, *Sukkah* 51b, be allowed significant resonance within the decision-making process of this paper?:

> "It has been taught that Rabbi Yehudah stated: He who has not seen the double colonnade of Alexandria in Egypt has never seen the glory of Israel. It was said to be like a huge basilica, one colonnade within the other, and sometimes held twice the number of people that left Egypt. Within were seventy-one golden chairs, corresponding to the seventy-one members of the Great Sanhedrin ... and a wooden platform in the middle upon which the synagogue's *shamas* stood, with a scarf in his hand. When the time came to answer Amen, he waved his scarf and all the congregation responded. And they did not occupy their seats at random. Goldsmiths sat separately, silversmiths sat separately, blacksmiths separately, weavers separately – so that when a poor man entered the synagogue he would recognize the members of his craft, and, approaching that group, could obtain a livelihood for himself and for the members of his family."

What would be the role of this next material?:

> "On November 22, 1909, the leadership of Local 25 of the ILGWU called a meeting of workers at Cooper Union. Thousands came, with crowds spilling over into other halls. Gompers spoke; so did Mary Dreier, head of the Women' Trade Union League; and, as usual at such meetings, Jacob Panken and Meyer London, the big guns of Jewish socialism. But no clear strategy had been worked out by the Local leadership, and the speakers, hesitating before the prospect of an ill-prepared general strike, could not quite decide between exhortation and caution. As the evening dragged along and speaker followed speaker, there suddenly raced up to the platform, from the depths of the hall, a frail teenage girl named Clara Lemlich, who had been picketing at the Leiserson plant day after day. She burst into a flow of passionate Yiddish which would remain engraved in thousands of memories: 'I am a working girl, one of those striking against intolerable conditions. I am tired of listening to speakers who talk in generalities. What we are here for is to decide wheth-

er or not to strike. I offer a resolution that a general strike be declared – now.'

A contagion of excitement swept the meeting, people screaming, stamping feet, waving handkerchiefs. The chairman, Benjamin Feigenbaum, stood on the platform trying to restore order, and when finally heard, asked for a second. Again pandemonium,the whole crowd shouting its second. Shaken by this outburst, Feigenbaum cried out: 'Do you mean it in good faith? Will you take the old Jewish oath?' Thousands of hands went up: 'If I turn traitor to the cause I now pledge, may this hand wither from the arm I raise!' Week after week the strike went on..."[85]

That's a movement. And deep in the site of a soul's commanded loyalties, where the value of rational discourse is limited to saying "Yes" as an immediate prelude to action, that movement has been my soul's potent inspiration. If our evolving system of responsa would grant this history formal influence in the decision-making process, then that movement would be a reason from which to project an ancient and vital halakhic reality as a metahalakhic ethical choice: Consciously, these Jews knew: Our labor union is the heart of our survival now. Emerging from a seriously observant world, many (and perhaps most) of them no longer as observant, not as Jewishly learned, also knew – sensed somehow – that labor unions, and the powers of a unified majority, had been central to the enduring halakhic structure of Jewish societies; that, in their essence, labor unions had expressed the imperative of Jewish communal survival.

Jews organized in common purpose are far more powerful than autonomous Jews, moderns with options, choosing self first. In this case, at least, the most significant choice of Jewish autonomy is to yield that autonomy for the collective benefit.

# Bibliography

Bleich, J. David. "Review of Recent Halakhic Periodical Literature," *Tradition* 19:261-272, Fall 1981.

Borowitz, Eugene B. "The Autonomous Jewish Self," *Modern Judaism*, Vol. 4, No. 1, February 1984.

Foulkes, Fred. "Large Nonunionized Employers," in *US Industrial Relations 1950-1980*.

Freeman, Richard B. and Medoff, James L. "The Impact of Collective Bargaining: Illusion or Reality?", in *US Industrial Relations 1950-1980*.

Hayek, F.A. *The Constitution of Liberty*, University of Chicago Press, 1979.

Howe, Irving. *World Of Our Fathers: The Journey of the East European Jews to America And The Life They Found And Made*, HBJ, New York and London, 1976.

Jung, Leo. *Business Ethics in Jewish Law*, New York: Hebrew Publishing Co., 1987.

Larson, Reed. "American Trade Unionism: The Shape of Things To Come", *American Review*, Summer, 1985 (Institute for American Studies, Rand Afrikaans University).

Larson, Reed. "Harry Beck's Earthquake," *Policy Review* 49, Summer, 1989.

Levine, Aaron. *Free Enterprise in Jewish Law*, New York: KTAV, 1980.

Mills, D. Quinn. "Management Performance," in *US Industrial Relations 1950-1980*.

*Primer of labor relations*, prepared by the staff of "The Labor Reporter," 19th edition, p.2, Bureau of National Affair, Washington, 1973.

Rice, Dr. Charles E. "The Constitution and the Right Not To Join," in *Compulsory Unionism in the Public Sector*, symposium proceedings of 4/6/79, Chicago, published by National Right To Work Committee, 1979.

St. Antoine, Theodore J., "The Role of Law," in *U.S. Industrial Relations 1950-1980: A Critical Assessment.* Industrial Relations Research Association, Madison, Wisconsin, 1981.

Steinsaltz, Rabbi Adin. *The Talmud: The Steinsaltz Edition*, Volume 1, Tractate *Baba Metzia*, Part 1.

Stieber, Jack. and Stieber, Richard. "Summary and Conclusions," citing Mills, in *US Industrial Relations 1950-1980*.

Tamari, Meir. *"With All Your Possessions,"* New York: The Free Press, 1987.

**Traditional Sources**

Moses ben Maimon, *Mishneh Torah* and commentaries

Joseph Karo, the *Shulḥan Arukh* and commentaries

Feinstein, Rabbi Moshe, *Iggerot Moshe.*

**Legal Sources and Personal Communications**

Algoma Plywood Co. v. Wisconsin Employment Relations Board (1949), as cited by Justice Brennan in Beck case, 128 LRRM 2733.

*Amicus curiae* brief by Senator Helms et al, Case No. 86-637, October Term 1987, printed in *Communication Workers of America versus Beck: Petitions and Briefs,* Labor Law Series, Volume 21, No.7. Law Reprints, 5442 30th Street NW, Washington, DC 20015.

Comments of Senator Taft, 93 Cong. Rec. 4887 (1947), Leg. Hist. 1422, as cited by Justice Brennan in Beck case, 128 LRRM 2734.

49 Stat. 449, section 1 (1935), as amended 29 U.S.C. section 151 (1976). For evidence of the House's state of mind, see HR 3020, 80th Congress, 1st Session, subsection 1(b), 101 (1947), as passed House; H. Conf. Rep. No. 510, 80th Congress, 1st Session, (1947); 93 Cong. Rec. 3968 (daily ed. April 17, 1947) (remarks of Rep. Celler); 93 Cong. Rec. 7690 (daily ed. June 23, 1947) (remarks of Senator Taft).

93 Cong. Rec. 7690 (daily ed. June 23, 1947), as cited by St. Antoine in "Role of Law."

S. Rep. No. 105, 80th Cong., 1st Sess., 6 (1947), as cited by Justice Brennan in Beck case, 128 LRRRM 2733.

Justice William Brennan in Beck case, 128 LRRM 2734.

NLRB v. General Motors, quoting S. Rep., at 6, Leg. Hist. 412, as cited by Justice Brennan in Beck case, 128 LRRM 2734.

Amendment to Florida's state constitution, as cited in printout "Background on Right To Work Laws", published by National Right To Work Committee, 4/5/85.

Lincoln Union v. Northwestern Company, 335 US 525, 531 (1949), 23 LRRM 2199,2204.

53 LRRM 2313, 53 LRRM 2318, 54 LRRM 2612.

29 U.S.C., section 158 (a)(3), as cited by Justice Brennan in Beck case, 128 LRRM 2732.

NLRB v. General Motors, as cited by Justice Brennan in Beck case, 128 LRRM 2732.

Communicated by Professor Michael Chernick in a conversation on March 4, 1990.

Communicated in telephone conversation by Douglas Levin, longtime manager of Local 99, ILGWU, vice-president of the ILG, who also headed the ILG's Central Organization Department from 1966-73.

Communicated in a converstion with Max Zimny on April 18. 1990.

Supreme Court Justice Harry Blackmun, in Beck case, 128 LRRM 2745.

# Notes

1. Communicated in a conversation in Max Zimny's office, 1710 Broadway, NYC, April 18. 1990.

2. *Amicus curiae* brief by Senator Helms et al, Case No. 86-637, October Term 1987, printed in *Communication Workers of America versus Beck: Petitions and Briefs,* Labor Law Series, Volume 21, No.7, p.5, Law Reprints, 5442 30th Street NW, Washington, DC 20015.

3. The twenty-one states with right-to-work statutes now in force are: Alabama, Arizona, Arkansas, Florida, Georgia, Idaho, Iowa, Kansas, Louisiana, Mississippi, Nebraska, Nevada, North Carolina, North Dakota, South Carolina, South Dakota, Tennessee, Texas, Utah, Virginia and Wyoming. The Idaho statute, the most recent, was passed on January 31, 1985. Seven states have right-to-work guarantess in their constitutions: Arizona, Arkansas, Florida, Kansas, Mississippi, Nebraska, South Dakota. Right-to-work laws do not protect employees of the federal government or employees covered by the Railway Labor Act. The fifth circuit has ruled that right-to-work laws do not apply to private sector employees working on federal properties in right-to-work states.

4. Helms brief, page 6, citing NLRB v. General Motors (1963).

5. *Primer of labor relations*, prepared by the staff of "The Labor Reporter", 19th edition, p.2, Bureau of National Affair, Washington, 1973.

6. See: Algoma Plywood Co. v. Wisconsin Employment Relations Board (1949), as cited by Justice Brennan in Beck case, 128 LRRM 2733.

7. St. Antoine, Theodore J., "The Role of Law" in *U.S. Industrial Relations 1950-1980: A Critical Assessment,* p.159, Industrial Relations Research Association, Madison, Wisconsin, 1981.

8. 49 Stat. 449, section 1 (1935), as amended 29 U.S.C. section 151 (1976). For evidence of the House's state of mind, see HR 3020, 80th Congress, 1st Session, subsection 1(b), 101 (1947), as passed House; H. Conf. Rep. No. 510, 80th Congress, 1st Session, pp.30-41 (1947); 93 Cong. Rec. 3968 (daily ed. April 17, 1947) (remarks of Rep. Celler); 93 Cong. Rec.7690 (daily ed. June 23, 1947) (remarks of Senator Taft).

9. 93 Cong. Rec. 7690 (daily ed. June 23, 1947) (remarks of Senator Taft), as cited by St. Antoine in "Role of Law".

10. S. Rep. No. 105, 80th Cong., 1st Sess., 6 (1947), as cited by Justice Brennan in Beck case, 128 LRRRM 2733.

11. Justice Brennan in Beck case, 128 LRRM 2734. See footnote on that page: "This sentiment was repeated throughout the hearings and lengthy debate that preceded passage of the bill."

12. NLRB v. General Motors, quoting S. Rep., at 6, Leg. Hist. 412, as cited by Justice Brennan in Beck case, 128 LRRM 2734.

13. *Primer*, p.51.

14. Amendment to Florida's state constitution, as cited in printout "Background on Right To Work Laws", published by National Right To Work Committee, 4/5/85.

15. See: Lincoln Union v. Northwestern Company, 335 US 525, 531 (1949), 23 LRRM 2199,2204.

16. For the three crucial decisions in this matter, see 53 LRRM 2313, 53 LRRM 2318, 54 LRRM 2612.

17. Helms brief, pp. 6-7.

18. 29 U.S.C., section 158 (a)(3), as cited by Justice Brennan in Beck case, 128 LRRM 2732.

19. Ibid.

20. Ibid.

21. NLRB v. General Motors, as cited by Justice Brennan in Beck case, 128 LRRM 2732.

22. Communicated by Professor Chernick in conversation, March 4, 1990. Cf. Leo Jung, *Business Ethics in Jewish Law*, New York: Hebrew Publishing Co., 1987, p. 180, and Meir Tamari, *"With All Your Possessions,"* New York: The Free Press, 1987, p. 149, for the general background.

23. In *Baba Metzia* 10a we read: "But surely Rav said: '*Hapoel* may retract – *lahzor* [meaning, leave the job, cancelling his commitment to work] — even in the middle of the day.'" In his notes to this sentence in *Baba Metzia* 10a, Rabbi Adin Steinsaltz comments: *"Tosafot* points out, in *Baba Metzia* 77a, where the *Gemara* deals with this question at length, there is no dispute that a worker may retract at any time." Why? We read on in *Baba Metzia* 7a: "...for it is written, 'For to Me the children of Israel are servants.' [Leviticus 25:55] They are My servants, and not the servants of servants." Rabbi Steinsaltz comments: "Some commentators interpret the verse as a warning, prohibiting a Jew from submitting himself to bondage. Indeed, this is Rav's main argument regarding the laborer's work. He explains that any absolute obligation to work for other people is in reality a situation of slavery, even if it only lasts for a short time. For that reason the worker has the right to stop working any time, and this is an expression of his status as a free man, bound only by his obligations to God." Commentary by Rabbi Adin Steinsaltz in *The Talmud: The Steinsaltz Edition*, Volume 1, Tractate *Baba Metzia*, Part 1, page 112. Rabbi Steinsaltz's note here continues: "However, there is a question whether the worker has any obligations to the employer if by unexpectedly leaving him he causes him finan-

cial loss." Cf. Jung, op. cit., p. 179, and Aaron Levine, *Free Enterprise in Jewish Law*, New York: KTAV, 1980, p. 44f.

24. Rashi *ad loc.* Professor Michael Chernick has said in conversation that this whole sentence in *Baba Batra* 7a can be interpreted as affirming the right of the townspeople to establish a tax policy. For the general talmudic and rabbinic law on taxes and other communal levies see Levine, op. cit., p. 136 ff.

25. Maimonides' *Mishneh Torah, Hilkhot Mekhira* 14:10.

26. *Maggid Mishneh ad loc.*

27. *Hatam Sofer, Helek Hoshen Mishpat*, 78.

28. Note the change in language from *Baba Batra's adam hashuv* – an important man – to Maimonides' *ḥaḥam hashuv*. Sephardic communities tended to turn to centralized authority, to a major sage, for legal decisions. According to Professor Michael Chernick, the legal processes of relatively few Ashkenazic communities were dominated by an *adam hashuv* or *ḥaḥam hashuv*. Ashkenazic communities dealt with their legal complexities on a more local and decentralized basis. In a majority of communities, craft guilds functioned without having to yield their legal authority to an individual of superior halakhic credentials and status. For detailed insights into the role of the *ḥakham hashuv* in relationship to *anshei umaniut*, see the commentaries of Bet Yosef (Josef Karo) to the *Tur, Hoshen Mishpat, Hilkhot Onaah Umekakh Taut* 231, and then follow the rich list of commentaries and responsa found in the commentary to the *Shulḥan Arukh* called *Pithei Tshuva*, under the same heading as cited for the *Tur*. See also the commentary of the Maggid Mishna to *Mishneh Torah, Hilkhot Mekhira* 14:11.

29. Jacob ben Asher's *Tur, Ḥoshen Mishpat, Hilkhot Onaah Umekakh Taot* 231.

30. Commentary of *Siftei Kohen* to *Shulḥan Arukh, Ḥoshen Mishpat, Hilkhot Onaah Umekakh Taut* 231.

31. I hope yet to study, in the sociohistorical context of each of the codes, why *poalim* are never specifically accorded the rights to establish guilds as are *b'nei umaniut*.

32. Note change in spelling here from *umaniut* to *umanut*.

33. Rabbi Moses Isserles (Rema) in central text of *Shulḥan Arukh, Ḥoshen Mishpat* 231.

34. Rabbi Moshe Feinstein in *Iggerot Moshe, Ḥoshen Mishpat* 59. In this connection, Rabbi Feinstein also cites *Yoreh Deah* 228:34 and the Rema in *Ḥoshen Mishpat* 163:1.

35. Rashdam, *Ḥoshen Mishpat* 406. The Rivash (Rabbi Yitzhak bar Sheshet,1326-1408, of Barcelona and, after 1391, North Africa), in answer-

ing a question in section 249 of his book of responsa, uses similar language (after citing the passage in *Baba Batra* 8b, ending with *l'hasiah al kitsatan*: "...and as the *beit din* of Israel was legally entitled to excommunicate and to banish, so is the legal authority with *anshei hair*. When all or a majority of them are in agreement with the position of *tovei hair*, all *b'nei hair* are obligated to behave according to the regulation which they have established."

36. Rabbi J. David Bleich, "Review of Recent Halakhic Periodical Literature", *Tradition* 19:261-272, Fall 1981.

37. Helms brief, p. 24.

38. Ibid, p. 6. See note 13 there.

39. Ibid., p. 24.

40. Ibid.

41. Comments of Senator Taft, 93 Cong. Rec. 4887 (1947), Leg. Hist. 1422, as cited by Justice Brennan in Beck case, 128 LRRM 2734.

42. In Beck case, 128 LRRM 2733.

43. Richard B. Freeman and James L. Medoff, "The Impact of Collective Bargaining: Illusion or Reality?", in *US Industrial Relations 1950-1980,* p. 49.

44. Ibid., p. 50, citing Ashenfelter (1976), Freeman and Medoff, Lewis (1980), Mellow 1981a), Oaxaca (1975), Welch (1980).

45. Ibid., citing Duncan (1976), Freeman (1981), Goldstein and Pauly (1976), Leigh (1979), Solnick (1978), Viscusi (1980).

46. Ibid., citing Freeman (1980c), Hyclak (1979, 1980), Plotnick (1981).

47. Ibid., citing Ashenfelter (1976), Bloch and Kuskin (1978), Johnson and Youmans (1971), Kiefer and Smith (1977), Leigh (1978), Pfeffer and Ross (1980), Schoeplein (1977), Shapiro (1978).

48. Ibid., citing Ashenfelter (1976), Hamermesh (1972), Johnson (1981), Lewis (1963), Medoff (1979), Mitchell (1980a, 1980b), Pierson (1968), Raisian (1979).

49. Ibid., citing Halasz (1980), Medoff and Abraham (1980b, 1981b), Yanker (1980).

50. Ibid., citing Blau and Kahn (1981), Block (1978a), Farber (OLS Results 1979), Freeman (1976,1980a, 1980b), Kahn (1977), Leigh (1979).

51. Ibid., citing Blau and Kahn (1981), Medoff and Abraham, (1981a, 1981b).

52. Ibid., pp. 58-9.

53. Ibid., p. 60.

54. D. Quinn Mills, "Management Performance," in *US Industrial Relations 1950-1980*, p. 112.

55. Ibid., p. 113.

56. Jack Stieber and Richard Block, "Summary and Conclusions," citing Mills, in *US Industrial Relations 1950-1980*, pp. 345-6.

57. Mills, pp. 115-16.

58. Fred Foulkes, "Large Nonunionized Employers," in *US Industrial Relations 1950-1980*, p. 156.

59. Ibid.

60. Stieber and Block, p. 346.

61. Justice Brennan in Beck case, 128 LRRM 2731.

62. Helms brief, p. 15, citing United Brotherhood of Carpenters versus Scott (1983).

63. Helms brief, p. 21, quoting Thomas Jefferson in: I. Brant, *James Madison: The Nationalist* (1948), cited in Abood.

64. Ibid.

65. Ibid., p. 30, from *The Writings of James Madison*, cited in Abood.

66. Reed Larson, "Harry Beck's Earthquake," *Policy Review* 49, Summer, 1989.

67. Dr. Charles E. Rice, "The Constitution and the Right Not To Join," in *Compulsory Unionism in the Public Sector*, symposium proceedings of 4/6/79, Chicago, published by National Right To Work Committee, 1979.

68. Ibid.

69. F.A. Hayek, *The Constitution of Liberty*, University of Chicago Press, 1979.

70. Helms brief, p. 18.

71. Ibid.

72. See note 36.

73. In his article in *Tradition* magazine (see note 36), Rabbi Bleich examines "(a) decision of the Rabbinical Administrative Board of Torah Umesorah, The National Association of Yeshivot and Day Schools, *prohibiting* teachers from joining national labor unions ...The statement is entirely declarative in nature and contains neither an analysis of halakhic issues nor citation of precedents ...This pronouncement, dated 2 Kislev 5741, is particularly

noteworthy since R. Moshe Feinstein, honorary chairman of the Rabbinical Administrative Board, in his *Iggerot Moshe, Ḥoshen Mishpat* 59, has sanctioned strike action by Yeshivah and Day School teachers, at least under limited circumstances." Rabbi Bleich concludes that "it is clear that the Torah Umesorah proclamation is not directed against unionization [for Torah Umesorah teachers] per se but against membership [for those teachers] in national unions whose actions and policies are not governed by halakhic considerations and constraints. Indeed, the text of the document bans [those teachers from] affiliation solely with 'secular' labor unions. Moreover, the same document calls for the formation of an '*Irgun haMorim*' (Teachers' Organization) under the aegis of Torah Umesorah for the purpose of 'advancing the status of Yeshivah teachers materially and professionally.' Such a body would undoubtedly enjoy the prerogatives which Jewish law conveys upon craft guilds and, to all intents and purposes, would function as a union without affiliation with any secular group." In the article, Rabbi Bleich notes Rabbi Feinstein's view that "(p)ersons earning a livelihood from the teaching of Torah are in a somewhat different position" from other workers who are entitled to join unions. "The compensation of (a teacher of Torah) is not in the form of a fee for services rendered but payment in lieu of not engaging in some other remunerative activity (*sekhar batalah*)."

74. Eugene B. Borowitz, "The Autonomous Jewish Self," *Modern Judaism*, 4.1, February 1984, p. 43.

75. Ibid., pp. 43-44.

76. Ibid., p. 44.

77. Ibid., idem.

78. See note 36.

79. Borowitz, ibid., p. 44.

80. Ibid., p. 45.

81. Reed Larson, "American Trade Unionism: The Shape of Things To Come," *American Review*, Summer, 1985 (Institute for American Studies, Rand Afrikaans University).

82. Communicated in telephone conversation by Douglas Levin, longtime manager of Local 99, ILGWU, vice-president of the ILG, who also headed the ILG's Central Organization Department from 1966-73.

83. Supreme Court Justice Harry Blackmun, in Beck case, 128 LRRM 2745.

84. Reed Larson, "American Trade Unionism: The Shape of Things To Come" (see note 81).

85. Irving Howe, *World Of Our Fathers: The Journey of the East European Jews to America And The Life They Found And Made*, HBJ, New York and London, 1976.

# Employee Rights in a Situation of Dismissal:

## A Liberal Jewish Perspective

Gayle Pomerantz
and David Stern

**O**ur initial task in writing this paper was to formulate a question that would help us understand the intersection of general ethics and Jewish law. We soon discovered, however, that the formation of our question would be part of our process of mediation, not prelude to it. As we learned more about elements as diverse as contract law, free enterprise, role morality, and the significance of human rights in the workplace, we decided upon our current question: what are the worker's rights in a situation of firing? By providing a basis for comparison that would be both inclusive and focused, this question provoked us to explore the ethical dimensions of the employment relationship.

## Dismissing An Employee: Halakhic Consideration

It turns out that our question, "what are the worker's rights in a situation of firing?" is somewhat of an anachronistic one when exploring halakhah. *Halakhah* focuses primarily on the rights and responsibilities of the employer, rather than on protecting the employee. So for purposes of examining *halakhah*, it is necessary to ask the mirror side of our original question: what are the employer's rights and responsibilities in a situation of firing? This question is fruitful for uncovering the layers of Jewish labor law. By concentrating on this question, halakhic attitudes toward job security, contracts, and employer/employee rights begin to be clarified.

However, even our question "what are the employer's rights

in a situation of firing?" is, as we discovered, not explicitly answered by the *halakhah*. The *halakhah* which we researched only answered the question, "what are the employer's rights in an extreme situation of firing?" We can, nevertheless, extrapolate from the *halakhah* regulating the extreme case of firing, i.e., firing without warning, to learn about the *halakhah* in the normal case of dismissal. The employer's right to summarily fire a contracted employee falls into three categories: "crime of the worker," "incompetency," and "improper behavior outside of the work place."[1]

## Crime of the Worker

The source for the first category, "crime of the worker," is *Baba Batra* 21b, which says:

> Rava said: A teacher of young children, a planter, a slaughterer, a bloodletter, and a town scribe are all liable to be dismissed immediately [literally: they are as if permanently warned]. The general principle is that anyone who causes an irretrievable loss is liable to be dismissed immediately.[2]

If an employee makes mistakes which can be rectified, the employer does not have the legal right to dismiss him summarily. However, if the employee causes an irretrievable loss to his employer, no matter how small it may be, his employer has the halakhic right to dismiss him immediately, i.e., without warning. The above talmudic statement teaches us that an employer may summarily dismiss an employee who has caused some form of irretrievable loss. From this we might deduce that there is another process of firing an employee who has not caused irretrievable loss, which would, perhaps, require the employer to go through a number of steps before he could legitimately fire an employee. Because the consequences for causing an irretrievable loss are so harsh, the commentators made efforts to define this term more precisely by providing examples of irretrievable loss in different professions. Teachers of Torah are regarded as having caused irretrievable loss when they make a mistake in their teaching and the students absorb the incorrect information,[3] or when they waste class time.[4] Rabbi Gershom, Maor HaGolah (960-1028), includes a teacher's negligence toward his own study of Torah among the justifiable reasons for firing a teacher.[5] In addition to the *halakhah* cited above, individual rabbis provide other legitimate reasons for dismissing teachers. Thus it appears that it is relatively easy to dismiss a teacher before his or her term is up. It's clear that the rabbis view Torah education as being of ultimate importance, even more important than job security for teachers.

The planter is considered to cause irretrievable loss when he plants trees or plants incorrectly, and they don't grow normally. Even though the planter can pay for the plants he planted incorrectly, he cannot pay for the fruit that would have already been growing on the trees if they had been planted correctly in the first place.[6]

A slaughterer or butcher who makes an animal ritually impure for consumption (*trefah*) causes irretrievable loss, because even though he can pay for the cost of the meat he has spoiled, he cannot, according to the *Maggid Mishneh* (second half of 14th century), pay for the shame he has caused his customers who had been planning on serving that meat to their guests, but now were left empty handed.[7]

Rashi (1040-1105) says that a scribe causes irretrievable loss when he makes a mistake in creating a Torah.[8] The Tosafot (12th-13th centuries) disagree with Rashi because they claim that these mistakes can be corrected. They say that irretrievable loss is caused when the scribe makes a mistake in a legal document, because the mistakes may cause the users of the document a financial loss, for which the scribe is not liable.[9] Rashi brings forth another interesting interpretation for an irretrievable loss caused by a "*sofer d'mata.*" He also reads "*sofer d'mata*" as "*sapar d'mata* – a town barber. A barber causes irretrievable loss when he cuts off more hair than he was supposed to, because there is no way to pay the customer for the embarrassment he has caused him [an embarrassment we all know too well!]. As Rashi's argument suggests, it can be relatively easy to make the case that an employee has caused irretrievable loss.[10]

There is a discussion among the rabbis as to whether Rava's statement in *Baba Batra* 21b about immediate dismissal applies only to public employees or includes private employees. According to the Rambam (1135-1204), the right to fire an employee without warning applies only to public employees. He reasons that since they are working for the public they have a greater obligation to fulfill their responsibilities in a suitable manner. "[All skilled persons] who cannot repair the damage caused by them, may be removed without warning because, having been appointed by the public, they have a standing warning to exert themselves in their work.[11] The Rabad (1125-1198), however, disagrees with the Rambam. The Rabad believes that there is no difference between the responsibilities of a public and a private employee, and that therefore they should both be dismissed without warning if they cause an irretrievable loss to their employers.[12]

The *Tur* (Ḥoshen Mishpat 306:12;14th century) accepts the Rabad's opinion and adduces the following story from *Baba Metzia* to support this theory:

Runya, who was Rabbina's planter, spoiled [a plant] and was dismissed. He went before Rava and said to him: 'Look at how he's treated me!' Rava said to him, 'He did the right thing.' Runya said to him, 'But he didn't warn me!' Rava said to him, 'He didn't have to warn. [As] Rava reasoned, 'A teacher of young children, a planter, a slaughterer, a bloodletter, and a town scribe are all liable to be dismissed immediately. ...'[13]

The *Tur* reasons that since Runya was Rabbina's private employee and Rabbina dismissed him without warning, Rava's statement in *Baba Batra* 21b applies to both public and private employees.

Over the centuries, the laws dealing with summary dismissal are interpreted more liberally by some halakhic commentators. These commentators limit an employer's right to summary dismissal by forcing an employer to warn an employee before firing him, or forcing the employer to allow the employee a second chance. The *Maggid Mishneh* states in Rabad's name: "Warning is not necessary except in the interest of certainty. Until he [the employer] is certain or he warned them, he cannot dismiss them."[14] In his commentary on the *Shulḥan Arukh* (16th century), *Ḥoshen Mishpat* 306:8, the Rema (1525-1572) states the same thing as the *Maggid Mishneh*, but limits the view to, "there are those who say..." The *Nimukei Yosef* (beginning of 15th century) to *Baba Metzia* 109b also utilizes Rabad's ruling and says that in order to be subject to immediate dismissal, the employee must repeat his mistake three times.

Sholem Warhaftig, the author of *Dinei Avodah B'mishpat Haivri*, (a contemporary compilation of *halakhah* dealing with employment), accepts a more liberal interpretation of the summary dismissal law, at least as seen from the employee's perspective. He says:

The law that the employer is able to dismiss an employee without warning when he causes him irretrievable loss, is applicable only when the employer is sure that the employee caused irreparable damage. That is to say, it is not enough that he has done it only once. Rather, the employee must repeat his mistake a number of times or continue in his [improper] behavior for a specific period of time in such a way that will prove that he treated his work irresponsibly. Otherwise the employer is not able to dismiss an employee unless he warned him first.[15]

One might make the following argument using the logic of *"kal v'ḥomer"*: since some commentators require that an employer warn an employee even in cases of irretrievable loss, when an employee has not caused irretrievable loss, how much the more so is the employer who wishes to fire him under obligation to warn him.

Both the issue of whether Rava's statement in *Baba Batra* 21b applies to both public and private employees, and the issue of whether some sort of warning is necessary before firing an employee who has caused irretrievable loss, illustrate the difficulty one has in determining what *halakhah* says about any issue. We conclude that the primary force of *halakhah* is that Rava's statement applies to public and private employees, and that warning is not necessary when firing an employee who has caused irretrievable loss. Yet there are later opinions which mitigate this view. Our tradition is rich with arguments, dissenting opinions and positions of compromise. The very dialectic of opinion testifies to the play of different hierarchies of values within the halakhic process. Thus when the contemporary Jew comes to mediate between *halakhah* and contemporary ethics, one may find more basis for an agreement and disagreement between them than a monolithic system would have made available. Through this process of unraveling employment *halakhah*, we learn not only about labor law, but also about the openness inherent in the rabbi's judicial-legislative process. Not only is the main thrust of the Law preserved, but also the dissenting opinions!

## Incompetency

The second category of the employer's right to summarily dismiss an employee is the employee's incompetency. Because an employee's incompetency is likely to cause his employer irretrievable loss, the employee falls into the category of being "permanently warned," thus his employer retains the right to dismiss him without warning. Therefore the source for this category of dismissal is also the passage in *Baba Batra* 21b: "The general principle is that anyone who causes an irretrievable loss is liable to be dismissed immediately." Within this category of incompetency there are two subdivisions. The first subdivision is an employee who claimed she was capable of fulfilling the job's tasks at the time she contracted, but once she was hired it was discovered that she could not. An example of this is a teacher who was hired to teach Torah, and after some time it was discovered that he was unable to teach Torah. The community was justified in dismissing him, thus reneging on its part of the contract, because the teacher was unable to fulfill his part of the contract. Since the contract could not be upheld by one party, *halakhah* allowed it to be dissolved.[16]

The second subdivision within this category is an employee whose incompetency develops only after many years on the job, usually because of sickness or old age. The rabbis did not legislate a mandatory retirement age, because they claimed that each field of work is different, and every person ages differently. An exception to this is a discussion about legislating a mandatory retirement age for the ritual slaughterer at age 70 or 80.[17]

While an employee's inability to fulfill her job responsibilities because of old age or sickness provides the employer with legal grounds for dismissing her, it does not eliminate the employer's financial responsibilities to her. When an employee has served an employer for many years, she deserves severance pay or a pension at the time of her dismissal. This understanding is based on the interpretation of the biblical requirement to give the Hebrew bondsman a final payment at the conclusion of his work: "You shall surely grant him from your flocks and your granary and your winepress, of that which the Lord your God has blessed you with" (Deut. 15:14). There is a question as to whether severance pay and pension funds are regulated by the law or are *"lifnim meshurat hadin –* beyond the letter of the law." Meir Tamari notes that the Rambam placed the information dealing with severance pay in his chapter dealing with *tzedakah*, thus implying that severance pay is not an obligation, but rather an act of good will.[18]

While the law in the private sector allows for dismissing an elderly employee who is no longer able to fulfill his responsibilities, in the public sector there are mechanisms for dealing with this situation. These flow from the general law requiring a Jewish community to maintain a public authority (*serarah*). The basis for this ruling is the passage in Deuteronomy 17:20 which says that the kingship is a hereditary function: "...to the end that he and his descendants may reign long in the midst of Israel." The *Sifre* (5th century) takes this passage about the hereditary function of the kingship and applies it to all Israelite administrators (*Sifre, Deut., Piska* 162).[19] In response to a question about tenure, Rabbi Moses ben Joseph Trani (1500-1580) explained that if the laws of succession apply to an Israelite administrator's son, all the more so they should apply to the administrator himself! He wrote, "'He and his descendants may reign long in the midst of Israel,' – How much the more so he himself who was appointed king or sage, they are not able to dismiss him!"[20] Therefore, a public official who was appointed for a long period of time has life tenure rights unless he causes irretrievable loss.

Realizing that a public official with life tenure rights may not remain able to fulfill all his job responsibilities, the Rashba (13th century) ruled that the community had to provide assistance to an aged or infirm employee, rather than dismiss him. In response to a question about an aged cantor, the Rashba wrote:

> Surely the congregation didn't believe that a man can maintain his strength and ability all his life without sickness or other difficulties suffered by all normal people. So the *ḥazzan* is entitled to have his

son assist him, since this was tacitly understood by both parties.[21]

Therefore, the community shows its respect and honor for the aged official by enabling him to maintain his position despite the setbacks of age. While this legal provision is not as economically efficient as dismissing an aged official, in this case honor for the official outweighs the criterion of productivity.

## Improper Behavior

The third reason for an employer to summarily fire an employee is improper behavior inside or possibly outside of the workplace. One example of improper behavior which could result in immediate dismissal is stealing. According to Rashi (*Baba Kama* 28a) all that is necessary to dismiss a servant is suspicion of stealing. Rabbi Moshe Shimshon of Crach (11th century) reasons that since a servant lives with his employer in the same house, it is impossible to always be on guard, therefore his employer may dismiss him.[22] Rabbi Yitzchak HaCohen Hasid (mid 19th century), however, disagrees with the above opinions. According to him, mere suspicion that an employee steals is not enough to fire him, because an employer may just use that as an excuse to fire an employee who he does not like. Rather, an employee must have a reputation for being a thief before an employer can fire him on the basis of suspicion.[23] Here, too, we see that over the centuries, an employer's right to dismiss an employee summarily has been scrutinized. Rabbi Yitzchak HaCohen Hasid attempts to limit the employer's right to dismiss an employee for improper behavior to only those cases where the employer is absolutely sure of the employee's misconduct. Since there needs to be a "reason" for firing a servant summarily, it is evident that the servant is considered to have a certain intrinsic human worth, and cannot be treated as a discarded object by her employee.

Another example of improper behavior which could result in summary dismissal for the public employee who is involved in holy service (e.g., the slaughterer, cantor, rabbi), is sexual impropriety, adultery, prostitution or lewd behavior. Rav Amram wrote in his *Siddur*, that a religious ministrant must be "*tzaddik, v'yashar, v'nakki* – righteous, upright and blameless," and if he isn't, he may be dismissed.[24] The Rambam ruled that a religious ministrant who is suspected of sexual misconduct because of a rumor may not be dismissed. In order to dismiss him, witnesses who can testify to his misconduct are necessary. (Even if he were guilty, the Rambam says that he may cleanse himself through sincere repentance and be restored to his former position.[25])

Private employees may also be dismissed for sexual misconduct if it in some way impinges on their ability to perform their job
properly or damages their employer's reputation. An example of
this is when a man discovers that his maidservant is a prostitute,
he may dismiss her because it may damage his reputation.[26] However, according to Warhaftig, if an employee engages in sexual misconduct which does not impinge on his ability to perform his job
and does not endanger the morals of co-workers, his employer may
not fire him.[27] As an example of this he cites a responsum from Rabbi
Moshe Minetz (15th century), who said that an adulterous person
could maintain his position as a scribe and *shoḥet*, but could not
maintain his position as a *shaliaḥ tzibur*.[28] Therefore, an employee
has a certain "right to privacy" as long as it does not interfere with
his ability to perform his job.

# Employee Rights
# In A Situation
# of Firing

Now that we have examined the legislation which protects an employer's rights to preserve his business, we will briefly examine the
legislation which protects an employee's right to maintain his job.
An employer may not fire an employee because he is able to replace
him with other employees for less money.[29] Thus it is evident once
again that, for *halakhah*, the profit motive cannot be the sole factor
which determines how one can run a business. Other considerations
must be employee rights and respect for contract.
       Another illegitimate reason for firing an employee is because
another, more qualified employee is found. The Rosh (1250-1327)
legislates this when he writes that if someone employs a teacher for
a year, and during that year another, more talented, teacher comes
along, he may not fire the first in order to hire the second unless
the first has caused irretrievable loss.[30] However, if the teacher is
not hired for a specific period of time, an employer may fire the first
teacher if a better one comes along.[31]
       According to *halakhah*, an employee cannot be fired because
his employer does not like him. This ruling has been deduced from
the Rema's comment: "When one lets a room to a friend whom he
once liked but now hates, he cannot evict him."[32] The policy which
seems to emerge from the above *halakhah* is that legitimate grounds
for dismissing a worker must be related to the worker's performance. Thus the contracted employee is protected by law from an
employer's bad temper, irrational prejudice, and greed for profit.

# Contract

According to *halakhah*, a labor contract is legally consummated through *kinyan sudar* when the employee begins her assigned work.[33] If either party reneges from the oral agreement before the labor contract is finalized, it is considered a breach of faith without legal sanctions: "If a man engages artisans and they deceive each other, they can only cherish resentment against each other (*Mishnah Baba Metzia* 76a)." However, the employer may be forced to compensate the worker if alternative sources of employment were available to the worker when he entered into the oral contract, but, at the time that the employer reneges, the worker is unable to find work or can only find a lower-paying job.[34]

After the contract has been finalized, the employer is discouraged from breaking it for unjustifiable reasons by financial penalties which *halakhah* imposes upon him. Many different factors are considered in determining what an employer owes an employee when he dismisses him unjustifiably before the contract has expired. If the worker makes no effort to find a new job, then it is presumed that he prefers leisure to work and is only entitled to half wages until the contracted period of service has expired.[35] However, if the dismissed employee prefers work to idleness, and is unable to find new employment, his employer is required to pay him his full wages until the contracted period expires.[36]

The employer's compensation obligations change if the worker is only able to find work which is identical to his former job but at lower wages, or if he is able to find work which is more difficult but pays the same wages as his former job. If the employee is able to find identical work at the same salary, the employer is excused from all compensation obligations.[37]

From the above discussion, we see that the rabbis took the notion of oral agreements and contracts very seriously. An employer was discouraged from making a commitment to an employee that he was not intending to uphold. When examining the penalties imposed upon an employee who reneges, we see that the employee, too, was discouraged from making a commitment to an employer that he was not intending to honor.

The rabbis considered both the employer and employee to be free agents who enter into contractual obligations freely. Therefore, rabbinic principles concerning the cancellation of contracts apply to both the employer and the employee. Thus the rabbis considered there to be somewhat of a balance of power between the employer and the employee. They recognized that when two parties enter into a contract, both parties are dependent on each other. Therefore, they thought it fit to punish whichever party violated the contract.

The rabbis regarded the employee's status as a free agent to be so important as to grant him the right to withdraw from work in the middle of the day, as it says in *Baba Metzia* 10a, "'For unto me the children of Israel are slaves (Lev. 25:55)' and not servants to servants..."[38] Since both the employer and the employee are servants of God, they cannot be servants of other people. Employment is therefore not considered to be an act of servitude, but rather an exchanging of goods.

An employee who takes advantage of his opportunity to withdraw from work before his contract expires may have to suffer certain consequences.[39] If his withdrawal results in an irretrievable loss for his employer, such as when a piper does not show up for a wedding ceremony or a funeral, his employer is entitled to hire another worker to finish the work. If he must pay more to the second worker, he may force the worker who reneged to pay the difference (but only up to the amount he earned from doing his part of the job). When there is the potential for an irretrievable loss, the employer is also permitted to induce the employee to return by making him false promises of higher wages; but after the labor is completed, the employer is permitted to pay him only the wages which he originally stipulated.[40]

If an employee withdraws from work in the middle of the day and it does not result in irretrievable loss, he is paid for the work he has already done, and the employer can do nothing but bear a grudge. The employee cannot be forced to work against his will because it would infringe upon his personal liberty and relegate him to the status of a slave.[41] The only time an employee can be forced to work is when it is a public employee whose withdrawal would result in harm to the public. In this case, the public employee would be compelled to stay until he finds someone to replace him.[42] Thus we see again Maimonides' notion that the public employee bears a greater responsibility to his employer, the public sector, than a private employee.

# Employer/Employee Rights and Obligations

In an employer/employee relationship, both parties have rights and obligations to each other. *Halakhah* considers the employee to be obligated to fulfill the responsibilities for which he was contracted. Indeed, not only is he committed to fulfill his tasks, but "...to work with all his strength."[43] Therefore the employee is not permitted to waste time at work, or to engage in additional employment since it may take away from his performance at his first job.[44] In return, the primary obligation of the employer to the employee is to pay his wages on time.[45]

As we have indicated, Jewish law focuses primarily on the employer's rights and responsibilities in the situation of summary dismissal, sometimes granting the employer considerable power. From the outset, however, even the consideration of summary dismissal focused upon performance related criteria. Furthermore, through the centuries, what begins as summary dismissal eventually becomes transformed to a system of warnings. Warhaftig's summary suggests that elements in the halakhic value system operated to enlarge the employee's rights. Moreover, having focused on issues of summary dismissal, we can learn something critical about the normal case of dismissal. If Jewish law imposes constraints on the employer even when an employee has caused irretrievable loss, then it most probably imposes similar regulations in less extreme cases of unsatisfactory performance.

# Dismissing An Employee: Contemporary Ethical Views

Both utilitarian and deontological perspectives influence the secular community's approach to business ethics. The utilitarian approach remains dominant; even as shifting trends reveal a greater concern for the abstract moral rights of the employee, deontologists seem compelled to defend the utility of their own arguments. Moreover, both the utilitarians and the deontologists present their positions as capitalist perspectives – each school insists that its views are consistent with, and most conducive to, the goals of capitalism in a democratic society.

Milton Friedman is the most prominent proponent of the classical theory of the corporation. The classical theory's utilitarian character reflects the influence of Adam Smith and Jeremy Bentham, and depends upon two premises: first, that individuals act in their own self-interest, and second, that the competitive process of self-interested actions yields the greatest public good. Since the corporation's striving for profit maximization thereby redounds to the good of society, the corporation is right when it seeks to maximize its profits.[46] Friedman's definition of business responsibility reflects the fundamental convictions of the classical position:

> There is one and only one social responsibility of business: to use its resources and engage in activities designed to increase its profits so long as it

> stays within the rules of the game, which is to say,
> engages in open and free competition without de-
> ception or fraud.[47]

According to the classical theory of capitalism, the rules of the game consist not of abstract moral rights, but of those limited regulations which permit the greatest opportunity for free and open competition. Freedom is Friedman's predominant value, and he defends free competition as an essential vehicle for both economic and political freedom in a democratic society: "The role of competitive capitalism – the organization of the bulk of economic activity through private enterprise operating in a free market is as a system of economic freedom and a necessary condition for political freedom."[48] Friedman argues his case, therefore, on the grounds that competitive capitalism provides greatest freedom to the individual, and thereby reflects and furthers values of a democratic society. Similarly, in Friedman's enunciation of the classical view of the employment relationship, unencumbered competition serves as an assurance of equal freedoms to both employer and employee. Friedman states the argument and its premises lucidly:

> Given competition among employers and employ-
> ees, there seems no reason why employers should
> not be free to offer any terms they want to their
> employees. ...So long as there are many employers,
> all employees who have particular kinds of wants
> will be able to satisfy them by finding employment
> with corresponding employers.[49]

Because workers possess the same right to quit as employers do to fire them, the absence of restrictions upon the employer preserves a balance of power between employer and employee, and maintains the competitive freedom of the marketplace.

This view of the employment relationship as granting equal freedom to both parties is the foundation for the traditional and prevailing common-law principle of employer-employee relations in the United States, the doctrine of "Employment at Will" (EAW). EAW applies to approximately two-thirds of the U.S. work force, those untenured workers who are non-government, non-union, and who have no specific term of contract. A widely cited definition of the at-will relationship appeared in an 1884 ruling in Tennessee, Payne v. Western and A.R.R. Co., in which the court held that an employer can terminate an employee for good cause, for no cause, or even for cause morally wrong without being thereby guilty of legal wrong.[50] In Adair v. U.S. (1908), the Supreme Court cited the equality of the relationship between employer and employee as an essential element of EAW:

> The right of a person to sell his labor upon such
> terms as he deems proper is ... the same as the
> right of the purchaser of labor to prescribe the con-
> ditions upon which he will accept such labor from
> the person. ...The employer and the employee have
> equality of right, and any legislation that disturbs
> that equality is an arbitrary interference with the
> liberty of contract.[51]

In a current example, EAW appears as an explicit doctrine in California Labor Code Section 2922: "An employment, having no specified term, may be terminated at the will of either party on notice to
the other.[52] EAW thereby emerges as the employment doctrine of
the classical position: the employer's right to dismiss an employee
at will is equal to the employee's right to resign; both these rights
preserve the freedom of the marketplace; and therefore, neither
can be considered an example of unjust or abusive exercise of power.

In arguing that EAW is fair, proponents like Friedman do
not claim that it will make all employees happy; Friedman, distin-
guishes, however, between "positive harm," such as physical force
or other coercion, and "negative harm," which results when two individuals are unable to find mutually acceptable contracts.[53] Thus,
Friedman argues, if a community seeking a blues singer refuses to
employ an opera singer, the harm that the opera singer experiences
due to the community's taste is merely "negative harm," and is,
therefore, no cause for government intervention; in fact, Friedman
claims, "such government intervention reduces freedom and limits
voluntary cooperation."[54] On these grounds, Friedman derides anti-
discriminatory Fair Employment Practice legislation:

> Such legislation clearly involves interference with
> the freedom of individuals to enter into voluntary
> contracts with one another. ...Thus it is directly an
> interference with freedom of the kind that we would
> object to in most other contexts.[55]

For Friedman, the content of the legislation is immaterial; it is the
state's power to regulate business which is dangerous – if it is appropriate for the state to insist upon non-discriminatory legislation,
then the state would be equally justified in insisting upon discriminatory legislation. The state cannot be vested with regulatory power
because the only trustworthy force is the force of the marketplace
itself. On what basis can one argue that free market forces provide
an ethical yardstick? For the advocate of the classical position, Adam
Smith's theory of the "invisible hand," as described in his *The Wealth
of Nations*, provides the answer:

> Each individual pursuing his own interest is led by
> an invisible hand to promote an end which was not
> part of his intention. ...By pursuing his own interest,
> he frequently promotes that of the society more effec-
> tually than when he really intends to promote it.[56]

The classical position is thereby utilitarian throughout: a measure
is defined as right if it preserves freedom of competition in the marketplace, because such freedom promotes not only the individual's
interest, but the interests of society as a whole.

The deontologist critique of the classical theory of the corporation argues that corporations have certain moral responsibilities above and beyond the pursuit of their utilitarian goals. Concepts
such as promises, contracts and relationships become especially
important for those who argue that corporations and businessper-
sons should make decisions by evaluating more than "which action
has the most desirable consequences."[57] Critics of the classical theory argue that corporations have a contract with society, and that
the corporation's existence would depend on its ability to further
the public good. More important, these critics deny Smith's 'invisible
hand'; they assert that the classically defined corporation, by acting
exclusively in the interests of its owners or stockholders, serves too
narrow a constituency: "the corporation must benefit not only those
who create it, it must benefit those who permit it."[58] While this
position still emphasizes consequences, it introduces the notion that
self-interest and societal interest cannot be assumed to be identical; moreover, by emphasizing that corporate activity takes place
within a social context, it leads to a more purely deontological argument: "business activity takes place within a social framework ...
hence business should conform to the laws and basic moral norms
of society."[59]

In his support of the deontological position, philosopher
Norman Bowie stresses the concept of role morality. With roots in
Platonic and Aristotelian ethical theory, role morality asserts that
positions in society impose duties which possess legal, customary
and moral dimensions: "a role ... is a cluster of rights and duties
with some sort of social function."[60] Thus the owner of a business or
the principal of a school has certain responsibilities by virtue of her
position: explicit and formal rules and regulations; informal matters of institutional tradition; and the moral obligations of employment, such as the sense that one should do the best job one can, or
that one should be loyal to one's institution. Role morality thereby
makes a significant break from the classical position: the link between a job and certain moral responsibilities contests the view that
one's job is simply an economic relation.[61]

Role morality, however, while justifiable on deontological
grounds, does not itself insure that business's self-interest will be

checked; one could argue that the businessperson's exclusive role is to maximize her company's profits, and that profit maximization can thereby serve as a worthy ethic. The deontologist, however, insists upon a morality beyond that dictated by the individual's role; Bowie relies upon Kant's formulation of the Categorical Imperative to expand the moral responsibilities of business. In particular, Bowie emphasizes two elements of Kant's theory: first, that one should never act unless one is willing to have the maxim on which one acts become a universal law; second, that one should treat all humankind as ends, and never as merely means.[62] On the basis of these principles, Bowie establishes what he terms "The Neoclassical Definition of the Function of the Corporation:" "The function of a corporation is to maximize profits consistent with universal moral norms of justice and with respect for legitimate individual rights."[63] Bowie thereby preserves the profit motive of business, while recognizing the profit motive's shortcomings as a guide for moral action; he qualifies both the classical definition and the role morality position by imposing the constraints of universal moral norms and the rights of the individual.

Bowie cites the importance of honoring contracts and promises as an example of the significance of the universalizability principle to business. While it may occasionally be in the interest of a given business to break a promise or renege on a contract, no executive would be willing to permit promise-breaking to be universalized. Without an element of trust in transactions, business would not be able to function; the success of the corporate enterprise depends upon parties' keeping their agreements. The executive who supports the existence of rules governing transactions but then chooses to break those rules is clearly inconsistent; similarly, to disregard rules while expecting others to keep them is patently unfair. Therefore, according to Kant's criterion, promise-breaking, even if quite profitable, cannot be considered an ethically permissible action for a businessperson.[64]

Kant's insistence on the unconditioned value of persons has particular relevance for employer-employee relations. According to Kant, it is inappropriate to view a human being as if he or she had only instrumental value. Such a view certainly militates against perceiving laborers only as instruments of capital; the unconditioned value of the employee is also important in considering contracts. Indeed, for a contract to be valid, both partners must be autonomous adults, moral agents capable of free and informed choice. In addition, as Bowie indicates, one can only be a moral agent if one has rights which one can press against others. By definition, then, "a person who enters a valid business contract is a person who has rights."[65] If a businessperson is to recognize the unconditioned value of an employee, then he cannot recognize that value only in order to effect a contract; he must recognize that value and its entailments (whatever they may be determined to be) in the varied contexts of the workplace.

Patricia Werhane, another proponent of the deontological perspective, derives important claims of reciprocity and accountability from Kant's second principle. If the employee's rights are inherent human moral rights, then the employer and the employee have equal claims to rights in the workplace, as well as equivalent responsibilities for honoring the rights of the other. Corporate handbooks frequently speak of "employee accountability;" if, however, the work relationship occurs between two unconditionally valued human beings, then accountability must itself represent a two-way relationship. Each partner in the employment relationship is a morally autonomous adult, deserving of the other's respect and fair treatment; to deny the rights of one party is to deny the validity, moral and practical, of the employment relationship:

> To deny employee rights in the workplace is to question the claim that employees can be held responsible to their employers ... role accountability is a correlative notion which entails the recognition of employee rights.[66]

On the basis of her assertion of a universal right to fair treatment, for example, Werhane defends the private worker's right to due process, an entitlement absent from the EAW doctrine and not treated explicitly in our halakhic investigation. While Werhane recognizes that the right to due process in the workplace "is not consistently protected by law," she supports it as "the right ... that every accused person has to a fair hearing and an objective evaluation of his or her guilt or innocence."[67] Because the right to due process stems from an obligation to respect employees as moral agents, T.S. Scanlon identifies it as "one of the conditions for the moral legitimacy of power-conferring institutions."[68] Finally, like Bowie, Werhane cites the important stabilizing force of trust in the corporate setting. She advocates the recognition of implied contracts as a function of "a moral contract or bond" between a long-term employee and his employer; at the same time, she notes that the moral quality of the employer-employee relationship influences loyalty, morale, and contract stability.[69]

Just as deontological perspectives such as those of Werhane and Bowie present a challenge to the traditional way of the classical theory of the corporation, recent court cases and arbitration decisions have evinced an increasing willingness to modify the doctrine of EAW with a more extensive recognition of employee rights. Employment law in the United States emerges largely through arbitration decisions, and sometimes through major court cases; it is rarely codified. Thus one can speak of shifting attitudes, but not of definitive transformations in perspective.

As Werhane's work suggests, one of the factors in the evolution of employee rights is a psychology of entitlement, a growing sense of the worker's dignity and of the worker's right to take part in decisions affecting his or her work. Notably, one of the doctrines that has emerged from the emphasis on worker's entitlement is the notion of a worker's property right in his or her job.

> By emphasizing the value of employer property and stockholder's interests, capitalism ... has promoted the idea that an employee has a kind of property right in his or her job. This idea ... leads to the conviction that a job is too precious to be destroyed by a capricious supervisor or oppressive department head.[70]

This changing perception of employee rights reflects a broader societal trend towards increased individual rights, as well as specific protections that already exist for union or government employees. Thus private employees have begun to claim a right to due process not only on the grounds that a morally autonomous worker deserves a fair hearing before being fired, but also by arguing that there is nothing intrinsic to private employment which should deprive the private employee of the rights enjoyed by civil servants and union members.

Perhaps the most significant factor in the changing attitudes towards EAW is the recognition of the essential inequality of the employer-employee relationship. EAW and the classical position which undergirds it are based upon the premise that the employment relationship in a free and competitive market provides employer and employee with equal measures of freedom and leverage. That premise has come under increasing attack as proponents of rights in the workplace emphasize the imbalance of the employment relationship as a primary rationale for seeking greater employee protections. One can no longer say accurately (if one ever could) that the employer who loses a worker suffers the same loss as an employee who loses a job:

> As a matter of practical common sense, the situation of the employer ... and that of one of its servants are very different. The loss or damage to the [employer] occasioned by the departures of one of its servants, would, save in very exceptional circumstances, be negligible. To a servant ... the security of employment ... is of immense value. [McClelland v. N.I. General Health Services Bd. (1957)][71]

Indeed, especially in the absence of due process protections, the employee might suffer long-term losses as the result of the stigma of being fired; even though prospective employers wish to retain the freedoms which EAW grants them, they still assume that a worker who was dismissed was dismissed for a reason, and might therefore be reluctant to hire him. Thus the damages to the worker dismissed under EAW might endure long after the dismissal itself

Though EAW remains the regnant doctrine in employment relationships in the private unorganized sector, employees have considerably more legal protections now than they did at the beginning of the century; moreover, a recent trend in some state courts towards recognizing the "wrongful discharge" actions brought by terminated employees has begun to make further inroads into the employer's absolute right to discharge.[72] In both the existing protections and the ones which have only begun to be granted, the underlying principle is that dismissal from employment must result from the consideration of performance related criteria. Policies currently in effect protect the employee from discriminatory firing and retaliatory firing (such as being dismissed for participating in union activity or for filing a safety complaint). Legislation also guarantees employees a safe workplace, and minimal economic protection through minimum wage and maximum hours laws.

Claims of "wrongful discharge," though not widely accepted, have begun to exert influence in a few states as a potent challenge to EAW. The most successful challenges to EAW have involved public policy considerations, as in Tameny v Atlantic Richfield Co. (CA, 1980), in which the dismissal of an employee for refusing to participate in a price-fixing scheme was deemed an unjust discharge: "The employer is not so absolute a sovereign of the job that there are not limits to his prerogative."[73] The second primary category of challenge to EAW under "wrongful discharge" involves the concept of "implied contract"; in these cases, courts have ruled that conditions other than a written contract create reasonable expectations of job security or due process on the part of the employee. Such conditions include satisfactory performance under long-term employment,[74] oral assurance of just cause criteria for dismissal,[75] and due process procedures communicated in employee handbooks.[76] The third major category of challenge is linked to implied contract, and is termed "the implied covenant of good faith and fair dealing;" the most widely cited ruling in this category is Fortune v NCR Co (MA, 1977), in which a Massachusetts court ruled against a company for dismissing a long-term employee just before he was due to receive a sizeable commission:

> The general requirement in this Commonwealth is that parties to contracts and commercial transactions must act in good faith toward one another. Good faith and fair dealing between parties are pervasive requirements in our law.[77]

Though these challenges represent limited exceptions to the dominance of EAW, they reflect both a discernible shift towards employee rights, and the potential influence of ethical claims for the value of the individual, reciprocal rights, and the significance of universalizable rules in creating trust and stability in the marketplace.

# Between Halakhah and General Ethics

Having examined both the halakhic and the general ethical response to our question, "what are the worker's rights in a situation of firing?", it is now our turn to respond. From the outset we observe that struggling at the intersection between ethics and Jewish law is itself a liberal Jew's quandary. We are trying to determine the extent to which *halakhah* will guide our decision-making. This task in and of itself can only be endeavored by one who does not feel obligated to live by *halakhah*. As liberal Jews who acknowledge sources of moral authority other than the *halakhah*, we allow *halakhah* to inform our decisions, but not to dictate them.

As we approach the intersection of general ethics and Jewish law in order to assert our own position regarding the dismissal of employees, we affirm certain fundamental ethical principles which shape our thinking. We believe especially in the human being's unconditional value, as propounded explicitly in Kant's Categorical Imperative, and implicitly in halakhic restrictions on the employer's right to dismiss a worker. Our conviction that the human being has implicit worth leads us to limit what we view as the abusive nature of unlimited employer discretion in firing. Unbridled employer power is inherently unjust because it relies upon a fallacy (one maintained in EAW as well as *halakhah*): the premise that employer and employee have equal power in the employment relationship. In the current context of American labor, the premise is alarmingly inaccurate. Employers may have once been more vulnerable to the decisions of their laborers, perhaps due to a smaller work force and a greater demand for labor. Now, however, in the age of assembly lines and mass production, the departure of an individual laborer rarely affects the manager or owner in any serious way; in contrast, as noted earlier, the discharged employee may suffer both financial and mental hardship. Given, therefore, that the employer already possesses more power than the employee, yet both have unconditional and therefore equal value, some constraints must be imposed upon the employer's untrammeled power of dismissal.

Another principle which shapes our conclusions is respect for contract, oral or written. This principle is reflected in Jewish law, where *halakhah* imposes penalties on the employer or employee who retracts from a contractual relationship and thereby causes irretrievable loss to the other party. Contract is important to us for both practical and deontological reasons. As Bowie indicates, dependable promise-keeping is essential to the business enterprise. Moreover, because our recognition of valid contracts acknowledges the moral agency of both parties, we again underscore the unconditional and therefore equal value of employer and employee.

These initial principles lead directly to our first policy conclusion: an employer can fire an employee only for just cause, i.e., only on the basis of performance-related criteria. This definition of just cause reflects both the growing trend in labor arbitration and the halakhic principles studied. The various challenges to EAW insist upon job-related criteria for dismissal: e.g employee's chronic absenteeism, disloyalty, dishonesty or repeated acts of incompetence. Similarly, Jewish law limits cause for dismissal to performance-related criteria. An employee can be dismissed summarily only for causing irretrievable loss to her employer through conditions such as incompetence or theft. Jewish law includes in this category actions which damage the employer's reputation; even though they may not occur as part of the labor activity itself, according to Jewish law they affect the course of the business enterprise and therefore qualify as an extension of performance-related criteria. (Contemporary secular trends make a different claim: that worker activity conducted while the worker is not on the job may be protected by the worker's right to privacy. The conflict of privacy rights with the possible impact of off-the-job activity on the reputation of an enterprise is complicated, and merits extensive analysis.) The requirement that an employer judge his employee's activity only according to job-related criteria demonstrates respect for the unconditional value of both employer and employee, and can begin to restore the balance of power between them. It endows the owner with the right and responsibility to make business decisions on the basis of business criteria, thereby protecting the worker from abusive or arbitrary judgments which might affect his livelihood. Similarly, a just-cause requirement stresses the binding nature of contract, and thereby the autonomous moral nature of employer and employee.

Our second policy conclusion is that employees have an inherent right to due process as part of their dismissal procedure. Like our call for a just-cause requirement, this assertion emerges from our convictions regarding the intrinsic value of human beings and of the contracts they create. By insuring the worker a fair hearing, due process protects her intrinsic worth, and protects her from being treated as a disposable commodity. Due process might include a hearing by an impartial third party, grievance procedures within a corporation or a system of warnings and opportunities for improvement before discharge. In whatever form, due process is a necessary partner to just cause. If a worker in fact has unconditioned value, and if an agreement between employer and employee has compelling force, then both employer and employee deserve the assurance that their intrinsic rights as human beings and as deciding moral agents will be protected – due process provides such protection. Given the imbalance of power between employer and employee, it insures that just cause is being justly determined. Furthermore, just as *halakhah* suggests elements of a just-cause principle in its emphasis on performance-related criteria, it also suggests the possibility of due process by implying that those workers who have not caused irretrievable loss require warning before dismissal, and by certain authorities' calling for warning of employees even in circumstances of irretrievable loss.

We have now examined our guiding principles: the unconditioned value of human beings; and its derivative principle, respect for contract. We have also noted manifestations of these principles in both halakhic and general ethical sources, and we have made two policy proposals which emerge from the guiding principles. Still, an essential question remains: what undergirds the guiding principles themselves? In addition to various historical and sociological factors which influence our choices, what convictions constitute the meta-ethical assumptions and foundations of our thought?

For us, those meta-ethical stances are fundamentally Jewish, and thereby meta-halakhic as well. The cornerstone of all of our thinking is the Jewish conviction that human beings are created *b'tzelem elohim*, "in the image of God." This core conviction, derived from Genesis 1:26-27, raises Kant's claims of human value to a transcendent level. While Kant asserted the unconditional value of human beings, Judaism roots that absolute value in God, the absolute source of all value: human beings possess implicit and unconditional worth because they are created in the image of God. Judaism insists upon the recognition of the transcendent dignity of every human being, no matter what the market conditions, no matter what the effect on profit or productivity. In fact, *b'tzelem elohim*, seems to be a guiding assumption of Jewish law itself, the meta-halakhic principle responsible for Jewish law's protecting the worker's status in the various circumstances reported above.

One might still argue, however, from the classical capitalist perspective, that the free market system provides for the utmost dignity of its participants by providing all with the utmost freedom. Another meta-halakhic principle, however, refutes this classical claim. Unlike classical free-market capitalism, Judaism does not enshrine freedom as an absolute value. The Jewish ethical tradition certainly relies significantly on the experience of and redemption from slavery: "You shall not oppress a stranger, for you know the feelings of the stranger, having yourselves been strangers in the land of Egypt" (Exodus 23:9). Nonetheless, *yetziat mitzrayim*, the exodus from Egypt, is the necessary means to an end: *matan torah*, the revelation of the Torah at Mt. Sinai. The Israelites were redeemed from slavery not to wander in the desert and make their own rules, but in order to accept the divine obligations presented to them at Sinai. This dual notion that freedom entails responsibility, and that responsibility requires freedom, is central to Jewish self-understanding (and corresponds to the more contemporary concept of moral agency); indeed, the acceptance of *mitzvot*, of deontological obligations, is the necessary basis for the halakhic system itself. The existence of the *halakhah* is evidence that Judaism, while valuing liberty, considers human freedom neither sufficient expression nor sufficient guarantee of human dignity. *Mitzvot* constitute an explicit, rigorous, and visible hand of guidance towards individual and collective well-being.

Finally, just as God and divinely-inspired obligation are the source and protection of the human being's unconditional value in Judaism, they also underlie the value of contract. In this case, *brit* emerges as a compelling concept. If *brit* is the Jewish people's (and the Jewish individual's) covenant with God, and human beings are created *b'tzelem elohim*, then the core concept of *brit* might also suggest the sanctity of commitments between human beings. Just as Werhane argued that the unconditional value of human beings undergirds the validity of contracts, so too from a Jewish perspective the divine element in human beings imposes upon human agreements some of the sacred responsibility of *brit*.

While principles such as *b'tzelem elohim* and *matan torah* undergird *halakhah*, *halakhah* does not always take these concepts as far as we would like. (Indeed, the need to resort to the term "meta-halakhic" suggests some of *halakhah*'s limitations.) Recent trends towards changing the structure and definition of the employment relationship, especially as already established in collective bargaining agreements and civil service professions, extend workers' rights farther than *halakhah* found necessary. Thus while meta-halakhic principles such as *b'tzelem elohim* have a primary role in shaping our conclusions, the further development of such principles in the general ethical literature and in court rulings (a development which derives in part from certain Constitutional protections) represents an enhancement of the halakhic position. By translating the concept of unconditional human value more extensively and explicitly into the realm of workers' rights, contemporary thought and policy regarding dismissal procedures have contributed to our conclusions.

The isolation and identification of core values is a complex and taxing process. That process itself, along with the very notion of mediation between halakhic and non-halakhic imperatives, is a result of our stance as liberal Jews, evidence of our connection to the present. The process also reveals, however, the power of the tradition we inherit. In fact, to stand at the intersection of Jewish law and general ethics is not only to stand along an historical continuum, but along a continuum of principles which resides wholly in the present. As we have learned from this consideration of the ethics of dismissing a worker, *halakhah* and current ethical thought can each exert a telling influence on the consideration of contemporary problems.

# Bibliography

Blades, Lawrence E. "Employment at Will v. Individual Freedom: On Limiting the Abusive Exercise of Employer Power," in Westin, Alan F. and Stephen Salisbury, eds., *Individual Rights in the Corporation: A Reader on Employee Rights* (New York: Pantheon Books, 1980). Excerpted from Columbia Law Review 67 (1967).

Bleich, David, *Contemporary Halakhic Problems* (New York: Yeshiva University Press, 1977).

Bowie, Norman. *Business Ethics* (New Jersey: Prentice-Hall, 1982).

Elon, Menahem. *The Principles of Jewish Law* (Jerusalem: Keter Publishing House, 1975)

Ewing, David W. *"Do It Mv Way – You're Fired": Employee Rights and the Changing Role of Management Prerogatives* (New York: John Wiley and Sons, Inc., 1983).

Falk, Zev. *Introduction to Jewish Law of the Second Commonwealth.* Leiden: E.J., Brill, 1972.

Friedman, Milton. "The Social Responsibility of Business," In Leube, Kurt R. ed. *The Essence of Friedman* (Stanford: Hoover Institution Press, 1987). Reprinted from *The New York Times Magazine*, September 13, 1970.

Friedman, Milton. *Capitalism and Freedom* (Chicago: The University of Chicago Press, 1982).

Levine, Aaron, *Economics and Jewish Law*, (Hoboken: Ktav Publishing House, Inc., 1987)

Hallock, Marcy M. "Implied Contracts," from a paper delivered at Executive Enterprises, 18th Employment Law Institute, March 34, 1988, Washington D.C. An unpublished paper received from Professor Oscar Ornati, New York University Graduate School of Business Administration.

Outen, Wayne N. with Noah A. Kinigstein, *The Rights of Employees: The Basic ACLU Guide to an Employee's Rights* (New York: Bantam Books, 1984)

Pastin, Mark. *The Hard Problems of Management: Gaining the Ethics Edge.* San Francisco: Jossey-Bass Publishers, 1986.

Stieber, Jack. "Protection Against Unfair Dismissal." Reprinted from Michigan State University, School of Labor and Industrial Relations Newsletter, Fall 1978. In Westin.

Susser, Peter A. "Wrongful Discharge Developments in California, Maryland, Michigan and New Jersey." Prepared for Keiler and Heckman; an unpublished paper received from Professor Oscar Ornati of the New York University Graduate School of Business Administration.

Tamari, Meir, *With All Your Possessions* (New York: The Free Press, A Division of MacMillan, Inc., and London, Collier MacMillan Publishers, 1987)

Warhaftig, Sholem, *Dinei Avodah Bamishpat Haivri* (Tel Aviv: Moreshet Publisher, 1969)

Werhane, Patricia H. *Persons. Rights. and Corporations* (New Jersey: Prentice-Hall, Inc., 1985).

# Notes

1. Dr. Sholem Warhaftig, *Dinei Avodah Bamishpat Haivri* (Tel Aviv: Moreshet Publisher, 1969), p. 549; these three categories are suggested by Dr. Warhaftig.

2. A near identical passage appears in the *Talmud Bavli. Baba Metzia* 109a and in Maimonides' *Mishneh Torah, Hilkhot Sekhirut* 10:7.

3. Rashi, *Baba Metzia* 109a.

4. The Tosafot, *Baba Metzia* 109b; also in Mordecai on *Baba Metzia* 109a, *Siman* 399. Maimonides in *Mishneh Torah, Hilkhot Sekhirut* 10:7, and Karo in *Shulḥan Arukh, Ḥoshen Mishpat, Siman* 306, Paragraph 8, support both Rashi and the Tosafot's arguments.

5. Rabeinu Gershom Maor HaGola, Edition S. Eidelberg, *Siman* 72; cited in *Dinei Avodah Bamishpat Haivri*, pp. 555-556.

6. The Tosafot, *Baba Batra* 21b; also in *Nimukei Yosef* on Baba Batra 21b.

7. The Maggid Mishneh, *Mishneh Torah, Hilkhot Sekhirut* 10:7.

8. Rashi, *Baba Batra* 21b.

9. The Tosafot, *Baba Batra* 21b; also in *Shittah Mekubetzet, Baba Metzia* 109a and *Baba Batra* 21b.

10. Rashi, *Baba Metzia* 97a; also in *Shittah Mekubetzet, Baba Metzia* 97a.

*All the Talmud citations are *Talmud Bavli*, unless otherwise stated.

11. Maimonides, *Mishneh Torah. Hilkhot Sekhirut* 10:7.

12. The Rabad, *Mishneh Torah, Hilkhot Sekhirut* 10:7; the Rema agrees with the Rabad in the *Shulḥan Arukh, Ḥoshen Mishpat, Siman* 306, Paragraph 8.

13. *Baba Metzia* 109a.

14. The Maggid Mishneh, *Mishneh Torah, Hilkhot Sekhirut* 10:7.

15. *Dinei Avodah Bamishpat Haivri*, p. 555.

16. *Lehem Rav, Siman* 70, 71; cited in *Dinei Avodah Bamishpat Haivri*, p. 568.

17. *Dinei Avodah Bamishpat Haivri*, p. 570.

18. For a more thorough discussion of severance pay and pension funds, see: Tamari, Meir, *With All Your Possessions* (New York: The Free Press, A Division of MacMillan, Inc., and London, Collier MacMillan Publishers, 1987), pp. 144-147. For some current Israeli rabbinic court decisions on this question, see Levine, Aaron, *Economics and Jewish Law*, (Hoboken: Ktav Publishing House, Inc., 1987), p. 31.

19. See also: *Mishneh Torah, Hilkhot Melakhim* 1:7.

20. *Responsa Mabit* 111:200.

21. *Teshuvot Harashba*, Part One, Section 300.

22. *Sheelot Uteshuvot Ḥut Hashani* 60:1; cited in *Dinei Avodah Bamishpat Haivri*, p. 574. The Rema agrees with Rabbi Shimshon; see, *Shulḥan Arukh, Ḥoshen Mishpat, Siman* 421, Paragraph 6.

23. The Ribash, *Ohel Yitzak, Ḥoshen Mishpat, Siman* 53, Page 67a; cited in *Dinei Avodah Bamishpat Haivri*. pp. 674-575.

24. *Seder Rav Amram*, cited in *Dinei Avodah Bamishpat Haivri*, p. 576.

25. *Teshuvot HaRambam, Siman* III.

26. *Dinei Avodah Bamishpat Haivri*, p. 580.

27. *Dinei Avodah Bamishpat Haivri*, p. 580.

28. *Sheelot Uteshuvot Maharam Minetz, Siman Yoreh Deah*, end: cited in *Dinei Avodah Bamishpat Haivri*, p. 580.

29. *Mishnah, Baba Metzia* 76a; also see Rashi and the Tosafot to *Baba Metzia* 67a.

30. *Sheelot Veteshuvot Harosh*, Rule 97, Question 4; cited in *Dinei Avodah Bamishpat Haivri*, p. 584.

31. *The Tur, Yoreh Deah, Siman* 246, Paragraph 18; also in *Shulḥan Arukh, Yoreh Deah, Siman* 246, Paragraph 18.

32. *Shulḥan Arukh, Ḥoshen Mishpat, Siman* 312, *Seif Katan* 9.

33. *Hidushei Haramban, Baba Metzia* 76b.

34. See also: Tosafot, *Baba Metzia* 76b; and, *Mishneh Torah, Hilkhot Sekhirut* 9. 27.

35. *Rashi Responsa,* #239; cited in Menahem Elon, *The Principles of Jewish Law* (Jerusalem: Keter Publishing House, 1975), p. 313. For a more thorough discussion, see: Aaron Levine, *Free Enterprise and Jewish Law* (New York: Yeshiva University Press, and Hoboken: Ktav Publishing House, Inc., 1980), pp. 4042.

36. *Baba Metzia* 77a.

37. *Hidushei Haramban, Baba Metzia* 76b.

38. See also: *Mishneh Torah, Hilkhot Sekhirut* 9:4.

39. This applies only to the hired worker (*poel*) who works for wages and not the independent contractor who works for a flat fee (*kabbelan*). The hired servant is hired for a specific period, whereas the independent contractor is hired to do a specific task Since the independent contractor may choose his own hours, there is no fear that he may feel like a slave. For a more thorough discussion, see: Elon, *The Principles of Jewish Law.* p. 310; or David Bleich, *Contemporary Halakhic Problems* (New York: Yeshiva University Press, 1977), pp. 132-133.

40. *Baba Metzia* 76a; also in *Mishneh Torah, Hilkhot Sekhirut* 9:4.

41. *Baba Metzia* 10a.

42. *The Tosefta, Baba Metzia* 11:13.

43. *Mishneh Torah, Hilkhot Sekhirut,* 13:7, see also: *Shulḥan Arukh, Ḥoshen Mishpat, Siman* 337, Paragraph 20.

44. *Mishneh Torah, Hilkhot Sekhirut,* 13:2,6.

45. *Baba Metzia* 65a.

46. Norman Bowie, *Business Ethics* (New Jersey: Prentice-Hall, 1982), p. 21.

47. Milton Friedman, "The Social Responsibility of Business," In Leube, Kurt R. ed. *The Essence of Friedman* (Stanford: Hoover Institution Press, 1987), p. 42. Reprinted from *The New York Times Magazine,* September 13, 1970.

48. Milton Friedman, *Capitalism and Freedom* (Chicago: The University of Chicago Press, 1982), p. 4.

49. Friedman, *Capitalism and Freedom*, pp. 115-116.

50. Peter A. Susser, "Wrongful Discharge Developments in California, Maryland, Michigan and New Jersey," p. 1. Prepared for Keiler and Heckman; an unpublished paper received from Professor Oscar Ornati of the New York University Graduate School of Business Administration.

51. Wayne N. Outen with Noah A. Kinigstein, *The Rights of Employees: The Basic ACLU Guide to an Employee's Rights* (New York: Bantam Books, 1984), p. 29.

52. Susser, p. 7.

53. Freidman, *Capitalism and Freedom*, p. 112.

54. Freidman, *Capitalism and Freedom*, pp. 112-113.

55. Freidman, *Capitalism and Freedom*, p. 111.

56. Freidman, *Capitalism and Freedom*, p. 133.

57. Bowie, p. 20.

58. Bowie, p.152.

59. Bowie, p. 50.

60. R.S. Downie, cited in Bowie, p. 3.

61. Bowie, p. 5.

62. Bowie, p. 40.

63. Bowie, p. 34.

64. Bowie, p. 42.

65. Bowie, p. 46.

66. Patricia H. Werhane, *Persons. Rights. and Corporations* (New Jersey: Prentice-Hall, Inc., 1985), p. 107.

67. Werhane, p.110.

68. Werhane, p. 111.

69. Werhane, p. 146.

70. David W. Ewing, *"Do It Mv Way – You're Fired": Employee Rights and the Changing Role of Management Prerogatives* (New York: John Wiley and Sons, Inc., 1983), pp. 8-9.

71. Lawrence E. Blades, "Employment at Will v. Individual Freedom: On Limiting the Abusive Exercise of Employer Power," in Westin, Alan F. and Stephen Salisbury, eds., *Individual Rights in the Corporation: A Reader on Employee Rights* (New York: Pantheon Books, 1980), p. 54. Excerpted from Columbia Law Review 67 (1967).

72. Susser, p. 2. (as per note 50).

73. Outen, p. 32. Susser and others cite at least a dozen more examples of the public policy challenge to EAW, Including dismissal for refusing to perjure oneself, for filing for workmen's compensation, for serving on jury duty. Rulings differ on what constitutes evidence of public policy (e.g., explicit statutes, constitutional guarantees, etc.)

74. Susser, p. 5. Susser cites several other cases of the implied contract challenge. While some rulings permit longevity of qualified service to be sufficient grounds for implied contract, most depend upon some other written or verbal assurance of job security by the employer.

75. Blades, p. 369.

76. Marcy M. Hallock, "Implied Contracts," from a paper delivered at Executive Enterprises, 18th Employment Law Institute, March 34,1988, Washington D.C., p. 2. An unpublished paper received from Professor Oscar Ornati, New York University Graduate School of Business Administration. Hallock cites numerous examples of the significance of employee handbooks in implied contract cases.

77. Ewing, p. 57. An excellent example of the implied covenant of good faith and fair dealing, and its relation to the principle of reciprocity, appeared in a front page article in the *Los Angeles Times* on May 10, 1988. The article reports Donald Regan's response when asked whether he thought that publication of his book, *For The Record*, was an act of disloyalty to Ronald Reagan: "I've always been taught in the Marine Corps, in Merrill Lynch, in management and I thought in this Administration that loyalty is a two-way street. You have to have loyalty down if you're going to have loyalty up."

# Should a Synagogue Accept Tainted Gifts?

Nancy Wiener
and Edward Elkin

In this paper, we propose to mediate an ethical problem in light of Jewish sources and modern ethical sources. Because we live in both worlds, we would like our decision to be informed by both. We realize, however, that the issues and concerns discussed in the two literatures are likely to use different categories and criteria. It will, therefore, be our task to present and explicate the central issues of each, to expose the tensions that are inherent in them, and to determine which categories and arguments are most compelling for us as modern American non-halakhically bound Jews.

The broad question that we will address is "May a synagogue accept a donation from an individual of ill-repute in the community?"

Before this question can be thoughtfully answered, a number of prior issues must be discussed. What is the nature of the donation, and under what circumstances was it acquired? What is the place of the synagogue in the community? How is the individual's "ill-repute" in the community to be defined? In other words, our question touches upon concerns about the gift, the community, and the individual involved.

## Jewish Sources

### The Principal Halakhic Category – *Etnan Zonah*

The principal halakhic category which bears on our question is called *etnan zonah*. This term is taken from Deuteronomy 23:19, which states

> You shall not bring an *etnan zonah* or the pay of a

> dog[1] into the house of the Lord your God in fulfill-
> ment of any vow, for both are abhorrent to the Lord
> your God.

The word "abhorrent" which is used in the verse conveys a particularly strong repugnance for the act in question. The problem for later
Jewish law is that the verse is not entirely clear. In order to determine how this biblical law should be applied, the *halakhah* had to
decide on the meaning of *etnan* and the meaning of *zonah*. Later, it
would need to determine whether the law, which is framed biblically as a temple cult issue, may be applied, in the post-temple era, to
the synagogue.

# Mishnaic Texts

The mishnaic stratum in the *halakhah* takes for granted who the
*zonah* is: the prostitute's status as an individual performing a legal
but disreputable service in the community is not questioned. Nor is
there halakhic debate over the definition of the "House of God" referred to in Deut. 23:19 – this is the Jerusalem temple. The primary concern of Jewish law in this period is the gift itself: what is its
nature, and under what circumstances was it acquired?

### To Define *Etnan*

> If one said to a prostitute, "Here is this lamb as your
> fee," even though [he had only stipulated one and]
> he gave her a hundred [lambs], they are all prohib-
> ited [to be offered on the altar]. And likewise, also,
> if one said to his fellow, "Here is this lamb for you;
> let your bondwoman lodge with my slave," Rabbi
> says: This is not deemed an *etnan*, but the Sages
> say: It is accounted an *etnan*. (*Temurah* 6:2)

This *mishnah* equates the words *etnan* and *sekhar*, the fee
which the prostitute receives for the services she renders. This fee
may not be brought to the altar for a sacrifice.

But the *mishnah* recognizes that the definitional problem
does not end there. There are cases in which the definition of "fee"
might not be so easily determined. What if the man specified one lamb
as the fee he would pay, but actually gave the prostitute one hundred
lambs? In this case, the *mishnah* decides that all one hundred lambs
are forbidden for the altar.

What if two slaveowners reach an agreement whereby one
would give the other a lamb so that his slave could have inter-

course with the other's slave? In this situation, where the fee is neither given nor received by the parties involved in the act of intercourse, there is a dispute. Rabbi[2] feels that the lamb in question
should not be considered an *etnan*, and therefore may be offered on
the altar. The sages, however, overrule him, declaring the lamb to
be in fact an *etnan*, and therefore prohibited. Both Rabbi and the sages
uphold the notion that an *etnan* is prohibited; the problem lies in a
disagreement over the extent to which this category may be applied.

The *Mishnah* also worries about other cases. What if the
man gave the prostitute money as her fee?

> If one gave money to [the prostitute], this [money]
> is permitted, but [if he gave to her] wine, oil, or
> meal, or anything the like of which is brought upon
> the altar, these are prohibited... (*Temurah* 6:4)

This *mishnah* recognizes that the fee exchanged for a prostitute's
services is not always something which would in itself be brought
to the temple as an offering. The decision rendered by the *mishnah*
in such a case is significant: the prohibited category *etnan* is restricted only to those things which may potentially be brought to the
altar as a sacrifice. Only if such a potential sacrifice is itself given
as the fee to a prostitute is there a restriction. Other types of fees
which a prostitute might receive, including money, are not prohibited as gifts for the temple.

## Main Concerns

The *Mishnah*'s main concern is to define the term *etnan*. Some
aspects of mishnaic law seem to interpret the term in a very inclusive way. The fact that the man going to the prostitute only specified one lamb doesn't matter – if he gave her one hundred lambs,
all fall under the category of *etnan* and are thus forbidden. The term
*etnan* thus goes beyond what was formally declared to be the prostitute's fee to include also anything she received, whether formally
declared payment or not.

On the other hand, *Mishnah Temurah* 6:4 restricts the
parameters of the term *etnan* by excluding money from the category, on the ground that money, qua money, cannot be offered on the
altar. The dispute between Rabbi and the sages over the fee paid
on behalf of one's slave reveals that the extent to which the Biblical
category might be applied was still open to debate in the mishnaic
period.

## Major Points

The most important points gleaned from the mishnaic material are:
- *Etnan zonah* is the fee received by a prostitute.
- All that a prostitute receives for the intercourse is

forbidden for the altar, whether or not the entire
quantity received was officially declared her fee.
- The acceptability on the altar of a fee received by a
master for letting his female slave have intercourse
was a subject of dispute.
- Only fees which are in the form of something which
may be offered on the altar are prohibited; money
is not prohibited.

## Gemara

The Talmudic discussion on this category continues with definitional concerns. The *Gemara*, in *Temurah* 29a-30b, adds a number of
important issues to the debate over the parameters of the forbidden
*etnan*. In a way, this section becomes the *locus classicus* for the
*halakhah* on this issue.

### Timing
The first concern is the timing of the payment in relation to the service rendered. The *Gemara* quotes a *baraita* which says

> If he gave [the prostitute] [her fee] but did not have
> intercourse with her, or if he had intercourse with
> her but did not give her [her fee], her etnan is per-
> mitted. (*Temurah* 29a)

This *baraita* contains a very important definitional shift. The phrase,
"her *etnan* is permitted" is surprising in light of the mishnaic passages just examined. The *Mishnah* assumed that the moment one
could define something as *etnan*, it was automatically forbidden –
the problem lay only in determining whether the gift in question was
in fact an *etnan*. The *baraita*, however, allows for something to be
declared a permissible *etnan*. This *baraita* renders the term *etnan*
ambiguous. It is this ambiguity that the Amoraim comment on.

> If he gave her [her fee] but did not have intercourse
> with her, can we call this an *etnan*? And moreover,
> regarding the case where he had intercourse with
> her but did not give her [her fee], what did he give
> her [that might possibly be permitted or forbidden]?
> What is meant is this: If he gave her [her fee] and
> afterwards had intercourse with her, or if he had
> intercourse with her, and afterwards gave her [her
> fee] her *etnan* is permitted. (*Temurah* 29a)

The Amoraim were troubled by the *baraita*. If no intercourse took
place, then can the *etnan* really be considered a fee? The implied

answer to this question is no. The entire category of *etnan zonah* does not come into play unless there took place a specific act of intercourse for which a fee was given.

This conclusion leaves the rabbis with another question, however. What is the *baraita* talking about? The answer, according to the *Gemara*, is that the *baraita* was really speaking about an issue of timing. When was payment made in relation to the time of intercourse? Both cases in the *baraita* involve the giving of a fee and the act of intercourse, the Amoraim say. The distinction is whether payment comes before or after the act.

But here the rabbis find themselves in another kind of bind: in explaining away one problem, they have boxed themselves into a corner. Since the *baraita* declares the *etnan* permissible, they have just declared both pre-payments and post-payments perfectly legitimate for the altar. In *Temurah* 29b, R. Elazar offers a solution which expresses his unwillingness to go that far. He refines the meaning of the *baraita* to resolve the pre-payment problem. For him, it still refers to the issue of timing, but the case is one in which the man gives the prostitute a lamb, and makes an appointment to come and visit her. He tells her that the lamb will not officially be considered hers until the time of intercourse. But if she needs it for a sacrifice in the meantime, she may consider it hers from the time he gave it to her. This is the situation spoken about in the *baraita*, according to R. Elazar.

Two interpretations may be offered with regard to R. Elazar's comments. First, R. Elazar can be understood as offering a case that is vague. In this interpretation, the *baraita*'s very permissive attitude would presumably not apply to cases where ownership and the way ownership was acquired were clear. Second, R. Elazar may be referring to the close identification of the fee with a specific act – the time delay reduces the stigma of the fee.

But R. Elazar has only helped clarify the decisive factor in the case of pre-payment. What about a case in which a man pays the prostitute her fee after the act of intercourse has taken place? Is this *etnan* to be forbidden? In this instance, there is a dispute. The *baraita* quoted above stated that the fee received under such circumstances is permissible as a gift for the altar. But further on in 29b another *baraita* is employed which claims that a prostitute's fee is forbidden, even if it paid up to twelve months after the act of intercourse.

R. Hanan b. Hisda resolves the apparent contradiction by explaining that in the one case, the man simply said that he would give her "a lamb" in exchange for her services. When he gives her a lamb, that lamb is permitted. In the other case, the man specified a particular lamb as "the lamb" with which he would pay her after the intercourse. When he gets around to giving her that particular lamb, even if it is a year later, that lamb is forbidden.

R. Hanan b. Hisda's solution may be seen as support for both or either of the interpretations discussed above. His comment substantiates the interpretation that there is a strong identification of the act with the item of exchange. It also may be seen as supporting the notion that it is important to determine whether or not the item(s) to be exchanged is clearly specified or left vague: where the lamb is specifically designated, it is forbidden. But where only a vague statement was made, the solution is to be lenient and allow the offering.

The discussion on *Temurah* 29b becomes rather intricate at this point, but the next important idea is that in the post-payment situation, the prostitute must have made a legal acquisition of the lamb for it to be considered forbidden. For Israelite prostitutes, *meshikhah* ("pulling, drawing") is required, but for non-Israelite prostitutes, payment alone makes it hers. This section teaches us that not only is timing important, but legal ownership of the item in question is also a crucial issue. For the fee to be forbidden, it must legally belong to the prostitute. This section also introduces the idea (which will be explicated later on by Abaye and Raba) that the category of *etnan zonah* applies to non-Israelite prostitutes as well as to Israelite prostitutes.

### Defining *Zenut*

In *Temurah* 29b the discussion focuses next on what kinds of activities are considered *zenut*, when considering the acceptability of *etnan zonah*. Rab teaches that the law of *etnan zonah* does apply in the case of a fee paid by a male to a male and to all forbidden relations (*'arayot*)[3] with one exception. The fee paid by a husband to a wife in exchange for intercourse during her menstrual period is not forbidden, because even though that act is prohibited, the wife is not considered a *zonah*. Levi disagrees; he includes in the prohibition the fee paid to a wife when she is a *niddah*.[4] This section reveals that the Amoraim were concerned not just with defining the *etnan*; they also understood that there was a problem in defining *zonah*.

### A Fee Whose Form Has Changed

The final major issue raised by the Amoraim is elaborated in

> Our rabbis taught, If he gave her wheat and she made it into flour; if he gave her olives, and she made them into oil; if he gave her grapes and she made them into wine; some say the [transformed product] is forbidden and others say it is permitted.

> Joseph said, Gurion of Asporak taught that the House of Shammai prohibits and the House of Hillel permits it. The House of Hillel thinks the word *shneihem* (in Deut. 23:19) means [the fee itself] but not its issues, [the fee itself] but not what it is trans-

formed into; whereas the House of Shammai infers
from the word *gam* that the subject is [the fee itself]
but not its issue, [the fee itself] and including what
it is transformed into.

Does not the House of Hillel see the word *gam*?
This is a difficulty for the House of Hillel.

Our rabbis taught, "The House of the Lord your
God"...The sages say that this includes the gold
plating [to cover the altar]. Whose opinion is that of
the sages? R. Hisda said that R. Yosi said it in the
name of R. Yehuda. It is a *baraita*: He gave her gold
– R. Yosi bar Yehuda says that they may not make
from it the beaten gold, even for the back wall of
the Holy of Holies. (*Temurah* 30b)

In this passage, the Amoraim raise a very serious question which
was hinted at in the mishnaic discussion about money as fee. What
if the man gives a prostitute a fee and she converts it into another
form? Is that new product considered a forbidden *etnan*? This issue
results in a dispute between the Houses of Hillel and Shammai.
The House of Hillel permits offerings such as wine made from grapes
which were given as a prostitute's fee, whereas the House of Shammai
would forbid the acceptance of such wine.

### A Non-Sacrificial *Etnan*
The beaten gold example raises two new issues almost as a throw-
away. When R. Yosi says that the beaten gold may not be used
"even for the back wall of the Holy of Holies," he seems to be indicating that the particular use for which the gift was intended should
not impact on the decision regarding whether or not it is acceptable. Even something which will be used for beautification[5] should
not be accepted if it has been given as a prostitute's fee. Perhaps
even more important, this example raises the issue of donations to
the temple which are not sacrificial. This shift is not underscored in
the *Gemara*, and no questions related to it are raised about its
appropriateness in a discussion about *etnan zonah*.

### Money As Fee
Significantly, the *Gemara* does not specifically raise the issue of
money in its discussion of transformation. Presumably, a common
enough case would have been a fee given in the form of money which
the prostitute then exchanges for an animal or some other gift for
the altar. The *Mishnah* permitted such a gift; the *Gemara* is silent.
    The parade example of the rabbis is that of an unconsecrat-
ed lamb given as payment by a man to a prostitute at the time of
the actual intercourse. The prohibition of this lamb is agreed to by

all. Once they depart from this example, however, the issue becomes
very murky. When it comes to deciding in questionable cases whether
or not a gift is forbidden, lenient authorities use a narrow definition of
*etnan zonah*, while more stringent authorities work with a broader,
more inclusive definition.

## Major Points

The *Gemara* raises a number of important new points in its discussion of M. *Temurah*.

- There is such a thing as a permissible *etnan*.
- In deciding whether or not a particular *etnan* is
  forbidden, the timing of the payment in relation
  to the deed is an important factor.
- Where the situation is clear, the fee should be
  prohibited; where the situation is vague, it
  should be permitted.
- If the *zonah* does not legally own what she is
  offer-ing, it cannot be prohibited.
- One's definition of the term *zonah* will have a
  great impact on one's ruling in unusual cases.
- The use to which the offering would be put
  should not impact upon one's decision.
- Non-sacrificial offerings to the temple may be
  included in the category *etnan zonah*.

### Mishneh Torah

In chapter four, *halakhot* 8-18, of *Sefer Avodah* (*Hilkhot Issurei
Mizbeaḥ*), Maimonides delineates his concerns regarding this issue.
Much of his contribution lies in his simplification of complex Talmudic
passages. But in this process of clarification, he also rendered some
important decisions.

Rambam's first order of business is to clarify just who and
what fall under the category of *etnan zonah*. He whittles down all
the talmudic discussion to the following statement:

> What is meant by the term *etnan*? If one said to a
> prostitute, "Here is this thing for you as your fee,"
> this refers either to a gentile prostitute [*zonah
> kutit*], or to a bondwoman [*shifḥah*], or an Israelite
> woman who is forbidden to him under the rule of in-
> cest [*ervah alav*] or because of a negative command-
> ment.

> But as for an unmarried girl [*penuyah*], even if the
> man is a priest, the *etnan* is permissible. And also,
> if his wife is menstruant, the *etnan* is permissible
> even though she is forbidden to him.

## Defining *Zonah*

Maimonides starts out by using the same type of language which the *Mishnah* had used in defining *etnan* as a prostitute's fee. But in the process of simplifying, the term *zonah* becomes restricted to the things which were considered only special cases in the Talmud. Maimonides indicates that, at least for the purposes of this area of *halakhah*, the term *zonah* only refers to the Gentile prostitute, the bondwoman, and Israelite women who are forbidden to a man under Jewish law. It is the *etnan* of these groups which is unacceptable. But, as for an ordinary unmarried Israelite girl who accepts a fee for having intercourse with a man, she is not a *zonah* and she may donate the fee she received to the temple. The *zonah*, for Maimonides, is not to be interpreted necessarily as a professional prostitute. The fee re-ceived by a free Israelite, *penuyah,* is, for Maimonides, a perfectly acceptable offering.

## Quantity Transferred

In *halakhah* 11, Maimonides repeats the strict ruling first found in the *Mishnah* that if the man specifies one lamb as the fee but gives her many, they are all forbidden, Maimonides even extends this principle – whereas the *Mishnah* expands the prohibition to one hun-dred lambs, Maimonides says even one thousand would not be allowed at the altar.

## Timing

Then Maimonides addresses the timing issue. Here he introduces a new and interesting variant to the discussion:

> If he gave her her fee, but did not have intercourse with her but rather said to her, "Let this fee be with you until we have intercourse," after they have inter-course it becomes forbidden. But if she offers it up before he comes to have intercourse with her, the offering is considered valid. And if the offering was a required offering, she is considered to have fulfilled her obligation...
>
> If she consecrates it before he comes to have inter-course with her, but afterwards he comes to have intercourse with her, there is doubtover whether it is forbidden inasmuch as the intercourse took place before the actual offering, or permitted inasmuch as she consecrated it before the intercourse. Therefore, it should not be offered, but if it was offered, it is con-sidered as having been accepted. (*Halakhot* 11-12)

Certain cases are clear – either the gift to the temple is prohibited or it is permitted. Other cases involve grey areas where there is doubt, and here Rambam stipulates, the gift should not be offered.

However, he continues, if a doubtful gift has already been offered, we should retroactively look upon it as having been a legitimate gift – the indication of this legitimacy being that the woman in question is considered *yotzeit* for her obligation to bring an offering. Although Maimonides himself does not use this language here, it appears that he is making a distinction between *lekhatḥilah* and *bediavad* situations. *Lekhatḥilah*, before the offering is made, a doubtful gift should be refused; but *bediavad*, if the gift was already made, we retroactively consider it as having been legitimate. This consideration was not raised at the talmudic level.

In *halakhah* 13, Maimonides looks at the second half of the timing issue raised in the *Gemara*. If a man has intercourse with a woman and sends her a gift afterwards, the *Gemara* said that this gift is forbidden even if it is sent up to a year later. Rambam extends this statute of limitations even further. Even if the gift is sent after many years, he rules it forbidden for the altar.

### The Fee Whose Form Has Changed

Finally, *halakhot* 14 and 15 relate to the issue of transformations, and Maimonides' rulings here help clarify the talmudic discussion.

> The prohibition on etnan falls only on the thing itself. Therefore, it only falls on something which is itself suitable to be offered on the altar. Examples include a clean animal, turtle doves, pigeons, wine, oil, and meat. If he gave her money, and she bought a sacrifice with the money, the offering is legitimate.
>
> If he gave her wheat and she made flour; if he gave her olives, and she made oil; if he gave her grapes, and she made wine — all of these are legitimate for the altar, because they have been transformed.
>
> If he gave her a consecrated animal as her fee, it did not become prohibited for the altar...
>
> If he gave her something which did not belong to him they should not invalidate the gift, because a man cannot render prohibited something which is not his, unless the owners have despaired of recovering it.
>
> But if he gave her birds, even if they have been consecrated they are forbidden – this is the tradition which has come down.

In this passage, Maimonides confirms the principle which appeared in the talmudic stratum: the prohibition of *etnan zonah* applies only to the actual fee which is exchanged for the *zonah*'s services. If he gives her something which could not potentially be offered, then this category has no relevance, and the fee is permitted as a temple offering. If the fee is a potential sacrifice, then even if he gives it to her years later, it would still be prohibited. But if it is not suitable for the altar, there are no restrictions.

## Money
This line of reasoning leads Maimonides to return to the issue of money originally raised in the *Mishnah*. Maimonides says explicitly that according to the principle that *etnan* applies only to the fee itself, a prostitute may buy a sacrifice permitted on the altar, with her monetary fee. And in accordance with the same principle, even if the *zonah* could make an offering from the fee he gives her, such as grapes from which she could make wine, the offering is not prohibited because the fee has been transformed.

## The Power of Tradition
After outlining his whole system so clearly, Maimonides' final comment in *halakhah* 15 is interesting. He brings the case of the consecrated birds given as a *zonah*'s fee, which should, according to everything he understands about the law, be permitted. But tradition says that these are indeed not to be accepted at the altar. This comment represents Rambam's acknowledgement that in some specific cases, a tradition can have more weight than the system one has worked out however painstakingly.

## Repair of Temple
One final *halakhah* of Rambam's is significant for our discussion. In *halakhah* 18 of the same chapter, he states that an *etnan zonah* is permitted for repair of the temple (*bedek habayit*), because this involves a transformation. Here Rambam raises the possibility, mentioned only briefly in the *Gemara*, that perhaps the gift brought to the temple might be used for something other than an actual sacrifice, namely, maintenance of the temple. In such a case, the fee was sure to be transformed, and therefore could be accepted. The exception is the beaten gold plates which were expressly forbidden in the *Gemara*. No explanation is given for this exception; it may be another case, like that of the consecrated birds, in which Maimonides bows to a tradition he does not fully understand.

# Major Points
Maimonides adds four major points to the discussions on this topic as they were presented by his predecessors.
  - The prohibition refers only to a fee earned through an act of intercourse which is expressly forbidden by Jewish law. The law does not apply to other kinds

of intercourse, which may be disreputable but are not forbidden.
- In cases of doubt, the offering should not be accepted *lekhathilahh*. But if already offered, they should be accepted *bediavad*.
- An offering which had been paid for with money earned through forbidden intercourse is not forbidden.
- Tradition must be respected, even if it prohibits an offering which should theoretically be acceptable.

# Toldot Adam Vehava:

## Etnan Zonah and The Synagogue

All of the above mentioned texts dealt with sacrifices or offerings brought to the Jerusalem temple. This is so even though all of these texts were written/compiled in the period after the destruction of that temple.

Does the *halakhah* apply the rule of *etnan zonah* to the Jewish institution which succeeded the temple, namely, the synagogue?

R. Jeroham b. Meshullam (1290-1350) was a Provence-born Spanish *posek* who wrote a work entitled *Toldot Adam Vehava*. In *Helek Hava*, Path 13, he makes the following comment:

> The Torah proscribed the bringing of an *etnan zonah* to the House of the Lord as a sacrifice. In this age, the law is that [it is forbidden] to make anything for the synagogue from [an *etnan zonah*] such as a Torah scroll or repairs or a lamp or oil or the like – anything for repair [*bedek habayit*] or for a *mitzvah* object [*davar mitzvah*].

With this one comment, R. Jeroham states that the laws related to *etnan zonah* extend to the synagogue. By using this language, it is not clear if R. Jeroham was the key decisor to make this determination or if he is upholding a generally accepted ruling. In either case, the result is that just as Jewish law forbids the offering of an *etnan zonah* at the Jerusalem Temple, so too does it forbid the acceptance of an *etnan zonah* at the synagogue as a gift either for a mitzvah object [*davar mitzvah*] such as a Torah scroll, or for synagogue maintenance [*bedek habayit*]. With the phrase "It is forbidden to make anything..." Jeroham makes his position on transformation clear. An item which results from a transformed *etnan* is forbidden.

## Money

Having just outlined a rather strict approach to the issue, R. Jeroham proceeds to pull back in two ways. First, he states that even regarding the synagogue, the restriction still only applies to fees which themselves might be offered on the altar in Jerusalem. But, if a man gives a *zonah* money, with which she buys something else for the synagogue, even a mitzvah object, that gift is permitted. Second, he seems to reverse himself toward the end of the discussion when he quotes Rambam as permitting *etnan zonah* for the purpose of *bedek habayit*.

## Defining *Zonah*

Finally, R. Jeroham emphasizes the point that *zonah* is here to be defined as someone who is *ervah alav*, someone with whom he is forbidden by the Torah to have intercourse. Thus *etnan zonah* is the fee received as a result of this prohibited intercourse. He notes that he has observed people interpreting the category as including penuyot and he wants to correct this misperception. A *zonah* is not just any unmarried Israelite girl who accepts a fee in exchange for intercourse.

## Timing

Interestingly, R. Jeroham reverses the position outlined in the Talmud and in the *Mishneh Torah*, saying that post-payments are acceptable as gifts to the synagogue, while pre-payments are forbidden.

## Major Points

R. Jeroham identified a number of issues as central to the question of the acceptability of an *etnan zonah*.

- The category of *etnan zonah* may be applied to thesynagogue.
- The use to which the gift would be put in the synagogue may or may not be a factor in deciding whether or not to accept it.
- A gift which is bought with money earned as a *zonah*'s fee is permissible.
- The *zonah* is defined as someone with whom the man is forbidden to have intercourse under Jewish law.
- Pre-payments are forbidden; post-payments are permitted.

## *Magen Avraham*

The *Magen Avraham* is a 17th century commentary on the *Shulḥan Arukh* written by the Polish authority Abraham Abele b. Hayim

HaLevi Gombiner. After reviewing Rambam's comments on *etnan zonah*, Gombiner makes one very important statement in his commentary on OH 153:21, which serves to cast doubt on much of R. Yeroham's position.

> And we must say that [when applying the rule of *etnan zonah*] to the synagogue, we should rule leniently [*l'kula*]. This is because the Bible speaks specifically only of the temple, as it is written, "the House of the Lord your God." And neither the Gemara nor any of the *poskim* mentioned [that it should be applied to the synagogue]. Only R. Yeroham took this position. We therefore rule leniently in situations of doubt. Moreover, Rambam ruled that if an *etnan* was sacrificed, we retroactively rule it to have been valid. Therefore, in the case of the synagogue, it should be valid even *lekhathilah*.

### Temple and Synagogue

Rabbi Gombiner accepts the fact that we can talk about *etnan zonah* in relation to the synagogue, but we must do so very gingerly. R. Yeroham's ruling is important, but without any other confirmation of his position, Rabbi Gombiner feels we should be extremely lenient when we must rule on the acceptability of such a gift in the synagogue. In fact, Rabbi Gombiner's second comment would seem to rule out any case where a gift to the synagogue should be rejected: if it is acceptable even *lekhathilah*, then it could never be unacceptable.[6]

### Major Points

The contribution of the *Magen Avraham* may be summarized as follows:

> – Because the application to the synagogue is not *d'oraita*, the decisor must be extremely lenient when using this principle with regard to the synagogue.

# Other Halakhic Categories

The major halakhic category which we examined was *etnan zonah*. However, there are other categories which do have some relevance to our topic.

### Presumed Stolen Money

In *Sefer Zeraim* of the *Mishneh Torah*, *Hilkhot Matanot Aniyim*, ch.7, *halakhah* 12, Maimonides declares the following:

> One does not exact charity from orphans, even for redemption of captives, and even if they have a lot of money. It is permissible for the judge to rule that charity should be exacted from them in order to give them [an honorable name].

> The charity collector [*gabbai*] takes only a small amount from women, slaves, and minors. He does not take a lot because the presumption would be that it was stolen. And what is a "small amount?" He judges according to the wealth or poverty of their masters/ husbands...

In this *halakhah*, Maimonides sets a precedent for refusing *tzedakah* on the grounds that the community suspects the money being offered to have been stolen.

In *Baba Kama* 113a, the following *mishnah* is quoted:

> No money may be taken in change either from the box of the customs collectors or from the purse of the tax-collectors, nor may charity be taken from them, though it may be taken from their [own coins which they have at] home or in the market place.

This ruling raises the notion that there are certain people in the community from whom charity should not be taken. The distinction made between money in the "box" and money they have at home seems to indicate that the issue here is that the former is presumed to be stolen.

## People of Ill-Repute

*Sanhedrin* 24b quotes the following *mishnah*:

> These are ineligible [to be witnesses or judges]: a gambler with dice, a usurer, a pigeon-trainer, and traders [in the produce] of the sabbatical year.

And in the *Gemara*, R. Sheshet explains the reason behind the exclusion of dice players:

> The reason is that they are not concerned with the general welfare [*ain oskin beyishuvo shel olam*].

Although this passage does not refer specifically to the issue of accepting *tzedakah* money, it does establish the idea that there are certain categories of people in the community whose ill-repute is such that they may not take part fully in its most important and honored activities and responsibilities.

# The Modern Ethical Literature

In order to fully appreciate the modern ethical considerations involved in the case of tainted gifts, certain definitions will be helpful. The case involves a donation given by a person of ill-repute. The word "donation" comes from the Latin root **donate**. The word donate means to give freely, to offer as a gift, to transfer the ownership of a thing from oneself to another as a free gift. The import of this for our situation is not felt unless one appreciates the difference between "donate" and other words such as "sell," "exchange," and "trade." When one donates, nothing is exchanged; neither money nor commodity nor honor. The donation is made without anticipated benefit for the donor.

The term "ill-repute" is derived from the word **reputation**. Reputation is defined as the estimation in which a person or thing is commonly held. The person of ill-repute is held in low esteem. He/she is not necessarily a tried or convicted criminal. Such a person's attitudes or behaviors are suspect, because they are believed to run counter to the established norms of the community.

Charities and non-profit organizations are supported by grants and donations from individuals and organizations; the flow of donations is their lifeline. A non-profit organization will generally not want to take actions which will limit its donations – such restrictive practices could prove life-threatening for the non-profit organization.

The most significant piece of information we gathered in our investigation of modern non-Jewish sources is that *there is virtually no written or oral material on the subject*. In the literature there are a few articles that are tangentially related. These articles addressed many different issues and demonstrated some intuitive, but not well-developed or articulated, ethical sensitivities. The variety of foci and concerns highlighted the fact that in addition to the dozen or so questions raised, an additional dozen or dozens of dozens could have been formulated.

Despite the lack of material addressing ethical issues related to donations made by people of ill-repute, there is an abundance of well-known historical precedents. In the last one hundred years in the United States, Rockefeller and Carnegie are only two of the better known "robber-baron" entrepreneurs of ill-repute, who made large donations to charities, or indeed established charitable institutions of their own.

At the Columbia University Seminar on Philanthropy held on February 8, 1989 the discussion focused on the philanthropic activities of the Russell Sage Foundation. At the seminar the positive achievements of the foundation were discussed. As for the man whose name is honored by the foundation it was said "Russell Sage himself was a notoriously stingy man, a son-of-a-bitch."[7] Professor Roger Shinn, Professor Emeritus of Christian Ethics at Union Theological Seminary, stated as a general rule "if you were to investigate most of the great foundations in this country, you would find that the money was acquired by ethically problematic methods."[8]

The ability to acknowledge the personality and behavioral "short-comings" of donors is not restricted to the historian. Fund-raising and charitable organizations today reluctantly admit that some donors may have less that ideal reputations. Nonetheless, *we were unable to find a single charitable or non-profit organization* that had specific written guidelines regarding the donor. Fundraisers received no training, nor specific instructions regarding the restrictions or standards that they should apply to potential donors.

Dr. Shinn said that he had "not found any materials on the ethics of accepting ill-gotten money."[9] He also said "of tainted money all they say is "tain't enough!"[10] The larger non-profit organizations that we contacted echoed these thoughts. A representative of the United Way[11] explained

> We never had a policy because the situation never arises. We solicit from large and medium size companies and their employees. We don't ask for character references. It wouldn't be appropriate.

A representative of the United Jewish Appeal[12] explained their policy in the following manner:

> There is no written policy; such matters are considered on a case-by-case basis. Our overriding concern is "who are we to judge what is ill-gotten or of ill-repute?"

Professors of communal service and social work felt that ours was a "fascinating question", but stated that they were not familiar with any material related to it.[13]

These statements and the paucity of material on this subject would indicate a general loathing to set standards. It appears that there is no sense of a shared "ultimate authority", no sense of communal or general norms. While there is no sense of "ultimate authority", there is also an absence of a conviction that anyone as an individual can make decisions about other individuals or for the community at large. This modern sensibility results in a passivity and reticence with regard to establishing norms.

# Main Concerns

At the start, it was mentioned that there are a number of articles on tangential subjects. The concerns raised in these articles may be divided into three categories: 1) issues concerned with public message; 2) issues related to the particular circumstances of a case; 3) issues related to the internal workings of the non-profit world.

### Public Message
Concerns about public message and acceptance of gifts were numerous and varied. The general consensus was that acceptance of a gift does convey a message. By and large, the message is seen as negative: the feeling was that acceptance of a gift from someone of ill-repute can have a deleterious effect. There were concerns that acceptance of such a gift could be unadvisable because

> We must not convey that ends justify means and that breaches of moral principle are unimportant.[14]

The public's association of donor with gift is powerful as the following attitude towards an endowed chair at a university attests:

> The imagery of a chair on a pedestal, supported by dishonest businessmen, is too obvious and too grotesque to be ignored.[15]

By contrast, for some, the notion that the public message could be transformed into something positive and, indeed, promote positive behavior is expressed in discussions related to the endowment of a Chair of Ethics in Business by a convicted criminal.[16] The Director of the Center of Business Ethics at Bentley College, W. Michael Hoffman, wrote

> the endowed chair of business ethics will hopefully serve to sensitize future business people with ethical integrity, thereby reducing such crimes in the future.[17]

Though questions related to the public message were addressed in these articles, other issues which seem central to this discussion were not found in the literature. One is still left with the questions: Does the acceptance of a gift convey a message of approval of the person? Does acceptance convey approval of a person's deed? Can a message of disapproval be conveyed with regard to a particular deed without conveying disapproval of the person? If such a separation is possible, is it desirable for us to promote it?

### Circumstances of Donation
Issues related to the particular circumstances of a donation can be

divided into two categories: 1) motivation for donation and 2) source of ill-repute. Questions related to motive primarily focused on the compensatory nature of some donations. It was widely recognized that donations are sometimes made as compensatory gestures and/or with the intent of improving one's reputation. Such was apparently the case with Rockefeller and Carnegie.

## Motivation

Given that gifts are often made as compensation, many questions arise: Who might benefit from the compensatory act? The ideal bene-ficiary of a compensatory act was not agreed upon. The range included general humanity,[18] an institution somehow connected to the source of the ill-repute such as a rapist giving to a rape counseling center,[19] and the defrauded person alone, not a second or third party.[20]

Can a later good compensate for a past error? There were no unqualified affirmative answers to this question. It was suggested that the compensation must be fitted to the crime – again, for example, the rapist making a donation of time or money to a rape counseling center: "such a well-suited penalty could potentially rehabilitate victim and perpetrator."[21]

A refocusing of this question was also suggested. Good does not negate or compensate for bad, as in a compensatory gesture, but neither does bad negate good.[22] Under this approach, each action must be viewed in a vacuum and no tally made. The person's crime should not be viewed as negating other aspects of his/her life, i.e. the fact that he is a good "family man" and a philanthropist.

## Source of Ill-Repute

In the area of the source of ill-repute, a variety of questions and concerns were raised. A broad question was asked: What was the perceived offense? This question engendered many subquestions: Should there be a distinction among different types of less-than-desirable behaviors? There was a suggestion that violent crimes committed against a person be considered in a separate category of its own.[23]

Was the money earned with the express purpose of being donated? For some, a negative answer to this question exonerated the donor and made acceptance of the money possible.[24] For others, the positive response made it acceptable, so that in essence the ends justified the means.

Should there be a close connection between the source of ill-repute/offense and the charity to which the donation is made? Opinions were split on these questions. Examples of contributions to rape-counseling centers by rapists or business swindlers donating to business schools are cited as creative and positive alternatives to conventional penalties.[25] Others saw such donations as unacceptable and ludicrous.[26]

# Inner Workings of the Non-Profit Organization

Finally, there were concerns about the inner working of the non-profit organization and the role of a dubious donor. Some suggested that there should be limitations and guidelines for money donated by people of ill or questionable repute. This indicates that the money once taken might be treated differently from other funds raised by the organization. A common suggestion is that the donor's name might not be made public in order to limit the honor given to the donor and to save the non-profit organization from possible embarrassment, if not guilt by association.[27]

A second common suggestion is that there be a limitation placed upon the individual's eligibility for a directorial position in the organization, or his/her having on-going influence upon the way in which the donation might be spent.[28]

It is noteworthy that none of the organizations suggested screening donors or rejecting donations. They focused, rather, on the ways in which to distinguish these funds, if necessary from all others.

Though many "watch-dog"agencies have been established in recent years, none has been established in this specific area. The National Charities Information Bureau [NCIB] does in depth studies of charities: their programs, management, and finances. It evaluates them in light of what it calls the NCIB Standards of Philanthropy. This service is provided because

> Donors needed to be better informed about now the charities spent contributed funds. Charities needed to know what kind of management and accountability was expected of them.[29]

However, the NCIB's concern for accountability does not extend to the area of donor reputation. None of its standards related to this issue in any way.

The variety of questions and the absence of any identified donor screening processes leads to the question of whether or not guidelines could be established, and if they could, whether such guidelines would be advisable? The absence of suggested guidelines, coupled with the oral data collected, indicate an attitude that establishing such guidelines would not be advisable.

# A Directive Approach to the Ethics of Giving

One non-profit institution deals directly with this issue. The Josephson Institute for the Advancement of Ethics differs from other non-profit organizations in that it disseminates its funds to support research and educational programs in the field of ethics.

The logo of the Josephson Institute is

> At a time when commitment to ethics can no longer be taken for granted in many segments of our society, creative and aggressive efforts advancing ethical principles are essential.[30]

Its brochure goes on to explain

> Ethical aspirations must be translated into operative principles and practical guidelines.[31]

In a recent article written by the director of the Josephson Foundation, the ethical issues that others seemed to avoid are dealt with directly. Mr. Josephson suggests that there are certain assumptions that the public has of charities and non-profit organizations. Among these are: a person or organization with integrity cannot be bought; the name and good-will of tax exempt non-profit organizations are a public trust; an organization will be judged by its standards; choices will be made by a non-profit organization without sacrificing principles or undermining the public trust. In light of these assumptions, he suggests that some gifts should be refused.[32]

Mr. Josephson suggests that the primary concern of an organization is one of public image. The public will weigh the acceptance of a dubious donation against the purposes and beliefs of the organization. Public image is the primary concern, and the decision about accepting money must be considered in light of the circumstances of the particular case and the source of ill-repute, to use the categories raised indirectly by the aforementioned articles.

Will the acceptance be contrary to the organization's integrity or its long-range interests?

> Gifts from adverse sources,... must be handled with great care so as to avoid the appearance that the organization either sanctions the donor's activities or that it might adjust its substantive or educational programs to accommodate the donor's interests.[33]

Mr. Josephson avoids two major concerns raised in the other articles; the role of the individual to make judgments; and fears that guidelines might restrict acceptance of donations and hence hinder fundraising efforts. These are the factors which have apparently led the non-profit organizations to conclude that the drafting of general guidelines would be impractical if not impossible to do.

Mr. Josephson, however, does suggest some guidelines. These guidelines seem broad enough so that they might be applied to a variety of organizations. The guidelines state that one must "Consider and involve all of the stakeholders... beneficiaries, other donors, employees, and volunteers and governing board." Each of these "stakeholders" must have a chance to share concerns and express opinions regarding the organization's mission.

Josephson also feels that one must consider what the donor wants in return. The suggested rule of thumb is "the less the charity has to give in return for a questionable gift, the better."[34] This, one would assume, includes fame and honor. One must realize that

> Need should not be a determining factor. ...The test of objectivity [is]: would you reject the gift if the amount were smaller or your need less?[35]

Finally, one should consider the nature of the negative evidence related to the potential donor. Mr. Josephson suggests that a decision should be based on more than rumor or guilt by association. The organization accepting a gift must be cognizant of its moral responsibility

> for embarrassment or harm caused to the donor and it ought to be very careful not to indirectly slander the name of any person or company.[36]

Mr. Josephson does not state that conviction by a court of law is an absolute prerequisite for rejecting a gift but he does emphasize that evidence is necessary. Therefore, judgment must be based upon more than rumor. Furthermore, the guiding consideration for Mr. Josephson is whether or not there is an appearance of betrayal of the organization's principles.

These suggestions are applicable in some cases, but not in others. The first guideline seems impractical for large non-profits which gather funds from a broad group. How practical would it be for UJA or United Way, the two major non-profit organizations appearing in this study, to solicit opinions and concerns from "all of the stakeholders", when a questionable donation arose? Though one might hold that in the best of all possible worlds this would be advisable, it is not likely to be adopted by these large non-profit organizations. It might be possible to place the decision in the hands of a committee that represents all stakeholders. But it should be noted that even the process of circulating and updating guidelines for potential donors might be potentially injurious to the non-profit organization's fund-raising efforts.

Some of the other guidelines which Mr. Josephson mentioned, however, might certainly be applicable for all non-profit organizations, no matter their size. All non-profit organizations, by law, must have a statement of purpose and principles. These could surely be referenced in cases of dubious donations. Furthermore, Mr. Josephson's "test of objectivity", which attempts to remove the temptation to screen large donors more leniently, would be efficacious for non-profit organizations which are concerned with maintaining the public trust.

# Religious Institutions

Religious institutions and groups seem to fall into a special category within the larger rubric of non-profit organizations in that they are associated with morality and a belief in a higher authority. They are viewed by members and non-members as constituting a special, "holy-community".

> Religious institutions must be extremely  careful lest by their excessive pragmatism – in the belief that the end justifies any means – they create the impression that moral impropriety is totally irrelevant to one's standing in the "holy community". But, it is one thing to open our doors and hearts even to a convict, and another to give the impression that we are indifferent even to the most flagrant breaches of moral principles.[37]

In the religious sphere, one writer has suggested that there is a difference between the Jewish and Roman Catholic responses to such questions. With regard to funerals, he notes that the Roman Catholic Dioceses of NY and Brooklyn have refused a public mass for a reputed mob leader. By contrast, Queens Borough President Donald Manes, who committed suicide during a public political scandal, received an "effusive eulogy" by a rabbi. This writer concluded:

> Indeed synagogues are usually the very last to censor their Jewish criminals.[38]

# Halakhah and Modern Ethics

We see two principal areas in which there is a dialectic between the concerns of the halakhic sources and the modern ethical sources.

The first revolves around questions of authority. Our Jewish sources possess confidence in their ability to judge in a particular case whether or not the offering may be accepted. The halakhic system, with its basis in the Revelation by God at Sinai, possesses explicitly stated laws which can be interpreted or applied to individual cases. The system can speak about issues such as timing, legal ownership, transformations. It understands as its mandate the setting of guidelines such that general laws can be carried out through specific actions.

By contrast, the modern ethicists do not share a common system or common sense of authority. Each may feel that its understanding and interpretations are valid, but most are reluctant to state or demonstrate that their system is superior to or preferable to all others and impose it on others.

Only one writer makes an initial attempt to suggest guidelines that could be applicable to many groups. Other individual institutions opt not to do this even for themselves, never mind other groups. They choose not to set such standards, saying, "Who are we to judge?" They do not see their institution or its directors as having authority to make such a decision because, perhaps, the multitude of considerations is overwhelming. Our society is accustomed to turning over judgments about offenses to a court; organizational boards do not perceive themselves as having the authority to judge.

The value of this is openness to varying values and situations. The curse is that it leads to relativism and a lack of standards.

One tension then, that exists between the Jewish and the modern ethical discussions, revolves around fundamental differences in their perception of the locus of authority, and their confidence in themselves as decisors.

The second major tension which appears to lie behind the Jewish and modern ethical discussions is that of the rights of the individual in relation to the community. The Jewish system is predicated on the existence of a community which lives by a common set of laws and recognizes common authority. Our Jewish sources do not speak of the rights of the individual. Their exclusive concern is that the communal laws be maintained with respect to Israel's religious or cultic institutions. The purpose of the individual in this system, then appears to be participation in and contribution to the community through adherence to its laws. While the individual is valued and has rights and merits respect, the integrity of the community cannot be compromised for the sake of the individual.

By contrast, most modern ethical discussions recognize a tension between individual and community, while tending to favor the rights of the individual over the community. This reflects the fundamental assumption that the community is a derivative of the individuals who comprise it.

Thus, in the modern world the individual is primary in the

decision making process. An institution is expected to take into account the individual's rights and needs when it makes decisions. For example, the individual's desire to give, the individual's personal need to make a compensatory gesture or exonerate his name, the potential embarrassment which might result for the individual – these and similar considerations must be weighed.

The modern writers, however, do not lose sight entirely of the norms and integrity of the community. The community in the modern world is a smaller, self-selected voluntary group which defines itself by common principles and concerns. As Daniel Elazar[39] points out the American Jewish community fits this description. A non-profit organization may also be considered a community which has its own principles, reputation, and integrity to consider and preserve. The tension between the needs of the individual and the community in the modern world is one of the factors which interferes with a non-profit organization's ability to decide questions that involve both individual and community.

This then is the second major tension between the two literatures: whereas the Jewish sources focus primarily on the needs of the community, the modern ethical sources are aware of a tension between the needs of the individual and the needs of the community.

## Similarities

As we have shown, there are important tensions between the Jewish and modern materials. However, one of the most interesting things that came to light during our investigation was that there are also some striking similarities between the Jewish and modern ethical discussions. With a little interpretation, one can find many common topics contained in the Jewish and modern ethical materials.

One commonality upon which all the others are predicated is the extra-ordinary nature of institutions in the life of the community. Jewish sources and modern ethical sources discuss entities, the Jewish temple/synagogue and the non-profit organization, which are perceived as occupying a category different from all others. Both the Jewish and modern ethical sources recognize a higher binding authority which uniquely informs the nature of the institution. In the Jewish system, as mentioned before, God is the authority. In the modern sources, there is an ethical imperative which is largely determined by the individual, but which in the case of non-profit institutions, has a more collective nature.

Discussion in the Jewish sources is inextricably linked with the maintenance of holiness.[40] In the modern, non-religious institution the concern for holiness is substituted with a concern for public trust. The institutions discussed are understood by the community to represent its highest values and ideals and they are believed to operate in a way such that their principles will not be compromised.

Other more specific concerns are shared. First, there are common concerns about limiting the influence that a gift's size might have on a potential recipient. In the Jewish sources, we find a stricture against accepting large amounts from people whose means appear to be limited or of dubious origin. In the modern ethical discussion, we are warned that a gift's size should not be a determining factor in deciding whether or not it is acceptable.

Second, there are common concerns about the source of ill-repute. The Jewish material focuses on defining a *zonah* not as a paid prostitute but as any woman who violates the laws of *arayot*. In the modern ethical literature this concern was expressed by the question: what was the perceived offense? Distinctions were made among different types of less-than-desirable behaviors.

Third, there are common concerns about what constitutes appropriate treatment of a person of ill-repute. The Jewish material allows the community to treat individuals differently based upon their reputations. People of ill-repute, for example, cannot freely give to charity or be witnesses in a court of law. The modern ethical material is concerned with whether or not a person of ill-repute could make donations as any other person might. Some suggest accepting gifts from disreputable donors, but placing certain conditions on the donation which do not apply to untainted gifts.

Fourth, both modern ethical and Jewish literature are concerned with the ultimate use to which the gift will be put. The Jewish sources sensed that there was some difference between *bedek habayit* and the actual sacrifice, but they remain equivocal on the issue. The modern ethical literature discusses the appropriateness of directing one's gift to a cause which is somehow related to the undesirable behavior, e.g. a chair of business ethics endowed by an embezzler or a donation by a rapist to a rape counseling center.

These similarities notwithstanding, the gulf between the worldview witnessed in the Jewish sources and that of modern ethical sources is large enough that if we want our decision on this issue to be informed by both literatures, we must find some way to mediate between them.

# Mediation

Mediation requires that we somehow in our decision making process consider both the differences between the two literatures which we have just outlined, and the similarities. In order to help us do so, we created the following test case which highlights what we feel are the most important ethical dilemmas.

# The Case

The synagogue is in need of a roof. A wealthy congregant sent a check to the temple maintenance committee for the entire amount needed for the roof. He attached a note saying that he looked forward to public acknowledgment of his gift at the upcoming High Holiday services. The committee contacts the rabbi with the "good news". The rabbi and the committee are aware that the donor is reputed to have amassed his fortune through his affiliation with the mob. How should the rabbi respond?

Before we can utilize our Jewish sources in our mediation, one issue must be clarified. We realize that there is nothing to mediate in our case if we do not accept the notion that the laws of *etnan zonah* can be extended to the synagogue. Therefore, we accept the decision of R. Yeroham in this matter, and feel free to use all of our Jewish sources. The synagogue, much as the temple, is a holy institution never to be profaned.

Similarly, we must determine from the start whether we will accept the exemption of money from the category of *etnan zonah*. In light of the fact that in the modern world virtually all gifts to a synagogue are monetary, we feel that to exclude money would mean deciding the case immediately, without ever facing the difficult issues which the literature raised.

We also wish to point out that we are aware that we are applying the Jewish category *etnan zonah* to types of disreputable conduct other than *zenut*. Just as we feel some of the laws of the temple can be extended to the synagogue, and just as our sources discussed the etnan in cases of *bedek habayit*, we feel the restrictions applied to *etnan zonah* can be extended to modern corollary behaviors.

Having laid out these provisos, we can say that our basic assumptions when mediating this case are derived from Jewish sources. Certain gifts must be rejected, and our role as decisors is to determine the guidelines for making such a ruling.

The first datum is that the synagogue is in need of a roof. Without a roof the community cannot meet to pray and study together, or even simply to enjoy each other's company at social events. The lack of a suitable structure could encourage congregants to seek affiliation elsewhere.

Nevertheless, in this area we find Josephson's argument compelling: need should not determine a gift's acceptability. Furthermore, we accept R. Yeroham's ruling that the intended use of a gift does not determine whether it should be accepted; the gift may not be used even for *bedek habayit*. We recognize that the Jewish sources had an eye to practicality and were writing in a time of poverty and persecution. Nevertheless and most fortunately, we are deciding in a time of relative plenty. We therefore choose to follow Josephson's guideline that the decision with regard to acceptance of a donation be made without regard for the recipient's need.

A donation made to "save" an institution should be accepted only in extraordinary circumstances and then only with the greatest self examination. At times, it may be advisable for an institution to close down rather than to continue due to support derived from sources inimicable to its values.

Our second datum is the fact that a check has already been received by the congregation's synagogue maintenance committee. Though our Jewish sources make a distinction between *bediavad* and *lekhathilah* we do not find this argument compelling. For us, the timing in such a case should not be a determining factor. For the congregant who views the synagogue as an institution that represents high moral principles, the application of *bediavad* and *lekhathilah* could be viewed as a cynical means to circumvent the very principles which the synagogue stands for. At a time when everything has its price, the synagogue must set a higher example.

Our third datum is that the donor anticipates something in exchange for his gift. He requests public honor on the day when the entire community assembles. For us, there are two important considerations. First, the synagogue should ideally not be modeling the idea that *tzedakah* is given in exchange for honor and status. Second, the particular compensation that he requests would convey a message of approval of a person whose activities are known to be antithetical to our community's values.

The Jewish sources place the needs and reputation of the community above those of the individual. In this case we feel that both the modern ethical sources and the Jewish sources support our rejection of the donor's request for public recognition.

One option might have been to tell the donor that the gift could be accepted anonymously. But because in our case the maintenance committee is already aware of the check, there is no longer a possibility for anonymity. Even if the check had not already been sent, however, we find this option problematic for two reasons: first, it is unrealistic to expect that in the typical synagogue community such information would not "leak" and then appear even more underhanded; and second, even an anonymous gift from such a source would not be consonant with the values of the synagogue.

Our fourth datum is that the congregant is a "reputed" mobster. We accept the modern notion that the rights of the individual must be taken into account. We have grown up in a culture that reveres the concept that "an individual is innocent until proven guilty", and we espouse this notion as our own. We are loathe to violate this principle. For this reason we found the ruling in *Matanot Aniyim* objectionable, as it promotes using reputation alone as a guide. We feel compelled, as does Josephson, to weigh this right against the rights and needs of the community. We, therefore, would want to look for evidence to determine whether or not the ill-repute was deserved.

In our particular case we as rabbis are dealing with a committee that has not expressed ethical concerns about the donation. As rabbis and administrators entrusted with maintaining the values of our institution and the community which it represents, we do feel that we can and should exercise the authority to determine whether the evidence is substantial enough to warrant rejection for the sake of promoting our core values.

It is at this point that the tension between public opinion and the rights of the individual become clearest. We can visualize a case in which the nature of the evidence does not substantiate the person's poor reputation and the rabbi might accept the money. However, in our case the knowledge of this man's illicit activities is so widespread that rejection of the gift, is, we feel, warranted.

# Process:
# At the Intersection
# of Halakhah
# and Ethics

As part of the process of researching and writing this paper, we have come to certain conclusions about liberal Jewish decision making. One of our purposes in writing this paper was to use this case as a model for future ethical dilemmas that will arise. We hoped that we would become more comfortable with using rabbinic materials and more sensitized to halakhic language and categories, and the meta-*halakhah* which informed them. We also hoped that we would begin to understand how we might integrate *halakhah* into our decision making process.

At the beginning of our study we both expressed our feeling that the acceptance of a tainted gift was undesirable. In light of the consonance between our final decision and our initial responses we are left with a disturbing question about the utilization of and manipulation of data. We learned a great deal about a variety of perspectives, and our own values and concerns. Yet, the data that we invoke as we present our decision is that which substantiates our viewpoint. We worry about the ability of a decisor to act in a way that does not merely reflect and find backing for a personal preference. We do not come into the problem as *tabula rasa* and we, quite honestly, do not know if that would be desirable. Nevertheless, we wonder if the process as a whole reflects the intellectual integrity that we would like it to.

Perhaps the liberal Jewish decisor should not enter the process with the goal of reaching an impartial decision based on sources. Rather, the goal might be familiarization with a variety of opinions in order 1) to clarify one's own values and concerns related to an impending decision, and 2) to become aware of the seriousness and integrity of opposing viewpoints.

Living in the modern world as Jews, our consciousness is a fusion of two distinct world views. Our thought processes and vocabulary are modern, as are many of our sensibilities. Nevertheless, there is a part of us, which often times is more difficult to delineate and articulate, that is unquestionably Jewish. This process has helped us to better understand which elements are "Jewish" and which are "modern". It has also helped us to enter the Jewish traditional sources in such a way that they can shed light on that part of us which is consonant with its values and world-view, if not its specific forms and behaviors.

Having said this, we are still unsure about what should ideally characterize the liberal Jewish decision making process. We do know that we do not exclusively follow either one of the systems available to us; we are neither strict halakhists nor avowed secularists. We want to make use of both Jewish and modern teachings as well as our own experience. In our attempt to do so we find ourselves taking bits and pieces from each system, where they confirm our instinct on the matter.

We find that after reviewing and analyzing all of the materials, we have not moved significantly from our initial responses. We found arguments and discussions in the two literatures which shed light for us on those factors which in an unarticulated and even unconscious manner led to our initial "gut" instinct on the issue. And, we have become aware of values and concerns that at first glance we were unable to identify as key factors or important considerations. Though our ultimate response to the problem was the same both before and after the process, our decision was markedly more self conscious after having made this study.

We see the value of this process in our heightened awareness that each system can provide a valuable perspective from which to conceive of and enter a problem, perspectives that generate issues and categories which should be considered in the decision-making process. (Our penchant for a variety of perspectives and interpretations is at first glance the modern in us, but, from a different perspective, perhaps it is the latent Talmudist in us!)

Having articulated our position in a newly self-conscious manner, we feel much more confident about voicing and implementing the decision which, prior to our study, we felt only instinctively.

# Bibliography

Brown, Driver, and Briggs. *Hebrew and English Lexicon of the Old Testament*

HaCohen, Aryeh Leib. *Avnei Miluim*, Responsum 27.

Columbia University Seminar on Philanthropy 2/17/89, speech delivered by Marshall A. Robinson, President Emeritus of the Russell Sage Foundation.

Conversation with Mr. Yacker, representative of the United Way.

Dresner, Samuel H. "For the Sin of Deadening Conscience," *Sh'ma*, October 3, 1986.

Elazar, Daniel. *Community and Polity*, (JPS) 1976.

Josephson, Michael. "Ethical Issues, Tainted Money, Sleazy Donors and Other Questionable Gifts", *NATA Journal*, Spring/Summer 1989.

Lubov, Rikki. Fundraiser, United Jewish Appeal, telephone conversation 3/16/89.

Neuman, Thomas. Director of Intergroup Relations, Anti-Defamation League, *Jewish Exponent*, June 19, 1987.

See symposium "Should Criminal Fines be Redeemed for Charity Gifts?" *Business and Society Review,*

"Should Criminal Fines Be Redeemed for Charity Gifts?" *Business and Society Review*, Summer 1984

Telephone conversations with Dr. Bernard Reisman, Director of School of Jewish Communal Service, Brandeis University; Dr. Norman Linzer, Wurzweiler School of Social Work, Yeshiva University; Dr. Gerald Bubis, founder of the School of Jewish Communal Service, Hebrew Union College, Los Angeles.

Wurzberger, Walter S. "For the Sins which we have committed," *Sh'ma*, October 3, 1986.

# Notes

1. The term "dog" is a reference to male cultic prostitutes, according to Brown, Driver, and Briggs *Hebrew and English Lexicon of the Old Testament*, p. 477.

2. There are variant texts attributing this opinion to R. Meir, rather than Rabbi.

3. This is an apparent reference to the prohibited relations specified in Leviticus 18.

4. There ensues an extensive discussion over whether the fee paid to a non-Israelite prostitute, to a widow by the High Priest, or to an unmarried woman by an unmarried man is forbidden. All of these cases are subjects for dispute among various authorities since they are not *d'oraita* ("Torah law").

5. It is not clear whether the "back wall of the Holy of Holies" is a phrase used to describe an especially sacred space for which a donation from the category *etnan zonah* would unquestionably be unfit, or a space that is hidden and inaccessible and therefore subject to fewer restrictions.

6. Further discussion on this topic can be found in *Avnei Miluim* by Aryeh Leib HaCohen, Responsum 27.

7. Columbia University Seminar on Philanthropy 2/17/89, speech delivered by Marshall A. Robinson, President Emeritus of the Russell Sage Foundation.

8. Letter dated April 27, 1989.

9. Ibid.

10. Telephone conversation on March 12, 1989.

11. Conversation with Mr. Yacker, representative of the United Way.

12. Rikki Lubov, Fundraiser, United Jewish Appeal, telephone conversation 3/16/89.

13. Telephone conversations with Dr. Bernard Reisman, Director of School of Jewish Communal Service, Brandeis University; Dr. Norman Linzer, Wurzweiler School of Social Work, Yeshiva University; Dr. Gerald Bubis, founder of the School of Jewish Communal Service, Hebrew Union College, Los Angeles.

14. Walter S. Wurzberger, "For the Sins which we have committed," *Sh'ma*, October 3, 1986.

15. "Should Criminal Fines Be Redeemed for Charity Gifts?" *Business and Society Review*, Summer 1984, pp. 41-45.

16. Ibid., p. 41. The case involved Peter Kiewit who was involved in highway bid-rigging and whose proposed punishment was to include a donation to the University of Nebraska to endow a Chair of Business Ethics.

17. Ibid., p. 42.

18. Hoffman, ibid., pp. 41-42.

19. Miller, ibid., p. 43.

19. Miller, ibid., p. 43.

20. Potter, ibid., p. 44.

21. Miller, ibid., p. 43.

22. Thomas Neuman, Director of Inter-group Relations Anti-Defamation League, *Jewish Exponent*, June 19, 1987.

23. See symposium "Should Criminal Fines be Redeemed for Charity Gifts?" *Business and Society Review,* p. 44. Mr. Potter made his comment with regard to the type of penalties that may be assigned to crimes and the possibilities for creative alternatives.

24. Neuman, *Jewish Exponent*, 6/19/87.

25. *Business and Society Review*, pp. 41-43.

26. See footnotes 7 and 8.

27. *Business and Society Review*, pp. 41-45.

28. Conversation with Rikki Lubov (UJA).

29. NCIB brochure.

30. From the Josephson Institute brochure.

31. Ibid.

32. Michael Josephson, "Ethical Issues, Tainted Money, Sleazy Donors and Other Questionable Gifts", *NATA Journal*, Spring/Summer 1989. pp 8-9, 22.

33. Ibid.

34. Ibid., p. 9.

35. Ibid., p. 9.

36. Ibid., p. 9.

37. Wurzberger.

38. Samuel H. Dresner, "For the Sin of Deadening Conscience," *Sh'ma*, October 3, 1986.

39. Daniel Elazar, *Community and Polity*, (JPS) 1976, p. xiii.

40. This emphasis on holiness led us to investigate traditional Jewish material on *hilul hashem* – profanation of God's name. Our preliminary study in this area showed hilul hashem to be a very narrowly defined cate-

# The Ethics of Hazardous Waste Disposal

## An Examination of the Ethics and Halakhah Concerning Hazardous Waste Disposal

Laurence Groffman
and Jordan Millstein

The proper disposal of hazardous wastes is one of the great challenges facing American society today. Many manufacturing plants, from paint factories to pharmaceutical labs, produce by-products which must be disposed of properly and safely so that they do not pose a threat to people or the environment.[1] Every year, American industries and businesses generate approximately 270 million tons of hazardous wastes.[2] In addition, common, everyday products may be classified as hazardous waste. For example, paint thinners, hair spray and house-hold cleaners can become hazardous wastes once they are no longer useful.[3]

A hazardous waste can be defined as a material that is potentially dangerous to human health or the environment based on the following criteria:

– It may ignite, easily posing a fire hazard

– It may be corrosive, capable of damaging materials or harming people

– It may be reactive, likely to explode, catch fire, or give off dangerous gases when in contact with water or other materials.

– It may be toxic, capable of causing illness or other health problems if handled incorrectly.

– It may be on a list of specific wastes which

the Environmental Protection Agency (EPA)
has determined to be hazardous.[4]

Clearly, the best way of managing hazardous waste
is to not produce waste in the first place. If wastes are not
generated from commercial and industrial activity, waste
management is a moot issue.[5] While some reduction in
waste creation is possible, in order to completely eliminate
the production of such waste we would have to give up
many, if not most, of the benefits of living in a modern,
industrial society. Since the ethics of the modern lifestyle
is not the topic of our paper, it must suffice to say that
such a drastic change in the world is not likely in the near
future. Consequently, ways must be found for dealing with
hazardous waste. Another method or approach is waste
minimization. This would include waste recovery or recy-
cling, wherein the potential waste is reused in the process
in which it is generated, or used for something else before
or after it is treated to lower its toxicity or harmful properties. This is an appealing alternative. However, even
with increasing efforts by industry to eliminate, reduce,
recover and recycle, a significant amount of hazardous
waste will continue to be produced.[6]

One method currently being advanced for ridding
ourselves of hazardous waste is high temperature incineration (HTI). In this process wastes are placed in what is
aptly called a high temperature incinerator, where they
are burned at a temperature of up to 2200 degrees fahren-
heit, with a proper amount of air, and with enough time to
ensure destruction of the wastes. In theory, HTI can thoroughly and permanently destroy hazardous wastes. If the
incinerator is well designed and run, HTI's emit only trace
elements of residual organic compounds and produce
small amounts of ash.[7]

High temperature incineration (HTI) is thought to
provide the highest level of control over toxic organic
material of all existing hazardous waste treatment methods. Land fills merely store the material and control the
danger as long as the wastes remain contained in the
landfill. But under current regulations, many hazardous
wastes must be treated to reduce toxicity before they can
be landfilled. HTI reduces both the toxicity and the volume of waste greatly.[8]

# Waste Technologies Industries, East Liverpool, Ohio

It is all well and good to discuss whether something is a good thing in theory. But, as has often been said, nothing exists "in theory." In order to truly understand the ethical issues surrounding hazardous waste incineration it is necessary to examine what occurs when there is an attempt to put it into practice. As it happens, it was not difficult for these authors to select a particular case for this study, since it was, in fact, the particular case which led us to choose this topic in the first place. As the student rabbi in East Liverpool, Ohio, a small town of about 25,000 on the banks of the Ohio river, this writer (Jordan Millstein) could not help but hear about "WTI." After all, "WTI" is the issue in the town of East Liverpool. "WTI" stands for Waste Technologies Industries, an American subsidiary of the Swiss firm, Von Roll, which has built several hazardous waste incinerators, most of them in Europe. It's building of just such an incinerator on the Columbiana County Port Authority site in East Liverpool has caused an extraordinary controversy in this midwestern town. *The Evening Review*, the town daily, is constantly filled with articles and letters to the editor about WTI, ranging from the technical to the emotional and vitriolic. It seems that almost every week there is some sort of protest at WTI, and a number of protestors, including actor Martin Sheen, have been arrested.[9] There have been countless meetings of the city council about this or that legal detail regarding the licensing and operation of WTI, with irate citizens blasting the mayor, the governor and the city council for not acting to stop it. And no local or state politicians, save one councilman, has even dared to take a stand on it, for fear of losing the votes of either the proponents or opponents of WTI.[10] Such a lively controversy seemed perfect grist for our ethical mill. Thus we posed our question: **Should Waste Technologies Industries (WTI) be allowed to continue building and operate a hazardous waste incinerator at the Columbiana County Port Authority site in East Liverpool, Ohio?**

## Historical Background

In the early 1980s WTI requested and received permission from the Port Authority of Columbiana County, Ohio to build a large hazardous waste incinerator on Port Authority land on the banks of the Ohio river.[11] It was no accident that Von Roll chose this site, for the Port Authority was actively seeking industrial firms to locate on this land. Indeed, the Port Authority of Columbiana County was formed for the express purpose of luring industry to this site, which was carved out of what is known as the "East End" of the city of East Liverpool, the poor area of town.[12]

For, by the late 1970s East Liverpool, like so many other towns of the Ohio Valley and midwest in general, was mired in a deep economic depression. The American steel industry had all but collapsed and many of the potteries (factories that make dishes and crockery), which had been the economic foundation of the East Liverpool area for decades, went bankrupt or moved away. Consequently, when WTI approached Port Authority officials with its project which, they claimed, would create 500 construction jobs and 100 permanent jobs, as well as attract other industry to the area, the Port Authority was eager to accept.[13]

At the same time, this was no offer of charity on the part of Von Roll. A large amount of hazardous waste is produced by industry in the Ohio valley, including steel mills, refineries, pharmaceutical plants and paint manufacturers.[14] It seemed likely that WTI would be able draw clients for their hazardous waste incinerator and turn a nifty profit. Thus, WTI leased the Ohio river site from the Columbiana County Port Authority, and WTI, the hazardous waste incinerator project, was born.[15]

During the early to mid-1980s WTI officials busied themselves getting building permits from the Ohio Environmental Protection Agency (OEPA) and its subdivision, the Ohio Hazardous Waste Facilities Board (OHWFB).[16] Permits were granted indicating that the WTI plant would produce air and water pollution below set standards and that the plant would be constructed to prevent washout of any hazardous waste from the facility by a 100-year-level flood. This last permit was necessary because the WTI plant is being built on a flood plain, i.e. an area that is expected to be flooded by the Ohio river every 100 years or so.[17]

According to Randy DeBee, recently elected city councilman and the only council member openly opposed to WTI, opposition to the plant already existed in the early 1980s and protests were heard when WTI was given it's building permits by the Ohio EPA. However, at that time, the mayor and the city council supported WTI. The vociferousness of opposition has ebbed and flowed during the past decade, becoming more intense recently as the plant nears completion.[18] (The plant is set to begin operation in the spring of 1992.) There are currently several groups actively opposing the opening of the WTI plant, including the midwest regional office of Greenpeace, and the more locally based Tri-State Environment Council and Save Our County.[19]

In the meantime, public officials have become more equivocal about the plant. For example, Ohio Governor Voinovich stated a few weeks ago that there is nothing he can do to stop the plant now but, had he been governor in the early 1980s and known as he does now that Ohio already has enough capacity to handle the hazardous waste it produces, he might have opposed WTI. Voinovich also recently declared a moratorium on the building of any new hazardous waste incinerators in Ohio.[20]

Another recent development of import was the release of the "draft" of a study conducted by environmental scientist Isaac Yomtovian of Enviro-Science Inc. This study was commissioned by the East Liverpool city council in order to get a more definitive, objective view of the dangers posed by WTI. The cost of the study was shared equally by the city and WTI.[21] Yomtovian's report was rather conservative in its findings, stating time and again that various issues needed more study. While he never says outright that WTI poses a serious danger to the citizens of East Liverpool, he does note that there is a small chance that the plant could cause significant harm[22] (see below). Thus, the controversy continues.

While there are many points of disagreement between supporters and opponents of the plant, the actual locus of the conflict in recent weeks has been over whether WTI is required to get a construction permit from the City of East Liverpool (it's current permits are state permits) to build within a flood plain. WTI and the OEPA claim that it does not, that the state permit is sufficient, while opponents say it does. The impetus for this conflict was a statement by a flood plain specialist at the Federal Emergency Management Agency to the effect that if state laws preempt local regulations, more than 500 communities across Ohio would be in jeopardy of losing flood insurance and federal assistance should a disaster occur.[23] The matter is already headed for court.[24]

**The Debate**

The debate over WTI in East Liverpool and the surrounding region would appear to be a debate over who has the correct facts. Greenpeace and WTI's other opponents say that the plant is dangerous to the environment and the surrounding communities. WTI and it's supporters say it's safe. Each side lobs mounds of data, allegedly accurate, in support of it's position. The question seems to be, which side is correct? A similar tit for tat argument exists over whether or not WTI will help the economy of the town and the region. WTI, of course, says it will, while the opposition debunks WTI's claim of more jobs and business for the area. Who is right? So, too, the question of whether there is a need for a high temperature incinerator in this locale. Each side hauls out its statistics to demonstrate definitively that there is or is not a need.

While an important aspect of this paper is to try to get at the truth behind the factual claims of each side, if that were all there was to discuss, there would be no point in presenting this as an ethics paper. These authors hold, however, that what is on the surface a clash of facts is, in fact, a clash of values. It is this clash of values that represents the ethical debate.

What follows is a presentation of the factual debate divided into the categories of mentioned above: the dangers of WTI, the economic benefits, and the need for WTI's services. In each case, there will be an attempt to extrapolate the values guiding each side in the debate. This will be followed by a discussion of the ethical conflicts that result from this clash of values and the conclusions drawn by the authors.

### The Dangers of WTI

There has been much debate about the hazards that WTI poses to East Liverpool. Naturally, WTI claims that it poses no significant threat to the community and the environment. Their opponents say that it will. Pursuant to the first category, WTI claims that its emissions are far below EPA limits, and in fact are less than the emissions of a typical power plant or steel mill. In a document, WTI details how their emissions of organic compounds, hydrogen chloride, sulfur, etc. are less than the Ohio EPA safe limits, using tons and pounds per year emitted as the unit of measurement.[25] The opposition does not lend these numbers much credence.

WTI claims that a minimum of 99.99% of organic wastes will be destroyed in its incineration process. Solids, (the only residuals) will be taken to EPA approved landfills.[26] Opponents point to the testimony of an expert environmental scientist, hired by the city council and WTI to study the matter. He states, "In the best case scenario, 0.01% of undestroyed waste will be emitted. But new chemicals will be formed. They are called dioxins and furans. They are also known as products of incomplete combustion (P.I.C.'s). They are made or synthesized during combustion or formed downstream of the furnace in the pollution control devices. Dioxin and furans are considered to be compounds that may be more deadly and complex than the original waste the incinerators are supposed to destroy."[27]

A second area of debate concerns water. WTI is situated on the Ohio River. In the event of a storm, hazardous waste can contaminate the water, possibly contaminating the water supply. WTI claims that they have elaborate spill containment systems, including dikes, curbs, sloped floors and sumps. They claim that storm water from areas where wastes are handled will be collected and tested for possible contamination. If it is contaminated, it will either be treated and recycled on site, incinerated or disposed of off site. The site is surrounded by an earthen berm which is at least 12" high, preventing storm water run-off and run-on. WTI claims that WTI can contain, at one time, the contents of all waste storage tanks, rain from the heaviest storm that occurred over the last 24 hour period in the past 25 years, plus six days of average rain during the maximum rainfall month.[28] The opponents claim that WTI's operational safety mechanisms have not yet been approved by the Federal EPA, and that it is not clear that an on-site spill would not ultimately find its way into the ground or the river.

Moreover, opponents say, in the event of flood, these safety precautions may well prove insufficient.

The third area concerns the threat to the surrounding community from an accident. Debate in this area centers around, among many things, the transportation of the waste (and possible accidents involving transportation) and accidents at the plant itself. WTI has always said, since the beginning of the project, that it would not use the Ohio river to transport hazardous wastes to the plant.[29] However, opponents have feared that once WTI received all of its permits and went into operation that, some time down the road, barges would begin slipping into dock at WTI carrying hazardous, pollution laden cargo. However, a permit modification granted WTI in December 1991 prohibits them from transporting wastes on barges on the Ohio River.[30]

Although WTI claims that the trucks carrying the waste are heavily regulated, their opponents point out that an accident (spill, explosion, etc.) could be catastrophic. The accident issue is particularly important since the trucks will travel on one residential street, and the plant is 1100 feet from an elementary school.[31] WTI counters that trucking companies that haul hazardous wastes are specially licensed and that they take special precautions when transporting such material.[32]

A flood is potentially dangerous, since WTI is located in a flood plain.[33] This means that every 100 or 500 years (depending on which report one reads) it is expected that the site upon which WTI is built will flood. WTI claims that they are prepared to deal with such an eventuality. Opponents say they do not even have a plan to deal such emergencies.

The same goes for an accident in the form of a fire and/or explosion. A fire could release toxic smoke into the air, which could lead to severe injury and illness to nearby residents. These fears are especially acute because of the presence of the elementary school nearby. Opponents point to such graphic descriptions as the one contained in the report of environmental scientist and expert Isaac Yomtovian:

> Dangerous emissions are accidentally released from the WTI/Von Roll hazardous waste incinerator. It is 10:30 on a school day morning. It is spring time. Children begin to complain to teachers. Remember, they are elementary school age. The younger children in kindergarten and first grade are not explaining their symptoms too well. A child collapses in the classroom. Other children in the same classroom begin to complain they don't feel well. Some say that they can't breathe very well. More children collapse. Some children are turning blue around the lips.[34]

WTI claims that extensive safety measures have been taken, including on-site safety teams, and an emergency response plan to be developed with local officials. Regarding the school, WTI says that it was granted its permit before a city law requiring the plant to be situated more than 2,000 feet from a school, and therefore it is unfair to require them to move now. Some people have proposed that if WTI does not move, then they should finance the school's relocation. In short, the possibility of an accident near the school is very disturbing to local residents and WTI's opponents have focused heavily on it.

The problem arises about how to best evaluate the factual claims and counterclaims. In light of the fact that the present writers' knowledge about hazardous waste and High Temperature Incinerators can at best be characterized as elementary, they consulted a third party expert, Dr. Peter Groffman, an environmental scientist with absolutely no connection whatsoever to the situation in East Liverpool, and the report of the consultant, Isaac Yomtovian, hired by the city (and paid for in part by WTI) to make recommendations to the city regarding WTI.

Dr. Groffman said that in fact that WTI's emissions numbers do not tell us much, since they do not tell us anything about the concentrations of these emissions in the air; density is the important factor, and merely telling us how many pounds of a material is released tells us little about how dangerous these emissions are to the environment. Our expert says that an earthen berm can be penetrated by water, and is not as secure as a concrete berm. However, Dr. Groffman seems satisfied with the overall precautions taken by WTI to deal with storm water contamination.[35]

One area which Dr. Groffman and Yomtovian agreed upon concerned the possibility of dioxin and furan production in the smokestacks, an issue discussed above. However, as of December 19, a stipulation was included in WTI's permit requiring it to install an automatic shut-off device which will stop wastes from entering the incinerator if the temperature in the kiln is such that dioxins could be formed.[36] Dr. Groffman feels that this appears to be an adequate precaution, and WTI seems to have adequately addressed the problem of dioxin and furan formation.[37]

However, Dr. Groffman did say that the transportation issue is a major concern, clearly surpassing air stack emissions as a threat. Nonetheless, Dr. Groffman said that a truck spill is something that can be cleaned up, and will not harm anyone.[38]

A flood, he said, presents a severe danger to the community, but he pointed out that there is plenty of warning for floods, allowing adequate time for evacuation if necessary. An explosion would also clearly be dangerous, but Dr. Groffman thinks that the chances of an explosion are not great, since not much of the waste is explosive. A fire, however, could release toxic smoke into the air. Accidents are obviously something that no one can insure will not occur, but our expert does not seem to think that the prospects of death or injury from an accident are very great.[39]

In sum, Dr. Groffman concluded that WTI does not pose a major threat to the environment or the citizens of East Liverpool in terms of the pollution it will emit, despite the fact that some of WTI's statistics are not very enlightening and do not help to make their case. WTI also seems to have addressed the problem of the possible formation of dioxins and furans in the smokestack, and the possibility of an accident appears to him to be of relatively minor concern.

Yomtovian concluded in his report that WTI will be built according to the legal requirements of U.S. and Ohio EPA regulations, and that WTI has invested millions of dollars to design and build what they think will be a state-of-the-art facility. However, he says that WTI "could significantly impact the environment, public health and economy of the region."[40] He claims that there has not been a comprehensive survey and study to determine the adverse effects of WTI and to determine the necessary protection measures (his report covers much more ground than reported here-he does indeed have other reservations about the WTI facility). Thus, Yomotovian seems to take a much more cautious view than Dr. Groffman about the WTI plant.

No matter which experts one listens to or how much expert testimony one reads, no expert will claim that WTI poses no threat at all to the environment or the residents of East Liverpool. From Dr. Yomtovian's perspective the threat seems to be greater than from Dr. Groffman's, but both fall somewhere in between the claims made by pro and anti WTI forces. Moreover, despite these authors' personal attachment to Groffman, they recognize that Yomtovian had access to much more information than Groffman and must be given more weight. Consequently, it seems that some degree of risk does exist, albeit quite small, in all of the areas discussed above. The possibility of an accident is the most daunting, but the dangers of air pollution and even, to a minor degree, water pollution, must be given some credence.

Given this small amount of risk one has a few choices. One can say that, given the consequences of an accident or pollution, any risk is too great and, thus, WTI should be stopped no matter what the alleged benefits to the community or region. In essence, this is the perspective of WTI's strongest opponents. On the other hand, one can say that the risk is so low that there really is no reason to oppose WTI, even if the benefit is very minimal. In between all those who would accept some level of risk if the benefits of WTI were significant enough. These are no longer factual questions, but questions of what one values. Opponents place a high value on their own health and safety, that of their children and/or other people who might be harmed. Other opponents, in particular Greenpeace protesters, place a high value on ensuring the safety or purity of the environment. We tend to call this value "environmentalism."

One might argue that this is not a question of values at all but of personality. If one is by nature cautious, fearful or paranoid, then one will magnify the risk and oppose WTI. This is what one hears from WTI supporters, that the protesters are "hysterical" or "crazy."[41] In the opinion of these authors, these personality traits can be understood in terms of values. If one is "cautious" vis a vis WTI, one values one's safety or that of the environment. If one is paranoid about the danger of WTI, one places extreme value on these things.

### The Economy

WTI claims that the building and operation of its plant will help the local and regional economy. They cite in support of this argument that 500 construction jobs have been created in order to build the WTI plant and that there will be about 100 permanent employees of WTI at the plant. Money will be pumped into the local economy through the purchase of goods and services for the operation of WTI. The firm will pay four million dollars in state and local taxes annually. Two hundred thousand dollars will go into city coffers each year. Moreover, WTI argues, other businesses, particularly those that need the services of WTI, will begin to move into the area as a result of WTI's presence.[42]

In contrast, WTI opponents say that the plant will do little for the local and regional economy. There will be only 55 permanent jobs and 35 of those will go to people out of state. Even if WTI does hire 100 people, this a mere drop in the bucket compared to the actual needs of the city. Opponents don't believe that much money will find its way from WTI into the local economy and they point sharply to the fact that, as of yet, no other businesses have chosen to locate in the area due to WTI. Finally, they argue that while WTI currently pays taxes to the city, it is not required to by law. Hence, as soon as the plant can no longer be stopped and protests die down they will cease to pay these taxes.[43]

Common sense tells these authors that some economic benefit will accrue to the residents of the town and region. The exact amount will never be known until many years after the plant goes into operation, and even then, it will never be totally clear. While there is some quibbling over the number of jobs that will actually exist at the plant and to whom they will go, there clearly have been temporary jobs created in construction (as all construction jobs are temporary by nature) and there will be permanent jobs at the plant. While it is hard to say whether WTI will continue to pay taxes in the long run to the City of East Liverpool, they clearly have paid some taxes to the city, will continue to pay taxes to the state and county, and fees to the Port Authority. As far as other business being drawn to the area, there is certainly some disappointment that this has not yet occurred, but this cannot be ruled out as a possibility.

The deeper conflict is really one of values. The pro-WTI forces place a high premium on jobs, taxes and other economic benefits. They tend to magnify those benefits because this is important to them, more important than the potential harm that the plant could cause to the environment. The exact opposite holds for the opposition to WTI. For them, the economic benefits seem puny, particularly when weighed against the possible damage the plant could do. How much value does one place on a job? Are 100 jobs a lot or a little? This is really an ethical question, one whose answer clearly depends upon one's point of view. Another ethical issue is who will benefit economically? The opponents clearly place no value on the prosperity of WTI's investors, but WTI obviously does. If someone living four towns down route 30 gets a job at the plant, is that of value to someone living in East Liverpool? A local vendor of materials which the plant uses will undoubtedly place higher premium on the economic benefits than would a person who does not stand to benefit directly.

**The Need**
WTI claims that there is a tremendous need for its services. Our nation in general and the Ohio Valley in particular produce a tremendous amount of hazardous waste that needs to be disposed of.[44] WTI recently signed contracts with Du Pont Co., BASF Corp. and Chemical Waste Management Inc. which will fill its capacity for burning waste for the next ten years. Ninety percent of the waste will come from Pennsylvania, Ohio and West Virginia.[45] WTI's opponents take a very different view of the need for the WTI plant. Two reports coming out of the OEPA (not exactly foes of WTI!) say that Ohio already has enough incineration capacity and will continue to have enough capacity through the year 2009, whether or not WTI ever goes into operation. At the same time only one-third of WTI's business will come from Ohio.[46] Consequently, if WTI comes on line, Ohio will become even more of a dumping ground for other people's waste than it already is.

A careful look at the debate over the need for WTI reveals surprisingly little factual difference. The difference lies in interpretation and values. While Ohio seems to have enough capacity already to burn its own hazardous waste, West Virginia and Pennsylvania, the other two states in the immediate vicinity of WTI, may not have adequate capacity. The Ohio Valley includes all three of these states. Perhaps, the Ohio Valley doesn't have enough capacity, although this is not known since the only known studies were conducted by the state of Ohio. Certainly, the nation as a whole does not have enough capacity. Thus, the question of need comes down to how one draws the borders of the relevant geographical area.

At the same time, this is a question of ethics. First of all, the "need" for WTI is a human and environmental one. If hazardous waste is not dealt with safely, an environmental disaster looms for this country. As mentioned above, the use of landfills alone to dispose of hazardous waste creates a serious environmental risk. Moreover, just as the landfilling of hazardous waste poses a danger to the environment it poses a danger to the health and safety of people who live near them. Water supplies may become contaminated and, in extreme cases communities could become uninhabitable. One well known situation in which such a catastrophe did occur is the famous case of "Love Canal." Valuing the safety of the environment and of people is mentioned in conjunction with the opponents of WTI. However, it would be just as valid to say that these may be values held by some proponents of WTI.

At the same time, there is the question of the fair distribution of hazardous waste disposal sites. "Why should we be dumped upon by the rest of the country?" is the cry of WTI opponents.[47] (It's interesting that Governor Voinovich, whose clearly delineated area of interest is Ohio and Ohio only, has raised this banner and banned any new hazardous waste incinerator projects in Ohio. Yet, he is not an opponent of WTI.)[48]

Yet, waste must be dealt with somewhere in particular. Why not in East Liverpool? WTI proponents have accused WTI foes of opposing the facility because they don't want it near them, even though it is beneficial. They would rather benefit, but have others take the risk of having the facility near them. This canard against the protesters is often referred to as "NIMBY" (Not In My Back Yard). Meanwhile, WTI opponents accuse WTI of profiting at the expense of the poor and disadvantaged. First, because they are falsely holding out the hope of prosperity to an economically desperate community. Secondly, because the WTI site is in the poorest part of town and, consequently, the poor, as usual, are forced to live near that which the wealthy would never allow near themselves.[49] An ethical position in support of this argument against WTI is that the poor as a class are generally taken advantage of and need to be specially protected. This liberal argument is akin to what our constitution says (or said, until recently) about the need to give blacks special protection against discrimination as a class of people.

## Ethical Conclusions

The ethical problem of whether WTI should be allowed to continue building and operate in East Liverpool can be approached from two, broadly different ethical mind sets: the deontological and the teleological. Given the authors' discussion of values above, it may have been apparent that they favor the teleological or consequentialist approach. Such an analysis might lead one to take the factual outcomes that would result from building and operating WTI, as far as such facts can be discerned, and then to apply one's values to them so that one comes out with a sense of how much one values a given outcome. Then, these results can be weighed against each other to determine whether one believes that WTI should be built. (This is actually an intuitive process which sounds much more complicated than it is.)

For example, it was determined above that WTI poses some potential risk to the health of the residents of the surrounding area. The risk of illness or injury resulting from WTI seems small, as far as the authors can tell. One can argue that a small risk of illness or death is still a major consideration, so much so that it overrides the benefits that could result from the plant. On the other hand, one can determine that the benefits to the environment of the region and nation that would result from building a large high temperature incinerator (e.g. less hazardous waste in landfills) outweigh the small potential risk to local residents. If one is greatly concerned with the economy of the region, one might consider the 100 or so permanent jobs that WTI offers, as well as the taxes and other business that they might generate, to be very significant. On the other hand, if one is greatly concerned about the risk to the health of the nearby school children one might argue that WTI is taking advantage of a poor neighborhood by locating there, while the benefit to the economy of the area pales in comparison. One can go on and on with this cost/benefit analysis ad infinitum.

Below is a short list of the authors' evaluation of the costs and benefits of WTI:

| value | cost | benefit |
|---|---|---|
| health/safety (Includes need for waste disposal) | small | small |
| clean environment (Includes need for waste disposal) | small | large |
| economic prosperity | none | small |
| equal/fair distribution of societal burdens | small | none |

This chart reveals that in the authors' balancing of the various goods, the benefits of WTI seem to slightly outweigh the costs. The operative word here, however, is "slightly," since, by and large the costs and benefits balance out. For example, while there is a small chance that the health of the local residents could be adversely effected, this is balanced out by the small benefit to the health of the residents of the larger region or country, whose health is also benefitted from the disposal of hazardous waste through the best technology available. Similarly, the unequal distribution of this small health risk among economic classes is balanced by the small benefit to the local economy, some of which should trickle down to the poor local residents.

The deontological school would demand, as it is typically phrased, that the "right" be placed ethically before the "good." In other words, there are certain inherent rights that individuals (or other entities) have which cannot be violated, whatever the ultimate policy goal or consequence might be. Within the values discussed above, there are several which have been and could be considered rights.

For example, one may claim that people have an inherent right to life, which broadly construed, would include health and safety. If one believes that there is such a right, then one could argue that WTI must not be built because there is at least some risk to the life and health of the nearby residents. This is an interesting position considering that the "right to life" is not usually applied to cases such as these, where clear, deliberate killing is not involved. Typically, the "right to life" is evoked in such debates as the one over the use of the death penalty or abortion.

These authors believe, as most people do, that there is an inherent right to life. Moreover, this right does indeed apply to the case at hand. However, the chances that an individual's right to life or health will be violated by WTI is very small. The right to life is usually asserted in situations where death or injury is fairly certain, such as abortion or the death penalty. In the case of WTI, precautions have been taken by the firm to greatly minimize this threat. In fact, the authors sense is that the current threat to life or health is very small, too small to assert that the right to life takes precedence over all other considerations in this case. On this basis alone it would not be ethical to stop WTI.

A right that may be asserted in favor of WTI is the right to free enterprise. Under this argument, WTI has a right to do with its property or money as it sees fit and not as others see fit. WTI chooses to use its money to establish a high temperature incinerator and other people, who have no economic investment in the firm, should not be allowed to prevent them from doing so. Thus, WTI should be built.

One of these authors completely opposes this ethical position, denying that there is an inherent right to property or a right to free enterprise (i.e. he holds a socialist position). The other author believes there is a right to free enterprise, but feels that, in a situation where this right may conflict with people's health and safety, it cannot be asserted as primary. In short, these authors do not feel that the right to free enterprise alone is enough to justify the building and operation of WTI.

Another possible economic right is the right to work, or the right to employment. While this is not openly asserted in this country as often as in the past, it is still a position worth reckoning with. One could argue that, since the building and operation of WTI provides jobs in a region in which jobs are scarce, the right to work takes precedence and, thus, WTI should be supported. One of these authors accepts the notion that there is an individual right to work, if he/she so desires. However, this stance is mitigated by the fact that WTI is not providing very many jobs. Thus, this author feels that the right to work does not take precedence in this case over other considerations and, at the very least, must be balanced against the right to life. The result is a conflict of rights in which neither is strong enough to override the other. The other author does not believe there truly is a right to work, though he values the need to provide jobs to the unemployed. Since this author does not consider employment to be a right, it cannot be used as the basis for opposing WTI from a deontological perspective.

The final right that must be considered is the right of the poor to special consideration in cases where a given action may harm this class of individuals while benefitting others. In *A Theory of Justice,* John Rawls includes the following in his "second principle" of justice: "Social and economic inequalities are to be arranged so that they are ... to the greatest benefit of the least advantaged. ..." (p. 302).[50] For Rawls, this must be considered a right that takes precedence over the good. In the case of WTI, this could translate into an argument against the plant on the grounds that it is located in a poor town and in the poorest part of that town. Any harm that might come to residents in the way of pollution or accidents would harm the poor more than the general population. While one of these authors strongly agrees with this right asserted by Rawls, he does not feel that the dangers involved in operating the plant are great enough to merit invoking this right over all other considerations. The other author is also sympathetic to this right, but does not give it primary consideration.

In sum, the authors did not find a review of this problem from the deontological perspective to be very helpful in coming to a decision. None of the rights relevant to this case seem to merit strong enough consideration to determine whether WTI should indeed be built.

# A Halakhic Approach

If any ethical problem is particular to the late twentieth century, it is our question about the building of a high temperature incinerator for hazardous wastes. One might be tempted to assume that the *halakhah* cannot speak to such a current, high-tech issue. But, in fact, as far back as the rabbinic period, the rabbis found themselves confronted with issues very much analogous to certain aspects of our modern day problem. For example, the *Mishnah* discusses the problem of the permanent threshing floor (*goren kavuah*) from which dust from chaff would rise and carry through the air. The dust might reach a populated area or a neighbor's property, damaging his seedlings or newly plowed fields. Consequently, the *Mishnah* indicates that a permanent threshing floor must be located at least 50 cubits from a town and 50 cubits from anyone else's property in order to avoid causing harm (*Baba Batra* 2:8). Similarly, tanneries, carcasses and graves must be 50 cubits from the town due to their obnoxious smell. Moreover, tanneries must be to the east of the town so that the prevailing winds will not carry the smell into the town. Rabbi Akiva argued that any side of the town except the west was acceptable, but the 50 cubits rule must be followed (*Baba Batra* 2:9). The *Mishnah* follows the discussion of tanneries with a discussion of other, related damages: A *mishrah* (a pool for the soaking of flax) must be kept at a distance from the vegetable garden of a neighbor, presumably because the tainted water from the *misrah* could travel through the ground and ruin the neighbor's vegetables. One must not grow leeks near a neighbor's onions, presumably because the taste of the onions would be affected. Mustard plants must be kept at a distance from bee hives for the same reason (*Baba Batra* 2:10). The common element in all of the above cases of industry or agriculture seems to be that the thing causing the damage does so without direct contact with the persons or things it damages. The harm is caused by something emitted from the source of the damage that travels to the thing it damages. In the opinion of these authors, modern pollution is a fitting analogue to these ancient forms of damage. Taken together, then, these *mishnahyot* provide us with a halakhic principle regarding pollution: Industrial or agricultural activities that cause pollution must be placed at prescribed distances from persons or property that might be damaged as a result of that pollution.

While this principle seems simple enough, an objection is raised in the *Mishnah* to the anonymous *mishnahic* statement (*stam mishnah*) that mustard must be distanced from bees. This objection, by Rabbi Yossi, becomes the basis, or *lacuna*, for major developments in the *halakhah*. The *Mishnah* states, "Rabbi Yossi permits it in the case of mustard." (*Baba Batra* 2:10) According to the classic commentary on the *Mishnah* of R. Ovadiah ben Avaraham of Bartenura, it seems that Rabbi Yossi felt that the grower of mustard plants should not be compelled to distance his mustard from a neighbor's bee hives. Bartenura reasons that the mustard grower had the same rights to his location as the bee keeper to his because bees eat the flowers of mustard plants and, consequently, the damage is reciprocal. In his commentary on the *Mishnah* (*Peirush Hamishnahyot L'harambam* on *Mishnah* 2:10), Maimonides takes a different approach. He argues that Rabbi Yossi actually felt that it was up to the bee keeper, the one sustaining the damage, to move away from the mustard plants or put up a partition between his bees and the mustard plants. He makes no mention of the reciprocal damage later cited by Bartenura. Moreover, Rambam states, Rabbi Yossi held the same position regarding the cases of the offending *mishrah* (flax pool) and leeks. In these cases, too, it is up the party sustaining harm to move out of harms way. However, Rambam notes, Rabbi Yossi believed that in cases where the damage (pollution) goes from the one causing it to the one sustaining it directly (*b'lo emtza'i*) then the one causing the damage must move. Rambam concludes that the *halakhah* is with Rabbi Yossi on these points.

Maimonides develops this notion further in the *Mishneh Torah*. After explaining how the flax pool in the *Mishnah* damages the neighbor's vegetables, the leeks damage the onions, and the mustard damages the honey produced by the bees, he states:

> With all of these and similar cases [the offender] does not have to move [the source of the damage] away in order to avoid causing damage. It is up to the one being harmed to move himself, if he wants, so that the damage doesn't reach him. For, he [the offender] is acting in his own domain and the damage is reaching [his neighbor] on its own (*mayaylav*). To what does this refer? When one doesn't distance [the source of the damage/pollution] and the damage reaches [his neighbor] on its own after the damaging activities have ceased. But, if the activities of the one who is acting in his own domain damage his neighbor at the time that they are being done (*b'shaat asiyato*), this is the same as one who commits the damage with his own hands. (*Mishneh Torah, Hilkhot Sh'khaynim* 10:5)

Thus, Maimonides develops the somewhat ambiguous statement of R. Yossi in the *Mishnah* into a principle for determining whether a "polluter" must distance his operation from one being harmed by the pollution. It seems, there are two variables one must know in order to make use of Maimonides' principle. One is whether the damage occurs *mayaylav*. This has been translated above as "on its own."

Alternatively, making use of the Rambam's commentary on the *Mishnah* to inform us about this term, we can translate *mayaylav* as "indirectly." The second variable has to do with the time when the damage occurs. Did the damage occur at the time that damaging/-polluting activity being done or did it occur after the activity was completed? If the damage occurs at the time that the activity is being done and that damage does not occur on its own, but is a direct damage, then the polluter must cease operating at his/her present location and distance him/herself from the neighbor being harmed. On the other hand, if the damage occurs indirectly/on its own, after the activity that caused the damage has ceased, then it is up to the one being harmed to move, if he/she desires.

Rambam offers a more concrete, descriptive explanation of these two halakhic categories for those (like these authors) who have trouble discerning exactly what types of cases fall into each of these categories. He compares the damage that occurs directly, at the time that the activity is being done, to the case of one who stands on his own property and shoots arrows into his neighbor's property and says, "I'm doing this in my own domain [so there is nothing wrong with it]." (ibid.) This person must cease his/her activities and distance him/herself from his/her neighbor. The damage that occurs indirectly/on it's own, after the time that the activity is completed, is compared to the case of one who has a tree close to the property of a neighbor and the roots of the tree have entered the cistern of the neighbor and damaged it. The neighbor cannot force him/her to get rid of the tree because this is damage that occurred *mayaylav* and "*aḥar z'man*" ("after time has passed"). (ibid 10:7). At the time that he was planting the tree he was not harming his neighbor. (ibid.)

It is illuminating to note how Rambam applies his principle in the *Mishneh Torah* to the cases of the flax pool, the leeks and the mustard. Instead of stating flatly, as he does in his commentary to the *Mishnah*, that it is up to the one being harmed to move, he applies both halakhic categories to these cases and comes up with the following: "Therefore, he must distance the flax pool from the vegetables, and the leeks from the onions, and the mustard from the bees, three handbreaths (or a little more), in order that the damage won't be by his own hands (*b'yadayim*). But, he does not have to distance [them] until damage no longer occurs on its own (*mayaylav*)." (ibid 10:5) It is crucial to note that the polluter may still be causing damage, but as soon as the pollution causing activity is far enough away so that the damage is only occurring *mayaylav*, the injunction against the polluter to distance him/herself ceases to operate.

Rambam also applies his principle to the cases of a permanent threshing floor (see above), a permanent latrine or outhouse (*beit hakisay*), and work which involves the creation of dust or ashes. These must be placed at a distance from neighbors so that the dust, ashes or smell of the latrine do not reach the neighbor and cause him/her harm or offense. If these are not placed at a distance and damage results it is like "one who causes damage with his arrows." (*Mishneh Torah, Hilkhot Sh'khaynim* 11:1) Rambam goes even farther to say that even if the dust, ashes, or smell are carried by an ordinary wind and harm a neighbor this is tantamount to one who causes damage with his arrows. (ibid.) While one might think that these damages fall into the *mayaylav* category because they seem indirect, they do not. It seems, then, that in determining whether a case fits the *mayaylav* category, it is crucial to determine if there is a significant time lag between the polluting activity and the damage it causes more than the time it takes the wind to carry dust or a smell to a neighbor's property. Furthermore, one can deduce from Rambam's use of the term "ordinary wind" (*ruah m'tzuyah*) that in a case where the pollution is carried by an unusual wind, then the damage would be considered *mayaylav*. If one extends this, one can say that where unusual circumstances cause pollution to harm a neighbor or his property, the one engaging in the pollution producing activity does not have to move and distance him/herself.

In order to apply Maimonides' principle[51] to WTI we must ask: Is the pollution damage which WTI may produce direct, occurring at the time that the activity is being done, or is it indirect, occurring after the activity is completed? Is WTI more like one who shoots arrows into a neighbor's property and injures him or more like one who plants a tree and, later, its roots grow into a neighbor's property and damage his cistern? Regarding WTI's smoke stack emissions one may argue as follows: If the emissions are such that there people nearby (such as the school children) get sick from them immediately or within a short time, then clearly WTI is too close to it's neighbors and must be shut down and moved. But, in the cases of illnesses such as cancer, which may result years after exposure to pollutants, one can use Rambam's halakhic principle to argue that this is *mayaylav* damage, occurring years after the actual pollution was spewed into the air. The counter argument to this is that such pollution reaches the individuals who are harmed within a very short time. It is simply that the illnesses occur later. What makes Rambam's principle difficult for these authors to apply to illnesses that occur long after a pollutant enters the body is that it is highly uncertain whether Rambam, being a physician during the premodern period, was aware of this kind of illness.

Nevertheless, in the case of WTI, where there is no clear evidence that their smokestack emissions would lead to such illnesses, it would seem appropriate to compare the building of their facility to the planting of a tree, wherein at the time of the planting it is not apparent that the roots will enter the neighbor's property and damage his/her cistern. Certainly, it is possible that damage or illness will result from the emissions from WTI's smokestacks, but it cannot be shown either that this damage will probably occur directly or within a short period of time. The analogy of the person standing on his property and shooting arrows into his neighbor's property does not apply at all. The risks of operating WTI, as far as these authors can tell, are simply not that high. One can add, moreover, that, at least insofar as the smokestack emissions are concerned, WTI has distanced itself more than the required "three handbreaths" from its neighbors (see the case of the flax pond, above). Their smokestacks are elevated and they even recently installed a special mechanism which will shut down the incinerator in the event that the temperature reaches the point at which dioxins or furans could be produced.

Insofar as the threat of water pollution resulting from storm runoffs from the grounds of the WTI facility, the case of the flax pond seems an appropriate analogy. WTI has placed an earthen berm around the facility to prevent runoff. It is possible that water could penetrate and pass through this berm causing damage to the river or the water supply. However, the berm seems to be a significant enough barrier to make this an unlikely scenario. If this does occur, it will happen *mayaylav*. That is, it will take some time for water to make it through the berm and reach a place where it will cause damage. Moreover, it is likely that such a seepage would be detected and stopped. In any event, in building the berm, WTI has distanced itself the requisite three handbreaths. Thus, there is no reason, on account of a direct and imminent threat of water pollution, to stop the plant from going into operation.

These authors did not investigate the *halakhah* on accidents. Thus, it is difficult to comment on the question of whether WTI should be stopped on the basis that there might be a fire, explosion or flood. It is possible to argue that there is no basis in the *halakhah* discussed above to consider a potential accident to be a reason for moving or closing the plant. An accident is, by definition, an unusual circumstance. Rambam did not require the fixed threshing floor, latrine or dust/ash producing enterprise to distance itself from a neighbor who might be harmed by an unusual wind, only in the case of an ordinary wind. Still, due to the lack of information on the *halakhah* on accidents, the *halakhah* cannot play a significant role in our decision when it comes to considering this risk.

While the conclusions reached above from the ethical and halakhic considerations are generally supportive of WTI, these conclusions are solidified by the fact that the project is nearing completion.

## Legitimate Expectations

WTI has worked for 12 years and invested $500 million dollars in the incinerator in East Liverpool. After all this time and money, is it right for the city of East Liverpool to protest and force WTI to move or shut down?

This has come to a head in a concrete way recently. The mayor of East Liverpool is threatening criminal action against WTI, claiming that WTI needs to have a local permit to build the incinerator on the flood plain, despite the fact that WTI received a state permit in 1984, at which time it was thought that the state permit overrode the need for a local permit.[52] Even if the mayor is right, why has he waited almost eight years to act? Did he not know that a local permit was necessary until now? If not, then his delay in taking criminal action is questionable. Although *halakhah* would seem to permit this, ethically it does not appear right. It is unfair to create the legitimate expectation for WTI that they have the necessary permit, to let them continue construction, only to take criminal action eight years later. This applies to the project as a whole. If WTI's opponents succeed in forcing WTI to relocate or shut down, much time, money and labor will have been wasted, which seems unfair. However, one might ask, "shouldn't have WTI stalled construction until everything was clear?" This way, they would not unnecessarily invest all the time and money that it has. On a certain level, it is a question of legitimate expectations. Has the government of East Liverpool in fact given WTI the impression that it approves of it (through silence, assisting WTI, etc.)? If so, the writers' interpretation of modern ethics would say that forcing WTI to close or move now would indeed be unethical.

## Halakhah on Permits

It is possible, however, for a "polluter" to operate at less than the prescribed distance under certain circumstances. According to Rambam, this applies if one "saw his neighbor and was quiet." (*Mishneh Torah, Hilkhot Sh'khaynim*, 11:4). That is to say, one saw his neighbor engaging in the polluting activity, and did not protest at the time of seeing it. Rambam clarifies this phrase with the following examples:

– one actually assisted the "polluter' in his/her activity

– one tells the "polluter" to go ahead and build

– one sees the "polluter" operating and keeps quiet.

However, none of the above applies in the case of "smoke, smell of the latrine, dust and the like, and significant vibrations of the ground, with every one of these, there is no *ḥazakah*" (*Mishneh Torah, Hilkhot Sh'khaynim*, 11:4). (acquisition of rights to continue the operation which cause the aforementioned effects; see *Baba Batra* 23a for the Talmudic basis of this principle). Even if the damaged party was quiet for several years, the party can compel the polluter to distance himself.

Thus, we see that silence constitutes a waiver of one's right to protest a "polluter's" operation and to compel him to move. The exception is in the case of smoke, smell, etc. Rambam explains that these cases are exceptions because "a person cannot suffer these damages." This is obviously relevant to WTI, which will emit smoke 24 hours a day.

However, there is an exception to all of the above mentioned according to Rambam. One does waive the right to protest if one waives their rights through a formal act of *kinyan*, or acquisition (*Mishneh Torah, Hilkhot Sh'khaynim*, 11:4). That is, a "polluter" may "purchase" a waiver from the potentially damaged parties through an act of *kinyan*.

Rabbi Meir of Rothenburg offers yet another qualification to the *Baba Batra* law in a responsum in which he notes that Rabbi Yitzhak, a Tosaphist, says that the law in *Baba Batra* refers to large furnaces which give off much smoke, and the nature of their damage is frequent and great. In the case that Rabbi Meir adjudicates, the complaint concerns a latrine whose smell is infrequent and therefore, there is *ḥazakah*.[53]

The applicability of this law to the WTI case is obvious. WTI will emit smoke 24 hours a day, seven days a week, which would certainly qualify as frequent smoke. Thus, on this basis, WTI cannot acquire the rights to operate.

Abraham ben ha-Rambam (1186-1237) affirms the principle that silence constitutes a waiver except in smoke cases, etc., in a responsum. In this case, Reuven complained to Shimon that the latter has a cloth-dyeing pit, and is lighting fires and causing smoke to be emitted in Reuven's direction, which is damaging his clothing and furniture. Reuven demands that Shimon remove the damage and stop lighting the fire. Shimon argued that he bought the house in which he operates his dye shop 15 years before Reuven bought his house, and the situation of which Reuven complains has obtained for 15 years. Furthermore, Levi, who owned the house before Reuven, did not complain. But the rabbi sides with Reuven, explaining that there is no *ḥazakah* in smoke damages, and that even if Levi wanted to file a complaint against Shimon, he could have done so, since Levi did not waive his right to complain via *kinyan*.[54]

Halakhically, despite the frequent nature of WTI's smoke emissions, which would seem to argue against their acquiring *ḥazakah*, the authors maintain that WTI in fact does have the right to operate, due to *kinyan*. It is our contention that the plethora of operating permits granted to WTI constitute a waiver of the right to force them to relocate and/or shut down. The *halakhah* is quite clear that even in smoke cases, an act of *kinyan* constitutes a waiver of the right to protest against a "polluter's" operations.

It is true that there is a current debate in East Liverpool about whether or not WTI needs a local permit, and one could argue that because this is a "smoke case" they have the right to protest despite the city's silence until now. Nevertheless, it is the author's opinion that WTI has obtained enough permits to constitute kinyan and it would be unfair to use this one questionable permit as the basis for blocking the entire project.

# Conclusion

After careful analysis of both general ethical and halakhic perspectives it is the opinion of the authors that Waste Technologies Industries should be allowed to build and operate their high temperature incinerator at the Columbiana County Port Authority site in East Liverpool, Ohio. Interestingly, while the halakhic and secular ethical approaches to the issue are radically different, they both lead the authors to similar conclusions. A teleological, cost/benefit analysis of WTI leads to a stance that is somewhat ambivalent, though mildly supportive of the plant. A deontological consideration reveals that no substantial violation of rights is likely to occur if the plant goes into operation. Similarly, the authors believe that the potential hazards that WTI poses would be categorized halakhically as *mayaylav* damages. Such damages do not require the source of the damage to move. Furthermore, the WTI plant is nearing completion. WTI has received numerous permits to build their facility and have invested millions of dollars to the same purpose. This creates a legitimate expectation on their part that they be allowed to complete and operate their high temperature incinerator. The *halakhah* provides that in the case where someone seeks to stop his/her neighbor from an activity that creates smoke, an act of *kinyan* would constitute a waiver of that person's right to do so. An application of this halakhic stance allows the authors to conclude that the permits that WTI has already received constitute *kinyan*, denying opponents the right to stop the plant at this late date.

# Bibliography

American Society of Mechanical Engineers, The. *Hazardous Waste Destruction By High Temperature Incineration*, (ASME, U.S.A., 1991).

"Council Members Rescind Support for WTI Spray Dryer," *The Evening Review*, December 17, 1991.

Interview with Randy DeBee, Member of East Liverpool City Council, October 27, 1991.

Interviews with Dr. Groffman, November and December 1991.

Interview with Hershel Rubin, long-time East Liverpool resident, November 8, 1991.

"Jury Trial asked by WTI Protesters: Sheen Returns for Hearing," East Liverpool's *The Evening Review*, November 8, 1991 and also "WTI Protestors Vow to Return to EPA Office," *The Evening Review*, December 18, 1991.

Ohio EPA, Waste Technologies Industries Permitting History, November 8, 1991

"Opinion Voiced," *The Evening Review*, October 24, 1991.

"Permit Exempts WTI from Local Requirements," *The Evening Review*, December 21, 1991.

Rawls, John. *A Theory of Justice*, (Cambridge, MA: Harvard University Press, 1971)

"Reports Ask: Do We or Don't We Need WTI?" *The Morning Journal*, December 8, 1991.

Responsa of Rabbi Abraham, son of Maimonides, no. 101.

Responsa of Rothenburg IV, (Prague Press).

"Scafide Says City Will File Suit Against WTI," *The Evening Review*, December 17, 1991.

STC Enviroscience, Inc., A Draft Report on Waste Technologies Industries and Von Roll, Inc., October 10, 1991.

"Voinovich Requests Incinerator Moratorium," *The Evening Review*, December 9, 1991.

Von Roll, Executive Summary – Waste Technologies Industries, August 1991.

Waste Technologies Industries, Facts About Waste Technologies Industries.

"Why WTI: Greenpeace Renews Verbal Attack on Need for ELO Incinerator," The Morning Journal, November 15, 1991.

WTI, Expected Stack Emissions at East Liverpoool, (WTI, East Liverpool, Ohio, September 1991).

WTI, Facts About Waste Technologies Industries, (WTI, East Liverpool, Ohio, May 1991).

"WTI Foes' Battle Cry:  Ban Liverpool's Burn" *The Evening Review*, December 11, 1991 and "WTI Foes' Battle Cry: Ban Liverpool's Burn" *The Morning Journal*, December 1991.

"WTI Has Customers Waiting in Line," *The Evening Review*, December 22, 1991.

"WTI Opponents question permit motives," *The Evening Review*, December 19, 1991.

Yomtovian, Isaac. A Draft Report On Waste Technologies Industries And Von Roll, Inc., (STC Enviroscience, Cleveland, Ohio, October 10, 1991).

# Notes

1. WTI, Facts About Waste Technologies Industries, (WTI, East Liverpool, Ohio, May 1991), p. 2.

2. Ibid.

3. Ibid.

4. The American Society of Mechanical Engineers, Hazardous Waste Destruction By High Temperature Incineration, (ASME, U.S.A., 1991), p. 2-3.

5. Ibid.

6. Ibid, p. 3

7. Ibid, p. 5.

8. Ibid, p. 4.

9. "Jury Trial asked by WTI Protesters: Sheen Returns for Hearing," East Liverpool's *The Evening Review*, November 8, 1991 and also "WTI Protestors Vow to Return to EPA Office", *The Evening Review*, December 18, 1991.

10. "Council Members Rescind Support for WTI Spray Dryer," *The Evening Review*, December 17, 1991.

11. Ohio EPA, Waste Technologies Industries Permitting History, November 8, 1991

12. Interview with Randy DeBee, Member of East Liverpool City Council, October 27, 1991.

13. Ibid.

14. Von Roll, Executive Summary – Waste Technologies Industries, August 1991.

15. *DeBee*, October 27, 1991.

16. Ohio EPA, Permitting History

17. "Permit Exempts WTI from Local Requirements," *The Evening Review*, December 21, 1991.

18. *DeBee*, October 27, 1991.

19. "WTI Foes' Battle Cry: Ban Liverpool's Burn" *The Evening Review*, December 11, 1991 and "WTI Foes' Battle Cry: Ban Liverpool's Burn" *The Morning Journal*, December 1991.

20. "Voinovich Requests Incinerator Moratorium," *The Evening Review*, December 9, 1991.

21. *DeBee*, October 27, 1991.

22. STC Enviroscience, Inc., A Draft Report on Waste Technologies Industries and Von Roll, Inc., October 10, 1991.

23. "Permit Exempts WTI from Local Requirements," *The Evening Review*, December 21, 1991.

24. "Scafide Says City Will File Suit Against WTI," *The Evening Review*, December 17, 1991.

25. WTI, Expected Stack Emissions at East Liverpoool, (WTI, East Liverpool, Ohio, September 1991), p. 1-2.

26. Facts About WTI, p.3.

27. Isaac Yomtovian, A Draft Report On Waste Technologies Industries And Von Roll, Inc., (STC Enviroscience, Cleveland, Ohio, October 10, 1991), p 13.

28. Facts About WTI, p. 4.

29. Facts About WTI, p. 6.

30. "WTI Opponents question permit motives," *The Evening Review*, December 19, 1991.

31. "Opinion Voiced," *The Evening Review*, October 24, 1991.

32. Facts About WTI, p. 6.

33. "Permit exemptes WTI from local requirements." *The Evening Review*, November (?) 21, 1991.

34. A Draft Report On Waste Technologies Industries And Von Roll, Inc., p. 28.

35. Interviews with Dr. Groffman, November and December 1991.

36. "WTI opponents question permit motives," *The Evening Review*, December 19, 1991.

37. Interview with Dr. Groffman, December 1991.

38. Interviews with Dr. Groffman, November and December 1991.

39. Interviews with Dr. Groffman, December 1991.

40. A Draft Report on Waste Technologies Industries and Von Roll Inc., p. 38

41. Interview with Hershel Rubin, long-time East Liverpool resident, November 8, 1991.

42. Waste Technologies Industries, Facts About Waste Technologies Industries, p. 5.

43. *DeBee*, October 27, 1991.

44. Waste Technologies Industries, Facts, pp. 1-2.

45. "WTI Has Customers Waiting in Line," *The Evening Review*, December 22, 1991.

46. "Reports Ask: Do We or Don't We Need WTI?" *The Morning Journal,* December 8, 1991.

47. "Why WTI: Greenpeace Renews Verbal Attack on Need for ELO Incinerator," The Morning Journal, November 15, 1991.

48. "Voinovich Requests Incinerator Moratorium," *The Evening Review*, December 9, 1991

49. *DeBee*, October 27, 1991.

50. John Rawls, *A Theory of Justice*, (Cambridge, MA: Harvard University Press, 1971) p. 302.

51. The discussion in the *Mishneh Torah* is the most thorough and clear of any of the halakhic codes. The *Shulḥan Arukh* deals with the same material and comes to essentially the same conclusions. However, it tends to leave out the reasoning in support of its positions.

52. "Scafide says city will file suit against WTI," *The Evening Review*, December 17, 1991.

53. Responsa of Rothenburg IV, (Prague Press), p. 233.

54. Responsa of Rabbi Abraham, son of Maimonides, no. 101.

# Political Hostage Taking: At the Intersection of Law and Ethics

Ronn S. Davids

The cast of characters is all too familiar: fanatical terrorists, determined to spill innocent American blood for political purposes, backed by Iran and given strategic depth by Syria's hold on Lebanon; a heart-rending pull on American compassion to save the hostages; an equally strong desire to exact justice and vengeance; justified fears about reentering the Lebanese quagmire; ambiguous intelligence information, or none at all.[1]

Shi'ite Muslim militants affiliated with Iran are presently holding twelve Westerners hostage in Lebanon. Of those twelve, six have been identified as American citizens. Letters and Op-Ed pieces frequently appear in our nation's newspapers, decrying the ineffectiveness of American policy and lashing out in frustration at the American government's inaction. Lucille Levin, wife of the Middle East bureau chief for the Cable News Network, Jeremy Levin, "defied State Department instructions to remain silent and raged publicly about U.S. indifference to the fate of her husband and the other "forgotten hostages.".…"We dealt for the hostages on the TWA flight last June," she says. "Why are these any different?"[2]

## A Political Crisis
Much may be learned of the immediacy and the complexity of the hostage situation through a careful definition of the phrase "political crisis."

"The term crisis in international relations refers to a specific event, such as the Berlin crisis of 1948-1949, the Taiwan Strait crisis of 1958, or the Cuban missile crisis of 1962. Although perhaps unalike in many ways, all shared certain common characteristics."[3] Oran Young argues that these common characteristics include: an increased level of interaction; a sharp break from normal events; a short duration; a rise in the prospect of violence; and significant implications for the stability of a given system.[4] Incidents of political hostage-taking share these traits.

## Interaction
On the most basic level, during hostage situations there is an increased level of interaction between the target and the offender. The offender has felt stymied in his/her attempt to communicate effectively with the target in the past and believes that the taking of hostages will increase the target's willingness to listen. Thus, a relationship which was previously marked by a lack of interaction is now one of increased interaction. It is important to note that this increased interaction is only relative to the previous situation, as encounters and contacts may still be quite infrequent.

## Intensity
The relationship now emphasizes confrontation rather than cooperation. This results from the offender's attempt to achieve a coercive value exchange. The ratio of intensity is directly proportional to the equivalent value which the target places upon the demands. If the target places a higher value on the hostage than on the demands, the target is likely to submit to the demands, thereby reducing the level of intensity. If the target places a higher value on the demands than on the hostage, the target is likely to refuse the demands, thereby increasing the level of intensity. If the target is the hostage, the target and the offender are likely to engage in a great deal of reciprocal cooperation, thereby reducing the level of intensity, as the target is wholly dependant upon the offender for survival, and the offender is wholly dependant upon the target for the achievement of his/her demands.

## Sharp Break from Normal Events
Hostage situations result in a sharp break from the normal flow of events. This break is distinguished by four distinct phases:

> **The initial phase.** The initial phase commences with the physical seizure of the hostage. During this stage, no one is aware of the seizure, with the possible exception of those in the immediate environs. When the authorities become aware of the seizure, either as a result of eyewitness reports or contact by the offender, the initial phase is complete and the next phase begins.

> **The negotiation phase.** The negotiation phase is marked by the offender's attempt to achieve a coer-

cive value exchange and the target's response to the potential exchange. Depending upon the equivalent value which the offender demands, this phase is usually the longest. It is marked by continuing cycles of demand and response.

**The termination of the incident.** The termination of the incident results in a significant change in the pattern of relationships which has been established. It results in the apprehension, death, or escape of the offender, and the release, death, or escape of the hostage. The increased level of interaction between the offender and the target significantly diminishes.

**The termination of the disruption.** The termination of the disruption relates to the domestic and international response to the target's handling of the situation. It is extremely difficult to place a timeframe on this phase, for the full ramifications may not become evident for years to come. Theoretically, the disruption would be terminated when the system returned to the status quo ante. With so many actors potentially involved, it is quite possible that a new status quo will be developed and this phase will never be fully completed (see Implications for Stability below).

## Shortness of Duration

While it is difficult to measure precisely the duration of a hostage situation when the termination of the incident phase is factored into the equation, political hostage-taking has been distinguished by its brevity. West European kidnappings have averaged 13.6 days, while sieges have averaged 4.7 days.[5] However, it should be noted that occurrences of political hostage-taking in the Middle East have been marked by their length. Not one day in the past thirteen years has passed without at least one Westerner being held hostage in Lebanon.

## Increase in the Prospect of Violence

Each of the four phases delineated above inherently includes an increase in the prospect of violence. The initial phase involves the direct use of threat in order to physically seize the hostage. During the negotiation phase, the threat of violence is consciously induced by the offender in order to reinforce his/her demands. Direct violence, usually aimed at the hostage, may also occur during this phase if the offender suddenly distrusts the motives or the actions of the target. While the termination of the incident suggests the end of violent confrontation, there is no guarantee that what has been agreed to will, in fact, occur. The promised capitulation of the target or compliance of the offender may evaporate at any point depending upon circumstances. It is also possible that this phase may be achieved by the target's use of force in order to secure release of the hostage. Finally, the termination of the dispute may also include outbursts of violence. This violence may erupt from many venues and may be exhibited in many forms simultaneously: riot against the host government by those disagreeing with the result, reaction by a third state disagreeing with the result, another attack by the same group of offenders in order to take advantage of increased media coverage or to re-assert its capabilities, or an attack by a different group of offenders who feel the need to respond to their own diminished sense of prestige.

## Implications
## for Stability

There are a number of factors which appear to determine the level of disruption within a given system.

The nature of the value demanded by the offender. The ensuing instability is directly proportional to the exchange value as perceived by the target. The more expensive the exchange value is to the target, the greater the potential for disruption within the system. Thus, if the exchange value involves an element fundamental to the normal functioning of the system (such as overturning the legal system in order to release prisoners from jail) the disruption will be higher. If the exchange value does not involve an element fundamental to the normal functioning of the system (such as a demand for improved working conditions), the disruption will be lower.

The nature of the seizure. The greater the amount of planning by the offender, the greater the potential for disruption. This is especially true when the offender has planned to manipulate the media.

The physical location of the seizure. The less decision-making authority that the target has over the incident because of location, the greater the potential for disruption. If the target is the sole decision-maker (the target is also the host, and the hostage is a citizen of the target country) the potential for disruption is lower. If the target must share decision-making responsibility with others (for example, the host country, the parent country of the hostage, etc...) there is a greater opportunity for disruption.

The nature of the hostage and his/her import to the functioning of the system. The higher the hierarchical position of the hostage within the system, the higher the potential for disruption. Conversely, the lower the hierarchical position of the hostage within the system, the lower the potential for disruption.

The legitimacy of the offender. The higher the perceived legitimacy of the offender, the higher the potential for instability. This dynamic is played out on two levels: perceptions internal to the system and perceptions external to the system.

> **Internal** – The more legitimate that the cause is perceived to be by those internal to the system, the more pressure there will be on the target to respond favorably. The less legitimate that the cause is perceived to be by those internal to the system, the more pressure there will be on the target to refuse to acquiesce. Thus, if the target's actions are out of sync with domestic perceptions of the legitimacy of the cause, the higher the potential for internal disruption. The more in sync the target's actions are with domestic perceptions, the lower the potential for internal disruption.

> **External** – The more legitimate that the cause is perceived to be by those external to the system, the more pressure there will be on the target to respond favorably. The less legitimate that the cause is perceived to be by those external to the system, the more pressure there will be on the target to refuse to acquiesce. Thus, if the target's actions are out of sync with international perceptions of the legitimacy of the cause, the higher the potential for disruption. The more in sync the target's actions are with international perceptions, the lower the potential for disruption. The relationship between the various international actors and the target may intensify the pressure to respond to international perceptions, whether the countries share a good relationship or whether the countries share a weak relationship with the target desiring an improvement in the relationship.

The nature of the host government. The potential for disruption will vary in direct proportion to the sanctity of any systematic norm violated by the response (for example, a bungled rescue attempt in a society which is contemptuous of military failures).

# A Conceptual Overview[6]

Now that it has been established that political hostage-taking is a form of political crisis, it is possible to present a conceptual overview of this crisis which will identify those actors who are potential stakeholders in a hostage situation.

**Offender.** The offender is the person who seizes the hostage. There are three distinct types of offender[7]:

> **Psycho/Sociopathic:** This offender is generally regarded as the most dangerous, for s/he is full of inner conflict and frustration which are transferred to his/her immediate reality and distorted to suit his/her illusions. The psycho/sociopathic individual derives pleasure from being the center of attention and may be motivated by a strong death wish.

> **Criminal** (professional kidnapper, or a criminal surprised during the commission of a crime who takes hostages): This offender is considered to be the easiest with whom to deal because s/he only desires personal gain. The criminal is usually a rational thinker who will take into account the odds and respond accordingly.

> **Political terrorist:** This offender is impossible to type due to the overwhelming number of variables at play. The terrorist's cause, which may be irrational in the eyes of outsiders, is the sine qua non of his/her actions and, except for this, s/he would be completely rational. Political terrorists usually operate on their home terrain or in a location where they have a network of supporters.

**Primary Victim (The Target).** The target possesses some value which the offender desires. It is sometimes difficult to discern who the target is, especially in cases of political hostage-taking when the action may stem primarily from internal considerations. The target is usually a government or business.

**Secondary Victim (The Hostage).** The hostage is the object which the offender attempts to exchange for a given value. This person or group of persons usually possess some symbolic value to the target.

**Inter-Victim Bond.** This is the relationship which exists between the victims. This relationship is vital for determining the outcome and must be carefully assessed by each of the actors. The offender must ensure that the relationship between the target and the hostage is sufficiently strong so that the target values the hostage. The hostage must rely upon the relationship which s/he has with the target in the hope that the target will respond quickly and with the intent to free the hostage. The target must determine the relative importance of its relationship with the hostage vis-a-vis the exchange demanded.

**Threat.** The threat is the means by which the offender attempts to coerce the target into compliance with his/her demands. This threat is one of direct violence and is the primary cause for the development of the Stockholm Syndrome.[8]

**Demand.** The demand specifies what must/must not be done by the target in order to secure the release of the hostage. Of recent politically motivated kidnappings, 14% had no demands, 36% had monetary demands, and 20% demanded the release of political prisoners.[9]

**Social Impact.** The social impact focuses upon internal and external responses to the incident. (see Implications for Stability above)

**Context.** The context, or physical location, determines how many actors will be directly involved in the incident. (see the physical location of the seizure above)

**Response.** How targets respond to hostage-taking is a highly controversial question. The response usually falls into one of two categories: hard or soft. This topic will be explained below in detail.

## Stakeholders

Stakeholders are those groups and individuals who benefit from, or who are harmed by, a given decision. Decision-makers are morally obligated to take stakeholders into account during the decision-making process.[10] Thus, in order to arrive at an ethical decision it is necessary for decision-makers to identify the major stakeholders and their interests, noting how their interests converge and compete.

**The hostage.** The hostage is potentially faced with two competing objectives: the desire to survive and the need to preserve cherished goals. The will to live is a basic human emotion which need not be examined in this context, but the role that cherished goals play is equally vital. A hostage who is forced to contradict beliefs fundamental to his/her being faces the possibility of incurring severe psychological trauma. Whether this involves signing manifestos attacking the target or agreeing to videotape requests that the ransom be paid despite a life-long stand against such actions, the hostage may come to decide that death is preferable than release under the imposed conditions (see the story of Rabbi Meir of Rothenburg below).

**The offender.** Hostage incidents do not necessarily evolve into zero-sum games. In many cases, especially with respect to political hostage-taking, the offender represents an organization. Thus, any decisions made must include the recognition that tomorrow is another day. That is to say, that the target will still face a potential threat from the offender following the completion of this specific incident. The offender also recognizes that all objectives need not be accomplished during this one incident. Thus, the offender must balance that which realistically can be achieved against his/her desire to survive. This equation is similar to that of the hostage - survival vs. cherished goals – and any decision regarding how to approach the incident must include an analysis of how the offender is likely to perceive and respond to the scenario.

**The family.** Frequently, the family of the hostage is less willing to abandon the victim's life than is the victim. Thus, cherished goals are relegated to a lower position on the hierarchy of priorities and the family will do anything in its power to achieve the release of its loved one. The moral suasion with which this arms the family is powerful. In fact, terrorism experts recommend that decision-makers, while taking family interests into account, avoid all direct contact with the family in the fear that this moral suasion will overwhelm the broader issues at stake.[11]

**The company (as target).** In hostage situations, companies are regularly faced with a major dilemma: they have a fiduciary obligation to their shareholders, and they have an ethical obligation to their employees. Thus, all decision-making must take these potentially conflicting obligations into account. For example, the payment of a large ransom to effect the release of an employee may successfully fulfill the company's obligation to its employees while simultaneously costing the stockholders millions of dollars of profit. Failure to pay the ransom may reduce employee moral, make recruiting and retention more difficult, and create a public relations problem, thus impairing the company's ability to conduct business, but payment may lead to further such incidents and a concomitant reduction of profits and image.

**The host government.** The government upon whose soil the hostage is being held also faces difficult decisions. The hostage is now primarily the responsibility of the host government. Anything which happens to the hostage will be held against the host. The host government is also interested in protecting its national interests and the rule of law. But the host also has international considerations. The host does not want to play this role again in the future, and all actions it takes will be carefully monitored by potential offenders in order to determine the host's ability to ward off such incidents. The host must also factor its relationship with the parent government into the equation. Finally, the host does not desire to expose its own citizens to violence and therefore must walk the fine line between opposition to the incident and treating the offenders with respect.

**The parent government (as target).** The parent government is the hostage's country of citizenship. This government is responsible for preventing harm to its citizens around the world. Thus, it must consider its relationship with host governments and with groups of potential offenders in order to prevent such incidents. However, this responsibility serves in contradistinction to its domestic considerations. Failure to act decisively on behalf of a citizen in danger puts the government in a difficult position with respect to its domestic constituency, especially when the parent government is a democracy. The parent country must also consider the impact of any decision it makes with respect to the rule of law, such as the overturning of a law in order to exchange arms for hostages.

**The media (as target).** While the media may not appear to be directly involved in a given incident, it is frequently the case that the attention of the media, especially with respect to political hostage-taking, is the primary target of the offender. The offender views the media as the way to get the message of his/her organization across to the international community. The media is also a business, and as such it is responsible to its shareholders. Thus, any event which will increase ratings is perceived as an opportunity to increase profits. On the other hand, as human beings, the members of the media must consider the ramifications of their coverage. Might they be encouraging further incidents? Might they someday be directly targeted? Will there be a backlash against the media for serving as the mouthpiece of the offenders? How will a backlash impact on ratings? Do the members of the media have responsibilities to their respective societies which are similar to those of other citizens, or does the nature of their job require them to function supra-nationally?[12]

# The Case[13]

A Shi'ite Muslim group said it was holding four Jews kidnapped in Lebanon and demanded the release of (300) prisoners held by Israel and its militia allies in southern Lebanon as the price of their freedom. The claim from the "Organization of the Oppressed on Earth" came in a typewritten Arabic statement delivered to a news agency in Beirut.[14]

An international Jewish organization appealed to the International Committee of the Red Cross Tuesday to seek the release of Lebanese Jews who have been kidnapped in Beirut... "On the occasion of the release of the American hostages in Lebanon, the World Organization of Jews from Arab Countries asks the ICRC to intervene for humanitarian reasons in order to secure the release of persons of Jewish faith kidnapped in Beirut because of their origins," the cable said.[15]

Despite the killing of a kidnapped Lebanese Jew in Beirut, Israel said Thursday it will not bow to blackmail from "those who turn Jews into hostages" to pressure the Jewish state. Foreign Minister Yitzhak Shamir said... that the killers of Jewish hostage Chaim Cohen-Halala were seeking "to turn all Jews, wherever they live, into hostages... to wrest concessions from Israel." Halala's body was found Tuesday in a bomb-shattered district of West Beirut, and a Moslem group... said it killed him in revenge for Israeli shelling of south Lebanon... Shamir said, "We will seek to protect Jews to the best of our ability, but we will not deal with those who turn them into hostages."[16]

Israel said today the killing of a second Lebanese Jew in Beirut by Shi'ite Muslim kidnappers was a criminal act that deserved worldwide condemnation. The self-styled "Organization of the Oppressed on Earth" said it killed hostage Isaac Tarrab to avenge raids by Israel... "This man was killed only because of one reason: because he was Jewish," Israeli Foreign Ministry Spokesman Avi Pazner said.[17]

Foreign Minister Yitzhak Shamir said today that Israel would not be coerced by Lebanese kidnappers holding Beirut Jews hostage and would strike back at them. "Israel will not tolerate Jews being taken hostage. Nothing can be obtained from us by following that route... The hand of Israel knows not only how to take note (of the perpetrators) but also how to reach out and get them," Shamir said.[18]

Lebanese Muslim extremists said they killed a 52-year-old Lebanese Jew kidnapped a year ago in retaliation for the current Israeli raids on Muslim villages in southern Lebanon. The Organization of the Oppressed on Earth... reported killing Elie Hallack, a physician and vice president of the Higher Council of Lebanon's Jews.[19]

Leading French Jews, saying that the Jews of Lebanon are

in imminent danger, called on them today to leave for other countries... Since December, extremist (Muslims) have announced the executions of four Jews in Lebanon... A group calling itself the Organization of the Oppressed on Earth has claimed responsibility for the abductions and the executions... A fourth Jewish hostage said to have been killed was Ibrahim Benesti, 34, a physician.[20]

A United Nations official briefed Israel today on his talks in Beirut on the fate of Lebanese Jews held hostage by extremist Muslim Shi'ites, Israeli officials said. Briton Marrack Goulding, newly appointed U.N. Under Secretary-General for Special Political Affairs, said he met with representatives of "all groups" to seek information on the missing Jews... Goulding later told Defence Minister Yitzhak Rabin that Israel's presence in its self-declared security zone in south Lebanon had caused the radicalization of Shi'ites there.[21]

What ought Israel to do when faced with political hostage – taking situations such as that outlined above? Four Jews were taken hostage in a foreign country. Demands were made upon Israel which challenged Israel's rule of law. Israel acknowledged its respon-sibility for the Jews, yet refused to negotiate on behalf of the hostages. Instead, Israel responded in a hard fashion, increasing its military activity in southern Lebanon.[22] Four of the hostages (it was never clear exactly how many Jews had been abducted in Lebanon) were killed.

## Responses – A Country-by-Country Analysis

Responses to political hostage-taking are generally divided into two categories: hard and soft. Hard responses are those which disdain acquiescence and which focus on the use of the military to thwart incidents. Soft responses favor negotiations and compromise in the effort to obtain the release of hostages. It should be noted that while no country fits neatly into either the hard or the soft format, it is possible to type countries by historical trends. Finally, when evaluating the various responses of individual countries, one must always remember that while:

> hostage-taking is only a small part of the terrorist problem confronting democratic societies, it has an impact completely out of proportion to its size. (For) one of the cornerstones of democratic thought is the worth and rights of the individual, (and) in this the Free World is at a serious disadvantage in the struggle with terrorists. Democratic governments are and must be concerned with individual lives, whereas terrorists can treat them as pawns to be sacrificed.[23]

The following countries will be used as examples of the hard and the soft approaches.

**Israel.** Israel provides us with the best example of a hard line approach. Beginning with the development of small anti-terrorist squads in the 1930s, Israel has maintained one the best trained and best equipped counter-terrorist units in the world. Known as Sayaret Matkal, this force has been regularly employed by the Israeli government not only in hostage situations (such as Ma'alot and Entebbe) but also in a constant world-wide preemptive battle against those terrorist forces which Israel perceives as a threat. This approach has worked, for Israelis are rarely taken hostage. Having little to gain from any other policy, Israel has generally remained steadfast in its refusal to negotiate with terrorists. However, the release of approximately 1,500 terrorists as part of the 1985 T.W.A. agreement and Israel's abduction of Sheik Obeid in Lebanon as a bargaining chip for the release of Israeli prisoners of war show that Israel is willing to moderate its posture when needed.

**U.S.S.R.** The Soviet Union also has a long history of combatting terrorists with force, but the Soviet stance tends to be ambivalent. This results from the fact that the Soviet Union has, historically, been directly involved in the training, equipping, and supporting of terrorist units. Recognizing the threat which terrorism poses to the Western world, the Soviets have engaged in this policy in order to further their long-term goals. (What impact the current political and economic situation in the Soviet Union will have on this program has yet to be determined.) However, when terrorists have turned on Soviet citizens, the Soviet response has been swift and hard. Hijacked Soviet airlines have been met with full assaults and high casualties (note the irony: the Soviet Union's suppression of domestic freedoms frees the government to respond with a latitude that would be completely unacceptable in a democracy and yet which terrorism experts claim is the most effective in preventing such incidents). In 1985 four Soviet diplomats were abducted in Lebanon. The Soviet counter-terrorism forces immediately identified the abductors. Then, they kidnapped a relative of one of the abductors and delivered his penis to them. Although one Soviet had already been killed, the others were immediately released.

**The United States.** The official policy of the United States has frequently been at odds with reality. Following the assassination of the U.S. Ambassador in Sudan during the Khartoum Embassy siege of 1973, "President Nixon made a public statement saying 'No negotiations' when an Assistant Secretary of State was on the plane to Khartoum to try to negotiate."[24] President Reagan, who came into office during the Iran hostage situation promising no more negotiations with hostages, left office in the midst of the Iran-Contra scandal. Thus, there has been a considerable amount of talk, but little consistent action. This probably results from "a rigid public policy and an internal dynamic which all but precludes timely action when risk is involved."[25] However, the U.S. has engaged in some successful hard responses to terrorism, such as the interception of the plane with the Achille Lauro hijackers and the raid on Libya. Nevertheless, despite the success of these actions, domestic response has been cool.

**France.** The French position exemplifies the soft approach.[26] France has a long tradition of providing political asylum to terrorists and respecting the "right" of the downtrodden to redress wrong through violence. The French have cut deals with terrorist organizations, allowing them bases in France in exchange for not attacking French interests. Thus, "France has, over the years, acquired an especially unsavory reputation for refusing to extradite terrorist suspects to other European countries while springing others from prison to buy domestic tranquility."[27] It should be noted that when various terrorist organizations have violated these agreements, France's security forces have responded quickly and forcefully.

**Japan.** The emergence of Japan as an economic superpower has led to the targeting of Japanese businesspeople around the world. However, as a result of Japan's unwillingness to assert itself as a political superpower, the Japanese have experienced few politically motivated abductions. When these incidents have occurred, the Japanese have overwhelmingly elected to employ the soft response - they pay the ransom demanded. This is justified by the Japanese as just another cost of doing business in certain areas of the world.

## Who is Obligated to Respond – An Ethical Decision

As noted above, it is frequently difficult to ascertain the target of a political hostage-taking incident. For example, who was the target of the T.W.A. hijacking in 1985? Was it the holding company which owned T.W.A.? Was it the United States government under whose flag the plane flew? Was it the government of Lebanon where the plane eventually came to rest? Was it the governments of Israel and Kuwait who were "asked" to release prisoners? Was it the "international citizen" who was called upon to respond sympathetically through the media circus which was conducted by the terrorists? Or was it some combination of the above? Given the difficulties inherent in identifying the target, it is necessary to ascertain who is morally obligated to respond before specifying the type of response to be employed.

Simon, Powers, and Gunneman[28] have developed a theory which aids us in determining an actor's minimum moral obligation. Using this theory we can establish who is morally obligated to prevent harm during a political hostage-taking crisis. This principle of preventing harm demands that one must act when four conditions are met (in order to clarify this point, the Israeli rescue mission to Entebbe will be explored):

**Proximity.** One must be within sufficient proximity so that one can respond effectively. (Despite the fact that Israel was over 1,000 miles away from the hostages, its airpower enabled it to be sufficiently proximate to respond effectively. That is, it was able to transport ample troops to achieve its goal.)

**Capability.** One must possess the capability necessary to achieve one's goal. (Israel's crack anti-terrorist units were well-trained for such an action and Israel had the hardware necessary to achieve the goal.)

**Need.** There must be a demonstrated need for action. (A plane transporting many Israeli citizens was hijacked. When Jewish passengers were separated from other passengers, the need for an immediate response became obvious.)

**Last Resort.** All other options must be exhausted before the obligation to prevent harm becomes incumbent upon an actor. (The host country – Uganda – became implicated on behalf of the terrorists. The company – Air France – pressured Israel to give in to the terrorists' demands. No other country was as prepared as Israel to take action and no other country could afford the political risk of failure. Thus, Israel remained as the last resort. Having fulfilled all of the conditions, Israel's rescue mission to Entebbe was morally justifiable. In fact, Israel was morally obligated to respond.)

Now that a framework has been presented by which to determine the actor obligated to respond, we must turn to defining the response.

## Hard vs. Soft Response - An Ethical Decision

James Tunstead Burchael[29] provides a useful paradigm by which to evaluate the ethical decision-making process for employing either a hard or a soft strategy vis-a-vis political hostage-taking. The core of the hard response is the capability of resorting to the use of force. Without this capability, the hard response remains merely another form of negotiation – the strategy of the bluff. Once uncovered, the strategy would be rendered as dangerous as a paper tiger. The core of the soft response is the belief that:

> bartering can lead to an appropriate solution that results in the freeing of hostages without the authorities either outrageously compromising themselves or having set a series of precedents that would make the next encounter more likely or more difficult. The value of negotiation becomes more evident if we can assume that the rationale behind hostage-taking extends beyond the immediate calculation of the likely capitulation of authorities to terrorist demands. If this is true, then possessing or not possessing an avowedly firm policy on negotiation may be largely irrelevant to whether or how frequently a government is a target of terrorist attack.[30]

Burchael's decision-making paradigm is based upon the question of what morally justifies going to war: "According to the Western tradition of justified warfare, there are five principal requisites for a war to be morally undertaken:

1. Action by a legitimate national authority.
2. A just grievance.
3. The exhaustion of other alternatives.
4. A reasonable likelihood of success.
5. More good foreseen than evil."[31]

Burchael now proceeds to exhibit how these criteria are to be applied when framing a moral response to terrorism.

> **Action by a legitimate national authority**. Of concern here is not the status of the government faced by terrorism, but of the terrorists themselves. International law clearly mandates that a country may only declare war on another country. This presents a difficulty, for terrorism, while in fact an act of war, is treated legally as if it were a criminal act. Thus, while the terrorist group is able to function as an organized body, those attacked respond as if they were merely facing an individual criminal. Burchael suggests that a new category of warfare be incorporated into international law which would enable those fighting terrorism to declare war upon terrorists as a collective. Thus, any member of a terrorist organization could be captured without proof of individual criminal wrongdoing. This concept becomes even more important when one recognizes

that many of those involved with terrorism are involved precisely because they have been denied the
right of self-determination.

Burchael notes that this classification is vital if any response to a
terrorist group is to be ethical. For example, while preemptive actions
against those believed to be contemplating criminal activities are
extremely difficult to justify, preemptive strikes against those with
whom one is already at war are morally acceptable. Thus, the ethical picture depends on the model which one applies. If terrorism is
a crime, then terrorists must be granted due process. If terrorism is
an act of war, then terrorism may be countered with acts appropriate
to warfare.

> **A just grievance.** As with the above, the condition of
> the just grievance refers not to the country facing
> terrorism, but to the terrorists themselves. Thus, a
> nation which desires to battle a terrorist organiza-
> tion is morally obligated to ensure that it has taken
> the time to appraise the grievances of its enemy
> before allowing itself to respond. Burchael demands
> that the attacked government employ patience and
> objectivity in its analysis of those grievances.

> **Exhaustion of other alternatives.** The first alterna-
> tive must always be the consideration of the demands
> of the terrorists. Burchael argues that this obliga-
> tion does not result from the terrorists' use of force,
> but rather from the reality that it is possible that
> these people are the victims of earlier injustices
> perpetrated by the government now under attack. If
> so, it may yet be possible for the government to alle-
> viate much of the pressure by addressing those
> grievances.

When there is no justice in terrorist demands, then the next alternative is measured retaliation: purposefully restrained, with the promise of harsher reprisal to follow. Should that not stay the hand of
terrorism, then is the time to declare that belligerency has begun.
After that, the strategy is not to await further strikes in order to
strike back, but to move to capture or to destroy the terrorists.[32]

> **Reasonable likelihood of success.** "The only success
> is peace, and the only steady ground under peace is
> justice. A nation must ask whether a belligerent
> response to a terrorist attack will quench hostility
> or only foment more determined resistance and
> widespread sympathy."[33] Thus, for Burchael, while
> it may be relatively easy to defeat a group of crimi-
> nals, it is far more difficult to defeat an adversarial
> nation. The nation must, in the long run, be rendered

peaceful. A hard response makes this outcome more difficult. Yet, war makes people prefer peace, and there will be no peace until both sides come to despise war so much that they will pay any price for hostilities to cease.

**More good foreseen than evil.** Burchael stresses that the primary risks of responding to terrorism with force are the impact on our characters from having succumbed to the use of force and, conversely, the impact on our characters from having stood idly by. The most difficult aspect of any assessment of good versus evil is the fact that the issues to be compared are incommensurables: life and property, short-term needs and long term values, the good of the individual and the good of the collective. Thus, it is vital that the goal always be before us: the achievement of peace. This goal serves to remind us that we cannot devastatingly assault the other side to the point of driving it to unrelenting hostility. Our goal mandates that we desire someday to live in peace with the other side. If the terrorists attacking a country are harbored by a country allied to the attacked country, is it worth harming that relationship in order to achieve justice? What response is strong enough for us to achieve our goal without recklessly endangering untold lives in a confrontation? Are there responses which would deliver the attacked country from the immediate threat, but which would render that country more vulnerable to attack in the future? These are questions which Burchael poses in order to draw out the ramifications of any action. A response is only ethically justifiable when it achieves more good in the long run than evil.

There is a double paradox about peace being the desired outcome of belligerency. On the one hand you may not be preserving the peace by refusing to fight. Thomas Jefferson, who had explicitly renounced any resort to warfare, eventually sent the navy to suppress the Barbary pirates. He explained, "Against such a banditti, war had become less ruinous than peace, for then peace was a war on one side only." Yet on the other hand, armed intervention can destroy the possibility of peace when its target is a resolute group of men and women who believe themselves to be defending their families, their homes and homeland, their faith and their freedom: in short, the precious things people are willing to die for. Every decision to use force or to abstain from force can be justified only by its realistic claim to make peace more possible.[34]

## A Utilitarian Perspective

Utilitarianism is committed to the maximization of the good and the minimization of harm and evil. It asserts that we ought always to produce the greatest possible balance of positive values for all persons affected, or the minimum balance of disvalue.[35]

Thus, the utilitarian's primary obligation is to weigh benefits against harms, benefits against other benefits, and harms against other harms.

Alexander Haig provides the following utilitarian lens through which to view our case. He claims that this approach, an approach which requires "cold, hard decisions on troubling problems,"[36] can be successful in the handling of a political hostage-taking incident:

> Terrorists manipulate our concern for the lives of individual hostages to overcome our natural instinct for self-defense. We also hesitate to retaliate for hostage-taking for fear of taking the lives of innocent civilians.
>
> We must understand, however, that these moral questions extend far beyond the immediate case. To ransom hostages through concessions is to exchange the immediate danger to them for an increasing danger to others later on. Successful terrorism only begets successful terrorism.
>
> And, as in any war, a commander-in-chief must also know that military operations can be designed to minimize civilian casualties but can never entirely avoid them. In other words, acceding to terrorists, no matter how politically disguised, is immoral.
>
> The test of our policy is not the morality of attacking the terrorists – that is always moral – but only prudence in doing so. And that test of prudence also extends to the issue of negotiations. For too long, we have sought to disguise the brittleness of our resistance by the seeming solidity of the oath never to negotiate. Our policy should be one of no concessions, not no negotiations.
>
> Terrorism has evoked from our military and civilian officials anger, frustration and often knee-jerk reactions that amount to paralysis. Too often, a brief intense crisis has been followed by the apparent return to normalcy. Relieved to be off the rollercoaster of emotions – however the crisis turns out – we turn our attention and our energies elsewhere, blocking out the awful memories. Then vigilance lapses, the terrorists attack on another front and we re-discover the problem all over again.

We need a better-balanced approach. We cannot allow a hostage crisis to paralyze the Government to the neglect of everything else; that only plays into the terrorists' hands. But it is crucial to realize that we are in a war – a twilight war, to be sure, a war of unusual tactics – but one that requires continuing, strenuous efforts, not just a spasmodic reaction to the headlines.

Are we to await the next blow at the time and place of the enemy's choosing? Or are we to strike when and where we can, even if no immediate incident arouses our indignation? To best the terrorists, we need a prolonged campaign, not just crisis management.[37]

Thus, while effectively maximizing utility, utilitarianism inherently engenders and tolerates the suffering of a certain number of stakeholders, including hostages, their families, and those members of the armed forces who are called upon to root out terrorists. While it is possible to understand how, in the long run, such suffering might be eliminated, in practice the course of action which professes to produce the greatest possible balance of positive values for the greatest number of people necessarily results in harm and disvalue to the minority. No where is it clear that this minority has any claim to protection in a utilitarian system. As long as the utilitarian is careful to include the long-term impact of such a "cold" approach, ransom payments, concessions, and negotiated settlements would be prohibited.

## A Deontological Perspective

"Deontological theories maintain that the concept of duty is in some respect independent of the concept of good and that some actions are right or wrong for reasons other than their consequences."[38] Immanuel Kant's categorical imperative further expresses this theory. The categorical imperative demands that one "(1) act only according to that maxim by which you can, at the same time, will that it should become a universal law; and (2) act so as to never treat another human being merely as a means to an end."[39]

As such, the deontologist would sharply disagree with Haig's position. Few would will that Haig's approach become a universal law when applied directly to themselves. This becomes evident in the results of a French public opinion poll. "The majority of those asked if the police should interfere in a barricade situation answered in the affirmative, while the majority said no to police involvement if their son or daughter were kidnapped."[40] Certainly, if one is to avoid using human beings merely as means to an end, one cannot place a human being in imminent danger in order to achieve a policy objective such as the one outlined by Mr. Haig. The danger to those individuals held hostage becomes readily apparent when one discovers that "of six hundred hostages held over a period of time, fifty had died but only three percent of those held (eighteen in total) had been killed by their captors, the remainder dying during the process of liberation."[41] Finally, it would be unconscionable for a deontologist to refuse to pay a ransom for a human being. A human being is priceless and must be redeemed at all costs. Thus, for the deontologist, a hard approach, while theoretically possible, would not be implementable once a political hostage-taking situation presented itself. The deontologist would prefer the soft response, placing a higher value on human life in real danger than on a theory which operates in the abstract.

## A Libertarian Perspective

The libertarian:

> promotes the minimal or night-watchman state, according to which government action is justified only if it protects the rights or entitlements of citizens. (S/)he argues that a theory of justice should work to protect our rights not to be coerced and should not propound a thesis intended to pattern society through arrangements such as those found in socialist and (impure) capitalist countries in which governments take pronounced steps to redistribute the wealth acquired by individuals acting in accordance with free-market laws.[42]

Thus, it becomes apparent that the libertarian would accept either the hard or the soft response. With respect to the hard approach, a government which acted in such a way so as to secure the rights of those deprived of their liberty would be acceptable as long as the individual – or someone acting on his/her behalf – agreed. However, the libertarian would strongly oppose any government ransom payment or acquiescence with respect to law and order on behalf of a citizen held hostage. That would obligate others to pay for an action of which they might disapprove. This would not preclude private efforts to come to some agreement with the offenders, including the payment of a ransom, providing that the money for such a payment be raised privately.

# The Ethical Perspective
# Vis-a-Vis The Case

## Stakeholders:

**The hostages.** Four Jews. Elie Hallack, a 52-year-old physician and Vice President of the Higher Council of Lebanon's Jews. Chaim Cohen-Halala, a 39-year-old merchant from Iran in Lebanon on business. Isaac Tarrab, a 70-year-old professor of mathematics at a Beirut University. Ibrahim Benesti, a 34-year-old physician.

**The offenders.** A secretive group called the Organization of the Oppressed on Earth (OOE) claimed responsibility for the abductions and the eventual executions (the threat). The OOE operates under the umbrella of the Islamic Holy War which, in turn, is connected with Hezbollah, a militant pro-Iranian Shi'ite Moslem group that has power in the southern suburbs of Beirut and in the Bekaa.

**The family.** Little reference is made to the families of the hostages, although Dr. Benesti's father and son were also abducted.

**The host government.** The "government" of Lebanon. At this time, Lebanon was in the midst of a civil war. Israeli and Syrian troops occupied the country.

**The parent government.** Three of the four hostages were Lebanese. One was Iranian. In this case, the parent governments were not the targets.

**The target government.** All demands were directed at Israel. This connection was established through the religion of those abducted (the inter-victim bond).

**The media.** All demands were transmitted through the media. In this case very little attention was given to the situation by the western media because the hostages were not western. Attempts were made by the OOE through the media to link the situation to the western hostages in an effort to force the United States to pressure Israel to release the 300 prisoners (the demand).

## Response:

Israel opted to employ a hard response. No other power was in proximity – Lebanon was in complete disarray and Israeli troops were already stationed in the vicinity. Israel possessed the requisite capability – Israeli prowess in such situations has been attested to above. There was a demonstrated need for action – the hostages lives were directly threatened, and, in fact, the hostages were murdered one after the other. Israel was the last resort – the French Jewish community merely recommended that all Lebanese Jews emigrate, the United Nations focused on blaming Israel for giving cause to the abductors, and the host government of Lebanon was incapacitated.

However, while Israel was morally obligated to respond, was a hard response ethically justifiable? This question remains open. Certainly the OOE, as a member of Hizbollah, was a legitimate national authority in Lebanon, and Israel was thereby in a position to declare war on that organization and its membership. An objective analysis of the grievances presented by the terrorists is difficult, but when one considers who was among the 300 prisoners who were to be released,[43] it seems plausible to deny the justice of their grievance. Israel and members of the French Jewish community were involved, indirectly, in negotiations with the offenders.[44] A representative of the United Nations was also involved in the process. Consideration was given to the demands of the terrorists. Thus, it appears that Israel did exhaust all of the possible alternatives. We now come to the final two aspects of Burchael's paradigm: reasonable likelihood of success and more good foreseen than evil. Burchael emphasizes the prospects for achieving peace, both in the short and in the long-term. The reasonable likelihood of success condition mandates that "a nation must ask whether a belligerent response to a terrorist attack will quench hostility or only foment more determined resistance." Thus, this condition focuses on the short-term. While hindsight makes the process of evaluating this condition rather easy, it is yet possible to surmise that Israel's response (an increase in military activity, especially bombing raids) was too broad-scale to effect the desired outcome. There was little likelihood of success, as defined by Burchael, so long as the response was not directed primarily at the offenders. The bombing raids only served to exacerbate the situation, as evidenced by the increasing hostility of the offenders. Negotiation became impossible, and the hostages were summarily killed. Long-term considerations are the focus of the more good foreseen than evil condition. Was more good achieved by the Israeli response? Apparently not. In fact, the situation worsened considerably. More Lebanese Jews were taken hostage. More Westerners were taken hostage. Two Israeli soldiers were taken hostage while on patrol in southern Lebanon. Israel kidnapped a Hizbollah cleric, Sheikh Abdel Karim Obeid, in an attempt to gain the freedom of the soldiers. Thus, it appears that the Israeli response failed the more good foreseen than evil test, as well. Of the five conditions suggested by Burchael's paradigm, Israel's hard response to the abduction of four Lebanese Jews fulfilled only three. Thus, Israel's military response cannot be morally defensible from this perspective.

## Utilitarianism:

The utilitarian argument, as presented by Alexander Haig, defends the position taken by Israel. Haig argues that "to ransom hostages through concession is to exchange the immediate danger to them for an increasing danger to others later on." Thus, Haig takes a long-term perspective which extends even beyond that taken by Burchael. Yes, it is possible that those immediately involved may have suffered as a result of Israel's hard response. But "the greatest possible balance of positive values for all persons affected" may have been achieved. While western hostages remain in Lebanon, there has been no recent word of either Israelis or Jews being held hostage in Lebanon. The Israeli response effectively convinced the offenders that the threat was insufficient to obtain the coercive value exchange desired. The secondary targets who were killed have no claim to protection under the utilitarian system as long as the target can maintain that its response created "the minimum balance of disvalue" possible.

## Deontology:

The deontologist would reject the legitimacy of Israel's hard response. By neglecting the implications of the categorical imperative, Israel opted to treat the lives of those human beings held hostage as means to achieving an end – a political victory. As such, the Israeli policy of refusing to negotiate with the offenders failed to consider the deontological perspective that "the concept of duty is in some respect independent of the concept of good and that some actions are right or wrong for reasons other than their consequences." The lives of the Jews held by the OOE could have been saved if the Israeli government had recognized their intrinsic value, a value which far exceeded any policy objectives desired by the Israelis.

## Libertarianism:

The libertarian would have a difficult time accounting for Israel's response to a situation which did not directly involve its citizens. If the kidnapped individuals had been Israeli citizens, then the libertarian would expect that the government would take all actions in its power to "protect the rights of (its) citizens." Whether a hard or a soft response would best achieve this goal in this case would determine the appropriate response, although it is vital to indicate that the libertarian would strongly oppose any action which would represent an overturn of the rule of law, such as the release of prisoners or the payment of ransom from public funds. However, the Israeli government's decision to respond when its citizens were not directly involved could not be countenanced by the libertarian. These individuals would be the responsibility of the parent governments, in this case Lebanon and Iran. Thus, the libertarian would oppose Israel's action.

# The Jewish Response

As a result of the Jewish experience over the years, the *halakhah* has much to offer with respect to the issue of hostage-taking. Confronted by a continuous onslaught of the taking of Jewish hostages, the Jewish legal tradition has developed a generally uniform approach to such incidents. This uniformity reflects two variables which remained constant until today: Jews were taken hostage primarily in the anticipation of ransom payments, and the Jewish people were rarely able to exercise force when faced with hostage-taking situations.

## Talmudic Texts

*Hullin* 7a. This section of *aggadah* highlights the Talmudic approach to the redemption of hostages:

> Once, R. Phinehas b. Jair was on his way to redeem captives, and came to the river Ginnai. "O Ginnai," said he, "divide thy water for me, that I may pass through thee." It replied, "Thou art about to do the will of thy Maker; I, too, am doing the will of my Maker. Thou mayest or mayest not accomplish thy purpose; I am sure of accomplishing mine." He said: "If thou wilt not divide thyself, I will decree that no waters ever pass through thee." It, thereupon, divided itself for him.

Thus, we learn that the Talmud takes the obligation to redeem hostages with the utmost seriousness: it is the will of God that hostages be redeemed.

*Baba Batra* 8b. The legal underpining for the aggadic tale of R. Phinehas is developed in this section:

> Raba asked Rabbah b. Mari: Whence is derived the maxim of the Rabbis that the redemption of captives is a religious duty of great importance? He replied: From the verse, "And it shall come to pass when they say unto thee, 'Whither shall go forth,' then thou shalt tell them, 'Thus saith the Lord, Such as are for death, to death, and such as are for the sword, to the sword, and such as are for famine, to the famine,

and such as are for captivity, to captivity."' (Jeremiah, 15:2) And [commenting on this] R. Johanan said: Each punishment mentioned in this verse is more severe than the one before. The sword is worse than death; this I can demonstrate either from Scripture, or, if you prefer, from observation. The proof from observation is that the sword deforms but death does not deform; the proof from Scripture is in the verse, "Precious in the eyes of the Lord is the death of his saints." (Psalms 116:15) Famine again is harder than the sword; this again can be demonstrated either by observation, the proof being that one causes [prolonged] suffering but the other not, or, if you prefer, from the Scripture, from the verse, "They that be slain with the sword are better than they that be slain with hunger." (Lamentations 4:9) Captivity is harder than all, because it includes the sufferings of all.

Thus, *Baba Batra* 8b establishes that the redemption of hostages is a religious duty of great importance. This will have broad implications as to how the Talmud will fashion its recommended response to hostage-taking situations.

*Baba Batra* 3b. Once the *mitzvah* of the redemption of hostages was established, it needed to be qualified vis-a-vis the other *mitzvot*. For example, the Talmud addresses the issue of whether funds collected for the building of a synagogue may be diverted in order to ransom a hostage:

Rabina asked R. Ashi: Suppose money for a synagogue has been collected and is ready for use, is there still a risk [that the building of the new one may be neglected]? He replied: They may be called upon to redeem captives and use it for that purpose. [Rabina asked further]: Suppose the bricks are already piled up and the lathes trimmed and the beams ready, what are we to say? He replied: It can happen that money is suddenly required for the redemption of captives, and they may sell the material for that purpose. If they could do that, [he said], could they do the same even if they had already built the synagogue? He answered: People do not sell their dwelling-places.

Thus, the Talmud teaches that the redemption of hostages takes precedence even over the building of a synagogue. However, once the synagogue building has been completed, it may not be sold in order to raise the necessary funds.

*Gittin* 45a-b. *Gittin* 45a-b assumes that hostages ought to be ransomed. The question which it raises focuses upon 392 how much one must be willing to pay in order to achieve this goal. Of prime concern are the ramifications of such payments:

> Captives should not be redeemed for more than their value, to prevent abuses (literally, "for the good order of the world"). Captives should not be helped to escape, to prevent abuses. Rabban Simeon B. Gamaliel says [that the reason is] to prevent the ill-treatment of fellow captives.

Thus, the Talmud recommends that ransom payments not exceed the value of the hostages in order to discourage offenders from engaging in hostage-taking. Also of interest in this section is the reference to helping hostages escape. It is not clear how this might be accomplished, but the Talmud indicates that because escape frequently leads to the imposition of even more stringent conditions on those who remain, it is forbidden to aid in the escape of a hostage.

*Ketubot* 52a-b. A husband has a special obligation to ransom his wife which is derived from the *k'tubah*. The question is raised as to whether this obligation requires the husband to pay in excess of the value of his wife in order to redeem her:

> Our Rabbis taught: [If a woman] was taken captive and a demand was made upon her husband for as much as ten times her value, he must ransom her the first time. Subsequently, however, he ransoms her only if he desired to do so but need not ransom her if he does not wish to do so. R. Simeon b. Gamaliel ruled: Captives must not be ransomed for more than their value, in the interests of the public. [This then implies] that they must be ransomed for their actual value even though the cost of a captive's ransom exceeds the amount of her *k'tubah*. Has not, however, the contrary been taught: [If a woman] was taken captive, and a demand was made upon her husband for as much as ten times the amount of her *k'tubah*, he must ransom her the first time. Subsequently, however, he ransoms her only if he desires to do so but need not ransom her if he does not wish to do so. R. Simeon b. Gamaliel ruled: If the price of her ransom corresponded to the amount of her *k'tubah* he must ransom her; if not, he need not ransom her.

This section of the Talmud introduces the concept that a higher ransom payment may be offered on behalf of certain, specified, people. For example, a husband may redeem his wife for up to ten times her value. An apparent conflict in the law is discussed: the husband's responsibility to his wife – which would mandate a larger payment – versus the husband's responsibility to his community which would mandate a smaller payment. Rabban Gamaliel rules that a husband may not pay more than either his wife's value or her *k'tubah* in order to effect her redemption.

*Gittin* 58a. Now that the principle of wives being ransomed for more than their value has been investigated, the Talmud introduces another group which may be ransomed for more than their value – scholars:

> Our Rabbis have taught: R. Joshua b. Hananiah once happened to go to the great city of Rome, and he was told there that there was in the prison a child with beautiful eyes and face and curly locks. He went and stood at the doorway of the prison and said, "Who gave Jacob a spoil and Israel to the robbers?" (Isaiah 42:24) The child answered, "Is it not the Lord, He against whom we have sinned and in whose ways they would not walk, neither were they obedient unto his law." (Isaiah 42:24) He said: I feel sure that this one will be a teacher in Israel. I swear that I will not budge from here before I ransom him, whatever price may be demanded. It is reported that he did not leave the spot before he had ransomed him at a high figure, nor did many days pass before he became a teacher in Israel. Who was he? He was R. Ishmael b. Elisha.

Thus, *Gittin* 58a introduces the concept that scholars may be ransomed at any price.

*Horayot* 13a. It has been assumed to this point that a community is able to raise all of the necessary funds, whether those funds exceed the value of the hostage or not. However, the Talmud recognized that a paucity of resources might require those paying the ransom to engage in a process of triage. The principles underpinning this triage are presented in this section:

> A man takes precedence over a woman in matters concerning the saving of life and the restoration of lost property, and a woman takes precedence over a man in matters of clothing and ransom from captivity. When both are exposed to immoral degradation in their captivity the man's ransom takes precedence over that of the woman.

> Our Rabbis taught: If a man and his father and his teacher were in captivity he takes precedence over his teacher and his teacher takes precedence over his father, while his mother takes precedence over all of them. A scholar takes precedence over a king of Israel, for if a scholar dies, all Israel are eligible for kingship.

> A priest takes precedence over a Levite, a Levite over

> an Israelite, an Israelite over a *mamzer*, a *mamzer* over
> a *natin*, a *natin* over a Proselyte, and a Proselyte
> over an Emancipated Slave. This order of precedence
> applies only when all these were in other respects
> equal. If the *mamzer*, however, was a scholar and the
> High Priest an ignoramus, the learned *Mamzer*
> takes precedence over the ignorant High Priest.

Thus, *Horayot* 13a teaches who must be ransomed before whom
and indicates the rationale behind this ordering. Of utmost importance is that the man not be exposed to homosexual acts by his captors. If that is not a concern, then the woman must be freed first in
order to prevent her sexual degradation. Once the issue of sexual
degradation has been addressed, the scholar takes precedence on
the belief that his scholarship is of irreplaceable value to the community. This system of triage then continues on to distinguish between
various other castes, ordering them according to the degrees of their
ritual purity.

**Summary.** The Talmud presents a concise and specific approach to
the issue of hostage-taking. It is a *mitzvah* of the highest degree to
obtain the release of captives, superseding even the *mitzvah* of building a synagogue. Apparently, perhaps as a result of the political situation of the Jews at the time, this release was to be effected through
the payment of ransoms. However, the Talmud warns the community not to offer excessive payments to offenders lest the offenders
be enticed to continue their hostage-taking. This requirement is qualified with respect to wives and scholars for whom excessive payments may be permitted. When faced with a paucity of resources, a
triage system was developed in order to direct the community
where to place their efforts, with the major emphasis on the avoiding of sexual degradation and the freeing of scholars.

## Geonic Texts

*Otzar Hageonim*, *Gittin*, *Teshuvah* 228. *Otzar Hageonim* reviews the
responsibility of the husband to the wife in cases of hostage-taking:

> And it was resolved according to the Tanna who ex-
> plained in the case of a young woman who was se-
> duced and taken captive, and a demand was made
> upon her husband for as much as ten times her value,
> that [he must ransom her] the first time, etc...
> Rabbi Simeon ben Gamaliel said: One does not ran-
> som captives for more than their value, in the
> interest of the public [order]. And we established it in
> that case, even though her ransom would equal her
> *k'tubah*, perhaps even though there is no [question of]
> public distress, one does not redeem [her for more
> than her value], etc...? But I found [a ruling accord-

ing] to Rabbi Chaninah and Rabbi Yitzchak (z"l) who determined the law there according to Rabbi Simeon ben Gamaliel... And thus Hannagid wrote in *Hikhata Gavrata* in an anonymous Mishnah the decision is according to Rashbag there. And the *halakhah* is according to him.

**Summary.** *Otzar Hageonim* determines that the *halakhah* is according to Rabbi Simeon ben Gamaliel. A husband is not obligated to redeem his wife for more than either her value or her *k'tubah*. This ruling is overturned by Maimonides in *Hilkhot Ishut*.

## Medieval Codes

*Mishneh Torah, Matanot Aniyim*, 8:10-15; 17-18. Building upon the Talmudic understanding of the importance of the *mitzvah* of redeeming hostages, Maimonides offers his view:

> The ransoming of captives has precedence over the feeding and clothing of the poor. Indeed, there is no religious duty more meritorious than the ransoming of captives, for not only is the captive included in the generality of the hungry, the thirsty, and the naked, but his very life is in jeopardy. He who turns his eyes away from ransoming him, transgresses the commandments, "Thou shalt not harden thy heart, nor shut thy hand" (Deut. 15:7), "Neither shalt thou stand idly by the blood of thy neighbor" (Lev. 19:16), and "He shall not rule with vigor over him in thy sight" (Lev. 25:23). Moreover, he nullifies the commandments, "Thou shalt surely open thy hand unto him (Deut. 15:8), "That thy brother may live with thee" (Lev. 25:36), "Thou shalt love thy neighbor as thyself" (Lev. 19:18), "Deliver them that are drawn unto death" (Proverbs 24:11), and many other admonitions like these. To sum up, there is no religious duty greater than the ransoming of captives.

Thus, Maimonides extends beyond the Talmudic declaration that redeeming hostages is of great importance, asserting that no religious duty supersedes this duty. He bases this claim on a different group of proof texts than the Talmud, involving both positive and negative commandments.

Maimonides then proceeds to codify much of the Talmudic legislation noted above, including the requirement that funds collected for the building of a synagogue be used for ransom payments as needed, the prohibition against ransoming hostages for more than their fair value, the precedence which women take over men except in cases of sexual degradation, the system of triage, and the precedence of the learned over the unlearned.

*Mishneh Torah, Hilkhot Ishut*, 14:19-20. In order to emphasize the serious nature of the husband's special obligation to the wife, Maimonides notes the following:

> (If) he says (of his captive wife), "I divorce her; here is her *k'tubah*, let her go and ransom herself," no attention need be paid to him, rather he must be forced to ransom her, even if her price is ten times the amount of her *k'tubah*, and even if his entire property is just sufficient to provide ransom.
>
> If the wife is made captive while her husband is away in a country beyond the sea, the court may seize his property, sell it at public auction, and ransom her, just as the husband would have done it.

Once again, the response is designed to effect the release of the hostage. Maimonides determines that the husband may not renege on this duty, no matter the price. If the husband is away, the court assumes the responsibility for redeeming the captive wife, even when fulfilling this responsibility requires selling the private property of another.

*Asheri, Gittin*, 4:44. Rabbenu Asher neatly summarizes the status of the legislation to this point:

> Captives should not be redeemed for more than their value, even by their relatives. And her husband is allowed to redeem her with all that he has. And so, too, with a scholar or even a sharp youngster, who may be redeemed for many times his value. One does not provide aid for captives and one does not advise them to flee away.

**Summary.** Thus, Rabbi Asher does not differ with the *halakhah* as established by Maimonides. Hostages must be redeemed at their value, except for wives and scholars for whom any price may be paid. This is the only type of aid which may be proffered to the victim.

*Tur, Yoreh Deah*, 252. The *Tur* also offers an understanding of the Talmudic legislation vis-a-vis hostage-taking:

> The ransoming of captives has precedence over the feeding and clothing of the poor. And there is no religious duty greater than the ransoming of captives. For whatever meritorious purpose money may have been collected it may be diverted in order to ransom captives, even money collected for the purpose of building a synagogue. Even after they bought the wood and the stones and cut them to the needs of the synagogue, which may not ordinarily be sold for an-

other *mitzvah*, it is permitted to sell them in order to redeem captives. But if it is already built, they shall not be sold. One does not redeem captives for more than their value for the sake of the social order, otherwise enemies would exact every effort to take captives, and even if their relatives want to redeem them for more than their value, you shall not permit them. But a man is permitted to redeem himself with all that he wants, and so, too, for his wife who is like his body, and so, too, for a scholar, or even if he is not [yet] a scholar and you see that he is succeeding and it is possible that he may be a scholar, you may redeem him with all that you can. Captives must not flee so the enemies will not increase their suffering and add more guards to their guards... The woman is freed before the man, and if the two of them are forced to engage in a sexual transgression, the man takes precedence for he is not used to this.

**Summary.** It is interesting to note that Maimonides does not alter the thrust of the Talmudic legislation with respect to hostage-taking, other than to increase the emphasis on the relative importance of redeeming the captive and deciding the question of the wife. Similarly, Rabbenu Asher merely codifies without additional comment. However, the *Tur* does place an extra emphasis on the fact that a person may redeem him/herself at whatever price s/he can afford. This is alluded to in the Talmud when justifying the man's obligation to redeem his wife no matter the cost – she is like his body. The *Tur* elects to clearly state the implication of this ruling: not only may the man pay any price for his wife, he may also pay any price for himself.

## Medieval Views
*Sefer Ḥasidim*, Paragraphs #15 and #16,148 (of the Parma MS). In this responsum, *Sefer Ḥasidim* makes very clear that a person who redeems hostages is praiseworthy because he has helped keep women from sexual degradation and men from transgressing the Torah and possible death:

And if a man considers his money to be of equal importance to him as his body, and he redeems hostages [only] because he desires to do so, this is also very meritorious for if he had not redeemed them, another would not have redeemed them. And if women were taken captive and not redeemed, they would engage in intercourse with them. And if they were men, they would force them to transgress the Torah or kill them. Behold, they have been saved from death.

Thus, *Sefer Ḥasidim* changes the focus from the obligation to redeem the hostage to praise for the redeemer, indicating the importance of this duty. Once again, the status of captive is unacceptable -the risks are too great – and therefore the captive must be ransomed. However, the *Sefer Ḥasidim* is careful to note that the ransom payment must not exceed the value of the hostage:

> "And I said to them, 'We have done our best to buy back our Jewish brothers who were sold to the nations.'" (Nehemiah 5:8) From here they said that captives should not be redeemed for more than their value. And there is a disagreement [in a case when the hostage] is wise or righteous and many different people need him.

*The Maharam, Ḥoshen Mishpat* #572 and #576. Rabbi Meir of Rothenburg presents an interesting case because he not only wrote responsa dealing with the issue of hostage-taking, but he also was taken hostage. Rabbi Meir was imprisoned by Rudolf I, who demanded 26,000 pieces of silver for his release. Rabbi Meir refused to be ransomed lest his freedom be purchased to the detriment of the community. Rabbi Meir spent seven years, from 1286 to his death in 1293, in the Rothenburg dungeon rather than permit the Jewish community to comply with Emperor Rudolf's excessive demands. Even his body was not released until fourteen years after his death, when Alexander ben Solomon Wimpfen paid a large sum so that his remains could be buried in Worms.[45]

His responsum includes the following statements:

> Had "A's" children protested against being ransomed, we would have paid no attention to them and would have effected their release even against their will, and then, we would have collected the ransom money from them; for we are obliged to ransom a Jew even against his will.

> A Jew should be ransomed even against his express will, and be charged with the expenses incurred. A captive in the hands of Gentiles is exposed to ruthless treatment and incessant flogging, and his very life is in danger. Therefore, anyone who effects the ransom of a Jew is praiseworthy and is entitled to the expenses incurred. Moreover, Jews threatened by a common danger may force one another to contribute of their means to the measures that will free them of that danger. "A" and "B" have to share the expenses in proportion to their wealth, since they were captured for the purpose of extorting money from them.

Thus, Meir of Rothenburg maintains that any Jew taken hostage must be redeemed, even if s/he does not desire to be redeemed. He justifies this by referring to the harsh treatment which a Jew held by Gentiles is purported to receive. Finally, he makes reference to the concept that those held ransom are obligated to pay back their redeemers "in proportion to their wealth." This, in effect, is treated as a tax. The *Maharam* expands upon this concept when he considers a general threat to the community. If necessary, the Jews are obligated to pay a community tax in order to alleviate the threat.

Note how Meir of Rothenburg's actions deviated from the established norms, including those norms perpetuated by his own responsa. He refused to allow the community, which had raised money through a special community tax, to ransom him on the grounds that it would result in the capture of other scholars. But as a scholar, the community had a special obligation to redeem him at all costs. Following this incident, many responsa appeared challenging Rothenburg's decision. One, *Yam Shel Shlomo*, Responsum #66, authored by Rabbi Solomon Luria, offers the following critique of Rothenburg's action:

> I have heard of the *Maharam* of Rothenburg who was held in a tower in agony for a number of years. And when they sought a large amount of money from the community, the community was prepared to redeem him. And he did not permit them to do so for he said that one does not redeem captives for more than their value. And I am surprised that a scholar was divided [about the proper response] for there was no equal to him in his generation in Torah and in loving-kindness and it was permitted to redeem him for all of the money in the world.

**Summary.** The medieval responsa literature is unified in its approach to hostage-taking incidents, and this approach follows the pattern established by the Talmud. Added to the now familiar obligation to redeem the hostage only at his/her worth are the praise which is garnered by the redeemer and the implicit system of taxation referred to by the *Maharam*. However, Rabbi Meir of Rothenburg's refusal to be redeemed stands in stark contrast to this unanimity. Despite his position as a scholar, he refused to be redeemed for what he obviously considered to be an exorbitant sum. His action, while sharply criticized by rabbis such as Solomon Luria, indicates that perhaps implicit parameters did exist. Certainly, it would be impossible for a community to exchange a scholar "for all of the money in the world." The Maharam believed that limits needed to be imposed, or Jews, and especially scholars, would become the constant victims and targets of hostage-taking incidents. This could not be countenanced as it would lead to the utter disruption of the Jewish communities of the time.

## Early Modern Texts

*Shulḥan Arukh, Yoreh Deah*, 252:1-5; 8-12. In this section of the *Shulḥan Arukh*, Karo simply repeats the earlier codes of Maimonides and the *Tur* concerning hostage-taking:[46]

> 1. Ransoming captives comes before feeding and clothing the poor for there is no greater *mitzvah* than to ransom captives. For whatever meritorious purpose money may have been collected, it may be diverted in order to ransom captives, even money collected for the purpose of building a synagogue. Even after the stone and wood had been bought and squared for a synagogue building, which materials may not ordinarily be sold for some other *mitzvah*, it is permitted to sell them for the purpose of redeeming captives. If, however, the structure is already erected, it may not be sold [for such purpose].
>
> 2. He who shuts his eyes against the ransoming of captives transgresses the negative commandments, "Thou shalt not harden thy heart, nor shut thy hand" (Deut. 15:7), "Neither shalt thou stand idly by the blood of thy neighbor" (Lev. 19:16), and "He shall not rule with vigor over him in thy sight" (Lev. 25:23). He also renders no effect the affirmative commandments, "Thou shalt surely open thy hand unto him" (Deut. 15:8), "That thy brother may live with thee" (Lev. 25:36), "Thou shalt love thy neighbor as thyself" (Lev. 19:18), and "Deliver them that are drawn unto death" (Proverbs 24:11).
>
> 3. Every moment that one delays unnecessarily the ransoming of a captive, it is as if he were to shed blood.
>
> 4. Captives are not be ransomed at an unreasonable price, for the welfare of society; otherwise enemies would exact every effort to take captives. But one may ransom himself at any price...
>
> 5. Captives should not be helped to escape, for the sake of public welfare, lest their captors treat them with greater severity and confine them in closer custody.
>
> 8. A woman is redeemed before a man; but where pederasty is common, the man is given precedence.
>
> 9. If he and his father and his teacher are captives,

he himself comes before his teacher, and his teacher before his father, but his mother comes before all.

10. If a man and his wife are captured, the wife is ransomed first, and the court may seize his property to ransom her. Even if he objects: "Do not ransom her with my property," no attention is paid to him.

11. If a captive has property but does not wish to ransom himself, his ransom is paid against his will.

12. A father is obliged to ransom his son if the father has the means and the son has not.

Thus, once again little has been added to the original legislation. The major distinction in this code is the inclusion of the concept of speed. One who delays in the ransoming of captives is to be considered as one who has shed blood. This serves to re-emphasize the important role which the redeemer plays as well as the legal presumption of the imminent danger of the hostage. This legal presumption becomes the cornerstone upon which most of the rulings are founded.

*Shulḥan Arukh, Even Haezer*, 78:2. Here Karo introduces a new concept which deviates from the previous norm. Isserles immediately challenges this deviation, as do the other commentators:

One does not obligate the husband to redeem his wife for more than her value. Rather, as if she were equal with the other captives.

Isserles' gloss then adds that "he may redeem her with all that he has." *Beit Shmuel* argues that Karo is attempting to respond to the direction not to ransom a person for more than his/her value, but that he has failed to take into account the understanding that "she is like his body." That is to say, that he must do all that is in his power to redeem her, including paying more than her value.

*Arukh Hashulḥan, Yoreh Deah*, 252:1-14. The *Arukh Hashulḥan* reviews the development of the Halakhic literature on hostage-taking, noting that while very little has changed, certain issues are no longer relevant. For example, of the commandment to free the scholar at all costs, the *Arukh Hashulḥan* comments, "and now, in those countries, none of this matters any longer." However, it does offer an interesting challenge to Maimonides' elevation of the Talmudic legislation requiring the redemption of captives to the highest level of *mitzvah*. After all, the *Arukh Hashulḥan* notes, even Maimonides claims that a Torah Scroll may only be sold for the study of Torah and for marriage. "And they did not say also for the redemption of captives."

Thus, the *Arukh Hashulḥan* comments that "all of this was from a previous time," while acknowledging that "even now, in the far-off outskirts of the deserts that are in Asia and Africa, bandits fall upon travelers, and take them into captivity until they are redeemed for a great deal of money." Not viewing hostage-taking as a direct threat, the author feels comfortable challenging the basic assumptions which survived from Talmudic times.

**Summary.** The *Shulḥan Arukh* crystallizes the halakhic response to hostage-taking in an easily understandable format without significantly altering that response, other than an attempt by Karo to diminish the responsibility of the husband vis-a-vis the wife, which is quickly rejected by the commentators. But it is in the period of the Early Modern Texts that a different perspective may finally be detected in the *halakhah*. The *Arukh Hashulḥan* changes the focus from the blueprint for problem-solving offered by the Talmud to a more analytical study. This more contemporary source obviously did not experience the immediacy of the threat and thus felt comfortable challenging even the most basic Talmudic assumptions, such as the degree of importance accorded to the redemption of hostages.

# The Jewish Perspective Vis-a-Vis The Case

## There is no greater mitzvah than to redeem captives:

This theme runs throughout the sources, except for the *Arukh Hashulḥan* which acknowledges the importance of redeeming hostages but questions whether such a broad-scale claim can be supported. The legal presumption is that hostages face imminent danger to their survival and must be redeemed at once. Delay in this matter is likened to the spilling of blood, as the danger may be of actual physical harm, such as flogging, sexual degradation, or even death. Thus, any response employed must consider this factor. The target would be prohibited from engaging in long-term negotiations designed to effect the release of the hostage. Too much time might pass during which the hostage would be exposed to an unacceptable level of risk. A hard response would have to be developed quickly, with little opportunity for practice. If the target must share decision-making responsibility with others, the increased potential for disruption would render the implementation of a hard response quite difficult as the time requisite for agreeing on a plan would be limited. Similarly, a soft response would be hamstrung by such a condition. A target with a reputation for settling quickly would be hard-pressed to negotiate an acceptable value exchange. Nevertheless, the target is mandated under Jewish law to redeem the hostages, and to do so as quickly as possible.

Determining the target is apparently of little issue under Jewish law. Instead, levels of responsibility are delineated which extend from the victim him/herself to the community as a whole. The victim must provide all of the resources which s/he has in order to pay-off the ransom. The victim has no choice in this matter, as the court is authorized to sell the victim's property to raise the needed money even over the objections of the victim. Likewise, the husband is obligated to redeem his wife at any price, and the court may sell the husband and wife's property to raise the needed money even over their objections. The next level of responsibility is the community at large. When faced with a threat, the community may tax itself, use monies donated for other charitable purposes, or even sell material designated for the building of a synagogue in order to raise the necessary funds. The primary obligation of the target must be the redemption of the hostage as quickly as possible.

Thus, the four Jews abducted in Lebanon must be ransomed. The target is the State of Israel, which the *halakhah* would recognize as the Jewish community-at-large. Israel is obligated to respond quickly on behalf of the captives in a manner designed to win their release from what the law presumes to be a perilous situation. Direct negotiations with the offenders would be mandated in an effort to gain the release of the hostages as soon as possible.

## Captives are not to be ransomed at an unreasonable price:

This condition prohibits the payment of inflated ransom payments on behalf of hostages for the welfare of society. Recognizing that if a target earned a reputation for paying any amount in order to effect the release of its hostages, offenders would stalk that target without mercy, the *halakhah* forbids targets from engaging in this practice with the exception of two cases: husbands on behalf of their wives, and communities on behalf of their scholars. While this second case appears to be rather self-serving, and is, in fact, challenged by Rabbi Meir of Rothenburg's actions, we learn from the *Arukh Hashulḥan* that by early modern days the question had ceased to be of issue. While it is difficult to ascertain what a reasonable price would be, the *halakhah* directs us that a reasonable price is that which could be obtained for the hostage on the open slave market. While such a market does not exist today, it is possible to extrapolate that human beings are presumably of equivalent value. Thus, with respect to the case at hand, a price of three hundred human beings in exchange for four human beings appears to be unbalanced. Such a payment would not be countenanced by the *halakhah*.

Israel would not be permitted to accept this price, and due to the conditions already established, would have to respond with a counteroffer designed to quickly effect the release of the hostages. As noted above, while conducting negotiations under these circumstances would be quite difficult, Israel's decision not to enter into any type of negotiations with the offenders would be soundly rejected by the *halakhah*. But Israel's refusal to trade three hundred terrorists for four Jews could be accepted as being too steep a price to pay.

## Captives should not be helped to escape:

Designed to prevent further abuse of the hostages, this stipulation effectively rules out any hard response under Jewish law. The primary consideration must always be the welfare of the hostages. This overwhelming concern is the impetus behind all of the halakhic legislation – the entire process was set up to safeguard the hostages, both physically and spiritually. Thus, Israel's decision to employ a military response would be rejected by the *halakhah*. The soft response, with its focus on negotiation and cooperation, would be favored as any other approach might lead directly to further harm to the hostages. In this case, the logic behind this line of reasoning becomes evident, at least in the short run, as Israel's use of the military directly resulted in the murder of the four hostages. Such an outcome would, perhaps, have been avoided if Israel had utilized a soft response.

## A Personal Perspective Vis-a-Vis the Case

The case of the four Jews taken hostage in Lebanon posits the question of what Israel ought to do when faced with such situations. Israel elected to employ a hard response in order to effect the release of the hostages. The ethical literature seems to indicate that, given the circumstances, this was not the ethical response. While fulfilling the requisite conditions justifying Israel's decision to respond as opposed to some other actor, the response did not have a reasonable likelihood of success and did not generate more good than evil. While the utilitarian would support Israel's decision, especially when one factors in the long-term benefits of such a decision, both the deontologist and the libertarian would reject the decision. The deontologist for its lack of concern for individual human beings, and the libertarian for its involvement on behalf of non-nationals. From the halakhic perspective, Israel's action failed two of the three conditions. Israel did not respond quickly in a manner which redeemed four Jews held hostage. Israel attempted, contrary to Jewish law, to help hostages escape from their captivity. While refusing to pay an unreasonable price for their lives was proper, the *halakhah* might also question Israel's decision to absolutely refuse to negotiate. Thus, Israel's response is difficult to justify from any theoretical angle we have investigated.

However, I am left to wonder how the various systems of ethical decision-making and how Jewish law would have responded had a rescue effort, in fact, succeeded. Setting aside, for the moment, the reality that Israel never truly engaged in a rescue mission, but rather increased its military activity in the area, striking at the military bases of those organizations believed to be responsible for the incident, what if Israel's hard response effected the release of the hostages?

A success, I believe, would radically alter the various equations. For example, it would be difficult to challenge the reasonable likelihood of success of a mission which has already succeeded. Likewise, if the hostages had been freed from their captivity, would not more good have been achieved than evil, both in the short and the long-run? Would the deontologist engage Israeli policy makers in debate over whether or not the hostages' lives had been used as a means to achieving an end if that end had been the saving of their lives? On the ethical side, the only remaining obstacle would be the libertarian whose argument was in no way contingent upon the success or the failure of the mission.

On the Jewish side, freeing the hostages would certainly fulfill the condition that the redemption of captives is of the greatest import, providing that the rescue mission occurred sooner rather than later. The second condition, too, would have been met, as no unreasonable price would have been paid on behalf of the hostages. The third condition, that which prohibits aiding hostages escape, appears less relevant in this case as it is difficult to ascertain how the condition of the four men in question could have been made more difficult. And their eventual murder enables us to assert, albeit retroactively, the condition of *pikuaḥ nefesh*, the saving of a life, for which all regulations save three may be overturned.[47]

The fact that the judgments which these systems render are so easily swayed by the eventual outcome, by the consequences, is vexing. I would prefer a system free of such flexibility. And yet, I am attracted to those systems which work when applied to specific cases.

Of the ethical systems, the utilitarian system remains, a system which focuses upon consequences. Alexander Haig's argument is enticing, and the long-term perspective which it offers appears useful. Although Israel's response in this case was misdirected – a hard response which was not a clear attempt to rescue the hostages' lives – a message was delivered to potential offenders: we will not negotiate with you, so hostage-taking will not aid you in achieving your objectives. The offenders, apparently, have listened, as there have been few attempts to take Jews or Israelis hostage since then. The Jewish response is more troubling, perhaps because, as Solomon Freehof notes:

> A sharp distinction must be made between the Jewish experience in the past and the modern situation. The earlier taking of captives was almost entirely the work of pirates for gain. Therefore, all that was needed was money to ransom the hostages. But the modern hijacking generally has a different purpose, not financial but political, i.e., to force a hated nation to suffer. Therefore the mere paying of money is no solution to the modern problem.[48]

Any target attempting to employ the Jewish system when faced with a political hostage-taking situation would be completely unable to function. The obligation to respond quickly without the use of military force, coupled with the obligation to avoid paying excessive ransoms, would render the target immobile. Times have changed to such an extent that the halakhic response, despite the Jewish people's thousands of years of experience with hostage-taking situations, and despite the many important lessons which the *halakhah* has to offer about our social responsibilities, has become irrelevant.

Thus, it would be my recommendation that Israel's response to political hostage-taking situations such as that delineated by the case be hard. The demands challenged Israel's system of law beyond its capacity to respond without doing great domestic damage. The threat was minor, from a utilitarian perspective, when compared with the possible ramifications of giving in to the demands. Offenders everywhere would have learned that taking Jewish hostages would best achieve their political goals. Israel's standing in the international community could, at that time, suffer no further significant damage, as its troops already occupied a great deal of Lebanon in defiance of numerous United Nations resolutions. Domestic public opinion was overwhelmingly opposed to any possible exchange. Israel was sufficiently proximate, possessed the military might, recognized the need, and was certainly the last resort for the survival of those four men. Given the training and track-record of Israel's anti-terrorist units, there was a high likelihood of success, a success which would have achieved more good than evil in both the short and the long run. The hostages served as both the means and the end of Israel's policy of no negotiation – we will not talk with you, but we will free our people. Finally, despite the objections of the libertarians, Israel recognized that it was morally beholden to those held hostage.

# Reflections on the Process

How does the modern Jew effectively straddle the two worlds in which s/he lives? One foot is firmly planted in the present, with its focus on logic and rationalism. The other planted in the past, with its focus on tradition and obligation. This effort at applied ethics has helped me to distinguish what my role is in this process. I mediate between the past and its mandates, and the present and its mandates. A case is presented. I investigate what the *halakhah* has to say. I am surprised to find a great deal of halakhic material, and surprised that the *halakhah* has, over the centuries, remained relatively uniform in its approach. I do not need to concern myself with choosing between differing halakhic norms. But somehow, in the final analysis, I am disappointed with what the *halakhah* has to offer. The claim is made that one can find all of life's answers in the *halakhah*, that one can live by its conditions. This is not true. The *halakhah* developed primarily in a different historical context from my own. It understands hostage-taking, but not political hostage-taking, a concept which was not relevant to the Jews of that day. And then I realize that unless the *halakhah* had provided that answer which I already believed to be true, or which the ethical literature of my day had convinced me was true, it would not be relevant for me. I would never accept the judgment of a rabbi from long ago over a contemporary thinker unless I was already predisposed to rejecting the contemporary thinker and was looking for support for my decision. But I do believe that I allowed the *halakhah* to speak for itself. I was not predisposed to rejecting the *halakhah qua halakhah*. I would have preferred to find that the halakhic approach matched my own. Yet I remain firm in my conviction that when a modern liberal Jew faces a decision, s/he must avail him/herself of all available sources, from the *halakhah* to the most recent ethical teachings of our day.

# Bibliography

Agus, Irving. *Rabbi Meir of Rothenburg.* New York: Ktav Publishing House, 1970.

Antokol, Norman, and Mayer Nudell. *No One A Neutral: Political Hostage-Taking in the Modern World.* Ohio: Alpha Publications of Ohio, 1990.

Aston, Clive. *A Contemporary Crisis: Political Hostage-Taking and the Experience of Western Europe.* Connecticut: Greenwood Press, 1982.

Beauchamp, Tom, and Norman Bowie. *Ethical Theory and Business.* Englewood Cliffs: Prentice Hall, 1988.

Bernstein, Richard. "Jews in Lebanon Urged to Get Out." *The New York Times,* February 24, 1986.

Boustany, Nora. "Three Hundred Prisoners are Released by Israel – Shi'ites Demand Freeing of Remaining Four Hundred Thirty-Five." *The Washington Post,* July 4, 1985.

Bowie, Norman, and Ronald Duska. *Business Ethics.* Englewood Cliffs: Prentice Hall, 1990.

Broder, Jonathan. "Israelis Sweep into Lebanon." *Chicago Tribune,* February 19, 1986.

Carlton, David, and Carlo Schaerf. *Contemporary Terror: Studies in Sub-State Violence.* New York: St. Marten's Press, 1981.

Dobson, Christopher, and Ronald Payne. *Terror! The West Fights Back.* London: MacMillan Press Limited, 1982.

Freedman, Lawrence Zelic, and Yonah Alexander. *Perspectives on Terrorism.* Wilmington: Scholarly Resources, 1983.

Freehof, Solomon. *Today's Reform Responsa.* USA: Hebrew Union College Press, 1990.

Friedman, Thomas. "Furor in Israel." *The New York Times,* May 22, 1985.

Haig, Alexander. "Seize the Initiative From Terrorists." *The New York Times,* August 15, 1989.

Horowitz, George. *The Spirit of Jewish Law.* New York, Central Book Company, 1963.

"International." United Press International, July 2, 1985, AM cycle.

"International." United Press International, December 26, 1985, AM cycle.

"International News." Reuters, January 2, 1986, AM cycle.

"International News." Reuters, January 6, 1986, AM cycle.

Kegley, Charles. *International Terrorism: Characteristics, Causes, Controls.* New York: St. Martin's Press, 1990.

Kupperman, Robert, and Jeff Kamen. "Greece, Haven for Terrorists." *The New York Times,* December 16, 1988.

Kupperman, Robert, and Darrell Trent. *Terrorism: Threat, Reality, Response.* Stanford: Hoover Institution Press, 1979.

"The Madrid Conference Demonstration Trial – Rescue of Hostages Case." *Israel Law Review,* April 1981.

Maher, George. Hostage: *A Police Approach to a Contemporary Crisis.* Illinois: Charles C. Thomas, 1977.

Markham, James. "Now It's Chirac Who Decides He Can Deal for Hostages." *The New York Times*, December 6, 1987.

McGrory, Mary. "Defying the Deadly Silence." *The Washington Post*, April 8, 1986.

Miller, Abraham. *Terrorism and Hostage Negotiations.* Boulder: Westview Press, 1980.

Miron, Murray, and Arnold Goldstein. *Hostage.* New York: Pergamon Press, 1979.

Netanyahu, Benjamin. *Terrorism: How the West Can Win.* New York: Avon Books, 1986.

Rapoport, David, and Yonah Alexander. *The Morality of Terrorism: Religious and Secular Justifications.* New York: Columbia University Press, 1989.

*Sefer Ḥasidim.* J. Wistinetski and J. Friedman (eds). Frankfurt: Wahrmann, 1924.

Segaller, Stephen. *Invisible Armies: Terrorism into the 1990s.* New York: Harcourt Brace Jovanovich, 1987.

Rivers, Gayle. *The War Against the Terrorists: How to Win It.* New York: Stein and Day, 1986.

"U.N. Official Reports to Israelis on Lebanese Jews." Reuters, March 11, 1986, AM cycle.

"The World." *The Los Angeles Times*, November 18, 1985.

Young, Oran. *The Politics of Force: Bargaining During International Crises.* Princeton: Princeton University Press, 1968.

# Notes

1. Alexander M. Haig Jr., "Seize the Initiative From Terrorists" *The New York Times*, August 15, 1989, Sec. A, p. 21, col. 2.

2. Mary McGrory, "Defying the Deadly Silence" *The Washington Post,* April 8, 1986, Sec. A, p. 2.

3. Clive Aston, *A Contemporary Crisis: Political Hostage-Taking and the*

*Experience of Western Europe* (Connecticut: Greenwood Press, 1982), p. 33. The analysis which follows is based upon Aston's approach.

4. Oran Young, *The Politics of Force: Bargaining During International Crises* (Princeton: Princeton University Press, 1968), p. 15.

5. Aston, p. 37.

6. The overview which follows is based upon the analysis of David Carlton and Carlo Schaerf, *Contemporary Terror: Studies in Sub-State Violence* (New York: St. Marten's Press, 1981), pp. 78-82.

7. For further information on this topic, see: George Maher, *Hostage: A Police Approach to a Contemporary Crisis* (Illinois: Charles C. Thomas, 1977), pp. 9-13.

8. For further information on the Stockholm Syndrome, see: Abraham Miller, *Terrorism and Hostage Negotiations* (Boulder: Westview Press, 1980), p. 46.

9. Carlton and Schaerf, p. 82.

10. For further information on the stakeholder theory, see: Tom Beauchamp and Norman Bowie, *Ethical Theory and Business* (Englewood Cliffs: Prentice Hall, 1988), pp. 100-105.

11. Thomas Friedman, "Furor in Israel." *The New York Times,* May 22, 1985, Sec. A, p. 1, col 2.

12. For further information on the role of the media, see: Charles Kegley, *International Terrorism: Characteristics, Causes, Controls* (New York: St. Marten's Press, 1990) pp. 241-244.

13. In order to facilitate a clear presentation, transliterations, titles, and translations have been rendered uniform by the author.

14. "The World," *The Los Angeles Times*, November 18, 1985, Sec. 1, p. 2, col. 1.

15. "International," United Press International, July 2, 1985, AM cycle.

16. "International," United Press International, December 26, 1985, AM cycle.

17. "International News," Reuters, January 2, 1986, AM cycle.

18. "International News," Reuters, January 6, 1986, AM cycle.

19. "The World," *The Los Angeles Times*, February 19, 1986, Sec. 1, p. 2, col. 1.

20. Richard Bernstein, "Jews in Lebanon Urged to Get Out" *The New York Times*, February 24, 1986, Sec. A, p. 3, col. 6.

21. "U.N. Official Reports to Israelis on Lebanese Jews," Reuters, March 11, 1986, AM cycle.

22. This was also occasioned by the abduction of two Israeli soldiers. See, Jonathan Broder, "Israelis Sweep into Lebanon" *Chicago Tribune,* February 19, 1986, Sec. News, p. 1, zone C.

23. Norman Antokol and Mayer Nudell, *No one a Neutral: Political Hostage-Taking in the Modern World* (Ohio: Alpha Publications of Ohio, 1990), p. 166. The analysis which follows is based upon Antokol and Nudell, pp. 167-172.

24. Stephen Segaller, *Invisible Armies: Terrorism into the 1990s* (New York: Harcourt Brace Jovanovich, 1987), p. 193.

25. Antokol and Nudell, p. 168.

26. Greece, too, has long been known for its soft approach. See, Robert Kupperman and Jeff Kamen, "Greece, Haven for Terrorists" *The New York Times,* December 16, 1988, Sec. A, p. 39, col. 1.

27. James Markham, "Now It's Chirac Who Decides He Can Deal for Hostages" *The New York Times,* December 6, 1987, Sec. 4, p. 2, col. 1.

28. Norman Bowie and Ronald Duska, *Business Ethics* (Englewood Cliffs: Prentice Hall, 1990), pp. 34-39.

29. The following is based upon the analysis of Kegley, pp. 213-218.

30. Miller, p. 25.

31. Kegley, p. 214.

32. Ibid., p. 216.

33. Ibid., p. 216.

34. Ibid., p. 218.

35. Beauchamp and Bowie, p. 26.

36. Haig, Sec. A, p. 21, col. 2.

37. Ibid., Sec. A, p. 21, col. 2.

38. Beauchamp and Bowie, p. 33.

39. Bowie and Duska, p. 46.

40. Carlton and Schaerf, p. 84.

41. Ibid., p. 7.

42. Beauchamp and Bowie, p. 556.

43. "Israeli authorities had evidence that the suspects had been involved in

anti-Israel attacks or were preparing for them." Nora Boustany, "Three Hundred Prisoners are Released by Israel – Shi'ites Demand Freeing of Remaining Four Hundred Thirty-Five." *The Washington Post*, July 4, 1985, Sec. A, p. 1.

44. "In the last few months, a few quiet efforts have been made here to win the release of the Jews being held prisoner. Catholic, Protestant, and Jewish spokesmen here have called on Muslim clerics in Lebanon to speak out against the taking of Jewish hostages. Serge Klarsfeld, a French lawyer who has tracked down former Nazis, went to West Beirut last week to appeal to local religious leaders to condemn the hostage seizures in Lebanon and to offer himself in exchange for the hostages." Bernstein, Sec . A, p. 3, col. 6.

45. For further information on Rabbi Meir of Rothenburg, see: Irving Agus, *Rabbi Meir of Rothenburg* (New York: Ktav Publishing House, 1970).

46. George Horowitz, *The Spirit of Jewish Law* (New York: Central Book Company, 1963), pp. 127-129.

47. *Pikuaḥ nefesh* – regard for human life – is the duty to save a person when that person's life is in danger. Only when the choice is between death and idolatry, unlawful intercourse, or murder is death preferred. (*Sanhedrin* 74a-b).

48. Solomon Freehof, *Today's Reform Responsa* (USA: Hebrew Union College Press, 1990), p. 116.

# Obedience to Which Commander ?

## An Examination of a Soldier's Right to Refuse Orders

Michael Feshbach
and Peter Schaktman

**D**iscipline is a necessary feature of any military organization. The goal of armies and other military institutions is to wage and win wars, "to compel our enemy to do our will,"[1] and this cannot take place but in the presence of a clearly-understood system of military discipline which calls upon officers to give orders to soldiers who can be counted upon to obey them. But how should a soldier, in particular a soldier wishing to realize the ethical imperatives of the Jewish tradition, respond when given an order that appears to be immoral? To what extent can a soldier be expected to resolve this apparent conflict between the demands of discipline and the dictates of conscience? This dilemma, posed here in abstract terms of the individual Jewish soldier, takes on dimensions that are far more acute when put into the context of the Israel Defense Forces, a military force which is presumed to be concerned with the preservation and actualization of Jewish values.

The aim of this study is the mediation of the classical halakhic response to this question on the one hand, and the contributions of general ethical theory toward its solution on the other. In the classical literature, the discussion revolves in the main around the notions of *shliḥut* (agency), in particular, the criminal liability of an appointed agent; and *ones* (compulsion), understood more specifically as *sakanat mavet* (upon threat of death).

In the general ethical material, the above issues are likewise of central importance, along with certain notions of international law such as manifest illegality, the personal knowledge principle and the doctrine of obedience to superior orders (*respondeat superior*). Then, freed of their limited jurisprudential definitions, they be-come elements of the analysis of our problem from within the basic moral theories of utilitarianism and non-consequentialism. The question of "evil intent" (*mens rea*) is also introduced in the contemporary literature.

## The Question in Jewish Tradition

The halakhic tradition reflects for the most part the concerns of the Jewish community out of which it grew. For some 2000 years, the exile and national powerlessness of the Jewish nation precluded the existence of any specifically Jewish military institutions. Hence the relative silence of the rabbis regarding the specific issues of war and warfare. Nevertheless, it is possible to deduce something of the meta-halakhic intent of the rabbis, by examining some of the halakhic texts and categories that are germane to our problem.

## On the Relation Between Commander and Commanded

The text of *Kiddushin* 41b details the legal status of a sacrifice per-formed by a *shohet* on behalf of the greater Jewish community and goes on to establish the principle of *shlihut*, whereby a person may legitimately engage another to act as an agent on his or her behalf:

> For Rabbi Joshua ben Karcha said: How do we know that a man's agent is as himself? Because it is said, "and the whole assembly of the congregation shall kill it [the Passover sacrifice] at even (Exodus 12:6); does then the whole assembly really slaughter? surely, only one person slaughters [an animal]; *hence it follows that a man's agent is as himself.*"[2]

In this case, any act performed by the *shaliah* (agent) in his role as such, has the same force as if it had been done by the *m'shaleiah* (solicitor) (*shluho shel adam kemoto*).

In *Baba Kama* 51a however, this concept of agency is seen to have a more limited scope. The example comes from a discussion of liability regarding a pit which is dug in public ground by an agent engaged to do so by two partners:

> "...how is it possible for a pit in public ground to be in charge of two partners? [For if you say that] both of them appointed an agent and said to him: 'Go forth and dig for us,' and he went and dug for them, [we reply that] *there can be no agency for a sinful act.*"

If someone falls into the pit, the agent, not the employer, is liable, based on the notion that *ein shaliah ledavar averah* – "there can be no agency for wrong-doing." In other words, a person, even when acting at the direction and as the agent of another, is held accountable for his or her own misdeeds, in this case, not covering a pit placed in public ground.

But what if the agent is not capable of responsibly carrying out an order? In *Kiddushin* 42b the situation described is that of a *heresh* (a deaf-mute), a *shoteh* (an incurably dull-witted person) or a *katan* (a child), all considered legally incompetent, being appointed as an agent to burn [a farmer's] fields:

> "He who sends forth a conflagration by a deaf-mute, idiot, or minor, is not liable [for the damage caused] by law of man, yet liable by the law of Heaven. But if he sends it by a normal person, the latter is [legally] liable. Yet why so? Let us say that a man's agent is as himself. There it is different, for there is no agent *for wrongdoing, for we reason: [When] the words of the master and the words of the pupil [are in conflict], whose words are obeyed?"*

In such a case, the agent, recognized to be incompetent, is not held responsible for the possible result of his action (i.e., the setting of a fire that gets out of control). Here, the principle that there is no agency for wrongdoing, and that each person is ultimately culpable for his own actions, relies on the presumption that the agent that is engaged is intellectually capable of such responsibility. If not, he is considered to be *patur* (released) from liability. His employer however, understood to be likewise *patur* from human justice (*dinei adam* – based on the notion that *ein shaliah ledavar averah)* is nonetheless held to bear responsibility before the court of Divine justice (*dinei shamayim)*, that is, to be culpable somehow in a moral sense.

This *Kiddushin* passage also contains an important statement of principle related to the issue of a *shaliah's* responsibility, namely, *"Divrei harav v'divrei talmid; divrei mi shomim? –"* [When] the words of the master and the words of the pupil [are in conflict], whose words are obeyed?" Clearly, when the commands of the temporal king (or government) come into conflict with the demands of the Divine King (i.e., the *mitzvot)*, it is the latter that take priority.

The notion that *ein shaliah ledavar averah* is further supported by the following section of *Kiddushin* 43a:

> "If he says to his agent, 'Go forth and slay a soul,' the latter is liable, and his sender is exempt. Shammai the Elder said on the authority of Haggai the Prophet:

His sender is liable, for it is said, 'thou hast slain
him with the sword of Ammon' (Samuel II 12:9). ...What
is meant by liable? He is liable by the laws of Heaven."

Again, when an agent is engaged for evildoing (in this case,
murder), the agent assumes full responsibility for the fulfillment of
his act. It should be noted that Shammai offers a counter-argument
here that in fact the sender is culpable, based on the passage from
Haggai. The later redactors of the Talmud however, in an apparent
attempt to preserve the original thrust of the *ein shaliaḥ ledavar
averah* principle, quickly assert that Shammai's statement refers to the
culpability of the sender according to *dinei shamayim* (i.e., unen-
forceable on earth), but not according to *dinei adam*.

In the later legal literature, the two principle of *shluho shel
adam kemoto* and *ein shaliaḥ ledavar averah* are both reaffirmed.
Thus the *Tur* states: "A man's agent is like himself in every way, except in the case of evildoing, for we hold that there is no agency for
wrongdoing."[3] Later, commenting on an almost identical passage in
the *Shulḥan Arukh*, Isserles ties the culpability of the *shaliaḥ* to
his awareness of the illegality of his appointed task:

After the thief hides that which he has stolen, he is
forced to leave the town such that he can no longer
smuggle the goods [himself]. Later, he sends another to bring him the goods. [Upon being discovered,]
The *shaliaḥ* is obliged to pay the fine for the theft,
because he knew the goods were stolen.[4]

Here, as in the passage from *Kiddushin* 42b, the issue of the
agent's cognizance is given great weight, but only to his detriment.
It is not at all clear whether this passage can be legitimately interpreted to mean that lack of cognizance absolves the *shaliaḥ* from
liability.

Returning to the Talmud, there is one case where the principle of *ein shaliaḥ ledavar averah* is absolutely rejected. The example involves the culpability of, as in the very first example, a
*shoḥet* slaughtering an animal, in this case, a stolen animal, on another's behalf:

If he stole [a sheep or an ox] and gave it to another
person who slaughtered it, or if he stole it and gave it
to another person who sold it,... he would have to
make four-fold and five-fold payments. What is this
meant to tell us? ... [this implies] that in this case the
law of agency has application even for a matter
involving transgression. Though in the whole of Torah
[there is] no [case of an] agent entrusted with a matter involving transgression [rendering the principle
liable], in this case an agent entrusted with a matter
involving transgression would render his principal

liable, the reason being [that Scripture says:] 'And he slaughter it or sell it,' implying *that just as a sale cannot be effected without the intervention of some other person, so also where the slaughter was effected [by some other person authorized by the thief to do so, the thief would be liable]."*[5]

Here, agency is assigned for the performance of an act which in and of itself requires both the agent and the solictor for its execution (i.e., the agent is not being solicited to perform an act that the solictor was capable of doing on his own).

Taken together, these texts reflect a generally consistent understanding of the relationship between the commander and the commanded.

Within a military context, a soldier is analogous to the *shaliah* of the Talmudic text; like a *shaliah*, the soldier is sent forth with a particular mission, that is, to perform a set of tasks on behalf of a military or political entity. But consistent with the *ein shaliah ledavar averah* principle, a *shaliah*-soldier may be presumed to be liable for performing an illegal act, even when acting in the context of executing a superior order. As stated in later legal literature, *respondeat superior non excusat* – "following orders is no excuse."

The question regarding the competence of the *shaliah* is a bit more complicated in this case. Clearly, an individual who is physically or mentally incompetent to be a soldier (by modern standards) would not be considered liable for negligence beyond his realistic control. But what of the individual whose training and/or ability in military and/or moral thinking is simply deficient? The voice of the rabbis is unclear on this point. Similarly, while it seems evident that a soldier who executes an order known to him to be illegal is culpable, it is yet unclear as to what responsibility is assigned to a soldier who obeys an order which he did not, at the time, know was illegal.

The final Talmud passage cited (*Baba Kama* 79a) leaves open yet another question. Namely, is the soldier as a *shaliah* called upon to perform actions that could be performed by his commanding officers (in which case the latter are exculpated for his wrongdoing, even if done while following their orders), or is the regressive chain of command in the military absolutely intrinsic to the functioning of the army (in which case we understand the illegal order to be a outgrowth of the system itself, implicating everyone who is a part of it)? As should already be apparent, the answers to this and other questions of liability for wrongdoing will ultimately play a critical role in solving our  original dilemma.

## Under What Circumstances
## Should An Illegal Order
## Be Disobeyed?

Sitting at an unusual session in Lydda, the rabbis determined when it was permissible to violate the *mitzvot* of the Torah, and when it was not:

> "Rabbi Johanan said in the name of Rabbi Simeon ben Jehozadak: ...in every [other] law of the Torah, if a man is commanded: 'Transgress and suffer not death' he may transgress and not suffer death, excepting idolatry, incest, [which includes adultery] and murder. Now may not idolatry be practiced [in these circumstances]? Has it not been taught: Rabbi Ishmael said: Whence do we know that if a man was bidden, 'Engage in idolatry and save your life', that he should do so, and not be slain? From the verse, ['Ye shall therefore keep my statutes and my judgments; which if a man do,] he shall live in them (Lev. 18:5):' but not die by them. I might think that it may even be openly practised, but Scripture teaches, 'Neither shall ye profane my holy name; but I will be hallowed (Lev. 22:32).'"[6]

They thus elucidated the principle that when faced with a *sakanat mavet* (threat of death), a Jew must violate the laws of the Torah rather than allow himself to be killed, except when ordered to violate the three *mitzvot hamurot* (cardinal sins): *avodah zarah* (idolatry), *gilui arayot* (sexual impropriety) and *sh'fikhut damim* (murder). In these cases, death is to be chosen over transgression. The doctrine of duress as a defense is thus stated, and then immediately limited.

Later Maimonides, in codifying this Talmudic concept, adds an important element to the halakhic perspective on this issue:

> Regarding one to whom it is said, "Transgress [a lesser commandment], lest you be killed," and who allows himself to be killed, behold, he is culpable for his own life. And regarding one to whom it is said, "Kill and do not disobey," and who dies rather than disobey [God], behold this is Sanctification of the Divine Name. ...And regarding one to whom it is said, "Kill and do not disobey," and who transgresses and is [therefore] not killed, behold he has desecrated the Divine Name. ...*But nevertheless, because he transgressed under duress (ones), we do not give him stripes; it needn't be added that a Beit Din does not sentence him to death, even though he killed, [for it was] under duress.*[7]

The charge to *Yehareg v'al ya'avor* (Be killed rather than

transgress) now takes on the character of a *l'khathilah/b'diavad* situation; *l'khathilah* (*a priori*), one must die rather than commit a *mitzvah hamurah*, but *b'diavad* (*ex post facto*), the sinner is understood to have been acting under *ones*, and is therefore exculpated. In his gloss to the same passage in Maimonides, Joseph Caro (a.k.a. *Kesef Mishneh*) seems to take the Talmudic thinking in just the opposite direction; he proposes that in cases where the morale of the Jewish community is at stake, even a "lesser" *mitzvah* should not be violated, even if the result is death.

Yet another source of insight regarding the abrogation of normative *mitzvot* is the so-called "law of pursuit" found in the Talmud: *Haba lehorgekha hashkem lehorgo* – "If one seeks to kill you, kill him first." The halakhic tradition, it should be noted, understands this principle to apply not only when one's own life is being threatened, but likewise when the threat is to another.[8] Also, while this principle applies mainly to situations where individuals are endangered, "[it] is certainly no less applicable when it is an entire community or nation, rather than an individual, which is pursued."[9]

We must also take into account the fact that Jewish tradition only recognizes two different categories of wars. Jews are permitted to engage in a *milhemet mitzvah,* an "obligatory war" and, under rare circumstances, a *milhemet reshut,* a "discretionary war." The first category solely involves situations in which the defense or survival of Judaism or the Jewish people is at stake, or other special circumstances specifically mandated by the Torah (e.g., the war against Amalek). A discretionary war, on the other hand, is a war fought in order to expand the boundaries of a Jewish state, or to increase the glory of a Jewish ruler. Because this latter category of war requires the approval of a Sanhedrin as well as the assent of the *urim* and *tumim*; in the absence of these institutions this kind of war is simply not possible today.

In discretionary wars, certain groups of potential soldiers are automatically exempted from military service. These include men who have recently married, built a home, or planted a vineyard. But these exemptions do not apply to the situation of an obligatory war, which is, it must be remembered, the only type of war that can legally take place since the demise of the Sanhedrin.[10] As J. David Bleich notes, "Under such circumstances any action – indeed any word – which gives support to the enemy is an action which endangers Jewish lives and as such is categorically forbidden by Jewish law."[11] Thus, it would seem to follow that in the case of wars fought under Jewish auspices, which are by definition "wars of obligation," any disobedience to the orders of a superior officer could be construed as giving suuport to the enemy, and therefore, "categorically forbidden by Jewish law."

With regard to when a soldier should disobey an illegal order then, our texts offer us a number of important guidelines. It seems clear, for example, that when an illegal order is accompanied by the threat, real or implied, of self-annihilation, a soldier is obligated by the Jewish tradition to violate all legal strictures, with the significant exception of orders calling for him to engage in murder (i.e., the wanton slaughter of civilians) or sexual violation (i.e., rape). It is not immediately clear how *avodah zarah* might be understood in the modern context; neither is the halakhic tradition of one mind about its character as a sin worthy of dying for.

The tradition does however appear to recognize the nature of duress implied by a threat of death upon disobedience. While not giving license to a soldier to engage in heinous sins like those mentioned above, it does acknowledge that a soldier cannot be punished following such a transgression in the way he might be punished were the act to have occurred off the battlefield.

Of possibly the greatest significance is the tradition's apparent call for soldiers to engage in critical reflection upon the legality of orders received, and upon the consistency of the orders with the mandates of the Jewish tradition. The following section explores this important principle with greater detail.

## The Ethics of Examination and Protest

An aggadic passage from the Talmud offers further insight into the question of refusing an illegal order:

> "'And the Lord will return his [Yoav's] blood upon his own head because he fell upon two men more righteous and better than he.' 'Better,' because they interpreted aright [the particles] *akh* and *rak* whilst he did not; 'More righteous,' because they were instructed verbally, yet did not obey, whereas he instructed in a letter, and nevertheless carried it out."[12]

In describing the source of Yoav's culpability for the deaths of Avner and Amasa, the text asserts that the latter two were "good and righteous;" their goodness came from their critical examination of the orders they were given in terms of their consistency with the laws of the Torah, and their righteousness derived from their immediate disobedience to Saul when he wrongly commanded them to kill the priests of Nob.

This passage accomplishes several things. It is, to be sure, a comment on a verse which seems to be unusual or surprising – and in its description of this unusual situation it affirms that obedience to orders is the generally expected norm. Beyond that, however, this passage acknowledges that there are times in which close scrutiny of instructions from a superior is the right course of action. We may not be able to demand this level of scrutiny from everyone, but the practice of such scrutiny is nevertheless a sign of righteousness.

A similar image of religiously-sanctioned disobedience to authority reappears in the *Mishneh Torah*, where Maimonides writes:

> "One who ignores the order of the king in order to busy himself in Torah, even a *mitzvah* of lesser gradation, is released [from his obligations to the king]. [For in the case of a conflict between] the words of the master and the words of a slave, the words of the master take priority. And there is no need to state that if the king's order [requires] that a *mitzvah* be violated, he is not listened to."13

Thus, we learn that a (civilian) subject may be expected to analyze the justice of the orders he is given, and that he will be considered praiseworthy if he refuses to obey orders that conflict with the principles of Torah.

Both of these passages, the aggadic and the legal, each affirm the primacy of Torah and the God who revealed it. They suggest to the modern soldier as well as the civilian, that he reflect upon the consistency of the orders he is given with the laws contained in the Torah, and to refuse to violate any order which conflicts with these laws. Furthermore, the soldier is urged to follow the examples of Avner and Amasa by refusing to obey such illegal orders with haste, that is, without even a thought toward sacrificing the Torah tradition.

An important question needs to be addressed at this point. Is it fair to apply this and similar texts, based as they are on civilian situations, to the military arena? We believe that, indirectly, such texts can be instructive for soldiers. Soldiers should reflect on the overall consistency of their orders with the primacy of a "higher" law, even if they cannot in practice ask such questions about every order.

## Excessive Violence and Proportionality

If the Jewish tradition guides us to examine and possibly disobey certain orders, it likewise proposes a means to evaluate what constitutes excessive violence in the military context. Maimonides, for example, offers this notion of proportionality:

> "Anyone who is able to rescue [a pursued person] by [attacking] a limb and does not make an effort to do so but instead rescues [a pursued person] by taking the purser's life, behold he has committed murder and is deserving of death, but a *Beit Din* does not execute him. But one who is able to rescue [a pursued person] and does not do so transgresses [the commandment] "You shall not stand idly while your fellow bleeds."14

One is clearly responsible for saving another who is in danger, even by killing their pursuer, if necessary. But excessive force is not permitted; one must use only that amount of force actually needed to stop the attacker.

Once again, we believe that this situation can give guidance in a military setting as well. If it is too much of an ideal to hope that every order will be questioned to determine if the amount of violence commanded is the minimum necessary, then at least we may hope that a certain sense of proportionality will be considered. We recognize as well that the category of war in which one is fighting (*milḥemet mitzvah* or *milḥemet reshut*) will affect the degree to which questions of proportionality are taken into account.

In strong contrast to the underlying ethic of the above passage, however, Maimonides elsewhere also has something to say about individual responsibility for violent action:

> "If he is beaten by ten persons using ten sticks so that he dies, either from being beaten by one after another, or from being beaten [by all ten acting] as one, all [ten] are absolved of execution by a *Beit Din*, as it is written 'Any man...' (Lev. 24:17), [meaning that] until one man takes the entire life of another, [there is no death penalty]. ...If ten people throw stones at him, one after another, and no one stone has the capability to kill him, and one throws the last stone and it has enough force to kill and he dies, the last person is executed on his [the victim's] account."[15]

Maimonides here affirms (unexpectedly) the notion of diffusion of responsibility. In cases where a number of people are all implicated in a murder, but no one can clearly be defined as the murderer, the entire group is absolved of liability, except for the "last person."

It would appear from the foregoing that a soldier, called upon to protect his country, must use whatever means necessary to accomplish this mission. He is not permitted, however, to do anything beyond what is necessary, i.e., to kill excessively for other than strategic reasons. The law also seems to offer an excuse for the sort of anonymous killing that armies are usually involved in. Killing that takes place in the context of group battle proceeds without questions of guilt. Out of this context, however, killing another human being leaves an individual soldier fully culpable for his actions.

## The Question
## in General Ethics

How should a soldier respond when given an immoral order? This is a question in the arena of "military ethics."

There are thinkers who believe that the term `military

ethics' is itself an oxymoron.[16] Von Clausewitz wrote in *On War* that "there is no logical limit to the application of force."[17] The goal is to disarm the enemy, and, since the enemy's goal is the same, this will be accomplished by ever increasing increments of force until the maximum effort of both sides is reached. Limitations are incompatible with the overall goal of victory.

Most thinkers, both legal and moral philosophers, do, however, believe that limitations on warfare can be expressed and maintained. It is the role of both military law and military ethics to define that line beyond which one must not go, to judge between actions, all of which are inconceivable in non-military situations, and say: this one is acceptable and appropriate, and this one is not. We will be looking to both legal and moral theorists to see how and where that line of demarcation has been drawn.

## Legal Expression of Ethics

Expressions of the ethical thinking of a society are found in many places. We will, in due course, turn to the general philosophical literature, to writings that deal directly with ethical questions in terms of their underlying moral theory. There are, however, ethical attitudes embedded in other areas as well. The legal system, for instance, is an example of a kind of codified morality; laws reflect a general level of ethical understanding in a society, and they change as ethical assumptions evolve.

Legal systems of modern societies, and legal theorists, have attempted to address our question directly. What, legally, should a soldier's options be when given an immoral order? (In this section, and for the reasons given in the above paragraph, we will be using the terms 'illegal' and 'immoral' interchangeably.) Before we address the question in terms of moral thinking, we will try to present solutions to the dilemma worked out by legal theorists.

## What can a soldier be expected to know?

War is a difficult and dangerous setting. It has, as was noted above, been questioned whether any ethical limitations can be placed on actions that occur during wars. And yet many legal systems do acknowledge a limit to what may be considered legitimate activity even in a military context.

If such a limit does exist, then the next question is what precisely is the limit, and how can this limit be ascertained? Whatever the legal line of demarcation is decided to be, how can soldiers in combat settings know, or be expected to know, when they have reached that line?

In his book *The Defense of 'Obedience to Superior Orders' in International Law,* the Israeli scholar, Yoram Dinstein, attempts to address this question. He notes that

> "the general rule is that a soldier committing an offense in obedience to superior orders is relieved of his responsibility for his wrongdoing. If, however, the illegality of the order is clear on the face of it, that is, manifestly and palpably, then the soldier must refuse to obey or else pay the penalty."[18]

This is known as the principle of "manifest illegality."[19] A soldier should therefore be aware that there is a serious problem with any action that is clearly and generally understood to be illegal, even if this action is ordered by a commanding officer.

There are several problems with this formulation as it stands, most of which relate to the fact that what is generally understood to be illegal may or may not correspond to what is understood by an individual soldier in question. Dinstein set the limits of the problem with two examples: suppose, in the first case, that an order is given that is illegal, but not manifestly so – and that the soldier who hears the order (who would normally not be culpable, since the order is not manifestly illegal) happens to be a draftee who was a professor of international law in civilian life, and who is quite aware of the fact that the order is illegal.[20] What would a court decide if this soldier committed the crime? Suppose, in the second case, that an order is manifestly illegal, but the particular soldier happens to be a man of subnormal intelligence, who did not in fact know that the action ordered was wrong.[21] What would a court decide in this case?

Dinstein handles this problem by subsuming the manifest illegality principle under a new category. He writes that

> "an accused should not be held responsible, under international law, for a criminal act executed in obedience to a superior order if he committed the act without being aware of its illegality. This is the substantive principle, to be termed hereinafter 'the personal knowledge principle;' and we can append subsidiary rules to it, including a rule of evidence to provide that, if the order was manifestly illegal, the defendant is presumed to have been aware of this illegality, and perhaps will not even be allowed to present proof in rebuttal of this presumption."[22]

We are, therefore, left with this situation: culpability is to be determined to some extent by the subjective knowledge on the part of the soldier that an action is question was illegal. A professor of international law would thus be found guilty, even though the action was illegal in a way that was not clear to the average person. In other situations, however, manifest illegality is taken as a minimum level of general knowledge with which all soldiers are assumed to be familiar. A person of subnormal intelligence would, therefore, not be allowed to give evidence for his subjective state of knowledge, since the general presumption of manifest illegality was in place.

A soldier can therefore be presumed to recognize as problematic any action that is manifestly illegal. Some soldiers, moreover, may be held to an even stricter account, if warranted by the situation of their subjective knowledge.

## How should a soldier act?

It is reasonably clear, then, that when an order given by a superior is blatantly illegal, the soldier can be assumed to have known that the order was problematic. Still, what should a soldier do with this awareness?

Some people have argued that the justifiable need for discipline within a military setting requires obedience to orders at any cost.[23] This is the pure doctrine of *respondeat superior*. Further, it is argued that in the heat of battle a soldier is neither an appropriate nor competent judge of the orders given to him, and that therefore obedience must be absolute.[24]

Dinstein notes however, even without referring to the ethical theories of a soldier as a moral agent which we will explore later, that soldiers are ethically expected to use their human judgement in evaluating orders.

> "Even the interests of military discipline itself require that the soldier will not act... as a machine, but... will use the glimmerings of understanding, intelligence, reasoning and will-power that were bestowed upon him."[25]

This is so because absolute obedience might lead a private to shoot a colonel on the order of a captain, or desert on the order of an immediate superior.[26] Soldiers must exercise judgement even within the argument for the preservation of military discipline.

If, therefore, soldiers can exercise judgement, and if, as we saw above, they can additionally be expected to know that certain things are manifestly illegal, it follows that a soldier, when given an order that is manifestly illegal, should disobey that order. This is the principle.

There are, however, problems with this formulation, as well. There are important circumstances in which *respondeat superior*, obedience to orders, *is* seen as a part of a valid defense. These circumstances involve both ignorance and duress (or compulsion).

Ignorance of the law, as we have already seen, may sometimes serve as a defense in international law. If a law is illegal but not manifestly illegal, and the soldier is not a professor of international law or the equivalent, then obedience to superior orders does, in fact, serve as a factor in a defense.

Further, if the order was accompanied by duress or compulsion, then following orders may be considered as a factor. There are times, for instance, when a soldier may feel that a real and present danger (originating from his side of the war) would be involved in disobeying an order. Dinstein notes that orders are often issues "at the point of the sword... and are accompanied... by the threat, explicit or implicit, that disobedience will entail capital punishment."[27] A soldier may know, in fact, that upon being given an illegal order he is automatically in a no-win situation, for he may well be shot by a court-martial if he disobeys such a command, or hanged by an international tribunal after the war if he obeys an order to commit a heinous crime, and his side loses.[28]

Thus, the presence of compulsion is, in legal terms, seen as a partially justifiable reason for obeying an order to commit even a manifestly illegal act.[29]

There is a question as to whether a situation of war in and of itself constitutes a situation of duress or compulsion. If threat and personal risk are so intrinsic to the waging of war as to be in-separable from it, then it follows that any order received in wartime has a high degree of compulsion on the individual soldier. If this is the case, then it would be hard to come up with a situation, in the heat of battle, in which a soldier would *not* be able to use the duress argument to justify obeying even a manifestly illegal order.

Michael Walzer, in his book *Just and Unjust Wars,* rejects the notion that war is always and inevitably a situation in which a soldier is compelled to obey orders and therefore not responsible for his actions in obedience.

> "Only a man with a gun at his head is not responsible... superior orders are not always enforced at the point of a gun. Army discipline in the actual context of war is often a great deal more haphazard than the firing squad example suggests."[30]

We see, then, that both ignorance and duress, in certain circumstances, can justify the obedience to certain superior orders. It is not, however, the fact of obedience that is a valid defense, but the reasons why that obedience occurred. Ignorance and duress, as defined here, have an element in common. Where orders are followed either out of real and present compulsion, or out of ignorance that the order is illegal, there is in the mind of the soldier a lack of *mens rea* (evil intent).[31] It is not the intention of the soldier to commit the act in question.

Dinstein concludes his survey with the following position:

"the fact of obedience to orders should be excluded
as a defense *per se*, but permitted to be taken into
account, among other circumstances of the case, for
the purpose of establishing a defense based on the
lack of *mens rea*."[32]

Legally, the intention of the soldier is the critical point. According to Dinstein's reasoning, soldiers can be expected to recognize blatantly immoral orders, and will be held accountable for those of their
actions which were within their power. This idea was, in fact, included in the seven general principles drafted (but not adopted) by the
International Law Commission of the United Nations:

"The fact that a person acted pursuant to an order of
his Government or of a superior does not relieve him
of responsibility under international law, *providing
a moral choice was in fact possible to him*."[33]

Thus, while some theorists emphasize an almost-unqualified
value of obedience, Dinstein represents the mainstream viewpoint
that in the face of an immoral order, understood as such, a soldier,
if at all possible, *should* disobey the order.

## Moral Theory
## Non-consequentialist
## ("absolutist") Ethics

The moral philosopher Thomas Nagel defines the approach of what he
calls absolutist (and others call non-consequentialist) ethics. In his
essay "War and Massacre," he writes that "Utilitarianism [consequen-
tialist ethics] gives primacy to a concern with what will happen. Absolutism gives primacy to a concern with what one is *doing*."[34] The
focus of concern in non-consequentialist ethics can, by definition, not
be on the consequences or end result of an act, but only on the act
as an independent arena. Morality is not relative; if an act is wrong
then no result-oriented reason should induce one to do it. There are
principles (a "moral teleology") which guide our behavior, helping
us to decide the framework in which some actions are wrong and
others are right.

The principle that applies to our question is the ethic of
personhood. Anthony Hartle, in his essay "Humanitarianism and
the Art of War," articulates the first humanitarian principle (HP1)
underlying the laws of war: "Individual persons deserve respect as
such."[35] By application of this principle, even during a war, people
should be treated as human beings, as ends in themselves, not as
objects or as means.

If all people are to be treated as people, this implies the
personhood of the soldiers themselves. Soldiers therefore *must* be

considered to be moral agents. A soldier in a combat situation is thought to be capable of making moral decisions, and is held responsible for the decisions that he makes.

Michael Walzer notes in this regard that even if it is true that actions we would consider to be immoral, such as the continued killing of enemy soldiers who are trying to surrender, often occur in war settings,

> "it is also true that a relatively small number of men do the 'extra' killing. The rest seem ready to stop as soon as they can, whatever the state of mind they had worked themselves into during the battle itself. This fact is morally decisive."[36]

Some of the soldiers at My Lai knew that what was happening was wrong; their ability to make this assessment is enough to indict the actions of their comrades.[37] If decisions can be made in difficult situations, then responsibility does not disappear in such settings.

Soldiers, however, are in a special category – to their disadvantage. While they remain fully *responsible* as persons and as moral agents, they are not as *privileged* as persons as the non-soldiers they encounter. Because soldiers, by the very nature of their jobs, themselves are "the immediate source of danger" in an area, they must "accept personal risk rather than kill innocent people."[38] In a conflict between the rights of soldiers to be treated as persons (and survive) and the rights of civilians to be treated as persons, the rights of the civilians take precedence, because the soldiers are the source of the conflict. Their job in and of itself involves danger; the job of being a civilian should not.

There remains a different question. How is it possible to use violent force at all, even between two groups of soldiers, in a way compatible with treating the people upon whom one is firing as human beings? Nagel addresses this question by delineating the areas in which violence may be compatible with an ethic of personhood.

> "Absolutist restrictions in warfare appear to be of two types: restrictions on the class of persons at whom aggression...may be directed, and restrictions on the manner of attack... These can be combined, however, under the principle that hostile treatment of any person must be justified by something about that person which makes the treatment appropriate. Hostility is a personal relation, and it must be suited to its target... Certain persons may not be subject to hostile treatment in war at all... Others will be proper objects of hostility only in certain circumstances."[39]

A distinction is made here, then, between innocent civilians, non-combatants, towards whom at no time and for no reason is violence justified, and enemy combatants, towards whom violence is justified only in the violent setting of battle, but not, for instance, while they are prisoners. Force may only be used against combatants engaged in combat. Violence is not totally incompatible with the ethics of personhood, but it is quite limited.

The distinction between combatants and non-combatants is not always as clear as we might like. In a situation of rioting by a civilian population, as, for instance, is occurring in Israel at the present time, it is not always clear that civilians are not also combatants. Nagel's distinctions above may be of some use here: violence is a possible response to violence demonstrated by a crowd of rioters (perhaps 'informal combatants'). This is an appropriate interpersonal response to that situation. Preventative beatings, on the other hand, are according to this ethic an inappropriate, even immoral use of force. Even assuming the people beaten were the previous afternoon informal combatants, there is nothing about their behavior at the moment of the night time beating that warrants such treatment.

Absolutist ethics poses absolute rules: certain actions are wrong and should not be done – whatever the warrant or however high the gain may seem. The higher the utilitarian gain seen in an immoral action, however, the harder this absolutist position becomes to maintain. Hartle writes of one such dilemma:[40] enemy soldiers are taken prisoner by a small force carrying out a mission behind enemy lines upon which the success of their war effort may depend. The mission would, if successful, bring victory easily, and by saving many lives. Yet the enemy prisoners would hinder the mission; they cannot be set free, nor is there the opportunity to send them back to prison camps. For the sake of minimizing the total amount of human suffering (his humanitarian principle number two, a consequentialist goal), may the prisoners be killed? HP2 would be accomplished in this way – but it would be at the expense of HP1, for killing the prisoners would be to treat them as object-means, not person-ends.

Hartle holds on to the primacy of the first principle, that people should be treated as persons, and that therefore the prisoners may not be killed.[41] Perhaps the reason for this is that the absolutist, non-consequentialist ethic would be immediately and certainly violated, whereas an ethic based on outcome (the supposed minimized amount of suffering) is far less certain. In any case, killing the prisoners here would be wrong – absolutely wrong – regardless of the consequences. The ethical position of the soldiers on that mission remains intact – even if their home cities do not.[42]

But what if the whole outcome of the war really does depend on the performance of some despicable deed? Where Hartle stands firm on his absolutist ground, both Nagel and Walzer are shakier.

Walzer discusses under the nature of necessity that "supreme emergency" in which, say, the very survival of a group or nation is at stake. If a resort to murder is all that is left to save the group, then murder will inevitably take place, political leaders being by nature utilitarian thinkers.[43] Here we have a situation in which there are murderers, albeit in "good cause." What is to be done? Walzer argues that "there is obviously no question here of legal punishment, but of some other way of assigning and enforcing blame."[44] He suggests the solution used by the British in handling a terror bomber who helped them win the war: we should dishonor (or at least refuse to honor) those who commit immoral acts, even if those actions help us to survive. The suggestion is bizarre. It amounts to, as Walzer admits,

> "a nation fighting a just war [which] when it is desperate and survival itself is at risk, must use unscrupulous or morally ignorant soldiers and, as soon as their usefulness is past, it must disown them."[45]

Something is wrong with the ethical system here! A nation acting in such a way would hardly be treating its own soldiers as anything more than means, to say nothing of the poor people against whom these hypothetical atrocities must be committed for the sake of the other group's survival. Consequences have crept in and taken over non-consequential thinking.

In the end, both Nagel and Walzer (quoting Nagel) are forced to acknowledge an unresolvable breakdown of their systems. Walzer writes that

> "in supreme emergencies, our judgments are doubled, reflecting the dualistic character of the theory of war, and the deeper complexities of our moral realism; we say yes and no, right and wrong. That dualism makes us uneasy; the world of war is not a fully comprehensible, let alone a morally satisfactory place."[46]

Nagel writes that

> "we must face the pessimistic alternative that these two forms of moral intuition are not capable of being brought together into a single, coherent moral system... We have always known that the world is a bad place. It appears that it may be an evil place as well."[47]

## Utilitarian Ethics

Basic to the moral theory known as utilitarianism is the goal of maximization of human welfare, and minimization of human suffering. There are two major subsets of utilitarianism, namely "act-utilitarianism" and "rule-utilitarianism." The former stresses the evaluation of an act in terms of how it will maximize benefit, while the latter aims to establish systems of rules which, when practiced consistently as a whole, bring about the greatest possible good.

With regard to the ethics of war in particular, utilitarian

theorists like R.B.Brandt reject the supremacy of so-called non-consequentialist ethics, such as the system of Thomas Nagel described above. Their major critique focuses on the often absolutist (Nagel's term) nature of this type of thought, which, by enshrining abstract principles, appears to permit absolutely no deviation from these principles, even when the universally acknowledged greater good is not being served.

Brandt notes that within rule-utilitarianism, it is possible to agree with thinkers like Nagel that certain types of actions are indeed morally untenable under any and all circumstances, for example, those actions prohibited by the laws of warfare. To the extent that utilitarian considerations cannot morally sanction an abandonment of these rules, they are understood to be absolute. But, Brandt adds, the moral justification of the rules themselves derive from utilitarian, and not deontological considerations, namely, the fact that the acceptance and enforcement of these rules will lead to greater long-range utility.[49]

Utilitarian thinkers like Brandt and R. M. Hare[50] object also to the "ethic of personhood" that Nagle uses to defend his thesis. Hare points out that such an ethic will be of little practical use, given the fact that opposing sides may reasonably invoke this principle to justify widely differing courses of action. Just as an ethic of personhood can lead to a response of love toward one's opponents, it can also legitimately (and in the war situation, more likely) lead to a response of hate toward them. Besides, notes Hare, exactly whose personhood does Nagel believe must be respected? In discussing the questions associated with the destruction of Hiroshima and Nagasaki, Nagel tellingly omits a consideration of the personhood of those who would have died had the war not ended quickly, jumping immediately to a concern for those annihilated by the bombs. Does an ethic of personhood not apply to the former group?[51]

Brandt, in objecting to Nagel's theory, actually co-opts his principle that an action may be justified by our ability to justify it to its victim. He notes, however, that there is an important difference between persuading a person to whom something horrible is going to happen to consent to its happening at that very time, and getting the same person to accept the justice of the action under different circumstances, that is, when he is in a position to be impartial and rational, and is able to choose what might be done (in the abstract) to someone in his original position.[52]

Brandt counters Nagel's "absolutism" with his own ethic of "rational contractors." In general, such a theory holds that the moral correctness of an action is derived from the presumed assent of rational, impartial persons choosing from among the available options, under a veil of ignorance regarding the possible advantages or disadvantages to their own side.[53] Applied to the situation of war, this ethic assumes 1) that rational and impartial persons would choose to establish certain rules of war, 2) that such rules are morally justified only if they would be chosen by such rational, impartial persons, and 3) that rational, impartial persons could be relied upon to choose rules that will maximize general long-range utility.[54]

Regarding this third point he elaborates: if such rational contractors happen to be self-interested, they will desire to maximize the expectable utility in general, in which case their chance for benefit is the greatest. If, on the other hand, they are altruistic, their concern for the welfare of others will again lead them to choose rules that maximize utility generally.[55]

Brandt is anxious to use his ethical framework to elucidate ethical limits on the waging of war. But he first must assert what might be called a "Serious War Doctrine," namely, that the rules of war may not limit the use of all force necessary to overcome the enemy. This doctrine acknowledges that nations fighting what they consider to be a "serious war" (it being understood that not all wars would be so self-defined) consider the defeat of the enemy to be so vital to their interests that they are often willing to stake their national survival on it. Thus, neither side in such a conflict will consent to rules of war that impair in a meaningful way the possibility of their side bringing the war to a victorious conclusion. Brandt quickly adds that this doctrine, derived as it is from a utilitarian understanding of "necessity," still permits a nation to use *only as much force as is necessary to win the war*, and no more.[56] Once this principle is established, Brandt is able to go on to enumerate, based on his rational contractor ethics, three types of rules which limit military activity in a war.

The first category of limitations are defined as "humanitarian restrictions of no cost to military operations." This means, for example, that the killing of prisoners whose deaths will bring no strategic benefit to the side doing the killing, cannot ethically take place. The justification of this limitation according to Brandt derives from the likely results of such wholesale slaughter, namely, the incitement of even greater resistance on the part of the enemy, including a desire to retaliate. On the other hand, reasons Brandt, obedience to such a guideline is likely to engender a greater respect for life in general on both sides.[57]

The second category of limitations relate to "humanitarian restrictions of possible cost to overall victory." That is, restrictions on actions that do not necessarily insure victory, but which may in fact involve a strategic cost. This category is the "home" of the proportionality principle, insofar as destruction is here permitted only when effected in proportion to the actual probability that victory will be enhanced.[58]

The third limitation that Brandt's system wishes to impose might be called "the acceptance of military losses for humanitarian reasons." In other words, in situations where the ultimate outcome of the war is not an issue, but there is the potential to inflict damage in order to cut one's losses (e.g., the dropping of the atomic bomb on the Japanese cities), Brandt holds that losses may be inflicted which are heavy enough to lead to the opponent's capitulation, but that are not so heavy as to be out of proportion to the cost to either side of continued struggle.[59]

Brandt's rule-utilitarianism leads him to create guidelines that, while appearing to constitute an almost deontological system of absolute duties, ultimately find their justification in the benevolent, clearly utilitarian outcomes they engender. Hare, rejecting also the absolutism of thinkers like Nagel, builds on Brandt's ethical system to create an ethic that learns from non-consequentialist thought, and recasts it in more authentic (for Hare) utilitarian form.

Hare's problem with the deontological ethics proposed by Nagel and others is its basis in simple moral principles, and its commitment to nothing greater than this. Philosophers, says he, are obliged to practice a style of thinking beyond this simple level, in order to determine whence these simplistic rules arose, and what to do when they come into conflict.[60]

His answer to the first question is that moral reasoning, even of the utilitarian sort, seems to begin with a number of *prima facie* considerations, that is, "sacred principles" held by the ordinary person. The rules of war are an attempt to apply these "sacred principles" practically. According to Hare, such principles play an important role in a "complete" theory of utilitarian ethics, but they are often de-emphasized (wrongly so) by utilitarians themselves. Their importance does not lie, of course, in their inherent "rightness;" this would strongly bring into question their utilitarian character. Instead, their significance grows out of their role in the moral education of potential moral agents (In this case, potential soldiers), that is, in their use in character formation. This is because, purely and simply, the principles being referred to are "sacred" insofar as their general acceptance will lead to the best consequences.[61]

Historically, the inculcation of certain basic principles was mainly the concern of religious authorities and, ironically, the army. The military has always had a stake in training its soldiers to value courage in attack, stubbornness in defense, the duty to obey orders, and not running away in battle.[62] These, it should be noted, are not moral duties *per se*, but rather values whose inculcation will lead to the effective performance or moral duty within the context of a just war (assuming the existence of such a thing). Without training in such principles, the soldier might simply flee from battle, believing this to be the best way of serving the greatest good of humankind (as well as saving his own life). Again, assuming that our discussion is limited to the context of a just war, that is a war with a just moral purpose, such conduct would in fact make the winning of the war impossible, and the greatest good for humanity unserved.

Hare notes, again making clear the distance of this theory from classical deontological thought, that while certain general principles may and should be affirmed, exceptions to these principles may be noted, and these exceptions do nothing to diminish the value of the principle itself. He cites as an example the principle that marital fidelity should generally be preserved, adding that this principle is in no way inconsistent with the admission that in certain cases, the practice of adultery would in fact serve the greatest good. The importance of affirming the principle however, is derived from the assumption that without such a general affirmation, every person who finds himself contemplating acting adulterously will immediately ask herself whether her situation is indeed one of the exceptional ones. Undoubtedly, without the affirmation of the general principle, many of these individuals will answer this question affirmatively, when in fact the answer is no. Thus our inculcation of the principle, while fully cognizant of the exceptions to it, still serves to promote the greatest good. This is what Hare calls "general rule-utilitarianism."[63]

But how do we go about determining the particular *content* of these principles? Hare posits that we utilize a notion he identifies as "specific rule-utilitarianism." Specific rule-utilitarianism permits us to examine our general rules in as minute detail as is necessary when they appear to conflict when a particular situation. The judgments at which we arrive through this process are understood to be universal, even as they are extremely specific. Ultimately, we employ specific rule-utilitarianism to reason at a higher level than is possible in general rule-utilitarianism, in order to determine the content of the general principles that comprise the lower-level ethic.[64] Thus in attempting to create an ethic of *jus in bello,* Hare's system recommends an ethic that, though much more complex, very closely resembles an act-utilitarian stance in its practical application. One does that act which on the whole, maximizes benefit and minimizes suffering. Furthermore, one attempts to establish rules that promote general principles, but which likewise address each specific exception in a meaningful way.

Finally, Hare notes one further (and important) objection to Nagel's position, specifically to Nagel's concern with guilt. One must separate, *feeling* guilty from *being guilty,* and in doing, distinguish between the issue of moral integrity and the issue of peace of mind.

> "If, say, we are theists and can convince ourselves that God has laid down some relatively simple rules and that by observing these we can keep ourselves unspotted and safe from hellfire, this may seem a good way of avoiding the agony of mind which comes, in difficult cases, from the calculation of the consequences of alternative actions."[65]

Responding to the moral *angst* expressed by Nagel, Hare thus states an important outgrowth of his ethical view. There are times, he notes, when the results of our moral decision-making leave us pained and full of despair. This not because our ethics have failed, but rather because our expectations of the goodness of the world were always too great.

## The Intersection of Jewish Law and General Ethics

We find the statement of the utilitarian positions here to be powerful. This, however, at least initially, presents us with something of a problem when we once again look at Jewish law. Utilitarianism is not a religiously based philosophy; we cannot expect it to be sympathetic to "ethics of faith" as we might of a religious tradition. The assumption underlying the traditional understanding of Jewish law, on the other hand, is that there are certain rules which we are unconditionally obliged to obey. This derives from the understanding that God is the source of these rules. Thus, the rules are to be followed, and God's law must be obeyed – period.[66]

This tension between tradition and utility is felt most acutely by Liberal Jews. For us to unquestioningly affirm a utilitarian viewpoint would be equivalent to rejecting the traditional conception of Jewish law as absolute. Clearly, this in and of itself is not a problem for liberal. Yet even if we feel no attachment to this absolutist interpretation of Jewish law, the tension nevertheless remains; our enduring predisposition to believe that transcendent values do in fact exist leaves us still with one foot in each view of the world.

In resolving this dilemma it is instructive to return to the question of the three cardinal sins in Judaism. Here, if anywhere, with the instruction to die before committing idolatry, sexual impropriety or murder, we seem to have an expression of an absolute limit: one may act to save his or her own life up to a point – but no further. These sins are absolute, and their violation is simply not tolerable, no matter what the cost or consequence.

And yet even here, loopholes remain. In proposing that idolatry in private might not require martyrdom, Caro (glossing Maimonides) seems to be focussing not on the act itself but on the outcome: Judaism and God will be disgraced if faith is lightly flung aside in public, but when challenged to show disrespect toward either in private, the value of life takes precedence. And according to Maimonides, if someone commits murder under a direct threat to their own life, the act is considered sinful, but the actor is not treated in quite the same way as a person who commits murder under other circumstances.

In the presence of these exemptions, Jewish law cannot remain completely immune from the claim that it is based in some measure upon a consideration of consequences. Over time and with development, considerations of outcome have entered into places where they may not have been before. Joseph Caro, by asserting that at times one must strictly follow the rule of dying rather than commit a sin, seems to be maintaining the original law. But here, the law is conditioned on context; what one should do depends on an analysis of the probable outcomes of the particular situation. Jewish law thus, on closer examination, seems to be closer in character to general rule utilitarian ethics than to absolutist, non-consequentialist ethics, than we would have supposed originally (if, that is, the utility is "holiness," not happiness).

We anticipated an underlying theoretical tension between Jewish law and those arguments of general ethics which we found to be the most powerful. It is possible that this tension is not as pronounced as we originally expected. If this is so, we can now turn to a consideration of specific scenarios.

A soldier is given an order that appears to be immoral. The situation is one of a "supreme emergency;" the outcome of a just cause is seen to hang on the performance or non-performance of this seemingly-heinous action. We have seen that, with considerable discomfort, several mostly non-consequentialist thinkers admit that in this case the heinous deed should be done, and the moral niceties worked out (if possible) later. Utilitarian thinkers say in such a situation that the moral choice is to follow the greater good; if greater good really would come from the performance of a seemingly despicable deed, then it would even be misguided to call such an act immoral. It is the right thing to do.

In Jewish law, we have seen the *Kesef Mishneh* argue that if a violation of even a *minor* commandment would result in the moral turpitude of the Jewish community, then the violation should not take place; this is all the more true if the violation of a *major* commandment would have such an outcome. But the same logic would lead us to say that if the result of not violating a commandment, major or minor, would be to deeply hurt the Jewish people, indeed, perhaps, if the survival of Judaism or the Jewish people as a whole might depend on this violation, than the violation should take place. Even if the act remains wrong, the outcome will (with Maimonides) force us to treat the offender differently than we would otherwise.

In all of these cases, the final decision about what we should do is at least strongly influenced, if not determined, by an analysis of outcome. Jewish law and consequentialist moral thought thus show a similarity in style.

The following seems to emerge out of both the Jewish and general literature: A soldier, when given an order that seems to be immoral, must make a decision. Even given the heat of a battle, blind obedience is not always an acceptable reaction. Our understanding of the metaethics of the *halakhah* leads us to affirm that the soldier remains a potentially culpable moral agent. As a result of this understanding, we maintain that some kind of analysis of the situation, even an imperfect one, must take place on the site. If the ultimate victory of an unambiguously just cause hangs in the balance, the soldier should follow the order. If the situation is not one of "greater good" or a "supreme emergency," the soldier definitely should disobey the order, *even* at great personal risk. If disobedience would be fatally dangerous (from his *own* side), then while the soldier *should* still disobey, the circumstances will be relevant in determining the extent of his culpability if he does not.

## Reactions

We believe that some problems remain with the picture presented above. First of all, the conclusions so far seem to point in the opposite direction from what we originally expected. Should a soldier disobey an order which appears to be immoral? We expected the answer to be yes – an immoral order should be disobeyed. We have learned, however, that deciding exactly what orders are immoral and when to disobey them may not be so simple.

We return to the example of prisoners of war. The survival of the state depends on the success of this mission. The prisoners can be neither guarded nor set free. Shall they, then, be killed? We do maintain our initial assumption that a soldier, as a moral agent, must be reflective and make a careful decision, even in a difficult situation like war. We realize, however, that no matter how morally necessary this reflection may be, a battlefield is not conducive to that kind of analysis. Therefore, systematic moral education before such situations arise is clearly called for.

In that careful analysis in which we would like the soldier to engage, we have so far said that the utilitarian arguments (again, maximizing holiness, not happiness) are more persuasive than we had anticipated. Acts that serve the long term greater good may in fact be moral even if they appear superficially immoral. For the soldier to preserve his own abstract moral purity at the expense of many other concrete lives, seems self-serving and almost obscene. Thus, though our conscience chafes at the suggestion of killing the prisoners in cold blood, our intellect persuades us that this may in fact be the only truly moral choice.

The direction of Jewish meta-ethics and certain schools of neo-Kantian absolutist thought might take us in another direction. We turn, instinctively at this point, to guidance from the meta-ethical tradition of Judaism, that is, those beliefs which underly, as best we can determine them, the *halakhah*. We are taught – and the teaching echoes deeply within us – that human beings are created *b'tzelem elohim*, in the image of God. If this is true, then each life is of inestimable value in and of itself. It follows that we cannot make quantitative analyses based on consequences. This principle appears in the *halakhah* as *ein dokhin nefesh mipnei nefesh* – "one life may not be taken to save another." Accordingly, we could not say that three killed now will save the lives of a hundred next week. This is partly because we cannot know the future for certain and we could not really balance numbers like this even if we could. The consequences may be dire – but (so far) we cannot act immorally in the present, to insure a better future. The internal moral mandate outweighs even the accusation that we are interested only in keeping our own souls pure at any price, even at the expense of all around us that we care for.

But this is not the whole picture. The Jewish tradition does call us to affirm certain values as absolute. Among these values are the notions of both preserving justice and preserving life. Although our heart leads us to want to preserve life at any cost, our minds must recognize that such absolutism, if it leads to losing, forces us to pay an absurd price in terms of justice – and sometimes, a higher price in life, as well. This is what Hare was referring to in urging us to disabuse ourselves of the romantic notion that that which appears superficially to be immoral neccessarily is immoral. In an obligatory war, in which survival of the nation is at stake, and on a mission in which, for example, captured prisoners could be neither guarded nor released nor otherwise disabled, the 'moral' thing to do would, in our opinion, be to shoot them.

We cannot help but remain troubled by this conclusion. In a world in which ethics is often defined by what makes us feel good, however, we are prepared to accept the fact the correct choice in a supremely difficult situation may not be the most pleasing choice. If this dissatisfaction is the inevitable result of competent moral thought, so be it.

# Bibliography

*The Babylonian Talmud*. London: The Soncino Press. 1938.

Bailey, Sydney D. *Prohibitions and Restrictions in War*. London: Oxford University Press. 1972.

Bleich, J. David. "The case for *glatt* silence on lebanon," *Sh'ma* 13/245.

– *Contemporary Halakhic Problems Vol. II* New York: Ktav. 1983.

Brandt, R.B. "Utilitarianism and the Rules of War," in *War and Moral Reasoning*. Cohen, Nagel and Scanlon, eds. Princeton, New Jersey: Princeton University Press. 1974.

Dinstein, Yoram. *The Defense of "Obedience to Superior Orders in International Law.* Leyden, Netherlands: A.W. Sijthoff. 1965.

Hare, R. M. "Rules of War and Moral Reasoning," in *War and Moral Responsibility*.

Hartle, Anthony. "Humanitarianism and the Laws of War," in *Philosophy* (Volume 61). 1986.

Nagel, Thomas. "War and Massacre," in *Mortal Questions*. Cambridge: Cambridge University Press. 1979.

Von Clausewitz, Carl. *On War*. Edited and translated by Howard, M. and Paret, P. Princeton, New Jersey: Princeton University Press. 1976.

Walzer, Michael. *Just and Unjust Wars: A Moral Argument With Historical Illustrations*. New York: Basic Books. 1977.

# Notes

1. Carl von Clausewitz, *On War*. Edited and translated by Michael Howard and Paret. (Princeton, New Jersey: Princeton University Press, 1976), p. 75.

2. All translations of Talmudic passages are from *The Babylonian Talmud* published by the Soncino Press (London, 1938).

3. *Hoshed Mishpat, Hilkhot Shluḥin* 182.

4. *Shulḥan Arukh, Hoshen Mishpat, Hilkhot G'nevah* 348.

5. *B.K.* 79a.

6. *Sanhedrin* 74a.

7. *Mishneh Torah, Yesodei Hatorah* 5:4.

8. Bleich, J. David. *Contemporary Halakhic Problems,* Vol. II (New York: Ktav, 1983), p. 160.

9. Ibid., p. 164

10. These categories are given in Deuteronomy 20.

11. See e.g., Maimonides, *Mishneh Torah, Hilkhot Melakhim* 7:4.

12. Bleich, "The case for glatt silence on lebanon," *Sh'ma* 13/245, p. 36.

13. *Sanhedrin* 49a.

14. *Mishneh Torah, Hilkhot Melakhim* 3:8-9.

15. *Mishneh Torah, Hilkhot Rotzeaḥ* 1:13.

16. *Mishneh Torah, Hilkhot Rotzeaḥ* 4:6-7.

17. "Ethics here refers to standards of behavior that embody a moral world-view. It is not to be understood here in its more technical sense, that is, as defining norms of conduct expected of people fulfilling a given professional or other role.

18. von Clausewitz, p. 77.

19. Yoram Dinstein, *The Defense of Obedience to Superior Orders in International Law* (Leyden, Netherlands: A.W. Sijthoff, 1965), p. 8.

20. Ibid., p. 9. Dinstein also notes on the same page that the manifest illegality principle has the "imprimatur of the legislation in force in Israel."

21. Ibid., p. 27, example (1).

22. Ibid., p. 27, example (2).

23. Ibid., p. 30.

24. Ibid., pp. 7 and 38f.

25. Ibid., p. 49, especially the expansion of Oppenhiem's theories by Renault, as quoted here by Dinstein.

26. Ibid., p. 53.

27. Citing examples from Stephen, *A History of Criminal Law in England* (1883), vol. 1., p. 205, in Dinstein. p. 53.

28. Dinstein, p. 53.

29. From Dicey, *Introduction to the Study of the Law of the Constitution* (1959, p. 303) in Dinstein, p. 7.

30. There is some question about what kind of manifestly illegal acts may be excuses in this manner. Dinstein, in a footnote, comments that the definition of constraint to perform an offense in Israeli law *excludes* :murder and offenses against the state punishable by death." There is a possibility that this comment has in mind the Jewish law on the subject.

31. Michael Walzer, *Just and Unjust Wars: A Moral Argument With Historical Illustrations* (New York: Basic Books, 1977) p. 314.

32. Dinstein, p. 77.

33. Ibid., p. 253.

34. Cited in Sydney D. Bailey, *Prohibitions and Restraints in War* (London: Oxford University Press, 1972), p. 44, emphasis added.

35. Thomas Nagel, "War and Massacre," *Moral Questions* (Cambridge University Press, 1979), p. 54.

36. Anthony Hartle, "Humanitarianism and the Laws of War," *Philosophy* (Volume 61, 1986), p. 109.

37. Walzer, p. 307.

38. Ibid., p. 313.

39. Ibid., pp. 306, 305.

40. Nagel, p. 64.

41. Hartle, pp. 109-110.

42. Ibid., p. 111.

43. It is, of course, far more likely that the orders to those on such an important mission would be to not take prisoners – the battle would simply continue until there were no prisoners left to take. So observed "Shal," a veteran of the Israel Defense Forces known to the authors.

44. Walzer, p. 326.

45. Ibid., p. 323.

46. Ibid., p. 325.

47. Ibid., pp. 326-7.

48. Nagel, pp. 73, 74.

49. "Utilitarianism and the Rules of War," *War and Moral Responsibility,* Marshall Cohen, Thomas Nagel and Thomas Scanlon, eds. (Princeton University Press, 1974), pp. 25-45.

50. Ibid., pp. 26-27.

51. "Rules of War and Moral Reasoning," *War and Moral Responsibility,* pp. 46-61.

52. Ibid., pp. 60-61.

53. Ibid., pp. 30-31.

54. Ibid., pp. 25, 29-30.

55. Ibid., p. 30.

56. Ibid., p. 32.

57.Ibid., p. 33-34.

58. Ibid., p. 34-35.

59. Ibid., pp. 35ff.

60. Ibid., pp. 40-41.

61. Ibid., p. 54.

62. Ibid., p. 54.

63. Ibid., p. 55.

64. Ibid., pp. 56-57.

65. Ibid., pp. 56-57.

66. Hare, p. 60.

67. We can sense the tension about the implications of consequentialist ethics for Jewish law in the fierce debate about investigation of *taamel hamitzvot,* the reasons for the commandments. Opposition of finding the 'real reasons' underlying the commandments was voiced because it was feared that if the reason was isolated, and the situation changed (i.e., the consequences of obedience would not produce the same result that originally motivated the law), the temptation – towards non-observance of that law would grow. Nevertheless and significantly, such investigation into the underlying reasons for the commandments never stopped completely.

# Toward
# A Postmodern
# Jewish Ethics

Eugene B. Borowitz

In hindsight it seems clear that differences in meta-ethics unconsciously make themselves felt in the different ways the student authors utilized the course model for decision-making. The schema itself, it now also seems clear, derived from my growing clarity about a postmodern theology of Jewish duty and I shall be using the term "postmodern" in that specific sense.[1] But other than the session introducing the course there was no time to explain the theological reasons I could now give for our proceeding as I proposed. I could only refer students to my early statement of my views[2] on what one needed to take into account when making a responsible non-Orthodox Jewish decision. Its mature exposition did not take place until the publication of *Renewing the Covenant*,[3] by which time all these papers had been written. It will clarify the situation in which liberal Jewish ethical thinkers now find themselves, as I see it, if I explain why I now consider the recommended schema postmodern and what I learned from the actual experience of having students work with it.

Four features of the model strike me, particularly in combination, as departures from various modern patterns of decision-making. First, as against an older liberal view that every rational person's access to the moral law has made possible a direct understanding of one's duty – popularly identified with the work of one's conscience – this schema calls for an elaborate examination of contemporary rational alternatives and historical material (*halakhah*). More specifically, thinkers of a prior generation could easily by-pass most of the study required here. Assuming the identity of Jewish and universal ethics, they only needed to refer to what conscientious (= liberal) general ethicians were advocating and know what Jews, too, ought to be doing. In the series of steps to be employed here, each requiring serious investigation of the available alternative views, a fundamentally different meta-ethical view is at work. The Kantian trust in human rationality and its view of moral law has now been so compromised that a more complex form of moral investigation is required.

Second, and related to the first, Jewish liberal religious ethicians of prior generations assumed that Jewish ethics customarily entailed liberal political stands. It is difficult to trace the source of this

■ **443**

assurance. It seems far more likely due to the social situation in which Jews found themselves than to their ethical philosophy. As a minority still seeking full equality in the general society Jews had both pragmatic and idealistic motives for identifying with the struggles of all outsiders for greater justice and opportunity. Rational, universal Jewish ethics then provided the theoretical foundation of this stance. In their eagerness to integrate, liberal Jewish ethicians ignored the possibility that particular Jewish needs might be lost in giving unrelenting priority to our universal obligations. They also so identified conservatism with the rights of privilege and the acceptance of prejudice that they could not conceive of it developing a more humane ethics. But gradually some conscientious Jews were attracted to it, at first because of its cogent criticism of liberalism's failings and then because of its thoughtful response to America and its Jewry's changed historical situation. The method recommended here was open to the possibility that the contemporary conscience might be as well expressed by a conservative as by a liberal political position.

Third, because reason or conscience provided their guidance, liberal Jewish thinkers had little interest in what classic Jewish literature might teach them ethically. The prophets, to whom they looked for inspiration, mainly served to validate their Kantian insight that ethics was to be distinguished from ritual with clear priority given to moral action. When the liberals did cite rabbinic literature, it was largely aggadic and educed to show that Judaism had some sources which agreed with the (normative) modern, rational temper. In contrast, the method called for here re-quires detailed attention to rabbinic views on a given issue, specifically, *halakhah lemaaseh*, authoritative rulings for action. Moreover, in following the dialectical development of halakhic views, students were asked to pay particular attention to the rabbinic views with which they disagreed. They were to be on guard against simply trying to find opinions which confirmed their contemporary moral intuitions and asked to develop a dialogic openness to what they might learn from our non-modern sages. When they could discipline themselves in this way, two intertwined results were likely to follow. First, the otherness of the *poskim*, the decisors, helped them gain radical insight into their modernist attitudes. Second, instead of resolutely reading the past by the standards of the present, they could amplify their moral probing by equally considering how the present might ethically gain from the wisdom of the past. Because postmodernity finds all universalism rooted in particularity – can any thinker or thought be anything other than particular? – it also takes our participation in the long chain of classic Jewish ethical reasoning as a sign of our Jewish authenticity even if our views ultimately differ with those of the tradition.

Fourth, having opened themselves to all these opinions, students were asked to render a decision, to give their reasons for deciding on just this course of action and, abstracting further from the process, to reflect on what they had learned about decision-making from their experience doing it. Despite all the study and reasoning, the six stages of this process tended to make students radically more self-consciousness about what they were doing in acting as ethical decisors. This emphasis on the personal involvement of the thinker in the thinking is characteristically postmodern. By contrast, moderns prided themselves on their clear, firm, essentially impersonal sense of duty. They considered moral disinterest a major sign of ethical probity and they deemed disciplining the self to the impartial demands of conscience a telling index of high character.

At the heart of this difference in approach is a meta-ethical divergence over human nature. Moderns had unlimited confidence in the enlightened human self, its reason and its moral capacity. Postmoderns have far less certainty about themselves and their abilities, on their own, to discern their responsibilities as they face complex challenges. So where moderns had little interest in what classic Jewish teaching might have to say to them, postmoderns are seriously open to our classic texts, specifically, the *halakhah*. This new found humility may be epitomized in saying that the rational, universal, Kantian self of Jewish modernity has now been displaced by the Jewish self, one which knows itself to be more fully personal than rational and more fundamentally particular than universal, though it remains significantly both rational and universal.

Permit me an aside at this point. I have been surprised by the way in which some otherwise astute readers of *Renewing the Covenant* have only recognized half its constructive argument. In keeping with the greater Jewish interest in spirituality today they have been reasonably receptive to its case for a greater place for God in our lives (chapters 1-10). Restoring a living relationship with a real God would at least bring us beyond the near-secularity of much modern Jewish religious thought. Yet that would only leave us *benei Noaḥ*, children of Noah, with only the duties of Noahides. We do not properly become authentic *benei Yisrael* and take up the fullness of Jewish living until we take our stand in the particular historic relationship of the people of Israel with God, the Covenant. If the task of a contemporary non-Orthodox Jewish theology is to explicate a theory of contemporary Jewish duty, its affirmation of God must be complemented by its equal affirmation of the people of Israel's true relationship with God. Postmodernity provides us with a language with which to affirm Jewish particularity by giving primary emphasis to the way our historicity, our race, our class, our gender, our language and other such specifics, necessarily shape our lives and thought. I draw on this to make a case for the ultimate particularity of the self[4] (chapters 11-13) which leads on then to a rethought doctrine of the people Israel (chapters 14-16) thus establishing the other side of the Covenant. The relationship then in place, a specific understanding of Jewish duty can then be educed from it.

This effort to situate the self primally in its Jewishness – what Louis Newman so nicely calls "Learning to be Led" – apparently troubled some of the authors of these papers. I had the feeling that some of them knew from the moment they decided on the question they would study what its answer had to be, so despite the recommended process, they were really only interested in texts which confirmed their views. Others may have been more open to the argument of the texts that opposed their ethical intuition but this seemed more an academic nicety they could live with since they knew they could always autonomously dismiss them. Perhaps they feared that taking the halakhic texts more seriously might impinge on their dedication to liberal Judaism and render them quasi-Orthodox. However, this fear receives no confirmation from the bulk of the papers for no author wound up agreeing with the dominant halakhic view simply because it was where "the" Jewish tradition stood. So too, none of those who most seriously engaged the *halakhah* evidenced a sacrifice of autonomy to the texts. The writers remained too modern for that.

This persistence of certain modern concerns amid the move to a pattern of decision-making I consider postmodern deserves some comment. It disconcerts some thinkers to be told that there remains a considerable overlap between modern and postmodern modes of ethical deliberation. It centers on the issue of autonomy. Few things if any are as religiously precious to our students as their right to self-determination in thought and action. Their intense concern for this value is confirmed by their deep devotion to compassionate human relations, individual and social. Ethical idealism has long been one of the two major motives bringing students to the rabbinate. (The other is a love of the Jewish people leading to the desire to serve it. How the two relate to one another varies widely.) They devoutly believe that autonomy is confirmed in ethics and this proposition is central to their understanding of non-Orthodox Judaism. I think the same is true of most caring American Jews and to that extent the modernization of Judaism has spoken truly and lastingly to a religious impulse basic to our people's lives.

Let me now qualify what I described above as the patronizing stance modern Jewish ethical thinkers took in relation to the Jewish tradition. Many of the writers and thinkers of prior generations were men (*sic*) of great Jewish learning and broad Jewish sympathies. While they were anxious to parade their broad humanity, much of their thinking was imbued with Jewish sensitivity and sympathy. It really is unfair to them to speak of their universalistic utterances as if there was nothing particularly Jewish in them, subterranean though it might be. Our students demonstrate this same interpenetration of the universal by the particular, perhaps even more intensely than did their liberal forebears. They are, after all, the offspring of some generations of American Jews who have enthusiastically identified the Jewish and the ethically universal. They and our community as a whole regularly show a devotion to justice and a concern for social betterment that cannot be termed distinctively Jewish. Yet the interpenetration of the two continually manifests itself in such odd indicators of continuing ethnicity as the heavy disproportion of Jews working to improve human welfare and voting for liberal social causes despite their contrary class interests. The result is that when American Jews assert their universal ethics without conscious regard for Jewish text or teaching, they are very often far more deeply grounded in their Jewishness than they take themselves to be. So I very often have sensed in these papers as their authors exercised their autonomy to universalize our tradition that there was something quite Jewish even about their reasons for transcending their particularity.

Despite my insistence on a certain Jewish particularity in modern Jewry's universalistic decision-making process, there remains a substantial difference between it and what follows from postmodern commitments. This is more than a matter of balance, the modern utterly subordinating its particularity, the postmodern glorying in it. The more critical issue is that postmodernity substantially transforms individual freedom in keeping with its different sense of the human situation. So to speak, moderns take the "auto[s]," the self, in autonomy quite seriously, individualizing judgment and legislation. In classic Kantian thought individuality quickly becomes socialized since one's autonomy ought to be guided by reason. Since rationality is common to all thinking-beings/moral-agents, a critical sign of proper moral reasoning is whether the duty one imposes upon oneself might be made a law for all humankind. Nonetheless, individual reason is the arbiter of that decision.

Postmodern thought does not have such confidence in the individual or in human rationality. In postmodern Jewish theology selfhood is indivisible from a relationship with that independent Other we call God and with the Jewish people, past, present and future. The "auto[s]" now validly exercises its power of self-legislation (auto-nomy) not as a quasi-monad but in intimate involvement with its relational-others, God and the Jewish people.

It may help to explain autonomy's overlap-with-transformation in directly religious terms. For all the postmodern critique of modernity, some postmoderns, I among them, acknowledge that part of its innovative religious insight remains valid. Modern thinkers tightly linked personal dignity with the right of self-determination in ways previously unknown and unacceptable to our tradition. For a religion based on a revealed text, our "orthodoxy" may have granted substantial individual freedom within the system. Moderns grandly expanded this. While postmoderns agree that they were right to do so, their chastened view of human capacity results in a newly contextualized and thereby delimited view of personal freedom.

Thus they affirm "autonomy" as moderns do but mean something significantly new by it.

These theoretical observations indicate something of what the teacher was learning from the students as they experimented with – as it turned out – applying a postmodern view of autonomy to some pressing ethical issues. (Of course, I was also working on *Renewing the Covenant* in this period. That, plus post-publication discussions concerning it refined my theoretical understanding.5) It came as little surprise that some students chafed at being asked to exercise their autonomy less independently than their upbringing and religiosity instructed them to do. Modernity remains the dominant Jewish community ideology (certainly its language) even though the signs of its intellectual collapse abound. What came as a pleasant surprise was how congenially most students took to this new (and demanding) schema. They knew that conservative ethicians were often quite cogent and while they might have preferred ignoring them they recognized that evasion was simple irresponsibility. More importantly, for Jewish and human reasons they wanted to know what the *halakhah* said on their topic so they avidly took to this aspect of our work (though it often involved them with texts for which they had received scant preparation). The two concluding, reflective steps – of decision in the face of alternatives and of personally reacting to the process – met with rather a more mixed response. I judged this to be less a resistance to postmodern self-consciousness than a preference for action over speculation as well as exhaustion at completing this paper in one semester. Considering that the students came to this effort with little conscious understanding of or commitment to my view of postmodern meta-ethics and thus the decision-making structure I imposed upon them, I found their general satisfaction with the method – albeit for major, not day-to-day, ethical deliberation – a confirmation of my analysis of our community's move toward postmodernity.6

I do not mean to suggest by these comments that these papers, for all their seriousness of intent and depth of research, fully present my ideal of postmodern decision-making. Sometimes their constricted method results from the specific issue being studied for then its particular contours will make one or another aspect of the procedure more or less valuable in dealing with it. However, here students were not asked to deal with three additional aspects of the postmodern decision-making process I deem significant.7 Two of these derive from standing in Covenant as one of the people of Israel: first, a concern for how our community today is facing up to a given issue, and, second, a consideration of the messianic future to which Jewish action ought to be directed. The third stems from the fact that our Covenant relationship is with God, no less, and so our decisions need to be made with intense regard for what we believe God now wants of us.

To some extent the first of these *desiderata*, the contemporary attitude, operates in these studies when they invoke the opinion of present day *poskim*, decisors. But that does not often yield what the mass of Jews themselves sense to be their present duty. Taken literally, this criterion self-destructs. The bulk of American Jewry is apathetic, ignorant and non-observant. Shall we really seek their guidance as to what God wants of the Covenant people? And if we limit ourselves to "caring" or "serious-minded" Jews, can we ever say just who they are? Nevertheless, the Covenant is made with the Jewish people and not simply its authorities. In recent generations the Jewish people has not infrequently been spiritually ahead of its leadership, as in their acceptance of responsible contraception, secular education and women's equality. Hence, with all its risks, a postmodern Jewish decisor must seek for what he understands to be the present trend or divisions in the Jewish community on a given issue.

The eye to the messianic future is not often found in these studies but it must have a place in any fully responsive Covenantal decision. At the least, the messianic consideration enters on two levels. The simpler one involves asking whether a given policy has redemptive features about it. So to speak, would instituting it serve to foreshadow the full redemption to which Jews aspire? I termed this the "simpler" level for people readily identify this purosiveness with their determination to be scrupulously moral in responding to an ethical challenge. High morality surely is redemptive. But even an intense dedication to ethics can easily become so time-and-culture-bound that it misses the grand sweep invoked by asking about ultimate redemption. Thus, on the second level one asks whether a given decision is likely to help the Jewish people endure the tests of history in holiness until the Messiah comes. Now Jewish continuity, the subject of so much communal discussion since the Jewish Population Survey of 1990, takes on its proper theological frame. On this level the speculative difficulties increase for no one can tightly connect specific Jewish duties with our people's survival to the end of history. But living messianism is indispensable to Jewish survival in faithfulness. Negatively, one cannot sanction an act which is unlikely to keep Jewry alive in long-term Covenant loyalty. So while we are not gifted with prophecy we must stretch our Jewish imaginations and seek in each decision to connect our deeds with the long passage to the end-time.

To suggest that our relationship with God also must play a direct role in our ethical deliberations often panics liberals. Adamant in their rejection of Orthodoxy, they worry lest religious leaders again be empowered to have God authorize ethical barbarities, the Crusades and Inquisition being quickly linked to Jonestown and the Waco Branch Davidians. They do not care that even in Jewish Orthodoxy God's authority is domesticated, as it were, by the halakhic tradition and community scrutiny. Among the non-Orthodox, of course, "God's authority" is even further conditioned by the emphasis on religion as substantially our human response to God and the resulting centrality of personal autonomy. But only in a thoroughgoing humanism would esteeming individual freedom require that God have no role at all in our decision-making.

Moderns, say those who thought of God as the organizing/integrating idea of their worldview, could easily equate being fully rational in their ethical judgment as attending to God's will. For the less philosophically inclined, this became simply listening to their conscience. For religious postmoderns, the self does not have such omnicompetence and the new humility induced by realism about our limits makes room for a relationship with a real God. "Listening" to that God, trying to discern what one's relationship with God entails, now claims a significant place in decision-making. Thus, traditional Jews not only expect exalted learning from their *posek*, decisor, but exemplary personal piety as well. Liberal Jews vary widely in their sense of God and what it means that they are involved with that God in the Covenant. But their faith always has a sense of our present, ongoing "listening/discerning" to God's "will," our equivalent of revelation, something we claim goes on today as in the past though not as spectacularly. One whose intimacy with God has grown over the years will "know" from time to time, with varying degrees of clarity, what God "demands" or "prohibits." At the very least, their ethical deliberations will be conducted with the seriousness befitting the One whom they seek to serve. I may only have been theologically wishful but I often found the depth of concern manifest in these papers to be the equivalent of the non-Orthodox piety I have in mind.

Even had these papers applied the fullest possible pattern of decision-making they would not likely have remedied an outcome that troubles some people: it may lead people to different results, as some papers indicate. Shouldn't a religion be giving unequivocal answers to questions of good and evil? and is that not a *desideratum* today in contrast to a liberal secularism that seems able to permit almost everything? I think there are many questions of morality where we could reach near unanimity but for pedagogic reasons we selected issues enveloped in controversy. We hoped that facing a clash of values would throw us back on our own (now richly informed) ethical intuition and bring many of our meta-ethical presumptions to consciousness. In any case, it seems strange for Jews to be asking for a more monolithic (applied) ethics when the *halakhah* regularly features differences of opinion. To be sure, the area of agreement as versus that of disagreement was much greater in our tradition than it is among liberals. Nonetheless, if even our "orthodoxy" tolerates diversity then surely non-Orthodox Judaism will do so to an even a greater extent.

The liberal Jewish proclivity for diversity stems from its recognition of the individual's right to self-determination. Once one's self is allowed a place in the decision-making process, a certain subjective variety acquires authority. Postmodern Jewish theology brings a considerable measure of order to bear on the threatened anarchy by requiring us to exercise our autonomy Covenantally, that is, out of our relationship with God as part of the people of Israel's past, present and messianically future involvement with God. But one thing more remains to be remarked upon: how a change in our actual pattern of contemporary Jewish existence would affect the single Jewish self. Today most caring Jews find themselves quite isolated among the masses of relatively indifferent Jews. Few people share their religious assumptions. So their efforts to determine just what constitutes their Covenant obligations must be pursued in a relatively solitary fashion. My comments here and in much of *Renewing the Covenant* have been addressed to such isolated, devoted Jews. But what if they were able to share in a community of Jews devoted like themselves to the imperatives of existence in Covenant? In that case, I suggest, the corporate patterns of this "mini-people-of-Israel" would have great sway in their lives (as a living extension of the communal criterion discussed above). Were we able to produce such small communities of shared faith/action – and then to link and enlarge them! – the threat of Jewish duty becoming radically subjective would diminish. And though this pattern of decision-making would always oscillate in avoidance of the dangers of anarchy and orthodoxy, its dedication to process over outcome would be less worrisome. Until such local communities of faith become realities, we will continue to suffer Jewishly from the residual effects of a modernization which has over-stressed the virtues of individuality to the point where we are now socially deprived. The postmodern understanding of the Covenant – and of the self which stands within it – restores a more recognizable Jewish balance.

If, indeed, our beliefs prevent our ever escaping the issue of subjectivity in our decision-making,[8] there is one further virtue of the scheme utilized in these papers: it forces us to confront the meta-ethical commitments in terms of which we read our various texts and construct our arguments. Having to make a case against people – whether halakhic or general ethical sages – with whose decisions one disagrees, eventually forces one back to the beliefs by which one hopes to live. Seeing their ethical consequences can strongly reenforce them; it may also suggest they need reconsideration. It takes a strong faith to live with such commitment/openness. I do not see that anything less would be adequate to what our ever renewing tradition requires of us today.

## Notes

1. "Postmodern" has turned out to be so useful in many venues of contemporary intellectual discussion that it permits of no reasonably clear definition. I use the term in a theological context worked out in *Renewing the Covenant* (Philadelphia: Jewish Publication Society, 1991). The standard,

Derridean understanding of the postmodern denies that such foundational terms like "self" and "God," which I employ, can still be meaningfully be used. But the philosophic/literary postmoderns then divide on whether any sort of reasonably didactic discourse remains possible or only educative forms of word-play. Other postmoderns seek to avoid this difficulty by new/ old modes of reading texts or their own lives, i. e., spiritual autobiography. For an early, 1990, statement of some Jewish varieties, see "A Symposium on Jewish Postmodernism," *Soundings, An Interdisciplinary Journal*, Vol. LXXVI, No. 1, Spring, 1993, with contributions by Edith Wyschogrod, Peter Ochs, Jose Faur, Robert Gibbs and Jacob Meskin.

2. "The Autonomous Jewish Self," *Modern Judaism*, 4.1, Feb., 1984.

3. This took place at the end of 1991. Its first nineteen chapters provide the basis for the culminating statement now significantly retitled, "The Jewish Self."

4. See, in particular, pp. 43-48 where, as part of the experiential exposition of American Jewry's postmodern situation, I explicate the socio-historic basis for my later polemic against the adequacy of the self before presenting my argument for the primacy of its particularity.

5. For the ongoing tri-partite split in my theological work – Jewish sources, apologetics, application – see *Renewing the Covenant*, pp. ix-xi. Note that I have been fairly consistent in using the realm of ethical duty as an academic means of exploring what my theological speculations entailed.

6. I refer to the analysis of "Jewish Religious Experience in Our Time" carried out in chapters 1-3 of *Renewing the Covenant*.

7. See chapter 20 of *Renewing the Covenant*, "The Jewish Self."

8. I believe this is as true of traditional *pesak*, decision-making, as it is of serious non-Orthodox ethical determinations, though there is an obvious difference of degree between the two modes. Thirty years ago, I devoted my column on "Contemporary Theological Literature" in *Judaism* to the topic, "Subjectivity and the Halachic Process" (Spring, 1964). I argued there that an examination of the current literature of each of the movements showed that decisors necessarily could not be fully "objective" about their decisions and that a certain measure of personal insight inevitably made itself felt in their work. This drew a rejoinder in a subsequent issue of *Tradition* (Vol. 7, No. 1, Winter, 1964-5) from Immanuel Jakobovits, the regular writer of its "Survey of Recent Halakhic Literature." He readily conceded that there were certain personal limitations involved in every human intellectual process and pointed out that only Moses knew God's will without distortion. But he then tried to make a case for the objectivity of halakhic *pesak*. I will still happily let readers decide for themselves on the basis of these two statements of the case whether subjectivity is not a significant factor in classic Jewish decision-making.

Were our culture now fully committed to the postmodern identification of text and reader we could simply abandon the pretense that there could be such a thing as an "objective" reading of a text and stop worrying that the reader necessarily is involved in giving meaning to any text. But for the time being, with modern as well as postmodern ways of approaching these issues being current, I shall continue to assume here that the reader is more influenced by the modern than the postmodern understanding of hermeneutics.

# The
# Contributors
# Today

Carole Balin is a rabbi, an Instructor at Hebrew Union College-Jewish Institute of Religion and a doctoral student in the Columbia University Graduate School of Arts and Sciences Department of History.

Eugene B. Borowitz is the Sigmund L. Falk Distinguished Professor of Education and Jewish Religious Thought at the New York School of Hebrew Union College-Jewish Institute of Religion.

Judith Brazen is a rabbi and Hillel director at Hunter College, City University of New York.

Daniel Cohen is a rabbi at Temple Sharey Tefilo-Israel, South Orange, NJ.

Faith Joy Dantowitz is a rabbi at Congregation B'nai Jeshurun, Short Hills, NJ.

Ronn S. Davids is a rabbi and a student at Columbia University Law School.

Edward Elkin is the rabbi of Congregation Iyr Ha-Melech, Kingston, Ontario and teaches at Bialk High School, Montreal.

Michael Feshbach is the rabbi at Temple Anshe Hesed, Erie, PA.

Susan Freeman is the rabbi-educator at Congregation B'nai Israel, Northhampton, MA.

Stuart Weinberg Gershon is the rabbi at Temple Sinai, Summit, NJ.

Laurence Groffman is a rabbi at Congregation B'nai Jeshurun, Short Hills, NJ.

Deborah Joselow is a rabbi at Temple Emanu-El, Westfield, NJ.

Karen Bookman Kaplan is the rabbi at Astoria Center of Israel, Long Island City, NY.

Jonathan Kraus is the rabbi at Beth El Temple Center, Belmont, MA.

Harry Levin is the rabbi at Congregation Beth Shalom, Clifton Park, NY.

Valerie Lieber is a student at the Hebrew Union College-Jewish Institute of Religion and will be ordained a rabbi with the class of 1995.

Amy Memis is a rabbi at Congregation B'nai Jehoshua Beth Elohim, Glenview, IL.

Jordan Millstein is a rabbi at North Shore Congregation Israel, Glencoe, IL.

Louis Newman is Associate Professor of Religion and Director of the Program in Judaic Studies, Carleton College, Northfield, MN.

Aaron Panken is a rabbi at Rodeph Sholom Congregation, New York, NY.

Gayle Pomerantz is a rabbi at Temple Beth Sholom, Miami Beach, FL.

Janise Poticha is a rabbi at Temple Shaaray Tefila, New York, NY.

Peter Schaktman is a rabbi at Congregation Emanu El, Houston, TX.

Janine Schloss is a rabbi at Congregation Shaare Emeth, St. Louis, MO.

David Stern is a rabbi at Temple Emanu-El, Dallas, TX.

Ariel Stone is a rabbi who most recently served a year in the former Soviet Union, with Congregation HaTikvah of Kiev, Ukraine.

Ronald B. B. Symons is Education Director/Assistant Rabbi at Larchmont Temple, Larchmont, NY.

Nancy Wiener is a rabbi and Field Work Coordinator and Instructor in Pastoral Counseling at the New York School of Hebrew Union College-Jewish Institute of Religion.

# Temple Israel
### Minneapolis, Minnesota

IN HONOR OF
THE BIRTH OF
LIORA DAVIDA LONDON
FROM
GEORGIA & IVAN KALMAN